2008
Senior
Biology 2

Student Workbook

Senior *Biology 2* 2008

Student Workbook

Previous annual editions 2002-2007
Seventh Edition 2008

ISBN 978-1-877329-93-7

Copyright © 2007 Richard Allan
Published by **BIOZONE International Ltd**

Printed by REPLIKA PRESS PVT LTD using paper
produced from renewable and waste materials

About the Writing Team

Tracey Greenwood joined the staff of Biozone at the beginning of 1993. She has a Ph.D in biology, specialising in lake ecology, and taught undergraduate and graduate biology at the University of Waikato for four years.

Lyn Shepherd joined as an author in 2003, bringing her 20 years experience as a secondary school biology teacher to Biozone.

Richard Allan has had 11 years experience teaching senior biology at Hillcrest High School in Hamilton, New Zealand. He attained a Masters degree in biology at Waikato University, New Zealand.

As always, the authors acknowledge and thank our graphic artist Dan Butler for his continued dedication to the job at hand.

Purchases of this workbook may be made direct from the publisher:

www.thebiozone.com

UNITED KINGDOM:

BIOZONE Learning Media (UK) Ltd.
P.O. Box 23698, Edinburgh EH5 2WX,
Scotland
Telephone: +44 (131) 557 5060
FAX: +44 (131) 557 5030
E-mail: sales@biozone.co.uk

ASIA & AUSTRALIA:

BIOZONE Learning Media Australia
P.O. Box 7523, GCMC 4217 QLD
Australia
Telephone: +61 (7) 5575 4615
FAX: +61 (7) 5572 0161
E-mail: info@biozone.com.au

NORTH & SOUTH AMERICA, AFRICA:

BIOZONE International Ltd.
P.O. Box 13-034, Hamilton, **New Zealand**
Telephone: +64 (7) 856 8104
FREE Fax: 1-800-717-8751 (USA-Canada)
FAX: +64 (7) 856 9243
E-mail: sales@biozone.co.nz

Preface to the 2008 Edition

This is the seventh edition of **Senior Biology 2**. It is designed to meet the needs of students in biology programs at grades 11 and 12 or equivalent. It is particularly well suited to students taking **International Baccalaureate** (IB) **Biology**, **Advanced Placement** (AP) **Biology**, or **Honors Biology**. Biozone's Senior Biology 1 and 2 workbooks cater for a wide audience and may contain more material than is required by any one particular biology program. The two compact softback volumes provide the ideal supplement to a compete biology program without the inconvenience of a single, large workbook. However, we would recommend purchasing both workbooks at the commencement of the teaching program to provide full flexibility and access to content. Previous editions have received very favorable reviews; see our web site: **www.thebiozone.com** for details.

There have been several organizational and content changes in this edition of Senior Biology 2, in line with the revisions to the **International Baccalaureate Biology program**. These changes involve the addition of a new chapter (*Microbes and Biotechnology*) and the division of the Plant Science chapter into two, more comprehensive sections. Details of these revisions are provided on a separate sheet supplied with the workbook and are also available on Biozone's web site. The current revisions should also improve the accessibility of material for other biology programs, especially for those teaching IB and AP programs concurrently. In addition to organizational revisions, we have continued to refine the stimulus material in the workbook to improve its accessibility, interest level, and appropriateness for student use. A new feature this year is the page tab identifying "**Related activities**" in the workbook and "**Web links**". These will help students to locate related material within the workbook and provides access to web links and activities (including animations) that will enhance their understanding of the topic. See page 11 to find out more about these. Supplementary material and extension activities continue to be available with a limited photocopy licence on Biozone's **Teacher Resource CD-ROM**. In addition, we continue to update all our lists of resources. These annual revisions are in keeping with our ongoing commitment to providing up-to-date, relevant, interesting, and accurate information to students and teachers.

A Note to the Teacher

This workbook has been produced as a student-centered resource, and benefits students by facilitating independent learning and critical thinking. Biozone's workbooks motivate and challenge a wide range of students by providing a highly visual format, a clear map through the course, and a synopsis of available supplemental resources. In modern biology, a single textbook may no longer provide all the information a student needs to grasp a topic. This workbook is a generic resource and **not a textbook**, and we make a point of referencing texts from other publishers. Above all, we are committed to continually revising and improving this resource **every year**. The price, at only US$18.95 for students, is a reflection of our commitment to providing high-quality, cost effective resources for biology. Please **do not photocopy** from this workbook. We cannot afford to supply single copies to schools and still provide annual updates as we intend. If you think it is worth using, then we recommend that the students themselves own this resource and keep it for their own use. A free model answer book is supplied with your **first order** of 5 or more workbooks.

How Teachers May Use This Workbook

This workbook may be used in the classroom to guide students through each topic. Some activities may be used to introduce topics while others may be used to consolidate and test concepts already covered by other means. The workbook may be used as the primary tool in teaching some topics, but it should not be at the expense of good, 'hands-on' biology. Students may attempt the activities on their own or in groups. The latter provides opportunities for healthy discussion and peer-to-peer learning. Many of the activities may be set as homework exercises. Each page is perforated, allowing for easy removal of pages to be submitted for marking. This has been facilitated this year by the back-to-back format of two page activities. Teachers may prescribe the activities to be attempted by the students (using the check boxes next to the objectives for each topic), or they may allow students a degree of freedom with respect to the activities they attempt. The objectives for each topic will allow students to keep up to date even if they miss lessons and teachers who are away from class may set work easily in their absence. I thank you for your support.

Richard Allan

Acknowledgements

We would like to thank the people who have contributed to this edition:
• Dan Butler for bravery in photographing his sword wound for the purposes of illustrating venous blood flow • David Brill for permission to produce an artist's rendering of his reconstructed skeleton of 'Lucy' • Dr Douglas Cooper and the University of California San Francisco, for the use of the SEM of a podocyte (http://www.sacs.ucsf.edu/home/cooper/Anat118/urinary/urinary98.htm) • Dr. John Green, University of Waikato, for his input to the evolution and human evolution sections • Dr. John Craig for permission to use his material on the behavior of swamphen • Dr. John Stencil for his data on the albino gray squirrel population • Mary McDougall and Sue FitzGerald for their efficient handling of the office • Jan Morrison for her diagrams • Raewyn Poole, University of Waikato, for information provided in her MSc thesis: Culture and transformation of *Acacia* • TechPool Studios, for their clipart collection of human anatomy: Copyright ©1994, TechPool Studios Corp. USA (some of these images were modified by R. Allan and T. Greenwood) • Totem Graphics, for their clipart collection • Corel Corporation, for use of their eps clipart of plants and animals from the Corel MEGAGALLERY collection • 3D modeling software, Poser IV (Curious Labs) and Bryce.

Photo Credits

Royalty free images purchased by Biozone International Ltd have been obtained from the following: **Corel** Corporation from titles in their Professional Photos CD-ROM collection; **IMSI** (International Microcomputer Software Inc.) images from IMSI's MasterClips® and MasterPhotosTM Collection, 1895 Francisco Blvd. East, San Rafael, CA 94901-5506, USA; ©1996 **Digital Stock**, Medicine and Health Care collection; ©**Hemera** Technologies Inc, 1997-2001; © 2005 JupiterImages Corporation www.clipart.com; ©Click Art, ©T/Maker Company; ©1994., ©**Digital Vision**; Gazelle Technologies Inc.; ©**istockphotos** (www.istockphoto.com); **PhotoDisc®**, Inc. USA, www.photodisc.com

We would like to thank the following individuals and institutions who kindly provided photographs: • Phil Camill, Carelton College, Minnesota for the photograph of mangrove pneumatophores • Grotte de Rouffignac, for drawings and photographs of the Rouffignac Cave • Dr. John Dale, Defenders Ltd., www.defenders.co.uk for the photos on biological pest control • Janice Windsor, for photographs taken 'on safari' in East Africa • LJ Grauke, USDA-ARS Pecan Breeding & Genetics, for his photograph of budscales in shagbark hickory • Simon Pollard, for his photograph of the naked mole rat • The late Ron Lind for his photograph of stromatolites • The late Dr. M. Soper, for his photograph of the waxeye feeding chicks • Stephen Moore, for his photo of a hydrophyte, *Myriophyllum* and for his photos of stream invertebrates • Dr Roger Wagner, Dept of Biological Sciences, University of Delaware, for the LS of a capillary. Contributors identified by coded credits are as follows: **BF**: Brian Finerran (Uni. of Canterbury), **BH**: Brendan Hicks (Uni. of Waikato), **BOB**: Barry O'Brien (Uni. of Waikato), **CDC**: Centers for Disease Control and Prevention, Atlanta, USA, **COD**: Colin O'Donnell, **DEQ**: Dept of Environment Queensland Ltd., **DoC**: Dept of Conservation (NZ), **EII**: Education Interactive Imaging, **EW**: Environment Waikato, **Eyewire**: Eyewire, Inc © 1998-2001, www.eyewire.com **FRI**: Forest Research Institute, **GW**: Graham Walker, **JR-PE**: Jane Roskruge, **JW**: Janice Windsor, **RA**: Richard Allan, **RCN**: Ralph Cocklin, **RM-DOC**: Rod Morris, **RL**: Ron Lind, **TG**: Tracey Greenwood, **VM**: Villa Maria Wines, **WBS**: Warwick Silvester (Uni. of Waikato), **WMU**: Waikato Microscope Unit.

Special thanks to all the partners of the Biozone team for their support.

Cover Photographs

Main photograph: The Siberian tiger (*P. t. altaica*) is the largest of several subspecies of *Panthera tigris*. Weighing up to 280 kg with a dense coat, Siberian tigers have been hunted almost to extinction and there are now estimated to be fewer than 400 left in the wild. PHOTO: Tim Davis/Stone©Gettyimages. **Background photograph:** Autumn leaves, Image ©2005 JupiterImages Corporation www.clipart.com

Contents

CODES: △ **Upgraded** this edition   ☆ **New** this edition   **Activity** is marked: ❑ to be done;   ☑ when completed

CONTENTS (continued)

CODES: △ **Upgraded** this edition   ☆ **New** this edition   **Activity** is marked: ● to be done; ✓ when completed

CONTENTS *(continued)*

CODES: △   **Upgraded** this edition   ☆   **New** this edition   **Activity** is marked: • to be done;   ✔ when completed

How to Use this Workbook

This workbook is designed to provide you with a resource that will make the study of biology more enjoyable. While this workbook meets the needs of most general biology courses, it also provides specific keyed objectives for the **International Baccalaureate** (IB) and **Advanced Placement** (AP) courses. Consult the Syllabus Guides on pages 12-14 of this workbook to establish where material for your syllabus is covered. It is hoped that this workbook will reinforce and extend the ideas developed by your teacher. It must be emphasized that this workbook is **not a textbook**. It is designed to complement the biology textbooks provided for your course. For each topic the workbook provides the following useful resources:

Introduction

Guidance Provided for Each Topic

Topic outcomes:
This panel identifies the learning objectives relevant to the topic for each designated course. Attempt only those objectives that relate to your course. See pages 12-14 for a listing of your syllabus requirements.

Learning objectives:
These provide a map of the topic content. Completing the relevant learning objectives will help you to satisfy the knowledge requirements of your course. Your teacher may add to or omit points from this list.

Key words:
Key words are displayed in **bold** type in the learning objectives and should be used to create a glossary as you study each topic. From your own reading and your teacher's descriptions, write your own definition for each word. Only the terms relevant to your learning objectives should be used to create your glossary. Free glossary worksheets are also available from our web site.

Use the check boxes to mark objectives to be completed.
Use a **dot** to be done (•).
Use a **tick** when completed (✓).

Comprehensive textbooks
The **Textbook Reference Grid** on pages 8-9 lists the major comprehensive textbooks available for your course (these are texts providing coverage of the majority of course topics). The grid provides the page or chapter numbers from each text relevant to each topic in the workbook.

Internet addresses:
Access our database of links to more than **800** web sites relevant to the topics covered. These are updated regularly. Go to **www.thebiozone.com** and link directly to these sites using the *BioLinks* button.

Supplementary texts:
References to supplementary texts, which have only a restricted topic coverage, are provided as appropriate in each topic.

Periodical articles:
Ideal for those seeking more depth or the latest research on a specific topic. Articles are sorted according to their suitability for student or teacher reference. Visit your school, public, or university library for these articles.

Supplementary resources from Biozone Supporting Presentation MEDIA are noted where appropriate. Computer software and videos relevant to every topic in the workbook are provided on the **Teacher Resource CD-ROM** (which may be purchased separately). See page 7 for details.

Activity Pages

The activities and exercises make up most of the content of this book. They are designed to reinforce the concepts you have learned about in the topic. Your teacher may use the activity pages to introduce a topic for the first time, or you may use them to revise ideas already covered. They are excellent for use in the classroom, and as homework exercises and revision. In most cases, the activities should not be attempted until you have carried out the necessary background reading from your textbook. Your teacher should have a model answer book with the answers to each activity. This workbook caters for the needs of more than one syllabus, and you will find some activities or even whole topics that may not be relevant to your course. Although you may miss out these pages, you will still find our workbooks to be exceptional value.

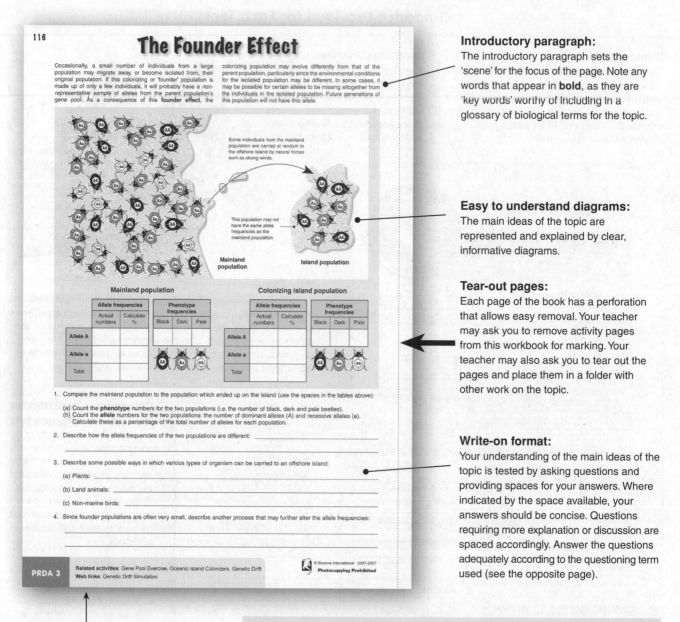

Introductory paragraph:
The introductory paragraph sets the 'scene' for the focus of the page. Note any words that appear in **bold**, as they are 'key words' worthy of including in a glossary of biological terms for the topic.

Easy to understand diagrams:
The main ideas of the topic are represented and explained by clear, informative diagrams.

Tear-out pages:
Each page of the book has a perforation that allows easy removal. Your teacher may ask you to remove activity pages from this workbook for marking. Your teacher may also ask you to tear out the pages and place them in a folder with other work on the topic.

Write-on format:
Your understanding of the main ideas of the topic is tested by asking questions and providing spaces for your answers. Where indicated by the space available, your answers should be concise. Questions requiring more explanation or discussion are spaced accordingly. Answer the questions adequately according to the questioning term used (see the opposite page).

Activity code and links:
Activity codes (explained right) help to identify the type of activities and the skills they require. Most activities require knowledge recall as well as the application of knowledge to explain observations or predict outcomes.

Use the **Related activities** indicated to visit pages that may help you with understanding the material or answering the questions.

Web links indicate additional material of assistance or interest (either web pages or pdf activities). You can access these from: *www.thebiozone.com/weblink/SB1-9665.html*

Activity Level

1	=	Simple questions not requiring complex reasoning
2	=	Some complex reasoning may be required
3	=	More challenging, requiring integration of concepts

PRDA 3

Related activities: Gene Pool Exercise, Oceanic Island Colonizers, Genetic Drift
Web links: Genetic Drift Simulation

Type of Activity

D	=	Includes some data handling and/or interpretation
P	=	includes a paper practical
R	=	May require research outside the page
A	=	Includes application of knowledge to solve a problem
E	=	Extension material

Explanation of Terms

Questions come in a variety of forms. Whether you are studying for an exam, or writing an essay, it is important to understand exactly what the question is asking. A question has two parts to it: one part of the question will provide you with information, the second part of the question will provide you with instructions as to how to answer the question. Following these instructions is most important. Often students in exams know the material but fail to follow instructions and therefore do not answer the question appropriately. Examiners often use certain key words to introduce questions. Look out for them and be absolutely clear as to what they mean. Below is a list of commonly used terms that you will come across and a brief explanation of each.

Commonly used Terms in Biology

The following terms are frequently used when asking questions in examinations and assessments. Most of these are listed in the IB syllabus document as action verbs indicating the depth of treatment required for a given statement. Students should have a clear understanding of each of the following terms and use this understanding to answer questions appropriately.

Account for: Provide a satisfactory explanation or reason for an observation.

Analyze: Interpret data to reach stated conclusions.

Annotate: Add **brief** notes to a diagram, drawing or graph.

Apply: Use an idea, equation, principle, theory, or law in a new situation.

Appreciate: To understand the meaning or relevance of a particular situation.

Calculate: Find an answer using mathematical methods. Show the working unless instructed not to.

Compare: Give an account of similarities and differences between two or more items, referring to both (or all) of them throughout. Comparisons can be given using a table. Comparisons generally ask for similarities more than differences (see contrast).

Construct: Represent or develop in graphical form.

Contrast: Show differences. Set in opposition.

Deduce: Reach a conclusion from information given.

Define: Give the precise meaning of a word or phrase as concisely as possible.

Derive: Manipulate a mathematical equation to give a new equation or result.

Describe: Give an account, including all the relevant information.

Design: Produce a plan, object, simulation or model.

Determine: Find the only possible answer.

Discuss: Give an account including, where possible, a range of arguments, assessments of the relative importance of various factors, or comparison of alternative hypotheses.

Distinguish: Give the difference(s) between two or more different items.

Draw: Represent by means of pencil lines. Add labels unless told not to do so.

Estimate: Find an approximate value for an unknown quantity, based on the information provided and application of scientific knowledge.

Evaluate: Assess the implications and limitations.

Explain: Give a clear account including causes, reasons, or mechanisms.

Identify: Find an answer from a number of possibilities.

Illustrate: Give concrete examples. Explain clearly by using comparisons or examples.

Interpret: Comment upon, give examples, describe relationships. Describe, then evaluate.

List: Give a sequence of names or other brief answers with no elaboration. Each one should be clearly distinguishable from the others.

Measure: Find a value for a quantity.

Outline: Give a brief account or summary. Include essential information only.

Predict: Give an expected result.

Solve: Obtain an answer using algebraic and/or numerical methods.

State: Give a specific name, value, or other answer. No supporting argument or calculation is necessary.

Suggest: Propose a hypothesis or other possible explanation.

Summarize: Give a brief, condensed account. Include conclusions and avoid unnecessary details.

In Conclusion

Students should familiarize themselves with this list of terms and, where necessary throughout the course, they should refer back to them when answering questions. The list of terms mentioned above is not exhaustive and students should compare this list with past examination papers and essays etc. and add any new terms (and their meaning) to the list above. The aim is to become familiar with interpreting the question and answering it appropriately.

Resources Information

Your set textbook should always be a starting point for information. There are also many other resources available, including scientific journals, magazine and newspaper articles, supplementary texts covering restricted topic areas, dictionaries, computer software and videos, and the internet.

A synopsis of currently available resources is provided below. Access the publishers of these resources directly from Biozone's web site through our resources hub: **www.thebiozonecom/resource-hub.html**. Most titles are also available through www.amazon.com (for supplementals, this is often the easiest way). Please note that our listing any product in this workbook does not, in any way, denote Biozone's endorsement of that product.

Comprehensive Biology Texts Referenced

Appropriate texts for this course are referenced in this workbook. Page or chapter references for each text are provided in the text reference grid on pages 8-9. These will enable you to identify the relevant reading as you progress through the activities in this workbook. Publication details of texts referenced in the grid are provided below and opposite. For further details of text content, or to make purchases, link to the relevant publisher via Biozone's resources hub or by typing:
www.thebiozone.com/resources/us-comprehensive-pg1.html

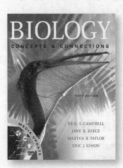

Campbell, N. A., J.B. Reece, M.R. Taylor, E.J. Simon, and L. Mitchell 2008
Biology: Concepts and Connections, Media Update 5 edn
Publisher: Benjamin Cummings
Pages: 781 plus appendices
ISBN: 978-0321512444
Comments: *Set at a more introductory level than Campbell and Reece, with a modular presentation that helps students to focus on main concepts. Comes with an interactive study partner on CD-ROM.*

Freeman, S., 2005
Biological Science
Publisher: Prentice Hall
Pages: 1392 incl. appendices and index
ISBN: 0-13-218746-9
Comments: *Aimed at Biology majors, and particularly the AP audience, this text includes an introductory chapter, and nine units covering core themes. Chapters conclude with a review, questions, and ideas for extra reading*

Allott, Andrew, 2001
Biology for the IB Diploma - Standard and Higher Level
Publisher: Oxford University Press
Pages: 192
ISBN: 0-19-914818-X
Comments: *Book structure mirrors that of the 2001 revised IB program. Includes core and option material.*

Mader, Sylvia, 2007
Biology, 9 edn
Publisher: McGraw Hill
Pages: 1040 including appendices
ISBN: 978-0072464634
Comments: *A revised edition, with updated content, covering concepts and principles of biology. An evolutionary theme continues to be central to its approach and modern ecological problems are stressed throughout.*

Bloom, M. and J. Greenberg, 2006
Biological Science: A Molecular Approach, (BSCS Blue Version), 9 edn
Publisher: Glencoe/McGraw Hill
Pages: 820+ including glossary
ISBN: 0-078-66427-6 (student edition)
Comments: *Aimed at gifted and honors biology students. A teacher's annotated edition, resource book, and overhead transparency booklet are also available.*

National Geographic Society, 2004
Biology: The Dynamics of Life
Publisher: Glencoe/McGraw-Hill
Pages: 1089 plus appendices
ISBN: 0-07-829900-4
Comments: *A highly colorful text, which uses a relatively large, easy-to-read format. Web site support is available for this text and English and Spanish glossaries are included.*

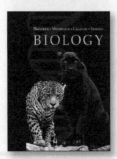

Brooker, R.J., Widmaier, E.P. L. Graham, and P. Stiling, 2008
Biology, 1 edn
Publisher: McGraw Hill
Pages: 1488
ISBN: 978-0073268071
Comments: *A comprehensive, modern text featuring an evolutionary focus with an emphasis on scientific inquiry, and especially critical thinking. Various electronic resources accompany the text.*

Raven, P.H., G.B. Johnson, K.A. Mason, and J. Losos, 2008
Biology, 8 edn
Publisher: McGraw-Hill
Pages: 1376 plus appendices
ISBN: 978-0072965810
Comments: *An authoritative majors text with a strong emphasis on evolution as a unifying theme. Content revision focuses on inheritance and evolution. A range of ancillary resources are also available.*

Campbell, N. A. and J.B. Reece, 2005
Biology, 7 edn
Publisher: Benjamin Cummings
Pages: 1312
ISBN: 0-8053-7146-X
Comments: *Written with a strong evolutionary perspective, and with CD-ROM and website support. Reviews are included for each chapter. A wide range of supplemental materials are also available for instructors and students.*

Sadava, D., H.C. Heller, G.H. Orians, W.K. Purves, and D. Hillis 2007
Life: The Science of Biology, 8 edn
Publisher: W.H. Freeman/Sinauer
Pages: 1121 plus appendices
ISBN: 978-0716776710
Comments: *Revised to include new content in key areas, with new illustrations and support resources. Also available in three softback volumes.*

Solomon, E., L. Berg, and D.W. Martin, 2008
Biology, 8 edn
Publisher: Brooks/Cole
Pages: 1376
ISBN: 978-0495317142
Comments: *A popular introductory majors text which has been substantially revised in key areas, including cell communication and genetics. Accompanied by online and multimedia resources.*

Starr, C., 2006
Biology: Concepts and Applications, 6 edn
Publisher: Brooks/Cole
Pages: 799
ISBN: 0-495-10296-3
Comments: *An introductory, issue-oriented approach for honor biology students. This text encourages critical thinking and includes overviews, chapter outlines, and multiple choice questions.*

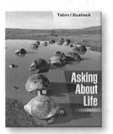

Starr, C. and R. Taggart, 2006
Biology: The Unity & Diversity of Life, 11 edn
Publisher: Brooks/Cole
Pages: 1056
ISBN: 0-495-01599-7
Comments: *A well illustrated, engaging majors text. As with earlier editions, this one emphasises the interconnectedness between structure, function, and evolution. Includes an interactive CD-ROM.*

Tobin, A.J. and J. Dusheck, 2005
Asking About Life, 3edn
Publisher: Brooks/Cole
Pages: 960
ISBN: 0-53-440653-X
Comments: *An important revision featuring streamlined coverage (this is a smaller text) and numerous examples. Evolution is the unifying theme throughout.*

Towle, Albert, 2006
Modern Biology, 11 edn
Publisher: Holt, Rinehart, and Winston
Pages: 53 chapters
ISBN: 0030651786
Comments: *Comprehensive and phylogeny-focused, providing sound, traditionally organized core content. A teacher's edition and a number of supporting resources are also available.*

Weem, M.P., 2001
Biology, 2 edn
Publisher: IBID Press
Pages: 494
ISBN: 1-876659-47-5
Comments: *Written specifically to support the 2001 revised IB course. Contains theory and worked examples.*

Supplementary Texts

For further details of text content, or to make purchases, link to the relevant publisher via Biozone's resources hub or by typing: **www.thebiozone.com/resources/us-supplementary-pg1.html**
All titles are available in North America unless indicated by (§).

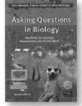

Barnard, C., F. Gilbert, F., and P. McGregor, 2007
Asking Questions in Biology: Key Skills for Practical Assessments & Project Work, 256 pp.
Publisher: Benjamin Cummings
ISBN: 978-0132224352
Comments: *Covers many aspects of design, analysis and presentation of practical work in senior level biology. Available in June 2007.*

Barnum, S.R., 2nd edn 2005
Biotechnology: An Introduction, 336 pp.
Publisher: Thomson Brooks/Cole
ISBN: 978-0495112051
Comments: *A broad view of biotechnology, integrating historical and modern topics. Processes and methods are described, and numerous examples describe applications.*

Cadogan, A. and Ingram, M., 2002
Maths for Advanced Biology
Publisher: NelsonThornes
ISBN: 0-7487-6506-9
Comments: *Provides coverage of basic mathematics requirements for biology at grades 11 and 12 (UK AS/A2). It includes worked examples.*

Helms, D.R., C.W. Helms, R.J. Kosinski, and J.C. Cummings, 3rd edn 1998
Biology in the Laboratory, 500 pp (paperback)
Publisher: W.H. Freeman
ISBN: 0-7167-3146-0
Comments: *A full lab program is covered in this text. Activities (#0-#45) are also available for purchase individually.*

Indge, B., 2003 (§)
Data and Data Handling for AS and A Level Biology, 128 pp.
Publisher: Hodder Arnold H&S
ISBN: 1340856475
Comments: *Examples and practice exercises to improve skills in data interpretation and analysis.*

Fullick, A., 1998
Human Health and Disease, 162 pp.
Publisher: Heinemann
ISBN: 0435570919
Comments: *An accompanying text for courses with modules in human health and disease. Covers both infectious and non-infectious disease.*

Jones, A., R. Reed, and J. Weyers, 3rd edn, 2003
Practical Skills in Biology, 488 pp.
Publisher: Prentice-Hall
ISBN: 978-0130451415
Comments: *Excellent, accurate guidance on study design, implementation, and data analysis. This edition includes several new chapters.*

Knisely, K., 2 edn, 2005
A Student Handbook for Writing in Biology, 224 pp.
Publisher: W.H. Freeman/Sinauer
ISBN: 0-7167-6709-0
Comments: *Practical advice covering writing, referencing, preparing lab reports, and poster and oral presentations. Includes appendices.*

Introduction

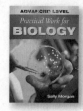

Morgan, S., 2002
Advanced Level Practical Work for Biology, 128 pp.
Publisher: Hodder and Stoughton
ISBN: 0-340-84712-3
Comments: *Caters for the practical and investigative requirements of biology at this level: experimental design, observations and measurement, and interpretation and analysis.*

Morton, D. & J.W. Perry, 1998
Photo Atlas for Anatomy & Physiology, 160 p.
Publisher: Brooks Cole. **ISBN**: 0-534-51716-1
Comments: *An excellent photographic guide to lab work. Also available are the PhotoAtlas for Botany (1998) ISBN: 0-534-52938-0 and Photo Atlas for Biology (1995) ISBN: 0-534-23556-5*

Taylor, J., 2001.
Microorganisms and Biotechnology, 192 pp.
Publisher: NelsonThornes. Available in Australia through Thomson Learning
ISBN: 0-17-448255-8
Comments: *Good coverage of this topic, including pathogens and disease, defence, and the use of microbes in industry and medicine.*

Collins Advanced Modular Sciences (HarperCollins)
Modular-style texts suitable as teacher reference and student extension reading for specific topic areas.

Hudson, T. and K. Mannion, 2001.
Microbes and Disease, 104 pp.
ISBN: 0-00-327742-9
Coverage of selected aspects of microbiology including the culture and applications of bacteria, and the role of bacteria and viruses in disease. Immunity, vaccination, and antimicrobial drug use are covered in the concluding chapter.

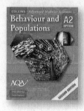

Behaviour & Populations, 82 pp.
ISBN: 0-00-327743-7
This text covers an eclectic range of topics including patterns of behavior, reproduction and its control, human growth and development, human populations, aspects of infectious disease, and issues related to health and lifestyle.

Illustrated Advanced Biology (John Murray Publishers)
Modular-style texts aimed as supplements to students of Grades 9-12 biology courses (AS and A2 level in the UK).

Clegg, C.J., 2003
Green Plants: The Inside Story, 96 pp.
ISBN: 0 7195 7553 2
The emphasis in this text is on flowering plants. Topics include leaf, stem, and root structure in relation to function, reproduction, economic botany, and sensitivity and adaptation.

Clegg, C.J., 2002
Microbes in Action, 97 pp.
ISBN: 0-71957-554-0
Microbes and their roles in disease and biotechnology. It includes material on the diversity of the microbial world, microbiological techniques, and enzyme technology.

Clegg, C.J., 1999
Genetics and Evolution, 96 pp.
ISBN: 0-7195-7552-4
Concise but thorough coverage of molecular genetics, genetic engineering, inheritance, and evolution. An historical perspective is included by way of introduction, and a glossary and a list of abbreviations used are included.

Clegg, C.J., 1998
Mammals: Structure & Function, 96 pp.
ISBN: 0-7195-7551-6
Excellent supplemental covering most aspects of basic mammalian anatomy and physiology. This text is now out of print from the publishers, but many schools will still have it and copies are still available from amazon books.

Advanced Biology Readers (John Murray Publishers)
Designed as supplementals supporting a range of specific topics in biology. Useful as teacher reference and student extension.

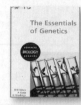

Jones, N., A. Karp., & G. Giddings, 2001.
Essentials of Genetics, 224 pp.
ISBN: 0-7195-8611-9
Thorough supplemental for genetics and evolution. Comprehensive coverage of cell division, molecular genetics, and genetic engineering. The application of new gene technologies to humans is also discussed.

Nelson Advanced Sciences (NelsonThornes)
Modular-style texts suitable as teacher reference and student extension reading for specific topics in grades 11 and 12 biology.

Adds, J., E. Larkcom & R. Miller, 2004.
Exchange and Transport, Energy and Ecosystems, revised edition 240 pp.
ISBN: 0-7487-7487-4
Includes exchange processes (gas exchanges, digestion, absorption), transport systems, adaptation, and sexual reproduction. Practical activities are included in several of the chapters.

Adds, J., E. Larkcom & R. Miller, 2004.
Genetics, Evolution, and Biodiversity, revised edition, 200 pp.
ISBN: 0-7487-7492-0
A range of topics including photosynthesis and the control of growth in plants, genetics and evolution, gene technology, and human evolution.

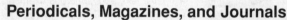

Periodicals, Magazines, and Journals
Periodical articles can be of great value in providing current information on specific topics. Periodicals may be accessed in your school, local, public, and university libraries. The periodicals referenced in this workbook are listed below. For general enquiries and further details regarding subscriptions, link to the relevant publisher via Biozone's resources hub or type: **www.thebiozone.com/resources/resource-journal.html**

Biological Sciences Review: *An excellent quarterly publication for all teachers and students of biology. The content is current and the language is accessible.* Subscriptions available from Philip Allan Publishers, Market Place, Deddington, Oxfordshire OX 15 OSE. **Tel.** 01869 338652 **Fax**: 01869 338803 **E-mail**: sales@philipallan.co.uk

New Scientist: *Published weekly, it often summarizes the findings published in other journals. Articles range from news releases to features.* Subscription enquiries:
Tel. (UK and international): +44 (0)1444 475636. (US & Canada) 1 888 822 3242.
E-mail: ns.subs@qss-uk.com

Scientific American: *A monthly magazine containing mostly specialist feature articles. Articles range in level of reading difficulty and assumed knowledge.* Subscription enquiries:
Tel. (US & Canada) 800-333-1199.
Tel. (outside North America): 515-247-7631
Web: www.sciam.com

The American Biology Teacher: *The peer-reviewed journal of the National Association of Biology Teachers. Published nine times a year and containing information and activities relevant to biology teachers.* Contact: NABT, 12030 Sunrise Valley Drive, #110, Reston, VA 20191-3409
Web: www.nabt.org

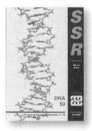

School Science Review: *A quarterly journal published by the ASE for science teachers in 11-19 education. SSR includes articles, reviews, and news on current research and curriculum development. Free to all Ordinary Members of the ASE or available on subscription.* Subscription enquiries:
Tel: 01707 28300
Email: info@ase.org.uk *or visit their web site.*

Biology Dictionaries

Access to a good biology dictionary is of great value when dealing with the technical terms used in biology. Below are some biology dictionaries that you may wish to locate or purchase. They can usually be sourced directly from the publisher or they are all available (at the time of printing) from www.amazon.com. For further details of text content, or to make purchases, link to the relevant publisher via Biozone's resources hub or by typing: **www.thebiozone.com/resources/dictionaries-pg1.html**

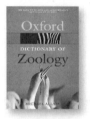

Allaby, M. (ed).
A Dictionary of Zoology 2 reissue ed., 2003, 608 pp. Oxford University Press.
ISBN: 019860758X
Wide coverage of terms in animal behavior, ecology, physiology, genetics, cytology, evolution, and zoogeography. Full taxonomic coverage of most phyla.

Bailey, J. (ed).
Facts on File Dictionary of Botany, 2002, 256 pp. Facts on File
ISBN: 0816049106
The definitions of some 2000 terms frequently used in botany. Topic coverage encompasses pure and applied plant science, classification, anatomy, morphology, and genetics.

Clamp, A.
AS/A-Level Biology. Essential Word Dictionary, 2000, 161 pp. Philip Allan Updates.
ISBN: 0-86003-372-4.
Essential words for AS and A2. Concise definitions are supported by further explanation and illustrations where required.

Hale, W.G. **Collins: Dictionary of Biology** 4 ed. 2005, 528 pp. Collins.
ISBN: 0-00-720734-4.
Updated to take in the latest developments in biology and now internet-linked. (§ This latest edition is currently available only in the UK. The earlier edition, ISBN: 0-00-714709-0, is available though amazon.com in North America).

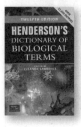

Henderson, I.F, W.D. Henderson, and E. Lawrence. **Henderson's Dictionary of Biological Terms**, 1999, 736 pp. Prentice Hall.
ISBN: 0582414989
An updated edition, rewritten for clarity, and reorganized for ease of use. An essential reference and the dictionary of choice for many.

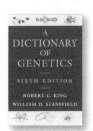

King, R.C. and W.D. Stansfield
A Dictionary of Genetics, 6 ed., 2002, 544 pp. Oxford University Press.
ISBN: 0195143256
A good source for the specialized terminology associated with genetics and related disciplines. Genera and species important to genetics are included, cross linked to an appendix.

Lincoln, R.J., G.A. Boxshall, & P.F. Clark.
A Dictionary of Ecology, Evolution, and Systematics, 2 ed., 1998, 371 pp. Cambridge Uni. Press. **ISBN**: 052143842X
6500 entries covering all major fields within biology, and recently expanded to reflect recent developments in the science. There are no pronunciation guidelines provided.

Market House Books (compiled by).
Oxford Dictionary of Biology 5 ed., 2004, 698 pp. Oxford University Press.
ISBN: 0198609175. *Revised and updated, with many new entries. This edition contains biographical entries on key scientists and comprehensive coverage of terms in biology, biophysics, and biochemistry.*

McGraw-Hill (ed). **McGraw-Hill Dictionary of Bioscience**, 2 ed., 2002, 662 pp. McGraw-Hill.
ISBN: 0-07-141043-0
22 000 entries encompassing more than 20 areas of the life sciences. It includes synonyms, acronyms, abbreviations, and pronunciations for all terms. Accessible, yet comprehensive.

Thain, M. and M. Hickman.
Penguin Dictionary of Biology 10/e (2000), 704 pp. Penguin (USA). **ISBN**: 0140513590
Pocket sized reference with definitions to more than 7500 terms, including more than 400 new entries. It includes explanations of fundamental concepts ad explorations of some of the more recent discoveries and developments in biology.

Internet Resources

The internet is a powerful tool for locating information. See pages 10-11 for details of how to access internet resources.

Teacher Resource CD-ROM

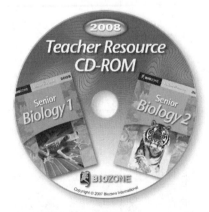

Biozone's **Teacher Resource CD-ROM** supports the content of the Senior Biology 1 and 2 workbooks with supplementary material and extension activities, worked statistical examples and worksheets, and comprehensive lists of available resources. The CD-ROM also includes glossary worksheets, crosswords and digital copies of the model answers for both workbooks. Contact Biozone for details.

Textbook Reference Grid

Guide to use:
Chapters or page numbers refer to the material in each text relevant to the stated topic in the workbook.

TOPIC IN WORKBOOK	Allott 2001	Bloom & Greenberg 2006	Brooker et al. 2008	Campbell & Reece 2005	Campbell et al. 2008	Freeman 2005	Mader 2007	National Geo. Soc. 2004
Pathogens and Disease	p. 49	Chpt. 23 as reqd	Chpt. 27-29 as reqd	Chpt. 18 & 27 as reqd	Chpt. 10, 16, & 24 (in part)	Chpt. 27-28, & 34	Chpt. 21-23 (in part)	Chpt. 18-19, 39
Defense Against Infectious Disease	pp. 50, 96-98	Chpt. 23 as reqd	Chpt. 53 as reqd	Chpt. 43	Chpt. 24	Chpt. 49	Chpt. 34- 35 in part	Chpt. 39
The Origin and Evolution of Life	pp. 124, 126-127	Chpt. 17 & 19 as reqd	Chpt. 22-23	Chpt. 26	Chpt. 15 & 16	Chpt. 1-4, 23 as reqd	Chpt.19	Chpt.14
Speciation	pp. 38, 125-126, 130, 132	Chpt. 17, 19-20 as reqd	Chpt. 22-23, & 25	Chpt. 22-24, & 34 as reqd	Chpt. 13 & 14	Chpt. 23-25 as reqd	Chpt. 17	Chpt. 15
Patterns of Evolution	p. 126	Chpt. 16 & 19	Chpt. 23	Chpt. 23 (in part)	Chpt. 13 & 15	Chpt 24	Chpt 17-18	Chpt 14-15 (in part)
Human Evolution	pp. 128-129	Chpt. 20 as reqd	Chpt. 25 (in part)	Chpt. 34 as reqd	Chpt. 19	Chpt. 33 as reqd	Chpt. 17-19 as reqd	Chpt. 16
Diet and Animal Nutrition	pp. 47, 112-17, 165-168	Chpt. 2 as reqd	Chpt. 40-41	Chpt. 41	Chpt. 21	Chpt. 45	Chpt. 36	Chpt. 35 (in part)
Gas Exchange in Animals	pp. 51, 171-72	Chpt. 3 as reqd	Chpt. 40, & 48	Chpt. 42 as reqd.	Chpt. 22	Chpt. 44 (in part)	Chpt. 37	Chpt. 37 (in part)
Animal Transport Systems	pp. 48, 169-70	Chpt. 7 as reqd	Chpt. 40 & 47	Chpt. 42 as reqd	Chpt. 23	Chpt. 44 (in part)	Chpt. 34	Chpt. 37 (in part)
Reproduction and Development	pp. 54-57, 90-94	Chpt. 12 as reqd	Chpt. 50-51	Chpt. 46 & 47 (in part)	Chpt. 27	Chpt. 48	Chpt. 43-44	Chpt. 38
Homeostasis and Excretion	pp. 53, 104-106, 164	Chpt. 3 as reqd	Chpt. 42, 49-50	Chpt. 44	Chpt. 25-26	Chpt. 41-42, 47	Chpt. 33 & 38	Chpt. 35 & 37 (both in part)
Nerves, Muscles, and Movement	pp. 99-102, 118-21, 135, 137, 140-41	Chpt. 21 as reqd	Chpt.40 & 46	Chpt.48-49	Chpt. 28 & 30	Chpt. 45-46 as reqd	Chpt. 39 & 41	Chpt. 34 & 36
Animal Behavior	pp. 134,136, 138-139	Chpt. 22 as reqd	Chpt. 55	Chpt. 51	Chpt.35	Chpt. 5	Chpt. 45	Chpt. 33
Plant Structure and Adaptation	pp. 107-109	Chpt. 7 & 11	Chpt. 8, 30-31, 35, 37-38	Chpt. 35-37	Chpt. 31-32	Chpt. 35-37	Chpt. 25	Chpt. 22-23
Plant Responses and Reproduction	pp. 110, 148, 151-152	Chpt. 11-12	Chpt. 39	Chpt. 38-39	Chpt. 32-33	Chpt. 38-40	Chpt. 27-28	Chpt. 24
Microbes and Biotechnology	p. 28	Chpt. 15	Chpt. 19-20	N/A	N/A	Chpt. 19-20 (in part)	Chpt. 16	Chpt. 13

Textbook Reference Grid

TOPIC IN WORKBOOK	Raven & Johnson 2008	Sadava et al. 2007	Solomon et al. 2008	Starr 2006	Starr & Taggart 2006	Tobin & Dusheck 2005	Towle 2005	Weem 2001
Pathogens and Disease	Chpt. 28, 30 & 50 (all in part)	Chpt. 30 (in part)	Chpt. 24-26 (in part) & 44	Chpt. 19-20 (in part)	Chpt. 21	Chpt. 12 & 20	Chpt. 23-26	pp. 123-124
Defense Against Infectious Disease	Chpt. 51	Chpt. 18	Chpt. 44	Chpt. 34	Chpt. 39	Chpt. 41	Chpt. 47	pp. 125-126, 214-219
The Origin and Evolution of Life	Chpt. 21 (in part)	Chpt. 21	Chpt. 21	Chpt. 18	Chpt. 20	Chpt. 18	Chpt. 14	pp. 314-328
Speciation	Chpt. 21	Chpt. 22-23	Chpt. 18-20	Chpt. 16	Chpt. 17-19	Chpt. 15-17 (in part)	Chpt. 15-16	pp. 98-100, 339-342
Patterns of Evolution	Chpt. 21	Chpt. 22-23	Chpt. 20	Chpt. 16-17	Chpt. 19	Chpt. 17	Chpt. 15-16	pp. 326-328, 321-332 & 339
Human Evolution	Chpt. 35 (in part)	Chpt. 31 (in part)	Chpt. 22	Chpt. 23 (in part)	Chpt. 26 (in part)	Chpt. 17 (in part)	Chpt. 16	pp. 329-335
Diet and Animal Nutrition	Chpt. 48	Chpt. 50	Chpt. 46	Chpt. 36	Chpt. 41	Chpt. 36	Chpt. 48	pp. 258-276, 431-438
Gas Exchange in Animals	Chpt. 49	Chpt. 48	Chpt. 45	Chpt. 35	Chpt. 40	Chpt. 39	Chpt. 46	pp. 127-131, 445-450
Animal Transport Systems	Chpt. 49	Chpt. 49	Chpt. 43	Chpt. 33	Chpt. 38	Chpt. 38	Chpt. 46	pp. 439-444
Reproduction and Development	Chpt. 52-53	Chpt. 42-43	Chpt. 49-50	Chpt. 38	Chpt. 43-44	Chpt. 44	Chpt. 51	pp. 136-143, 204-209
Homeostasis and Excretion	Chpt. 43, 46, & 50	Chpt. 40 & 51	Chpt. 47	Chpt. 28	Chpt. 33 (in part), 36, 42	Chpt. 37 (in part), & 40	Chpt. 5, 48 & 50	pp. 132-136, 234-239
Nerves, Muscles, and Movement	Chpt. 44 & 47	Chpt. 44, 46 -47	Chpt. 39-41	Chpt. 29 & 32	Chpt. 34-35, 37	Chpt. 34-35 & 42-43	Chpt. 45 & 49	pp. 222-230, 278-292, 349-354, 364-368
Animal Behavior	Chpt. 54	Chpt. 53	Chpt. 51	Chpt. 38	Chpt. 49	Chpt. 29	Chpt. 44	pp. 346-348, 355-363
Plant Structure and Adaptation	Chpt. 36, 38	Chpt. 34-36	Chpt. 27-28, 33-34	Chpt. 25 - 26	Chpt. 29-30	Chpt. 30-31	Chpt. 29-30	pp. 242-250, 373-375
Plant Responses and Reproduction	Chpt. 41-42	Chpt. 38-39	Chpt. 36	Chpt. 27	Chpt. 32-33	Chpt. 32-33	Chpt. 30-31	pp. 251-255, 382-384
Microbes and Biotechnology	Chpt. 17	Chpt. 16	Chpt. 15	N/A	N/A	N/A	Chpt. 13	N/A

Using the Internet

The internet is a powerful resource for locating information. There are several key areas of Biozone's web site that may be of interest to you. Go to the **BioLinks** area to browse through the hundreds of web sites hosted by other organizations. These sites provide a supplement to the activities provided in our workbooks and have been selected on the basis of their accurate, current, and relevant content. We have also provided links to biology-related **podcasts** and **RSS newsfeeds**. These provide regularly updated information about new discoveries in biology; perfect for those wanting to keep abreast of changes in this dynamic field.

The BIOZONE website: www.thebiozone.com

The current internet address (URL) for the web site is displayed here. You can type a new address directly into this space.

Use Google to search for web sites of interest. The more precise your search words are, the better the list of results. EXAMPLE. If you type in "biotechnology", your search will return an overwhelmingly large number of sites, many of which will not be useful to you. Be more specific, e.g. "biotechnology medicine DNA uses".

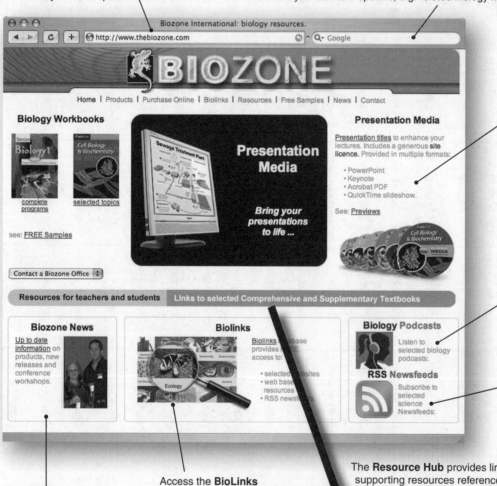

Find out about our superb **Presentation Media**. These slide shows are designed to provide in-depth, highly accessible illustrative material and notes on specific areas of biology.

Podcasts: Access the latest news as audio files (mp3) that may be downloaded to your ipod (mp3 player) or played directly off your computer.

RSS Newsfeeds: See breaking news and major new discoveries in biology directly from our web site.

Access the **BioLinks** database of web sites related to each major area of biology.

News: Find out about product announcements, shipping dates, and workshops and trade displays by Biozone at teachers' conferences around the world.

The **Resource Hub** provides links to the supporting resources referenced in the workbook. These resources include comprehensive and supplementary texts, biology dictionaries, computer software, videos, and science supplies.

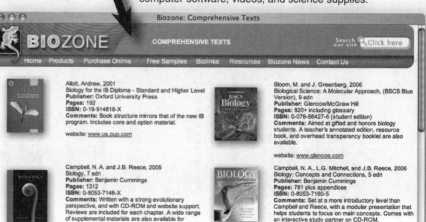

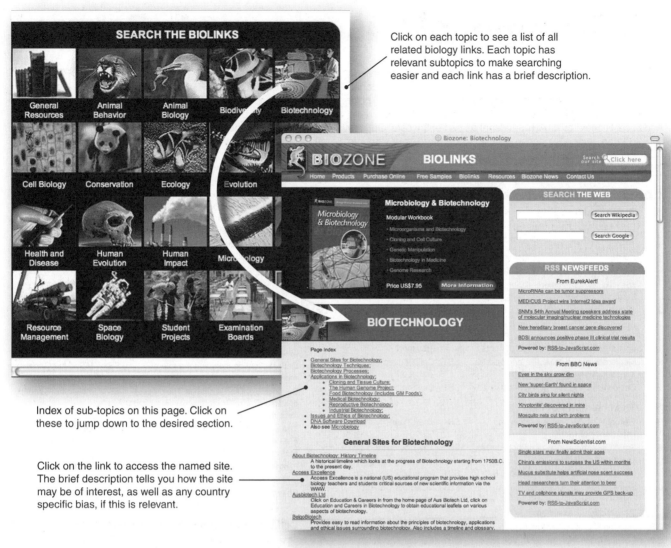

Click on each topic to see a list of all related biology links. Each topic has relevant subtopics to make searching easier and each link has a brief description.

Index of sub-topics on this page. Click on these to jump down to the desired section.

Click on the link to access the named site. The brief description tells you how the site may be of interest, as well as any country specific bias, if this is relevant.

Weblinks:

Go to: **www.thebiozone.com/weblink/SB1-9665.html**

Throughout this workbook, some pages make reference to additional or alternative activities, as well as web sites that have particular relevance to the activity. See example of page reference below:

Related activities: Plant Cells, Animal Cells
Web links: Eukaryotic Cells Interactive Animation   **RA 2**

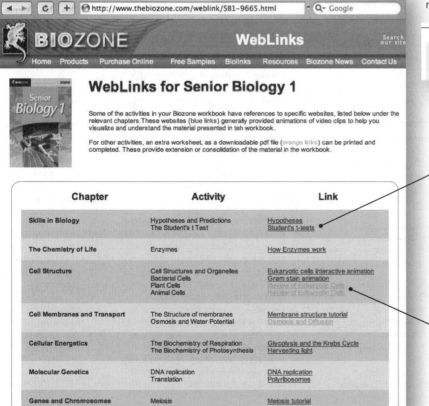

Web Link: provides a link to an **external web site** with supporting information for the activity

Web Link: provides a link to a downloadable **Acrobat (PDF) file** which may provide an additional activity or a different activity with an alternative set of features.

International Baccalaureate Course

The International Baccalaureate (IB) diploma biology course is divided into three sections: core, additional higher level material, and option material. All **IB candidates** must complete the **core** topics. Higher level students are also required to undertake Additional Higher Level (**AHL**) material as part of the core. Options fall into three categories: those specific to standard level students (**OPT-SL**), those specific to higher level students (**OPT-HL**), and those offered to both (**OPT-SL/HL**). All candidates are required to study two options. All candidates must also carry out **practical work** and must participate in the **group 4 project**. In the guide below, we have indicated where the relevant material can be found: SB1 for Senior Biology 1 and SB2 for Senior Biology 2.

Topic		See workbook
CORE:	*(All students)*	
1	**Statistical analysis**	
1.1	Error bars. Mean and standard deviation. Comparing means, t-test, correlation.	SB1 Skills in Biology
2	**Cells**	
2.1	Cell theory. Cell and organelle sizes. Cell specialization and differentiation. SA:V. Emergent properties. Stem cells.	SB1 Cell Structure, Cell Membranes and Transport
2.2	Prokaryotic cells: ultrastructure & function.	SB1 Cell Structure
2.3	Eukaryotic cells: ultrastructure & function. Prokaryotic vs eukaryotic cells. Plant vs animal cells. Extracellular components.	SB1 Cell Structure, Cell Membranes and Transport
2.4	Membrane structure. Active and passive transport. Diffusion and osmosis.	SB1 Cell Membranes and Transport
2.5	Cell division and the origins of cancer.	SB1 Cell Structure
3	**The chemistry of life**	
3.1	Elements of life. The properties and importance of water.	SB1 The Chemistry of Life
3.2	Structure and function of carbohydrates, lipids, and proteins.	SB1 The Chemistry of Life
3.3	Nucleotides and the structure of DNA.	SB1 Molecular Genetics
3.4	Semi-conservative DNA replication.	SB1 Molecular Genetics
3.5	RNA and DNA structure. The genetic code. Transcription. Translation.	SB1 Molecular Genetics
3.6	Enzyme structure and function.	SB1 The Chemistry of Life
3.7	Cellular respiration and ATP production.	SB1 Cellular Energetics
3.8	Biochemistry of photosynthesis. Factors affecting photosynthetic rates.	SB1 Cellular Energetics
4	**Genetics**	
4.1	Eukaryote chromosomes. Genomes. Gene mutations and consequences.	SB1 Genes and Chromosomes
4.2	Meiosis and non-disjunction. Karyotyping and pre-natal diagnosis.	SB1 Genes and Chromosomes
4.3	Theoretical genetics: alleles and single gene inheritance, sex linkage, pedigrees.	SB1 Inheritance
4.4	Genetic engineering and biotechnology: PCR, gel electrophoresis, DNA profiling. HGP. Transformation. GMOs. Cloning.	SB1 Gene Technology
5	**Ecology and evolution**	
5.1	Ecosystems. Food chains and webs. Trophic levels. Ecological pyramids. The role of decomposers in recycling nutrients.	SB1 Ecosystems, Energy Flow and Nutrient Cycles
5.2	The greenhouse effect. The carbon cycle. Precautory principle. Global warming.	SB1 Human Impact and Conservation
5.3	Factors influencing population size. Population growth.	SB1 The Dynamics of Populations
5.4	Genetic variation. Sexual reproduction as a source of variation in species. Evidence for evolution: natural selection. Evolution in response to environmental change.	SB1 Genes and Chromosomes, SB2 The Origin and Evolution of Life, Speciation
5.5	Classification. Binomial nomenclature. Features of plant & animal phyla. Keys.	SB1 Classification
6	**Human health and physiology**	
6.1	Role of enzymes in digestion. Structure and function of the digestive system.	SB2 Diet and Animal Nutrition
6.2	Structure and function of the heart. The control of heart activity. Blood & vessels.	SB2 Animal Transport Systems
6.3	Pathogens and their transmission. Antibiotics. Role of skin as a barrier to infection. Role of phagocytic leucocytes. Antigens & antibody production. HIV/AIDS.	SB2 Pathogens and Disease, Defense Against Infectious Disease
6.4	Gas exchange. Ventilation systems. Control of breathing.	SB2 Gas Exchange in Animals

Topic		See workbook
6.5	Principles of homeostasis. Control of body temperature and blood glucose. Diabetes. Role of the nervous and endocrine systems in homeostasis. Nervous system.	SB2 Homeostasis and Excretion, Nerves, Muscles and Movement
6.6	Human reproduction: urinogenital systems. Role of hormones in the menstrual cycle. Testosterone roles in males. Reproductive technologies and ethical issues.	SB2 Reproduction and Development
COMPULSORY:	**AHL Topics** *(HL students only)*	
7	**Nucleic acids and proteins**	
7.1	DNA structure: nucleosomes, purines, pyrimidines. Exons & introns ('junk' DNA)	SB1 Molecular Genetics
7.2	DNA replication including the role of enzymes and Okazaki fragments.	SB1 Molecular Genetics
7.3	Sense and antisense strands. The process of transcription. The removal of introns to form mature mRNA.	SB1 Molecular Genetics
7.4	The structure of tRNA and ribosomes. Free and bound ribosomes. The process of translation. Peptide bond.	SB1 Molecular Genetics, The Chemistry of Life
7.5	Protein structure and function. Fibrous and globular proteins.	SB1 The Chemistry of Life
7.6	Enzymes: induced fit model. Inhibition. Allostery in the control of metabolism.	SB1 The Chemistry of Life
8	**Cell respiration and photosynthesis**	
8.1	Structure and function of mitochondria. Biochemistry of cellular respiration.	SB1 Cellular Energetics
8.2	Chloroplasts, the biochemistry of photosynthesis, chemiosmosis. Action and absorption spectra. Limiting factors.	SB1 Cellular Energetics
9	**Plant science**	
9.1	Structure and growth of a dicot plant. Function and distribution of tissues in leaves. Dicots vs monocots. Plant modifications. Auxins.	SB2 Plant Structure and Adaptation, Plant Responses and Reproduction
9.2	Support in terrestrial plants. Transport in angiosperms: ion movement through soil, active ion uptake by roots, transpiration, translocation. Abscisic acid. Xerophytes.	SB2 Plant Structure and Adaptation
9.3	Dicot flowers. Pollination and fertilization. Seeds: structure, germination, dispersal. Flowering and phytochrome.	SB2 Plant Responses and Reproduction
10	**Genetics**	
10.1	Meiosis, and the process of crossing over. Mendel's law of independent assortment.	SB1 Genes and Chromosomes
10.2	Dihybrid crosses in unlinked and linked genes. Autosomes and sex chromosomes.	SB1 Inheritance
10.3	Polygenic inheritance.	SB1 Inheritance
11	**Human health and physiology**	
11.1	Blood clotting. Clonal selection. Acquired immunity. Antibodies and monoclonal antibodies. Vaccination.	SB2 Defense Against Infectious Disease
11.2	Locomotion in animals. Roles of nerves, muscles, and bones in movement. Joints. Skeletal muscle and contraction.	SB2 Nerves, Muscles and Movement
11.3	Excretion. Structure and function of the human kidney. Urine production. Diabetes.	SB2 Homeostasis and Excretion
11.4	Testis structure and spermatogenesis. Ovarian structure and oogenesis. Fertilization and embryonic development. Structure and function of the placenta. Birth. Role of hormones.	SB2 Reproduction and Development

Topic		See workbook

OPTIONS: OPT - SL (SL students only)

A   Human nutrition and health

A.1 Main constituents of diet. Balanced diet. Malnutrition. Deficiency diseases. Dietary supplements.
PKU.

SB2 Diet and Animal Nutrition
SB1 Molecular Genetics

A.2 Energy content of food types. BMI. Obesity and anorexia. Appetite control center.

SB2 Diet and Animal Nutrition

A.3 Special issues include breastfeeding vs bottle-feeding, type II diabetes, vegans, unhealthy cholesterol, food miles.

SB2 Aspects covered in Diet and Animal Nutrition

B   Physiology of exercise

B.1 Locomotion in animals. Roles of nerves, muscles, and bones in movement. Joints. Skeletal muscle and contraction.

SB2 Nerves, Muscles and Movement

B.2 Training and the pulmonary system.
SB2 Gas Exchange

B.3 Training and the cardiovascular system.
SB2 Transport Systems

B.4 Respiration and exercise intensity. Roles of myoglobin and adrenaline. Oxygen debt and lactate in muscle fatigue.

SB2 Nerve, Muscles and Movement, Gas Exchange

B.5 Exercise induced injuries and treatment.
Not yet covered

C   Cells and energy

C.1 Protein structure and function. Fibrous and globular proteins.

SB1 The Chemistry of Life

C.2 Enzymes: induced fit model. Inhibition. Allostery in the control of metabolism.

SB1 The Chemistry of Life

C.3 Biochemistry of cellular respiration.
SB1 Cellular Energetics.

C.4 The biochemistry of photosynthesis including chemiosmosis. Action and absorption spectra. Limiting factors.

SB1 Cellular Energetics

OPTIONS: OPT - SL/HL (SL and HL students)

D   Evolution

D.1 Prebiotic experiments. Comets. Protobionts and prokaryotes. Endosymbiotic theory.

SB2 The Origin and Evolution of Life

D.2 Species and gene pools. Speciation. Divergent and convergent evolution. Pace of evolution. Transient vs balanced polymorphism.

SB2 Speciation, Patterns of Evolution

D.3 Fossil dating. Primate features. Hominid features. Diet and brain size correlation. Genetic and cultural evolution.

SB2 Patterns of Evolution

D.4-D.5 is extension for HL only

D.4 The Hardy-Weinberg principle.
SB2 Speciation

D.5 Classification. Biochemical evidence for evolution. Biochemical variations indicating phylogeny. Cladistics and cladograms.

SB1 Classification
SB2 The Origin and evolution of Life

E   Neurobiology and behavior

E.1 Stimuli, responses and reflexes in the context of animal behavior. Animal responses and natural selection.

SB2 Nerves, Muscles and Movement, Animal Behavior

E.2 Sensory receptors. Structure and function of the human eye and ear.

SB2 Nerves, Muscles and Movement

E.3 Innate vs learned behavior and its role in survival. Types of learned behavior. Development of birdsong.

SB2 Animal Behavior

E.4 Presynaptic neurons at synapses. Examples of excitatory and inhibitory psychoactive drugs. Effects of drugs on synaptic transmission. Causes of addiction.

SB2 Aspects covered in Nerves, Muscles and Movement

E.5-E.6 is extension for HL only

E.5 Structure and function of the human brain. ANS control. Pupil reflex and its use in testing for death. Hormones as painkillers.

SB2 Aspects covered in Nerves, Muscles and Movement

E.6 Social behavior and organization. The role of altruism in sociality. Foraging behavior. Mate selection. Rhythmical behavior.

SB2 Animal Behavior

F   Microbes and Biotechnology

F.1 Classification. Diversity of Archaea and Eubacteria. Diversity of viruses. Diversity of microscopic eukaryotes.

SB1 Classification, Cell Structure

F.2 Roles of microbes in ecosystems. Details of the nitrogen cycle including the role of bacteria. Sewage. Biofuels.

SB1 Energy Flow and Nutrient Cycles, Human Impact and Conservation

F.3 Reverse transcription. Somatic vs germ line gene therapy. Viral vectors.

SB1 Aspects of Gene Technology

F.4 Microbes involved in food production of beer, wine, bread, and soy sauce. Food preservation. Food poisoning.

SB1 Aspects of Gene Technology,
SB2 Pathogens & Disease

F.5-F.6 is extension for HL only

F.5 Metabolism of microbes. Modes of nutrition. Cyanobacterium. Bioremediation.

SB2 Diet and Animal Nutrition

F.6 Pathogens and disease: influenza virus, malaria, bacterial infections. Controlling microbes. Epidemiology. Prion hypothesis.

SB2 Pathogens & Disease, Defense Against Infectious Disease

G   Ecology and conservation

G.1 Factors affecting plant and animal distribution. Sampling. Ecological niche and the competitive exclusion principle. Species interactions. Measuring biomass.

SB1 Ecosystems, The Dynamics of Populations, Practical Ecology

G.2 Trophic levels. Ecological pyramids. Primary vs secondary succession. Biome vs biosphere. Plant productivity (includes calculating gross and net production, and biomass).

SB1 Ecosystems, Energy Flow and Nutrient Cycles
SB2 Plant Structure and Adaptation

G.3 Conservation of biodiversity. The Simpson diversity index. Human impact on ecosystems: alien species. Biological control. Effect of CFCs on ozone layer. UV radiation absorption.

SB1 Ecosystems, Human Impact and Conservation

G.4-G.5 is extension for HL only

G.4 Monitoring environmental change. Conservation of biodiversity. Endangered species. Nature reserves. Monitoring environmental change.
Extinction.

SB1 Human Impact and Conservation

SB2 Patterns of Evolution

G.5 *r*-strategies and K-strategies. Mark-and-recapture sampling. Fisheries conservation.

SB1 The Dynamics of Populations, Practical Ecology, Human Impact and Conservation

OPTION: OPT - HL (HL students only)

H   Further human physiology

H.1 Hormones and their modes of action. Hypothalamus and pituitary gland. Control of ADH secretion.

SB2 Homeostasis and Excretion

H.2 Digestion and digestive juices. Stomach ulcers and stomach cancers. Role of bile.

SB2 Diet and Animal Nutrition

H.3 Structure of villus. Absorption of nutrients and transport of digested food.

SB2 Diet and Animal Nutrition

H.4 The structure and function of the liver (including role in nutrient processing and detoxification). Liver damage from alcohol.

SB2 Homeostasis and Excretion, also Diet and Animal Nutrition

H.5 The cardiac cycle and control of heart rhythm. Atherosclerosis, coronary thrombosis and coronary heart disease.

SB2 Animal Transport System

H.6 Gas exchange: oxygen dissociation curves and the Bohr shift. Ventilation rate and exercise. Breathing at high altitude.

SB2 Gas Exchange in Animals

Causes and effects of asthma.

SB2 Defense Against Infectious Disease

Practical Work (All students)

Practical work consists of short and long term investigations, and an interdisciplinary project (The Group 4 project). Also see the "Guide to Practical Work" on the last page of this introductory section.

Short and long term investigations

Investigations should reflect the breadth and depth of the subjects taught at each level, and include a spread of content material from the core, options, and AHL material, where relevant.

The Group 4 project

All candidates must participate in the group 4 project. In this project it is intended that students analyze a topic or problem suitable for investigation in each of the science disciplines offered by the school (not just in biology). This project emphasizes the processes involved in scientific investigations rather than the products of an investigation.

Introduction

Advanced Placement Course

The Advanced Placement (AP) biology course is designed to be equivalent to a college introductory biology course. It is designed to be taken by students after successful completion of first courses in high school biology and chemistry. In the guide below, we have indicated where the relevant material can be found: SB1 for Senior Biology 1 and SB2 for Senior Biology 2. Because of the general nature of the AP curriculum document, the detail given is based on the content of the workbooks.

Topic	See workbook

Topic I: Molecules and Cells

A   Chemistry of life

1	The chemical & physical properties of water. The importance of water to life.	SB1	The Chemistry of Life
2	The role of carbon. Structure and function of carbohydrates, lipids, nucleic acids, and proteins. The synthesis and breakdown of macromolecules.	SB1	The Chemistry of Life, Molecular Genetics, Cell Membranes and Transport
3	The laws of thermodynamics and their relationship to biochemical processes. Free energy changes.	SB1	The Chemistry of Life
4	The action of enzymes and their role in the regulation of metabolism. Enzyme specificity. Factors affecting enzyme activity. Applications of enzymes.	SB1	The Chemistry of Life

B   Cells

1	Comparison of prokaryotic and eukaryotic cells, including their evolutionary relationships.	SB1 SB2	Cell Structure, The Origin and Evolution of Life
2	Membrane structure: fluid mosaic model. Active and passive transport.	SB1	Cell Membranes and Transport
3	Structure and function of organelles. Organization of cell function. Comparison of plant and animal cells. Cell size and surface area: volume ratio.	SB1	Cell Structure, Cell Membranes and Transport
4	Mitosis and the cell cycle. Mechanisms of cytokinesis. Cancer (tumor formation) as the result of uncontrolled cell division.	SB1	Cell Structure

C   Cellular energetics

1	Nature and role of ATP. Anabolic and catabolic processes. Chemiosmosis.	SB1	Cellular Energetics
2	Structure and function of mitochondria. Biochemistry of cellular respiration, including the role of oxygen in energy yielding pathways. Anaerobic generation of ATP.	SB1	Cellular Energetics
3	Structure and function of chloroplasts. The biochemistry of photosynthesis. Adaptations for photosynthesis in different environments.	SB1	Cellular Energetics

Topic II: Heredity and Evolution

A   Heredity

1	The importance of meiosis in heredity. Gametogenesis. Similarities and differences between gametogenesis in animals and plants.	SB1 SB2	Genes and Chromosomes Reproduction and Development, Plant Responses and Reproduction
2	Structure of eukaryotic chromosomes. Heredity of genetic information.	SB1	Genes and Chromosomes
3	Mendel's laws. Inheritance patterns.	SB1	Inheritance

B   Molecular genetics

1	RNA and DNA structure and function. Eukaryotic and prokaryotic genomes.	SB1	Molecular Genetics
2	Gene expression in prokaryotes and eukaryotes. The *Lac* operon model.	SB1	Molecular Genetics
3	Causes of mutations. Gene mutations (e.g. sickle cell disease). Chromosomal mutations (e.g. Down syndrome).	SB1	Genes and Chromosomes
4	Viral structure and replication.	SB2	Pathogens and Disease
5	Nucleic acid technology and applications. legal and ethical issues.	SB1	Gene Technology

Topic	See workbook

C   Evolutionary biology

1	The origins of life on Earth. Prebiotic experiments. Origins of prokaryotic cells. Endosymbiotic theory.	SB2	The Origin and Evolution of Life
2	Evidence for evolution: comparative anatomy, vestigial organs, biochemistry, biogeography. Dating of fossils.	SB2	The Origin and Evolution of Life
3	Mechanisms of evolution: natural selection, speciation, macroevolution. The species concept.	SB2 SB1	Speciation, Patterns of Evolution Classification

Topic III: Organisms and Populations

A   Diversity of organisms

1	Evolutionary patterns: major body plans of plants and animals.	SB1	Classification
2	Diversity of life: representative members from the five kingdoms Monera (=Prokaryotae), Fungi, Protista (=Protoctista), Animalia and Plantae.	SB1	Classification
3	Phylogenetic classification. Binomial nomenclature. Five kingdom classification. Use of dichotomous keys.	SB1	Classification
4	Evolutionary relationships: genetic and morphological characters. Phylogenies.	SB1 SB2	Classification The Origin and Evolution of Life

B   Structure and function of plants and animals

1	Plant and animal reproduction and development (includes humans). Adaptive significance of reproductive features and their regulation.	SB2	Reproduction and Development, Plant Responses and Reproduction
2	Organization of cells, tissues & organs.	SB1	Cell Structure
	The structure and function of animal and plant organ systems. Adaptive features that have contributed to the success of plants and animals in occupying particular terrestrial niches.	SB2	Plant Structure and Adaptation, Diet and Animal Nutrition, Animal Transport Systems, Homeostasis and Excretion, Gas Exchange in Animals
3	Plant and animal responses to environmental cues. The role of hormones in these responses.	SB2	Animal Behavior, Plant Responses and Reproduction

C   Ecology

1	Factors influencing population size. Population growth curves.	SB1	The Dynamics of Populations
2	Abiotic and biotic factors: effects on community structure and ecosystem function. Trophic levels: energy flows through ecosystems and relationship to trophic structure. Nutrient cycles.	SB1	Ecosystems, Energy Flow and Nutrient Cycles
3	Human influence on biogeochemical cycles: (e.g. use of fertilizers).	SB1	Human Impact and Conservation

Practical Work

Integrated practicals as appropriate: see Senior Biology 1: Skills in Biology. Also see the page "Guide to Practical Work" on the last page of this introductory section.

Guide to Practical Work

A practical or laboratory component is an essential part of any biology course, especially at senior level. It is through your practical sessions that you are challenged to carry out experiments drawn from many areas within modern biology. Both AP and IB courses have a strong practical component, aimed at providing a framework for your laboratory experience. Well executed laboratory and field sessions will help you to understand problems, observe accurately, make hypotheses, design and implement controlled experiments, collect and analyze data, think analytically, and communicate your findings in an appropriate way using tables and graphs. The outline below provides some guidelines for AP and IB students undertaking their practical work. Be sure to follow required safety procedures at all times during practical work.

International Baccalaureate Practical Work

The practical work carried out by IB biology students should reflect the depth and breadth of the subject syllabus, although there may not be an investigation for every syllabus topic. All candidates must participate in the group 4 project, and the internal assessment (IA) requirements should be met via a spread of content from the core, options and, where relevant, AHL material. A wide range of IA investigations is possible: *short laboratory practicals and longer term practicals or projects, computer simulations, data gathering and analysis exercises, and general laboratory and field work.*

Suitable material, or background preparation, for this component can be found in this workbook and its companion title, Senior Biology 2.

College Board's AP® Biology Lab Topics

Each of the 12 set laboratory sessions in the AP course is designed to complement a particular topic area within the course. The basic structure of the lab course is outlined below:

LAB 1: Diffusion and osmosis
Overview: To investigate diffusion and osmosis in dialysis tubing. To investigate the effect of solute concentration on water potential (ψ) in plant tissues.
Aims: An understanding of passive transport mechanisms in cells, and an understanding of the concept of water potential, solute potential, and pressure potential, and how these are measured.

LAB 2: Enzyme catalysis
Overview: To investigate the conversion of hydrogen peroxide to water and oxygen gas by catalase.
Aims: An understanding of the effects of environmental factors on the rate of enzyme catalyzed reactions.

LAB 3: Mitosis and meiosis
Overview: To use prepared slides of onion root tips to study plant mitosis. To simulate the phases of meiosis by using chromosome models.
Aims: Recognition of stages in mitosis in plant cells and calculation of relative duration of cell cycle stages. An understanding of chromosome activity during meiosis and an ability to calculate map distances for genes.

LAB 4: Plant pigments and photosynthesis
Overview: To separate plant pigments using chromatography. To measure photosynthetic rate in chloroplasts.
Aims: An understanding of Rf values. An understanding of the techniques used to determine photosynthetic rates. An ability to explain variations in photosynthetic rate under different environmental conditions.

LAB 5: Cell(ular) respiration
Overview: To investigate oxygen consumption during germination (including the effect of temperature).
Aims: An understanding of how cell respiration rates can be calculated from experimental data. An understanding of the relationship between gas production and respiration rate, and the effect of temperature on this.

LAB 6: Molecular biology
Overview: To investigate the basic principles of molecular biology through the transformation of *E.coli* cells. To investigate the use of restriction digestion and gel electrophoresis.
Aims: An understanding of the role of plasmids as vectors, and the use of gel electrophoresis to separate DNA fragments of varying size. An ability to design appropriate experimental procedures and use multiple experimental controls.

LAB 7: Genetics of organisms
Overview: Use *Drosophila* to perform genetic crosses. To collect and analyze the data from these crosses.
Aims: An understanding of the independent assortment of two genes and an ability to determine if genes are autosomal or sex linked from the analysis of the results of multigeneration genetic crosses.

LAB 8: Population genetics and evolution
Overview: To learn about the Hardy-Weinberg law of genetic equilibrium and study the relationship between evolution and changes in allele frequency.
Aims: An ability to calculate allele and genotype frequencies using the Hardy-Weinberg formula. An understanding of natural selection and other causes of microevolution.

LAB 9: Transpiration
Overview: To investigate transpiration in plants under controlled conditions. To examine the organization of plant stems and leaves as they relate to this.
Aims: An understanding of the effects of environmental variables on transpiration rates. An understanding of the relationship between the structure and function of the tissues involved.

LAB 10: Physiology of the circulatory system
Overview: To measure (human) blood pressure and pulse rate under different conditions. To analyze these variables and relate them to an index of fitness. To investigate the effect of temperature on heart rate in *Daphnia*.
Aims: An understanding of blood pressure and pulse rate, and their measurement and significance with respect to fitness. An understanding of the relationship between heart rate and temperature in a poikilotherm.

LAB 11: Animal behavior
Overview: To investigate responses in pillbugs (woodlice). To investigate mating behavior in fruit flies.
Aims: To understand and describe aspects of animal behavior. To understand the adaptiveness of appropriate behaviors.

LAB 12: Dissolved oxygen & aquatic primary productivity
Overview: To measure & analyze dissolved oxygen concentration in water samples. To measure and analyze the primary productivity of natural waters or lab cultures.
Aims: An understanding of primary productivity and its measurement. To use a controlled experiment to investigate the effect of changing light intensity on primary productivity.

Pathogens and Disease

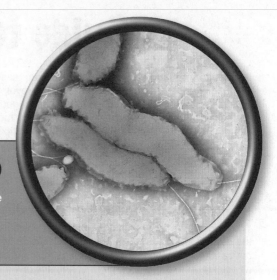

IB SL

Complete:
1-2, 5, 11-12, 29-30
Extension: 3-4, 8-10,
21-26, 31
as appropriate

IB HL

Complete:
1-2, 5, 11-12, 29-30
Extension: 3-4, 8-10,
21-26, 31
as appropriate

IB Options

Complete:
Option F:
HL: 3, 7, 10-11,
23, 27, 33

AP Biology

Not applicable
to AP biology

Learning Objectives

☐ 1. Compile your own glossary from the **KEY WORDS** displayed in **bold type** in the learning objectives below.

Infection and Disease

☐ 2. Distinguish between **infectious disease** and **non-infectious disease**. Define the terms **pathogen** and **infection**. Identify pathogens in different taxa including the bacteria, viruses, fungi, and protists.

Patterns of disease *(pages 20-21)*

☐ 3. Recognise patterns of disease distribution: **pandemic**, **epidemic**, and **endemic diseases**. Distinguish between **etiology** and **epidemiology**. Explain the role of health statistics (e.g. **incidence** and **mortality**) in predicting and managing disease outbreaks.

☐ 4. Describe and explain differences in the standards of health in developed and developing countries.

Treatment of disease *(pages 41-44)*

☐ 5. Understand the role of the following in the treatment or prevention of disease: **antibiotics**, therapeutic **anti-microbial drugs** (other than antibiotics), **hygiene**, **diet**. Discuss these in the context of a case study (#14-20).

Infectious Disease *(pages 18-19)*

☐ 6. Identify one example of a disease caused by a pathogenic member of each of the following taxa: **bacteria**, **viruses**, **fungi**, **protozoa**, **flatworms**, and **roundworms** (cross ref. with case studies).

☐ 7. List methods by which pathogens are **transmitted** and gain entry to the body. Identify the role of better hygiene and sanitation in controlling some infectious diseases.

Bacterial Diseases *(pages 29-33, 41-44)*

☐ 8. Recognize that bacteria are widespread and only a small proportion ever cause disease. Identify the ways in which pathogenic bacteria cause disease. Giving examples, identify the ways in which bacterial diseases are transmitted. Relate the type and incidence of bacterial disease to the prevailing social conditions.

☐ 9. Describe factors affecting bacterial **pathogenicity**, including features of the cell wall and capsule, **toxin** production, **infectivity**, and **invasiveness**.

☐ 10. Distinguish between different types of bacterial toxins and their actions: **exotoxins** (e.g. *Staphylococcus*) and **endotoxins** (e.g. *Salmonella*). Recognize **enterotoxins** as exotoxins that affect the gastrointestinal tract.

☐ 11. With reference to **disinfectants**, **antiseptics**, and **antibiotics**, explain how bacterial pathogens are controlled and treated.

☐ 12. Understand why antibiotics are not effective against viruses. Identify the ways in which different antibiotics work against specific bacteria. Describe the role of antibiotics in medicine and discuss the current problems associated with their use.

☐ 13. Describe the cause, transmission, and effects of one bacterial disease affecting humans. You could choose from the case studies below (#14-20), or use an example of a locally occurring disease.

Case study: tuberculosis (TB)

☐ 14. Describe the causes and modes of transmission of TB. Assess the global importance of TB and understand its history in the human population, including reference to its **prevalence**, decline, and reemergence.

☐ 15. Discuss the factors important in the prevalence of TB in a population. Define the term **carrier** and explain the importance of carriers in the spread of TB.

☐ 16. Discuss the treatment of TB, including the significance of increasing antibiotic resistance in *Mycobacterium*. Describe the roles of social, economic, and biological factors in the control and prevention of TB.

Contamination of food and water

☐ 17. Identify factors important in transmitting food and water-borne pathogens. Examples spread by the **fecal-oral route** include: *Salmonella* (e.g. *Salmonella typhi*), *Vibrio cholerae*, and *E. coli* (including *E. coli* O157:H7).

Case study: food poisoning

☐ 18. Describe the causes and modes of transmission of **salmonellosis** and/or **staphylococcal food poisoning**. Describe factors governing the occurrence, prevention, and severity of these diseases.

Case study: cholera

☐ 19. Describe the agent involved and modes of transmission of **cholera**. Assess the past and current global importance of cholera and relate its distribution to factors such as levels of sanitation and general poverty.

☐ 20. Describe the roles of social, economic, and biological factors in the control and prevention of cholera. Explain clearly how cholera of different severities is treated.

Fungal Diseases *(page 34)*

☐ 21. Only a few fungi are pathogenic to humans and most of the diseases they cause tend to be superficial diseases of the skin and nails. List and describe some common fungal diseases, identifying the pathogen in each case.

Protozoan Diseases *(pages 35-36)*

☐ 22. *Background:* Describe the nature of protozoa (ciliates, amoebae, sporozoans, and flagellates). Explain how some pathogenic **protozoans** are also parasites with part of their life cycle occurring within a human.

Case study: malaria

☐ 23. Describe the agent involved and modes of transmission of **malaria**. Assess the global importance of malaria and describe factors in its distribution.

☐ 24. Describe the roles of social, economic, and biological factors in the treatment, control, and prevention of malaria. Comment on the adequacy of these methods with reference to the difficulties associated with developing drugs against protozoans.

Multicellular Pathogens

(see the TRC: Multicellular Parasites)

☐ 25. Describe infection by a multicellular parasite e.g. *Schistosoma* or the hookworm *Necator*. Include reference to modes of transmission and life cycle.

☐ 26. Describe a modern example of an insect-carried infection of humans. Name some ectoparasites and the conditions or diseases for which they are responsible.

Viral Diseases *(pages 22-28 also see pages 61-62 and the TRC: Replication in Bacteriophages)*

☐ 27. Describe the host-specific, parasitic nature of viral pathogens. Using examples, describe how **viral diseases** are transmitted and how they cause disease.

☐ 28. Identify globally important viral diseases and their causative agents. Describe the role of **vaccination** in the past and present control of viral disease.

Case study: HIV/AIDS

☐ 29. Describe the cause, transmission, and social implications of **HIV/AIDS**. In your account:
  - Assess the global importance of HIV/AIDS and describe factors in its distribution and future spread.
  - Identify the role of social, economic, and biological factors in treating, controlling, and preventing AIDS.
  - Discuss the economic impact of the disease on the countries where incidence rates are very high.

☐ 30. Identify stages in the development of an HIV infection, including the effect of HIV on the immune system (cross ref. with *Defense Against Infectious Disease*).

☐ 31. Describe the probable origins of the two strains of HIV as cross species transfers (**zoonoses**).

Emerging Diseases *(pages 37-40)*

☐ 32. Explain what is meant by an **emerging disease**. Describing an appropriate example, identify factors important in the emergence, spread, and **virulence** of an emerging disease.

☐ 33. Describe the nature of **prion diseases**, identifying the feature that distinguishes them from other pathogens. Describe how prions are thought to cause disease. Give examples of prion diseases, describing their mode of transmission, incubation period, and mortality.

See the 'Textbook Reference Grid' on pages 8-9 for textbook page references relating to material in this topic.

Supplementary Texts
See pages 5-6 for additional details of these texts:

■ Clegg, C.J., 2002. **Microbes in Action**, (John Murray), chpt 1-5, and chpt 10.

■ Fullick, A., 1998. **Human Health and Disease** (Heinemann), pp. 2-26, 36-53 as required.

■ Helms, D.R. *et al.*, 1998. **Biology in the Laboratory** (W.H. Freeman), #6.

■ Hudson, T. & K. Mannion, 2001. **Microbes and Disease** (Collins), pp. 48-69, 82-85.

■ Murray, P. & N. Owens, 2001. **Behaviour and Populations** (Collins), pp. 72-95.

■ Taylor, J. 2001. **Microorganisms and Biotechnology** (NelsonThornes), chpt. 8.

See page 6 for details of publishers of periodicals:

STUDENT'S REFERENCE

■ **War on Disease** National Geographic 201(2) Feb. 2002, pp. 4-31. *An excellent update on the global importance of a range of infectious diseases.*

■ **Rules of Contagion** New Scientist, 28 Oct. 2006, pp. 44-47. *The different levels of virulence of infectious diseases and which are the most deadly.*

■ **Viral Plagues** Biol. Sci. Rev., 17(3) Feb. 2005, pp. 37-41. *The nature of viruses and viral transmission, how viral infections are diagnosed, and what we can do to combat them.*

■ *Campylobacter jejuni* Biol. Sci. Rev., 15(1) Sept. 2002, pp. 26-28. *An account of the diseases caused by Campylobacter, an increasingly common contaminant. Preventative measures are discussed.*

■ **Campylobacter ...on the Run!** Biol. Sci. Rev., 19(3) Feb. 2007, pp. 7-9. *A look at the physical characteristics of this food-contaminating bacterium.*

■ **Koch's Postulates** Biol. Sci. Rev., 15(3) Feb. 2003, pp. 24-25. *Koch's postulates and the diagnosis of infectious disease.*

■ **HIV and AIDS Update** Biol. Sci. Rev., 14(1) Sept. 2001, pp. 37-40. *A summary of the recent knowledge on HIV/AIDS.*

■ **Search for a Cure** National Geographic 201(2) Feb. 2002, pp. 32-43. *A current account of the global status of the AIDS epidemic, and an examination of the measures to stop it.*

■ **New Medicines for the Developing World** Biol. Sci. Rev., 14(1) Sept. 2001, pp. 22-26. *The challenges of controlling and treating infectious disease in the developing world.*

■ **Food / How Safe?** National Geographic, May 2002, pp. 2-31. *An excellent account of the issue of food safety and bacterial contamination of food.*

■ **The White Plague** New Scientist (Inside Science), 9 Nov. 2002. *The causes and nature of TB, an update on the global incidence of this disease, and a discussion of the implications of increasing drug resistance to TB treatment.*

■ **Tuberculosis** Biol. Sci. Rev., 14(1) Sept. 2001, pp. 30-33. *Despite vaccination, TB has become more common recently. Why has it returned?*

■ **Beating the Bloodsuckers** Biol. Sci. Rev., 16(3) Feb. 2004, pp. 31-35. *The global distribution of malaria, the current state of malaria research, and an account of the biology of the Plasmodium parasite and the body's immune response to it.*

■ **Malaria** Biol. Sci. Rev., 15(1) Sept. 2002, pp. 29-33. *An account of the the world's most important parasitic infection of humans. Symptoms, prevention and control, and treatment options are discussed.*

■ **Global BSE Crisis: Special Report** New Scientist, 7 Aug. 2004, pp. 32-41. *A series of short articles examining the current state of the BSE epidemic: threats to humans and known and likely distributions of the disease globally.*

TEACHER'S REFERENCE

■ **Positive Progress** New Scientist, 8 Feb. 2003, pp. 33-45. *A series of articles focusing on current issues in HIV research: the latest in vaccine development, and new measures against infection.*

■ **Hope in a Vial** Scientific American, June 2002, pp. 28-35. *The search for an AIDS vaccine, current research and the status of global infection rates.*

■ **Will there ever be a Malaria Vaccine** Biol. Sci. Rev., 19(1), Sept. 2006, pp. 24-28. *Outline of the three categories of malarial vaccine development.*

■ **To Kill a Superbug** New Scientist, 13 Feb. 1999, pp. 34-37. *New technology to counter the increasing antibiotic resistance in bacteria.*

■ **Epidemiology: Teaching the Fundamentals** The Am. Biology Teacher, 62(1), Jan. 2000, pp. 8-17. *Using computer simulations to model patterns of infection and spread of disease.*

■ **Is TB in your Curriculum?** The Am. Biology Teacher, 64(4), April 2002, pp. 280-284. *A look at TB: symptoms, epidemiology, and treatment.*

■ **The Infection Dynamics of a Hypothetical Virus in a High School: Use of an Ultraviolet Detectable Powder** The Am. Biology Teacher, 69(2), Feb. 2007, pp. 99-103. *Using a hypothetical virus to study disease transmission in populations.*

See pages 10-11 for details of how to access **Bio Links** from our web site: **www.thebiozone.com** From Bio Links, access sites under the topics:
GENERAL BIOLOGY ONLINE RESOURCES > Online Textbooks and Lecture Notes • An online biology book • Learn.co.uk *... and others*
HEALTH & DISEASE: • CDC disease links • WHO/OMS: health > **Infectious Diseases:** • Centers for Disease Control and Prevention (CDC) • Cholera and epidemic dysentery • Disease-causing bacteria • Emerging infectious diseases • HIV Insite: gateway to AIDS knowledge • Koch's postulates • Public Health Laboratory Service: Disease facts • The science of HIV... *and others* > **Prevention and Treatment:** • Antimicrobial agents • Inducible defenses against pathogens • Monoclonal antibodies *... and others*

Presentation MEDIA to support this topic:
HEALTH & DISEASE:
• Infectious Disease

Infection and Disease

Infectious disease refers to disease caused by a **pathogen** (an infectious agent). In 1861, **Louis Pasteur** demonstrated experimentally that microorganisms can be present in non-living matter and can contaminate seemingly sterile solutions. He also showed conclusively that microbes can be destroyed by heat; a discovery that formed the basis of modern-day **aseptic** **technique**. The development of the germ theory of disease followed Pasteur's discoveries and, in 1876-1877, **Robert Koch** established a sequence of experimental steps (known as **Koch's postulates**) for directly relating a specific microbe to a specific disease. During the past 100 years, the postulates have been invaluable in determining the specific agents of many diseases.

Infectious Disease

Pathogens and Parasites

Pathogens are organisms that cause disease. Some pathogens are also (intra- or extracellular) parasites and seek to exploit the rich food resources of the host and use the host's tissues as incubators for their own reproduction. The invasion of the body by pathogens is called **infection**. Pathogens can be classified as microorganisms (bacteria, fungi, and viruses) or macroorganisms (i.e. organisms visible to the naked eye, such as worms, ticks, and mites). Macroorganisms can cause disease as a direct result of their activity, or they can serve as **vectors** for the transmission of other infectious agents.

Robert Koch

In 1876-1877, the German physician Robert Koch demonstrated that a specific infectious disease (anthrax) was caused by a specific micro-organism (*Bacillus anthracis*). From his work he devised what are now known as **Koch's postulates**.

Koch's postulates

1. The same pathogen must be present in every case of the disease.
2. The pathogen must be isolated from the diseased host and grown in pure culture.
3. The pathogen from the pure culture must cause the disease when it is introduced by inoculation into a healthy, but susceptible organism (usually animal).
4. The pathogen must be isolated from the inoculated animal and be shown to be the original organism.

Exceptions to Koch's Postulates

- Some bacteria and viruses cannot be grown on artificial media (they multiply only within cells).
- Some pathogens cause several disease conditions (e.g. *Mycobacterium tuberculosis*, *Streptococcus pyogenes*).

Types of Pathogens

Bacteria: All bacteria are prokaryotes, but they are diverse in both their structure and metabolism. Bacteria are categorized according to the properties of their cell walls and characteristics such as cell shape and arrangements, oxygen requirement, and motility. Many bacteria are useful, but the relatively few species that are pathogenic are responsible for enormous social and economic cost.

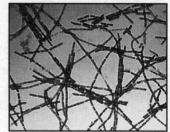

Bacillus anthracis: the rod-shaped bacterial pathogen that causes anthrax

Eukaryotic pathogens: Eukaryotic pathogens (fungi, algae, protozoa, and parasitic worms) include the pathogens responsible for malaria and schistosomiasis. Many are highly specialized parasites with a number of hosts. Serious fungal diseases are also more prevalent now than in the past, affecting those with compromised immune systems, such as AIDS patients.

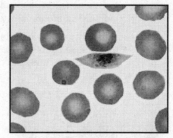

The malarial parasite, *Plasmodium*, seen in a red blood cell smear.

Viral pathogens: Viruses are responsible for many of the everyday diseases with which we are familiar (e.g. the common cold), as well as rather more alarming and dangerous diseases, such as Ebola. Viruses were first distinguished from other pathogens because of their small size and because they are obligate intracellular parasites and need living host cells in order to multiply.

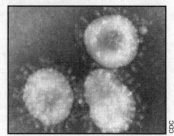

The *Coronavirus* responsible for the 2003 global epidemic of SARS.

1. Using a named example, explain what is meant by a **pathogen**: _____

_____

2. Explain the contribution of Robert Koch to the **etiology** of disease: _____

_____

_____

3. Suggest why diseases caused by **intracellular protozoan parasites** can be particularly difficult to control and treat:

_____

_____

_____

Related activities: Patterns of Disease, Protozoan Diseases

Transmission of Disease

The human body, like that of other large animals, is under constant attack by a wide range of potential parasites and pathogens. Once inside us, these organisms seek to reproduce and exploit us for food. Pathogens may be transferred from one individual to another by a number of methods (below). The transmission of infectious diseases can be virtually eliminated by observing appropriate personal hygiene procedures, and by chlorinating drinking water and providing adequate sanitation.

Portals of Entry

Respiratory tract
The mouth and nose are major entry points for pathogens, particularly airborne viruses, which are inhaled from other people's expelled mucus.

Examples: diphtheria, meningococcal meningitis, tuberculosis, whooping cough, influenza, measles, German measles (rubella), chickenpox.

Gastrointestinal tract
The mouth is one of the few openings where we deliberately place foreign substances into our body. Food is often contaminated with microorganisms, but most of these are destroyed in the stomach.

Examples: cholera, typhoid fever, mumps, hepatitis A, poliomyelitis, bacillary dysentery, salmonellosis.

Breaking the skin surface
The skin provides an effective barrier to the entry of most pathogens. However, a cut or abrasion will allow easy entry for pathogens. Some parasites and pathogens have adaptive features that allow them to penetrate the skin surface.

Examples: tetanus, gas gangrene, bubonic plague, hepatitis B, rabies, malaria, leptospirosis, and HIV.

Urinogenital openings
The urinogenital openings provide entry points for the pathogens responsible for sexually transmitted infections (STIs) and other opportunistic infections (i.e. thrush).

Examples: gonorrhea, syphilis, HIV, and *E. coli* (a cause of urinary tract infections).

The Body Under Assault

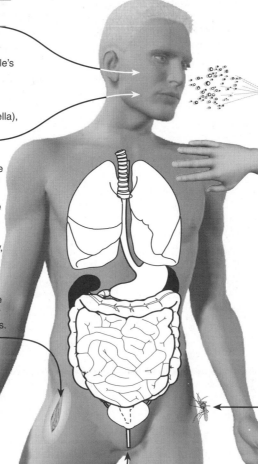

Modes of Transmission

Contact transmission
The agent of disease may occur by contact with other infected humans or animals:

Droplet transmission: Mucus droplets are discharged into the air by coughing, sneezing, laughing, or talking within a radius of 1 m.

Direct contact: Direct transmission of an agent by physical contact between its source and a potential host. Includes touching, kissing, and sexual intercourse. May be person to person, or between humans and other animals.

Indirect contact: Includes touching objects that have been in contact with the source of infection. Examples include: eating utensils, drinking cups, bedding, toys, money, and used syringes.

Vehicle transmission
Agents of disease may be transmitted by a medium such as food, blood, water, intravenous fluids (e.g. drugs), and air. Airborne transmission refers to the spread of fungal spores, some viruses, and bacteria that are transported on dust particles.

Animal Vectors
Some pathogens are transmitted between hosts by other animals. Bites from arthropods (e.g. mosquitoes, ticks, fleas, and lice) and mammals (e.g. rodents) may introduce pathogens, while flies can carry pathogens on their feet.

Pathogens and Disease

1. State how pathogens benefit from invading a host: _____

_____

2. Describe two personal hygiene practices that would minimize the risk of transmitting an infectious disease:

(a) _____

(b) _____

3. Identify the common **mode of transmission** and the **portal of entry** for the following pathogens:

(a) Protozoan causing malaria: _____

(b) Tetanus bacteria: _____

(c) Cholera bacteria: _____

(d) Common cold virus: _____

(e) Tuberculosis bacteria: _____

(f) HIV (AIDS) virus: _____

(g) Gonorrhea bacteria: _____

Related activities: Bacterial Diseases, Cholera, Tuberculosis, Malaria, Viral Diseases, HIV and AIDS, The Control of Disease

RA 2

Patterns of Disease

Diseases present in low levels of a population at any time are known as **endemic** diseases. Occasionally there may be a sudden increase in the **prevalence** of a particular disease. On a local level this is known as an **outbreak**. Such an increase in prevalence on a national scale is called an **epidemic**. An epidemic occurs when an infectious disease spreads rapidly through a population and affects large numbers of people. One example is influenza, epidemics of which are relatively common and occur every two to three years. On rare occasions an epidemic disease will spread to other countries throughout the world. This is known as a **pandemic**. Examples of diseases that are known to have caused pandemics are bubonic plague, cholera, tuberculosis, HIV/AIDS, and influenza. **Epidemiologists** gather data on the number of infected people (**morbidity**) and the number of people that have died (**mortality**) within a population. These data help to establish the **incidence** (number of new cases per unit time) and **prevalence** (number of infected people expressed as a proportion of the population) of the disease in the population at any given time. **Etiology** is the study of the cause of a disease. It can assist in pinpointing the origin of new diseases as they arise in populations. One example is the respiratory disease SARS, which arose in 2003 and spread globally before being contained.

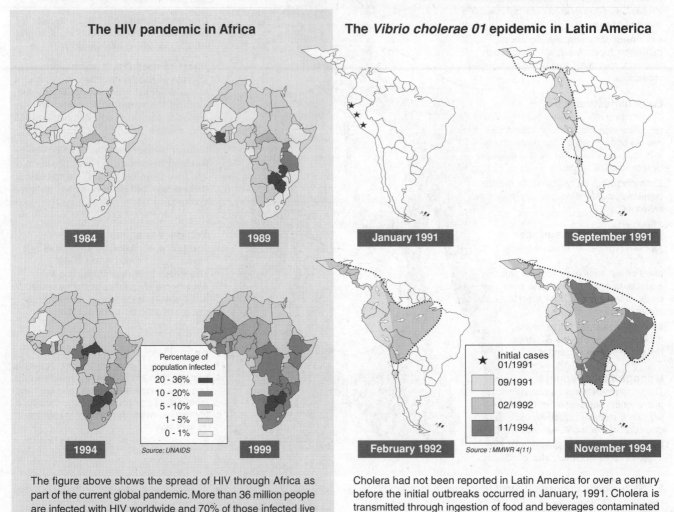

The HIV pandemic in Africa

1984   1989

1994   1999

Percentage of population infected
20 - 36%
10 - 20%
5 - 10%
1 - 5%
0 - 1%
Source: UNAIDS

The *Vibrio cholerae 01* epidemic in Latin America

January 1991   September 1991

February 1992   November 1994

★ Initial cases 01/1991
09/1991
02/1992
11/1994
Source : MMWR 4(11)

The figure above shows the spread of HIV through Africa as part of the current global pandemic. More than 36 million people are infected with HIV worldwide and 70% of those infected live in sub-Saharan Africa. In this region, seven countries have an adult prevalence of 20% or higher, including Botswana where 36% of the population is infected.

Cholera had not been reported in Latin America for over a century before the initial outbreaks occurred in January, 1991. Cholera is transmitted through ingestion of food and beverages contaminated with feces, or by bathing in fecally contaminated water. By the time the epidemic began to subside in 1994, more than 1 million cases and nearly 10 000 deaths had been reported. Death rates were high as a result of inadequate provision for oral rehydration.

1. Using examples, distinguish between different patterns of disease (epidemic, pandemic, and endemic disease):

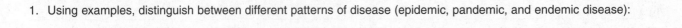

_____

_____

_____

_____

2. Suggest why it is important to establish the **incidence** of a disease when it begins to spread through a community:

_____

_____

Related activities: Cholera, Epidemiology of AIDS, Emerging Diseases

The Role of Health Statistics

Health is difficult to define and to measure, and most of the information about the state of health of a nation's population comes from studying disease. **Epidemiology** is the study of the occurrence and the spread of disease. The **health statistics** collected by epidemiologists are used by health authorities to identify patterns of disease in their country. These patterns, including the **incidence** and **prevalence** of a disease are important in planning health services and investigating causes of disease. Health statistics enable the effectiveness of health policies and practices, such as vaccination programs, to be monitored. The World Health Organization (WHO) gathers data on an international basis to identify global patterns.

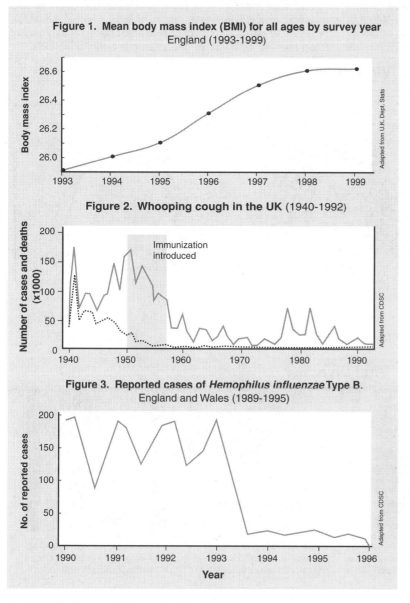

The causes of illness and death for people in developing countries are very different from those in affluent societies.

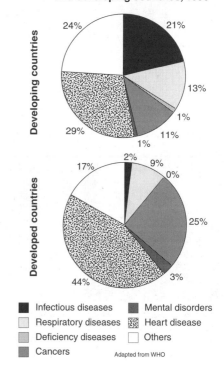

Figure 4. The causes of death in developed and developing countries, 1998

1. Explain the contribution of epidemiologists to monitoring public health: _____

2. Describe the trend in BMI between 1993 and 1999 (Figure 1): _____

3. (a) Suggest a probable reason for the pattern of reported cases of *Hemophilus influenzae* (Figure 3) prior to 1993:

   (b) Suggest a possible cause for the decline in the incidence of *Hemophilius influenzae* after 1993:

4. (a) Identify a difference between the cause of death between developed and developing countries:

   (b) Suggest a reason for this difference: _____

The Structure of Viruses

Viruses are non-cellular **obligate intracellular parasites**, requiring a living host cell in order to reproduce. The traditional view of viruses is as a minimal particle, containing just enough genetic information to infect a host and highjack the host's machinery into replicating more viral particles. The identification in 2004 of a new family of viruses, called **mimiviruses**, is forcing a rethink of this conservative view. Mimiviruses overlap with parasitic cellular organisms in terms of both size (400 nm) and genome complexity (over 1000 genes) and their existence suggests a fourth domain of life. A typical, fully developed viral particle (**virion**) lacks the metabolic machinery of cells, containing just a single type of nucleic acid (DNA or RNA) encased in a protein coat or **capsid**. Being non-cellular, they do not conform to the existing criteria upon which a five or six kingdom classification system is based. Viruses can be distinguished by their structure (see below) and by the nature of their genetic material (single or double stranded DNA or RNA). Those that use bacterial cells as a host (**bacteriophages**) can be grown on bacterial cultures, but other viruses are more difficult to study because they require living animals, embryos, or cell cultures in order to replicate.

Viral Structure

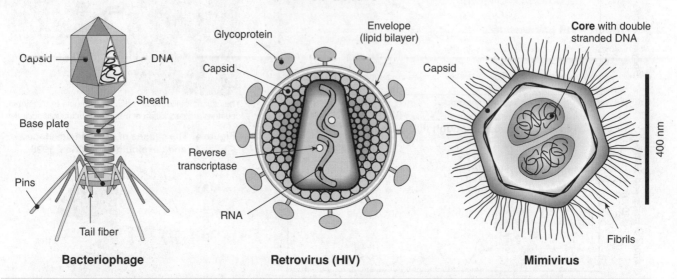

Bacteriophage — Capsid, DNA, Sheath, Base plate, Pins, Tail fiber

Retrovirus (HIV) — Glycoprotein, Capsid, Envelope (lipid bilayer), Reverse transcriptase, RNA

Mimivirus — Core with double stranded DNA, Capsid, 400 nm, Fibrils

Viral Diversity

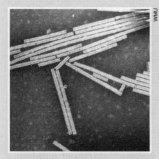

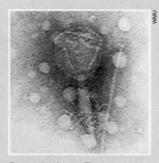

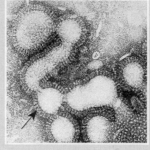

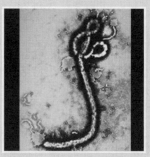

Tobacco Mosaic Virus (TMV): A single stranded RNA plant virus, with a helical capsid.

Bacteriophage T4: A complex virus that uses its contractile tail region to inject DNA into its host.

Influenzavirus has a flexible helical capsid and many glycoprotein spikes (arrowed).

Ebola virus: A helical shaped, RNA filovirus. *Ebola* causes severe hemorrhagic disease (Ebola).

1. Describe the basic structure of a generalized virus particle (virion): _____
_____
_____

2. Explain why viruses are such a difficult group to classify conventionally: _____
_____

3. State whether you regard viruses as living or non-living. Give a reason for your answer: _____
_____

4. Outline why viruses are classified as obligate intracellular parasites: _____
_____

5. Explain why viruses are difficult to culture: _____
_____

Related activities: Viral Diseases, HIV and AIDS

Viral Diseases

Viruses are found as parasites in all kinds of organisms including humans and other animals, plants, fungi, bacteria, and protists. Some crop and livestock diseases, and many diseases of humans are caused by viruses. Antiviral drugs are difficult to design because they must kill the virus without killing the host cells. Moreover, viruses cannot be attacked when in an inert state. Antiviral drugs work by preventing entry of the virus into the host cell or by interfering with their replication. There are only a few antiviral drugs currently in use and immunisation is still regarded as the most effective way in which to control viral disease. However immunisation does not necessarily provide lifelong immunity. New viral strains develop as preexisting strains acquire mutations. These mutations allow the viruses to change their surface proteins and thus evade detection by the host's immune system.

Coronaviruses
Associated with upper respiratory infections and responsible for ~20% of colds. A coronavirus is responsible for the disease SARS.

Rhinoviruses
More than 100 rhinoviruses exist and are the most common cause of colds.

HIV (*Lentivirus*)
The human immunodeficiency virus causes AIDS; a complex assortment of secondary infections that result after HIV has weakened the immune system.

Influenzavirus
This virus causes influenza (the flu) in humans. The ability of this virus to rapidly mutate results in many strains.

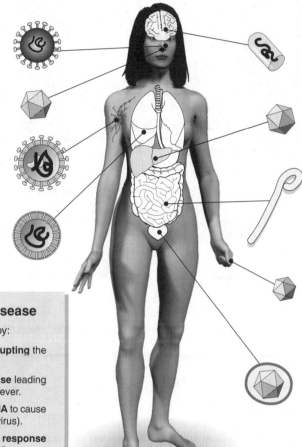

How Viruses Cause Disease
Viruses cause disease by:

- **Invading, destroying, or disrupting** the activities of the host cells.
- Triggering an **immune response** leading to symptoms of infection, e.g. fever.
- **Interacting with the host's DNA** to cause cancer (e.g. human papillomavirus).
- **Disrupting the cell-mediated response** of the immune system (e.g. HIV).

Human Viral Pathogens

Lyssavirus
This bullet-shaped virus causes rabies and is usually contracted from a bite by a rabid dog or fox.

Hepatitis viruses
The viruses responsible for hepatitis A, B, and C are not related and are from different viral families. Symptoms include liver damage.

Filoviruses
Filoviruses, also called thread-viruses, includes the Marburg and Ebola viruses. They are spread by contact with contaminated blood or tissue and cause severe, usually fatal, internal bleeding.

Papillomavirus
This virus causes warts in humans. Some strains also transform cells and are implicated in causing cervical cancer. Host cells may reproduce rapidly, resulting in a tumor.

Herpesviruses
Nearly 100 herpesviruses are known. Types found in humans include those that cause cold sores, chickenpox, shingles, infectious mononucleosis, and genital herpes. They have also been linked to a type of human cancer called Burkitt's lymphoma.

Pathogens and Disease

1. Summarise important features of each of the following viral pathogens. For disease symptoms, consult a textbook, the internet, a good dictionary, or an encyclopedia:

(a) HIV causes the disease: _____

　　Natural reservoir: _____ Symptoms: _____

　　_____

　　_____

(b) Coronaviruses cause: _____

　　Natural reservoir: _____ Symptoms: _____

　　_____

　　_____

(c) *Influenzavirus* causes the disease: _____

　　Natural reservoir: _____ Symptoms: _____

　　_____

　　_____

Related activities: Immunization, HIV and AIDS
Web links: Viral Infection

RA 2

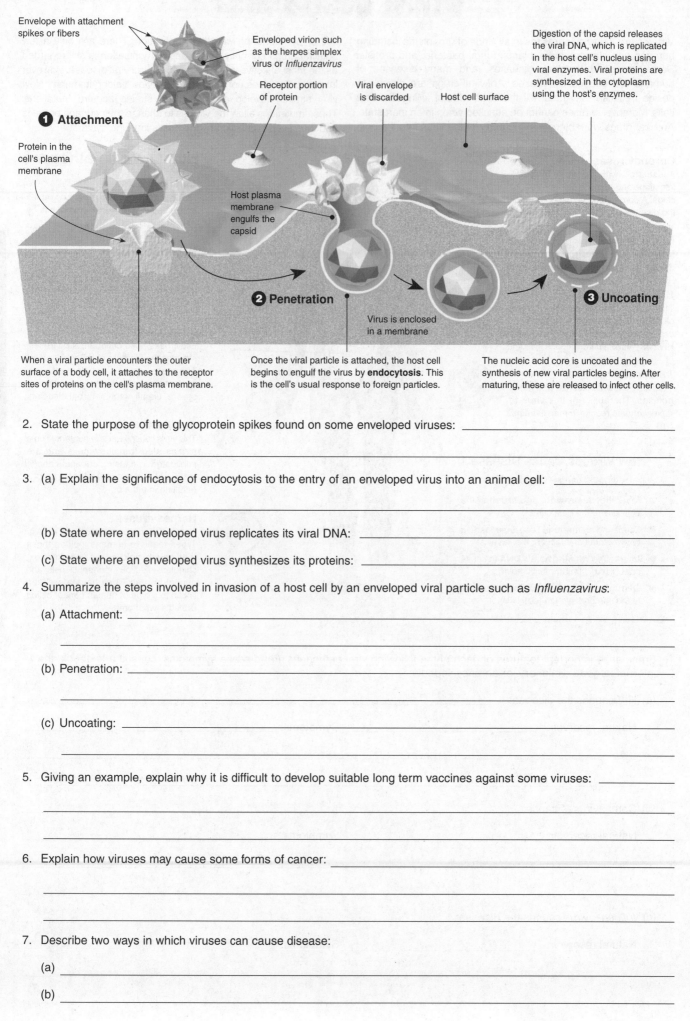

Envelope with attachment spikes or fibers

Enveloped virion such as the herpes simplex virus or *Influenzavirus*

Receptor portion of protein

Viral envelope is discarded

Host cell surface

Digestion of the capsid releases the viral DNA, which is replicated in the host cell's nucleus using viral enzymes. Viral proteins are synthesized in the cytoplasm using the host's enzymes.

1 Attachment

Protein in the cell's plasma membrane

Host plasma membrane engulfs the capsid

2 Penetration

Virus is enclosed in a membrane

3 Uncoating

When a viral particle encounters the outer surface of a body cell, it attaches to the receptor sites of proteins on the cell's plasma membrane.

Once the viral particle is attached, the host cell begins to engulf the virus by **endocytosis**. This is the cell's usual response to foreign particles.

The nucleic acid core is uncoated and the synthesis of new viral particles begins. After maturing, these are released to infect other cells.

2. State the purpose of the glycoprotein spikes found on some enveloped viruses: _____

_____

3. (a) Explain the significance of endocytosis to the entry of an enveloped virus into an animal cell: _____

_____

(b) State where an enveloped virus replicates its viral DNA: _____

(c) State where an enveloped virus synthesizes its proteins: _____

4. Summarize the steps involved in invasion of a host cell by an enveloped viral particle such as *Influenzavirus*:

(a) Attachment: _____

_____

(b) Penetration: _____

_____

(c) Uncoating: _____

_____

5. Giving an example, explain why it is difficult to develop suitable long term vaccines against some viruses: _____

_____

_____

6. Explain how viruses may cause some forms of cancer: _____

_____

_____

7. Describe two ways in which viruses can cause disease:

(a) _____

(b) _____

HIV and AIDS

AIDS (acquired immune deficiency syndrome) first appeared in the news in 1981, with cases being reported in Los Angeles, in the United States. By 1983, the pathogen causing the disease had been identified as a retrovirus that selectively infects **helper T cells**. The disease causes a massive deficiency in the immune system due to infection with **HIV** (human immunodeficiency virus). HIV is a retrovirus (RNA, not DNA) and is able to splice its genes into the host cell's chromosome. As yet, there is no cure or vaccine, and the disease has taken the form of a **pandemic**, spreading to all parts of the globe and killing more than a million people each year. It has now been established that HIV arose by the recombination of two simian viruses. It has probably been endemic in some central African regions for decades, as HIV has been found in blood samples from several African nations from as early as 1959. HIV's mode of infection is described on the next page and its origin and prevalence are covered in the next activity.

Capsid
Protein coat that protects the nucleic acids (RNA) within.

Viral envelope
A piece of the cell membrane budded off from the last human host cell.

Nucleic acid
Two identical strands of RNA contain the genetic blueprint for making more HIV viruses.

Reverse transcriptase
Two copies of this important enzyme convert the RNA into DNA once inside a host cell.

Surface proteins
These spikes allow HIV to attach to receptors on the host cells (T cells and macrophages).

The structure of HIV

Pathogens and Disease

HIV/AIDS

Individuals affected by the human immunodeficiency virus (HIV) may have no symptoms, while medical examination may detect swollen lymph glands. Others may experience a short-lived illness when they first become infected (resembling infectious mononucleosis). The range of symptoms resulting from HIV infection is huge, and is not the result of the HIV infection directly. The symptoms arise from an onslaught of secondary infections that gain a foothold in the body due to the suppressed immune system (due to the few helper T cells). These infections are from normally rare fungal, viral, and bacterial sources. Full blown AIDS can also feature some rare forms of cancer. Some symptoms are listed below:

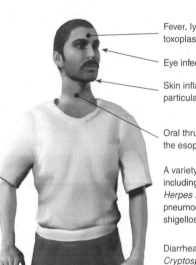

Fever, lymphoma (cancer) and toxoplasmosis of the brain, dementia.

Eye infections (*Cytomegalovirus*).

Skin inflammation (dermatitis) particularly affecting the face.

Oral thrush (*Candida albicans*) of the esophagus, bronchi, and lungs.

A variety of opportunistic infections, including: chronic or persistent *Herpes simplex*, tuberculosis (TB), pneumocystis pneumonia, shingles, shigellosis and salmonellosis.

Diarrhea caused by *Isospora* or *Cryptosporidium*.

Marked weight loss.
A number of autoimmune diseases, especially destruction of platelets.

Kaposi's sarcoma: a highly aggressive malignant skin tumor consisting of blue-red nodules, usually start at the feet and ankles, spreading to the rest of the body later, including respiratory and gastrointestinal tracts.

Category A: HIV positive with little or no symptoms	Category B: Some symptoms, low helper T cell count	Category C: Clinical AIDS symptoms appear

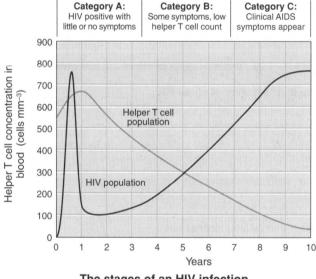

Helper T cell concentration in blood (cells mm⁻³)

Helper T cell population

HIV population

Years

The stages of an HIV infection

AIDS is actually only the end stage of an HIV infection. Shortly after the initial infection, HIV antibodies appear within the blood. The progress of infection has three clinical categories shown on the graph above.

1. Explain why the HIV virus has such a devastating effect on the human body's ability to fight disease:

_____

_____

_____

2. Consult the graph above showing the stages of HIV infection (remember, HIV infects and destroys helper T cells).

(a) Describe how the virus population changes with the progression of the disease: _____

_____

_____

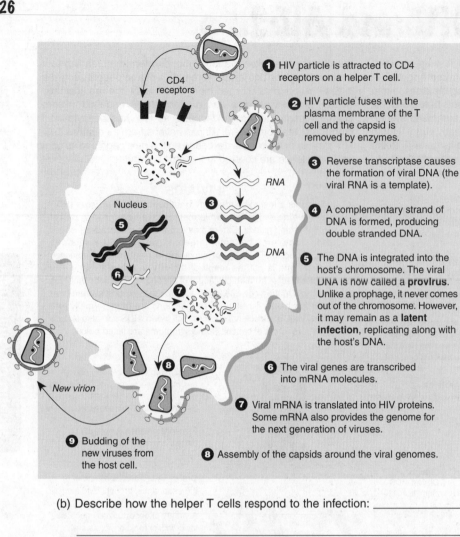

1 HIV particle is attracted to CD4 receptors on a helper T cell.

2 HIV particle fuses with the plasma membrane of the T cell and the capsid is removed by enzymes.

3 Reverse transcriptase causes the formation of viral DNA (the viral RNA is a template).

4 A complementary strand of DNA is formed, producing double stranded DNA.

5 The DNA is integrated into the host's chromosome. The viral DNA is now called a **provirus**. Unlike a prophage, it never comes out of the chromosome. However, it may remain as a **latent infection**, replicating along with the host's DNA.

6 The viral genes are transcribed into mRNA molecules.

7 Viral mRNA is translated into HIV proteins. Some mRNA also provides the genome for the next generation of viruses.

8 Assembly of the capsids around the viral genomes.

9 Budding of the new viruses from the host cell.

Modes of Transmission

1. HIV is transmitted in blood, vaginal secretions, semen, breast milk, and across the placenta.

2. In developed countries, blood transfusions are no longer a likely source of infection because blood is tested for HIV antibodies.

3. Historically, transmission of HIV in developed countries has been primarily through intravenous drug use and homosexual activity, but heterosexual transmission is increasing.

4. Transmission via heterosexual activity is important in Asia and Africa.

Treatment and Prevention

HIV's ability to destroy, evade, and hide inside cells of the human immune system make it difficult to treat. Research into conventional and extremely unconventional approaches to **vaccination** and **chemotherapy** is taking place. The first chemotherapy drug to show promise was *AZT*, which is a nucleotide analogue that inhibits reverse transcriptase. Protease inhibitors (Saquinavir, Ritonavir, Indinavir) are drugs that work by blocking the HIV protease. Once this is blocked, HIV makes copies of itself that cannot infect other cells. These drugs seem to be less toxic and to have less severe side effects than other anti-AIDS drugs. Subunit vaccines *HIVAC-1e* and *gp160* are being tested that use HIV glycoproteins inserted into other viruses.

(b) Describe how the helper T cells respond to the infection: _____

_____

3. (a) Explain the role of the reverse transcriptase in the life cycle of a retrovirus such as HIV: _____

_____

_____

(b) Explain the significance of the formation of a provirus: _____

_____

4. Name three common ways in which HIV can be transmitted from one person to another: _____

_____

5. Explain what is meant by the term **HIV positive**: _____

_____

6. In the years immediately following the discovery of the HIV pathogen, there was a sudden appearance of AIDS cases amongst **hemophiliacs** (people with an inherited blood disorder). State why this group was being infected with HIV:

_____

_____

7. State why it has been so difficult to develop a **vaccine** for HIV: _____

_____

8. In a rare number of cases, people who have been HIV positive for many years still have no apparent symptoms. Explain the significance of this observation and its likely potential in the search for a cure for AIDS:

_____

_____

Epidemiology of AIDS

In many urban centers of sub-Saharan Africa, Latin America, and the Caribbean, AIDS has already become the leading cause of death for both men and women aged 15 to 49 years. AIDS kills people in their most productive years and ranks as the leading cause of potential healthy life-years lost in sub-Saharan Africa. Within the next decade, crude death rates in some countries will more than double, and infant and child mortality rates will increase markedly. Perhaps the most significant impact will be seen in projected life expectancies due to the increased mortality of young adults. The AIDS pandemic has lowered the estimated world population level for the year 2050 from 9.4 billion to 8.9 billion, mostly caused by the massive toll of AIDS in Africa.

Regional HIV Statistics and Figures, December 2006

North America
People living with HIV / AIDS¶: 1.4 million
Adult prevalence rate*: 0.8%
People newly infected with HIV: 43 000
Deaths of people from AIDS: 18 000
Main modes of transmission**: MSM, IDU, Hetero

Western & Central Europe
People living with HIV / AIDS¶: 740 000
Adult prevalence rate*: 0.3%
People newly infected with HIV: 22 000
Deaths of people from AIDS: 12 000
Main modes of transmission**: Hetero, MSM, IDU

Eastern Europe & Central Asia
People living with HIV / AIDS¶: 1.7 million
Adult prevalence rate*: 0.9%
People newly infected with HIV: 270 000
Deaths of people from AIDS: 84 000
Main modes of transmission**: IDU, Hetero

Caribbean
People living with HIV / AIDS¶: 250 000
Adult prevalence rate*: 1.2%
People newly infected with HIV: 27 000
Deaths of people from AIDS: 19 000
Main modes of transmission**: Hetero, MSM, IDU

Latin America
People living with HIV / AIDS¶: 1.7 million
Adult prevalence rate*: 0.5%
People newly infected with HIV: 140 000
Deaths of people from AIDS: 65 000
Main modes of transmission**: Hetero, MSM, IDU

North Africa and Middle East
People living with HIV / AIDS¶: 460 000
Adult prevalence rate*: 0.2%
People newly infected with HIV: 68 000
Deaths of people from AIDS: 36 000
Main modes of transmission**: Hetero, IDU, MSM

Sub-Saharan Africa
People living with HIV / AIDS¶: 24.7 million
Adult prevalence rate*: 5.9%
People newly infected with HIV: 2.8 million
Deaths of people from AIDS: 2.1 million
Main modes of transmission**: Hetero

Oceania
People living with HIV / AIDS¶: 81 000
Adult prevalence rate*: 0.4%
People newly infected with HIV: 7100
Deaths of people from AIDS: 4000
Main modes of transmission**: MSM, Hetero, IDU

South & South East Asia
People living with HIV / AIDS¶: 7.8 million
Adult prevalence rate*: 0.6%
People newly infected with HIV: 860 000
Deaths of people from AIDS: 590 000
Main modes of transmission**: Hetero, IDU

East Asia
People living with HIV / AIDS¶: 750 000
Adult prevalence rate*: 0.1%
People newly infected with HIV: 100 000
Deaths of people from AIDS: 43 000
Main modes of transmission**: IDU, Hetero, MSM

Estimated percentage of adults (15-49) living with HIV/AIDS

- >15%
- 5 – 15%
- 0 – 5%

Source: UNAIDS, WHO

* The proportion of adults (15 to 49 years of age) living with HIV/AIDS in 2006   ¶ People includes adults & children
** Modes of transmission: **Hetero**: heterosexual sex; **IDU**: injecting drug use; **MSM**: sex between men

The origins of HIV

AIDS researchers have confirmed that the two strains of HIV each originated from cross-species transmission (**zoonosis**) from other primates. HIV-1, responsible for the global pandemic, arose as a result of recombination between two separate strains of simian immunodeficiency virus (SIV) in infected **common chimpanzees** in west-central Africa. HIV-2 is less virulent than HIV-1 and, until recently, was restricted to West Africa. It originated from a strain of SIV found in **sooty mangabey** monkeys in that region. The killing of primates as "bushmeat" for human consumption allows the virus to transmit to human hunters when they handle infected carcasses with cuts or other open wounds on their hands. Such cross-species transmissions could be happening every day.

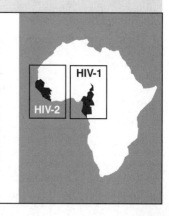

Related activities: HIV and AIDS   DA 2

Factors in the spread of HIV

Epidemiologists cannot predict with certainty how rapidly a given epidemic will expand or when it will peak, although short term predictions can be made on the basis of trends in HIV spread and information on risk behavior. Fortunately, there is strong evidence showing that countries will ultimately reduce their new infections if they carry out effective prevention programs encouraging abstinence, or fidelity and safer sex. A crucial factor is promoting the acceptance and use of condoms, both the traditional kind and the female condom. Condoms are protective irrespective of age, the scope of sexual networks, or the presence of other sexually transmitted infections. There is evidence from around the world that many factors play a role in starting a sexually transmitted HIV epidemic or driving it to higher levels. Some of these risk factors are listed below.

In many African communities, men travel from rural settlements into the cities in search of work. These men often develop sexual networks while they are away and bring HIV with them when they return.

Social and behavioral risk factors
- Little or no condom use.
- Large proportion of the adult population with multiple partners.
- Overlapping (as opposed to serial) sexual partnerships. Individuals are highly infectious when they first acquire HIV and are more likely to infect any concurrent partners.
- Large sexual networks which are often seen in individuals who move back and forth between home and a far off work place.
- Women's economic dependence on marriage or prostitution, robbing them of control over the circumstances or safety of sex.

Biological risk factors
- High rates of sexually transmitted infections, especially those causing genital ulcers.
- Low rates of male circumcision (for poorly understood reasons, circumcised males have a reduced risk of contracting HIV).
- High viral load (HIV levels in the blood is typically highest when a person is first infected and again in the late stages of illness).

1. Comment on the social, economic, and biological factors involved in the prevalence of HIV in many of the **rural** communities of sub-Saharan Africa:

   _____

   _____

   _____

   _____

2. Describe the effects of AIDS on the countries of sub-Saharan Africa with respect to the following:

   (a) Age structure of their populations: _____

   _____

   (b) Their local economies: _____

   _____

3. Effective antiviral therapies have reduced deaths from HIV/AIDS in developed countries. Suggest why a similar reduction has not occurred in the countries of sub-Saharan Africa:

   _____

   _____

4. Briefly state the origin of the two main strains of HIV:

   HIV-1: _____

   _____

   HIV-2 _____

   _____

5. Using the information provided on the previous page and your own graph paper, plot a column graph of the number of people living with HIV/AIDS for each region. Staple the completed graph into this workbook.

Bacterial Diseases

Of the many species of bacteria that exist in the world, relatively few cause disease in humans, other animals, plants or any other organisms. The diagram below shows four adaptive features that help bacteria infect host tissue and cause disease. Bacteria infect a host to exploit the food potential of the host's body tissues. The fact that this exploitation causes disease is not in the interest of the bacteria; a healthy host is better than a sick one. Some well-known human diseases caused by bacteria are illustrated in the diagram below. The natural reservoir (source of infection) of a disease varies from species to species, ranging from humans, insects, and other animals, to sewage and contaminated water.

Bacterial Infection

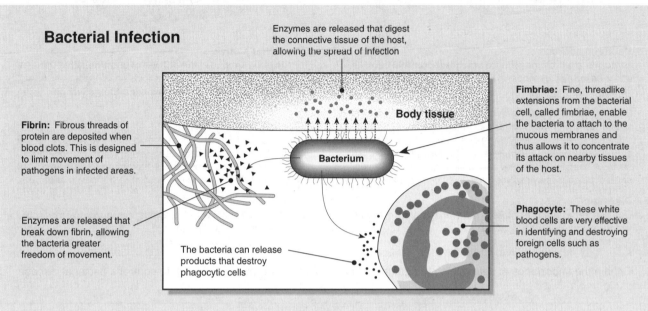

Enzymes are released that digest the connective tissue of the host, allowing the spread of infection

Fibrin: Fibrous threads of protein are deposited when blood clots. This is designed to limit movement of pathogens in infected areas.

Enzymes are released that break down fibrin, allowing the bacteria greater freedom of movement.

Body tissue

Bacterium

The bacteria can release products that destroy phagocytic cells

Fimbriae: Fine, threadlike extensions from the bacterial cell, called fimbriae, enable the bacteria to attach to the mucous membranes and thus allows it to concentrate its attack on nearby tissues of the host.

Phagocyte: These white blood cells are very effective in identifying and destroying foreign cells such as pathogens.

Examples of Bacterial Diseases

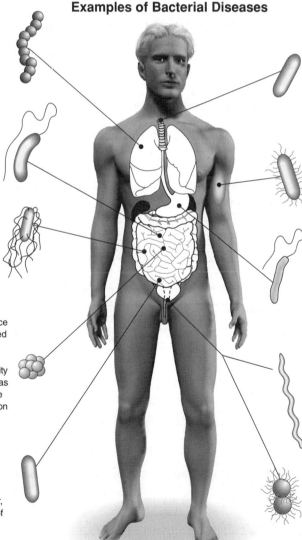

Streptococcus bacteria
These bacteria can cause scarlet fever, sore throats (pharyngitis) and a form of pneumonia. They exist as chains or in pairs. They cause more illness than any other group of bacteria.

Vibrio cholerae
These bacteria cause cholera, a disease common in Asia, caused by a temporary lapse in sanitation (where drinking water is contaminated with human waste).

Salmonella bacteria
This group is not divided up into species, but comprises over 2,000 varieties (called *serovars*). They cause gastrointestinal diseases such as typhoid.

Staphylococcus aureus
This bacterium inhabits noses, the surface of skin, and is also found growing in cured meats such as ham. One of the most common causes of food poisoning, it produces many toxins that increase its ability to invade the body or damage tissue. It has the ability to develop antibiotic resistance very quickly and for this reason is a common problem in hospitals.

Enterobacter cloacae
This bacterium can cause urinary tract infections and is widely distributed in humans and animals, as well as in water, sewage and soil. It is a common source of hospital-acquired infection.

Hemophilus influenzae
Despite its name, this bacterium does not cause influenza. This organism inhabits the mucous membranes of the upper respiratory tract and mouth. It causes the most common form of meningitis in young children and is a frequent cause of earaches. It can also cause epiglottitis, bronchitis and pneumonia.

Yersinia pestis
This bacterium caused the Black Death or the bubonic plague of medieval Europe. Fleas from urban rats and ground squirrels transmit the bacteria among animals and to humans. Direct contact with animals and respiratory droplets from infected people can be involved in transmission.

Helicobacter pylori
H. pylori is a helical bacterium that infects various regions of the stomach and duodenum. *Helicobacter* spp. are the only know microbes to thrive in the highly acidic environment of the stomach and are responsible for many cases of peptic and duodenal ulcers as well as gastritis.

Treponema pallidum
This spirochete bacterium causes syphilis and is transmitted through sexual intercourse. The helical shape allows it to move by a corkscrew rotation.

Neisseria gonorrheae
This bacterium causes the sexually transmitted disease gonorrhea. The fimbriae enable the organism to attach to the mucous membranes of the vagina and urethra of the penis.

Related activities: Foodborne Disease, The Control of Disease
Web links: Microbiology in Action

RA 2

Properties of Exotoxins

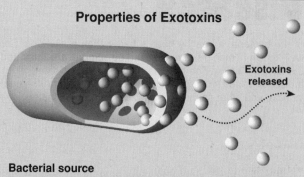

Exotoxins released

Properties of Endotoxins

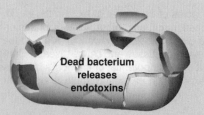

Dead bacterium releases endotoxins

Bacterial source

Exotoxins are proteins produced by **gram-positive** bacteria and released as part of normal bacterial growth and metabolism.

Toxicity and lethal dose

Exotoxins are amongst the most toxic compounds known. Due to their solubility they can diffuse easily into the circulatory system and are then easily transported around the body. They are unstable and can usually (but not always) be destroyed easily by heat. However, they have a high infectivity and a very small dose causes symptoms in the infected person.

Diseases

Gas gangrene, tetanus, botulism, diphtheria, scarlet fever, and various staphylococcal infections.

Bacterial source

Endotoxins are part of the cell wall of **gram-negative** bacteria. They are composed primarily of lipids (in contrast to exotoxins, which are proteins). Endotoxins exert their effect only when the bacteria die.

Toxicity and lethal dose

Although endotoxins are less toxic than exotoxins, they are heat stable and withstand autoclaving (121°C for one hour). The dose required to produce symptoms is relatively high, but the immune system cannot neutralize them with antitoxins.

Diseases

Typhoid fever, urinary tract infections, meningococcal meningitis, and *Salmonella* food poisoning.

1. Explain the importance of determining the natural reservoir of infection when attempting to control a bacterial disease:

_____

_____

2. Distinguish between exotoxins and endotoxins, identifying the role of each in disease: _____

_____

_____

3. Evaluate the evidence for the link between *Helicobacter pylori* infection and the incidence of peptic ulcers:

_____

_____

4. Summarise important features of each of the following bacterial pathogens. For disease symptoms, consult a textbook, the internet, a good dictionary, or an encyclopedia:

   (a) *Salmonella* bacteria cause the disease: _____

   Natural reservoir: _____ Symptoms: _____

   _____

   (b) *Clostridium botulinum* causes the disease: _____

   Natural reservoir: _____ Symptoms: _____

   _____

   (c) *Staphylococcus aureus* causes the disease: _____

   Natural reservoir: _____ Symptoms: _____

   _____

5. Identify three common features of the three bacterial pathogens identified in the previous question:

   (a) _____

   (b) _____

   (c) _____

Cholera

Cholera is an acute intestinal infection caused by the bacterium *Vibrio cholerae*. The disease has a short incubation period, from 1-5 days. The bacterium produces an enterotoxin that causes a copious, painless, watery diarrhea that can quickly lead to severe dehydration and death if treatment is not promptly given. Most people infected with *V. cholerae* do not become ill, although the bacterium is present in their feces for 7-14 days. When cholera appears in a community it is essential to take measures against its spread. These include: hygienic disposal of human feces, provision of an adequate supply of safe drinking water, safe food handling and preparation (e.g. preventing contamination of food and cooking food thoroughly), and effective general hygiene (e.g. hand washing with soap). Cholera has reemerged as a global health threat after virtually disappearing from the Americas and most of Africa and Europe for more than a century. Originally restricted to the Indian subcontinent, cholera spread to Europe in 1817 in the first of seven pandemics. The current pandemic shows no sign of abating in developing countries with the actual number of cases known to be much higher than reported.

Symptoms

More than 90% of cases are of mild or moderate severity and are difficult to distinguish from other types of acute diarrhea. Less than 10% of ill people develop typical cholera with signs of moderate or severe dehydration.

Treatment

Most cases of diarrhea can be treated by giving a solution of oral rehydration salts. During an epidemic, 80-90% of diarrhea patients can be treated by oral rehydration alone, but patients who become severely dehydrated must be given intravenous fluids. In severe cases, antibiotics can reduce the volume and duration of diarrhea and reduce the presence of *V. cholerae* in the feces.

Transmission

Cholera is spread by contaminated water and food. Sudden large outbreaks are usually caused by a contaminated water supply. *Vibrio cholerae* is often found in the aquatic environment and is part of the normal flora of brackish water and estuaries. Human beings are also one of the reservoirs of the pathogenic form of *Vibrio cholerae*.

The Cholera Pandemic: Reported Cases and Deaths (2005)

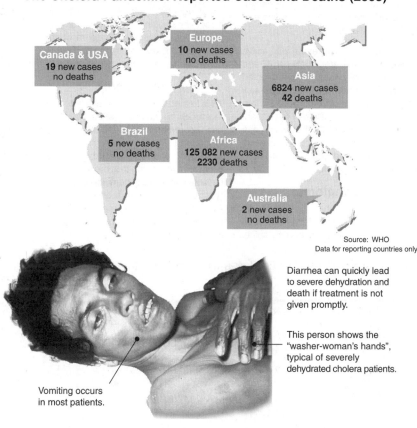

Canada & USA 19 new cases, no deaths
Europe 10 new cases, no deaths
Asia 6824 new cases, 42 deaths
Brazil 5 new cases, no deaths
Africa 125 082 new cases, 2230 deaths
Australia 2 new cases, no deaths

Source: WHO
Data for reporting countries only

Diarrhea can quickly lead to severe dehydration and death if treatment is not given promptly.

This person shows the "washer-woman's hands", typical of severely dehydrated cholera patients.

Vomiting occurs in most patients.

1. Identify the pathogen that causes cholera: _____

2. Describe the symptoms of cholera and explain why these symptoms are so dangerous if not treated quickly:

_____

_____

_____

3. State how cholera is transmitted between people: _____

_____

4. Describe the effective treatment of cholera at the following stages in the progression of the disease:

(a) Mild onset of dehydration: _____

(b) Severe symptoms: _____

5. Identify the risk factors associated with the incidence of cholera and relate these to social and economic conditions:

_____

_____

_____

Tuberculosis

Tuberculosis (TB) is a contagious disease caused by the *Mycobacterium tuberculosis* bacterium (**MTB**). The breakdown in health services in some countries, the spread of HIV/AIDS, and the emergence of **multi-drug resistant TB** are contributing to the increasingly harmful impact of this disease. In 1993, the World Health Organization (WHO) responded to the growing pandemic and declared TB a global emergency. By 1998, the WHO estimated that about a third of the world's population were already infected with MTB. They estimate that 8 million new cases are added annually and that TB causes about 2 million deaths each year (note that in the figures given below, only notified cases are reported). WHO implemented a new global plan in 2006 to stop TB and aims to achieve the Millennium Development Goal to have halted and begun to reverse the incidence of TB by 2015.

Infection and Transmission

TB is a contagious disease, and is spread through the air when infectious people cough, sneeze, talk, or spit. A person needs only to inhale a small number of MTB to be infected.

Left untreated, each person with active TB will infect on average between 10 and 15 people every year. People infected with MTB will not necessarily get sick with the disease; the immune system 'walls off' the MTB which can lie dormant for years, protected by a thick waxy coat. When the immune system is weakened, the chance of getting sick (showing symptoms) is greater.

Symptoms

TB usually affects the lungs, but it can also affect other parts of the body, such as the brain, the kidneys, and the spine.

The general symptoms of TB disease include weakness and nausea, weight loss, fever, and night sweats. The symptoms of TB of the lungs include coughing, chest pain, and coughing up blood. The bacteria can spread from the bronchioles to other body systems, where the symptoms depend on the part of the body that is affected.

Treatment

TB is treated with an aggressive antibiotic regime. Since the early 1990s, the WHO has recommended the DOTS (Directly Observed Therapy, Short-course) strategy to control TB worldwide. This program improves the proportion of patients successfully completing therapy (taking their full course of antibiotics). Proper completion of treatment is the most effective way in which to combat increasing drug resistance.

The Pathogenesis of Tuberculosis

The series below illustrates stages in MTB infection.

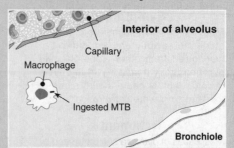

MTB enter the lung and are ingested by macrophages (phagocytic white blood cells).

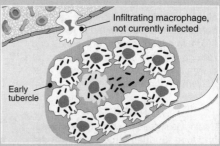

The multiplying bacteria cause the macrophages to swell and rupture. The newly released bacilli infect other macrophages. At this stage a tubercle may form and the disease may lie dormant.

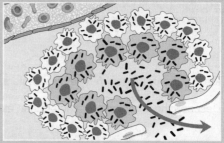

Eventually the tubercle ruptures, allowing bacilli to spill into the bronchiole. The bacilli can now be transmitted when the infected person coughs.

Estimated TB Incidence Rates in 2006 (cases per 100 000)

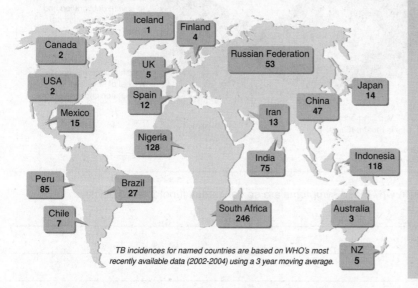

TB incidences for named countries are based on WHO's most recently available data (2002-2004) using a 3 year moving average.

1. Identify the pathogen that causes tuberculosis (TB): _____

2. Explain how MTB may exist in a dormant state in a person for many years without causing disease symptoms:

3. Explain how TB is transmitted between people: _____

4. Suggest how some strains of MTB have acquired **multi-drug resistance**: _____

Related activities: Evolution of Bacteria
Web links: Microbiology in Action

Foodborne Disease

Foodborne disease is caused by consuming contaminated foods or beverages. More than 250 food and waterborne diseases have been identified. The symptoms and severity of these diseases vary according to the infectious agent, however diarrhea and vomiting are two universal symptoms. Food and waterborne diseases cause an estimated 76 million illnesses annually in the USA alone. Food poisoning is a common cause of **gastroenteritis**; the inflammation of the stomach and intestines. Food poisoning is a term used for any gastrointestinal illness with sudden onset, usually accompanied by stomach pain, diarrhea, and vomiting, caused by eating **contaminated food**. Food poisoning usually results from food contaminated with viruses, or bacteria or their toxins. It may also result from contamination of food or water by chemicals such as nitrates.

Common Sources of Bacterial Food Poisoning

Salmonella Infections

Most serotypes of *Salmonella* bacteria are pathogenic. **Endotoxins** released from dead bacteria are a likely (but not proven) cause of the symptoms associated with infection.

Salmonella enteritidis can spread to humans via a variety of foods of animal origin (especially poultry products) and is the cause of **salmonellosis** (*Salmonella* food poisoning). Typical symptoms include fever, accompanied by diarrhea and abdominal cramps.

Salmonella typhi is a highly pathogenic *Salmonella* serotype and causes the life threatening disease, **typhoid fever**. *S.typhi* lives in humans and is shed in the feces. Transmission occurs through the ingestion of food or drink that has been handled by a person shedding the bacterium, or when water used to prepare or wash food is contaminated with sewage containing the pathogen. Recovered patients can become carriers and continue to shed the bacteria and spread infection. Typhoid fever is common in most regions of the world except in industrialized nations such as the USA, Canada, and western Europe.

Fecal contamination of the hands at meal times is a common cause of gastroenteritis.

Sharing food and utensils may transmit foodborne pathogens between individuals.

Inadequate supply of clean drinking water is a major problem in many parts of the world.

E. coli Gastroenteritis

Escherichia coli is the most common form of infantile and travellers' diarrhea in developing countries. *E. coli* is the most abundant microbe in the intestinal tract and is normally harmless. However, certain strains are pathogenic and have specialized fimbriae allowing them to bind to the intestinal epithelial cells. They also release **exotoxins** which cause the production of copious watery diarrhea and symptoms similar to mild cholera. *E. coli* infection is caused by poor sanitation and can be very difficult to avoid in developing countries.

Staphylococcus aureus

S. aureus is a normal inhabitant of human nasal passages. From here, it can contaminate the hands, where it may cause skin lesions and/or contaminate food. Contaminated food held at room temperature will rapidly produce a population of about 1 million bacteria per gram of food and enough **exotoxin** to cause illness. Unusually, the toxin is heat stable and can survive up to 30 minutes of boiling. Reheating the contaminated food may destroy the bacteria but not the toxin itself.

1. Describe three ways in which food can become contaminated by *E. coli*: _____

_____

_____

2. Explain why food poisoning is more prevalent in developing countries than in developed countries: _____

_____

_____

3. Outline the basic precautions that should be taken with drinking water when traveling to developing countries:

_____

_____

4. (a) Describe the symptoms of salmonellosis: _____

_____

(b) Identify the method of transmission of this disease: _____

5. Explain why reheating food will still cause food poisoning if the food is contaminated with *Staphylococcus aureus*:

_____

Fungal Diseases

The study of fungi (molds, yeasts, and fleshy fungi) is called **mycology**. All fungi are chemoheterotrophs, requiring organic compounds for energy and carbon. Most fungi are saprophytes, and are found in the soil and water, where they decompose organic matter using extracellular enzymes. Of the 100 000 species of fungi, only about 100 species are pathogenic to humans and other animals, although thousands of fungal species are pathogenic to plants. Any fungal infection is called a **mycosis**. They are generally **chronic** (long-lasting) infections because fungi grow slowly. Fungal infections are divided into three groups according to the degree of tissue involvement and the mode of entry into the host. Characteristics of these groups are summarized below. Some of these infections (e.g. candidiasis) can also be classed opportunistic, because they occur when the host is immune depressed or weakened in some way.

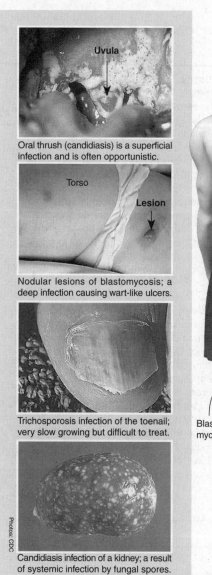

Oral thrush (candidiasis) is a superficial infection and is often opportunistic.

Nodular lesions of blastomycosis; a deep infection causing wart-like ulcers.

Trichosporosis infection of the toenail; very slow growing but difficult to treat.

Candidiasis infection of a kidney; a result of systemic infection by fungal spores.

Photos: CDC

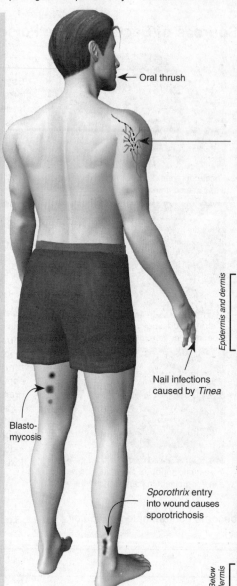

Oral thrush

Nail infections caused by *Tinea*

Blasto-mycosis

Sporothrix entry into wound causes sporotrichosis

Systemic infection

Infection occurring deep inside the body, affecting internal organs, such as the lungs, bones, lymph nodes, heart, and urinary tract. Often starting in the lungs and spreading throughout the body.

Depth of tissue affected: Internal tissues.

Transmission: Usually through inhalation of spores.

Examples: Histoplasmosis; a disease endemic to northern and central USA and parts of South America and Africa. Blastomycosis; a disease affecting various internal organs as well as the skin.

Cutaneous (superficial) infection

Infection affecting the skin, hair, nails, genital organs, and the inside of the mouth.

Epidermis and dermis

Depth of tissue affected: Superficial (affecting epidermis and dermis). Some more persistent infections (e.g. of the toenails) require long treatment with systemic, oral antifungal drugs.

Transmission: By contact with an infected person or spores.

Examples: Candidiasis (thrush) and *Tinea* (ringworm and athlete's foot)

Subcutaneous infection

Rare infections caused by direct implantation of spores into the skin via a scratch or puncture wound.

Depth of tissue affected: Subcutaneous, i.e. beneath the dermis, affecting the layer of fatty connective tissue beneath the skin.

Transmission: Contact with plant material or soil (gardeners are at risk).

Examples: Sporotrichosis is the most common. Other conditions of this type occur mainly in tropical countries.

Below dermis

1. Distinguish between cutaneous and subcutaneous fungal infections, identifying why subcutaneous infections are rarer:

_____

_____

2. Suggest which individuals would be at greatest risk from systemic fungal infections and why: _____

_____

_____

3. Explain why fungal infections tend to be **chronic**: _____

_____

4. Suggest how the spread of athlete's foot (*Tinea pedis*) can be limited by thorough drying of the feet: _____

_____

Protozoan Diseases

Protozoa are one-celled, eukaryotic organisms that belong to the Kingdom Protista. Among the protozoans, there are many variations on cell structure. While most inhabit water and soil habitats, some are part of the natural microbiota of animals (i.e. they are microorganisms that live on or in animals). Relatively few of the nearly 20 000 species of protozoans cause disease; those that do are often highly specialized, intracellular parasites with complex life cycles involving one or more hosts. Under certain adverse conditions, some protozoans produce a protective capsule called a **cyst**. A cyst allows the protozoan to survive conditions unsuitable for survival. For specialized parasitic species, this includes survival for periods outside a host.

AMOEBAE

Amoebae move by extending projections of their cytoplasm. Several pathogenic amoebae infect humans and feed mainly on red blood cells. *Entamoeba* is transmitted through ingestion of cysts that are passed in the feces. People become infected with *Naegleria* while swimming, when the waterborne cysts pass across mucous membranes and infect blood, brain, and spinal cord.

Pathogen	Disease
Naegleria fowleri	Microencephalitis
Entamoeba histolytica	Amoebic dysentery

MICROSPORA

This unusual group of protozoans lack mitochondria and live as intracellular parasites (within cells). They were first reported to cause human diseases in 1984.

Pathogen	Disease
Nosema	Chronic diarrhea, kerato-conjunctivitis (in AIDS patients)

FLAGELLATES

Flagellates are usually spindle-shaped, with flagella projecting from the front end. The whiplike motion of the flagella pulls the cells through their environment. *Giardia* is found in the small intestine of mammals. It is passed in the feces and survives in the environment as a cyst until ingested by the next host. *Trichinomas* moves using an undulating membrane. It is unable to form a cyst and must be transferred directly from host to host quickly (e.g. during sexual intercourse or via toilet facilities or towels). Various *Trypanosoma* species, which cause African sleeping sickness, are spread by the tsetse fly.

Pathogen	Disease
Giardia lamblia	Giardia enteritis
Trichinomas vaginalis	Urethritis, vaginitis
Trypanosoma (in tsetse fly vector)	Sleeping sickness (African trypanosomiasis)

APICOMPLEXA

These protozoans are not mobile and tend to be intracellular parasites. They use special enzymes to penetrate the host's tissues. They have complex life cycles involving transmission between several host species.

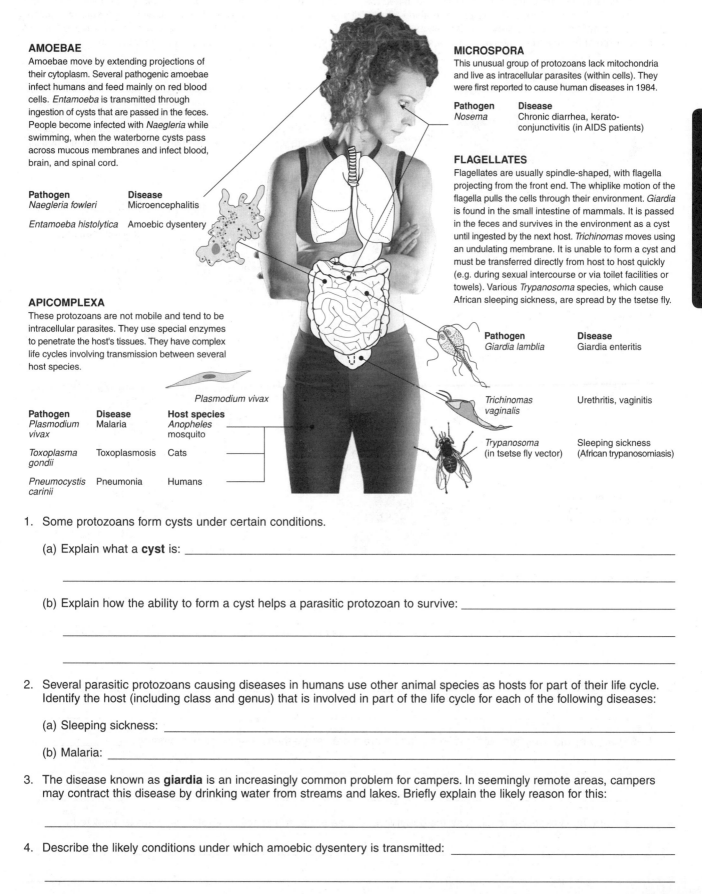

Plasmodium vivax

Pathogen	Disease	Host species
Plasmodium vivax	Malaria	*Anopheles* mosquito
Toxoplasma gondii	Toxoplasmosis	Cats
Pneumocystis carinii	Pneumonia	Humans

1. Some protozoans form cysts under certain conditions.

   (a) Explain what a **cyst** is: _____

   _____

   (b) Explain how the ability to form a cyst helps a parasitic protozoan to survive: _____

   _____

   _____

2. Several parasitic protozoans causing diseases in humans use other animal species as hosts for part of their life cycle. Identify the host (including class and genus) that is involved in part of the life cycle for each of the following diseases:

   (a) Sleeping sickness: _____

   (b) Malaria: _____

3. The disease known as **giardia** is an increasingly common problem for campers. In seemingly remote areas, campers may contract this disease by drinking water from streams and lakes. Briefly explain the likely reason for this:

   _____

4. Describe the likely conditions under which amoebic dysentery is transmitted: _____

   _____

Malaria

Malaria is a serious parasitic disease, spread by bites of **Anopheles mosquitoes**, affecting up to 300 million people in the tropics each year. The parasites responsible for malaria are protozoa known as **plasmodia**. Four species can cause the disease in humans. Each spends part of its life cycle in humans and part in *Anopheles* mosquitoes. Even people who take antimalarial drugs and precautions against being bitten may contract malaria. Malaria, especially *falciparum* malaria, is often a medical emergency that requires hospitalization. Treatment involves the use of antimalarial drugs and, in severe cases, blood transfusions may be necessary. Symptoms, which appear one to two weeks after being bitten, include headache, shaking, chills, and fever. *Falciparum* malaria is more severe, with high fever, coma, and convulsions, and it can be fatal within a few days of the first symptoms. These more severe symptoms result from this plasmodium's ability to infect all ages of red blood cells (whereas other species attack only young or old cells). Destruction of a greater proportion of blood cells results in **hemolytic anemia**. The infected blood cells become sticky and block blood vessels to vital organs such as the kidneys and the brain.

Malaria

Malaria occurs in over 100 countries and territories. More than 40% of the people in the world are at risk. Large areas of Central and South America, Hispaniola (Haiti and the Dominican Republic), Africa, the Indian subcontinent, Southeast Asia, the Middle East, and Oceania are considered malaria-risk areas (an area of the world that has malaria).

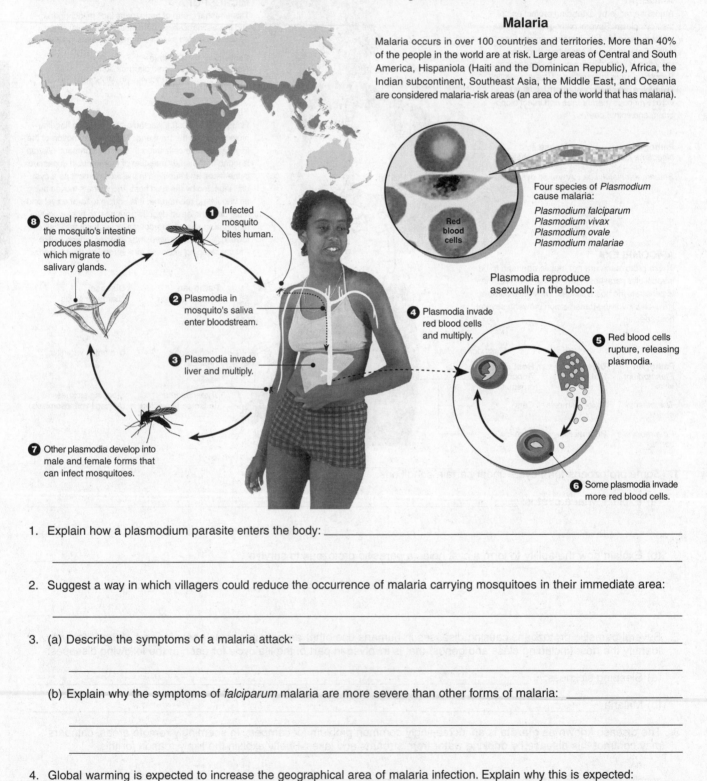

Four species of *Plasmodium* cause malaria:

Plasmodium falciparum
Plasmodium vivax
Plasmodium ovale
Plasmodium malariae

Plasmodia reproduce asexually in the blood:

8 Sexual reproduction in the mosquito's intestine produces plasmodia which migrate to salivary glands.

1 Infected mosquito bites human.

2 Plasmodia in mosquito's saliva enter bloodstream.

3 Plasmodia invade liver and multiply.

7 Other plasmodia develop into male and female forms that can infect mosquitoes.

4 Plasmodia invade red blood cells and multiply.

5 Red blood cells rupture, releasing plasmodia.

6 Some plasmodia invade more red blood cells.

Red blood cells

1. Explain how a plasmodium parasite enters the body: _____

_____

2. Suggest a way in which villagers could reduce the occurrence of malaria carrying mosquitoes in their immediate area:

_____

3. (a) Describe the symptoms of a malaria attack: _____

_____

   (b) Explain why the symptoms of *falciparum* malaria are more severe than other forms of malaria: _____

_____

_____

4. Global warming is expected to increase the geographical area of malaria infection. Explain why this is expected:

_____

_____

Related activities: The Control of Disease
Web links: Malaria Animation

Prion Diseases

Until recently, all pathogens were thought to contain some form of nucleic acid. It now seems that a protein alone can be an infectious agent. Called **prions**, they are capable of replication and of causing infection. Prions have been spread by eating contaminated meat and, because they resist normal sterilization methods, they can also be spread on surgical instruments. Prions are produced by mutations in the gene coding for a normal cell protein (PrP). They cause a group of degenerative nervous diseases in mammals called transmissible spongiform encephalopathies (TSEs). These include scrapie in sheep, bovine spongiform encephalopathy (**BSE**) in cattle, and variant **Creutzfeldt-Jakob disease** and **kuru** in humans. Different mutations of the PrP gene are thought to be responsible in each case.

Kuru is the condition which first brought prion diseases to prominence in the 1950s. Found in the geographically isolated tribes in the Fore highlands of Papua New Guinea. Researchers discovered that these people were eating the brain tissue of dead relatives for religious reasons. They ground up the brain into a pale gray soup, heated it and ate it. Clinically, the disease resembles CJD.

The Infectious Nature of Prion Proteins

A shape change transforms the harmless protein into its infectious 'prion' form. This shape change may be caused by a point mutation in the gene that codes for it.

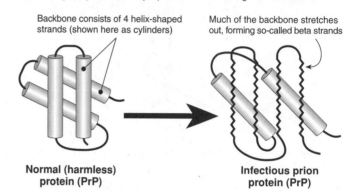

Backbone consists of 4 helix-shaped strands (shown here as cylinders)

Much of the backbone stretches out, forming so-called beta strands

Normal (harmless) protein (PrP) → **Infectious prion protein (PrP)**

Propagation of the Prion Protein

Infectious protein (prion) has an unusual shape allowing it to bind to the normal form of the protein.

The normal (harmless) protein is converted into the infectious prion form.

The original and newly formed prions attack other normal proteins nearby. Those molecules, in turn, attack other normal molecules, until the prions accumulate to dangerous levels.

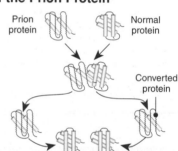

Prion diseases of selected mammals

Mammal	Disease
Sheep	Scrapie
Mink	Transmissible Mink Encephalopathy (TME)
Mule deer, elk	Chronic Wasting Disease (CWD)
Cattle	Bovine Spongiform Encephalopathy (BSE)

Prion Diseases of Humans

Disease	Typical symptoms	Acquisition of disease	Distribution	Span of overt illness
Kuru	Loss of coordination, often followed by dementia.	Infection probably through cannibalism (which stopped in 1958).	Known only in highlands of Papua New Guinea; some 2600 cases have been identified since 1957.	Three months to one year
"Classical" Creutzfeldt-Jakob Disease (CJD)	Dementia, followed by loss of coordination, although sometimes this sequence is reversed.	Usually unknown (in "sporadic" disease). In 10-15% of cases, inheritance of a mutation in the gene coding for the prion protein. Infection as an accidental consequence of surgery, as well as growth hormone injections, corneal transplants from dead donors (not blood transfusions).	*Sporadic form:* 1 person per million worldwide. *Inherited form:* some 100 extended families have been identified. *Infectious form:* 80 cases from medical procedures (e.g. injection of human growth hormone from pituitary of dead people).	Typically about one year; the range is one month to more than 10 years
Mad Cow Disease or Variant Creutzfeldt-Jakob Disease (vCJD)	Dementia, shaky movements, unsteady gait, sudden, jerky, involuntary movements of head, face, or limbs.	Infection by eating beef products from cattle infected with bovine spongiform encephalopathy (BSE).	By June 1999, 43 people had been identified as being infected from BSE cattle in the UK.	Unknown but probably between 2 and 30 years
Gerstmann-Straussler-Scheinker Disease (GSS)	Loss of coordination, often followed by dementia.	Inheritance of a mutation in the gene coding for the prion protein (PrP).	Some 50 extended families have been identified.	Typically about two to six years
Fatal Familial Insomnia	Trouble sleeping and disturbance of the autonomic nervous system, followed by insomnia and dementia.	Inheritance of a mutation in the gene coding for the prion protein (PrP).	Nine extended families have been identified.	Typically about one year

Source: Modified after Scientific American, January 1995, p. 32.

Reported incidence of scrapie and BSE in the UK

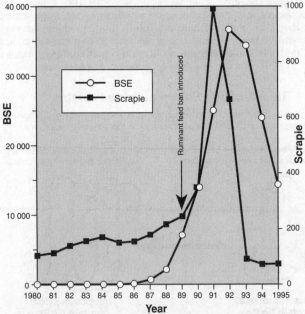

The first cases of Bovine Spongiform Encephalopathy (BSE) were seen at the end of 1986. The disease had spread because meat and bone meal (MBM) rendered from the bodies of infected cows and sheep (infected with a similar disease, scrapie), were used in feeds given to other cattle. On the 18th July 1988, Britain banned ruminant-to-ruminant feeding. By the end of 1998, approximately 170 000 cases had been confirmed and another 100 000 cattle were culled in an attempt to stop the spread of the disease. BSE very nearly destroyed the British beef industry.

Deaths of human prion disease cases in the UK

Year	Sporadic	Iatrogenic	Familial	GSS	vCJD	Total¶
1992	45	2	5	1	-	53
1993	37	4	3	2	-	46
1994	53	1	4	3	-	61
1995	35	4	2	3	3	47
1996	40	4	2	4	10	60
1997	60	6	4	1	10	81
1998	63	3	3	2	18	89
1999	62	6	2	0	15	85
2000	50	1	2	1	28	82
2001	58	4	3	2	20	87
2002	72	0	4	1	17	94
2003	79	5	4	2	18	108
2004	51	2	4	1	9	67
2005	65	3	7	6	5	86
2006	57	1	6	3	5	72
2007*	7	2	0	1	2	12

Source: Department of Health, United Kingdom: www.cjd.ed.ac.uk/figures.htm

Sporadic: Classic CJD cases that appear to occur spontaneously with no definite cause and account for 85% of all cases.

Iatrogenic: Classic CJD cases resulting from a medical procedure. All UK cases have resulted from treatment with human derived pituitary growth hormones or from grafts using dura mater (a membrane lining the skull).

Familial: Cases occurring in families associated with mutations in the PrP gene (10-15% of cases).

GSS: *Gertsmann-Straussler-Scheinker syndrome;* an extremely rare inherited autosomal dominant disease that causes shaky movements and terminal dementia.

vCJD: Variant CJD (originally named *new variant* CJD). Hitherto unrecognized variant of CJD discovered in April 1996.

Total¶: Includes all confirmed cases.

* Incomplete data (as to 4 May 2007)

1. Describe the main feature of prions that distinguishes them from other infectious agents: _____

_____

2. Explain briefly how a prion is able to replicate inside a mammal's body: _____

_____

_____

_____

3. In 1988, the British government introduced a ban on feeding cattle with meat and bone meal.

   (a) Explain the purpose of this ban: _____

   _____

   (b) Suggest why the incidence of **BSE** continued to increase for a number of years after the ban: _____

   _____

   _____

4. State the source of infection for people with **variant CJD**: _____

5. Describe the cultural practice of highland tribes of Papua New Guinea that spread the prion disease known as **kuru**:

_____

_____

6. Name a prion disease that affects the following mammals:

   (a) Sheep: _____ (b) Cattle: _____ (c) Humans: _____

7. Identify three medical procedures that have been known to accidentally introduce CJD into patients:

_____

Emerging Diseases

A host of infectious diseases new to humans have affected millions of people world-wide. These **emerging diseases** pose a real threat to the human population, particularly in some countries. Emerging diseases are so named because they have no previous history in the human population. Often, as with **AIDS** and **SARS**, they are **zoonoses** (animal diseases that cross to humans). Zoonoses are capable of causing highly lethal **pandemics** (world-wide epidemics) amongst an unprepared population. The increasing incidence of **drug-resistance** in pathogens (including those that cause tuberculosis, malaria, pneumonia, gonorrhea,

and cholera) has led to the **re-emergence** of diseases that were previously thought to be largely under control. Foodborne diseases are also on the rise, despite improved hygiene. Even diseases once thought to be non-infectious (e.g. stomach ulcers and cervical cancer) are now known to be linked to infectious agents. In the 1940s, many common and lethal diseases (e.g. scarlet fever and diphtheria) were conquered using antibiotics. It is now evident that antibiotics are not only losing their power, but they are encouraging the emergence of deadly and potentially untreatable infections.

E. coli 0157:H7

A highly pathogenic form of a normally harmless human intestinal bacterium, *Escherichia coli* (below), which causes diarrhea, sweating, vomiting, and sometimes death. Past sources of contamination include meats (Scotland) and apple juice (western US). Several deaths in New York and Canada were caused by outbreaks of this pathogen in 1999-2000.

BSE and CJD

Investigation into the appearance of a new form of **Creutzfeldt-Jakob Disease** (vCJD) in Britain in 1994-1995 established a link with **Mad Cow Disease** or BSE (**bovine spongiform encephalopathy**). This **prion** disease is spread through the consumption of contaminated beef.

Severe Acute Respiratory Syndrome (SARS)

The first case of this respiratory illness was reported 16 November 2002, in China. Initially, epidemiologists thought that people were contracting SARS from eating masked palm civet and racoon-dogs infected with the virus. It is now known that the reservoir for the disease is a bat, which passes the infection to other mammals. Once in the human population, SARS spread rapidly via close contact (e.g. sneezing). The virus belongs to a group called Coronaviruses (right). SARS had a mortality of about 10%, with 50% for people aged 60+ (see the next page).

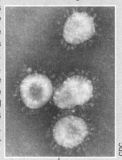

Resistant Tuberculosis

The reappearance of TB as a virulent disease is the result of an increasing multi-drug resistance to antibiotics and fewer people being immunized.

Hantavirus

An outbreak in Argentina of *hantavirus pulmonary syndrome* in 1996 caused 9 deaths from 17 cases. The source of infection was contact with rodent feces. A recent outbreak in Panama caused 3 deaths.

Avian influenza A(H5N1)

In January 2004, a new strain of 'bird flu' (H5N1) spread rapidly through 8 Asian countries. Outbreaks occurred again in 2005, each time with high human mortality. It is now continuing its spread through Africa and Europe. Because it mutates rapidly and appears to easily cross the species barrier, this disease poses a considerable public health threat.

West Nile Virus

A sometimes fatal encephalitis caused by a flaviviral infection. Most of those infected have no symptoms, but 20% will have some symptoms and a small proportion (less than 1%) will develop severe infection. Symptoms of severe infection include high fever, coma, convulsions, and paralysis. In 2002, there were 277 deaths from West Nile fever in the US, with infection rates concentrated in certain states. The disease is transmitted to humans via **mosquitoes** (below), which are infected with the virus when feeding on bird **reservoir hosts**. Over 110 bird species are known to have been infected with West Nile virus, and bird deaths are closely monitored in the US as indicators of West Nile outbreaks.

Hemorrhagic Fevers: Ebola & Marburg

Viral hemorrhagic fevers are a group of diseases from four distinct families of viruses. The two best known examples are the filoviruses **Ebola** (below) and **Marburg**. Outbreaks of Ebola have occurred sporadically: in 1976 and 1979, and again in 1995-1996 and 2001-2003. Marburg virus erupted in Angola early in 2005 and was still continuing in May of this year. Mortality was high at 87%, with a total of 276 of 316 reported cases being fatal.

HIV and AIDS

The AIDS pandemic is set to have a lasting effect on the world population. At least two strains are recognized: the deadly **HIV-1 virus** is more widespread than the slightly more benign **HIV-2 strain**. **HIV viruses** (arrowed) are shown below emerging from a human T cell. HIV is responsible for the massive AIDS pandemic that some claim to be species threatening.

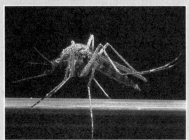

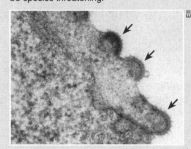

Related activities: HIV & AIDS, The Control of Disease, Antimicrobial Drugs

ERA 2

The Initial Spread of SARS in Toronto, Canada
(February – April, 2003)

Kwan Sui-Chu travels to Hong Kong in February, contracts **Severe Acute Respiratory Syndrome** (SARS) at the Metropole Hotel from a "super spreader", and returns home to Toronto where she infects her family. She later dies of SARS on March 5.

Kwan's Family

Tse Chi Kwai (son)

Wife of **Tse's** doctor

Scarborough Grace Hospital

Joseph Pollack

Tse shares a room with other patients, infecting two of them: "**Mr. D.**" and **Joseph Pollack**

"**Mr. D.**"

Pollack's wife, **Rose**, is infected while in waiting room

"**Mr. D.**" is transferred to York Central

Rose sits next to a prayer group **patriarch** and his **two sons**

In addition, at least 14 hospital staff develop symptoms

Mount Sinai Hospital

A patient had visited a Scarborough clinic; four on Mount Sinai staff develop symptoms

Filipino Prayer Group
(Bukas Loob Sa Diyos)

York Central Hospital

Health officials say "**Mr. D.**" could have exposed dozens. Two other patients die at York

One son travels to a Montreal conference

Patriarch's sons attend father's funeral and two other group functions. At least 30 members are infected.

One son travels to Pennsylvania

Source: "How One Case Spawned Dozens More", TIME Magazine, May 5, 2003, page 36-37.

KEY: Infected — Known dead

The Containment of an Epidemic

The global SARS outbreak in 2003 developed quickly and dramatically. Its containment required heroic efforts and extraordinary measures. Health systems at every major outbreak site were strained to the limits of their capacity. The last reported case of SARS from this initial epidemic was detected and isolated, in Taiwan, on 15 June 2003.

Health authorities rapidly introduced a series of sweeping measures, including:

- Vigorous tracing of every possible contact with a SARS patient.

- Immediate quarantine of individuals suspected (but not confirmed) of having SARS (enforced with the threat of execution in the case of mainland China).

- Surveillance systems were upgraded and began to deliver the kind of information needed for prompt and targeted action.

- Hospital procedures for infection control were tightened, and procedures were developed to ensure the efficient delivery of protective equipment and other supplies.

- Mass education campaigns persuaded the population to check frequently for fever and report promptly at fever clinics. This greatly reduced the time between onset of symptoms and isolation of patients.

- A mechanism was established for coordinating the response of all relevant agencies.

- WHO issued rare travel advisories as evidence mounted that SARS was spreading by air travel along international routes. WHO recommended that persons traveling to certain regions/cities consider postponing all but essential travel until further notice. This was the most stringent travel advisory issued by WHO in its 55-year history.

- WHO set up three networks of leading laboratories around the world to investigate:

  - speeding up detection of the causative agent and developing a diagnostic test;

  - pooling clinical knowledge on symptoms, diagnosis, and management (treatment);

  - SARS epidemiology (how the disease is spread through a population).

Source: World Health Organisation (WHO)

1. Describe the biological and social factors important in the emergence and spread of a named **emerging disease**:

_____

_____

_____

_____

_____

_____

2. Explain the role of **zoonoses** in the emergence of new diseases: _____

_____

3. Using an example, explain what a **re-emerging disease** is: _____

_____

4. The Spanish influenza pandemic of 1917-18 was made worse by the return of troops from World War I to their home countries. More than 20 million people died in the pandemic, which had a death rate of about 3%. Explain how this pandemic differed from that of SARS in 2003, in terms of its **global spread** and **death rate**:

_____

The Control of Disease

Many factors can influence the spread of disease, including the social climate, diet, general health, and access to medical care. Human intervention and modification of behavior can reduce the transmission rate of some diseases and inhibit their spread. Examples include the use of personal physical barriers, such as condoms, to prevent sexually transmitted infections (STIs), and the use of **quarantine** to ensure that potential carriers of disease are isolated until incubation periods have elapsed. Cleaning up the environment also lowers the incidence of disease by reducing the likelihood that pathogens or their vectors will survive. The effective control of infectious disease depends on knowing the origin of the outbreak (its natural reservoir), its mode of transmission within the population, and the methods that can be feasibly employed to contain it. Diseases are often classified according to how they behave in a given population. Any disease that spreads from one host to another, either directly or indirectly, is said to be a **communicable disease**. Those that are easily spread from one person to another, such as chicken pox or measles, are said to be **contagious**. Such diseases are a threat to **public health** and many must be notified to health authorities. **Noncommunicable diseases** are not spread from one host to another and pose less of a threat to public health. A disease that occurs only occasionally and is usually restricted in its spread is called a **sporadic disease**.

Methods For Controlling the Spread of Disease

Transmission of disease can be prevented or reduced by adopting 'safe' behaviors. Examples include using condoms to reduce the spread of STIs, isolation of people with a specific illness (such as SARS), or establishing quarantine procedures for people who may be infected, but are not yet ill.

The development of effective sanitation, sewage treatment, and treatment of drinking water has virtually eliminated dangerous waterborne diseases from developed countries. These practices disrupt the normal infection cycle of pathogens such as cholera and giardia.

Appropriate personal hygiene practices reduce the risk of infection and transmission. Soap may not destroy the pathogens but washing will dilute and remove them from the skin. Although popular, antibacterial soaps encourage development of strains resistant to antimicrobial agents.

The environment can be made less suitable for the growth and transmission of pathogens. For example, spraying drainage ditches and draining swamps eliminates breeding habitats for mosquitoes carrying diseases such as malaria and dengue fever.

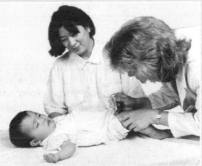

Immunization schedules form part of public health programs. If most of the population is immune, 'herd immunity' limits outbreaks to sporadic cases. In such populations there are too few susceptible individuals to support the spread of an epidemic.

Disinfectants and sterilization techniques, such as autoclaving, destroy pathogenic microbes before they have the opportunity to infect. The use of these techniques in medicine has significantly reduced post operative infections and associated deaths.

1. Distinguish between contagious and non-communicable diseases, providing an example of each:

   _____

   _____

2. (a) Explain the difference between **isolation** and **quarantine**: _____

   _____

   _____

   _____

Related activities: HIV and AIDS, Malaria, Emerging Diseases, Immunization

RA 2

(b) Using the recent example of SARS, explain how isolation and quarantine operate to prevent the spread of disease:

_____

_____

3. Explain how the use of condoms reduces the spread of the human immunodeficiency virus (HIV) that causes AIDS:

_____

_____

4. Explain how the drainage of stagnant water in tropical regions may reduce the incidence of malaria in those countries:

_____

_____

5. Describe how each of the following methods is used to control the **growth** of disease-causing microbes:

(a) Disinfectants: _____

_____

(b) Antiseptics: _____

_____

(c) Heat: _____

_____

(d) Ionizing radiation (gamma rays): _____

_____

(e) Desiccation: _____

_____

(f) Cold: _____

_____

6. The **Human Genome Project** (HGP) was launched in 1990 and completed in 2003, two years ahead of schedule. Its achieved aim was to sequence the entire human genome, but much of the research since has focused on determining the various roles of the (expressed) gene products. It is hoped that a more complete understanding the human genome will revolutionize the treatment and prevention of disease. Briefly discuss how the HGP will facilitate:

(a) Diagnosis of disease: _____

_____

_____

(b) Treatment of disease: _____

_____

_____

7. The first measles vaccine was introduced to Britain in 1964. However, in 1993 there were 9000 cases of measles notified to the health authorities in England and Wales.

(a) Suggest why measles has not been eliminated in Britain: _____

_____

(b) Explain how vaccination interrupts the transmission of measles within a population: _____

_____

_____

Antimicrobial Drugs

Antimicrobial drugs include synthetic (manufactured) **drugs** as well as drugs produced by bacteria and fungi, called **antibiotics**. Antibiotics are produced naturally by these microorganisms as a means of inhibiting competing microbes around them (a form of antibiosis, hence the name antibiotic). The first antibiotic, called penicillin, was discovered in 1928 by Alexander Fleming. Since then, similar inhibitory reactions between colonies growing on solid media have been commonly observed. Antibiotics are actually rather easy to discover, but few of them are of medical or commercial value. Many antibiotics are toxic to humans or lack any advantage over those already in use. More than half of our antibiotics are produced by species of filamentous bacteria that commonly inhabit the soil, called *Streptomyces*. A few antibiotics are produced by bacteria of the genus *Bacillus*. Others are produced by molds, mostly of the genera *Cephalosporium* and *Penicillium*. Antimicrobial drugs are used in **chemotherapy** programs to treat infectious diseases. Like disinfectants, these chemicals interfere with the growth of

microorganisms (see diagram below). They may either kill microbes directly (**bactericidal**) or prevent them from growing (**bacteriostatic**). To be effective, they must often act inside the host, so their effect on the host's cells and tissues is important. The ideal antimicrobial drug has **selective toxicity**, killing the pathogen without damaging the host. Some antimicrobial drugs have a narrow **spectrum of activity**, and affect only a limited number of microbial types. Others are **broad-spectrum drugs** and affect a large number of microbial species (see the table below). When the identity of a pathogen is not known, a broad-spectrum drug may be prescribed in order to save valuable time. There is a disadvantage with this, because broad spectrum drugs target not just the pathogen, but much of the host's normal microflora also. The normal microbial community usually controls the growth of pathogens and other microbes by competing with them. By selectively removing them with drugs, certain microbes in the community that do not normally cause problems, may flourish and become **opportunistic pathogens**.

How Antimicrobial Drugs Work

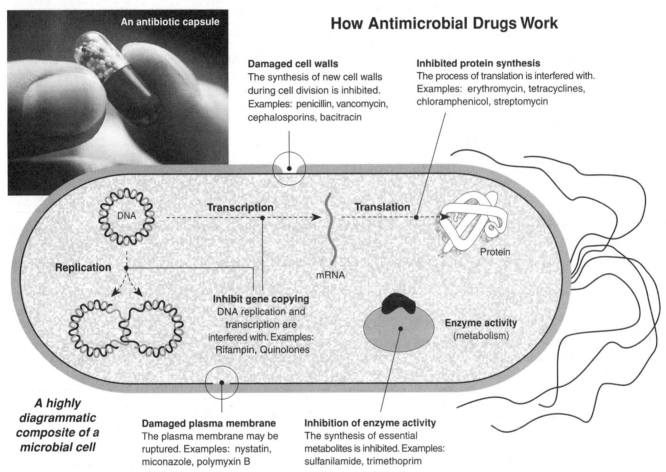

Damaged cell walls
The synthesis of new cell walls during cell division is inhibited. Examples: penicillin, vancomycin, cephalosporins, bacitracin

Inhibited protein synthesis
The process of translation is interfered with. Examples: erythromycin, tetracyclines, chloramphenicol, streptomycin

Inhibit gene copying
DNA replication and transcription are interfered with. Examples: Rifampin, Quinolones

Enzyme activity
(metabolism)

A highly diagrammatic composite of a microbial cell

Damaged plasma membrane
The plasma membrane may be ruptured. Examples: nystatin, miconazole, polymyxin B

Inhibition of enzyme activity
The synthesis of essential metabolites is inhibited. Examples: sulfanilamide, trimethoprim

An antibiotic capsule

Spectrum of antimicrobial activity of a number of chemotherapeutic drugs

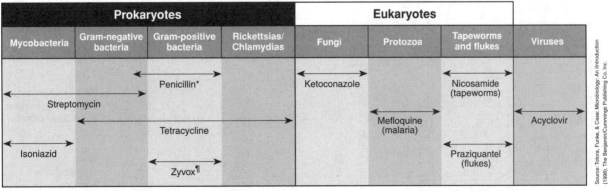

Prokaryotes				Eukaryotes			
Mycobacteria	Gram-negative bacteria	Gram-positive bacteria	Rickettsias/ Chlamydias	Fungi	Protozoa	Tapeworms and flukes	Viruses

Penicillin*

Streptomycin

Tetracycline

Isoniazid

Zyvox¶

Ketoconazole

Nicosamide (tapeworms)

Mefloquine (malaria)

Acyclovir

Praziquantel (flukes)

Source: Totora, Funke, & Case: Microbiology: An Introduction (1998) The Benjamin/Cummings Publishing Co. Inc.

* There are some synthetic derivatives of penicillin that act effectively against gram-negative bacteria.
¶ The first new class of antibiotics to be used in 35 years.

1. Discuss the requirements of an "ideal" anti-microbial drug, and explain in what way antibiotics satisfy these requirements:

_____

_____

_____

_____

2. Some bacteria have ways of tolerating treatment by antibiotics, and are termed 'superbugs'.

   (a) Explain what is meant by **antibiotic resistance** in bacteria: _____

   _____

   _____

   (b) Explain why a course of antibiotics should be finished completely, even when the symptoms of infection have gone:

   _____

   _____

3. (a) Explain the advantages and disadvantages of using a **broad-spectrum drug** on an unidentified bacterial infection:

   _____

   _____

   (b) Identify two groups of broad spectrum drugs: _____

4. Although there are a few drugs that have some success in controlling viruses, antibiotics are ineffective. Explain why antibiotics do not work against viruses:

   _____

   _____

5. Describe four ways in which antimicrobial drugs kill or inhibit the growth of microbes: _____

   _____

   _____

6. The diagram below shows an experiment investigating the effectiveness of different antibiotics on a pure culture of a single species of bacteria. Giving a reason, state which antibiotic (A-D) is most effective in controlling the bacteria:

   _____

   _____

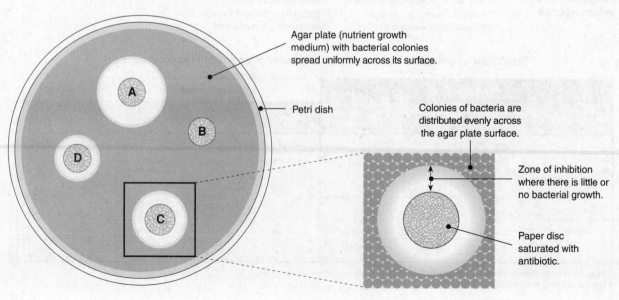

Agar plate (nutrient growth medium) with bacterial colonies spread uniformly across its surface.

Petri dish

Colonies of bacteria are distributed evenly across the agar plate surface.

Zone of inhibition where there is little or no bacterial growth.

Paper disc saturated with antibiotic.

Defense Against Infectious Disease

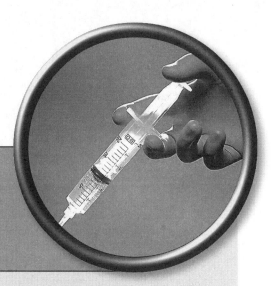

IB SL	IB HL	IB Options	AP Biology
Complete: 1, 7(a)-(b), (f), 19-21, 24 *Extension:* 7(c)-(e), 8-10	**Complete:** 1, 6-7(a)-(b), (f), 8-9, 11-16, 19-24, 27-29, 33, 35	**Not applicable to options**	**Complete:** 1-35 *Some numbers extension as appropriate*

Learning Objectives

☐ 1. Compile your own glossary from the **KEY WORDS** displayed in **bold type** in the learning objectives below.

Recognizing Self and Non-self *(pages 49-50)*

☐ 2. Explain how a body is able to distinguish between self and non-self and comment on the importance of this.

☐ 3. Appreciate the nature of **major histocompatibility complex (MHC)** and its role in self-recognition and in determining tissue compatibility in transplant recipients.

☐ 4. Explain the basis of the **Rh** and **ABO blood group systems** in humans. Explain what is meant by **agglutination** and how this reaction forms the basis of blood grouping. Explain the consequences of blood type incompatibility in **blood transfusions**.

☐ 5. Discuss the physiological basis of **transplant rejection** and suggest how it may be avoided. Explain why it is so difficult to find compatible tissue and organ donors and suggest how this problem may be solved in the future.

Defense Mechanisms

Blood clotting *(page 51)*

☐ 6. Describe the process of **blood clotting**, including the role of **clotting factors**, **thrombin**, and **fibrin**. Appreciate the role of blood clotting in the resistance of the body to infection by sealing off damage and restricting invasion of the tissues by microorganisms.

Non-specific defenses *(pages 47-48, 52-54)*

☐ 7. Explain what is meant by a **non-specific defense mechanism**. Distinguish between first and second lines of defense. Describe the nature and role of each of the following in protecting against pathogens:
   (a) Skin (including sweat and sebum production).
   (b) Mucus-secreting and ciliated membranes.
   (c) Body secretions (tears, urine, saliva, gastric juice).
   (d) Natural anti-bacterial and anti-viral proteins such as **interferon** and **complement.**
   (e) The **inflammatory response**, **fever**, and cell death.
   (f) **Phagocytosis** by phagocytes. Recognize the term phagocyte as referring to any of a number of phagocytic leukocytes (e.g. macrophages).

Specific defenses *(pages 47-48, 55-56)*

☐ 8. Identify the role of **specific resistance** in the body's resistance to infection. Contrast specific and non-specific defenses in terms of time for activation and specificity towards a pathogen.

☐ 9. Explain what is meant by an **immune response**. Explain how the immune response involves recognition and response to foreign material. Explain the significance of the immune system having both specificity and memory. Providing examples, distinguish between **naturally acquired** and **artificially acquired immunity** and between **active** and **passive immunity**. Compare the duration of the immunity gained by active and passive means.

☐ 10. Recognize the role of the **lymphatic system** in the production and transport of leukocytes.

The Immune System *(pages 57-60)*

☐ 11. Distinguish between **cell-mediated immunity** and **humoral (antibody-mediated) immunity**, identifying the speciifc white blood cells involved in each case.

☐ 12. Recall that other types of white blood cells are involved in non-specific defense mechanisms.

☐ 13. Explain the role of the **thymus** in the immune response. Describe the nature, origin, and role of **macrophages** (a type of phagocyte). Appreciate the role of macrophages in processing and presenting foreign antigens and in stimulating lymphocyte activity.

☐ 14. Explain the origin and maturation of **B lymphocytes** (cells) and **T lymphocytes** (cells). Describe and distinguish between the activities of the B and T lymphocytes in the immune response.

☐ 15. With reference to immune system function, outline the principle of challenge and response. Outline **clonal selection** and the basis of **immunological memory**. Explain how the immune system is able to respond to the large and unpredictable range of potential antigens.

☐ 16. Appreciate that self-tolerance occurs during development as a result of the selective destruction of the B cells that react to self-antigens.

Cell-mediated immunity

☐ 17. T cells are responsible for **cell-mediated immunity**. Describe how T cells recognize **specific** foreign antigens. Describe the roles of named T cells, including **cytotoxic** (killer) **T cells** (T_C) and **helper T cells** (T_H). Identify the organisms against which these T cells act.

☐ 18. Appreciate the role of T lymphocytes in the rejection of transplanted tissues and organs.

Humoral immunity

☐ 19. Define the terms: **antibody** (immunoglobulin), and **antigen**. Name some common antigens and explain their role in provoking a specific immune response.

☐ 20. Describe the structure of an antibody identifying the constant and variable regions, and the antigen binding site. Relate the structure of antibodies to their function.

☐ 21. Explain antibody production, including how B cells bring about **humoral (antibody-mediated) immunity** to specific antigens. If required, provide an explanation of how antigens are presented, the role of **helper T cells**, and the activation and differentiation of B-cells.

22. Contrast the roles of **plasma cells** and **memory cells**. Discuss the role of **immunological memory** in long term immunity.

23. Describe the methods by which antibodies inactivate antigens and facilitate their destruction.

Immune Dysfunction *(pages 25-26, 66 and the TRC: Autoimmune Diseases)*

24. Outline the effects of **HIV** on the immune system, including reference to the reduction in the number of active lymphocytes and the loss of immune function.

25. Explain what is meant by an **autoimmune disease** and describe examples. Identify common triggers for autoimmune diseases and suggest how they can be managed (see the TRC.)

26. With reference to **asthma** or **hayfever**, outline the role of the immune system in **allergies**. Identify common triggers for allergic reactions in susceptible people.

Immunization *(pages 61-65 and the TRC: Edible Vaccines)*

27. Recognize that vaccination provides **artificially acquired immunity**. Recall the difference between **passive** and **active immunity**.

28. Outline the principle of **vaccination**. Explain what is meant by a **primary** and a **secondary response** to infection and identify the role of these, and the immune system memory, in the success of vaccines.

29. Appreciate that **immunization** involves the production of immunity by artificial means and that **vaccination** usually refers to immunization by inoculation. Know that these terms are frequently used synonymously.

30. Explain the role of **vaccination** programs in preventing disease. Discuss the role of **vaccination programs** in the eradication of some (named) infectious diseases.

31. Outline the vaccination schedule for your country or state, identifying critical times for vaccination against specific diseases. Comment on the role of effective vaccination programs in public health.

32. Describe the principles involved in vaccine production. Distinguish between **subunit** and **whole-agent vaccines** and between **inactivated** (dead) and **live** (attenuated) **vaccines**. Contrast the risks and benefits associated with live and dead vaccines.

33. Discuss the benefits and risks of vaccination against bacterial and viral infection. Include reference to the MMR vaccine and two other examples. Evaluate the risks associated with immunization relative to the risks associated with contracting the disease itself.

34. Describe the role of genetic engineering in the development of new vaccines. *Some of this material is covered in an activity on the TRC: Edible Vaccines.*

Monoclonal antibodies *(page 65)*

35. Describe the production of **monoclonal antibodies**. Explain why they are so useful in medicine and outline some of their applications. Describe one use of them in diagnosis and one use in treatment.

See the 'Textbook Reference Grid' on pages 8-9 for textbook page references relating to material in this topic.

Supplementary Texts

See pages 5-6 for additional details of these texts:

■ Clegg, C.J., 1998. **Mammals: Structure and Function** (John Murray), pp. 40-41.

■ Fullick, A., 1998. **Human Health and Disease** (Heinemann), pp. 27-36.

■ Helms, D.R. *et al.*, 1998. **Biology in the Laboratory** (W.H. Freeman), #19.

■ Hudson, T. & K. Mannion, 2001. **Microbes and Disease** (Collins), pp. 70-86.

■ Taylor, J. 2001. **Microorganisms and Biotechnology** (NelsonThornes), chpt. 7.

See page 6 for details of publishers of periodicals:

STUDENT'S REFERENCE

Self-recognition & the immune system

■ **Red Blood Cells** Biol. Sci. Rev., 11(2) Nov. 1998, pp. 2-4. *The function of red blood cells, including their role in antigenic recognition.*

■ **Beware! Allergens** New Scientist, 22 Jan. 2000 (Inside Science). *The allergic response: sensitization and the role of the immune system.*

Presentation MEDIA to support this topic:

HEALTH & DISEASE:
• **Defense & Immunity**

■ **Anaphylactic Shock** Biol. Sci. Rev., 19(2) Nov. 2006, pp. 11-13. *Describes anaphylactic shock, a severe allergic reaction caused by a massive overreaction of the body's immune system.*

■ **Skin, Scabs and Scars** Biol. Sci. Rev., 17(3) Feb. 2005, pp. 2-6. *The many roles of skin, including its importance in wound healing and the processes involved in its repair when damaged.*

■ **Intestinal Worms - Can they keep you Healthy?** Biol. Sci. Rev., 19(2) Nov. 2006, pp. 2-6. *Having intestinal worms appears to suppress inappropriate allergic responses.*

■ **Antibodies** Biol. Sci. Rev., 11(3) Jan. 1999, pp. 34-35. *The operation of the immune system and the production of antibodies (including procedures for producing monoclonal antibodies).*

■ **Lymphocytes - The Heart of the Immune System** Biol. Sci. Rev., 12 (1) Sept. 1999, pp. 32-35. *An excellent account of the role of lymphocytes in the immune response (includes the types and actions of different lymphocytes).*

Vaccines and vaccine development

■ **HIV Focus** New Scientist, 8 Feb. 2003, pp. 33-44. *A special issue covering HIV research: why the immune system responds in different ways in different individuals, new hope in vaccine development, and use of protective microbiocides.*

■ **Immunotherapy** Biol. Sci. Rev., 15(1), Sept. 2002, pp. 39-41. *Medical research is uncovering ways in which our immune system can be used in developing vaccines for cancer.*

TEACHER'S REFERENCE

■ **Inside Trading** New Scientist, 26 June 1999, pp. 42-46. *How do we maintain a stable relationship with our microflora and protect ourselves from attack by pathogens?*

■ **The Long Arm of the Immune System** Sci. American, Nov. 2002, pp. 34-41. *The role of dendritic cells, a class of leukocyte with a role in activating the immune system (good extension).*

■ **Disarming Flu Viruses** Scientific American, Jan. 1999, pp. 56-65. *The influenza virus, its life cycle, and vaccine development for its control.*

■ **Filthy Friends** New Scientist, 16 April 2005, pp. 34-39. *Early contact with a range of harmless microbes helps in reducing the risk of allergy.*

■ **Let Them Eat Dirt** New Scientist, 18 July 1998, pp. 26-31. *Effective, normal immune system function may require a certain level of early exposure to bacteria and microorganisms.*

■ **Edible Vaccines** Scientific American, Sept. 2000, pp. 48-53. *Vaccines in food may be the way of future immunization programs.*

■ **How Interferons Fight Disease** Scientific American, May 1994, pp. 40-47. *The active role of interferons in human immune system function.*

■ **Preparing for Battle** Scientific American, Feb. 2001, pp. 68-69. *Preparation and mode of action of the influenza vaccine.*

■ **Genetic Vaccines** Scientific American, July 1999, pp. 34-41. *This excellent article includes a description of how these vaccines work and a table of specific diseases treatable by this method.*

■ **Peacekeepers of the Immune System** Scientific American, Oct. 2006, pp. 34-41. *Regulatory T cells suppress immune activity and combat autoimmunity.*

■ **ABORh Blood-Typing Model: a Problem Solving Activity** The Am. Biology Teacher, March 2005, pp. 158-162. *Using an easy to make blood-typing model kit to practise problem solving skills.*

See pages 10-11 for details of how to access **Bio Links** from our web site: **www.thebiozone.com** From Bio Links, access sites under the topics:

GENERAL BIOLOGY ONLINE RESOURCES > Online Textbooks and Lecture Notes: • S-Cool! A level biology revision guide • Learn.co.uk • Mark Rothery's biology web site *... and others*

ANIMAL BIOLOGY: • Anatomy and physiology • Human physiology lecture notes *... and others*

HEALTH & DISEASE > Defense and the Immune System: • Blood group antigens • Inducible defenses against pathogens • Microbiology and immunology • Primary immunodeficiency diseases • The immune system: An overview • Understanding the immune system *... and others*

The Body's Defenses

If microorganisms never encountered resistance from our body defenses, we would be constantly ill and would eventually die of various diseases. Fortunately, in most cases our defenses prevent this from happening. Some of these defenses are designed to keep microorganisms from entering the body. Other defenses remove the microorganisms if they manage to get inside. Further defenses attack the microorganisms if they remain inside the body. The ability to ward off disease through the various defense mechanisms is called **resistance**. The lack of resistance, or vulnerability to disease, is known as **susceptibility**. One form of defense is referred to as **non-specific resistance**, and includes defenses that protect us from any pathogen. This includes a first line of defense such as the physical barriers to infection (skin and mucous membranes) and a second line of defense (phagocytes, inflammation, fever, and antimicrobial substances). **Specific resistance** is a third line of defense that forms the **immune response** and targets specific pathogens. Specialized cells of the immune system, called lymphocytes, produce specific proteins called antibodies which are produced against specific antigens.

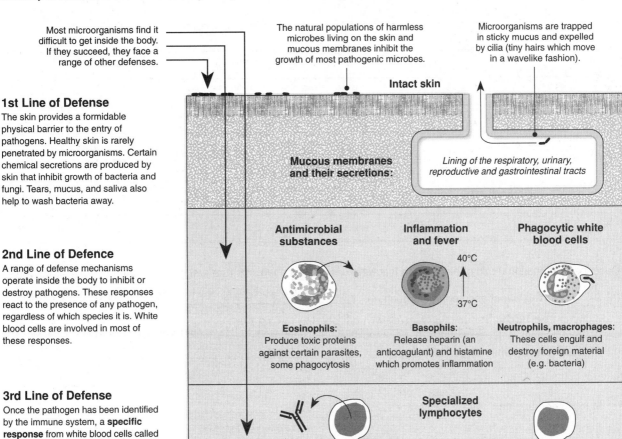

Most microorganisms find it difficult to get inside the body. If they succeed, they face a range of other defenses.

The natural populations of harmless microbes living on the skin and mucous membranes inhibit the growth of most pathogenic microbes.

Microorganisms are trapped in sticky mucus and expelled by cilia (tiny hairs which move in a wavelike fashion).

Intact skin

Mucous membranes and their secretions:

Lining of the respiratory, urinary, reproductive and gastrointestinal tracts

Antimicrobial substances

Eosinophils:
Produce toxic proteins against certain parasites, some phagocytosis

Inflammation and fever
40°C
↑
37°C

Basophils:
Release heparin (an anticoagulant) and histamine which promotes inflammation

Phagocytic white blood cells

Neutrophils, macrophages:
These cells engulf and destroy foreign material (e.g. bacteria)

Specialized lymphocytes

B cell:
Antibody production

T cell:
Cell-mediated immunity

1st Line of Defense
The skin provides a formidable physical barrier to the entry of pathogens. Healthy skin is rarely penetrated by microorganisms. Certain chemical secretions are produced by skin that inhibit growth of bacteria and fungi. Tears, mucus, and saliva also help to wash bacteria away.

2nd Line of Defence
A range of defense mechanisms operate inside the body to inhibit or destroy pathogens. These responses react to the presence of any pathogen, regardless of which species it is. White blood cells are involved in most of these responses.

3rd Line of Defense
Once the pathogen has been identified by the immune system, a **specific response** from white blood cells called lymphocytes occurs. Lymphocytes coordinate a range of specific responses to the pathogen.

Defense Against Infectious Disease

1. Compare and contrast the type of response against pathogens carried out by each of the three levels of defense:

_____

_____

_____

_____

_____

_____

_____

_____

_____

_____

_____

_____

Related activities: Targets for Defense, The Action of Phagocytes, Inflammation, Fever, The Immune System
Web links: Immunoanimations

RA 2

2. Distinguish between specific and non-specific resistance: _____

_____

_____

_____

_____

3. Describe features of the different types of white blood cells and explain how these relate to their role in the second line of defense:

_____

_____

_____

_____

_____

_____

_____

_____

_____

_____

4. Describe the functional role of each of the following defense mechanisms (the first one has been completed for you):

   (a) Skin (including sweat and sebum production): _Skin helps to prevent direct entry of pathogens into the body. Sebum slows growth of bacteria and fungi._

   (b) Phagocytosis by white blood cells: _____

   _____

   (c) Mucus-secreting and ciliated membranes: _____

   _____

   (d) Body secretions: tears, urine, saliva, gastric juice: _____

   _____

   (e) Natural antimicrobial proteins (e.g. interferon): _____

   _____

   (f) Antibody production: _____

   _____

   (g) Fever: _____

   _____

   (h) Cell-mediated immunity: _____

   _____

   (i) The inflammatory response: _____

   _____

5. Infection with HIV results in the progressive destruction of T lymphocytes. Suggest why this leads to an increasing number of opportunistic infections in AIDS sufferers:

   _____

   _____

Targets for Defense

In order for the body to present an effective defense against pathogens, it must first be able to recognize its own tissues (self) and ignore the body's normal microflora (e.g. the bacteria of the skin and gastrointestinal tract). In addition, the body needs to be able to deal with abnormal cells which, if not eliminated, may become cancerous. Failure of self/non-self recognition can lead to autoimmune disorders, in which the immune system mistakenly attacks its own tissues. The body's ability to recognize its own molecules has implications for procedures such as tissue grafts, organ transplants, and blood transfusions. Incompatible tissues (identified as foreign) are attacked by the body's immune system (**rejected**). Even a healthy pregnancy involves suppression of specific features of the self recognition system, allowing the mother to tolerate a nine month gestation with the fetus.

The Body's Natural Microbiota

After birth, normal and characteristic microbial populations begin to establish themselves on and in the body. A typical human body contains 1×10^{13} body cells, yet harbors 1×10^{14} bacterial cells. These microorganisms establish more or less permanent residence but, under normal conditions, do not cause disease. In fact, this normal microflora can benefit the host by preventing the overgrowth of harmful pathogens. They are not found throughout the entire body, but are located in certain regions.

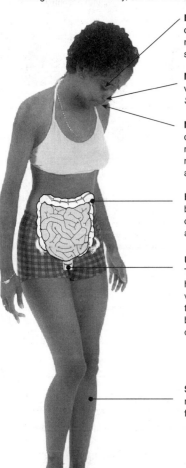

Eyes: The conjuctiva, a continuation of the skin or mucous membrane, contains a similar microbiota to the skin.

Nose and throat: Harbors a variety of microorganisms, e.g. *Staphylococcus spp.*

Mouth: Supports a large and diverse microbiota. It is an ideal microbial environment; high in moisture, warmth, and nutrient availability.

Large intestine: Contains the body's largest resident population of microbes because of its available moisture and nutrients.

Urinary and genital systems: The lower urethra in both sexes has a resident population; the vagina has a particular acid-tolerant population of microbes because of the low pH nature of its secretions.

Skin: Skin secretions prevent most of the microbes on the skin from becoming residents.

Distinguishing Self from Non-Self

The human immune system achieves self-recognition through the **major histocompatibility complex** (MHC). This is a cluster of tightly linked genes on chromosome 6 in humans. These genes code for protein molecules (MHC antigens) that are attached to the surface of body cells. They are used by the immune system to recognize its own or foreign material. **Class I MHC** antigens are located on the surface of virtually all human cells, but **Class II MHC** antigens are restricted to macrophages and the antibody-producing B-lymphocytes.

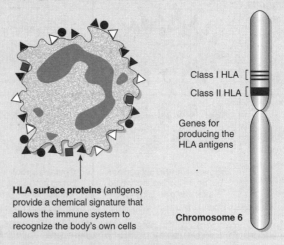

Class I HLA [

Class II HLA [

Genes for producing the HLA antigens

Chromosome 6

HLA surface proteins (antigens) provide a chemical signature that allows the immune system to recognize the body's own cells

Tissue Transplants

The MHC is responsible for the rejection of tissue grafts and organ transplants. Foreign MHC molecules are antigenic, causing the immune system to respond in the following way:

- T cells directly lyse the foreign cells

- Macrophages are activated by T cells and engulf foreign cells

- Antibodies are released that attack the foreign cell

- The complement system injures blood vessels supplying the graft or transplanted organ

To minimize this rejection, attempts are made to match the MHC of the organ donor to that of the recipient as closely as possible.

Defense Against Infectious Disease

1. Explain why it is healthy to have a natural population of microbes on and inside the body: _____

_____

2. (a) Explain the nature and purpose of the **major histocompatibility complex** (MHC): _____

_____

_____

_____

(b) Explain the importance of such a self-recognition system: _____

_____

3. Identify two situations when the body's recognition of 'self' is undesirable: _____

Blood Group Antigens

Blood groups classify blood according to the different marker proteins on the surface of red blood cells (RBCs). These marker proteins act as **antigens** and affect the ability of RBCs to provoke an immune response. The **ABO blood group** is the most important blood typing system in medical practice, because of the presence of anti-A and anti-B antibodies in nearly all people who lack the corresponding red cell antigens (these antibodies are carried in the plasma and are present at birth). If a patient is to receive blood from a blood donor, that blood must be compatible otherwise the red blood cells of the donated blood will clump together (agglutinate), break apart, and block capillaries. There is a small margin of safety in certain blood group combinations, because the volume of donated blood is usually relatively small and the donor's antibodies are quickly diluted in the plasma. In practice, blood is carefully matched, not only for ABO types, but for other types as well. Although human RBCs have more than 500 known antigens, fewer than 30 (in 9 blood groups) are regularly tested for when blood is donated for transfusion. The blood groups involved are: *ABO, Rh, MNS, P, Lewis, Lutheran, Kell, Duffy,* and *Kidd*. The ABO and rhesus (Rh) are the best known. Although blood typing has important applications in medicine, it can also be used to rule out individuals in cases of crime (or paternity) and establish a list of potential suspects (or fathers).

	Blood Type A	Blood Type B	Blood Type AB	Blood Type O
Antigens present on the *red blood cells*	antigen *A*	antigen *B*	antigens *A* and *B*	Neither antigen *A* nor *B*
Anti-bodies present in the *plasma*	Contains **anti-B** antibodies; but no antibodies that would attack its own antigen *A*	Contains **anti-A** antibodies; but no antibodies that would attack its own antigen *B*	Contains neither **anti-A** nor **anti-B** antibodies	Contains both **anti-A** and **anti-B** antibodies

Blood type	Frequency in US *Rh+*	*Rh−*	Antigen	Antibody	Can donate blood to:	Can receive blood from:
A	34%	6%	*A*	*anti-B*	A, AB	A, O
B	9%	2%				
AB	3%	1%				
O	38%	7%				

1. Complete the table above to show the antibodies and antigens in each blood group, and donor/recipient blood types:

2. In a hypothetical murder case, blood from both the victim and the murderer was left at the scene. There were five suspects under investigation:

   (a) Describe what blood typing could establish about the guilt or innocence of the suspects: _____

   _____

   (b) Identify what a blood typing could not establish: _____

   _____

   (c) Suggest how the murderer's identity could be firmly established (assuming that s/he was one of the five suspects): _____

   _____

   (d) Explain why blood typing is not used forensically to any great extent: _____

   _____

3. Explain why the discovery of the ABO system was such a significant medical breakthrough: _____

Related activities: Blood
Web links: Blood Typing Game

Blood Clotting and Defense

Apart from its transport role, **blood** has a role in the body's defense against infection and **hemostasis** (the prevention of bleeding and maintenance of blood volume). The tearing or puncturing of a blood vessel initiates **clotting**. Clotting is normally a rapid process that seals off the tear, preventing blood loss and the invasion of bacteria into the site. Clot formation is triggered by the release of clotting factors from the damaged cells at the site of the tear or puncture. A hardened clot forms a scab, which acts to prevent further blood loss and acts as a mechanical barrier to the entry of pathogens.

Blood Clotting

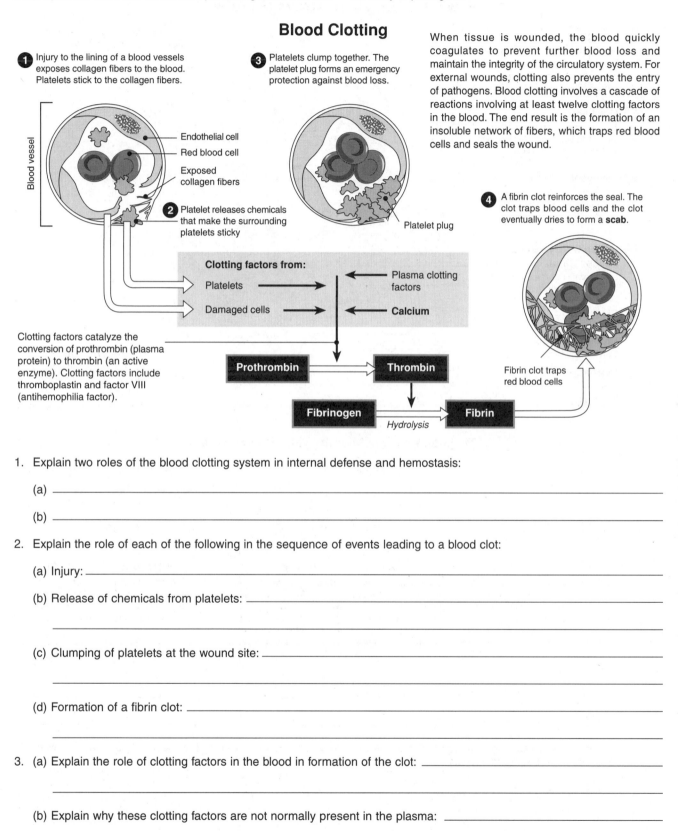

1 Injury to the lining of a blood vessels exposes collagen fibers to the blood. Platelets stick to the collagen fibers.

3 Platelets clump together. The platelet plug forms an emergency protection against blood loss.

When tissue is wounded, the blood quickly coagulates to prevent further blood loss and maintain the integrity of the circulatory system. For external wounds, clotting also prevents the entry of pathogens. Blood clotting involves a cascade of reactions involving at least twelve clotting factors in the blood. The end result is the formation of an insoluble network of fibers, which traps red blood cells and seals the wound.

Blood vessel

Endothelial cell
Red blood cell
Exposed collagen fibers

2 Platelet releases chemicals that make the surrounding platelets sticky

Platelet plug

4 A fibrin clot reinforces the seal. The clot traps blood cells and the clot eventually dries to form a **scab**.

Clotting factors from:
Platelets
Damaged cells

Plasma clotting factors
Calcium

Clotting factors catalyze the conversion of prothrombin (plasma protein) to thrombin (an active enzyme). Clotting factors include thromboplastin and factor VIII (antihemophilia factor).

Fibrin clot traps red blood cells

Prothrombin → **Thrombin**

Fibrinogen → **Fibrin**
Hydrolysis

1. Explain two roles of the blood clotting system in internal defense and hemostasis:

(a) _____

(b) _____

2. Explain the role of each of the following in the sequence of events leading to a blood clot:

(a) Injury: _____

(b) Release of chemicals from platelets: _____
_____

(c) Clumping of platelets at the wound site: _____
_____

(d) Formation of a fibrin clot: _____
_____

3. (a) Explain the role of clotting factors in the blood in formation of the clot: _____
_____

(b) Explain why these clotting factors are not normally present in the plasma: _____
_____

4. (a) Name one inherited disease caused by the absence of a clotting factor: _____

(b) Name the clotting factor involved: _____

Related activities: Blood
Web links: Hemostasis

RA 2

Defense Against Infectious Disease

The Action of Phagocytes

Human cells that ingest microbes and digest them by the process of **phagocytosis** are called **phagocytes**. All are types of white blood cells. During many kinds of infections, especially bacterial infections, the total number of white blood cells increases by two to four times the normal number. The ratio of various white blood cell types changes during the course of an infection.

How a Phagocyte Destroys Microbes

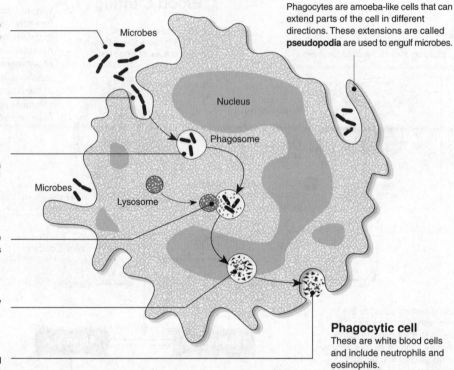

1 Detection
Phagocyte detects microbes by the chemicals they give off (chemotaxis) and sticks the microbes to its surface.

2 Ingestion
The microbe is engulfed by the phagocyte wrapping pseudopodia around it to form a vesicle.

3 Phagosome forms
A phagosome (phagocytic vesicle) is formed, which encloses the microbes in a membrane.

4 Fusion with lysosome
Phagosome fuses with a lysosome (which contains powerful enzymes that can digest the microbe).

5 Digestion
The microbes are broken down by enzymes into their chemical constituents.

6 Discharge
Indigestible material is discharged from the phagocyte cell.

Phagocytes are amoeba-like cells that can extend parts of the cell in different directions. These extensions are called **pseudopodia** are used to engulf microbes.

Microbes

Nucleus

Phagosome

Microbes

Lysosome

Phagocytic cell
These are white blood cells and include neutrophils and eosinophils.

The Interaction of Microbes and Phagocytes

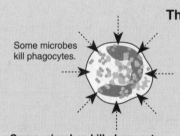

Some microbes kill phagocytes.

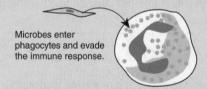

Microbes enter phagocytes and evade the immune response.

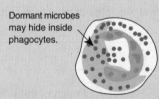

Dormant microbes may hide inside phagocytes.

Some microbes kill phagocytes
Some microbes produce toxins that can actually kill phagocytes, e.g. toxin-producing staphylococci and the dental plaque-forming bacteria *Actinobacillus*.

Microbes evade immune system
Some microbes can evade the immune system by entering phagocytes. The microbes prevent fusion of the lysosome with the phagosome and multiply inside the phagocyte, almost filling it. Examples include *Chlamydia, Mycobacterium tuberculosis, Shigella*, and malarial parasites.

Dormant microbes hide inside
Some microbes can remain dormant inside the phagocyte for months or years at a time. Examples include the microbes that cause brucellosis and tularemia.

1. Identify the white blood cells capable of phagocytosis: _____

_____

2. Describe how a blood sample from a patient may be used to determine whether they have a microbial infection (without looking for the microbes themselves):

_____

_____

_____

3. Explain how some microbes are able to overcome phagocytic cells and use them to their advantage:

_____

_____

Related activities: The Body's Defenses, Blood

Inflammation

Damage to the body's tissues can be caused by physical agents (e.g. sharp objects, heat, radiant energy, or electricity), microbial infection, or chemical agents (e.g. gases, acids and bases). The damage triggers a defensive response called **inflammation**. It is usually characterized by four symptoms: pain, redness, heat and swelling. The inflammatory response is beneficial and has the following functions: (1) to destroy the cause of the infection and remove it and its products from the body; (2) if this fails, to limit the effects on the body by confining the infection to a small area; (3) replacing or repairing tissue damaged by the infection. The process of inflammation can be divided into three distinct stages. These are described below.

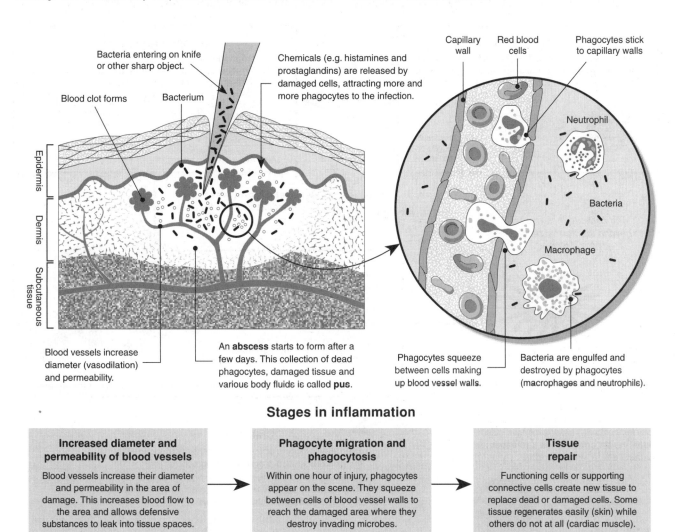

Bacteria entering on knife or other sharp object.

Chemicals (e.g. histamines and prostaglandins) are released by damaged cells, attracting more and more phagocytes to the infection.

Blood clot forms

Bacterium

Capillary wall

Red blood cells

Phagocytes stick to capillary walls

Neutrophil

Bacteria

Macrophage

Epidermis

Dermis

Subcutaneous tissue

Blood vessels increase diameter (vasodilation) and permeability.

An **abscess** starts to form after a few days. This collection of dead phagocytes, damaged tissue and various body fluids is called **pus**.

Phagocytes squeeze between cells making up blood vessel walls.

Bacteria are engulfed and destroyed by phagocytes (macrophages and neutrophils).

Stages in inflammation

Increased diameter and permeability of blood vessels	**Phagocyte migration and phagocytosis**	**Tissue repair**
Blood vessels increase their diameter and permeability in the area of damage. This increases blood flow to the area and allows defensive substances to leak into tissue spaces.	Within one hour of injury, phagocytes appear on the scene. They squeeze between cells of blood vessel walls to reach the damaged area where they destroy invading microbes.	Functioning cells or supporting connective cells create new tissue to replace dead or damaged cells. Some tissue regenerates easily (skin) while others do not at all (cardiac muscle).

1. Outline the three stages of inflammation and identify the beneficial role of each stage:

(a) _____

_____

(b) _____

_____

(c) _____

_____

2. Identify two features of phagocytes important in the response to microbial invasion: _____

_____

3. State the role of histamines and prostaglandins in inflammation: _____

4. Explain why pus forms at the site of infection: _____

_____

Defense Against Infectious Disease

Fever

To a point, fever is beneficial, because it assists a number of the defense processes. The release of the protein **interleukin-1** helps to reset the thermostat of the body to a higher level and increases production of **T cells** (lymphocytes). High body temperature also intensifies the effect of **interferon** (an antiviral protein) and may inhibit the growth of some bacteria and viruses. Because high temperatures speed up the body's **metabolic** **reactions**, it may promote more rapid tissue repair. Fever also increases heart rate so that white blood cells are delivered to sites of infection more rapidly. The normal body temperature range for most people is 36.2 to 37.2°C. Fevers of less than 40°C do not need treatment for **hyperthermia**, but excessive fever requires prompt attention (particularly in children). Death usually results if body temperature rises above 44.4 to 45.5°C.

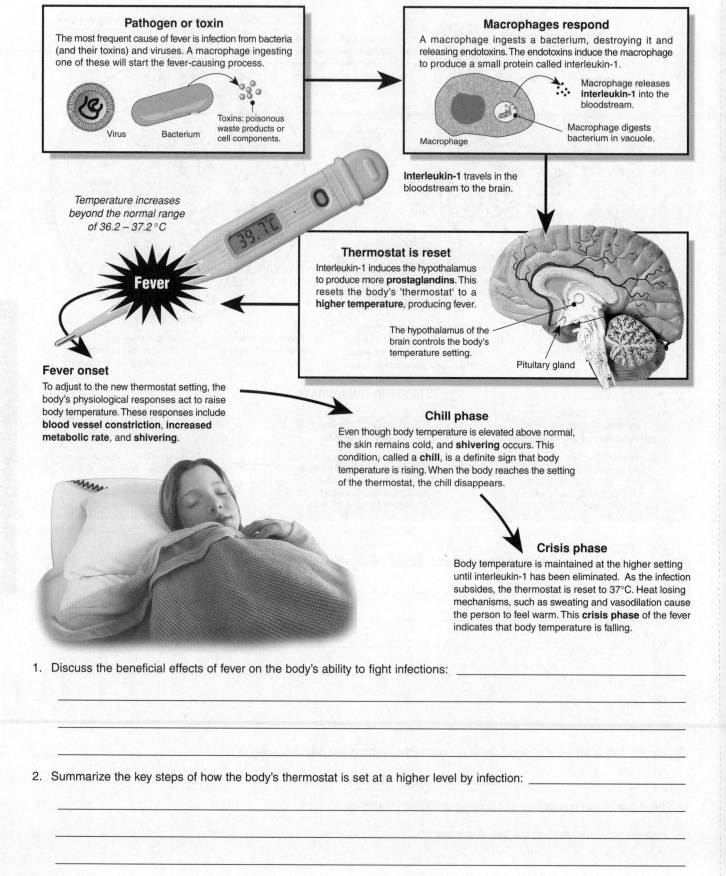

Pathogen or toxin

The most frequent cause of fever is infection from bacteria (and their toxins) and viruses. A macrophage ingesting one of these will start the fever-causing process.

Virus   Bacterium   Toxins: poisonous waste products or cell components.

Macrophages respond

A macrophage ingests a bacterium, destroying it and releasing endotoxins. The endotoxins induce the macrophage to produce a small protein called interleukin-1.

Macrophage releases **interleukin-1** into the bloodstream.

Macrophage digests bacterium in vacuole.

Macrophage

Interleukin-1 travels in the bloodstream to the brain.

Temperature increases beyond the normal range of 36.2 – 37.2 °C

Fever

39.7℃

Thermostat is reset

Interleukin-1 induces the hypothalamus to produce more **prostaglandins**. This resets the body's 'thermostat' to a **higher temperature**, producing fever.

The hypothalamus of the brain controls the body's temperature setting.

Pituitary gland

Fever onset

To adjust to the new thermostat setting, the body's physiological responses act to raise body temperature. These responses include **blood vessel constriction**, **increased metabolic rate**, and **shivering**.

Chill phase

Even though body temperature is elevated above normal, the skin remains cold, and **shivering** occurs. This condition, called a **chill**, is a definite sign that body temperature is rising. When the body reaches the setting of the thermostat, the chill disappears.

Crisis phase

Body temperature is maintained at the higher setting until interleukin-1 has been eliminated. As the infection subsides, the thermostat is reset to 37°C. Heat losing mechanisms, such as sweating and vasodilation cause the person to feel warm. This **crisis phase** of the fever indicates that body temperature is falling.

1. Discuss the beneficial effects of fever on the body's ability to fight infections: _____

_____

_____

_____

2. Summarize the key steps of how the body's thermostat is set at a higher level by infection: _____

_____

_____

_____

Related activities: The Body's Defenses

The Lymphatic System

Fluid leaks out from capillaries and forms the tissue fluid, which is similar in composition to plasma but lacks large proteins. This fluid bathes the tissues, supplying them with nutrients and oxygen, and removing wastes. Some of the tissue fluid returns directly into the capillaries, but some drains back into the blood circulation through a network of lymph vessels. This fluid, called **lymph**, is similar to tissue fluid, but contains more leukocytes. Apart from its circulatory role, the lymphatic system also has an important function in the immune response. Lymph nodes are the primary sites where the destruction of pathogens and other foreign substances occurs. A lymph node that is fighting an infection becomes swollen and hard as the lymph cells reproduce rapidly to increase their numbers. The thymus, spleen, and bone marrow also contribute leukocytes to the lymphatic and circulatory systems.

Tonsils: Tonsils (and adenoids) comprise a collection of large lymphatic nodules at the back of the throat. They produce lymphocytes and antibodies and are well-placed to protect against invasion of pathogens.

Thymus gland: The thymus is a two-lobed organ located close to the heart. It is prominent in infants and diminishes after puberty to a fraction of its original size. Its role in immunity is to help produce **T cells** that destroy invading microbes directly or indirectly by producing various substances.

Spleen: The oval spleen is the largest mass of lymphatic tissue in the body, measuring about 12 cm in length. It stores and releases blood in case of demand (e.g. in cases of bleeding), produces mature **B cells**, and destroys bacteria by phagocytosis.

Bone marrow: Bone marrow produces red blood cells and many kinds of leukocytes: monocytes (and macrophages), neutrophils, eosinophils, basophils, and lymphocytes (B cells and T cells).

Lymphatic vessels: When tissue fluid is picked up by lymph capillaries, it is called **lymph**. The lymph is passed along lymphatic vessels to a series of lymph nodes. These vessels contain one-way valves that move the lymph in the direction of the heart until it is reintroduced to the blood at the subclavian veins.

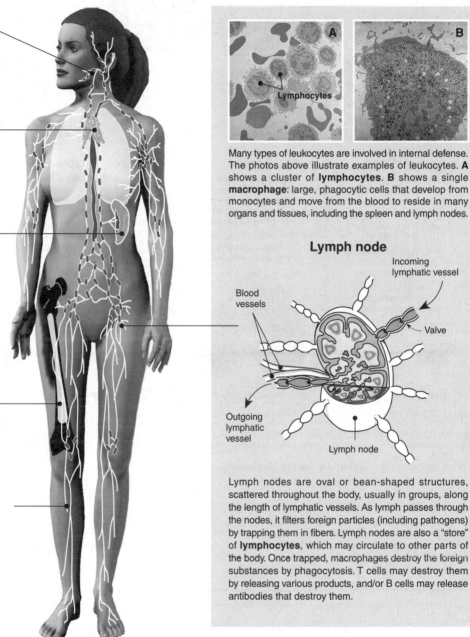

Many types of leukocytes are involved in internal defense. The photos above illustrate examples of leukocytes. **A** shows a cluster of **lymphocytes**. **B** shows a single **macrophage**: large, phagocytic cells that develop from monocytes and move from the blood to reside in many organs and tissues, including the spleen and lymph nodes.

Lymph node

Lymph nodes are oval or bean-shaped structures, scattered throughout the body, usually in groups, along the length of lymphatic vessels. As lymph passes through the nodes, it filters foreign particles (including pathogens) by trapping them in fibers. Lymph nodes are also a "store" of **lymphocytes**, which may circulate to other parts of the body. Once trapped, macrophages destroy the foreign substances by phagocytosis. T cells may destroy them by releasing various products, and/or B cells may release antibodies that destroy them.

Defense Against Infectious Disease

1. Briefly describe the composition of lymph: _____

_____

2. Discuss the various roles of lymph: _____

_____

_____

3. Describe one role of each of the following in the lymphatic system:

   (a) Lymph nodes: _____

   (b) Bone marrow: _____

Related activities: Capillaries and Tissue Fluid

RA 2

Acquired Immunity

We have natural or **innate resistance** to certain illnesses: examples include most diseases of other animal species. **Acquired immunity** refers to the protection an animal develops against certain types of microbes or foreign substances. Immunity can be acquired either passively or actively and is developed during an individual's lifetime. **Active immunity** develops when a person is exposed to microorganisms or foreign substances and the immune system responds. **Passive immunity** is acquired when antibodies are transferred from one person to another. Recipients do not make the antibodies themselves and the effect lasts only as long as the antibodies are present; usually several weeks or months. Immunity may also be **naturally acquired**, through natural exposure to microbes, or **artificially acquired** as a result of medical treatment.

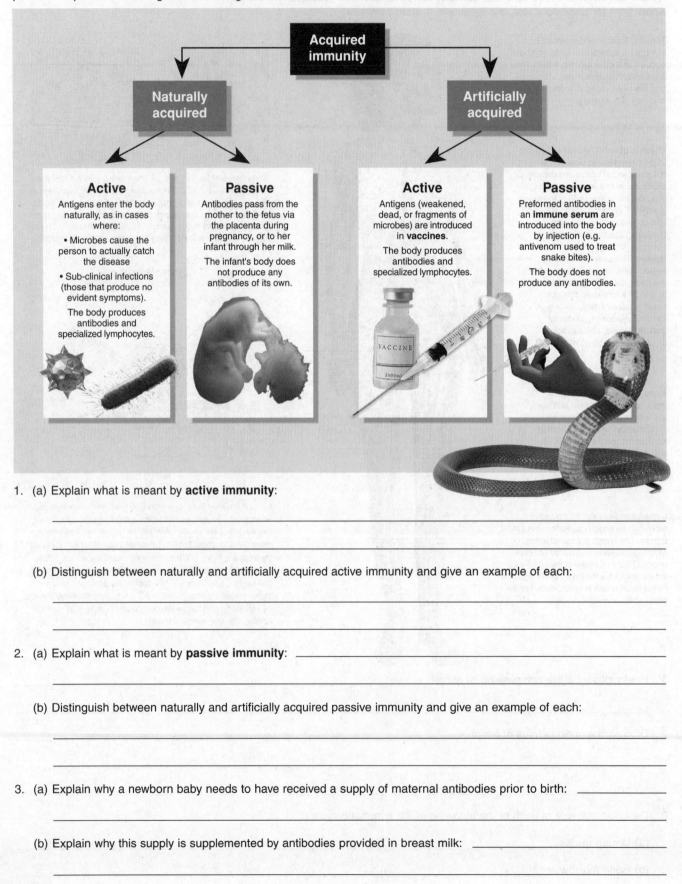

1. (a) Explain what is meant by **active immunity**:

   _____

   _____

   (b) Distinguish between naturally and artificially acquired active immunity and give an example of each:

   _____

   _____

2. (a) Explain what is meant by **passive immunity**: _____

   _____

   (b) Distinguish between naturally and artificially acquired passive immunity and give an example of each:

   _____

   _____

3. (a) Explain why a newborn baby needs to have received a supply of maternal antibodies prior to birth: _____

   _____

   (b) Explain why this supply is supplemented by antibodies provided in breast milk: _____

   _____

Related activities: Immunization

The Immune System

The efficient internal defense provided by the immune system is based on its ability to respond specifically against a foreign substance and its ability to hold a memory of this response. There are two main components of the immune system: the humoral and the cell-mediated responses. They work separately and together to protect us from disease. The **humoral immune response** is associated with the serum (non-cellular part of the blood) and involves the action of **antibodies** secreted by B cell lymphocytes. Antibodies are found in extracellular fluids including lymph, plasma, and mucus secretions. The humoral response protects the body against circulating viruses, and bacteria and their toxins. The **cell-mediated immune response** is associated with the production of specialized lymphocytes called **T cells**. It is most effective against bacteria and viruses located within host cells, as well as against parasitic protozoa, fungi, and worms. This system is also an important defense against cancer, and is responsible for the rejection of transplanted tissue. Both B and T cells develop from stem cells located in the liver of fetuses and the bone marrow of adults. T cells complete their development in the thymus, whilst the B cells mature in the bone marrow.

Lymphocytes and their Functions

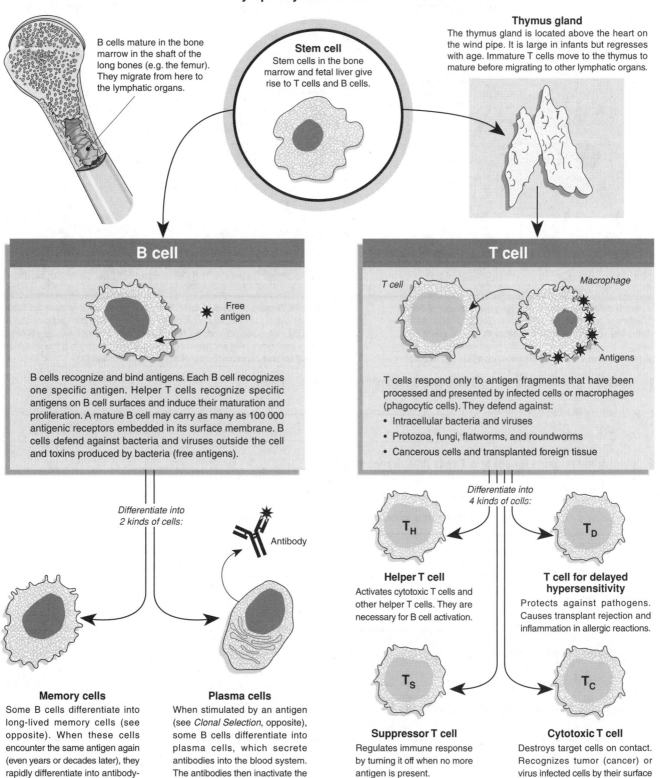

B cells mature in the bone marrow in the shaft of the long bones (e.g. the femur). They migrate from here to the lymphatic organs.

Stem cell
Stem cells in the bone marrow and fetal liver give rise to T cells and B cells.

Thymus gland
The thymus gland is located above the heart on the wind pipe. It is large in infants but regresses with age. Immature T cells move to the thymus to mature before migrating to other lymphatic organs.

B cell

Free antigen

B cells recognize and bind antigens. Each B cell recognizes one specific antigen. Helper T cells recognize specific antigens on B cell surfaces and induce their maturation and proliferation. A mature B cell may carry as many as 100 000 antigenic receptors embedded in its surface membrane. B cells defend against bacteria and viruses outside the cell and toxins produced by bacteria (free antigens).

T cell

T cell   Macrophage

Antigens

T cells respond only to antigen fragments that have been processed and presented by infected cells or macrophages (phagocytic cells). They defend against:
• Intracellular bacteria and viruses
• Protozoa, fungi, flatworms, and roundworms
• Cancerous cells and transplanted foreign tissue

Differentiate into 2 kinds of cells:

Antibody

Differentiate into 4 kinds of cells:

T_H

T_D

Helper T cell
Activates cytotoxic T cells and other helper T cells. They are necessary for B cell activation.

T cell for delayed hypersensitivity
Protects against pathogens. Causes transplant rejection and inflammation in allergic reactions.

T_S

T_C

Memory cells
Some B cells differentiate into long-lived memory cells (see opposite). When these cells encounter the same antigen again (even years or decades later), they rapidly differentiate into antibody-producing plasma cells.

Plasma cells
When stimulated by an antigen (see *Clonal Selection*, opposite), some B cells differentiate into plasma cells, which secrete antibodies into the blood system. The antibodies then inactivate the circulating antigens.

Suppressor T cell
Regulates immune response by turning it off when no more antigen is present.

Cytotoxic T cell
Destroys target cells on contact. Recognizes tumor (cancer) or virus infected cells by their surface (antigens and MHC markers).

Defense Against Infectious Disease

Related activities: The Lymphatic System, Allergies and Hypersensitivity
Web links: Introducing... Specific Immunity, The Immune System Overview

A 2

The immune system has the ability to respond to the large and unpredictable range of potential antigens encountered in the environment. The diagram below explains how this ability is based on **clonal selection** after antigen exposure. The example illustrated is for B cell lymphocytes. In the same way, a T cell stimulated by a specific antigen will multiply and develop into different types of T cells. Clonal selection and differentiation of lymphocytes provide the basis for **immunological memory**.

Five (a-e) of the many, randomly generated B cells. Each one can recognize only one specific antigen.

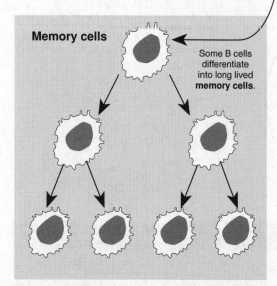

This B cell encounters and binds an antigen. It is then stimulated to proliferate.

Clonal Selection Theory

During development, millions of randomly generated B cells are formed. These are able to recognize many different antigens, including those never before encountered. Each B cell has one specific type of antigenic receptor on its surface whose shape is identical to the antibodies that the cell can make. The receptor will react only to a single antigen. When a B cell encounters its specific antigen, it responds by proliferating into a large clone of cells, all with the same genetic material and the same kind of antibody. This is called **clonal selection** because the antigen selects the B cells that will proliferate.

Memory cells

Some B cells differentiate into long lived **memory cells**.

Some B cells differentiate into **plasma cells**.

Plasma cells

Antibodies inactivate antigens

Some B cells differentiate into long lived **memory cells**. These are retained in the lymph nodes to provide future immunity (**immunological memory**). In the event of a second infection, B-memory cells react more quickly and vigorously than the initial B-cell reaction to the first infection.

Plasma cells secrete antibodies specific to the antigen that stimulated their development. Each plasma cell lives for only a few days, but can produce about 2000 antibody molecules per second. Note that during development, any B cells that react to the body's own antigens are selectively destroyed in a process that leads to **self tolerance** (acceptance of the body's own tissues).

1. State the general action of the two major divisions in the immune system:

    (a) Humoral immune system: _____

    (b) Cell-mediated immune system: _____

2. Identify the origin of B cells and T cells (before maturing): _____

3. (a) State where B cells mature: _____ (b) State where T cells mature: _____

4. Briefly describe the function of each of the following cells in the immune system response:

    (a) Memory cells: _____

    (b) Plasma cells: _____

    (c) Helper T cells: _____

    (d) Suppressor T cells: _____

    (e) Delayed hypersensitivity T cells: _____

    (f) Cytotoxic T cells: _____

5. Explain the basis of **immunological memory**: _____

    _____

    _____

    _____

Antibodies

Antibodies and antigens play key roles in the response of the immune system. Antigens are foreign molecules that are able to bind to antibodies (or T cell receptors) and provoke a specific immune response. Antigens include potentially damaging microbes and their toxins (see below) as well as substances such as pollen grains, blood cell surface molecules, and the surface proteins on transplanted tissues. **Antibodies** (also called immunoglobulins) are proteins that are made in response to antigens. They are secreted into the plasma where they circulate and can recognize, bind to, and help to destroy antigens. There are five classes of **immunoglobulins**. Each plays a different

role in the immune response (including destroying protozoan parasites, enhancing phagocytosis, protecting mucous surfaces, and neutralizing toxins and viruses). The human body can produce an estimated 100 million antibodies, recognizing many different antigens, including those it has never encountered. Each type of antibody is highly specific to only one particular antigen. The ability of the immune system to recognize and ignore the antigenic properties of its own tissues occurs early in development and is called **self-tolerance**. Exceptions occur when the immune system malfunctions and the body attacks its own tissues, causing an **autoimmune disorder**.

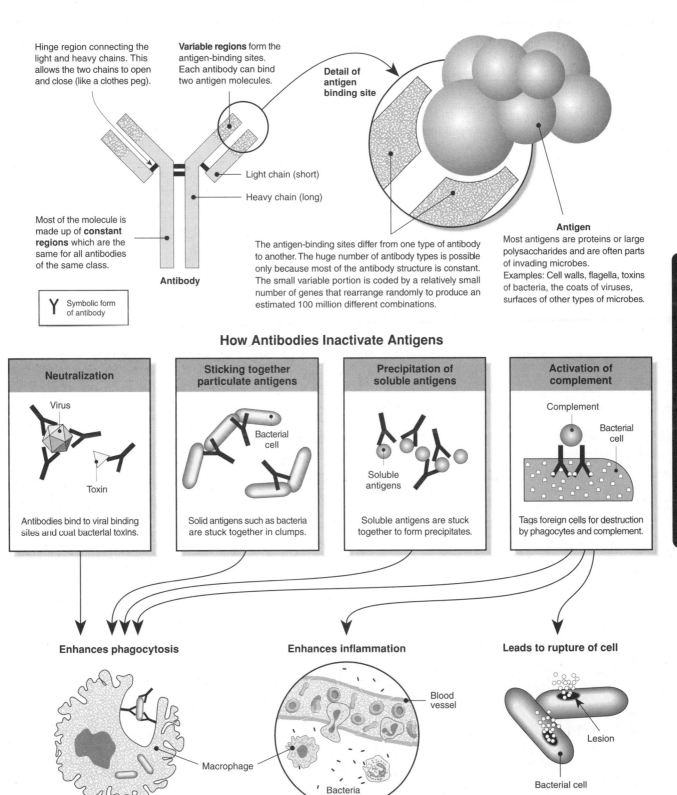

Hinge region connecting the light and heavy chains. This allows the two chains to open and close (like a clothes peg).

Variable regions form the antigen-binding sites. Each antibody can bind two antigen molecules.

Detail of antigen binding site

Light chain (short)

Heavy chain (long)

Most of the molecule is made up of **constant regions** which are the same for all antibodies of the same class.

Antibody

Y Symbolic form of antibody

The antigen-binding sites differ from one type of antibody to another. The huge number of antibody types is possible only because most of the antibody structure is constant. The small variable portion is coded by a relatively small number of genes that rearrange randomly to produce an estimated 100 million different combinations.

Antigen
Most antigens are proteins or large polysaccharides and are often parts of invading microbes.
Examples: Cell walls, flagella, toxins of bacteria, the coats of viruses, surfaces of other types of microbes.

How Antibodies Inactivate Antigens

Neutralization

Virus

Toxin

Antibodies bind to viral binding sites and coat bacterial toxins.

Sticking together particulate antigens

Bacterial cell

Solid antigens such as bacteria are stuck together in clumps.

Precipitation of soluble antigens

Soluble antigens

Soluble antigens are stuck together to form precipitates.

Activation of complement

Complement

Bacterial cell

Tags foreign cells for destruction by phagocytes and complement.

Enhances phagocytosis

Macrophage

Enhances inflammation

Blood vessel

Bacteria

Leads to rupture of cell

Lesion

Bacterial cell

Defense Against Infectious Disease

Related activities: Targets for Defense, The Immune System

RA 2

1. Distinguish between an antibody and an antigen: _____

_____

_____

_____

_____

_____

2. It is necessary for the immune system to clearly distinguish cells and proteins made by the body, from foreign ones.

   (a) Explain why this is the case: _____

   _____

   _____

   (b) In simple terms, explain how **self tolerance** develops (see the activity *The Immune System* if you need help):

   _____

   _____

   (c) Name the type of disorder that results when this recognition system fails: _____

   (d) Describe two examples of disorders that are caused in this way, identifying what happens in each case:

   _____

   _____

   _____

   _____

3. Discuss the ways in which antibodies work to inactivate antigens: _____

_____

_____

_____

_____

_____

_____

_____

_____

4. Explain how antibody activity enhances or leads to:

   (a) Phagocytosis: _____

   _____

   (b) Inflammation: _____

   _____

   (c) Bacterial cell lysis: _____

   _____

Immunization

A vaccine is a suspension of microorganisms (or pieces of them) that protects against disease by stimulating the production of antibodies and inducing **immunity**. **Vaccination** (often used synonymously with **immunization**) is a procedure that provides **artificially acquired active immunity** in the recipient. A concerted vaccination campaign led to the eradication (in 1977) of **smallpox**, the only disease to have been eradicated in this way. Once eradicated, a pathogen is no longer present in the environment and vaccination is no longer necessary. Features of smallpox made it particularly suitable for complete eradication. It was a very recognizable and visible disease, with no long-term, human carriers and no non-human carriers. In addition, people who had not been vaccinated against the disease were identifiable by the absence of a vaccination scar on the upper arm. Disease control (as opposed to eradication) does not necessarily require that everyone be immune. **Herd immunity**, where most of the population is immune, limits outbreaks to sporadic cases because there are too few susceptible individuals to support an epidemic. Vaccination provides effective control over many common bacterial and viral diseases. Viral diseases in particular are best prevented with vaccination, as they cannot be effectively treated once contracted.

Primary and Secondary Responses to Antigens

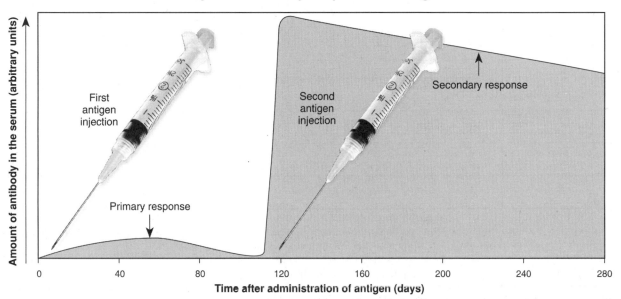

Vaccines to protect against common diseases are administered at various stages during childhood according to an immunization schedule.

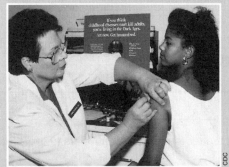

While most vaccinations are given in childhood, adults may be vaccinated against specific diseases (e.g. tuberculosis) if they are in a high risk group or if they are traveling to a region in the world where a disease is prevalent.

Selected Vaccines Used To Prevent Diseases In Humans		
Disease	**Type of vaccine**	**Recommendation**
Diphtheria	Purified diphtheria toxoid	From early childhood and every 10 years for adults
Meningococcal meningitis	Purified polysaccharide of *Neisseria menigitidis*	For people with substantial risk of infection
Whooping cough	Killed cells or fragments of *Bordetella pertussis*	Children prior to school age
Tetanus	Purified tetanus toxoid	14-16 year olds with booster every 10 years
Meningitis caused by *Hemophilus influenzae* b	Polysaccharide from virus conjugated with protein to enhance effectiveness	Early childhood
Influenza	Killed virus (vaccines using genetically engineered antigenic fragments are also being developed)	For chronically ill people, especially with respiratory diseases, or for healthy people over 65 years of age
Measles	Attenuated virus	Early childhood
Mumps	Attenuated virus	Early childhood
Rubella	Attenuated virus	Early childhood; for females of child-bearing age who are not pregnant
Polio	Attenuated or killed virus (enhanced potency type)	Early childhood
Hepatitis B	Antigenic fragments of virus	Early childhood

Defense Against Infectious Disease

Related activities: Acquired Immunity

RDA 2

1. After consulting your family doctor, medical centre or other medical authority, complete the table below, by:

   (a) Listing the vaccines administered to infants and young adults in your area.

   (b) Stating the diseases that each vaccine protects against.

   (c) Determining the ages at which each vaccine should be given. Place a tick (✔) in each age column as appropriate.

Vaccination Schedule								
Vaccine	**Diseases protected from**	**Age (months)**				**Age (years)**		

2. The graph at the top of the previous page illustrates how a person reacts to the injection of the same antibody on two separate occasions. This represents the initial vaccination followed by a booster shot.

   (a) State over what time period the antigen levels were monitored: _____

   (b) State what happens to the antibody levels after the first injection: _____

   _____

   (c) State what happens to the antibody levels after the booster shot: _____

   _____

   (d) Explain why the second injection has a markedly different effect: _____

   _____

3. The whole question of whether young children should be immunized has been a point of hot debate with some parents. The parents that do not want their children immunized have strongly held reasons for doing so. In a balanced way, explore the arguments for and against childhood immunization:

   (a) State clearly the benefits from childhood immunization: _____

   _____

   _____

   (b) Explain why some parents are concerned about immunizing their children: _____

   _____

   _____

4. Consult your family doctor or medical centre and list three vaccinations that are recommended for travelers to overseas destinations with high risk of infectious disease:

   (a) Country/region: _____ Vaccine required: _____

   (b) Country/region: _____ Vaccine required: _____

   (c) Country/region: _____ Vaccine required: _____

Types of Vaccine

There are two basic types of vaccine: subunit vaccines and whole-agent vaccines. **Whole-agent vaccines** contain complete nonvirulent microbes, either **inactivated** (killed), or alive but **attenuated** (weakened). Attenuated viruses make very effective vaccines and often provide life-long immunity without the need for booster immunizations. Killed viruses are less effective and many vaccines of this sort have now been replaced by newer subunit vaccines. **Subunit vaccines** contain only the parts of the pathogen that induce the immune response. They are safer than attenuated vaccines because they cannot reproduce in the recipient, and they produce fewer adverse effects because they contain little or no extra material.

Subunit vaccines can be made using a variety of methods, including cell fragmentation (*acellular vaccines*), inactivation of toxins (*toxoids*), genetic engineering (*recombinant vaccines*), and combination with antigenic proteins (*conjugated vaccines*). In all cases, the subunit vaccine loses its ability to cause disease but retains its antigenic properties so that it is still effective in inducing an immune response. Some of the most promising types of vaccine under development are the DNA vaccines, consisting of naked DNA which is injected into the body and produces an antigenic protein. The safety of DNA vaccines is uncertain but they show promise for use against rapidly mutating viruses such as influenza and HIV.

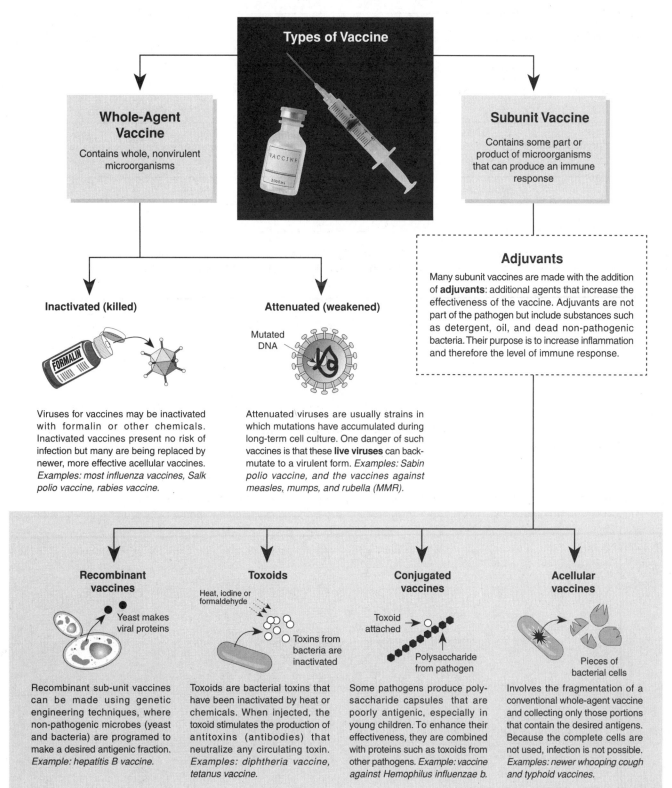

Types of Vaccine

Whole-Agent Vaccine

Contains whole, nonvirulent microorganisms

Subunit Vaccine

Contains some part or product of microorganisms that can produce an immune response

Adjuvants

Many subunit vaccines are made with the addition of **adjuvants**: additional agents that increase the effectiveness of the vaccine. Adjuvants are not part of the pathogen but include substances such as detergent, oil, and dead non-pathogenic bacteria. Their purpose is to increase inflammation and therefore the level of immune response.

Inactivated (killed)

Viruses for vaccines may be inactivated with formalin or other chemicals. Inactivated vaccines present no risk of infection but many are being replaced by newer, more effective acellular vaccines. *Examples: most influenza vaccines, Salk polio vaccine, rabies vaccine.*

Attenuated (weakened)

Mutated DNA

Attenuated viruses are usually strains in which mutations have accumulated during long-term cell culture. One danger of such vaccines is that these **live viruses** can back-mutate to a virulent form. *Examples: Sabin polio vaccine, and the vaccines against measles, mumps, and rubella (MMR).*

Recombinant vaccines

Yeast makes viral proteins

Recombinant sub-unit vaccines can be made using genetic engineering techniques, where non-pathogenic microbes (yeast and bacteria) are programed to make a desired antigenic fraction. *Example: hepatitis B vaccine.*

Toxoids

Heat, iodine or formaldehyde

Toxins from bacteria are inactivated

Toxoids are bacterial toxins that have been inactivated by heat or chemicals. When injected, the toxoid stimulates the production of antitoxins (antibodies) that neutralize any circulating toxin. *Examples: diphtheria vaccine, tetanus vaccine.*

Conjugated vaccines

Toxoid attached

Polysaccharide from pathogen

Some pathogens produce poly-saccharide capsules that are poorly antigenic, especially in young children. To enhance their effectiveness, they are combined with proteins such as toxoids from other pathogens. *Example: vaccine against Hemophilus influenzae b.*

Acellular vaccines

Pieces of bacterial cells

Involves the fragmentation of a conventional whole-agent vaccine and collecting only those portions that contain the desired antigens. Because the complete cells are not used, infection is not possible. *Examples: newer whooping cough and typhoid vaccines.*

Defense Against Infectious Disease

Related activities: Immunization, The Structure of Viruses

RA 3

1. Describe briefly how each of the following types of vaccine are made and name an example of each:

   (a) Whole-agent vaccine: _____

   _____

   (b) Subunit vaccine: _____

   _____

   (c) Inactivated vaccine: _____

   _____

   (d) Attenuated vaccine: _____

   _____

   _____

   (e) Recombinant vaccine: _____

   _____

   (f) Toxoid vaccine: _____

   _____

   (g) Conjugated vaccine: _____

   _____

   (h) Acellular vaccine: _____

   _____

2. **Attenuated viruses** provide long term immunity to their recipients and generally do not require booster shots. Suggest a possible reason why attenuated viruses provide such effective long-term immunity when inactivated viruses do not:

   _____

   _____

3. Bearing in mind the structure of viruses, explain why heat cannot be used to kill viruses to make **inactivated vaccines**:

   _____

   _____

4. (a) Vaccines may now be produced using **recombinant DNA technology**. Describe an advantage of creating vaccines using these methods:

   _____

   (b) Draw a simple diagram to illustrate the use of the recombinant method to manufacture a vaccine:

Monoclonal Antibodies

A **monoclonal antibody** is an artificially produced antibody that neutralises only one specific protein (antigen). Monoclonal antibodies are produced in the laboratory by stimulating the production of B-lymphocytes in mice injected with the antigen. These B-lymphocytes produce an antibody against the antigen. When isolated and made to fuse with immortal tumour cells, they can be cultured indefinitely in a suitable growing medium (as illustrated below). Monoclonal antibodies are useful for three reasons: they are totally uniform (i.e. clones), they can be produced in large quantities, and they are highly specific. The uses of antibodies produced by this method have ranged from diagnostic tools to treatments for infections and cancer. The therapeutic use of monoclonal antibodies has been limited because the antibodies are currently produced by non-human cells. The immune systems of some people have reacted against the foreign proteins (the antibodies themselves). It is hoped in the future to produce monoclonal antibodies derived from human cells, which will probably cause fewer reactions.

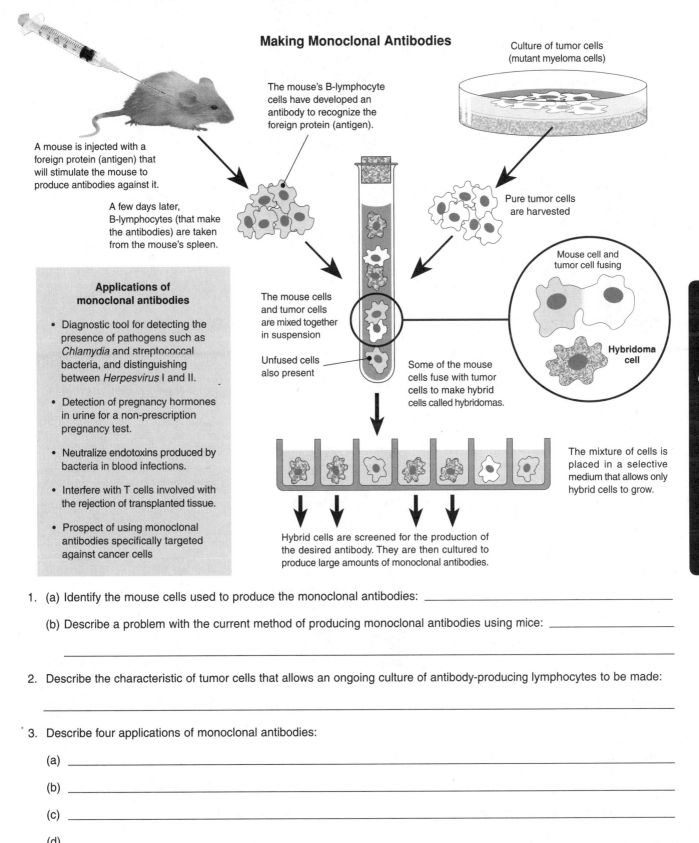

Making Monoclonal Antibodies

Culture of tumor cells
(mutant myeloma cells)

A mouse is injected with a foreign protein (antigen) that will stimulate the mouse to produce antibodies against it.

The mouse's B-lymphocyte cells have developed an antibody to recognize the foreign protein (antigen).

A few days later, B-lymphocytes (that make the antibodies) are taken from the mouse's spleen.

Pure tumor cells are harvested

The mouse cells and tumor cells are mixed together in suspension

Unfused cells also present

Some of the mouse cells fuse with tumor cells to make hybrid cells called hybridomas.

Mouse cell and tumor cell fusing

Hybridoma cell

The mixture of cells is placed in a selective medium that allows only hybrid cells to grow.

Hybrid cells are screened for the production of the desired antibody. They are then cultured to produce large amounts of monoclonal antibodies.

Applications of monoclonal antibodies

- Diagnostic tool for detecting the presence of pathogens such as *Chlamydia* and streptococcal bacteria, and distinguishing between *Herpesvirus* I and II.

- Detection of pregnancy hormones in urine for a non-prescription pregnancy test.

- Neutralize endotoxins produced by bacteria in blood infections.

- Interfere with T cells involved with the rejection of transplanted tissue.

- Prospect of using monoclonal antibodies specifically targeted against cancer cells

Defense Against Infectious Disease

1. (a) Identify the mouse cells used to produce the monoclonal antibodies: _____

    (b) Describe a problem with the current method of producing monoclonal antibodies using mice: _____

    _____

2. Describe the characteristic of tumor cells that allows an ongoing culture of antibody-producing lymphocytes to be made:

    _____

3. Describe four applications of monoclonal antibodies:

    (a) _____

    (b) _____

    (c) _____

    (d) _____

RA 2

Allergies and Hypersensitivity

Sometimes the immune system may overreact, or react to the wrong substances instead of responding appropriately. This is termed **hypersensitivity** and the immunological response leads to tissue damage rather than immunity. Hypersensitivity reactions occur after a person has been **sensitized** to an antigen. In some cases, this causes only localized discomfort, as in the case of hayfever. More generalized reactions (such as anaphylaxis from insect venom or drug injections), or localized reactions that affect essential body systems (such as asthma), can cause death through asphyxiation and/or circulatory shock.

Hypersensitivity

A person becomes **sensitized** when they form antibodies to harmless substances in the environment such as pollen or spores (steps 1-2 right). These substances, termed **allergens**, act as antigens to induce antibody production and an allergic response. Once a person is sensitized, the antibodies respond to further encounters with the allergen by causing the release of **histamine** from mast cells (steps 4-5). It is histamine that mediates the symptoms of hypersensitivity reactions such as hay fever and asthma. These symptoms include wheezing and airway constriction, inflammation, itching and watering of the eyes and nose, and/or sneezing.

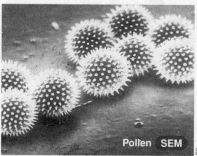

Pollen SEM | **Ragweed**

Hay fever (allergic rhinitis) is an allergic reaction to airborne substances such as dust, molds, pollens, and animal fur or feathers. Allergy to wind-borne pollen is the most common, and certain plants (e.g. ragweed and privet) are highly allergenic. There appears to be a genetic susceptibility to hay fever, as it is common in people with a family history of eczema, hives, and/or asthma. The best treatment for hay fever is to avoid the allergen, although anti-histamines, decongestants, and steroid nasal sprays will assist in alleviating symptoms.

Asthma is a common disease affecting more than 15 million people in the US. It usually occurs as a result of an allergic reaction to allergens such as house dust and the feces of house dust mites, pollen, and animal dander. As with all hypersensitivity reactions, it involves the production of histamines from mast cells (far right). The site of the reaction is the respiratory bronchioles where the histamine causes constriction of the airways, accumulation of fluid and mucus, and inability to breathe. During an attack, sufferers show labored breathing with overexpansion of the chest cavity (photo, right).

Asthma attacks are often triggered by environmental factors such as cold air, exercise, air pollutants, and viral infections. Recent evidence has also indicated the involvement of a bacterium: *Chlamydia pneumoniae*, in about half of all cases of asthma in susceptible adults.

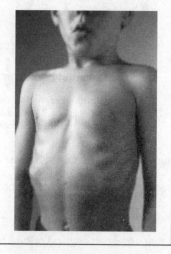

The Basis of Hypersensitivity

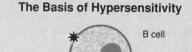
B cell

1 B cell encounters the allergen and differentiates into plasma cells

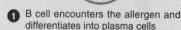
Plasma cell

Antibodies

2 The plasma cell produces antibodies

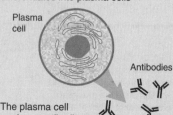
Mast cell

3 Antibodies bind to specific receptors on the surface of the mast cells

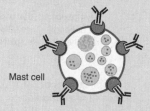
Vesicles with histamine

4 The mast cell binds the allergen when it encounters it again.

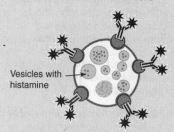

5 The mast cell releases histamine and other chemicals, which together cause the symptoms of an allergic reaction.

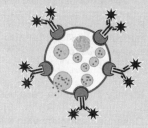

1. Explain the role of histamine in hypersensitivity responses: _____

_____

2. Explain what is meant by becoming **sensitized** to an allergen: _____

_____

3. Explain the effect of **bronchodilators** and explain why they are used to treat asthma: _____

_____

The Origin and Evolution of Life

IB SL	IB HL	IB Options	AP Biology
Complete: 1, 14-19 & see #28 (cross ref: Speciation)	Complete: 1, 14-19 & see #28 (cross ref: Speciation)	Complete: Option D: SL/HL: 1-3, 5, 7-8, 12 HL: 19-22	Complete: 1-28 Some numbers extension as appropriate

Learning Objectives

☐ 1. Compile your own glossary from the **KEY WORDS** displayed in **bold type** in the learning objectives below.

The Origin of Life on Earth

The prebiotic world *(pages 69-71, and see the TRC: Life in the Universe)*

☐ 2. Outline the conditions of **prebiotic Earth**, including reference to the role of the following: *high temperature, lightning, ultraviolet light penetration, and reducing atmosphere.* Explain the probable events that lead to the formation of life on Earth.

☐ 3. Recognize major stages in the evolution of life on Earth. Summarize the main ideas related to where life originated: ocean surface, extraterrestrial (**panspermia**), and deep sea thermal vents.

☐ 4. Describe some of the geological and paleontological evidence that suggests when life originated on Earth.

☐ 5. Outline the experiments (in particular the experiments of **Miller** and **Urey**) that have attempted to simulate the **prebiotic environment** on Earth. Describe their importance in our understanding of the probable origin of organic compounds.

☐ 6. Discuss the hypothesis that the first catalysts responsible for **polymerization reactions** were clay minerals and RNA.

The first cells *(pages 69-70 also SB1: page 329)*

☐ 7. Describe the possible role of RNA as the first self-replicating molecule. Discuss its role as an enzyme and its role in the origin of the first self-replicating cells.

☐ 8. Discuss the possible origin of membranes and the first prokaryotic cells.

☐ 9. Describe the evidence in the **geological record** for the first aquatic **prokaryotes**. Discuss the importance of these early organisms to the later evolution of diversity.

☐ 10. Distinguish between the **Eubacteria**, the **Archaea**, and the **Eukarya** with respect to their features and the environments in which they live. Explain what the current ecology of some bacterial groups tells us about the probable conditions of early life on Earth.

The origin of eukaryotes *(page 72)*

☐ 11. Recall how eukaryotes differ from prokaryotes. Explain why the evolution of eukaryotic cells is regarded as a milestone in the development of complexity in living things.

☐ 12. Discuss the **endosymbiotic** (endosymbiont) **theory** for the evolution of eukaryotic cells. Summarize the evidence in support of this theory.

☐ 13. Summarize the main ideas about the evolution of multicellular life. Describe the benefits gained by the evolution of multicellularity (multicellular life).

The Evidence for Evolution

Background: The greatest obstacle to the establishment of evolutionary theory has been the difficulty in observing evolution in the time scales within which humans operate. Although more recently there have been direct observations made of populations evolving within observable time periods (flour beetles, bacteria, viruses, <u>Drosophila</u>), much of the evidence for evolution is indirect or circumstantial. The weight of accumulated evidence from many fields of science is overwhelmingly in support of evolution. The way in which organisms are classified reflects their evolutionary development (phylogeny) and degree of relatedness. Students should be aware that the scientific debate of evolution has centered on hypotheses for the evolutionary processes, <u>not</u> on the phenomenon of evolution itself.

The fossil record *(pages 73-80 and the TRC: Dating Fossils)*

☐ 14. State the conditions under which different **fossils** form. Include reference to **petrified remains**, **prints** and **molds**, and preservation in **amber**, **tar**, **peat**, and **ice**.

☐ 15. Outline the methods for dating rocks and fossils using **radioisotopes**, with specific reference to ^{14}C and ^{40}K. Appreciate the degree of accuracy achieved by different dating methods and how the choice of isotope to use is made. Define the term: **half-life** and deduce the approximate age of materials based on a simple **decay curve** for a radioisotope.

☐ 16. Describe relative dating techniques using fossil sequence in strata. Distinguish between **relative dating** and **absolute dating** methods. Identify the different methods by which fossil remains are dated and describe when each of the dating methods is appropriate.

☐ 17. Appreciate that the dating of the main fossil-bearing rocks has provided the data for dividing the history of life on Earth into **geological periods**, which collectively form the geological time scale. Explain the system used to describe the age of rock strata (*era, period, epoch*).

☐ 18. Explain what is meant by **transitional forms** and explain their significance. Offer an explanation for the apparent lack of transitional forms in the fossil record. Using examples, describe the trends that fossils indicate in the evolution of related groups.

☐ 19. Outline the **paleontological evidence** for evolution using one example, e.g. evolution of horses or birds.

Comparative biochemistry *(pages 81-83)*

☐ 20. Explain the biochemical evidence by the universality of DNA, amino acids, and protein structures (e.g. cytochrome C) for the common ancestry of living organisms. Describe how comparisons of specific molecules between species are used as an indication of relatedness or phylogeny. Examples could include comparisons of DNA, amino acid sequences, or blood proteins (see #21).

21. Describe how **immunology** provides a method of quantifying the relatedness of species. Describe the basic principles and techniques involved.

22. Discuss how biochemical variations can be used as an **evolutionary** (molecular) **clock** to determine probable dates of divergence from a common ancestor.

Anatomical comparisons *(pages 83-84, 128)*

23. In a general way, describe how **comparative anatomy**, **embryology**, and physiology have contributed to an understanding of evolutionary relationships.

24. Explain how the contemporary field of evolutionary developmental biology (**evo-devo**) has provided some of the strongest evidence for the mechanisms of evolution, particularly for the evolution of novel forms. Appreciate that evo-devo compares the developmental processes of different organisms in an attempt to establish phylogenies and determine how developmental processes evolved.

25. Discuss the significance of **vestigial organs** as indicators of evolutionary trends in some groups.

Biogeography *(pages 87-92)*

26. Using named examples, explain how the geographical distribution of plants and animals (both living and extinct), provides evidence of dispersal of organisms from a point of origin across pre-existing barriers.

27. Outline the evidence for the occurrence of crustal movements by plate tectonics.

Modern examples of evolution *(pages 99-104 and see the following topic: Speciation)*

28. Outline two modern examples of observed evolution. For each example, identify the species involved, the selective pressures thought to be operating, common ancestor(s) if known, and (if appropriate) the species diversity that has arisen as a result of the evolution. One example should be the changes to the size and shape of the beaks of **Galapagos finches**. Other examples could include:
    (a) Development of **antibiotic resistance** in bacteria.
    (b) Development of **pesticide resistance** in insects.
    (c) **Heavy metal tolerance** in plants.
    (d) Selective predation on moths by birds.
    (e) The sickle cell trait as the basis for **balanced poly-morphism** in regions where malaria is prevalent.

Textbooks

See the 'Textbook Reference Grid' on pages 8-9 for textbook page references relating to material in this topic.

Supplementary Texts

The following references for teachers provide detailed material on life's origins:

■ **The Molecular Origins of Life** (1998) Brack, A. (ed). Cambridge U.P. ISBN: 0-521-56475-1. *A thought provoking summary of this topic.*

■ **Biogenesis: Theories of Life's Origin** (1999) Lahav, N. Oxford University Press. ISBN: 0-19-511755-7. *A critical discussion of the study of the origin of life (detailed with good diagrams).*

Periodicals

See page 6 for details of publishers of periodicals:

STUDENT'S REFERENCE

■ **Desert Island** Scientific American, June 2005, pp. 11-12. *A new study suggests that climate can effectively isolate organisms and thereby foster endemism.*

■ **The Golden Age of Dinosaurs** New Scientist, 21 May 2005, pp. 34-51. *A series of articles in a special issue exploring the discoveries that have transformed our understanding of dinosaurs.*

■ **How Old is...** National Geographic, 200(3) Sept. 2001, pp. 79-101. *A comprehensive discussion of dating methods and their application.*

■ **Primeval Pools** New Scientist, 2 July 2005, pp. 40-43. *An ecosystem where microbes still dominate as they did millions of years ago.*

■ **Meet your Ancestor** New Scientist, 9 Sept. 2006, pp. 35-39. *The significance of a recent fossil find: the missing link between fish and tetrapods.*

Presentation MEDIA to support this topic:

EVOLUTION:
• **The Origin of Life**
• **Evolution**

■ **Earth in the Beginning** National Geographic, 210(6) Dec. 2006, pp. 58-67. *Modern landscapes offer glimpses of the way Earth may have looked billions of years ago.*

■ **A Cool Early Life** Scientific American, Oct. 2005, pp. 40-47. *Discovery of ancient zircon crystals suggest that the earth cooled far sooner than once thought; as early as 4.4 bya. These cooler, wet surroundings were necessary for life to evolve.*

■ **Was Darwin Wrong?** National Geographic, 206(5) Nov. 2004, pp. 2-35. *Portrayal of the overwhelming scientific evidence for evolution.*

■ **An RNA World** Biol. Sci. Rev., 11(3) January 1999, pp. 2-6. *An experiment to reproduce the prebiotic conditions on Earth suggests that RNA evolved before DNA as an early enzyme.*

TEACHER'S REFERENCE

■ **Proof of Life** New Scientist, 22 Feb. 2003, pp. 28-31. *Recent studies of microfossils suggest that life on Earth may be much younger than thought.*

■ **The Rise of Life on Earth (series)** National Geographic, 193(3) March 1998, pp. 54-81. *Series of excellent, readable articles covering the theories for the origins of life on Earth, the evolution of life's diversity, and the origin of eukaryotic cells.*

■ **For a Handful of Dust** New Scientist, 28 Oct. 2006, pp. 48-52. *Soil from Chile's Atacama desert is being used to better understand the origin of life as it reacts very similarly to Martian soil.*

■ **Born Lucky** New Scientist, 12 July 2003, pp. 32-35. *This article discusses how, against all odds, life established itself quickly on Earth, and suggests that this can tell us something about where life began. One of a series in this issue.*

■ **Life's Rocky Start** Sci. American, April 2001, pp. 62-71. *The origins of life: prebiotic experiments & the role of minerals in early reactions on Earth.*

■ **The Ice of Life** Scientific American, August 2001, pp. 37-41. *Space ice may promote organic molecules and may have seeded life on Earth.*

■ **Putting Together Fossil Collections for 'Hands On' Evolution Laboratories** The Am. Biology Teacher, 63(1), January 2001, pp. 16-19. *How to put together a fossil lab: types of fossils (species) and contacts for material.*

■ **Resources for Teaching Evolution** The Am. Biology Teacher, 66(2), Feb. 2004, pp. 109-113. *The latest approaches to teaching evolution in the classroom, with reference to sample activities.*

■ **Building a Phylogenetic Tree of the Human & Ape Superfamily Using DNA-DNA Hybridisation Data** The Am. Biology Teacher, 66(8), Oct. 2004, pp. 560-566. *A how-to-do-it activity determining genetic differences between species.*

■ **Astrobiology: Using Research to Investigate Science Curricula** The Am. Biology Teacher, 68(1), Jan. 2006, pp. 7-12. *The outline of a curriculum unit developed on astrobiology which focuses on current research into origins of life on earth and on other planets.*

■ **Using Inquiry and Phylogeny to Teach Comparative Morphology** The Am. Biology Teacher, 67(6), Aug. 2005, pp. 412-417. *A hands-on, inquiry based approach to teaching comparative vertebrate skeletal morphology.*

Case study in transitional fossils: birds

■ **Winging It** New Scientist, 28 Aug. 1999, pp. 28-32. *Update on the evidence for the origin of bird flight.*

■ **Dinosaurs and Birds** The Am. Biology Teacher, 61(9), Nov. 1999, pp. 701-705. *A look at the bird-dinosaur link and the origins of flight.*

■ **Dinosaurs take Wing** National Geographic, 194(1) July 1998, pp. 74-99. *The evolution of birds from small theropod dinosaurs. Explores the homology between the typical dinosaur limb and the wing of the modern bird. An excellent article.*

■ **The Origin of Birds and their Flight** Scientific American, Feb. 1998, pp. 28-37. *Excellent article on avian evolution. The central idea is that birds are as much dinosaurs as humans are mammals.*

Internet

See pages 10-11 for details of how to access **Bio Links** from our web site: **www.thebiozone.com** From Bio Links, access sites under the topics:

GENERAL BIOLOGY ONLINE RESOURCES > Online Textbooks and Lecture Notes.

EVOLUTION: • A history of evolutionary thought • Evolution • The Talk.Origins archive ... *and others* > **Evolution: Theory and Evidence:** • Evidence for evolution: an eclectic survey • Transitional vertebrate fossils FAQ ... *and others* > **The Fossil Record:** • Geological time scale • Geology and geologic time ... *and others* > **The Origins of Life on Earth:** • From primordial soup to prebiotic beach • Miller/Urey experiment • Origin of life • Origin of life on Earth

SPACE BIOLOGY > Exobiology: • Archaea in space • Cosmic ancestry • Evidence of primitive life from Mars • NASA's exobiology... *and others*

The Origin of Life on Earth

Recent discoveries of **prebiotic** conditions on other planets and their moons has rekindled interest in the origin of life on primeval Earth. Experiments demonstrate that both peptides and nucleic acids may form polymers naturally in the conditions that are thought to have existed in a primitive terrestrial environment. RNA has also been shown to have enzymatic properties (**ribozymes**) and is capable of self-replication. These discoveries have removed some fundamental obstacles to creating a plausible scientific model for the origin of life from a prebiotic soup. Much research is now underway and space probes have been sent to Mercury, Venus, Mars, Pluto and its moon, Charon. They will search for evidence of prebiotic conditions or primitive microorganisms. The study of life in such regions beyond our planet is called **exobiology**.

Steps Proposed in the Origin of Life

The appearance of life on our planet may be understood as the result of evolutionary processes that involve the following major steps:

1. Formation of the Earth (4600 mya) and its acquisition of volatile organic chemicals by collision with comets and meteorites, which provided the precursors of biochemical molecules.

2. Prebiotic synthesis and accumulation of amino acids, purines, pyrimidines, sugars, lipids, and other organic molecules in the primitive terrestrial environment.

3. Prebiotic condensation reactions involving the synthesis of polymers of peptides (proteins), and nucleic acids (most probably just RNA) with self-replicating and catalytic (enzymatic) abilities.

4. Synthesis of lipids, their self-assembly into double-layered membranes and liposomes, and the 'capturing' of prebiotic (self-replicating and catalytic) molecules within their boundaries.

5. Formation of a **protobiont**; an immediate precursor to the first living systems. Such protobionts would exhibit cooperative interactions between small catalytic peptides, replicative molecules, proto-tRNA, and protoribosomes.

An RNA World

RNA has the ability to act as both genes and enzymes and offers a way around the "chicken-and-egg" problem: genes require enzymes to form; enzymes require genes to form. The first stage of evolution may have proceeded by RNA molecules performing the catalytic activities necessary to assemble themselves from a nucleotide soup. At the next stage, RNA molecules began to synthesize proteins. There is a problem with RNA as a prebiotic molecule because the ribose is unstable. This has led to the idea of a pre-RNA world (PNA).

These living **stromatolites** from a beach in Western Australia are created by mats of bacteria. Similar, fossilized stromatolites have been found in rocks dating back to 3500 million years ago.

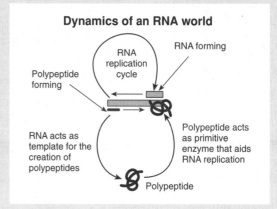

Dynamics of an RNA world

Scenarios for the Origin of Life on Earth

The origin of life remains a matter of scientific speculation. Three alternative views of how the key processes occurred are illustrated below:

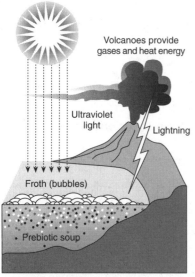

Ocean surface (tidal pools)
This popular theory suggests that life arose in a tidepool, pond or on moist clay on the primeval Earth. Gases from volcanoes would have been energized by UV light or electrical discharges to form the prebiotic molecules in froth.

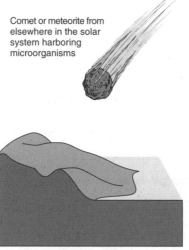

Panspermia
Cosmic ancestry (panspermia) is a serious scientific theory that proposes living organisms were 'seeded' on Earth as 'passengers' aboard comets and meteors. Such incoming organisms would have to survive the heat of re-entry.

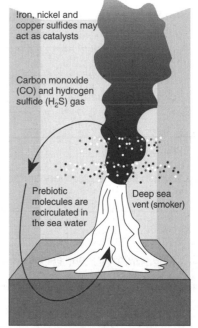

Undersea thermal vents
A recently proposed theory suggests that life may have arisen at ancient volcanic vents (called smokers). This environment provides the necessary gases, energy, and a possible source of catalysts (metal sulfides).

Related activities: Prebiotic Experiments
Web links: 4 Billion Years of Evolution

A 2

The Origin and Evolution of Life

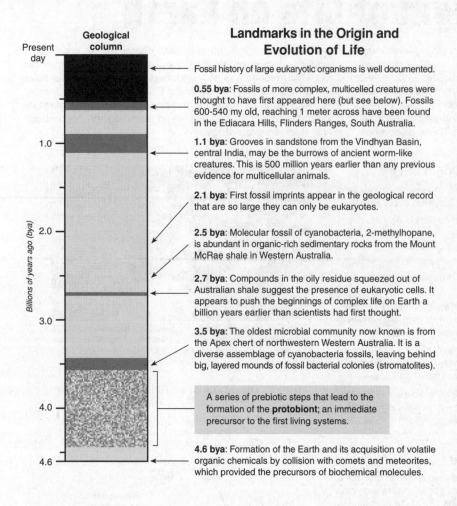

Landmarks in the Origin and Evolution of Life

Geological column

Present day

Billions of years ago (bya)

Fossil history of large eukaryotic organisms is well documented.

0.55 bya: Fossils of more complex, multicelled creatures were thought to have first appeared here (but see below). Fossils 600-540 my old, reaching 1 meter across have been found in the Ediacara Hills, Flinders Ranges, South Australia.

1.1 bya: Grooves in sandstone from the Vindhyan Basin, central India, may be the burrows of ancient worm-like creatures. This is 500 million years earlier than any previous evidence for multicellular animals.

2.1 bya: First fossil imprints appear in the geological record that are so large they can only be eukaryotes.

2.5 bya: Molecular fossil of cyanobacteria, 2-methylhopane, is abundant in organic-rich sedimentary rocks from the Mount McRae shale in Western Australia.

2.7 bya: Compounds in the oily residue squeezed out of Australian shale suggest the presence of eukaryotic cells. It appears to push the beginnings of complex life on Earth a billion years earlier than scientists had first thought.

3.5 bya: The oldest microbial community now known is from the Apex chert of northwestern Western Australia. It is a diverse assemblage of cyanobacteria fossils, leaving behind big, layered mounds of fossil bacterial colonies (stromatolites).

A series of prebiotic steps that lead to the formation of the **protobiont**; an immediate precursor to the first living systems.

4.6 bya: Formation of the Earth and its acquisition of volatile organic chemicals by collision with comets and meteorites, which provided the precursors of biochemical molecules.

A black smoker: In 1977, a vent was discovered at the Galapagos spreading center (mid-oceanic ridge), out of which gushed hot water laden with dissolved minerals. Since this discovery, hydrothermal venting has been found to be common along the length of the 55 000 km ridge crest system. Such black smokers are named after the dirty looking, high temperature water (350°C) that gushes from the chimney structures that they form. Such an environment is thought to be a possible site for prebiotic synthesis of life molecules.

1. Summarize the main features of the three most accepted scientific models for the origin of life on Earth:

   (a) Ocean surface: _____

   _____

   _____

   (b) Panspermia: _____

   _____

   _____

   (c) Undersea thermal vents: _____

   _____

   _____

2. Explain how the discovery of ribozymes has assisted in creating a plausible model for the prebiotic origin of life:

   _____

   _____

3. State how old the earliest fossils of microscopic life are known to be: _____

4. Scientists are seriously looking for evidence of life on other planets of our solar system, as well as some of their moons.

   (a) Name a planet or a moon that are pending targets for such spacecraft missions: _____

   (b) Explain how the discovery of life elsewhere in our solar system may affect the explanations for the origin of life:

   _____

   _____

Prebiotic Experiments

In the 1950s, Stanley Miller and Harold Urey used equipment (illustrated below) to attempt to recreate the conditions on the primitive Earth. They hoped that the experiment might give rise to the biological molecules that were forerunners to the development of the first living organisms. Researchers at the time believed that the Earth's early atmosphere was made up of methane, water vapor, ammonia, and hydrogen gas. Many variations on this experiment, using a variety of recipes, have produced similar results. It seems that the building blocks of life are relatively easy to create. Many types of organic molecules have even been detected in deep space.

The Miller-Urey Experiment

The experiment (right) was run for a week after which samples were taken from the collection trap for analysis. Up to 4% of the carbon (from the methane) had been converted to amino acids. In this and subsequent experiments, it has been possible to form all 20 amino acids commonly found in organisms, along with nucleic acids, several sugars, lipids, adenine, and even ATP (if phosphate is added to the flask). Researchers now believe that the early atmosphere may be similar to the vapors given off by modern volcanoes: carbon monoxide (CO), carbon dioxide (CO_2), and nitrogen (N_2). Note the absence of free atmospheric oxygen.

Iron pyrite, or 'fools gold' (above), has been proposed as a possible stabilizing surface for the synthesis of organic compounds in the prebiotic world.

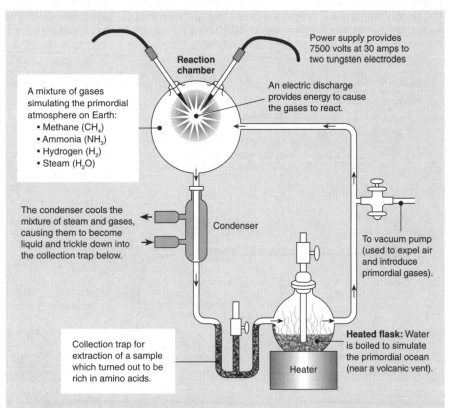

Reaction chamber

Power supply provides 7500 volts at 30 amps to two tungsten electrodes

A mixture of gases simulating the primordial atmosphere on Earth:
- Methane (CH_4)
- Ammonia (NH_3)
- Hydrogen (H_2)
- Steam (H_2O)

An electric discharge provides energy to cause the gases to react.

The condenser cools the mixture of steam and gases, causing them to become liquid and trickle down into the collection trap below.

Condenser

To vacuum pump (used to expel air and introduce primordial gases).

Collection trap for extraction of a sample which turned out to be rich in amino acids.

Heater

Heated flask: Water is boiled to simulate the primordial ocean (near a volcanic vent).

Some scientists envisage a global winter scenario for the formation of life. Organic compounds are more stable in colder temperatures and could combine in a lattice of ice. This frozen world could be thawed later.

Lightning is a natural phenomenon associated with volcanic activity. It may have supplied a source of electrical energy for the formation of new compounds (such as oxides of nitrogen) which were incorporated into organic molecules.

The early Earth was subjected to volcanism everywhere. At volcanic sites such as deep sea hydrothermal vents and geysers (like the one above), gases delivered vital compounds to the surface, where reactions took place.

1. In the Miller-Urey experiment simulating the conditions on primeval Earth, identify parts of the apparatus equivalent to:

   (a) Primeval atmosphere: _____

   (b) Primeval ocean: _____

   (c) Lightning: _____

   (d) Volcanic heat: _____

2. Name the organic molecules that were created by this experiment: _____

   _____

3. (a) Suggest a reason why the Miller-Urey experiment is not an accurate model of what happened on the primeval Earth:

   _____

   (b) Suggest changes to the experiment that could help it to better fit our understanding of the Earth's primordial conditions:

   _____

Related activities: The Origin of Life on Earth

A 3

The Origin and Evolution of Life

The Origin of Eukaryotes

The first firm evidence of eukaryote cells is found in the fossil record at 540-600 mya. It is thought that eukaryote cells evolved from large prokaryote cells that ingested other free-floating prokaryotes. They formed a symbiotic relationship with the cells they engulfed (**endosymbiosis**). The two most important organelles that developed in eukaryote cells were mitochondria, for aerobic respiration, and chloroplasts, for photosynthesis in aerobic conditions. Primitive eukaryotes probably acquired mitochondria by engulfing purple bacteria. Similarly, chloroplasts may have been acquired by engulfing primitive cyanobacteria (which were already capable of photosynthesis). In both instances the organelles produced became dependent on the nucleus of the host cell to direct some of their metabolic processes. The sequence of evolutionary change shown below suggests that the lines leading to animal cells diverged before those leading to plant cells, but the reverse could also be true. Animal cells might have evolved from plant-like cells which subsequently lost their chloroplasts.

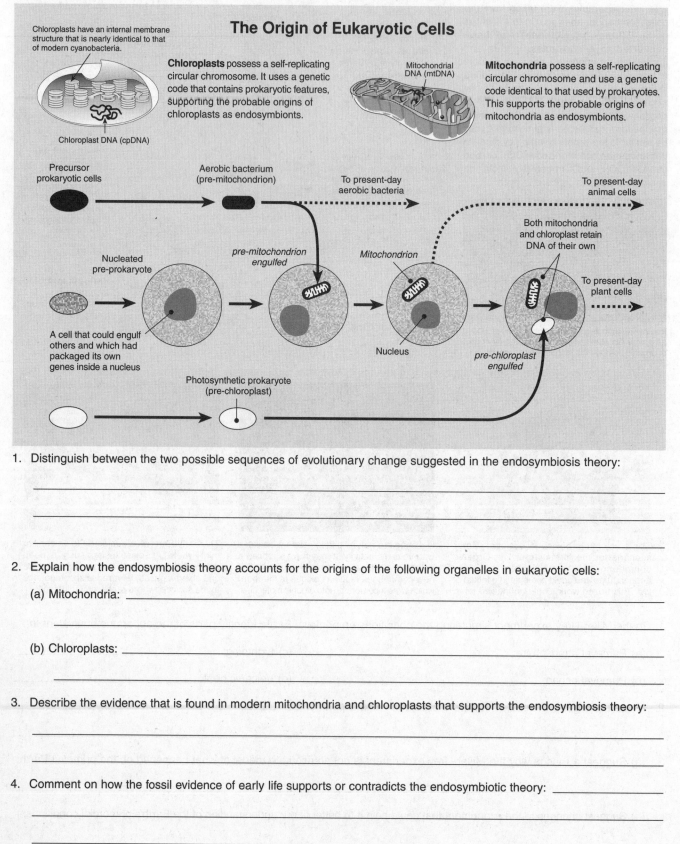

The Origin of Eukaryotic Cells

Chloroplasts have an internal membrane structure that is nearly identical to that of modern cyanobacteria.

Chloroplast DNA (cpDNA)

Chloroplasts possess a self-replicating circular chromosome. It uses a genetic code that contains prokaryotic features, supporting the probable origins of chloroplasts as endosymbionts.

Mitochondrial DNA (mtDNA)

Mitochondria possess a self-replicating circular chromosome and use a genetic code identical to that used by prokaryotes. This supports the probable origins of mitochondria as endosymbionts.

Precursor prokaryotic cells

Aerobic bacterium (pre-mitochondrion)

To present-day aerobic bacteria

To present-day animal cells

Nucleated pre-prokaryote

pre-mitochondrion engulfed

Mitochondrion

Both mitochondria and chloroplast retain DNA of their own

A cell that could engulf others and which had packaged its own genes inside a nucleus

Nucleus

To present-day plant cells

pre-chloroplast engulfed

Photosynthetic prokaryote (pre-chloroplast)

1. Distinguish between the two possible sequences of evolutionary change suggested in the endosymbiosis theory:

_____

_____

_____

2. Explain how the endosymbiosis theory accounts for the origins of the following organelles in eukaryotic cells:

(a) Mitochondria: _____

_____

(b) Chloroplasts: _____

_____

3. Describe the evidence that is found in modern mitochondria and chloroplasts that supports the endosymbiosis theory:

_____

_____

4. Comment on how the fossil evidence of early life supports or contradicts the endosymbiotic theory: _____

_____

_____

Related activities: The Origin of Life on Earth

© Biozone International 2001-2007
Photocopying Prohibited

The History of Life on Earth

The scientific explanation the origin of life on Earth is based soundly on the extensive fossil record, as well as the genetic comparison of modern life forms. Together they clearly indicate that modern life forms arose from ancient ancestors that have long since become extinct. These ancient life forms themselves originally arose from primitive cells living some 3500 million years ago in conditions quite different from those on Earth today. The earliest fossil records of living things show only simple cell types. It is believed that the first cells arose as a result of evolution at the chemical level in a 'primordial soup' (a rich broth of chemicals in a warm pool of water, perhaps near a volcanic vent). Life appears very early in Earth's history, but did not evolve beyond the simple cell stage until much later, (about 600 mya). This would suggest that the development of complex life forms required more difficult evolutionary hurdles to be overcome. The buildup of free oxygen in the atmosphere, released as a by-product from photosynthesizing organisms, was important for the evolutionary development of animal life.

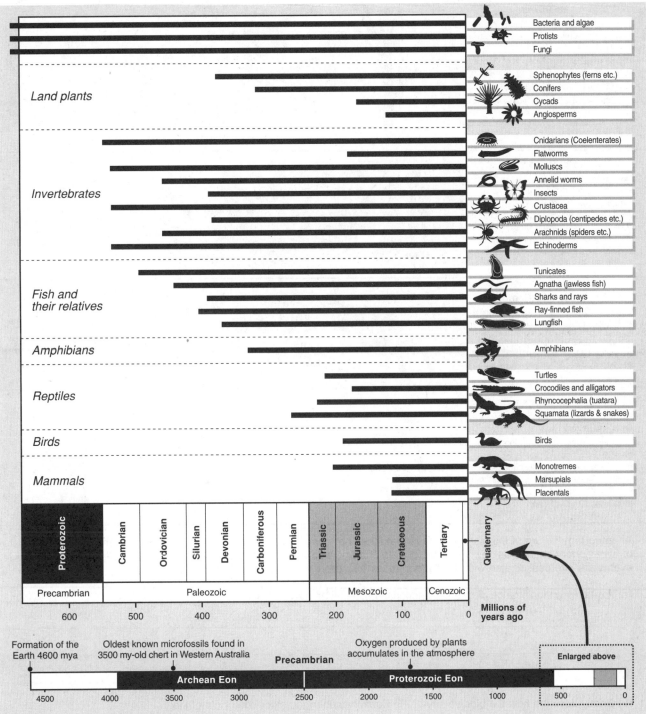

1. Explain the importance of the buildup of free oxygen in the atmosphere for the evolution of animal life:

_____

_____

2. Using the diagram above, determine how many millions of years ago the fossil record shows the first appearance of:

(a) Invertebrates: _____   (b) Fish (ray-finned): _____   (c) Land plants: _____

(d) Reptiles: _____   (e) Birds: _____   (f) Mammals: _____

Related activities: The Origin of Life on Earth, The Origin of Eukaryotes, Extinction
Web links: Deep Time, A Brief History of Life

A 2

Cenozoic

1.65 mya: Modern humans evolve and their hunting activities, starting at the most recent ice age, cause the most recent mass extinction.

3-5 mya: Early humans arise from ape ancestors

65-1.65 mya: Major shifts in climate. Major adaptive radiations of angiosperms (flowering plants), insects, birds and mammals.

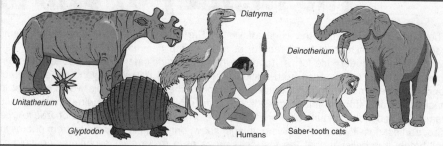

Mesozoic

65 mya: Apparent asteroid impact causes mass extinctions of many marine species and all dinosaurs.

135-65 mya: Major radiations of dinosaurs, fishes, and insects. Origin of angiosperms.

181-135 mya: Major radiations of dinosaurs.

240-205 mya: Recoveries, adaptive radiation of marine invertebrates, dinosaurs and fishes. Origin of mammals Gymnosperms become dominant land plants.

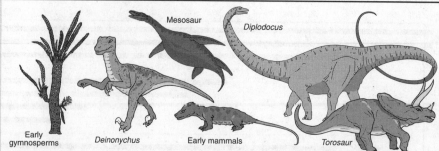

Later Paleozoic

240 mya: Mass extinction of nearly all species on land and in the sea.

435-280 mya: Vast swamps with the first vascular plants. Origin and adaptive radiation of reptiles, insects and spore bearing plants (including gymnosperms).

500-435 mya: Major adaptive radiations of marine invertebrates and early fishes.

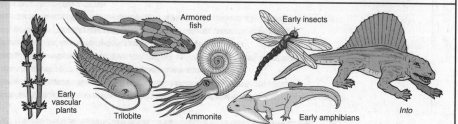

Early Paleozoic (Cambrian)

550-500 mya: Origin of animals with hard parts (appear as fossils in rocks). Simple marine communities. A famous Canadian site with a rich collection of early Cambrian fossils is known as the Burgess Shale deposits; examples are shown on the right.

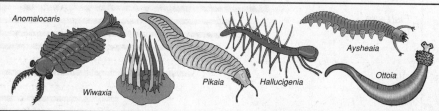

Precambrian

2500–570 mya: Origin of protists, fungi, algae and animals.

3800–2500 mya: Origin of photosynthetic bacteria.

4600–3800 mya: Chemical and molecular evolution leading to origin of life; protocells to anaerobic bacteria.

4600 mya: Origin of Earth.

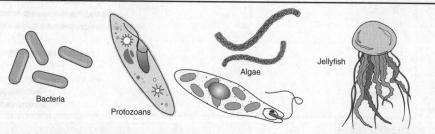

3. An important feature of the history of life is that it has not been a steady progression of change. There have been bursts of evolutionary change as newly evolved groups undergo **adaptive radiations** and greatly increase in biodiversity. Such events are often associated with the sudden mass extinction of other, unrelated groups.

(a) Explain the significance of mass extinctions in stimulating new biodiversity: _____

_____

_____

_____

(b) Briefly describe how the biodiversity of the Earth has changed since the origin of life:

_____

_____

_____

_____

_____

_____

Fossil Formation

Fossils are the remains of long-dead organisms that have escaped decay and have, after many years, become part of the Earth's crust. A fossil may be the preserved remains of the organism itself, the impression of it in the sediment (cast), or marks made by it during its lifetime (called trace fossils). For fossilization to occur, rapid burial of the organism is required (usually in water-borne sediment). This is followed by chemical alteration, where minerals are added or removed. Fossilization

requires the normal processes of decay to be permanently arrested. This can occur if the remains are isolated from the air or water and decomposing microbes are prevented from breaking them down. Fossils provide a record of the appearance and extinction of organisms, from species to whole taxonomic groups. Once this record is calibrated against a time scale (by using a broad range of dating techniques), it is possible to build up a picture of the evolutionary changes that have taken place.

Modes of preservation

Silicification: Silica from weathered volcanic ash is gradually incorporated into partly decayed wood (also called petrification).

Phosphatization: Bones and teeth are preserved in phosphate deposits.

Pyritization: Iron pyrite replaces hard remains of the dead organism.

Tar pit: Animals fall into and are trapped in mixture of tar and sand.

Trapped in amber: Gum from conifers traps insects and then hardens.

Limestone: Calcium carbonate from the remains of marine plankton is deposited as a sediment that traps the remains of other sea creatures.

Brachiopod (lamp shell), Jurassic (New Zealand)

Cast: This impression of a lamp shell is all that is left after the original shell material was dissolved after fossilization.

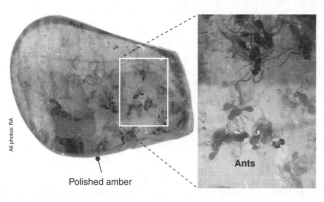

All photos: RA

Polished amber

Ants

Insects in amber: The fossilized resin or gum produced by some ancient conifers trapped these insects (including the ants visible in the enlargement) about 25 million years ago (Madagascar).

Ray structure

Bark

Growth rings largely destroyed

Petrified wood: A cross-section of a limb from a coniferous tree (Madagascar).

Rock phosphate matrix

Shark tooth: The tooth of a shark *Lamna obliqua* from phosphate beds, Eocene (Khouribga, Morocco).

Shell

Stone interior

Ammonite: This ammonite still has a layer of the original shell covering the stone interior, Jurassic (Madagascar).

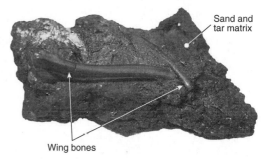

Sand and tar matrix

Wing bones

Bird bones: Fossilized bones of a bird that lived about 5 million years ago and became stuck in the tar pits at la Brea, Los Angeles, USA.

Shell and chambers replaced by iron pyrite

Ammonite: This ammonite has been preserved by a process called pyritization, late Cretaceous (Charmouth, England).

Fossil fern: This compression fossil of a fern leaf shows traces of carbon and wax from the original plant, Carboniferous (USA).

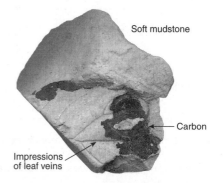

Soft mudstone

Carbon

Impressions of leaf veins

Sub-fossil: Leaf impression in soft mudstone (can be broken easily with fingers) with some of the remains of the leaf still intact (a few thousand years old, New Zealand).

The Origin and Evolution of Life

Related activities: Dating a Fossil Site

A 1

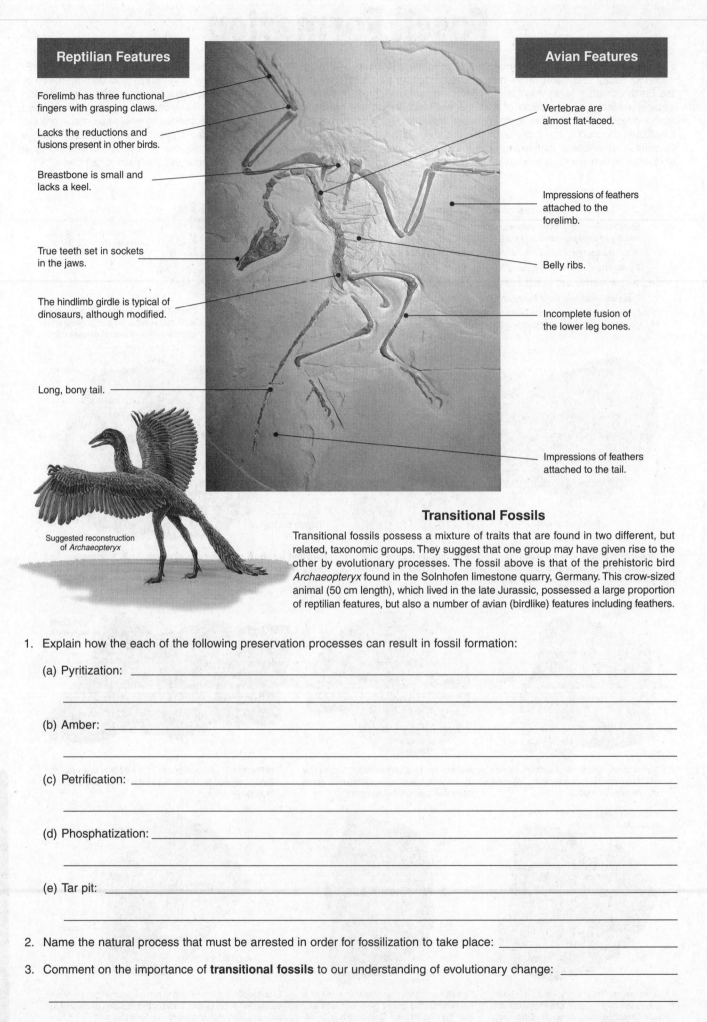

Reptilian Features

Forelimb has three functional fingers with grasping claws.

Lacks the reductions and fusions present in other birds.

Breastbone is small and lacks a keel.

True teeth set in sockets in the jaws.

The hindlimb girdle is typical of dinosaurs, although modified.

Long, bony tail.

Suggested reconstruction of *Archaeopteryx*

Avian Features

Vertebrae are almost flat-faced.

Impressions of feathers attached to the forelimb.

Belly ribs.

Incomplete fusion of the lower leg bones.

Impressions of feathers attached to the tail.

Transitional Fossils

Transitional fossils possess a mixture of traits that are found in two different, but related, taxonomic groups. They suggest that one group may have given rise to the other by evolutionary processes. The fossil above is that of the prehistoric bird *Archaeopteryx* found in the Solnhofen limestone quarry, Germany. This crow-sized animal (50 cm length), which lived in the late Jurassic, possessed a large proportion of reptilian features, but also a number of avian (birdlike) features including feathers.

1. Explain how the each of the following preservation processes can result in fossil formation:

   (a) Pyritization: _____

   _____

   (b) Amber: _____

   _____

   (c) Petrification: _____

   _____

   (d) Phosphatization: _____

   _____

   (e) Tar pit: _____

   _____

2. Name the natural process that must be arrested in order for fossilization to take place: _____

3. Comment on the importance of **transitional fossils** to our understanding of evolutionary change: _____

   _____

   _____

The Fossil Record

The diagram below represents a cutting into the earth revealing the layers of rock. Some of these layers may have been laid down by water (sedimentary rocks) or by volcanic activity (volcanic rocks). Fossils are the actual remains or impressions of plants, animals, or other organisms that become trapped in the sediments after their death. Layers of sedimentary rock are arranged in the order that they were deposited, with the most recent layers near the surface (unless they have been disturbed).

Profile with Sedimentary Rocks Containing Fossils

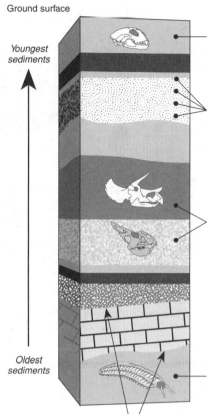

Ground surface

Youngest sediments

Recent fossils are found in more recent sediments
The more recent the layer of rock, the more resemblance there is between the fossils found in it and living forms.

Numerous extinct species
The number of extinct species is enormously greater than the number living today.

Fossil types differ in each sedimentary rock layer
Fossils found in a given layer of sedimentary rock generally differ in significant respects from those in other layers.

Only primitive fossils are found in older sediments
Phyla are represented by more generalized forms in the older layers, and not by specialized forms (such as those alive today).

Oldest sediments

New fossil types mark changes in environment
In the rocks marking the end of one geological period, it is common to find many new fossils that become dominant in the next. Each geological period had an environment very different from those before and after. Their boundaries coincided with drastic environmental changes and the appearance of new niches. These produced new selection pressures resulting in new adaptive features in the surviving species, as they responded to the changes.

The rate of evolution can vary

According to the fossil record, rates of evolutionary change seem to vary. There are bursts of species formation and long periods of relative stability within species (stasis). The occasional rapid evolution of new forms apparent in the fossil record, is probably a response to a changing environment. During periods of stable environmental conditions, evolutionary change may slow down.

The Fossil Record of Proboscidea

African and Indian elephants have descended from a diverse group of animals known as **proboscideans** (named for their long trunks). The first pig-sized, trunkless members of this group lived in Africa 40 million years ago. From Africa, their descendants invaded all continents except Antarctica and Australia. As the group evolved, they became larger; an effective evolutionary response to deter predators. Examples of extinct members of this group are illustrated below:

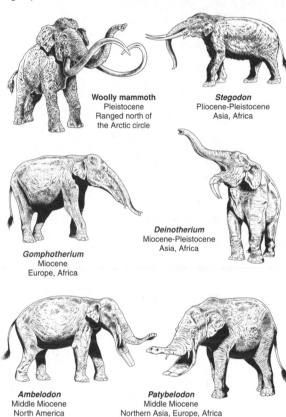

Woolly mammoth
Pleistocene
Ranged north of the Arctic circle

Stegodon
Pliocene-Pleistocene
Asia, Africa

Gomphotherium
Miocene
Europe, Africa

Deinotherium
Miocene-Pleistocene
Asia, Africa

Ambelodon
Middle Miocene
North America

Patybelodon
Middle Miocene
Northern Asia, Europe, Africa

- **Modern day species can be traced:** The evolution of many present-day species can be very well reconstructed. For instance, the evolutionary history of the modern elephants is exceedingly well documented for the last 40 million years. The modern horse also has a well understood fossil record spanning the last 50 million years.

- **Fossil species are similar to but differ from today's species:** Most fossil animals and plants belong to the same major taxonomic groups as organisms living today. However, they do differ from the living species in many features.

1. Name an animal or plant taxon (e.g. family, genus, or species) that has:

   (a) A good fossil record of evolutionary development: _____

   (b) Appeared to have changed very little over the last 100 million years or so: _____

2. Discuss the importance of **fossils** as a record of evolutionary change over time: _____

   _____

   _____

   _____

The Origin and Evolution of Life

Related activities: Dating a Fossil Site

RA 2

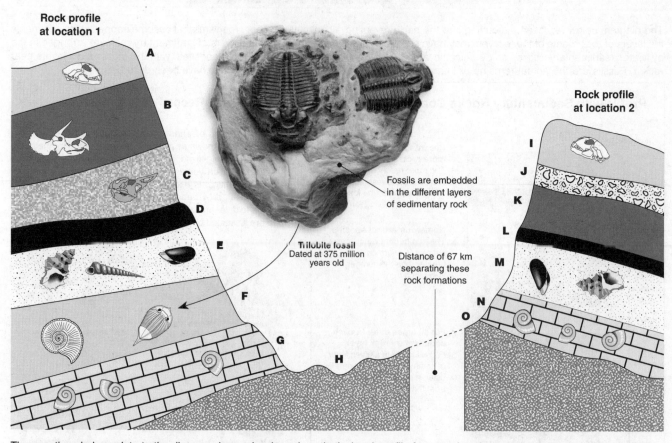

Rock profile at location 1

A
B
C
D
E
F
G
H

Rock profile at location 2

I
J
K
L
M
N
O

Fossils are embedded in the different layers of sedimentary rock

Trilobite fossil
Dated at 375 million years old

Distance of 67 km separating these rock formations

The questions below relate to the diagram above, showing a hypothetical rock profile from two locations separated by a distance of 67 km. There are some differences between the rock layers at the two locations. Apart from layers D and L which are volcanic ash deposits, all other layers are comprised of sedimentary rock.

3. Assuming there has been no geological activity (e.g. tilting or folding), state in which rock layer (**A-O**) you would find:

   (a) The youngest rocks at Location 1: _____   (c) The youngest rocks at Location 2: _____

   (b) The oldest rocks at Location 1: _____   (d) The oldest rocks at Location 2: _____

4. (a) State which layer at location 1 is of the same age as layer M at location 2: _____

   (b) Explain the reason for your answer above: _____

   _____

5. The rocks in layer H and O are sedimentary rocks. Explain why there are no visible fossils in layers:

   _____

   _____

6. (a) State which layers present at location 1 are missing at location 2: _____

   (b) State which layers present at location 2 are missing at location 1: _____

7. Describe three methods of dating rocks: _____

   _____

   _____

8. Using radiometric dating, the trilobite fossil was determined to be approximately 375 million years old. The volcanic rock layer (D) was dated at 270 million years old, while rock layer B was dated at 80 million years old. Give the approximate **age range** (i.e. greater than, less than or between given dates) of the rock layers listed below:

   (a) Layer A: _____   (d) Layer G: _____

   (b) Layer C: _____   (e) Layer L: _____

   (c) Layer E: _____   (f) Layer O: _____

Dating a Fossil Site

The diagram below shows a rock shelter typical of those found in the Dordogne Valley of Southwest France. Such shelters have yielded a rich source of Neanderthal and modern human remains. It illustrates the way in which hominin activity is revealed at archaeological excavations. Occupation sites included shallow caves or rocky overhangs of limestone. The floors of these caves accumulated the debris of natural rockfalls, together with the detritus of human occupation at various layers, called **occupation horizons**. A wide array of techniques can be used for dating, some of which show a high degree of reliability (see the table below). The use of several appropriate techniques to date material improves the reliability of the date determined.

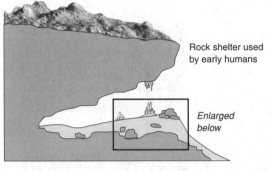

Rock shelter used by early humans

Enlarged below

Dating method	Dating range (years ago)	Datable materials
Radiocarbon (^{14}C)	1000 - 50 000+	Bone, shell, charcoal
Potassium-argon (K/Ar)	10 000 - 100 million	Volcanic rocks and minerals
Uranium series decay	less than 1 million	Marine carbonate, coral, shell
Thermoluminescence	less than 200 000	Ceramics (burnt clay)
Fission track	1000 - 100 million	Volcanic rock, glass, pottery
Electron spin resonance	2000 - 500 000	Bone, teeth, loess, burnt flint

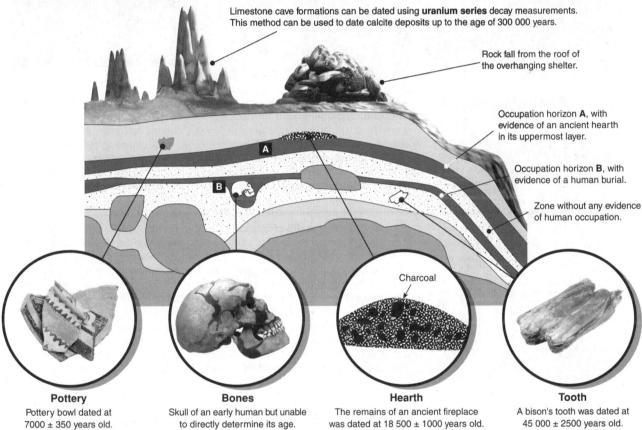

Limestone cave formations can be dated using **uranium series** decay measurements. This method can be used to date calcite deposits up to the age of 300 000 years.

Rock fall from the roof of the overhanging shelter.

Occupation horizon **A**, with evidence of an ancient hearth in its uppermost layer.

Occupation horizon **B**, with evidence of a human burial.

Zone without any evidence of human occupation.

Charcoal

Pottery
Pottery bowl dated at 7000 ± 350 years old.

Bones
Skull of an early human but unable to directly determine its age.

Hearth
The remains of an ancient fireplace was dated at 18 500 ± 1000 years old.

Tooth
A bison's tooth was dated at 45 000 ± 2500 years old.

1. Discuss the significance of **occupation horizons**: _____

_____

_____

_____

2. Determine the approximate date range for the items below: (Hint: take into account layers/artifacts with known dates)

   (a) The skull at point B: _____

   (b) Occupation horizon A: _____

3. Name the dating methods that could have been used to date each of the following, at the site above:

   (a) Pottery bowl: _____ (c) Hearth: _____

   (b) Skull: _____ (d) Tooth: _____

Related activities: The Fossil Record

RDA 2

The Origin and Evolution of Life

Interpreting Fossil Sites

Human skull

Charcoal fragments (possible evidence of fire use and excellent for radiocarbon dating).

Bones from a large mammal with evidence of butchering (cut and scrape marks from stone tools). These provide information on the past ecology and environment of the hominins in question.

Excavation through rock strata (layers). The individual layers can be dated using both chronometric (absolute) and relative dating methods.

Stone tools

Photo: RA

istock

Searching for ancient human remains, including the evidence of culture, is the work of **paleoanthropologists**. Organic materials, such as bones and teeth, are examined and analyzed by physical anthropologists, while cultural materials, such as tools, weapons, shelters, and artworks, are examined by archaeologists. Both these disciplines, **paleoanthropology** and **archeology**, are closely associated with other scientific disciplines, including **geochemistry** (for **chronometric dates**), **geology** (for reconstructions of past physical landscapes), and **paleontology** (for knowledge of the past species assemblages).

The reconstruction of a **dig site**, pictured above, illustrates some of the features that may be present at a site of hominin activity. Naturally, the type of information recovered from a site will depend on several factors, including the original nature of the site and its contents, the past and recent site environment, and earlier disturbance by people or animals. During its period of occupation, a site represents an interplay between additive and subtractive processes; building vs destruction, growth vs decay. Organic matter decays, and other features of the site, such as tools, can be disarranged, weathered, or broken down. The archaeologists goal is to maximize the recovery of information, and recent trends have been to excavate and process artifacts immediately, and sometimes to leave part of the site intact so that future work, perhaps involving better methodologies, is still possible.

4. Explain why paleoanthropologists date and interpret all of the remains at a particular site of interest (e.g. animal bones, pollen, and vegetation, as well as hominin remains):

_____

_____

_____

_____

5. Discuss the importance of involving several scientific disciplines when interpreting a site of hominin activity:

_____

_____

_____

_____

_____

DNA Hybridization

The more closely two species are related, the fewer differences there will be in the exact sequence of bases. This is because there has been less time for the point mutations that will bring about these changes to occur. Modern species can be compared to see how long ago they shared a **common ancestor.** This technique gives a measure of 'relatedness', and can be calibrated as a **molecular clock** against known fossil dates. It is then possible to give approximate dates of common origin to species with no or poor fossil data. This method has been applied to primate DNA samples to help determine the approximate date of human divergence from the apes, which has been estimated to be between 10 and 5 million years ago.

DNA Hybridization

1. Blood samples from each species are taken, from which the DNA is isolated.

2. The DNA from each species is made to unwind into single strands by applying heat (both human and chimpanzee DNA unwinds at 86°C).

3. Enzymes are used to snip the single strands of DNA into smaller pieces (about 500 base pairs long).

4. The segments from human and chimpanzee DNA are combined to see how closely they bind to each other (single strand segments tend to find their complementary segments and rewind into a double helix again).

5. The greater the similarity in DNA base sequence, the stronger the attraction between the two strands and therefore they are harder to separate again. By measuring how hard this hybrid DNA is to separate, a crude measure of DNA 'relatedness' can be achieved.

6. The degree of similarity of the hybrid DNA can be measured by finding the temperature that it unzips into single strands again (in this case it would be 83.6°C).

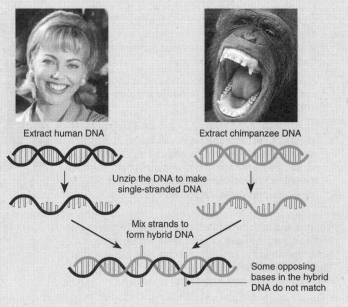

Extract human DNA   Extract chimpanzee DNA

Unzip the DNA to make single-stranded DNA

Mix strands to form hybrid DNA

Some opposing bases in the hybrid DNA do not match

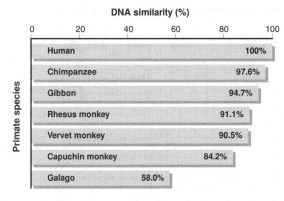

Flamingo   Ibis   Shoebill   Pelican   Stork   New World vulture

DNA difference score

Millions of years ago

The relationships among the **New World vultures** and **storks** have been determined using DNA hybridization. It has been possible to estimate how long ago various members of the group shared a common ancestor.

Similarity of human DNA to that of other primates

DNA similarity (%)

Primate species	DNA similarity
Human	100%
Chimpanzee	97.6%
Gibbon	94.7%
Rhesus monkey	91.1%
Vervet monkey	90.5%
Capuchin monkey	84.2%
Galago	58.0%

The genetic relationships among the **primates** has been investigated using DNA hybridization. Human DNA was compared with that of the other primates. It largely confirmed what was suspected from anatomical evidence.

1. Explain how **DNA hybridization** can give a measure of genetic relatedness between species:

_____

_____

_____

2. Study the graph showing the results of a DNA hybridization between human DNA and that of other primates.

(a) Identify which is the most closely related primate to humans: _____

(b) Identify which is the most distantly related primate to humans: _____

3. State the DNA difference score for: (a) Shoebills and pelicans: _____   (b) Storks and flamingos: _____

4. On the basis of DNA hybridization, state how long ago the ibises and New World vultures shared a common ancestor:

_____

The Origin and Evolution of Life

DA 2

Immunological Studies

Immunological studies provide a method of indirectly estimating the degree of similarity of proteins in different species. If differences exist in the proteins, then there must also be differences in the DNA that codes for them. The evolutionary relationships of a large number of different animal groups have been established on the basis of immunology. The results support the phylogenies developed from other areas: biogeography, comparative anatomy, and fossil evidence.

Method for Immunological Comparison

1. Blood serum (containing blood proteins but no cells) is collected from a human and is injected into a rabbit. This causes the formation of antibodies in the rabbit's blood. These identify human blood proteins, attach to them and render them harmless.

2. A sample of the rabbit's blood is taken and the rabbit's antibodies that recognize human blood proteins are extracted.

3. These anti-human antibodies are then added to blood samples from other species to see how well they recognize the proteins in the different blood. The more similar the blood sample is to original human blood, the greater the reaction (which takes the form of creating a precipitate, i.e. solids).

The five blood samples that were tested (on the right) show varying degrees of precipitate (solid) formation. Note that when the anti-human antibodies are added to human blood there is a high degree of affinity. There is poor recognition when added to rat blood.

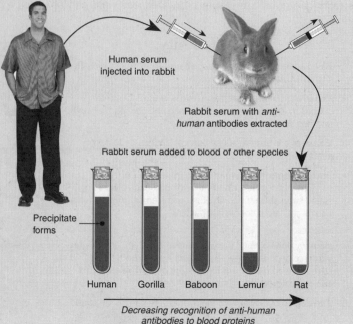

Human serum injected into rabbit

Rabbit serum with *anti-human* antibodies extracted

Rabbit serum added to blood of other species

Precipitate forms

Human · Gorilla · Baboon · Lemur · Rat

Decreasing recognition of anti-human antibodies to blood proteins

Immunological Comparison of Tree Frogs

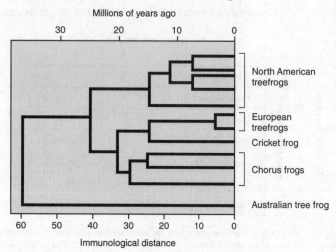

Millions of years ago

North American treefrogs

European treefrogs

Cricket frog

Chorus frogs

Australian tree frog

Immunological distance

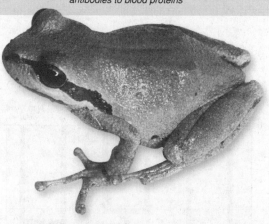

The relationships among **tree frogs** have been established by immunological studies. The immunological distance is a measure of the number of amino acid substitutions between two groups. This, in turn, has been calibrated to provide a time scale showing when the various related groups diverged.

1. Briefly describe how **immunological studies** have contributed evidence that the process of evolution has taken place:

_____

_____

_____

_____

2. Study the graph above showing the immunological distance between tree frogs. Determine the immunological distance between the following frogs:

(a) Cricket frog and the Australian tree frog: _____ (b) The various chorus frogs: _____

3. Describe how closely the Australian tree frog is related to the other frogs shown:

_____

4. State when the North American tree frogs became separated from the European tree frogs: _____

Related activities: The Fossil Record, Biogeographical Evidence, Comparative Anatomy

Other Evidence for Evolution

Amino Acid Sequences

Each of our proteins has a specific number of amino acids arranged in a specific order. Any differences in the sequence reflect changes in the DNA sequence. The hemoglobin beta chain has been used as a standard molecule for comparing the precise sequence of amino acids in different species. Hemoglobin is the protein in our red blood cells that is responsible for carrying oxygen around our bodies. The hemoglobin in adults is made up of four polypeptide chains: two alpha chains and two beta chains. Each is coded for by a separate gene.

Example right: When the sequence of human hemoglobin, which is 146 amino acids long, was compared with that of five other primate species it was found that chimpanzees had an identical sequence while those that were already considered less closely related had a greater number of differences. This suggests a very close genetic relationship between humans, chimpanzees and gorillas, but less with the other primates.

Amino Acid Differences Between Humans and Other Primates

The *'position of changed amino acid'* is the point in the protein, composed of 146 amino acids, at which the **different** amino acids occurs

Primate	No. of amino acids different from humans	Position of changed amino acids
Chimpanzee	Identical	–
Gorilla	1	104
Gibbon	3	80 87 125
Rhesus monkey	8	9 13 33 50 76 87 104 125
Squirrel monkey	9	5 6 9 21 22 56 76 87 125

Comparative Embryology

By comparing the development of embryos from different species, Ernst von Bayer in 1828 noticed that animals are more similar during early stages of their embryological development than later as adults. This later led to Ernst Haeckel (1834-1919) to propose his famous principle: *ontogeny recapitulates phylogeny*. He claimed that the development of an individual (ontogeny) retraces the stages through which the individual species has passed during its evolution (phylogeny). This idea is now known to be an oversimplification and is misleading. Although early developmental sequences between all vertebrates are similar, there are important deviations from the general developmental plan in different species. Notice the gill slits that briefly appear in the human embryo (arrowed). The more closely related forms of the monkey and humans continue to appear similar until a later stage in development, compared to more distantly related species. From the study of fetal development it is possible to find clues as to how evolution generates the diversity of life forms through time, but 'ontogeny does not recapitulate phylogeny'.

Developmental stage	Amphibian	Bird	Monkey	Human
Fertilized egg				
Late cleavage				
Body segments				Gill slits
Limb buds				
Late fetal				

1. Study the table of data showing the differences in **amino acid sequences** for selected primates. Explain why chimpanzees and gorillas are considered most closely related to humans, while monkeys are less so:

_____

_____

_____

2. Briefly describe how **comparative embryology** has contributed evidence to support the concept of evolution:

_____

_____

3. Describe a commonly used biochemical method for precisely analyzing the genes in organisms to determine their evolutionary relationships:

_____

_____

Related activities: Respiratory Pigments

RDA 2

The Origin and Evolution of Life

Vestigial Organs

Some classes of characters are more valuable than others as reliable indicators of common ancestry. Often, the less any part of an animal is used for specialized purposes, the more important it becomes for classification. This is because common ancestry is easier to detect if a particular feature is unaffected by specific adaptations arising later during the evolution of the species. Vestigial organs are an example of this because, if they have no clear function and they are no longer subject to natural selection, they will remain unchanged through a lineage. It is sometimes argued that some vestigial organs are not truly vestigial, i.e. they may perform some small function. While this may be true in some cases, the features can still be considered vestigial if their new role is a minor one, unrelated to their original function.

Ancestors of Modern Whales

1.8 m long

Pakicetus (early Eocene) a carnivorous, four limbed, early Eocene whale ancestor, probably rather like a large otter. It was still partly terrestrial and not fully adapted for aquatic life.

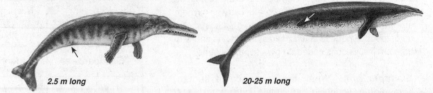

2.5 m long

Protocetus (mid Eocene). Much more whale-like than *Pakicetus*. The hind limbs were greatly reduced and although they still protruded from the body (arrowed), they were useless for swimming.

20-25 m long

Basilosaurus (late Eocene). A very large ancestor of modern whales. The hind limbs contained all the leg bones, but were vestigial and located entirely within the main body, leaving a tissue flap on the surface (arrowed).

Vestigial organs are common in nature. The vestigial hind limbs of modern whales (right) provide anatomical evidence for their evolution from a carnivorous, four footed, terrestrial ancestor. The oldest known whale, *Pakicetus*, from the early Eocene (~54 mya) still had four limbs. By the late Eocene (~40 mya), whales were fully marine and had lost almost all traces of their former terrestrial life. For fossil evidence, see *Whale Origins* at: www.neoucom.edu/Depts/Anat/whaleorigins.htm

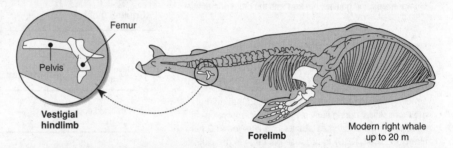

Femur

Pelvis

Vestigial hindlimb

Forelimb

Modern right whale up to 20 m

RM-DoC

Vestigial organs in birds and reptiles

In all snakes (far left), one lobe of the lung is vestigial (there is not sufficient room in the narrow body cavity for it). In some snakes there are also vestiges of the pelvic girdle and hind limbs of their walking ancestors. Like all ratites, kiwis (left) are flightless. However, more than in other ratites, the wings of kiwis are reduced to tiny vestiges. Kiwis evolved in the absence of predators to a totally ground dwelling existence.

1. In terms of natural selection explain how structures, that were once useful to an organism, could become vestigial:

_____

_____

_____

_____

2. Suggest why a vestigial structure, once it has been reduced to a certain size, may not disappear altogether:

_____

_____

3. Whale evolution shows the presence of **transitional forms** (fossils that are intermediate between modern forms and very early ancestors). Suggest how vestigial structures indicate the common ancestry of these forms:

_____

_____

_____

Related activities: Natural Selection, Fossil Formation

The Evolution of Novel Forms

The relatively new field of **evolutionary developmental biology** (or evo-devo) addresses the origin and evolution of embryonic development and looks at how modifications of developmental processes can lead to novel features. Scientists now know that specific genes in animals, including a subgroup of genes called *Hox* genes, are part of a basic **'tool kit'** of genes that control animal development. Genomic studies have shown that these genes are **highly conserved** (i.e. they show little change in different lineages). Very disparate organisms share the same **tool kit** of genes, but regulate them differently. The implication of this is that large changes in morphology or function are associated with changes in gene regulation, rather than the evolution of new genes, and natural selection associated with gene switches plays a major role in evolution.

The Role of *Hox* Genes

Hox genes control the development of back and front parts of the body. The same genes (or homologous ones) are present in essentially all animals, including humans.

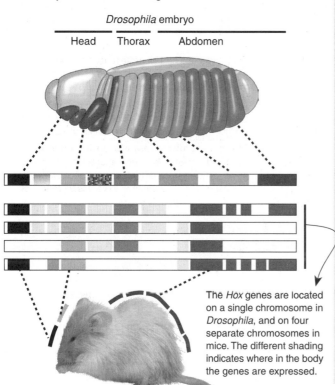

Drosophila embryo

Head | Thorax | Abdomen

The *Hox* genes are located on a single chromosome in *Drosophila*, and on four separate chromosomes in mice. The different shading indicates where in the body the genes are expressed.

The Evolution of Novel Forms

Even very small changes (mutations) in the *Hox* genes can have a profound effect on morphology. Such changes to the genes controlling development have almost certainly been important in the evolution of novel structures and body plans. Four principles underly the evo-devo thinking regarding the evolution of novel forms:

- **Evolution works with what is already present**: New structures are modifications of pre-existing structures.

- **Multifunctionality** and **redundancy**: Functional redundancy in any part of a multifunctional structure allows for specialisation and division of labour through the development of two separate structures.

  Example: the diversity of appendages (including mouthparts) in arthropods.

- **Modularity**: Modular architecture in animals (arthropods, vertebrates) allows for the modification and specialisation of individual body parts. Genetic switches allow changes in one part of a structure, independent of other parts.

Shifting *Hox* Expression

Huge diversity in morphology in organisms within and across phyla could have arisen through small changes in the genes controlling development.

Differences in neck length in vertebrates provides a good example of how changes in gene expression can bring about changes in morphology. Different vertebrates have different numbers of neck vertebrae. The boundary between neck and trunk vertebrae is marked by expression of the **Hox c6 gene** (c6 denotes the sixth cervical or neck vertebra) in all cases, but the position varies in each animal relative to the overall body. The forelimb (arrow) arises at this boundary in all four-legged vertebrates. In snakes, the boundary is shifted forward to the base of the skull and no limbs develop. As a result of these differences in expression, mice have a short neck, geese a long neck, and snakes, no neck at all.

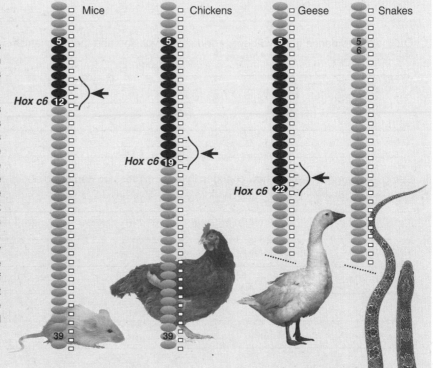

Mice   Chickens   Geese   Snakes

Hox c6 **12**   Hox c6 **19**   Hox c6 **22**

Related activities: Other Evidence for Evolution, The Modern Theory of Evolution
Web links: Genetic Tool Kit

A 3

The Origin and Evolution of Life

Genetic Switches in Evolution

The *Hox* genes are just part of the collection of genes that make up the genetic tool kit for animal development. The genes in the tool kit act as switches, shaping development by affecting how other genes are turned on or off. The distribution of genes in the tool kit indicates that it is ancient and was in place before the evolution of most types of animals. Differences in form arise through changes in genetic switches. One example is the evolution of eyespots in butterflies:

■ The ***Distal-less*** gene is one of the important **master body-building genes** in the genetic tool kit. Switches in the *Distal-less* gene control expression in the embryo (E), larval legs (L), and wing (W) in flies and butterflies, but butterflies have also evolved an extra switch (S) to control eyespot development.

■ Once *Distal-less* spots evolved, changes in *Distal-less* expression (through changes in the switch) produced more or fewer spots.

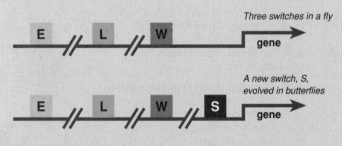

Three switches in a fly

A new switch, S, evolved in butterflies

Changes in *Distal-less* regulation were probably achieved by changing specific sequences of the *Distal-less* gene eyespot switch. The result? Changes in eyespot size and number.

Same Gene, New Tricks

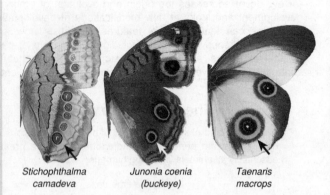

Stichophthalma camadeva

Junonia coenia (buckeye)

Taenaris macrops

■ The action of a tool kit protein depends on context: where particular cells are located at the time when the gene is switched on.

■ Changes in the DNA sequence of a genetic switch can change the zone of gene expression without disrupting the function of the tool kit protein itself.

■ The spectacular **eyespots** on butterfly wings (arrowed above) represent different degrees of a basic pattern, from virtually all eyespot elements expressed (*Stichophthalma*) to very few (*Taenaris*).

1. Explain what is meant by "evo-devo" and state its aims: _____

_____

_____

2. Briefly describe the role of *Hox* genes in animal development: _____

_____

_____

_____

3. Outline the evidence that evo-devo provides for evolution and the mechanisms by which it occurs: _____

_____

_____

_____

_____

4. Using an example, discuss how changes in gene expression can bring about changes in morphology:

_____

_____

_____

_____

_____

_____

_____

Biogeographical Evidence

The distribution of organisms around the world lends powerful support to the idea that modern forms evolved from ancestral populations. **Biogeography** is the study of the geographical distribution of species, both present-day and extinct. It stresses the role of dispersal of species from a point of origin across pre-existing barriers. Studies from the island populations (below) indicate that flora and fauna of different islands are more closely related to adjacent continental species than to each other.

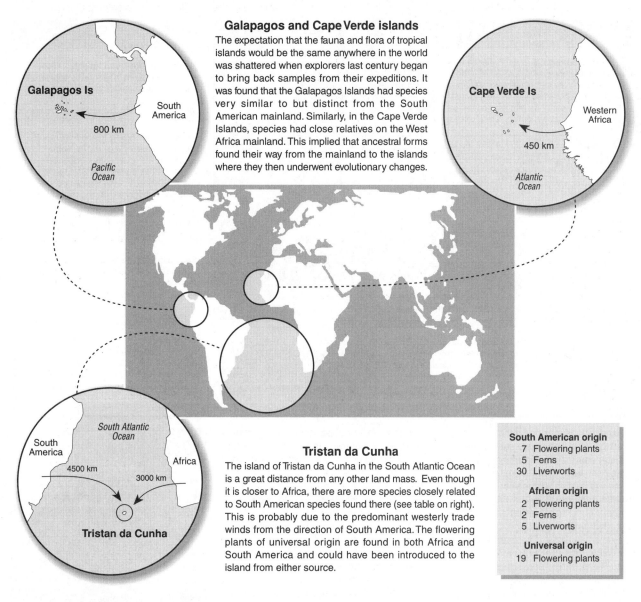

Galapagos and Cape Verde islands

The expectation that the fauna and flora of tropical islands would be the same anywhere in the world was shattered when explorers last century began to bring back samples from their expeditions. It was found that the Galapagos Islands had species very similar to but distinct from the South American mainland. Similarly, in the Cape Verde Islands, species had close relatives on the West Africa mainland. This implied that ancestral forms found their way from the mainland to the islands where they then underwent evolutionary changes.

Galapagos Is
South America
800 km
Pacific Ocean

Cape Verde Is
Western Africa
450 km
Atlantic Ocean

South Atlantic Ocean
South America
Africa
4500 km
3000 km
Tristan da Cunha

Tristan da Cunha

The island of Tristan da Cunha in the South Atlantic Ocean is a great distance from any other land mass. Even though it is closer to Africa, there are more species closely related to South American species found there (see table on right). This is probably due to the predominant westerly trade winds from the direction of South America. The flowering plants of universal origin are found in both Africa and South America and could have been introduced to the island from either source.

South American origin
7 Flowering plants
5 Ferns
30 Liverworts

African origin
2 Flowering plants
2 Ferns
5 Liverworts

Universal origin
19 Flowering plants

1. The Galapagos Islands and the Cape Verde Islands are tropical islands close to the equator. These islands have plants and animals that are very different from each other. Explain why this is so:

_____

_____

2. The island of Tristan da Cunha is situated in the South Atlantic Ocean remote from any other land. Identify the origin of the majority of the plant species that are found there, and explain why this is so:

_____

_____

3. Using one or more specific examples, describe how biogeography provides support for the theory of evolution:

_____

_____

_____

_____

Related activities: Ocean Island Colonizers

A 2

The Origin and Evolution of Life

Oceanic Island Colonizers

Oceanic islands have a **unique biota** because only certain groups of plants and animals tend to colonize them, while others are just not able to do so. The animals that successfully colonize oceanic islands have to be marine in habit, or able to survive long periods at sea or in the air. This precludes large numbers from ever reaching distant islands. Plants also have limited capacity to reach distant islands. Only some have fruits and seeds that are salt tolerant. Many plants are transferred to the islands by wind or migrating birds. The biota of the **Galapagos islands** provide a good example of the results of such a colonization process.

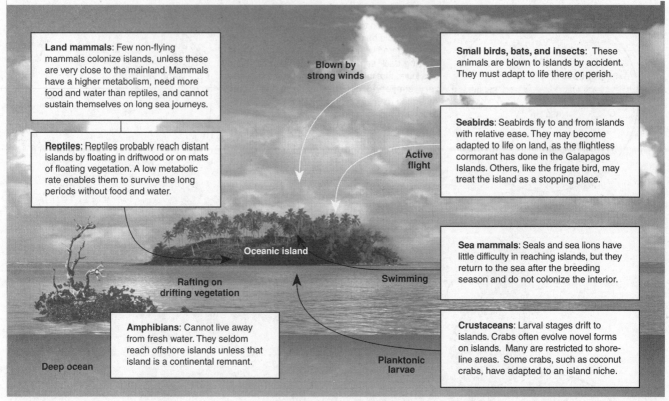

Land mammals: Few non-flying mammals colonize islands, unless these are very close to the mainland. Mammals have a higher metabolism, need more food and water than reptiles, and cannot sustain themselves on long sea journeys.

Reptiles: Reptiles probably reach distant islands by floating in driftwood or on mats of floating vegetation. A low metabolic rate enables them to survive the long periods without food and water.

Small birds, bats, and insects: These animals are blown to islands by accident. They must adapt to life there or perish.

Seabirds: Seabirds fly to and from islands with relative ease. They may become adapted to life on land, as the flightless cormorant has done in the Galapagos Islands. Others, like the frigate bird, may treat the island as a stopping place.

Sea mammals: Seals and sea lions have little difficulty in reaching islands, but they return to the sea after the breeding season and do not colonize the interior.

Amphibians: Cannot live away from fresh water. They seldom reach offshore islands unless that island is a continental remnant.

Crustaceans: Larval stages drift to islands. Crabs often evolve novel forms on islands. Many are restricted to shore-line areas. Some crabs, such as coconut crabs, have adapted to an island niche.

Blown by strong winds

Active flight

Oceanic island

Rafting on drifting vegetation

Swimming

Deep ocean

Planktonic larvae

The oldest islands making up the Galapagos archipelago appeared above sea level some 3-4 million years ago. The photographs on this page show some of the features typical of animals that colonize oceanic islands. The **flightless cormorant** (below left) is one of a number of bird species that have lost the power of flight once they had taken up residence on an island. The **giant tortoises** of the Galapagos (below Centrex) are not unique. There were other, almost identical, giant tortoise subspecies living on islands in the Indian Ocean including the Seychelles archipelago, Reunion, Mauritius, Farquhar, and Diego Rodriguez. These were almost completely exterminated by early Western sailors, although a small population remained untouched on the island of Aldabra. Another feature of oceanic islands is the 'adaptive radiation' (diversification) of colonizing species into different specialist forms. The two forms of Galapagos iguana almost certainly arose, through diversification, from a hardy traveler from the South American mainland. The **marine iguana** (below right) feeds on the seaweeds of the shoreline and is adept at swimming. The **land iguana** (right) feeds on cacti, which are numerous.

Land iguana feeding on cactus

Flightless cormorant

Giant Galapagos tortoise

Marine iguana feeding on seaweed

1. Explain why the flora and fauna of the Galapagos Archipelago must be relatively recent arrivals:

_____

2. Describe how the marine iguana and the land iguana have become different: _____

_____

Related activities: Biogeographical Evidence

Continental Drift and Evolution

Continental drift is a measurable phenomenon; it has happened in the past and continues today. Movements of up to 2-11 cm a year have been recorded between continents using laser technology. The movements of the Earth's 12 major crustal plates are driven by thermal convection currents in the mantle; a geological process known as **plate tectonics.** Some continents appear to be drifting apart while others are on a direct collision course. Various lines of evidence show that the modern continents were once joined together as 'supercontinents'. One supercontinent, called **Gondwana**, was made up of the southern continents some 200 million years ago. The diagram below shows some of the data collected that are used as evidence to indicate how the modern continents once fitted together.

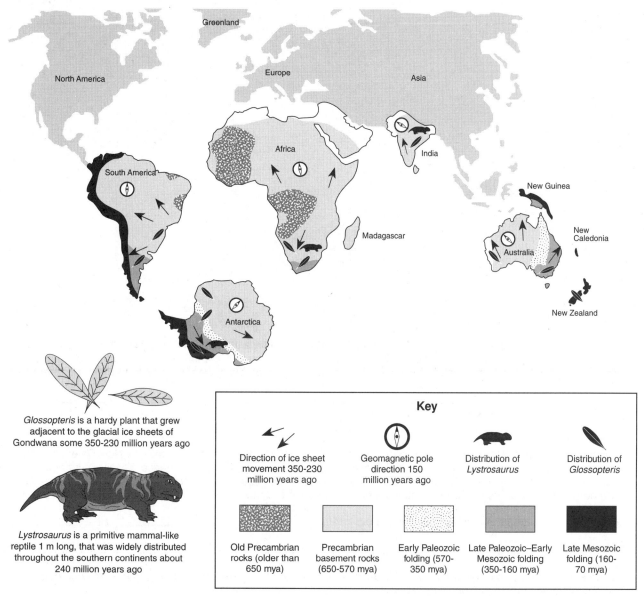

Glossopteris is a hardy plant that grew adjacent to the glacial ice sheets of Gondwana some 350-230 million years ago

Lystrosaurus is a primitive mammal-like reptile 1 m long, that was widely distributed throughout the southern continents about 240 million years ago

Key

Direction of ice sheet movement 350-230 million years ago

Geomagnetic pole direction 150 million years ago

Distribution of *Lystrosaurus*

Distribution of *Glossopteris*

Old Precambrian rocks (older than 650 mya)

Precambrian basement rocks (650-570 mya)

Early Paleozoic folding (570-350 mya)

Late Paleozoic–Early Mesozoic folding (350-160 mya)

Late Mesozoic folding (160-70 mya)

1. Name the modern landmasses (continents and large islands) that made up the supercontinent of Gondwana:

   _____

2. Cut out the southern continents on page 91 and arrange them to recreate the supercontinent of Gondwana. Take care to cut the shapes out close to the coastlines. When arranging them into the space showing the outline of Gondwana on page 90, take into account the following information:
   (a) The location of ancient rocks and periods of mountain folding during different geological ages.
   (b) The direction of ancient ice sheet movements.
   (c) The geomagnetic orientation of old rocks (the way that magnetic crystals are lined up in ancient rock gives an indication of the direction the magnetic pole was at the time the rock was formed).
   (d) The distribution of fossils of ancient species such as *Lystrosaurus* and *Glossopteris*.

3. Once you have positioned the modern continents into the pattern of the supercontinent, mark on the diagram:
   (a) The likely position of the South Pole 350-230 million years ago (as indicated by the movement of the ice sheets).
   (b) The likely position of the geomagnetic South Pole 150 million years ago (as indicated by ancient geomagnetism).

4. State what general deduction you can make about the position of the polar regions with respect to land masses:

   _____

The Origin and Evolution of Life

PDA 3

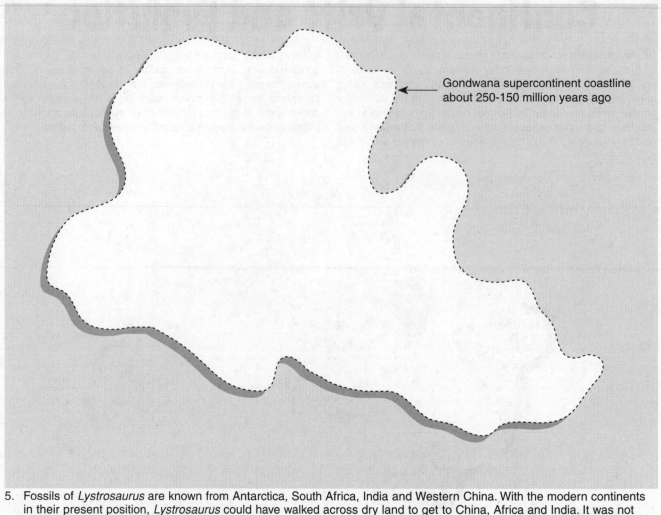

Gondwana supercontinent coastline about 250-150 million years ago

5. Fossils of *Lystrosaurus* are known from Antarctica, South Africa, India and Western China. With the modern continents in their present position, *Lystrosaurus* could have walked across dry land to get to China, Africa and India. It was not possible for it to walk to Antarctica, however. Explain the distribution of this ancient species in terms of continental drift:

_____

_____

6. The southern beech (*Nothofagus*) is found only in the southern hemisphere, in such places as New Caledonia, New Guinea, eastern Australia (including Tasmania), New Zealand, and southern South America. Fossils of southern beech trees have also been found in Antarctica. They have never been distributed in South Africa or India. The seeds of the southern beech trees are not readily dispersed by the wind and are rapidly killed by exposure to salt water.

(a) Suggest a reason why *Nothofagus* is not found in Africa or India: _____

_____

(b) Use a colored pen to indicate the distribution of *Nothofagus* on the current world map (on the previous page) and on your completed map of Gondwana above.

(c) State how the arrangement of the continents into Gondwana explains this distribution pattern:

_____

_____

7. The Atlantic Ocean is currently opening up at the rate of 2 cm per year. At this rate in the past, calculate how long it would have taken to reach its current extent, with the distance from Africa to South America being 2300 km (assume the rate of spreading has been constant):

_____

8. Explain how continental drift provides evidence to support evolutionary theory: _____

_____

_____

_____

_____

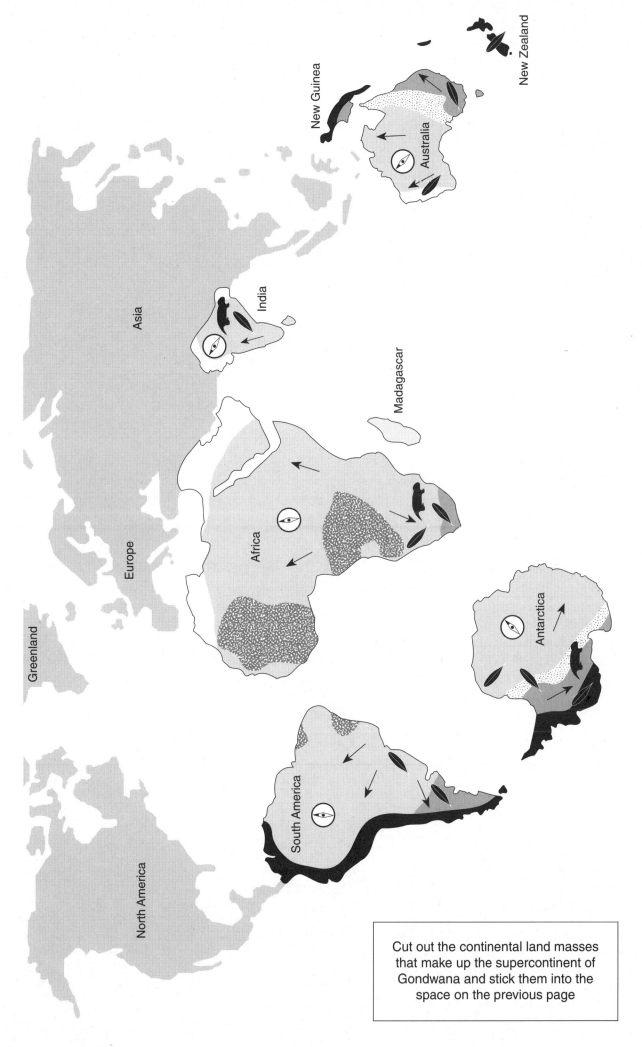

New Guinea

New Zealand

Australia

India

Asia

Madagascar

Europe

Africa

Antarctica

Greenland

South America

North America

Cut out the continental land masses that make up the supercontinent of Gondwana and stick them into the space on the previous page

The Origin and Evolution of Life

Speciation

Learning Objectives

☐ 1. Compile your own glossary from the **KEY WORDS** displayed in **bold type** in the learning objectives below.

Modern Synthesis of Evolution *(pages 69, 95-97)*

☐ 2. Give a precise definition of the term **evolution**, explaining how evolution is a feature of **populations** and not of individuals.

☐ 3. Identify some of the main contributors to the modern theory of evolution. Include:
   • An outline of Lamarck's theory of evolution by the inheritance of acquired characteristics. Include reference to the mechanism of, and lack of evidence for, inheritance of acquired characteristics.
   • An explanation of the Darwin-Wallace theory of evolution by natural selection (cross ref. with #5-6).

☐ 4. Discuss the evidence for various theories for the origin of species, including the theories of Darwin and Wallace, and Lamarck, and the theories of **panspermia** and evolution by special creation. Discuss the applicability of the scientific method to each.

☐ 5. Outline the fundamental ideas in Darwin's theory of evolution by natural selection. Include reference to:
   • The tendency of populations to overproduce.
   • The fact that overproduction leads to competition.
   • The fact that members of a species show variation, that sexual reproduction promotes variation, and that variation is (usually) heritable.
   • The differential survival and reproduction of individuals with favorable, heritable variations.

☐ 6. Discuss the (Darwin-Wallace) theory that species evolve by natural selection. Appreciate how Darwin's original theory has been modified in the **new synthesis** to incorporate our current understanding of genetics and inheritance.

☐ 7. Understand the term **fitness** and explain how evolution, through **adaptation**, equips species for survival. Recognize structural and physiological adaptations of organisms to their environment.

Concept of the Gene Pool *(pages 105-114 and the TRC: Genes and Evolution)*

☐ 8. Understand the concept of the **gene pool** and explain the term **deme**. Recognize that populations may be of various sizes and geographical extent.

☐ 9. Explain the term **allele frequency** and describe how allele frequencies are expressed for a population.

☐ 10. State the Hardy-Weinberg principle (of **genetic equilibrium**). Understand the criteria that must be satisfied in order to achieve genetic equilibrium in a population. Identify the consequences of the fact that these criteria are rarely met in reality.

☐ 11. Explain how the **Hardy-Weinberg equation** provides a simple mathematical model of genetic equilibrium in a population. Demonstrate an ability to use the Hardy-Weinberg equation to calculate the allele, genotype, and phenotype frequencies from appropriate data.

Microevolution *(page 107)*

☐ 12. Recognize that changes occur in gene pools (**microevolution**) when any or all of the criteria for genetic equilibrium are not met. Appreciate that populations, not individuals, evolve.

☐ 13. Recognize the forces in microevolution that may alter allele frequencies: **natural selection**, **genetic drift**, **gene flow**, and **mutation**. Identify processes that increase genetic variation and those that decrease it.

Natural selection *(pages 96, 98-110)*

☐ 14. Recall that individuals within a species show **variation** and that heritable variation is the raw material for natural selection. Explain how **natural selection** is responsible for most evolutionary change by selectively changing genetic variation through differential survival and reproduction. Interpret data to explain how natural selection produces change in a population (see #16).

☐ 15. Describe three types of natural selection: **stabilizing**, **directional**, and **disruptive selection**. Describe the outcome of each type in a population exhibiting a normal curve in phenotypic variation.

☐ 16. As required, describe examples of evolution including:
   (a) **Transient polymorphism**, e.g. **industrial melanism** in peppered moths (*Biston betularia*).
   (b) The sickle cell trait as the basis for **balanced polymorphism** in malarial regions.
   (c) Changes to the size and shape of the beaks of **Galapagos finches** (cross ref. with the topic *The Origin and Evolution of Life*, Option D.3).
   (d) The development of **multiple antibiotic resistance** in bacteria and one other example of evolution in response to environmental change.
   (e) The development of **pesticide resistance** in insects or **heavy metal tolerance** in plants.

The effects of genetic drift, mutation, and gene flow *(pages 107-109, 118)*

☐ 17. Define the term **genetic drift** and describe the conditions under which it is important. Explain, using diagrams or a gene pool model, how genetic drift may lead to loss or **fixation of alleles** (where a gene is represented in the population by only one allele).

18. Recognize **mutations** as the source of all new alleles. Use a diagram to explain how mutations alter the genetic equilibrium of a population. Recall that recombination during meiosis reshuffles alleles and increases variation, but it does not create new alleles.

19. Explain how **migration** leads to **gene flow** between natural populations, and may affect allele frequencies.

Special Events in Gene Pools *(pages 107, 116-18)*

20. Explain the **founder effect**, including reference to its genetic and evolutionary consequences.

21. Explain the **population bottleneck effect**, including reference to its genetic and evolutionary consequences.

22. Appreciate how the founder effect and population (genetic) bottlenecks may accelerate the pace of evolutionary change. Explain the importance of **genetic drift** in populations that undergo these events.

Sexual Selection *(page 115)*

23. Discuss the role of **sexual selection** in affecting anatomy and behavior. Suggest how sexual selection may lead to the evolution of elaborate secondary sexual characteristics, particularly in males.

Speciation *(pages 119-124, also see page 139 and the TRC: The Species Concept)*

24. Recall your definition of **evolution** and distinguish clearly between **microevolution** and **macroevolution**.

25. Define **species**. Describe how the nature of some species can create problems for our definition.

26. Recognize the role of **natural selection** and **isolation** in **speciation**. Discuss speciation in terms of migration, geographical or ecological isolation (see #26-27) and adaptation (see #7), leading to reproductive or genetic isolation of gene pools.

27. Explain what is meant by **reproductive isolation**. Describe the mechanisms through which populations may become reproductively isolated. If required, distinguish between **prezygotic** and **postzygotic** reproductive isolating mechanisms (RIMs).

28. Contrast **allopatric** and **sympatric speciation**, identifying the situations in which each is most likely to occur. Explain why RIMs tend to be more pronounced between sympatric (as opposed to allopatric) species. Explain the role of **polyploidy** in **instant speciation**.

29. Recognize stages in species development, including reference to the reduction in gene flow as populations become increasingly isolated.

 See the 'Textbook Reference Grid' on pages 8-9 for textbook page references relating to material in this topic.

Supplementary Texts

See pages 5-6 for additional details of these texts:
■ Adds, J., *et al.*, 2004. **Genetics, Evolution and Biodiversity**, (NelsonThornes), chpt. 8.

■ Clegg, C.J., 1999. **Genetics and Evolution**, (John Murray), pp. 60-78.

■ Helms, D.R. *et al.*, 1998. **Biology in the Laboratory** (W.H. Freeman), #20, #21.

■ Jones, N., *et al.*, 2001. **The Essentials of Genetics**, pp. 190-232.

See page 6 for details of publishers of periodicals:

STUDENT'S REFERENCE

■ **The Species Enigma** New Scientist, 13 June 1998 (Inside Science). *The nature of species, ring species, and the status of hybrids.*

■ **Speciation** Biol. Sci. Rev., 16(2) Nov. 2003, pp. 24-28. *An excellent account of speciation. It covers the nature of species, reproductive isolation, how separated populations diverge, and sympatric speciation. Case examples include the cichlids of Lake Victoria and the founder effect in mynahs.*

■ **Optimality** Biol. Sci. Rev., 17(4), April 2005, pp. 2-5. *Environmental stability and optimality of structure and function can explain evolutionary stasis in animals. Examples are described.*

■ **Plants on the Move** New Scientist, 20 March 1999 (Inside Science). *Glaciation and warming have evolutionary consequences for flora.*

■ **Polymorphism** Biol. Sci. Rev., 14(1), Sept. 2001, pp. 19-21. *An account of polymorphism in populations, with several case studies (including Biston moths) provided as illustrative examples.*

■ **Together We're Stronger** New Scientist, 15 March 2003. (Inside Science). *The mechanisms behind the evolution of social behaviour in animals. The evolution of eusociality in hymenopteran insects is the case study provided.*

■ **Listen, We're Different** New Scientist, 17 July 1999, pp. 32-35. *An excellent account of speciation in periodic cicadas as a result of behavioural and temporal isolating mechanisms.*

■ **How Life Branches Out** New Scientist, 24 June 2006, pp. 50-53. *The origin of Amazonia's spectacular biodiversity is attributable to sympatric speciation, not the Pleistocene refugia hypothesis.*

TEACHER'S REFERENCE

■ **15 Answers to Creationist Nonsense** Scientific American, July 2002, pp. 62-69. *A synopsis of the common arguments presented by Creationists and the answers offered by science.*

■ **Evolution: Five Big Questions** New Scientist, 14 June 2003, pp. 32-39, 48-51. *A discussion of the most covered points regarding evolution and the mechanisms by which it occurs.*

■ **The Hardy-Weinberg Principle** Biol. Sci. Rev., 15(4), April 2003, pp. 7-9. *A succinct explanation of the basis of the Hardy-Weinberg principle, and its uses in estimating genotype frequencies and predicting change in populations.*

■ **Cichlids of the Rift Lakes** Scientific American, Feb. 1999, pp. 44-49. *An excellent account of the recent speciation events in cichlid fishes in Lake Victoria, as revealed through mitochondrial DNA.*

■ **How are Species Formed?** New Scientist, 14 June 2003, pp. 36-37. *Part of an in-depth examination of evolution, this article discusses how ideas about speciation have moved away from chance and small populations. New species may be the result of parallel evolution (ecological selection), sexual selection, or hybridizaton.*

■ **How the Species Became** New Scientist, 11 Oct. 2003, pp. 32-35. *Stability in species and new ideas on speciation. Species are stable if changes in form or behavior are damped down, but unstable if the changes escalate as new generations shuffle parental genes and natural selection discards the allele combinations that do not work well.*

■ **Live and Let Live** New Scientist, 3 July 1999, pp. 32-36. *Recent research suggests that hybrids are intact entities subject to the same evolutionary pressures as pure species.*

■ **Fair Enough** New Scientist, 12 Oct. 2002, pp. 34-37. *Skin color in humans: this article examines the argument for there being a selective benefit to being dark or pale in different environments.*

■ **Skin Deep** Scientific American, Oct. 2002, pp. 50-57. *This article presents powerful evidence for skin color ("race") being the end result of opposing selection forces. Clearly written and of high interest, this is a perfect vehicle for student discussion and for examining natural selection.*

■ **Desert Island** Scientific American, June 2005, pp. 11-12. *A new study suggests that climate can effectively isolate organisms and foster endemism.*

■ **Replaying Life** New Scientist, 13 February 1999, pp. 29-33. *Rapid evolution in bacteria driven by habitat diversity and niche differentiation.*

■ **The Challenge of Antibiotic Resistance** Scientific American, March 1998, pp. 32-39. *The rise in antibiotic resistance: how it arises and the threat it poses to the treatment of bacterial disease.*

■ **The American Biology Teacher** contains many excellent articles covering the teaching of basic evolutionary principles. A list of recent articles in this topic area is provided on the TRC.

See pages 10-11 for details of how to access **Bio Links** from our web site: www.thebiozone.com From Bio Links, access sites under the topics:
GENERAL BIOLOGY ONLINE RESOURCES > Online Textbooks and Lecture Notes: • An online biology book... *and others* > **General Online Biology resources:** • Ken's Bioweb resources ... *and others* > **Glossaries:** • Evolutionary biology and genetics glossary... *and others*

EVOLUTION: • Enter evolution: theory & history • BIO 414 evolution • Evolution • Evolution on the web for biology students • Harvard University biology links: evolution • The Talk.Origins archive ... *and others* > **Charles Darwin:** • Darwin and evolution overview • What is Darwinism? ... *and others*

GENETICS > Population Genetics: • Introduction to evolutionary biology • Industrial melanism in *Biston betularia* • Micro-evolution and population genetics • Random genetic drift • Population genetics: lecture notes ... *and others*

Presentation MEDIA to support this topic:
EVOLUTION:
• **Population Genetics**
• **Evolution**

Evolution

The Modern Theory of Evolution

Although **Charles Darwin** is credited with the development of the theory of evolution by natural selection, there were many people that contributed ideas upon which he built his own. Since Darwin first proposed his theory, aspects that were problematic (such as the mechanism of inheritance) have now been explained. The development of the modern theory of evolution has a history going back at least two centuries. The diagram below illustrates the way in which some of the major contributors helped to form the currently accepted model, or **new synthesis**. Understanding of evolutionary processes continued to grow through the 1980s and 1990s as comparative molecular sequence data were amassed and understanding of the molecular basis of developmental mechanisms improved. Most recently, in the exciting new area of evolutionary developmental biology (**evo-devo**), biologists have been exploring how developmental gene expression patterns explain how groups of organisms evolved.

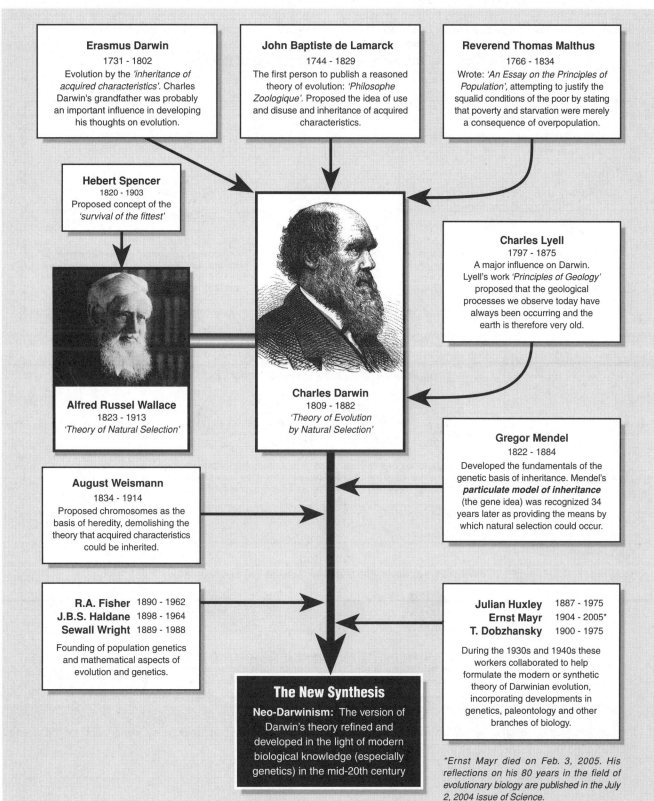

Erasmus Darwin
1731 - 1802
Evolution by the *'inheritance of acquired characteristics'*. Charles Darwin's grandfather was probably an important influence in developing his thoughts on evolution.

John Baptiste de Lamarck
1744 - 1829
The first person to publish a reasoned theory of evolution: *'Philosophe Zoologique'*. Proposed the idea of use and disuse and inheritance of acquired characteristics.

Reverend Thomas Malthus
1766 - 1834
Wrote: *'An Essay on the Principles of Population'*, attempting to justify the squalid conditions of the poor by stating that poverty and starvation were merely a consequence of overpopulation.

Hebert Spencer
1820 - 1903
Proposed concept of the *'survival of the fittest'*

Charles Lyell
1797 - 1875
A major influence on Darwin. Lyell's work *'Principles of Geology'* proposed that the geological processes we observe today have always been occurring and the earth is therefore very old.

Alfred Russel Wallace
1823 - 1913
'Theory of Natural Selection'

Charles Darwin
1809 - 1882
'Theory of Evolution by Natural Selection'

Gregor Mendel
1822 - 1884
Developed the fundamentals of the genetic basis of inheritance. Mendel's *particulate model of inheritance* (the gene idea) was recognized 34 years later as providing the means by which natural selection could occur.

August Weismann
1834 - 1914
Proposed chromosomes as the basis of heredity, demolishing the theory that acquired characteristics could be inherited.

R.A. Fisher 1890 - 1962
J.B.S. Haldane 1898 - 1964
Sewall Wright 1889 - 1988
Founding of population genetics and mathematical aspects of evolution and genetics.

Julian Huxley 1887 - 1975
Ernst Mayr 1904 - 2005*
T. Dobzhansky 1900 - 1975
During the 1930s and 1940s these workers collaborated to help formulate the modern or synthetic theory of Darwinian evolution, incorporating developments in genetics, paleontology and other branches of biology.

The New Synthesis
Neo-Darwinism: The version of Darwin's theory refined and developed in the light of modern biological knowledge (especially genetics) in the mid-20th century

Ernst Mayr died on Feb. 3, 2005. His reflections on his 80 years in the field of evolutionary biology are published in the July 2, 2004 issue of Science.

1. From the diagram above, choose one of the contributors to the development of evolutionary theory (excluding Charles Darwin himself), and write a few paragraphs discussing their role in contributing to Darwin's ideas. You may need to consult an encyclopedia or other reference to assist you.

Darwin's Theory

In 1859, Darwin and Wallace jointly proposed that new species could develop by a process of natural selection. Natural selection is the term given to the mechanism by which better adapted organisms survive to produce a greater number of viable offspring. This has the effect of increasing their proportion in the population so that they become more common. It is Darwin who is best remembered for the theory of evolution by natural selection through his famous book: **'On the origin of species by means of natural selection'**, written 23 years after returning from his voyage on the Beagle, from which much of the evidence for his theory was accumulated. Although Darwin could not explain the origin of variation nor the mechanism of its transmission (this was provided later by Mendel's work), his basic theory of evolution by natural selection (outlined below) is widely accepted today. The study of population genetics has greatly improved our understanding of evolutionary processes, which are now seen largely as a (frequently gradual) change in allele frequencies within a population. Students should be aware that scientific debate on the subject of evolution centers around the relative merits of various alternative hypotheses about the nature of evolutionary processes. The debate is not about the existence of the phenomenon of evolution itself.

Darwin's Theory of Evolution by Natural Selection

Overproduction
Populations produce too many young: many must die

Populations tend to produce more offspring than are needed to replace the parents. Natural populations normally maintain constant numbers. There must therefore be a certain number dying.

Variation
Individuals show variation: some are more favorable than others

Individuals in a population vary in their phenotype and therefore, their genotype. Some variants are better suited to the current conditions than others and find it easier to survive and reproduce.

Natural Selection
Natural selection favors the best suited at the time

The struggle for survival amongst overcrowded individuals will favor those variations which have the best advantage. This does not necessarily mean that those struggling die, but they will be in a poorer condition.

Inherited
Variations are Inherited. The best suited variants leave more offspring.

The variations (both favorable and unfavorable) are passed on to offspring. Each new generation will contain proportionally more descendents from individuals with favorable characters than those with unfavorable.

1. In your own words, describe how Darwin's theory of evolution by natural selection provides an explanation for the change in the appearance of a species over time:

_____

_____

_____

_____

Related activities: The Modern Theory of Evolution

Adaptations and Fitness

An **adaptation**, is any heritable trait that suits an organism to its natural function in the environment (its niche). These traits may be structural, physiological, or behavioral. The idea is important for evolutionary theory because adaptive features promote fitness. **Fitness** is a measure of how well suited an organism is to survive in its habitat and its ability to maximize the numbers of offspring surviving to reproductive age. Adaptations are distinct from *properties* which, although they may be striking, cannot be described as adaptive unless they are shown to be functional in the organism's natural habitat. Genetic adaptation must not be confused with **physiological adjustment** (acclimatization), which refers to an organism's ability to adapt during its lifetime to changing environmental conditions. The physiological changes that occur when a person spends time at altitude provide a good example of acclimatization. Examples of adaptive features arising through evolution are illustrated below.

Ear Length in Rabbits and Hares

The external ears of many mammals are used as important organs to assist in thermoregulation (controlling loss and gain of body heat). The ears of rabbits and hares native to hot, dry climates, such as the jack rabbit of south-western USA and northern Mexico, are relatively very large. The Arctic hare lives in the tundra zone of Alaska, northern Canada and Greenland, and has ears that are relatively short. This reduction in the size of the extremities (ears, limbs, and noses) is typical of cold adapted species.

Arctic hare: *Lepus arcticus*

Black-tail jackrabbit: *Lepus californicus*

Body Size in Relation to Climate

Regulation of body temperature requires a large amount of energy and mammals exhibit a variety of structural and physiological adaptations to increase the effectiveness of this process. Heat production in any endotherm depends on body volume (heat generating metabolism), whereas the rate of heat loss depends on surface area. Increasing body size minimizes heat loss to the environment by reducing the surface area to volume ratio. Animals in colder regions therefore tend to be larger overall than those living in hot climates. This relationship is know as **Bergman's rule** and it is well documented in many mammalian species. Cold adapted species also tend to have more compact bodies and shorter extremities than related species in hot climates.

Fennec fox

The **fennec fox** of the Sahara illustrates the adaptations typical of mammals living in hot climates: a small body size and lightweight fur, and long ears, legs, and nose. These features facilitate heat dissipation and reduce heat gain.

Arctic fox

The **Arctic fox** shows the physical characteristics typical of cold-adapted mammals: a stocky, compact body shape with small ears, short legs and nose, and dense fur. These features reduce heat loss to the environment.

Number of Horns in Rhinoceroses

Not all differences between species can be convincingly interpreted as adaptations to particular environments. Rhinoceroses charge rival males and predators, and the horn(s), when combined with the head-down posture, add effectiveness to this behavior. Horns are obviously adaptive, but it is not clear that the possession of one (Indian rhino) or two (black rhino) horns is necessarily related directly to the environment in which those animals live.

Great Indian rhino

African black rhino

1. Distinguish between adaptive features (genetic) and acclimatization: _____

_____

_____

2. Explain the nature of the relationship between the length of extremities (such as limbs and ears) and climate:

_____

_____

3. Explain the adaptive value of a larger body size at high latitude: _____

_____

_____

Related activities: The Effects of High Altitude

A 2

Natural Selection

Natural selection operates on the phenotypes of individuals, produced by their particular combinations of alleles. In natural populations, the allele combinations of some individuals are perpetuated at the expense of other genotypes. This differential survival of some genotypes over others is called **natural selection**. The effect of natural selection can vary; it can act to maintain the genotype of a species or to change it. **Stabilizing** **selection** maintains the established favorable characteristics and is associated with stable environments. In contrast, **directional selection** favors phenotypes at one extreme of the phenotypic range and is associated with gradually changing environments. **Disruptive selection** is a much rarer form of selection favoring two phenotypic extremes, and is a feature of fluctuating environments.

Stabilizing Selection

Extreme variations are culled from the population (there is selection against them). Those with the established (middle range) adaptive phenotype are retained in greater numbers. This reduces the variation for the phenotypic character. In the example right, light and dark snails are eliminated, leaving medium colored snails. Stabilizing selection can be seen in the selection pressures on human birth weights.

Directional Selection

Directional selection is associated with gradually changing conditions, where the adaptive phenotype is shifted in one direction and one aspect of a trait becomes emphasized (e.g. coloration). In the example right, light colored snails are eliminated and the population becomes darker. Directional selection was observed in peppered moths in England during the Industrial Revolution. They responded to the air pollution of industrialization by increasing the frequency of darker, melanic forms.

Disruptive or Diversifying Selection

Disruptive selection favors two extremes of a trait at the expense of intermediate forms. It is associated with a fluctuating environment and gives rise to **balanced polymorphism** in the population. In the example right, there is selection against medium colored snails, which are eliminated. There is considerable evidence that predators, such as insectivorous birds, are more likely to find and eat common morphs and ignore rare morphs. This enables the rarer forms to persist in the population.

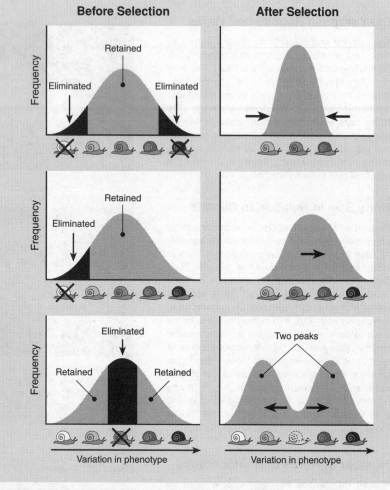

1. (a) Distinguish between directional selection and disruptive selection, identifying when each is likely to operate:

_____

_____

_____

(b) Identify which of the three types of selection described above will lead to evolution, and explain why:

_____

_____

2. Explain how a change in environment may result in selection becoming directional rather than stabilizing:

_____

_____

3. Explain how, in a population of snails, through natural selection, shell color could change from light to dark over time:

_____

_____

_____

Related activities: Industrial Melanism
Web links: Natural Selection in Populations, Changes in a Gene Pool

Industrial Melanism

Natural selection may act on the frequencies of phenotypes (and hence genotypes) in populations in one of three different ways (through stabilizing, directional, or disruptive selection). Over time, natural selection may lead to a permanent change in the genetic makeup of a population. The increased prevalence of melanic forms of the peppered moth, *Biston betularia*, during the Industrial Revolution, is one of the best known examples of directional selection following a change in environmental conditions. Although the protocols used in the central experiments on *Biston*, and the conclusions drawn from them, have been queried, it remains one of the clearest documented examples of phenotypic change in a polymorphic population.

Industrial Melanism in Peppered Moths, *Biston betularia*

The **peppered moth**, *Biston betularia*, occurs in two forms (morphs): the gray mottled form, and a dark melanic form. Changes in the relative abundance of these two forms was hypothesized to be the result of selective predation by birds, with pale forms suffering higher mortality in industrial areas because they are more visible. The results of experiments by H.D. Kettlewell supported this hypothesis but did not confirm it, since selective predation by birds was observed but not quantified. Other research indicates that predation by birds is not the only factor determining the relative abundance of the different color morphs.

Gray or mottled morph: vulnerable to predation in industrial areas where the trees are dark.

Melanic or carbonaria morph: dark color makes it less vulnerable to predation in industrial areas.

Museum collections of the peppered moth made over the last 150 years show a marked change in the frequency of the melanic form. Moths collected in 1850 (above left), prior to the major onset of the industrial revolution in England. Fifty years later (above right) the frequency of the darker melanic forms had greatly increased. Even as late as the mid 20th century, coal-based industries predominated in some centers, and the melanic form occurred in greater frequency in these areas (see map, right).

Frequency of peppered moth forms in 1950

This map shows the relative frequencies of the two forms of peppered moth in the UK in 1950; a time when coal-based industries still predominated in some major centers.

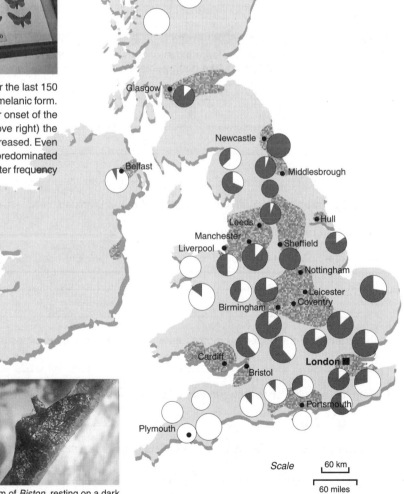

Glasgow
Newcastle
Belfast
Middlesbrough
Hull
Leeds
Manchester
Liverpool
Sheffield
Nottingham
Leicester
Birmingham
Coventry
Cardiff
London
Bristol
Portsmouth
Plymouth

Scale

60 km

60 miles

Key to frequency graphs

- Gray or speckled form
- Melanic or carbonaria form

Industrial areas

Non-industrial areas

A gray (mottled) form of *Biston*, camouflaged against a lichen covered bark surface. In the absence of soot pollution, mottled forms appear to have the selective advantage.

A melanic form of *Biston*, resting on a dark branch, so that it appears as part of the branch. Note that the background has been faded out so that the moth can be seen.

Related activities: Natural Selection, Artificial Selection

RDA 2

Changes in frequency of melanic peppered moths

In the 1940s and 1950s, coal burning was still at intense levels around the industrial centers of Manchester and Liverpool. During this time, the melanic form of the moth was still very dominant. In the rural areas further south and west of these industrial centers, the gray or speckled forms increased dramatically. With the decline of coal burning factories and the Clean Air Acts in cities, the air quality improved between 1960 and 1980. Sulfur dioxide and smoke levels dropped to a fraction of their previous levels. This coincided with a sharp fall in the relative numbers of melanic moths.

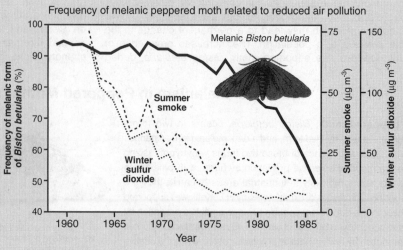

Frequency of melanic peppered moth related to reduced air pollution

1. The populations of peppered moth in England have undergone changes in the frequency of an obvious phenotypic character over the last 150 years. Describe the phenotypic character that changed in its frequency:

2. (a) Identify the (proposed) selective agent for phenotypic change in *Biston*: _____

   (b) Describe how the selection pressure on the light colored morph has changed with changing environmental conditions over the last 150 years:

3. The industrial centers for England in 1950 were located around London, Birmingham, Liverpool, Manchester, and Leeds. Glasgow in Scotland also had a large industrial base. Comment on how the relative frequencies of the two forms of peppered moth were affected by the geographic location of industrial regions:

4. The level of pollution dropped around Manchester and Liverpool between 1960 and 1985.

   (a) State how much the pollution dropped by: _____

   (b) Describe how the frequency of the darker melanic form changed during the period of reduced pollution:

5. In the example of the peppered moths, state whether the selection pressure is disruptive, stabilizing, or directional:

6. Outline the key difference between natural and artificial selection: _____

7. Discuss the statement "the environment directs natural selection": _____

Heterozygous Advantage

There are two mechanisms by which natural selection can affect allele frequencies. Firstly, there may be selection against one of the homozygotes. When one homozygous type (for example, aa), has a lower fitness than the other two genotypes (in this case, Aa or AA), the frequency of the deleterious allele will tend to decrease until it is completely eliminated. In some situations, both homozygous conditions (aa **and** AA) have lower fitness than the heterozygote; a situation that leads to **heterozygous advantage** and may result in the stable coexistence of both alleles in the population (**balanced polymorphism**). There are remarkably few well-documented examples in which the evidence for heterozygous advantage is conclusive. The maintenance of the sickle cell mutation in malaria-prone regions is one such example.

The Sickle Cell Allele (Hb^S)

Sickle cell disease is caused by a mutation to a gene that directs the production of the human blood protein called hemoglobin. The mutant allele is known as **Hb^S** and produces a form of hemoglobin that differs from the normal form by just one amino acid in the β-chain. This minute change however causes a cascade of physiological problems in people with the allele. Some of the red blood cells containing mutated hemoglobin alter their shape to become irregular and spiky; the so-called **sickle cells**.

Sickle cells have a tendency to clump together and work less efficiently. In people with just one sickle cell allele plus a normal allele (the heterozygote condition **Hb^{S}Hb**), there is a mixture of both red blood cell types and they are said to have the sickle cell trait. They are generally unaffected by the disease except in low oxygen environments (e.g. climbing at altitude). People with two Hb^S genes (**Hb^{S}Hb^S**) suffer severe illness and even death. For this reason Hb^S is considered **a lethal gene**.

Heterozygous Advantage in Malarial Regions

Falciparum malaria is widely distributed throughout central Africa, the Mediterranean, Middle East, and tropical and semi-tropical Asia (Fig. 1). It is transmitted by the *Anopheles* mosquito, which spreads the protozoan *Plasmodium falciparum* from person to person as it feeds on blood.

SYMPTOMS: These appear 1-2 weeks after being bitten, and include headache, shaking, chills, and fever. Falciparum malaria is more severe than other forms of malaria, with high fever, convulsions, and coma. It can be fatal within days of the first symptoms appearing.

THE PARADOX: The Hb^S allele offers considerable protection against malaria. Sickle cells have low potassium levels, which causes plasmodium parasites inside these cells to die. Those with a normal phenotype are very susceptible to malaria, but heterozygotes (**Hb^{S}Hb**) are much less so. This situation, called **heterozygous advantage**, has resulted in the Hb^S allele being present in moderately high frequencies in parts of Africa and Asia despite its harmful effects (Fig. 2). This is a special case of balanced polymorphism, called a **balanced lethal system** because neither of the homozygotes produces a phenotype that survives, but the heterozygote is viable.

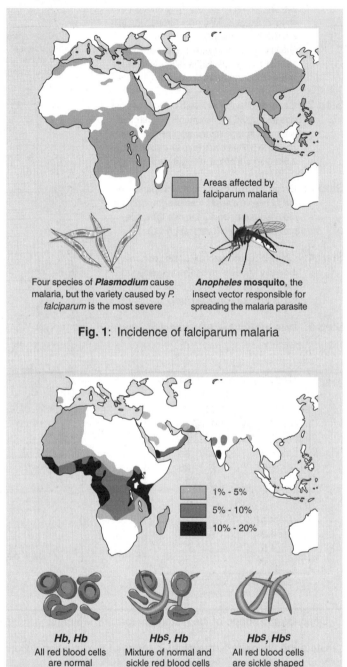

Four species of *Plasmodium* cause malaria, but the variety caused by *P. falciparum* is the most severe

Anopheles mosquito, the insect vector responsible for spreading the malaria parasite

Fig. 1: Incidence of falciparum malaria

Areas affected by falciparum malaria

1% - 5%
5% - 10%
10% - 20%

Hb, Hb
All red blood cells are normal

Hb^S, Hb
Mixture of normal and sickle red blood cells

Hb^S, Hb^S
All red blood cells are sickle shaped

Fig. 2: Frequency of the sickle cell allele

1. With respect to the sickle cell allele, explain how **heterozygous advantage** can lead to **balanced polymorphism**:

_____

_____

_____

_____

_____

EA 3

Selection for Human Birth Weight

Selection pressures operate on populations in such a way as to reduce mortality. For humans, giving birth is a special, but often traumatic, event. In a study of human birth weights it is possible to observe the effect of selection pressures operating to constrain human birth weight within certain limits. This is a good example of **stabilizing selection**. This activity explores the selection pressures acting on the birth weight of human babies. Carry out the steps below:

Step 1: Collect the birth weights from 100 birth notices from your local newspaper (or 50 if you are having difficulty getting enough; this should involve looking back through the last 2-3 weeks of birth notices). If you cannot obtain birth weights in your local newspaper, a set of 100 sample birth weights is provided in the Model Answers booklet.

Step 2: Group the weights into each of the 12 weight classes (of 0.5 kg increments). Determine what percentage (of the total sample) fall into each weight class (e.g. 17 babies weigh 2.5-3.0 kg out of the 100 sampled = 17%)

Step 3: Graph these in the form of a histogram for the 12 weight classes (use the graphing grid provided right). Be sure to use the scale provided on the left vertical (y) axis.

Step 4: Create a second graph by plotting percentage mortality of newborn babies in relation to their birth weight. Use the scale on the right y axis and data provided (below).

Step 5: Draw a line of 'best fit' through these points.

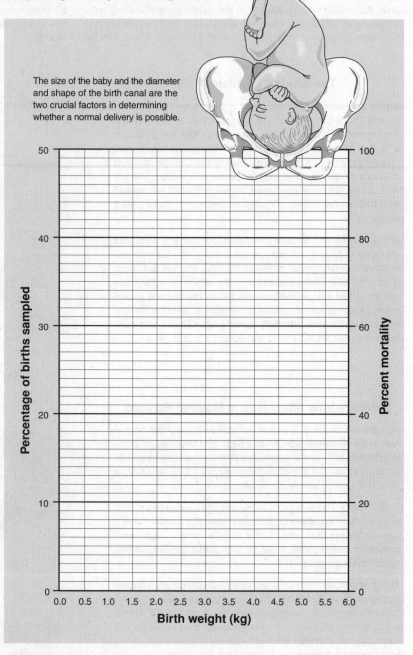

The size of the baby and the diameter and shape of the birth canal are the two crucial factors in determining whether a normal delivery is possible.

Mortality of newborn babies related to birth weight

Weight (kg)	Mortality (%)
1.0	80
1.5	30
2.0	12
2.5	4
3.0	3
3.5	2
4.0	3
4.5	7
5.0	15

Source: Biology: The Unity & Diversity of Life (4th ed), by Starr and Taggart

1. Describe the shape of the histogram for birth weights: _____

2. State the optimum birth weight in terms of the lowest newborn mortality: _____

3. Describe the relationship between newborn mortality and birth weight: _____

_____

4. Describe the selection pressures that are operating to control the range of birth weight: _____

_____

_____

5. Describe how medical intervention methods during pregnancy and childbirth may have altered these selection pressures:

_____

_____

Related activities: Natural Selection

Darwin's Finches

The Galapagos Islands, 920 km off the west coast of Ecuador, played a major role in shaping Darwin's thoughts about evolution. While exploring the islands in 1835, he was struck by the unique and peculiar species he found there, in particular, the island's finches. The Galapagos group is home to 13 species of finches in four genera. This variety has arisen as a result of evolution from one ancestral species. Initially, a number of small finches, probably grassquits, made their way from South America to the Galapagos Islands. In the new environment, which was relatively free of competitors, the colonizers underwent an adaptive radiation, producing a range of species each with its own unique feeding niche. Although similar in their plumage, nest building techniques, and calls, the different species can be distinguished by the size and shape of their beaks. Each species has a beak adapted for a different purpose, such as crushing seeds, pecking wood, or probing flowers. Between them, the 13 species of this endemic group fill the roles of seven different families of South American mainland birds. DNA analyses have confirmed Darwin's insight and have shown that all 13 species evolved from a flock of about 30 birds arriving a million years ago.

The Evolution of Darwin's Finches

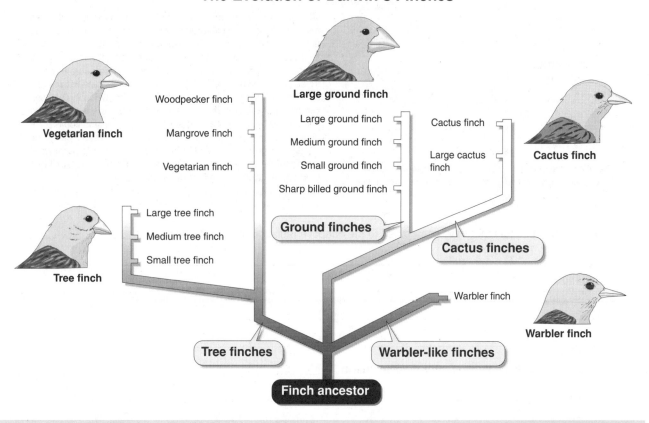

Vegetarian finch

Woodpecker finch
Mangrove finch
Vegetarian finch

Large ground finch

Large ground finch
Medium ground finch
Small ground finch
Sharp billed ground finch

Cactus finch
Large cactus finch

Cactus finch

Large tree finch
Medium tree finch
Small tree finch

Tree finch

Ground finches

Cactus finches

Warbler finch

Warbler finch

Tree finches

Warbler-like finches

Finch ancestor

Small tree finch

Large tree finch

As the name implies, **tree finches** are largely arboreal and feed mainly on insects. The bill is sharper than in ground finches and better suited to grasping insects. Paler than ground or cactus finches, they also have streaked breasts.

There are four species of **ground finches** with crushing-type bills used for seed eating. On Wolf Island, they are called vampire finches because they peck the skin of animals to draw blood, which they then drink (see left).

Cactus finches have most probably descended from ground finches. They have a probing beak and feed on insects on the cactus or the cactus itself. On islands where there are no ground finches, there is more variation in beak size than on the islands where the species coexist.

The **warbler finch** is named for its resemblance to the unrelated warblers. The beak of the warbler finch is the thinnest of the Galapagos finches. It is also the most widespread species, found throughout the archipelago. Warbler finches prey on flying and ground dwelling insects.

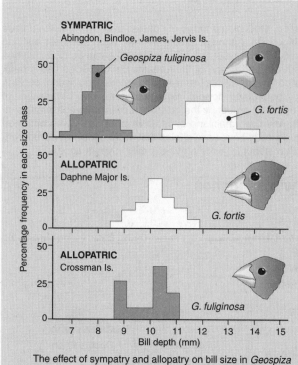

SYMPATRIC
Abingdon, Bindloe, James, Jervis Is.

Geospiza fuliginosa

G. fortis

ALLOPATRIC
Daphne Major Is.

G. fortis

ALLOPATRIC
Crossman Is.

G. fuliginosa

Percentage frequency in each size class

Bill depth (mm)

The effect of sympatry and allopatry on bill size in *Geospiza fuliginosa* (small ground finch) and *G. fortis* (medium ground finch)

Sympatry and Character Displacement

There is good evidence that finch evolution appears to be driven by a combination of allopatric and sympatric events. Coexisting species of ground finches on four islands (top graph) show large differences in bill sizes, enabling each species to feed on different sized seeds. However when either species exists in the absence of the other on different islands (lower graphs), it possesses intermediate bill sizes (about 10 mm) enabling it to feed without partitioning seed resources. This phenomenon, whereby competition causes two closely related species to become more different in regions where their ranges overlap, is referred to as **character displacement**.

Character displacement is evident in other populations of finches as well. There are well-studied populations of the large cactus finch (*G. conirostris*) on Genovesa and Espanola Islands, but their bill sizes are quite different. On Genovesa, the large ground finch (*G. magnirostris*) coexists with the large cactus finch. In these sympatric populations, the variability in bill size *within* each species is minimal but there is little overlap *between* the species with respect to this trait. On Espanola, where the large ground finch either never arrived, or became extinct, the situation is quite different. With no competition on Espanola, the large cactus finch displays a greater variability in bill size. Its bill is somewhat intermediate between the two finches on Genovesa, and it can feed equally well in both niches all year round.

Data based on an adaptation by Strickberger (2000)

1. Describe the main factors that have contributed to the adaptive radiation of Darwin's finches: _____

_____

_____

_____

2. (a) Explain what is meant by **character displacement**: _____

_____

_____

(b) Discuss how the incidence of character displacement observed in the Galapagos finches supports the view that their adaptive radiation from a common ancestor has been driven by a combination of allopatric and sympatric events:

_____

_____

_____

_____

3. The range of variability shown by a phenotype in response to environmental variation is called **phenotypic plasticity**.

(a) Discuss the evidence for phenotypic plasticity in Galapagos finches: _____

_____

_____

(b) Explain what this suggests about the biology of the original finch ancestor: _____

_____

_____

Gene Pool Exercise

Cut out each of the beetles on this page and use them to reenact different events within a gene pool as described in this topic (see *Gene Pools and Evolution, Changes in a Gene Pool, Founder Effect, Population Bottlenecks, Genetic Drift*).

Related activities: Gene Pools and Evolution, Changes in a Gene Pool, The Founder Effect, Population Bottlenecks, Genetic Drift

P

Gene Pools and Evolution

The diagram below illustrates the dynamic nature of **gene pools**. It portrays two imaginary populations of one beetle species. Each beetle is a 'carrier' of genetic information, represented here by the alleles (A and a) for a single **codominant gene** that controls the beetle's color. Normally, there are three versions of the phenotype: black, dark, and pale. Mutations may create other versions of the phenotype. Some of the **microevolutionary processes** that can affect the genetic composition (**allele frequencies**) of the gene pool are illustrated. See the activity *Gene Pool Exercise* for cut-out beetles to simulate this activity.

Immigration: Populations can gain alleles when they are introduced from other gene pools. Immigration is one aspect of gene flow.

Mutations: Spontaneous mutations can develop that alter the allele frequencies of the gene pool, and even create new alleles. Mutation is very important to evolution, because it is the original source of genetic variation that provides new material for natural selection.

Emigration: Genes may be lost to other gene pools.

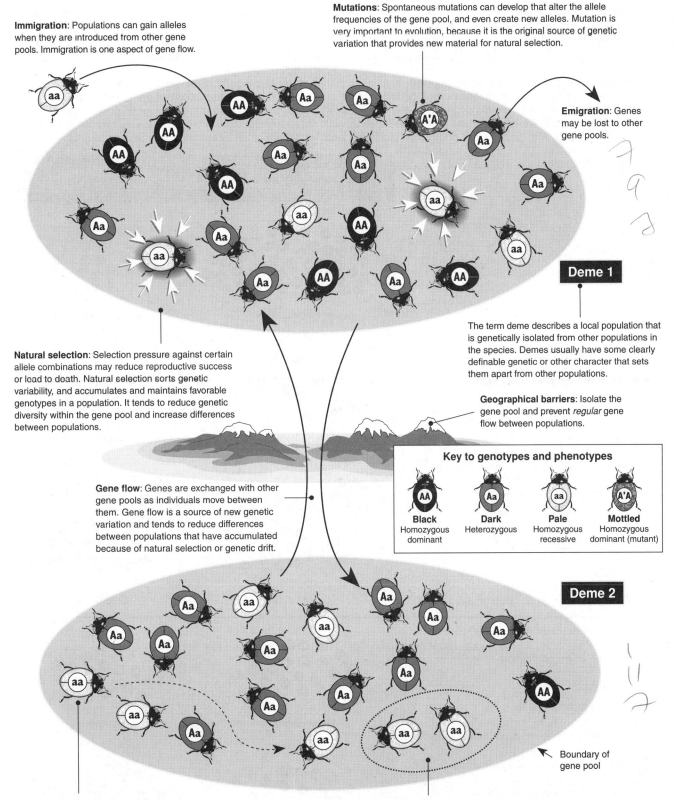

Natural selection: Selection pressure against certain allele combinations may reduce reproductive success or load to death. Natural selection sorts genetic variability, and accumulates and maintains favorable genotypes in a population. It tends to reduce genetic diversity within the gene pool and increase differences between populations.

Deme 1

The term deme describes a local population that is genetically isolated from other populations in the species. Demes usually have some clearly definable genetic or other character that sets them apart from other populations.

Geographical barriers: Isolate the gene pool and prevent *regular* gene flow between populations.

Gene flow: Genes are exchanged with other gene pools as individuals move between them. Gene flow is a source of new genetic variation and tends to reduce differences between populations that have accumulated because of natural selection or genetic drift.

Key to genotypes and phenotypes

Black Homozygous dominant	**Dark** Heterozygous	**Pale** Homozygous recessive	**Mottled** Homozygous dominant (mutant)
AA	Aa	aa	A'A

Deme 2

Boundary of gene pool

Mate selection (non-random mating): Individuals may not select their mate randomly and may seek out particular phenotypes, increasing the frequency of these "favored" alleles in the population.

Genetic drift: Chance events can cause the allele frequencies of small populations to "drift" (change) randomly from generation to generation. Genetic drift can play a significant role in the microevolution of very small populations. The two situations most often leading to populations small enough for genetic drift to be significant are the **bottleneck effect** (where the population size is dramatically reduced by a catastrophic event) and the **founder effect** (where a small number of individuals colonize a new area).

1. For each of the 2 demes shown on the previous page (treating the mutant in deme 1 as a AA):

   (a) Count up the numbers of **allele types** (**A** and **a**).

   (b) Count up the numbers of **allele combinations** (**AA, Aa, aa**).

2. Calculate the frequencies as percentages (%) for the allele types and combinations:

Deme 1		Number counted	%	Deme 2		Number counted	%
Allele types	A	23	64	Allele types	A	13	34
	a	13	36		a	25	66
Allele combinations	AA	7	39	Allele combinations	AA	1	5
	Aa	9	50		Aa	11	57
	aa	2	11		aa	7	38

3. One of the fundamental concepts for population genetics is that of **genetic equilibrium**, stated as: *"For a very large, randomly mating population, the proportion of dominant to recessive alleles remains constant from one generation to the next"*. If a gene pool is to remain unchanged, it must satisfy all of the criteria below that favour gene pool stability. Few populations meet all (or any) of these criteria and their genetic makeup must therefore by continually changing. For each of the five factors (a-e) below, state briefly **how** and **why** each would affect the allele frequency in a gene pool:

   (a) Population size: A small population does not allow for enough variety or diversity so a large population is needed

   (b) Mate selection: Random mating allows for the upkeep of the HWE since its random and can maintain the numbers

   (c) Gene flow between populations: If two populations have differing genes, then mixing would effect equilibrium

   (d) Mutations: mutations make abnormal DNA unlike other DNA so it effects the equilibrium

   (e) Natural selection: Natural selection takes unfavorable genes and is not random thus throws off equilibrium

4. Identify the factors that tend to:

   (a) Increase genetic variation in populations: crossover, random mating, gene flow

   (b) Decrease genetic variation in populations: assortive mating, natural selection, no gene flow.

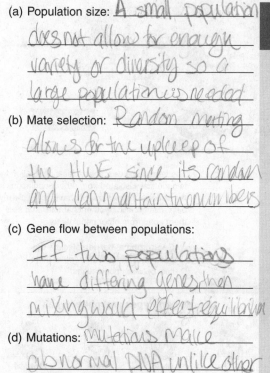

Factors Favoring Gene Pool Stability	Factors Favoring Gene Pool Change
LARGE POPULATION	SMALL POPULATION
RANDOM MATING	ASSORTATIVE MATING
NO GENE FLOW	GENE FLOW
NO MUTATION	MUTATIONS
NO NATURAL SELECTION	NATURAL SELECTION

Changes in a Gene Pool

The diagram below shows an imaginary population of beetles undergoing changes as it is subjected to two 'events'. The three phases represent a progression in time, i.e. the same gene pool, undergoing change. The beetles have three phenotypes determined by the amount of pigment deposited in the cuticle. Three versions of this trait exist: black, dark, and pale. The gene controlling this character is represented by two alleles **A** and **a**. Your task is to analyze the gene pool as it undergoes changes.

Phase 1: Initial gene pool

Calculate the frequencies of the *allele types* and *allele combinations* by counting the actual numbers, then working them out as percentages.

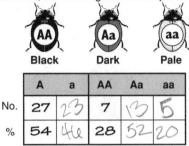

Black   Dark   Pale

	A	a	AA	Aa	aa
No.	27	23	7	13	5
%	54	46	28	52	20

Allele types   *Allele combinations*

Phase 2: Natural selection

In the same gene pool at a later time there was a change in the allele frequencies. This was due to the loss of certain allele combinations due to natural selection. Some of those with a genotype of aa were eliminated (poor fitness).

Calculate as for above. Do not include the individuals surrounded by small white arrows in your calculations; they are dead!

	A	a	AA	Aa	aa
No.	27	19	7	13	3
%	59	41	30	57	13

Phase 3: Immigration and emigration

This particular kind of beetle exhibits wandering behavior. The allele frequencies change again due to the introduction and departure of individual beetles, each carrying certain allele combinations.

Calculate as above. In your calculations, include the individual coming into the gene pool (AA), but remove the one leaving (aa).

	A	a	AA	Aa	aa
No.	29	17	8	13	2
%	63	37	35	57	8

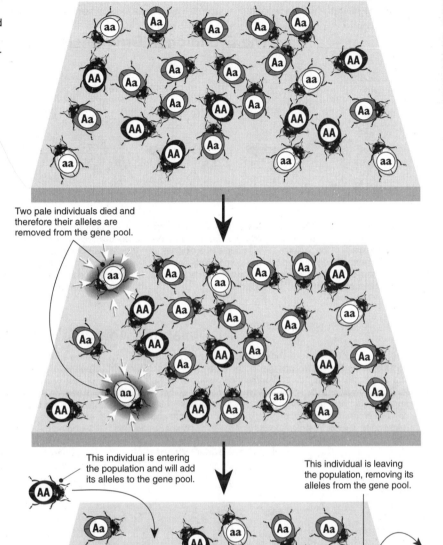

Two pale individuals died and therefore their alleles are removed from the gene pool.

This individual is entering the population and will add its alleles to the gene pool.

This individual is leaving the population, removing its alleles from the gene pool.

1. Explain how the number of dominant alleles (A) in the genotype of a beetle affects its phenotype:

Since every beetle with a (A) allele will show the (A) phenotype regardless of the other allele then having more (A) alleles will make more beetles displaying the (A) phenotype

2. For each phase in the gene pool above (place your answers in the tables provided; some have been done for you):

    (a) Determine the relative frequencies of the two alleles: A and a. Simply total the **A** alleles and **a** alleles separately.

    (b) Determine the frequency of how the alleles come together as allele pair combinations in the gene pool (AA, Aa and aa). Count the number of each type of combination.

    (c) For each of the above, work out the frequencies as percentages:

Allele frequency = Number of counted alleles ÷ Total number of alleles × 100

Evolution in Bacteria

As a result of their short **generation times**, bacterial populations can show significant evolutionary change within relatively short periods of time. The development of **antibiotic resistance** is one such evolutionary change and it arises and spreads within and between bacterial populations with frightening ease. A variety of human practices have led to antibiotic resistance and have increased the rate at which bacterial strains acquire new properties.

These practices include the overuse and misuse of antibiotics by physicians, the use of antibiotics by immunosuppressed patients to prevent infection, the use of antibiotics in animal feed, and the spread of resistant bacteria to new areas because of air travel. For many strains of pathogenic bacteria, resistant mutants are increasingly replacing susceptible normal populations. This makes the search for new types of antibiotics increasingly urgent.

The Evolution of Drug Resistance in Bacteria

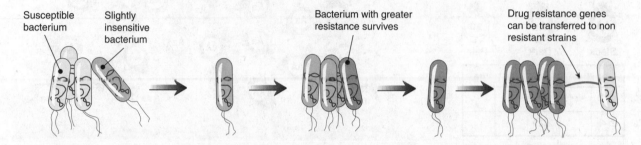

Susceptible bacterium | Slightly insensitive bacterium | Bacterium with greater resistance survives | Drug resistance genes can be transferred to non resistant strains

Within any population, there is genetic variation. In this case, the susceptibility of the bacterial strain is normally distributed, with some cells being more susceptible than others.

If the amount of antibiotic delivered is too low, or the full course of antibiotics is not completed, only the most susceptible bacteria will die.

Now a population of insensitive bacteria has developed. Within this population there will also be variation in the susceptibility to antibiotics. As treatment continues, some of the bacteria may acquire greater resistance.

A highly resistant population has evolved. The resistant cells can exchange genetic material with other bacteria, passing on the resistance genes. The antibiotic that was initially used against this bacterial strain will now be ineffective against it.

Observing Adaptive Radiation

Recently, scientists have demonstrated rapid evolution in bacteria. *Pseudomonas fluorescens* was used in the experiment and propagated in a simple heterogeneous environment consisting of a 25 cm³ glass container containing 6 cm³ of broth medium. Over a short period of time, the bacteria underwent morphological diversification, with a number of new morphs appearing. These morphs were shown to be genetically distinct. A striking feature of the evolved species is their niche specificity, with each new morph occupying a distinct habitat (below, left). In a follow up experiment (below, right), the researchers grew the same original bacterial strain in the same broth under identical incubation conditions, but in a homogeneous environment (achieved by shaking the broth). Without the different habitats offered by an undisturbed environment, no morphs emerged. The experiment illustrated the capacity of bacteria to evolve to utilize available niches.

Heterogeneous environment

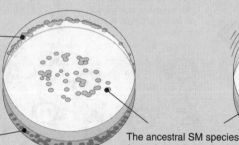

WS bacteria (wrinkly morphology) evolved to colonize the air-broth interface.

The FS species (fuzzy morphology) colonized the bottom of the container.

Homogeneous environment

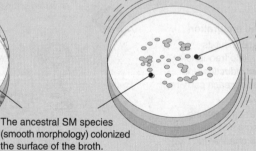

Because there is only one niche, no adaptive radiation occurs.

The ancestral SM species (smooth morphology) colonized the surface of the broth.

1. Using an illustrative example, explain why evolution of new properties in bacteria can be very rapid: Due to the fact that bacteria can reproduce rapidly and DNA can be transfered between bacteria, a favorable gene surfaces among bacteria it can spread quickly

2. (a) In the example above, suggest why the bacteria evolved when grown in a heterogeneous environment: Because when there is multiple genes there can be favorable traits thus it can evolve while when all the genes are the same there is no difference therefore no evolution

   (b) Predict what would happen if the FS morph was cultured in the homogeneous environment: No change would occur if the FS morph it was cultured in the homogeneous environment

Related activities: Antimicrobial Drugs

Population Genetics Calculations

The **Hardy-Weinberg equation** provides a simple mathematical model of genetic equilibrium in a gene pool, but its main application in population genetics is in calculating allele and genotype frequencies in populations, particularly as a means of studying changes and measuring their rate. The use of the Hardy-Weinberg equation is described below.

Punnett square

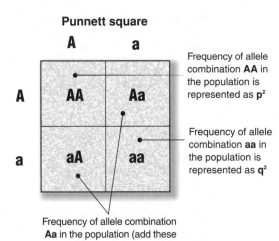

Frequency of allele combination **AA** in the population is represented as **p^2**

Frequency of allele combination **aa** in the population is represented as **q^2**

Frequency of allele combination **Aa** in the population (add these together to get **2pq**)

$$(p + q)^2 = p^2 + 2pq + q^2 = 1$$

Frequency of allele types

p = Frequency of allele A

q = Frequency of allele a

Frequency of allele combinations

p^2 = Frequency of AA (homozygous dominant)

2pq = Frequency of Aa (heterozygous)

q^2 = Frequency of aa (homozygous recessive)

The Hardy-Weinberg equation is applied to populations with a simple genetic situation: dominant and recessive alleles controlling a single trait. The frequency of all of the dominant (A) and recessive alleles (a) equals the total genetic complement, and adds up to 1 or 100% of the alleles present.

How To Solve Hardy-Weinberg Problems

In most populations, the frequency of two alleles of interest is calculated from the proportion of homozygous recessives (q^2), as this is the only genotype identifiable directly from its phenotype. If only the dominant phenotype is known, q^2 may be calculated (1 – the frequency of the dominant phenotype). The following steps outline the procedure for solving a Hardy-Weinberg problem:

Remember that all calculations must be carried out using proportions, NOT PERCENTAGES!

1. Examine the question to determine what piece of information you have been given about the population. In most cases, this is the percentage or frequency of the homozygous recessive phenotype q^2, or the dominant phenotype $p^2 + 2pq$ (see note above).

2. The first objective is to find out the value of p or q, If this is achieved, then every other value in the equation can be determined by simple calculation.

3. Take the square root of q^2 to find q.

4. Determine p by subtracting q from 1 (i.e. p = 1 – q).

5. Determine p^2 by multiplying p by itself (i.e. $p^2 = p \times p$).

6. Determine 2pq by multiplying p times q times 2.

7. Check that your calculations are correct by adding up the values for $p^2 + q^2 + 2pq$ (the sum should equal 1 or 100%).

Worked example

In the American white population approximately 70% of people can taste the chemical phenylthiocarbamide (PTC) (the dominant phenotype), while 30% are non-tasters (the recessive phenotype).

Determine the frequency of:	**Answers**
(a) Homozygous recessive phenotype(q^2).	30% - provided
(b) The dominant allele (**p**).	45.2%
(c) Homozygous tasters (p^2).	20.5%
(d) Heterozygous tasters (**2pq**).	49.5%

Data: The frequency of the dominant phenotype (70% tasters) and recessive phenotype (30% non-tasters) are provided.

Working:

Recessive phenotype:	q^2 =	30% *use 0.30 for calculation*
therefore:	q =	0.5477 *square root of 0.30*
therefore:	p =	0.4523 *1 – q = p* *1 – 0.5477 = 0.4523*

Use p and q in the equation (top) to solve any unknown:

Homozygous dominant	p^2 =	0.2046 *(p × p = 0.4523 x 0.4523)*
Heterozygous:	**2pq** =	0.4953

1. A population of hamsters has a gene consisting of 90% M alleles (black) and 10% m alleles (gray). Mating is random.

   Data: Frequency of recessive allele (10% m) and dominant allele (90% M).

   Determine the proportion of offspring that will be black and the proportion that will be gray (show your working):

   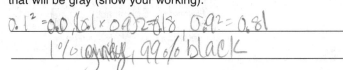

   $0.1^2 = 0.0.01 \times 0.9 = 0.18$ $0.9^2 = 0.81$

   1% gray, 99% black

Recessive allele:	q =	.1
Dominant allele:	p =	.9
Recessive phenotype:	q^2 =	.01
Homozygous dominant:	p^2 =	.18
Heterozygous:	2pq =	.81

Related activities: Analysis of a Squirrel Gene Pool

RDA 2

2. You are working with pea plants and found 36 plants out of 400 were dwarf.
   Data: Frequency of recessive phenotype (36 out of 400 = 9%)

   (a) Calculate the frequency of the tall gene: _____.7_____

   (b) Determine the number of heterozygous pea plants:

   _____ 196 _____

   _____

Recessive allele:	q	=	.3
Dominant allele:	p	=	.7
Recessive phenotype:	q^2	=	.09
Homozygous dominant:	p^2	=	.49
Heterozygous:	2pq	=	.42

3. In humans, the ability to taste the chemical phenylthiocarbamide (PTC) is inherited as a simple dominant characteristic. Suppose you found out that 360 out of 1000 college students could not taste the chemical.
   Data: Frequency of recessive phenotype (360 out of 1000).

   (a) State the frequency of the gene for tasting PTC:

   _____.4_____

   (b) Determine the number of heterozygous students in this population:
   _____ 480 _____

Recessive allele:	q	=	.6
Dominant allele:	p	=	.4
Recessive phenotype:	q^2	=	.36
Homozygous dominant:	p^2	=	.16
Heterozygous:	2pq	=	.48

4. A type of deformity appears in 4% of a large herd of cattle. Assume the deformity was caused by a recessive gene.
   Data: Frequency of recessive phenotype (4% deformity).

   (a) Calculate the percentage of the herd that are carriers of the gene:
   _____ 8% _____

   (b) Determine the frequency of the dominant gene in this case:
   _____ .8 _____

Recessive allele:	q	=	.2
Dominant allele:	p	=	.8
Recessive phenotype:	q^2	=	.04
Homozygous dominant:	p^2	=	.64
Heterozygous:	2pq	=	.32

5. Assume you placed 50 pure bred black guinea pigs (dominant allele) with 50 albino guinea pigs (recessive allele) and allowed the population to attain genetic equilibrium (several generations have passed).
   Data: Frequency of recessive allele (50%) and dominant allele (50%).

   Determine the proportion (%) of the population that becomes white:
   _____ 25% _____

Recessive allele:	q	=	.5
Dominant allele:	p	=	.5
Recessive phenotype:	q^2	=	.25
Homozygous dominant:	p^2	=	.25
Heterozygous:	2pq	=	.5

6. It is known that 64% of a large population exhibit the recessive trait of a characteristic controlled by two alleles (one is dominant over the other).
   Data: Frequency of recessive phenotype (64%). Determine the following:

   (a) The frequency of the recessive allele: _____.8_____

   (b) The percentage that are heterozygous for this trait: _____ 32% _____

   (c) The percentage that exhibit the dominant trait: _____ 36% _____

   (d) The percentage that are homozygous for the dominant trait: _____ 4% _____

   (e) The percentage that has one or more recessive alleles: _____ 68% _____

7. Albinism is recessive to normal pigmentation in humans. The frequency of the albino allele was 10% in a population.
   Data: Frequency of recessive allele (10% albino allele).

   Determine the proportion of people that you would expect to be albino:
   _____ $.1^2 = 0.01 = 1\%$ _____

   _____

Recessive allele:	q	=	.8
Dominant allele:	p	=	.2
Recessive phenotype:	q^2	=	.64
Homozygous dominant:	p^2	=	.04
Heterozygous:	2pq	=	.32

Analysis of a Squirrel Gene Pool

In Olney, Illinois, in the United States, there is a unique population of albino (white) and gray squirrels. Between 1977 and 1990, students at Olney Central College carried out a study of this population. They recorded the frequency of gray and albino squirrels. The albinos displayed a mutant allele expressed as an albino phenotype only in the homozygous recessive condition. The data they collected are provided in the table below. Using the **Hardy-Weinberg equation** for calculating genotype frequencies, it was possible to estimate the frequency of the normal 'wild' allele (G) providing gray fur coloring, and the frequency of the mutant albino allele (g) producing white squirrels. This study provided real, first hand, data that students could use to see how genotype frequencies can change in a real population.

Thanks to **Dr. John Stencel**, Olney Central College, Olney, Illinois, US, for providing the data for this exercise.

Gray squirrel, usual color form

Albino form of gray squirrel

Speciation

Population of gray and white squirrels in Olney, Illinois (1977-1990)

Year	Gray	White	Total	GG	Gg	gg	Freq. of g	Freq. of G
1977	602	182	784	26.85	49.93	23.21	48.18	51.82
1978	511	172	683	24.82	50.00	25.18	50.18	49.82
1979	482	134	616	28.47	49.77	21.75	46.64	53.36
1980	489	133	622	28.90	49.72	21.38	46.24	53.76
1981	536	163	699	26.74	49.94	23.32	48.29	51.71
1982	618	151	769	31.01	49.35	19.64	44.31	55.69
1983	419	141	560	24.82	50.00	25.18	50.18	49.82
1984	378	106	484	28.30	49.79	21.90	46.80	53.20
1985	448	125	573	28.40	49.78	21.82	46.71	53.29
1986	536	155	691	27.71	49.86	22.43	47.36	52.64
1987	No data collected this year							
1988	652	122	774	36.36	47.88	15.76	39.70	60.30
1989	552	146	698	29.45	49.64	20.92	45.74	54.26
1990	603	111	714	36.69	47.76	15.55	39.43	60.57

1. **Graph population changes**: Use the data in the first 3 columns of the table above to plot a line graph. This will show changes in the phenotypes: numbers of gray and white (albino) squirrels, as well as changes in the total population. Plot: **gray**, **white**, and **total** for each year:

   (a) Determine by how much (as a %) total population numbers have fluctuated over the sampling period:

   _9 %_

   (b) Describe the overall trend in total population numbers and any pattern that may exist:

   Generally dependent on the grey population as it changes dramatically while the white population remains somewhat constant

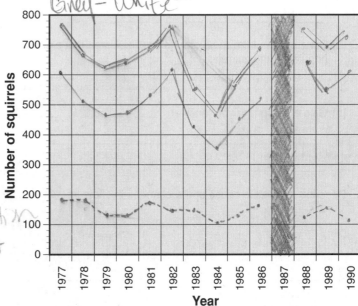

Related activities: Population Genetics Calculations

DA 3

2. **Graph genotype changes**: Use the data in the genotype columns of the table on the opposite page to plot a line graph. This will show changes in the allele combinations (**GG**, **Gg**, **gg**). Plot: **GG**, **Gg**, and **gg** for each year:

Describe the overall trend in the frequency of:

(a) Homozygous dominant (**GG**) genotype:

no trend

(b) Heterozygous (**Gg**) genotype:

remaind constant

(c) Homozygous recessive (gg) genotype:

no trend

3. **Graph allele changes**: Use the data in the last two columns of the table on the previous page to plot a line graph. This will show changes in the *allele frequencies* for each of the dominant (**G**) and recessive (**g**) alleles.
Plot: the frequency of **G** and the frequency of **g**:

(a) Describe the overall trend in the frequency of the dominant allele (**G**):

Changes as the allelic frequency
allele does

(b) Describe the overall trend in the frequency of the recessive allele (**g**):

Changes as the allelic
frequency of the g
allele does

4. (a) State which of the three graphs best indicates that a significant change may be taking place in the gene pool of this population of squirrels:

The graph of allelic frequencies

(b) Give a reason for your answer: _Because it is directly related to the_
gene pool

5. Describe a possible cause of the changes in allele frequencies over the sampling period: _____

Sexual Selection

The success of an individual is measured not only by the number of offspring it leaves, but also by the quality or likely reproductive success of those offspring. This means that it becomes important who its mate will be. It was Darwin (1871) who first introduced the concept of sexual selection; a special type of natural selection that produces anatomical and behavioral traits that affect an individual's ability to acquire mates. Biologists today recognise two types: **intrasexual selection** (usually male-male competition) and **intersexual selection** or mate selection. One result of either type is the evolution of **sexual dimorphism**.

Intrasexual Selection

Intrasexual selection involves competition within one sex (usually males) with the winner gaining access to the opposite sex. Competition often takes place before mating, and males compete to establish dominance or secure a territory for breeding or mating. This occurs in many species of ungulates (**deer**, antelope, cattle) and in many birds. In deer and other ungulates, the males typically engage in highly ritualized battles with horns or antlers. The winners of these battles gain dominance over rival males and do most of the mating.

In other species, males compete vigorously for territories. These may contain resources or they may consist of an isolated area within a special arena used for communal courtship display (a **lek**). In lek species, males with the best territories on a lek (the dominant males) are known to get more chances to mate with females. In some species of grouse (right), this form of sexual selection can be difficult to distinguish from intersexual selection, because once males establish their positions on the lek the females then choose among them. In species where there is limited access to females and females are promiscuous, **sperm competition** (below,center) may also be a feature of male-male competition.

Intersexual Selection

In intersexual selection (or **mate choice**), individuals of one sex (usually the males) advertise themselves as potential mates and members of the other sex (usually the females), choose among them. Intersexual selection results in development of exaggerated ornamentation, such as elaborate plumages. Female preference for elaborate male ornaments is well supported by both anecdotal and experimental evidence. For example, in the **long-tailed widow bird** (*Euplectes progne*), females prefer males with long tails. When tails are artificially shortened or lengthened, females still prefer males with the longest tails; they therefore select for long tails, not another trait correlated with long tails.

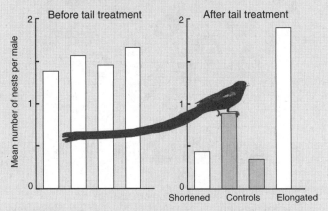

As shown above, there was no significant difference in breeding success between the groups before the tails were altered. When the tails were cut and lengthened, breeding success went down and up respectively.

In male-male competition for mates, ornamentation is used primarily to advertise superiority to rival males, and not to mortally wound opponents. However, injuries do occur, most often between closely matched rivals, where dominance must be tested and established through the aggressive use of their weaponry rather than mere ritual duels.

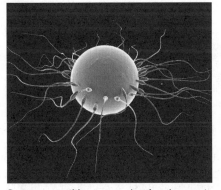

Sperm competition occurs when females remate within a relatively short space of time. The outcome of sperm competition may be determined by mating order. In some species, including those that guard their mates, the first male has the advantage, but in many the advantage accrues to the sperm of the second or subsequent males.

How do male features, such as the extravagant plumage of the peacock, persist when increasingly elaborate plumage must become detrimental to survival at some point? At first, preference for such traits must confer a survival advantage. Male adornment and female preference then advance together until a stable strategy is achieved.

1. Explain the difference between **intrasexual selection** and **mate selection**, identifying the features associated with each:

   _____

   _____

2. Suggest how sexual selection results in marked **sexual dimorphism**: _____

   _____

   _____

Related activities: Breeding Behavior

The Founder Effect

Occasionally, a small number of individuals from a large population may migrate away, or become isolated from, their original population. If this colonizing or 'founder' population is made up of only a few individuals, it will probably have a *non-representative sample* of alleles from the parent population's gene pool. As a consequence of this **founder effect**, the colonizing population may evolve differently from that of the parent population, particularly since the environmental conditions for the isolated population may be different. In some cases, it may be possible for certain alleles to be missing altogether from the individuals in the isolated population. Future generations of this population will not have this allele.

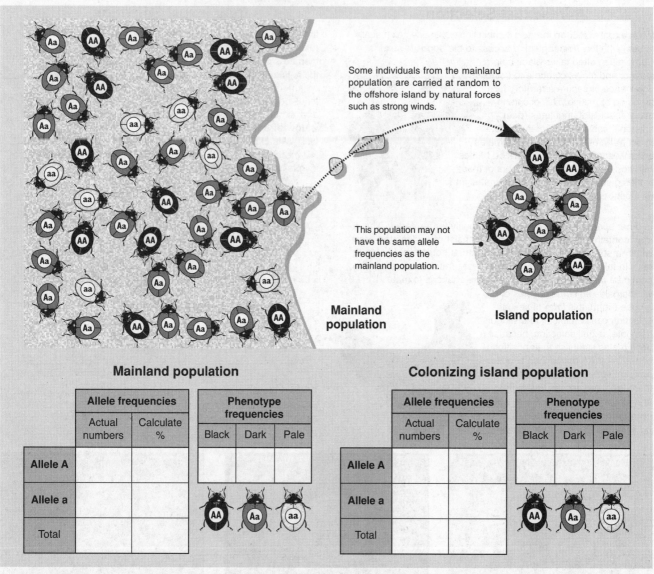

Some individuals from the mainland population are carried at random to the offshore island by natural forces such as strong winds.

This population may not have the same allele frequencies as the mainland population.

Mainland population

Island population

Mainland population

	Allele frequencies		Phenotype frequencies		
	Actual numbers	Calculate %	Black	Dark	Pale
Allele A					
Allele a					
Total					

Colonizing island population

	Allele frequencies		Phenotype frequencies		
	Actual numbers	Calculate %	Black	Dark	Pale
Allele A					
Allele a					
Total					

1. Compare the mainland population to the population which ended up on the island (use the spaces in the tables above):

   (a) Count the **phenotype** numbers for the two populations (i.e. the number of black, dark and pale beetles).
   (b) Count the **allele** numbers for the two populations: the number of dominant alleles (A) and recessive alleles (a). Calculate these as a percentage of the total number of alleles for each population.

2. Describe how the allele frequencies of the two populations are different: _____

   _____

3. Describe some possible ways in which various types of organism can be carried to an offshore island:

   (a) Plants: _____

   (b) Land animals: _____

   (c) Non-marine birds: _____

4. Since founder populations are often very small, describe another process that may further alter the allele frequencies:

   _____

   _____

Related activities: Gene Pool Exercise, Oceanic Island Colonizers, Genetic Drift
Web links: Genetic Drift Simulation

Population Bottlenecks

Populations may sometimes be reduced to low numbers by predation, disease, or periods of climatic change. A population crash may not be 'selective': it may affect all phenotypes equally. Large scale catastrophic events (e.g. fire or volcanic eruption) are examples of such non-selective events. Humans may severely (and selectively) reduce the numbers of some species through hunting and/or habitat destruction. These populations may recover, having squeezed through a 'bottleneck' of low numbers.

The diagram below illustrates how population numbers may be reduced as a result of a catastrophic event. Following such an event, the small number of individuals contributing to the gene pool may not have a representative sample of the alleles in the pre-catastrophe population, i.e. the allele frequencies in the remnant population may be altered. Genetic drift may cause further changes to allele frequencies. The small population may return to previous levels but with a reduced genetic diversity.

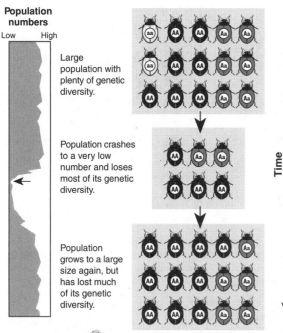

Population numbers

Low ——— High

Large population with plenty of genetic diversity.

Population crashes to a very low number and loses most of its genetic diversity.

Population grows to a large size again, but has lost much of its genetic diversity.

Time

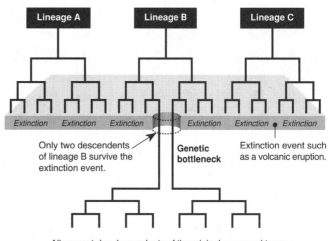

The original gene pool is made up of the offspring of many lineages (family groups and sub-populations).

Lineage A   **Lineage B**   **Lineage C**

Extinction   Extinction   Extinction   Genetic bottleneck   Extinction   Extinction   Extinction

Only two descendents of lineage B survive the extinction event.

Extinction event such as a volcanic eruption.

All present day descendents of the original gene pool trace their ancestry back to individual B and therefore retain only a small sample of genes present in the original gene pool.

Modern Examples of Population Bottlenecks

Cheetahs: The world population of cheetahs currently stands at fewer than 20 000. Recent genetic analysis has found that the entire population enhibits very little genetic diversity. It appears that cheetahs may have narrowly escaped extinction at the end of the last ice age, about 10-20 000 years ago. If all modern cheetahs arose from a very limited genetic stock, this would explain their present lack of genetic diversity. The lack of genetic variation has resulted in a number of problems that threaten cheetah survival, including sperm abnormalities, decreased fecundity, high cub mortality, and sensitivity to disease.

Illinois prairie chicken: When Europeans first arrived in North America, there were millions of prairie chickens. As a result of hunting and habitat loss, the Illinois population of prairie chickens fell from about 100 million in 1900 to fewer than 50 in the 1990s. A comparison of the DNA from birds collected in the mid-twentieth century and DNA from the surviving population indicated that most of the genetic diversity has been lost.

Photo: Dept. of Natural Resources, Illinois

1. Endangered species are often subjected to population bottlenecks. Explain how population bottlenecks affect the ability of a population of an endangered species to recover from its plight:

_____

_____

_____

2. Explain why the lack of genetic diversity in cheetahs has increased their sensitivity to disease:

_____

_____

3. Describe the effect of a population bottleneck on the potential of a species to adapt to changes (i.e. its ability to evolve):

_____

_____

Related activities: Gene Pool Exercise, Genetic Drift

Genetic Drift

Not all individuals, for various reasons, will be able to contribute their genes to the next generation. **Genetic drift** (also known as the Sewell-Wright Effect) refers to the *random changes in allele frequency* that occur in all populations, but are much more pronounced in small populations. In a small population, the effect of a few individuals not contributing their alleles to the next generation can have a great effect on allele frequencies. Alleles may even become **lost** from the gene pool altogether (frequency becomes 0%) or **fixed** as the only allele for the gene present (frequency becomes 100%).

The genetic makeup (allele frequencies) of the population changes randomly over a period of time

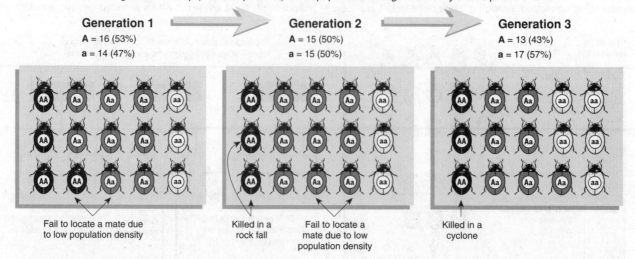

Generation 1
A = 16 (53%)
a = 14 (47%)

Generation 2
A = 15 (50%)
a = 15 (50%)

Generation 3
A = 13 (43%)
a = 17 (57%)

Fail to locate a mate due to low population density

Killed in a rock fall

Fail to locate a mate due to low population density

Killed in a cyclone

This diagram shows the gene pool of a hypothetical small population over three generations. For various reasons, not all individuals contribute alleles to the next generation. With the random loss of the alleles carried by these individuals, the allele frequency changes from one generation to the next. The change in frequency is directionless as there is no selecting force. The allele combinations for each successive generation are determined by how many alleles of each type are passed on from the preceding one.

Computer Simulation of Genetic Drift

Below are displayed the change in allele frequencies in a computer simulation showing random genetic drift. The breeding population progressively gets smaller from left to right. Each simulation was run for 140 generations.

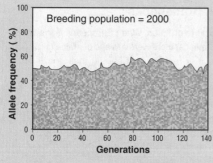

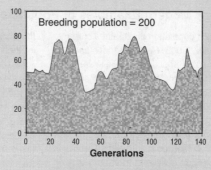

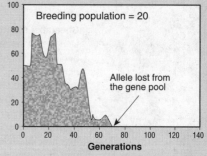

Large breeding population
Fluctuations are minimal in large breeding populations because the large numbers buffer the population against random loss of alleles. On average, losses for each allele type will be similar in frequency and little change occurs.

Small breeding population
Fluctuations are more severe in smaller breeding populations because random changes in a few alleles cause a greater percentage change in allele frequencies.

Very small breeding population
Fluctuations in very small breeding populations are so extreme that the allele can become fixed (frequency of 100%) or lost from the gene pool altogether (frequency of 0%).

1. Explain what is meant by **genetic drift**: _____

_____

2. Describe how genetic drift affects the amount of genetic variation within very small populations: _____

_____

_____

_____

3. Identify a small breeding population of animals or plants in your country in which genetic drift could be occurring:

_____

Related activities: Gene Pool Exercise, The Founder Effect
Web links: Genetic Drift Simulation

Reproductive Isolation

The concept of a biological species is based in **reproductive isolation**, with each species isolated by factors (barriers) that prevent interbreeding (and therefore gene flow) with other species. Any factor that impedes two species from producing viable, fertile hybrids contributes to reproductive isolation. Single barriers may not completely stop gene flow, so most species have more than one type of barrier. Geographical barriers are not always classified as reproductive isolating mechanisms (RIMs) because they are not part of the species' biology. Such barriers often precede the development of other reproductive isolating mechanisms, which can operate before fertilization (prezygotic RIMs) or after fertilization (postzygotic RIMs).

Prezygotic Isolating Mechanisms

Spatial (geographical)

Includes physical barriers such as: mountains, rivers, altitude, oceans, isthmuses, deserts, ice sheets. There are many examples of speciation occurring as a result of isolation by oceans or by geological changes in lake basins (e.g. the proliferation of cichlid fish species in Lake Victoria). The many species of iguana from the Galapagos Islands are now quite distinct from the Central and South American species from which they arose.

Land iguana: Galapagos Is.

Galapagos Is

South America

800 km

Pacific Ocean

Temporal (including seasonal)

Timing of mating activity for an organism may prevent contact with closely related species: nocturnal, diurnal, spring, summer, fall, spring tide etc. Plants flower at different times of the year or even at different times of the day. Closely related animals may have quite different breeding seasons.

Breeding season for species B

J F M A M J J A S O N D

Breeding season for species A

J F M A M J J A S O N D

Ecological (habitat)

Closely related species may occupy different habitats even within the same general area. In the USA, geographically isolated species of antelope squirrels occupy different ranges either side of the Grand Canyon. The white tailed antelope squirrel inhabits the desert to the north of the canyon, while the smaller Harris's antelope squirrel has a much more limited range to the south of the canyon.

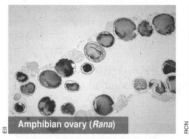

Grand Canyon

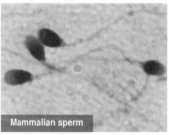

Harris's antelope squirrel

Gamete mortality

Sperm and egg fail to unite. Even if mating takes place, most gametes will fail to unite. The sperm of one species may not be able to survive in the reproductive tract of another species. Gamete recognition may be based on the presence of species specific molecules on the egg or the egg may not release the correct chemical attractants for sperm of another species.

Amphibian ovary (*Rana*)

Mammalian sperm

Behavioral (ethological)

Animals attract mates with calls, rituals, dances, body language, etc. Complex displays, such as the flashes of fireflies, are quite specific. In animals, behavioral responses are a major isolating factor, preserving the integrity of mating within species. Birds exhibit a remarkable range of courtship displays that are often quite species-specific.

Peacock display of tail

Blue footed boobies courtship

Structural (morphological)

Shape of the copulatory (mating) apparatus, appearance, coloration, insect attractants. Insects have a lock-and-key arrangement for their copulatory organs. Pheromone chemical attractants, which may travel many kilometers with the aid of the wind, are quite specific, attracting only members of the same species.

Beetles mating

Damselflies mating

Related activities: Stages in Species Development

A 2

Postzygotic Isolating Mechanisms

Hybrid sterility

Even if two species mate and produce hybrid offspring that are vigorous, the species are still reproductively isolated if the hybrids are sterile (genes cannot flow from one species' gene pool to the other). Such cases are common among the horse family (such as the zebra and donkey shown on the right). One cause of this sterility is the failure of meiosis to produce normal gametes in the hybrid. This can occur if the chromosomes of the two parents are different in number or structure (see the "**zebronkey**" karyotype on the right). The **mule**, a cross between a donkey stallion and a horse mare, is also an example of **hybrid vigor** (they are robust) as well as **hybrid sterility**. Female mules sometimes produce viable eggs but males are infertile.

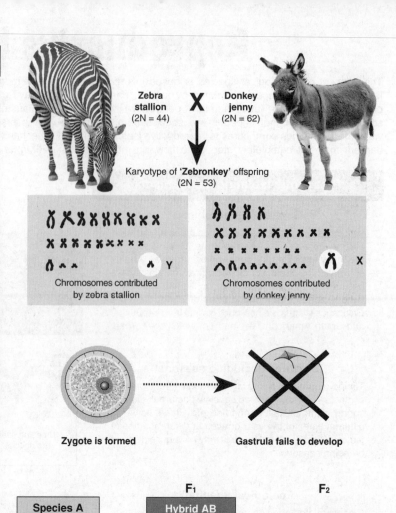

Zebra stallion (2N = 44) X Donkey jenny (2N = 62)

Karyotype of 'Zebronkey' offspring (2N = 53)

Chromosomes contributed by zebra stallion   Y

Chromosomes contributed by donkey jenny   X

Hybrid inviability

Mating between individuals of two different species may sometimes produce a zygote. In such cases, the genetic incompatibility between the two species may stop development of the fertilized egg at some embryonic stage. Fertilized eggs often fail to divide because of unmatched chromosome numbers from each gamete (a kind of aneuploidy between species). Very occasionally, the hybrid zygote will complete embryonic development but will not survive for long.

Zygote is formed   **Gastrula fails to develop**

Hybrid breakdown

First generation (F$_1$) are fertile, but the second generation (F$_2$) are infertile or inviable. Conflict between the genes of two species sometimes manifests itself in the second generation.

		F$_1$	F$_2$
Species A Viable		**Hybrid AB** Reduced viability	**Hybrid AB** Non-viable or sterile
X	X		
Species B Viable		**Hybrid AB** Reduced viability	

1. In general terms, explain the role of reproductive isolating mechanisms in maintaining the integrity of a species:

_____

_____

2. In the following examples, classify the reproductive isolating mechanism as either **prezygotic** or **postzygotic** and describe the mechanisms by which the isolation is achieved (e.g. temporal isolation, hybrid sterility etc.):

(a) Some different cotton species can produce fertile hybrids, but breakdown of the hybrid occurs in the next generation when the offspring of the hybrid die in their seeds or grow into defective plants:

Prezygotic / postzygotic (delete one)   Mechanism of isolation: _____

(b) Many plants have unique arrangements of their floral parts that stops transfer of pollen between plants:

Prezygotic / postzygotic (delete one)   Mechanism of isolation: _____

(c) Three species of orchid living in the same rainforest do not hybridize because they flower on different days:

Prezygotic / postzygotic (delete one)   Mechanism of isolation: _____

(d) Several species of the frog genus *Rana*, live in the same regions and habitats, where they may occasionally hybridize. The hybrids generally do not complete development, and those that do are weak and do not survive long:

Prezygotic / postzygotic (delete one)   Mechanism of isolation: _____

3. Postzygotic isolating mechanisms are said to reinforce prezygotic ones. Explain why this is the case:

_____

_____

Allopatric Speciation

Allopatric speciation is a process thought to have been responsible for a great many instances of species formation. It has certainly been important in countries which have had a number of cycles of geographical fragmentation. Such cycles can occur as the result of glacial and interglacial periods, where ice expands and then retreats over a land mass. Such events are also accompanied by sea level changes which can isolate populations within relatively small geographical regions.

Stage 1: Moving into new environments

There are times when the range of a species expands for a variety of different reasons. A single population in a relatively homogeneous environment will move into new regions of their environment when they are subjected to intense competition (whether it is interspecific or intraspecific). The most severe form of competition is between members of the same species since they are competing for identical resources in the habitat. In the diagram on the right there is a 'parent population' of a single species with a common gene pool with regular 'gene flow' (theoretically any individual has access to all members of the opposite sex for mating purposes).

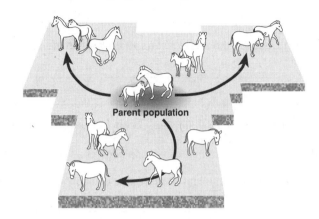

Stage 2: Geographical isolation

Isolation of parts of the population may occur due to the formation of physical barriers. These barriers may cut off those parts of the population that are at the extremes of the species range and gene flow is prevented or rare. The rise and fall of the sea level has been particularly important in functioning as an isolating mechanism. Climatic change can leave 'islands' of habitat separated by large inhospitable zones that the species cannot traverse.

Example: In mountainous regions, alpine species are free to range widely over extensive habitat during cool climatic periods. During warmer periods, however, they may become isolated because their habitat is reduced to 'islands' of high ground surrounded by inhospitable lowland habitat.

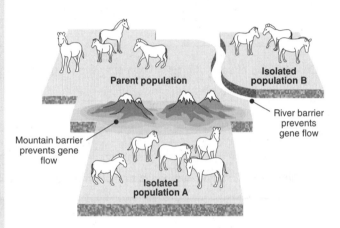

Stage 3: Different selection pressures

The isolated populations (A and B) may be subjected to quite different selection pressures. These will favor individuals with traits that suit each particular environment. For example, population A will be subjected to selection pressures that relate to drier conditions. This will favor those individuals with phenotypes (and therefore genotypes) that are better suited to dry conditions. They may for instance have a better ability to conserve water. This would result in improved health, allowing better disease resistance and greater reproductive performance (i.e. more of their offspring survive). Finally, as allele frequencies for certain genes change, the population takes on the status of a subspecies. Reproductive isolation is not yet established but the subspecies are significantly different genetically from other related populations.

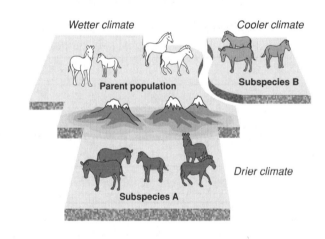

Stage 4: Reproductive isolation

The separated populations (isolated subspecies) will often undergo changes in their genetic makeup as well as their behavior patterns. These ensure that the gene pool of each population remains isolated and 'undiluted' by genes from other populations, even if the two populations should be able to remix (due to the removal of the geographical barrier). Gene flow does not occur. The arrows (in the diagram to the right) indicate the zone of overlap between two species after the new Species B has moved back into the range inhabited by the parent population. Closely-related species whose distribution overlaps are said to be sympatric species. Those that remain geographically isolated are called allopatric species.

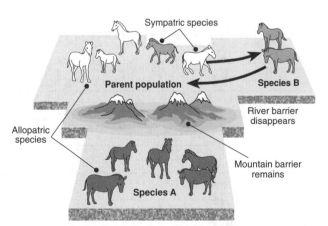

Related activities: Reproductive Isolation, Stages in Species Development
Web links: Mechanisms of Speciation, Allopatric Speciation

RA 2

1. Describe why some animals, given the opportunity, move into new environments: _____

_____

2. (a) Plants are unable to move. State how plants might disperse to new environments: _____

_____

   (b) Describe the amount of **gene flow** within the parent population prior to and during this range expansion:

_____

_____

_____

3. Identify the process that causes the formation of new mountain ranges: _____

4. Identify the event that can cause large changes in sea level (up to 200 meters): _____

5. Describe six **physical barriers** that could isolate different parts of the same population: _____

_____

_____

_____

_____

6. Describe the effect that physical barriers have on **gene flow**: _____

_____

_____

_____

7. (a) Describe four different types of **selection pressure** that could have an effect on a gene pool: _____

_____

_____

_____

   (b) Describe briefly how these selection pressures affect the isolated gene pool in terms of **allele frequencies**:

_____

_____

_____

_____

8. Describe two **prezygotic** and two **postzygotic** reproductive isolating mechanisms (see the previous activity for help):

   (a) Prezygotic: _____

_____

   (b) Postzygotic: _____

_____

9. Distinguish between **allopatry** and **sympatry** in populations: _____

_____

_____

_____

_____

_____

_____

Sympatric Speciation

New species may be formed even where there is no separation of the gene pools by physical barriers. Called **sympatric speciation**, it is rarer than allopatric speciation, although not uncommon in plants which form **polyploids**. There are two situations where sympatric speciation is thought to occur. These are described below:

Speciation Through Niche Differentiation

Niche isolation

In a heterogeneous environment (one that is not the same everywhere), a population exists within a diverse collection of **microhabitats**. Some organisms prefer to occupy one particular type of 'microhabitat' most of the time, only rarely coming in contact with fellow organisms that prefer other microhabitats. Some organisms become so dependent on the resources offered by their particular microhabitat that they never meet up with their counterparts in different microhabitats.

Reproductive isolation

Finally, the individual groups have remained genetically isolated for so long because of their microhabitat preferences, that they have become reproductively isolated. They have become new species that have developed subtle differences in behavior, structure, and physiology. Gene flow (via sexual reproduction) is limited to organisms that share a similar microhabitat preference (as shown in the diagram on the right).

Example: When it is time for them to lay eggs, some beetles preferentially locate the same plant species as they grew up on. Individual beetles of the same species have different preferences.

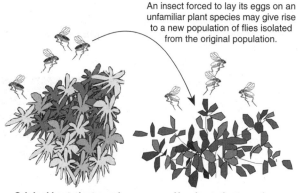

An insect forced to lay its eggs on an unfamiliar plant species may give rise to a new population of flies isolated from the original population.

Original host plant species   **New host plant species**

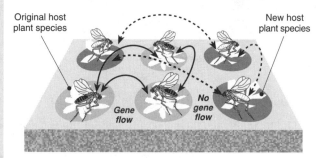

Original host plant species

New host plant species

Gene flow

No gene flow

Instant Speciation by Polyploidy

When polyploidy occurs, it is possible to form a completely new species without isolation from the parent species. This type of malfunction during the process of meiosis produces sudden reproductive isolation for the new group. Because the sex-determining mechanism is disturbed, animals are rarely able to achieve new species status this way (they are effectively sterile e.g. tetraploid XXXX). Many plants, on the other hand, are able to reproduce vegetatively, or carry out self pollination. This ability to reproduce on their own enables such polyploid plants to produce a breeding population.

Speciation by allopolyploidy

This type of polyploidy usually arises from the doubling of chromosomes in a hybrid between two different species. The doubling often makes the hybrid fertile.

Examples: Modern wheat. Swedes are polyploid species formed from a hybrid between a type of cabbage and a type of turnip.

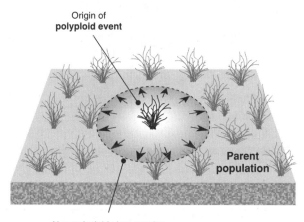

Origin of **polyploid event**

Parent population

New polyploid plant species spreads outwards through the existing parent population

1. Explain what is meant by **sympatric speciation** and identify the mechanisms by which it can occur:

_____

_____

2. Explain briefly how polyploidy may cause the formation of a new species: _____

_____

_____

3. Identify an example of a species that has been formed by polyploidy: _____

4. Explain how niche differentiation may cause the formation of a new species: _____

_____

_____

Related activities: Allopatric Speciation, The Domestication of Wheat
Web links: Sympatric Speciation

A 2

Stages in Species Development

The diagram below represents a possible sequence of genetic events involved in the origin of two new species from an ancestral population. As time progresses (from top to bottom of the diagram) the amount of genetic variation increases and each group becomes increasingly isolated from the other. The mechanisms that operate to keep the two gene pools isolated from one another may begin with **geographical barriers**. This may be followed by **prezygotic** mechanisms which protect the gene pool from unwanted dilution by genes from other pools. A longer period of isolation may lead to **postzygotic** mechanisms (see the page on reproductive isolating mechanisms). As the two gene pools become increasingly isolated and different from each other, they are progressively labeled: population, race, and subspecies. Finally they attain the status of separate species.

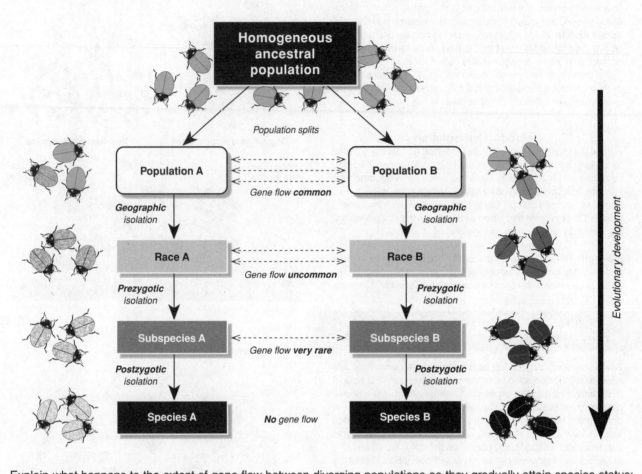

1. Explain what happens to the extent of gene flow between diverging populations as they gradually attain species status:

_____

_____

2. Early human populations about 500 000 ya were scattered across Africa, Europe, and Asia. This was a time of many regional variants, collectively called archaic *Homo sapiens*. The fossil skulls from different regions showed mixtures of characteristics, some modern and some 'primitive'. These regional populations are generally given subspecies status. Suggest reasons why gene flow between these populations may have been rare, but still occasionally occurred:

_____

_____

_____

3. In the USA, the species status of several duck species, including the black duck (*Anas rubripes*) and the mottled duck in Florida (*A. fulvigula*) is threatened by interbreeding with the now widespread and very adaptable mallard duck (*A. platyrhynchos*). Similar threatened extinction though hybridization has occurred in New Zealand, where the native gray duck has been virtually eliminated as a result of interbreeding with the introduced mallard.

   (a) Suggest why these hybrids threaten the Species status of some native duck species: _____

   _____

   (b) Suggest what factor may deter mallards from hybridizing with other duck species: _____

   _____

Related activities: Reproductive Isolation

Patterns of Evolution

IB SL	IB HL	IB Options	AP Biology
Complete: 1, 5, 8	Complete: 1, 5, 8	Complete: Option D: SL/HL: 1,3, 6 HL: 5	Complete: 1-9 Some numbers extension as appropriate

Learning Objectives

☐ 1. Compile your own glossary from the **KEY WORDS** displayed in **bold type** in the learning objectives below.

Patterns of Evolution *(pages 83, 126-136, 141 and the TRC: Genes in Evolution, Adaptive Radiation in Ratites, and Mass Extinctions)*

☐ 2. Describe the major stages in a **species life cycle** extending from origin to extinction.

☐ 3. Using examples, distinguish patterns of species formation: **sequential (phyletic) speciation, coevolution, divergent evolution, adaptive radiation** (dichotomous) speciation. Recognise adaptive radiation as a form of divergent evolution. Explain how evolutionary change over time has resulted in a great diversity of forms among living organisms. Appreciate that some biologists also recognize **parallel evolution** (as distinct from convergence) to indicate evolution along similar lines in closely related groups.

☐ 4. Describe examples of **coevolution**, including in flowering plants and their pollinators, parasites and their hosts, and predators and their prey (including herbivory). Discuss the evidence for coevolution in species with close ecological relationships.

☐ 5. Distinguish between **homologous** structures and **analogous structures** arising as a result of **convergent evolution**. Give examples of **homology**.

Explain the evidence for evolution provided by homologous anatomical structures, including: the vertebrate pentadactyl limb and vertebrate embryos. Note: Recognize that although vertebrate embryos may pass through similar stages during their development, ontogeny does not recapitulate phylogeny; Haeckel's original drawings were inaccurate and misleading.

☐ 6. Distinguish between the two models for the pace of evolutionary change: **punctuated equilibrium** and **gradualism**. Discuss the evidence for each model.

☐ 7. Explain what is meant by **extinction**, identifying it as part of of the **species life cycle**. Describe the role of extinction in evolution. Distinguish clearly between **background extinction rates** and **mass extinction**. Identify the major **mass extinctions** and discuss the theories for their causes.

Artificial Selection *(pages 137-140)*

☐ 8. Explain the genetic basis of **artificial selection (selective breeding)**. Describe examples of artificial selection, explaining how the selection process has led to the development of particular traits:
- Crop plants, e.g. brassicas, wheat, maize.
- Companion animals (e.g. dogs).

☐ 9. Using examples, explain the terms **outbreeding, inbreeding**, interspecific **hybridisation**, and **polyploidy**. Using examples, explain what is meant by F_1 **hybrid vigor** and explain its genetic basis.

 See the 'Textbook Reference Grid' on pages 8-9 for textbook page references relating to material in this topic.

Supplementary Texts

See pages 5-6 for additional details of these texts:

■ Adds, J., *et al.,* 2004. **Genetics, Evolution and Biodiversity**, (NelsonThornes), chpt. 8.

■ Clegg, C.J., 1999. **Genetics and Evolution**, (John Murray), pp. 60-78.

■ Helms, D.R. *et al.,* 1998. **Biology in the Laboratory** (W.H. Freeman), #20, #21.

■ Jones, N., *et al.,* 2001. **The Essentials of Genetics**, pp. 190-232.

Evolution — Presentation MEDIA to support this topic:

EVOLUTION:
- **Population Genetics**
- **Evolution**

See page 6 for details of publishers of periodicals:

STUDENT'S REFERENCE

■ **The Rise of Mammals** National Geographic, 203(4), pp. April 2003, p. 2-37. *An account of the adaptive radiation of mammals and the significance of the placenta in mammalian evolution.*

■ **Mass Extinctions** New Scientist, 11 Dec. 1999 (Inside Science). *The nature and causes of the five mass extinctions of the past. A discussion of the current sixth extinction is included.*

■ **The Sixth Extinction** National Geographic, 195(2) Feb. 1999, pp. 42-59. *High rates of extinction have occurred five times in the past. The sixth extinction is nigh, driven by human impact.*

■ **A Fin is a Limb is a Wing - How Evolution Fashioned its Masterworks** National Geographic, 210(5) Nov. 2006, pp. 110-135. *The evolution of complex organs and structures in animals.*

■ **Impact from the Deep** Scientific American, Oct. 2006, pp. 42-49. *Strangling heat and gases from the earth and sea, not asteroids, most likely caused several ancient mass extinctions.*

■ **Big, Bad and Furry** New Scientist, 3 Feb. 2007, pp. 32-35. *Mesozoic mammals were large and unusual at a time when dinosaurs ruled the world, and not tiny, primitive and shrew-like.*

■ **In the Blink of an Eye** New Scientist, 9 July 2005, pp. 28-31. *Rapid contemporary evolution may be widespread and humans may be unwittingly helping it along.*

See pages 10-11 for details of how to access **Bio Links** from our web site: **www.thebiozone.com** From Bio Links, access sites under the topics: **GENERAL BIOLOGY ONLINE RESOURCES > Online Textbooks and Lecture Notes:** • An on-line biology book... *and others* > **General Online Biology resources:** • Ken's Bioweb resources ... *and others* > **Glossaries:** • Evolutionary biology and genetics glossary... *and others*

EVOLUTION: • BIO 414 evolution • Evolution • Evolution on the web for biology students • Harvard University biology links: evolution • The Talk.Origins archive ... *and others*

Patterns of Evolution

The diversification of an ancestral group into two or more species in different habitats is called **divergent evolution**. This process is illustrated in the diagram below, where two species have diverged from a **common ancestor**. Note that another species budded off, only to become extinct. Divergence is common in evolution. When divergent evolution involves the formation of a large number of species to occupy different niches, this is called an **adaptive**

radiation. The example below (right) describes the radiation of the mammals that occurred after the extinction of the dinosaurs; an event that made niches available. Note that the evolution of species may not necessarily involve branching: a species may accumulate genetic changes that, over time, result in the emergence of what can be recognized as a different species. This is known as **sequential evolution** (below, left).

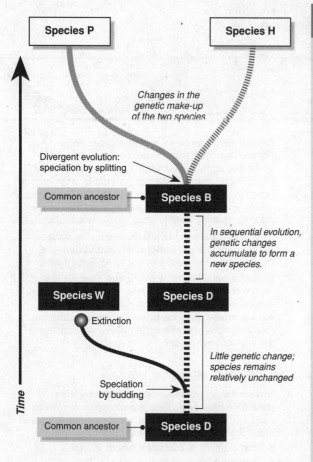

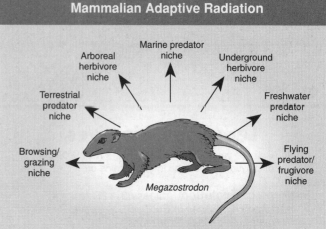

Mammalian Adaptive Radiation

Megazostrodon

Megazostrodon: one of the first mammals

Megazostrodon (above) is known from fossil remains in South Africa. This shrew-like animal first appeared in the Early Jurassic period (about 195 million years ago) and probably had an insectivorous diet.

The earliest true mammals evolved about 195 million years ago, long before they underwent their major adaptive radiation some 65-50 million years ago. These ancestors to the modern forms were very small (12 cm), many were nocturnal and fed on insects and other invertebrate prey. It was climatic change as well as the extinction of the dinosaurs (and their related forms) that suddenly left many niches vacant for exploitation by such an adaptable 'generalist'. All modern mammal orders developed very quickly and early.

1. In the hypothetical example of divergent evolution illustrated above, left:

   (a) Classify the type of evolution that produced species B from species D: _____

   (b) Classify the type of evolution that produced species P and H from species B: _____

   (c) Name all species that evolved from: **Common ancestor D**: _____ **Common ancestor B**: _____

   (d) Suggest why species B, P, and H all possess a physical trait not found in species D or W: _____

   _____

2. (a) Explain the distinction between **divergence** and **adaptive radiation**: _____

   _____

   _____

   (b) Discuss the differences between **sequential evolution** and **divergent evolution**: _____

   _____

   _____

   _____

   _____

   _____

   _____

Related activities: Adaptive Radiation in Mammals

The Rate of Evolutionary Change

The pace of evolution has been much debated, with two models being proposed: **gradualism** and **punctuated equilibrium**. Some scientists believe that both mechanisms may operate at different times and in different circumstances. Interpretations of the fossil record will vary depending on the time scales involved. During its formative millennia, a species may have accumulated its changes gradually (e.g. over 50 000 years). If that species survives for 5 million years, the evolution of its defining characteristics would have been compressed into just 1% of its (species) lifetime. In the fossil record, the species would appear quite suddenly.

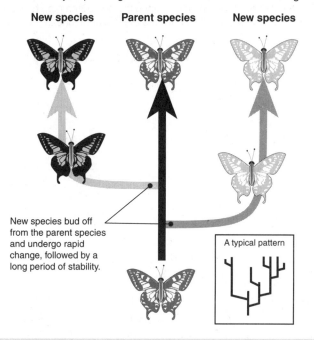

New species bud off from the parent species and undergo rapid change, followed by a long period of stability.

A typical pattern

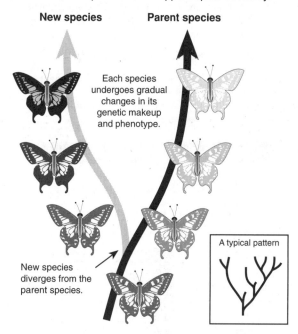

Each species undergoes gradual changes in its genetic makeup and phenotype.

New species diverges from the parent species.

A typical pattern

Punctuated Equilibrium

There is abundant evidence in the fossil record that, instead of gradual change, species stayed much the same for long periods of time (called stasis). These periods were punctuated by short bursts of evolution which produce new species quite rapidly. According to the punctuated equilibrium theory, most of a species' existence is spent in stasis and little time is spent in active evolutionary change. The stimulus for evolution occurs when some crucial factor in the environment changes.

Gradualism

Gradualism assumes that populations slowly diverge from one another by accumulating adaptive characteristics in response to different selective pressures. If species evolve by gradualism, there should be transitional forms seen in the fossil record, as is seen with the evolution of the horse. Trilobites, an extinct marine arthropod, are another group of animals that have exhibited gradualism. In a study in 1987 a researcher found that they changed gradually over a three million year period.

1. Suggest the kinds of environments that would support the following paces of evolutionary change:

   (a) Punctuated equilibrium: _____

   _____

   _____

   (b) Gradualism: _____

   _____

   _____

2. In the fossil record of early human evolution, species tend to appear suddenly, linger for often very extended periods before disappearing suddenly. There are few examples of smooth inter-gradations from one species to the next. Explain which of the above models best describes the rate of human evolution:

   _____

3. Some species apparently show little evolutionary change over long periods of time (hundreds of millions of years).

   (a) Name two examples of such species: _____

   (b) State the term given to this lack of evolutionary change: _____

   (c) Suggest why such species have changed little over evolutionary time: _____

   _____

Comparative Anatomy

The evolutionary relationships between groups of organisms is determined mainly by structural similarities called **homologous structures** (homologies), which suggest that they all descended from a common ancestor with that feature. The bones of the forelimb of air-breathing vertebrates are composed of similar bones arranged in a comparable pattern. This is indicative of a common ancestry. The early land vertebrates were amphibians and possessed a limb structure called the **pentadactyl limb**: a limb with five fingers or toes (below left). All vertebrates that descended from these early amphibians, including reptiles, birds and mammals, have limbs that have evolved from this same basic pentadactyl pattern. They also illustrate the phenomenon known as **adaptive radiation**, since the basic limb plan has been adapted to meet the requirements of different niches.

Generalized Pentadactyl Limb

The forelimbs and hind limbs have the same arrangement of bones but they have different names. In many cases bones in different parts of the limb have been highly modified to give it a specialized locomotory function.

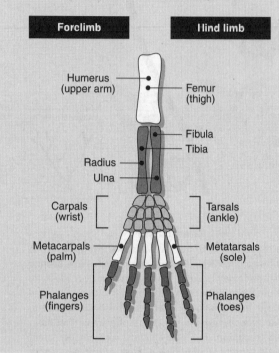

Forelimb

Hind limb

Humerus (upper arm)
Femur (thigh)
Fibula
Tibia
Radius
Ulna
Carpals (wrist)
Tarsals (ankle)
Metacarpals (palm)
Metatarsals (sole)
Phalanges (fingers)
Phalanges (toes)

Specializations of Pentadactyl Limbs

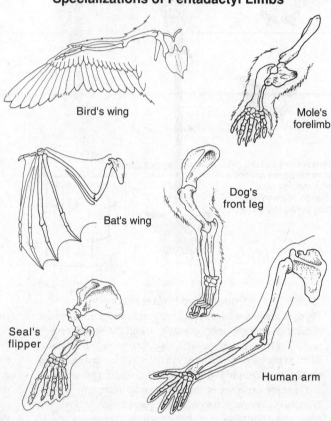

Bird's wing

Mole's forelimb

Bat's wing

Dog's front leg

Seal's flipper

Human arm

1. Briefly describe the purpose of the major anatomical change that has taken place in each of the limb examples above:

   (a) Bird wing: _Highly modified for flight. Forelimb is shaped for aerodynamic lift and feather attachment._

   (b) Human arm: _____

   (c) Seal flipper: _____

   (d) Dog foot: _____

   (e) Mole forelimb: _____

   (f) Bat wing: _____

2. Describe how homology in the pentadactyl limb is evidence for adaptive radiation: _____

   _____

   _____

   _____

3. Homology in the behavior of animals (for example, sharing similar courtship or nesting rituals) is sometimes used to indicate the degree of relatedness between groups. Suggest how behavior could be used in this way:

   _____

   _____

   _____

Related activities: Patterns of Evolution
Web links: All in the Family

Convergent Evolution

Not all similarities between species are a result of common ancestry. Species from different evolutionary lines may come to resemble each other if they have similar ecological roles and natural selection has shaped similar adaptations. This is called **convergent evolution** (**convergence**). Similarity of form due to convergence is called **analogy**.

Convergence in Swimming Form

Although similarities in body form and function can arise because of common ancestry, it may also be a result of **convergent evolution**. Selection pressures in a particular environment may bring about similar adaptations in unrelated species. These selection pressures require the solving of problems in particular ways, leading to the similarity of body form or function. The development of succulent forms in unrelated plant groups (*Euphorbia* and the cactus family) is an example of convergence in plants. In the example (right), the selection pressures of the aquatic environment have produced a similar **streamlined** body shape in unrelated vertebrate groups. Icthyosaurs, penguins, and dolphins each evolved from terrestrial species that took up an aquatic lifestyle. Their general body form has evolved to become similar to that of the shark, which has always been aquatic. Note that flipper shape in mammals, birds, and reptiles is a result of convergence, but its origin from the pentadactyl limb is an example of **homology**.

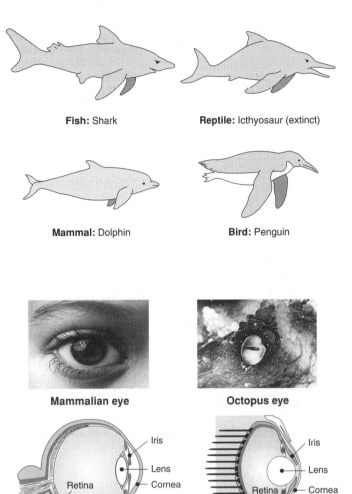

Fish: Shark

Reptile: Icthyosaur (extinct)

Mammal: Dolphin

Bird: Penguin

Mammalian eye

Octopus eye

Iris

Lens

Retina — Cornea

Iris

Lens

Retina — Cornea

Analogous Structures

Analogous structures are those that have the same function and often the same basic external appearance, but **quite different origins**. The example on the right illustrates how a complex eye structure has developed independently in two unrelated groups. The appearance of the **eye** is similar, but there is no genetic relatedness between the two groups (mammals and cephalopod molluscs). The **wings** of birds and insects are also an example of analogy. The wings perform the same function, but the two groups share no common ancestor. *Longisquama*, a lizard-like creature that lived about 220 million years ago, also had 'wings' that probably allowed gliding between trees. These 'wings' were not a modification of the forearm (as in birds), but highly modified long scales or feathers extending from its back.

1. In the example above illustrating convergence in swimming form, describe two ways in which the body form has evolved in response to the particular selection pressures of the aquatic environment:

   (a) _____

   _____

   (b) _____

   _____

2. Describe two of the selection pressures that have influenced the body form of the swimming animals above:

   (a) _____

   (b) _____

3. Early taxonomists, when encountering new species in the Pacific region and the Americas, were keen to assign them to existing taxonomic families based on their apparent similarity to European species. In recent times, many of the new species have been found to be quite unrelated to the European families they were assigned to. Explain why the traditional approach did not reveal the true evolutionary relationships of the new species:

   _____

   _____

   _____

   _____

4. For each of the paired examples (b)-(f), briefly describe the adaptations of body shape, diet and locomotion that appear similar in both forms, and the likely selection pressures that are acting on these mammals to produce similar body forms:

Convergence Between Marsupials and Placentals

Australia

Marsupials and **placental** mammals were separated from each other very early in mammalian evolution (about 120 mya). Marsupials were initially widely distributed throughout the ancient supercontinent of Gondwana, and there are some modern species still living in the American continent. Gondwana split up about 100 million years ago. As the placentals developed, they displaced the marsupials in most habitats around the world. The island continent of Australia, because of its early isolation by the sea, escaped this competition and placentals did not reach the continent until the arrival of humans 35 000 to 50 000 years ago. The Australian marsupials evolved into a wide variety of forms (below left) that bear a remarkable resemblance to ecologically equivalent species of North American placentals (below right).

North America

Marsupial mammals

Placental mammals

Marsupial		Placental
Wombat	(a) Adaptations: Both have rodent-like teeth, eat roots and above ground plants, and excavate burrows. Selection pressures: Diet requires chisel-like teeth for gnawing. The need to seek safety from predators on open grassland.	Wood chuck
Flying phalanger	(b) Adaptations: Selection pressures:	Flying squirrel
Marsupial mole	(c) Adaptations: Selection pressures:	Mole
Marsupial mouse	(d) Adaptations: Selection pressures:	Mouse
Tasmanian wolf (tiger)	(e) Adaptations: Selection pressures:	Wolf
Long-eared bandicoot	(f) Adaptations: Selection pressures:	Jack rabbit

Coevolution

The term **coevolution** is used to describe cases where two (or more) species reciprocally affect each other's evolution. Each party in a coevolutionary relationship exerts selective pressures on the other and, over time, the species develop a relationship that may involve mutual dependency. Coevolution is a likely consequence when different species have close ecological interactions with one another. These ecological relationships include predator-prey and parasite-host relationships and mutualistic relationships such as those between plants and their pollinators (see *Pollination Syndromes*). There are many examples of coevolution amongst parasites or pathogens and their hosts, and between predators and their prey, as shown on the following page.

Photo courtesy of Alex Wild

Swollen-thorn *Acacia* lack the cyanogenic glycosides found in related *Acacia* spp. and the thorns are large and hollow, providing living space for the aggressive, stinging *Pseudomyrmex* ants which patrol the plant and protect it from browsing herbivores. The *Acacia* also provides the ants with protein rich food.

Hummingbirds (above) are important pollinators in the tropics. Their needle-like bills and long tongues can take nectar from flowers with deep tubes. Their ability to hover enables them to feed quickly from dangling flowers. As they feed, their heads are dusted with pollen, which is efficiently transferred between flowers.

Butterflies find flowers by vision and smell them after landing to judge their nectar source. Like bees, they can remember characteristics of desirable flowers and so exhibit constancy, which benefits both pollinator and plant. Butterfly flowers are very fragrant and are blue, purple, deep pink, red, or orange.

Bees are excellent pollinators; they are strong enough to enter intricate flowers and have medium length tongues which can collect nectar from many flower types. They have good colour vision, which extends into the UV, but they are red-blind, so bee pollinated flowers are typically blue, purplish, or white and they may have nectar guides that are visible as spots.

Beetles represent a very ancient group of insects with thousands of modern species. Their high diversity has been attributed to extensive coevolution with flowering plants. Beetles consume the ovules as well as pollen and nectar and there is evidence that ovule herbivory by beetles might have driven the evolution of protective carpels in angiosperms.

NZ's short tailed bat pollinates *Dactylanthus* flowers on the forest floor

DoC

Bats are nocturnal and colour-blind but have an excellent sense of smell and are capable of long flights. Flowers that have coevolved with bat pollinators are open at night and have light or drab colours that do not attract other pollinators. Bat pollinated flowers also produce strong fragrances that mimic the smell of bats and have a wide bell shape for easy access.

1. Using examples, explain what you understand by the term coevolution: _____

   _____

   _____

   _____

   _____

2. Describe some of the strategies that have evolved in plants to attract pollinators: _____

   _____

   _____

   _____

   _____

   _____

Predators, Parasites, and Coevolution

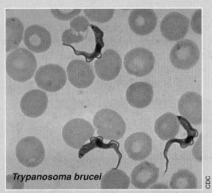

Trypanosoma brucei

Predators have obviously evolved to exploit their prey, with effective offensive weapons and hunting ability being paramount. Prey have evolved numerous strategies to protect themselves from predators, including large size and strength, protective coverings, defensive weapons, and toxicity. Lions have evolved the ability to hunt cooperatively to increase their chance of securing a kill from swift herding species such as zebra and gazelles.

Female *Helicornius* butterflies will avoid laying their eggs on plants already occupied by eggs, because their larvae are highly cannibalistic. Passionfruit plants (*Passiflora*) have exploited this by creating fake, yellow eggs on leaves and buds. *Passiflora* has many chemical defences against herbivory, but these have been breached by *Heliconius*. It has thus counter-evolved new defences against this herbivory by this genus.

Trypanosomes provide a good example of **host-parasite coevolution**. Trypanosomes must evolve strategies to evade their host's defences, but their virulence is constrained by needing to keep their host alive. Molecular studies show that *Trypanosoma brucei* coevolved in Africa with the first hominids around 5 mya, but *T. cruzi* contact with human hosts occurred in South America only after settlements were made by nomadic cultures.

3. Explain how coevolution could lead to an increase in biodiversity: _____

_____

_____

_____

_____

_____

4. Discuss some of the possible consequences of species competition: _____

_____

_____

_____

_____

_____

_____

_____

5. The analogy of an "arms race" is often used to explain the coevolution of exploitative relationships such as those of a parasite and its host. Form a small group to discuss this idea and then suggest how the analogy is flawed:

_____

_____

_____

_____

_____

_____

_____

Pollination Syndromes

The mutualistic relationship between plants and their pollinators represents a classic case of coevolution. Flower structure has evolved in many different ways in response to the many types of animal pollinators. Flowers and pollinators have coordinated traits known as **pollination syndromes**. This makes it relatively easy to deduce pollinators type from the appearance of flowers (and vice versa). Plants and animals involved in such pollination associations often become highly specialized in ways that improve pollination efficiency: innovation by one party leads to some response from the other.

Controlling Pollinator Access

Flowers control pollinator access by flower shape and position.

Dandelion

Rigid inflorescences offer a stable landing platform to small or heavy insects, such as bumblebees.

Fuschia

Only animals that can hover can collect rewards from and pollinate flowers that hang upside down.

Attracting Pollinators

Flowers advertise the presence of nectar and pollen, with colour, scent, shape, and arrangement.

Rose

While many flowers, like roses, are fragrant, flowers pollinated by flies (right) can give off dung or rotten meat smells.

Daisy

Nectar guides help the pollinator to locate nectar and pollen. In this flower, the inner petals reflect UV.

Common Pollination Syndromes: Insects

Beetles

Ancient insect group
Good sense of smell
Hard, smooth bodies

Beetle-pollinated flowers

Ancient plant groups
Strong, fruity odours
Large, often flat, with easy access

Nectar-feeding flies

Sense nectar with feet
Tubular mouthparts

Nectar-feeding fly-pollinated flowers

Simple flowers with easy access
red or light colour, little odour

Moths

Many active at night
Good sense of smell
Feed with long, narrow tongues
Some need landing platforms

Moth-pollinated flowers

Flowers may be open at night
Fragrant; with heavy, musky scent
Nectar in narrow, deep tubes
landing platforms often provided

Carrion flies

Attracted by heat, odours, or
or colour of carrion or dung.
Food in the form of nectar or
pollen not required.

Carrion fly-pollinated flowers

Coloured to resemble dung or carrion
Produce heat or foul odours
No nectar or pollen reward offered

Common Pollination Syndromes: Vertebrates

Birds

Most require a perching site
Good colour vision, including red
Poor sense of smell
Feed during daylight
High energy requirements

Bird-pollinated flowers

Large and damage resistant
Often red or other bright colours
Not particularly fragrant
Open during the day
Copious nectar produced

Bats

Active at night
High food requirements
Colour blind
Good sense of smell
Cannot fly in foliage
High blossom intelligence

Bat-pollinated flowers

Open at night
Plentiful nectar and pollen offered
Light or dingy colours
Strong, often bat-like odours
Open shape, easy access
Pendulous or on the trunks of trees

Non-flying mammals

Relatively large size
High energy requirements
Colour vision may be lacking
Good sense of smell

Non-bat mammal-pollinated flowers

Robust, damage resistant
Copious, sugar-rich nectar
Dull coloured
Odorous, but not necessarily fragrant

1. (a) Describe a common pollination syndrome of an insect: _____

_____

(b) Describe a common pollination syndrome of a vertebrate: _____

_____

2. Suggest how knowledge of pollination syndromes might be used to develop testable predictions about plant and animal pollination relationships:

_____

_____

_____

_____

_____

Geographical Distribution

The camel family, Camelidae, consists of six modern-day species that have survived on three continents: Asia, Africa and South America. They are characterized by having only two functional toes, supported by expanded pads for walking on sand or snow. The slender snout bears a cleft upper lip. The recent distribution of the camel family is fragmented. Geophysical forces such as plate tectonics and the ice age cycles have controlled the extent of their distribution. South America, for example, was separated from North America until the end of the Pliocene, about 2 million years ago. Three general principles about the dispersal and distribution of land animals are:

- When very closely related animals (as shown by their anatomy) were present at the same time in widely separated parts of the world, it is highly probable that there was no barrier to their movement in one or both directions between the localities in the past.
- The most effective barrier to the movement of land animals (particularly mammals) was a sea between continents (as was caused by changing sea levels during the ice ages).
- A scattered distribution of modern species may be explained by the movement out of the area they originally occupied, or by extinction in those regions between modern species.

Origin and Dispersal of the Camel Family

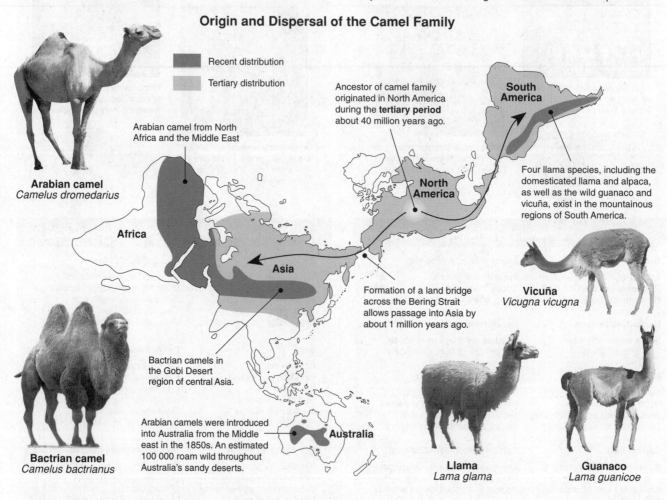

Recent distribution
Tertiary distribution

Ancestor of camel family originated in North America during the **tertiary period** about 40 million years ago.

Arabian camel from North Africa and the Middle East

Arabian camel
Camelus dromedarius

Africa

Asia

Formation of a land bridge across the Bering Strait allows passage into Asia by about 1 million years ago.

North America

South America

Four llama species, including the domesticated llama and alpaca, as well as the wild guanaco and vicuña, exist in the mountainous regions of South America.

Vicuña
Vicugna vicugna

Bactrian camels in the Gobi Desert region of central Asia.

Bactrian camel
Camelus bactrianus

Arabian camels were introduced into Australia from the Middle east in the 1850s. An estimated 100 000 roam wild throughout Australia's sandy deserts.

Australia

Llama
Lama glama

Guanaco
Lama guanicoe

1. The early camel ancestors were able to move into the tropical regions of Central and South America. Explain why this did not happen in southern Asia and southern Africa:

2. Arabian camels are found wild in the Australian Outback. Explain how they got there and why they were absent during prehistoric times:

3. The camel family originated in North America. Explain why there are no camels in North America now:

4. Suggest how early camels managed to get to Asia from North America:

5. Describe the present distribution of the camel family and explain why it is scattered (discontinuous):

Adaptive Radiation in Mammals

Adaptive radiation is diversification (both structural and ecological) among the descendants of a single ancestral group to occupy different niches. Immediately following the sudden extinction of the dinosaurs, the mammals underwent an adaptive radiation. Most of the modern mammal groups became established very early. The diagram below shows the divergence of the mammals into major orders; many occupying niches left vacant by the dinosaurs. The vertical extent of each gray shape shows the time span for which that particular mammal order has existed (note that the scale for the geological time scale in the diagram is not linear). Those that reach the top of the chart have survived to the present day. The width of a gray shape indicates how many species were in existence at any given time (narrow means there were few, wide means there were many). The dotted lines indicate possible links between the various mammal orders for which there is no direct fossil evidence.

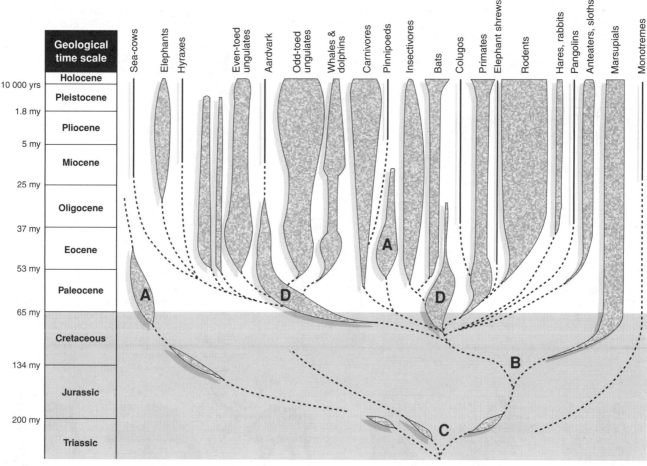

Patterns of Evolution

1. In general terms, discuss the **adaptive radiation** that occurred in mammals: _____

_____

_____

2. Name the term that you would use to describe the animal groups at point **C** (above): _____

3. Explain what occurred at point **B** (above): _____

_____

4. Describe two things that the animal orders labeled **D** (above) have in common:

    (a) _____

    (b) _____

5. Identify the two orders that appear to have been most successful in terms of the number of species produced:

_____

6. Explain what has happened to the mammal orders labeled **A** in the diagram above: _____

_____

7. Identify the **epoch** during which there was the most adaptive radiation: _____

Related activities: Patterns of Evolution   RDA 3

8. Describe two key features that distinguish mammals from other vertebrates:

(a) _____ (b) _____

9. Describe the principal reproductive features distinguishing each of the major mammalian lines (sub-classes):

(a) Monotremes: _____

(b) Marsupials: _____

(c) Placentals: _____

10. There are 18 orders of placental mammals (or 17 in schemes that include the pinnipeds within the Carnivora). Their names and a brief description of the type of mammal belonging to each group is provided below. Identify and label each of the diagrams with the correct name of their Order:

Orders of Placental Mammals

1 _____ 2 _____ 3 _____

4 _____ 5 _____ 6 _____

Order	Description
Insectivora	Insect-eating mammals
Macroscelidae	Elephant shrews (formerly classified with insectivores)
Chiroptera	Bats
Cetacea	Whales and dolphins
Pholidota	Pangolins
Rodentia	Rodents
Probiscidea	Elephants
Sirenia	Sea-cows (manatees)
Artiodactyla	Even-toed hoofed mammals
Dermoptera	Colugos
Primates	Primates
Xenarthra	Anteaters, sloths, and armadillos
Lagomorpha	Pikas, hares, and rabbits
Carnivora	Flesh-eating mammals (canids, raccoons, bears, cats)
Pinnipedia	Seals, sealions, walruses. (Often now included as a sub-order of Carnivora).
Tubulidentata	Aardvark
Hyracoidea	Hyraxes
Perissodactyla	Odd-toed hoofed mammals

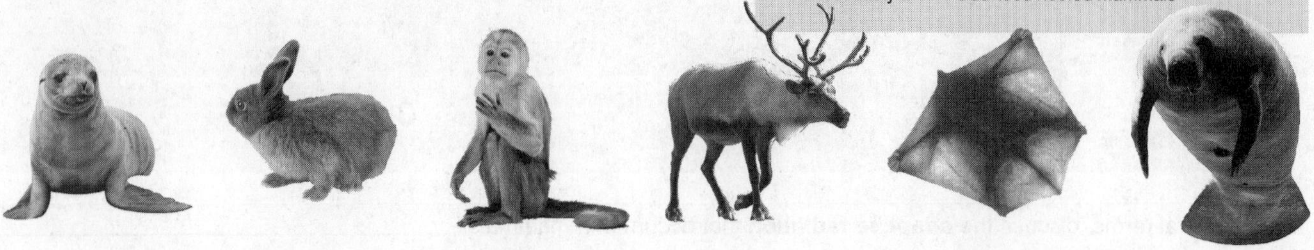

7 _____ 8 _____ 9 _____ 10 _____ 11 _____ 12 _____

13 _____ 14 _____ 15 _____ 16 _____ 17 _____ 18 _____

11. For each of three named **orders** of placental mammal, describe one **adaptive feature** that allows it to exploit a different niche from other placentals, and describe a **biological advantage** conferred by the adaptation:

(a) Order: _____ Adaptive feature: _____

Biological advantage: _____

(b) Order: _____ Adaptive feature: _____

Biological advantage: _____

(c) Order: _____ Adaptive feature: _____

Biological advantage: _____

Artificial Selection

The ability of people to control the breeding of domesticated animals and crop plants has resulted in an astounding range of phenotypic variation over relatively short time periods. Most agricultural plants and animals, as well as pets, have undergone **artificial selection** (selective breeding). The dog is a striking example of this, as there are now over 400 different breeds. Artificial selection involves breeding from individuals with the most desirable phenotypes. The aim of this is to alter the average phenotype within the species. As well as selecting for physical characteristics, desirable behavioral characteristics (e.g. the ability to 'read' the body language of humans) has also been selected for in dogs. All breeds of dog are members of the same species, **Canis familiaris**. This species descended from a single wild species, the gray wolf **Canis lupus**, over 15 000 years ago. Five ancient dog breeds are recognized, from which all other breeds are thought to have descended by artificial selection.

Gray wolf *Canis lupus pallipes*

The gray wolf is distributed throughout Europe, North America, and Asia. Amongst members of this species, there is a lot of variation in coat coloration. This accounts for the large variation in coat colors of dogs today.

Gray Wolf: Ancestor of Domestic Dogs

Until recently, it was unclear whether the ancestor to the modern domestic dogs was the desert wolf of the Middle East, the woolly wolf of central Asia, or the gray wolf of Northern Hemisphere. Recent genetic studies (mitochondrial DNA comparisons) now provide strong evidence that the ancestor of domestic dogs throughout the world is the gray wolf. It seems likely that this evolutionary change took place in a single region, most probably China.

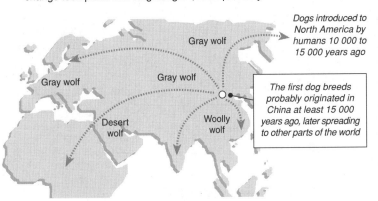

Dogs introduced to North America by humans 10 000 to 15 000 years ago

Gray wolf

Gray wolf

Gray wolf

Desert wolf

Woolly wolf

The first dog breeds probably originated in China at least 15 000 years ago, later spreading to other parts of the world

Patterns of Evolution

Mastiff-type
Canis familiaris inostranzevi
Originally from Tibet, the first records of this breed of dog go back to the Stoneage.

Greyhound
Canis familiaris leineri
Drawings of this breed on pottery dated from 8000 years ago in the Middle East make it one of the oldest.

Pointer-type
Canis familiaris intermedius
Probably derived from the greyhound breed for the purpose of hunting small game.

Sheepdog
Canis familiaris metris optimae
Originating in Europe, this breed has been used to guard flocks from predators for thousands of years.

Wolf-like
Canis familiaris palustris
Found in snow covered habitats in northern Europe, Asia (Siberia), and North America (Alaska)

1. Explain how artificial selection can result in changes in a gene pool over time: _____

_____

_____

_____

2. Describe the behavioral tendency of wolves that predisposed them to becoming a domesticated animal: _____

_____

3. List the physical and behavioral traits that would be desirable (selected for) in the following uses of a dog:

(a) Hunting large game (e.g. boar and deer): _____

(b) Game fowl dog: _____

(c) Stock control (sheep/cattle dog): _____

(d) Family pet (house dog): _____

(e) Guard dog: _____

Related activities: The Domestication of Wheat
Web links: Dog and More Dogs

RA 2

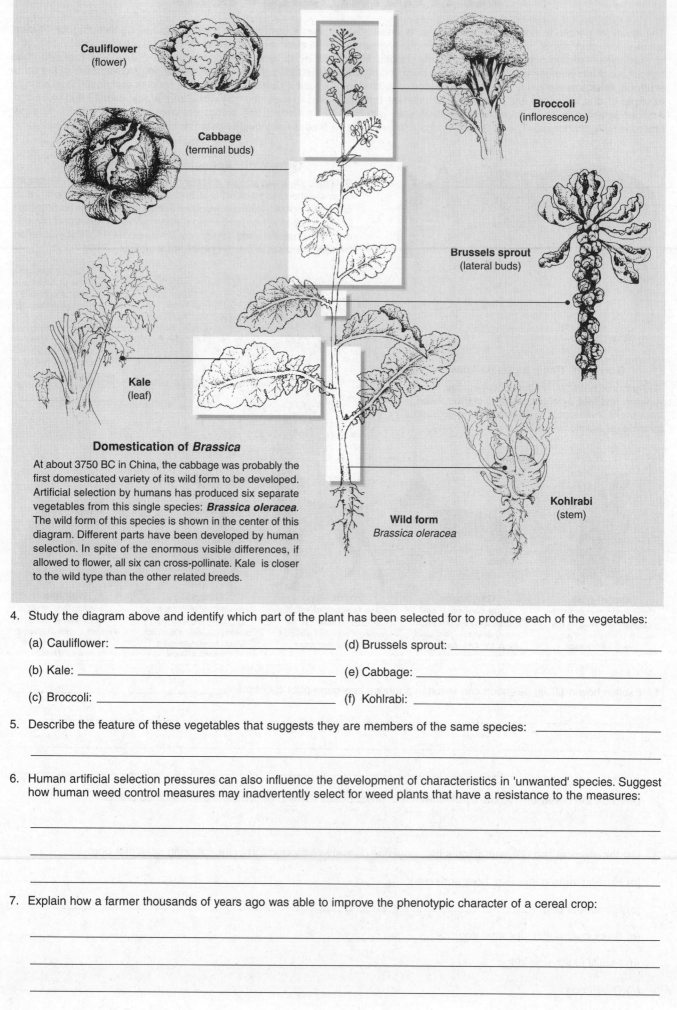

Cauliflower
(flower)

Cabbage
(terminal buds)

Broccoli
(inflorescence)

Brussels sprout
(lateral buds)

Kale
(leaf)

Kohlrabi
(stem)

Wild form
Brassica oleracea

Domestication of *Brassica*

At about 3750 BC in China, the cabbage was probably the first domesticated variety of its wild form to be developed. Artificial selection by humans has produced six separate vegetables from this single species: ***Brassica oleracea***. The wild form of this species is shown in the center of this diagram. Different parts have been developed by human selection. In spite of the enormous visible differences, if allowed to flower, all six can cross-pollinate. Kale is closer to the wild type than the other related breeds.

4. Study the diagram above and identify which part of the plant has been selected for to produce each of the vegetables:

(a) Cauliflower: _____ (d) Brussels sprout: _____

(b) Kale: _____ (e) Cabbage: _____

(c) Broccoli: _____ (f) Kohlrabi: _____

5. Describe the feature of these vegetables that suggests they are members of the same species: _____
_____

6. Human artificial selection pressures can also influence the development of characteristics in 'unwanted' species. Suggest how human weed control measures may inadvertently select for weed plants that have a resistance to the measures:
_____
_____
_____

7. Explain how a farmer thousands of years ago was able to improve the phenotypic character of a cereal crop:
_____
_____

The Domestication of Wheat

Wheat has been cultivated for more than 9000 years and has undergone many changes during the process of its domestication. The evolution of wheat involved two natural hybridization events, accompanied by **polyploidy**. **Hybrids** are the offspring of genetically dissimilar parents. They are important because they recombine the genetic characteristics of (often inbred) parental lines and show increased **heterozygosity**. This is associated with greater adaptability, survival, growth, and fertility in the offspring; a phenomenon known as **hybrid vigor** or heterosis. There is evidence to show that **interspecific hybridization** (i.e. between species) was an important evolutionary mechanism in the domestication of wheat. **Polyploidy** has also played a major role in the evolution of crop plants. Most higher organisms are

diploid, i.e. two sets of chromosomes (2N), one set derived from each parent. If there are more than two sets, the organism is said to be **polyploid**. Diploids formed from hybridization of genetically very dissimilar parents, e.g. from different species, are often infertile because the two sets of chromosomes are not able to pair properly at meiosis. In such hybrids, there are no gametes produced or the gametes are abnormal. In some cases of **allopolyploidy**, the chromosomes can be doubled and a tetraploid is formed from the diploid. This restores fertility to a hybrid, because each of the original chromosome sets can pair properly with each other during meiosis. These processes are outlined in the diagram below showing the history of domestication in wheat.

Polyploidy Events in the Evolution of Wheat

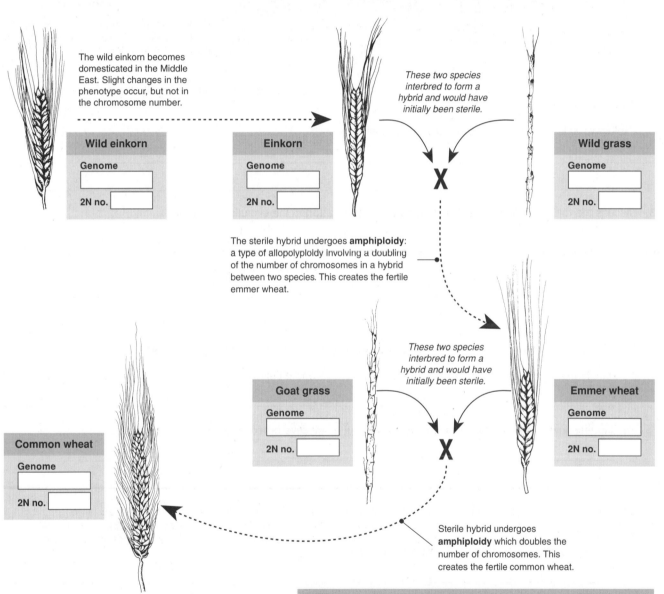

The wild einkorn becomes domesticated in the Middle East. Slight changes in the phenotype occur, but not in the chromosome number.

Wild einkorn
Genome
2N no.

Einkorn
Genome
2N no.

These two species interbred to form a hybrid and would have initially been sterile.

Wild grass
Genome
2N no.

The sterile hybrid undergoes **amphiploidy**: a type of allopolyploidy involving a doubling of the number of chromosomes in a hybrid between two species. This creates the fertile emmer wheat.

These two species interbred to form a hybrid and would have initially been sterile.

Goat grass
Genome
2N no.

Emmer wheat
Genome
2N no.

Common wheat
Genome
2N no.

Sterile hybrid undergoes **amphiploidy** which doubles the number of chromosomes. This creates the fertile common wheat.

The table on the right and the diagram above show the evolution of the common wheat. Common wheat is thought to have resulted from two sets of crossings between different species to produce hybrids. Wild einkorn (14 chromosomes, genome AA) evolved into einkorn, which crossed with a wild grass (14 chromosomes, genome BB) and gave rise to emmer wheat (28 chromosomes, genome AABB). Common wheat arose when emmer wheat was crossed with another type of grass (goat grass).

Common name	Species	Genome	Chromosomes N
Wild einkorn	*Triticum aegilopiodes*	**AA**	7
Einkorn	*Triticum monococcum*	**AA**	7
Wild grass	*Aegilops speltoides*	**BB**	7
Emmer wheat	*Triticum dicoccum*	**AABB**	14
Goat grass	*Aegilops squarrosa*	**DD**	7
Common wheat	*Triticum aestivum*	**AABBDD**	21

Ancient cereal grasses had heads which shattered readily so that seeds would be scattered widely.

Modern wheat has been selected for its non shattering heads, high yield, and high gluten content.

Teosinte

Modern corn

Corn has also evolved during its domestication. Teosinte is thought to be the ancestor to both corn and maize.

1. Using the table on the previous page, label each of the wheats and grasses in the diagram with the correct **genome** and **2N** chromosome number for each plant.

2. Explain what is meant by **F₁ hybrid vigor** (heterosis): _____

_____

_____

3. Discuss the role of **polyploidy** and **interspecific hybridization** in the evolution of wheat: _____

_____

_____

_____

_____

4. Cultivated wheat arose from wild, weedy ancestors through the selection of certain characters.

   (a) Identify the phenotypic traits that are desirable in modern wheat cultivars: _____

   _____

   (b) Suggest how ancient farmers would have carried out a selective breeding program: _____

   _____

   _____

5. Cultivated American cotton plants have a total of 52 chromosomes (2N = 52). In each cell there are 26 large chromosomes and 26 small chromosomes. Old World cotton plants have 26 chromosomes (2N = 26), all large. Wild American cotton plants have 26 chromosomes, all small. Briefly explain how cultivated American cotton may have originated from Old World cotton and wild American cotton:

_____

_____

_____

6. Discuss the need to maintain the biodiversity of wild plants and ancient farm breeds: _____

_____

_____

_____

Extinction

Extinction is an important process in evolution as it provides opportunities, in the form of vacant niches, for the development of new species. Most species that have ever lived are now extinct. The species alive today make up only a fraction of the total list of species that have lived on earth throughout its history. Extinction is a natural process in the life cycle of a species. Background extinction is the steady rate of species turnover in a taxonomic group (a group of related species). The duration of a species is thought to range from as little as 1 million years for complex larger organisms, to as long as 10-20 million years for simpler organisms. Superimposed on this constant background extinction are catastrophic events that wipe out vast numbers of species in relatively brief periods of time in geological terms. The diagram below shows how the number of species has varied over the history of life on Earth. The number of species is indicated on the graph by **families** (a taxonomic group comprising many genera and species). There have been five major extinction events and two of these have been intensively studied by paleontologists.

Major Mass Extinctions

The Permian extinction
(225 million years ago)
This was the most devastating mass extinction of all. Nearly all life on Earth perished, with 90% of marine species and probably many terrestrial ones also, disappearing from the fossil record. This extinction event marks the **Paleozoic-Mesozoic** boundary.

The Cretaceous extinction
(65 million years ago)
This extinction event marks the boundary between the **Mesozoic** and **Cenozoic** eras. More than half the marine species and many families of terrestrial plants and animals became extinct, including nearly all the dinosaur species (the birds are now known to be direct descendants of the dinosaurs).

Megafaunal extinction
(10 000 years ago)
This mass extinction occurred when many giant species of mammal died out. This is known as the 'Pleistocene overkill' because their disappearance was probably hastened by the hunting activities of prehistoric humans. Many large marsupials in Australia and placental species elsewhere became extinct.

The sixth extinction
(present day)
The current mass extinction is largely due to human destruction of habitats (e.g. coral reefs, tropical forests) and pollution. It is considered far more serious and damaging than some earlier mass extinctions because of the speed at which it is occurring. The increasing human impact is making biosphere recovery difficult.

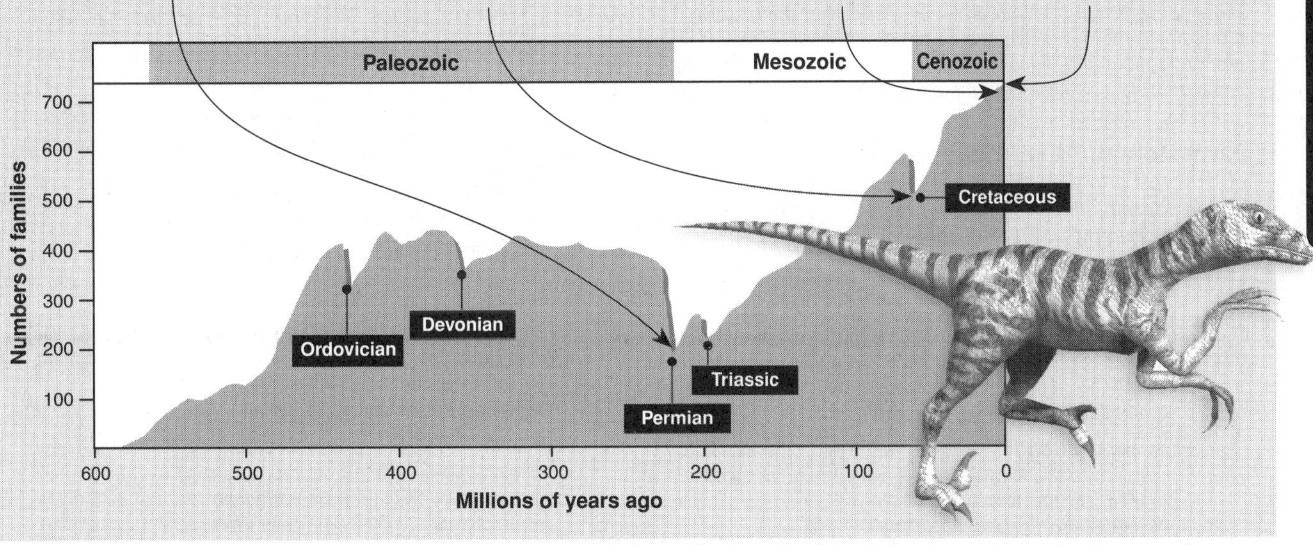

Patterns of Evolution

1. Describe the main features (scale and type of organisms killed off) of each of the following major extinction events:

(a) Permian extinction: _____

(b) Cretaceous extinction: _____

(c) Megafaunal extinction: _____

2. Explain how human activity has contributed to the most recent mass extinction: _____

3. In general terms, describe the effect that past mass extinctions had on the way the surviving species **further evolved**: _____

Related activities: The History of Life on Earth

A 2

Human Evolution

IB SL	IB HL	IB Options	AP Biology
Not applicable to core	Not applicable to core	Complete: Option D: 1-4(a),(b), 5(c), 7-8(a),(b),(d),(e), 10-13	Applicable to AP Biology as an exemplar for evolution

Learning Objectives

☐ 1. Compile your own glossary from the **KEY WORDS** displayed in **bold type** in the learning objectives below.

NOTE: Since the mid-1990s, new fossil finds have overturned earlier ideas about hominin evolution. Altogether the picture is becoming more complicated as new finds uncover more information, e.g. the discovery of *Homo floresiensis*. Be aware that older textbooks will not reflect these recent developments.

Early Hominin Evolution *(pages 143-148, 151-152 and the TRC: Primates, Hominin Skull Identification, Bipedalism and Nakedness and Hominin Evolution Supplements)*

☐ 2. Identify and describe the major physical features that define humans as **primates**.

☐ 3. Describe the anatomical features that are associated with **bipedalism**. Discuss the origin and consequences of bipedalism in human evolution, identifying when significant developments occurred.

☐ 4. Identify the **trends** and **main features** of the biological evolution of the following three early hominin species:
(a) *Australopithecus afarensis*
(b) *Australopithecus africanus*
(c) *Australopithecus (Paranthropus) robustus*

NOTE: There is a growing consensus that the robust **australopithecines** (which includes *A. robustus*) should be placed in a separate genus: *Paranthropus*.

☐ 5. Be aware that a complete listing of early hominin species appearing in the scientific literature includes:
(a) *Sahelanthropus tchadensis* ("Toumai")
(b) *Orrorin tugenensis* ("Millennium Man")
(c) *Ardipithecus ramidus* (two subspecies)
(d) *Australopithecus anamensis, A. bahrelghazali,* **A. afarensis, A. africanus**, *A. garhi*
(e) *Kenyanthropus platyops*
(f) **Paranthropus boisei, P. robustus**

☐ 6. Explain the terms: **robust** and **gracile** used to describe early hominin body shapes. Explain how the evolution of the early hominins was a response to habitat change and a shift in the resources they exploited.

Genus *Homo* *(pages 144-150, 153-156 and the TRC)*

☐ 7. Identify **distinguishing characteristics** of the genus *Homo* (features that are unique to them).

☐ 8. Identify the **trends** and **main features** of the biological and cultural evolution of the following genus *Homo*:
(a) **Homo habilis** *(also H. rudolfensis)*
(b) **H. erectus** *(also H. ergaster)*
(c) **H. heidelbergensis** (Archaic *H. sapiens*)
(d) **H. neanderthalensis** (**Neanderthals**)
(e) **H. sapiens** (anatomically modern humans)

☐ 9. Suggest reasons why all hominin species, apart from our own, became extinct and identify those species that may have coexisted, Discuss the two main hypotheses for the origin and dispersal of modern humans: **replacement** and **multiregional hypotheses**.

☐ 10. Discuss the trends in the development of brain size and intelligence during the course of human evolution and identify the selection pressures involved in this. Identify when significant developments in increasing brain size and intelligence occurred.

☐ 11. Identify **specific trends** and consequences of brain development such as continued brain expansion, the development of the **Broca's** and **Wernicke's** areas (speech production and recognition).

☐ 12. Distinguish between **cultural evolution** and **biological evolution** (genetically transmitted changes) and their relative importance in the evolution of humans.

☐ 13. Discuss trends in the evolution of complex behaviors (namely the use of tools, fire, clothing, beliefs). Explain how the development of these behaviors was aided by a growing capacity for learning and communication.

 **Textbooks**

 **Periodicals**

 **Internet**

See the 'Textbook Reference Grid' on pages 8-9 for textbook page references relating to material in this topic.

Supplementary Texts

■ **The First Humans** 1993.University of Queensland Press, St. Lucia, QL. *A superb text that has an excellent section on primate evolution covering some of the current ideas.* ISBN: 0-7022-2676-9.

■ **The Cambridge Encyclopedia of Human Evolution** 1992. Cambridge University Press, Cambridge. *An outstanding reference for teachers and keen students.* ISBN: 0-521-46786-1.

See page 6 for details of publishers of periodicals:
■ **Lucy's Baby** Scientific American, Dec. 2006 pp. 56-63. *An amazing A. afarensis skeleton from 3.3 mya renews debate over the evolution of upright walking.*
NEW LOOK AT HUMAN EVOLUTION Scientific American **SPECIAL ISSUE** 13(2) July 2003. *A collection of twelve features (some of which are new and some are updated from previous issues).*
BECOMING HUMAN Scientific American **SPECIAL ISSUE** 16(2) 2006. *A collection of features (previously published) covering aspects of primate behavior and evolution.*

See pages 10-11 for details of how to access **Bio Links** from our web site: **www.thebiozone.com** From Bio Links, access sites under the topics:
HUMAN EVOLUTION > Primates > Cultural Evolution > Human Fossil Record: • **Becoming Human** • **Early Human Evolution...** *and others*

Presentation MEDIA to support this topic:
HUMAN EVOLUTION

General Primate Characteristics

Primates have a combination of features unique to their group. All primates retain five digits in the hands and feet (pentadactyly) although some have one digit markedly reduced (e.g. thumb in spider monkeys). **Nails** are found on at least some digits in all modern primates. Climbing is achieved by grasping (not by using claws) and is aided by tactile pads at the end of the digits. Primates have flexible hands and feet with a good deal of **prehensility** (grasping ability). They have a tendency toward **erectness**, particularly in the upper body. This is associated with sitting, standing, leaping, and (in some) walking. The **collarbone** (clavicle) has been retained, allowing more flexibility in the shoulder joint (the clavicle has been lost in many other quadrupedal mammals as an adaptation to striding). Primates have a generalized **dental pattern**. This has enabled primates to adopt a flexible omnivorous diet. The snout is reduced along with the olfactory regions of the brain. Baboons go against this trend, with a secondary increase in muzzle length. There is an emphasis on **vision**, with visual areas of the brain enhanced, and well developed binocular, stereoscopic vision to provide overlapping visual fields and good depth perception. Color vision is probably present in all primates, except specialized nocturnal forms. The **brain** is large and generally more complex than in other mammals. Fetal nourishment is more efficient and **gestation** is longer than in most other mammals. Single births are the norm. Infancy is prolonged with longer periods of infant dependency and a large **parental investment** in each offspring. Life span is generally longer than most other mammals and there is a greater dependency on highly flexible **learned** behavior. Unusually for mammals, adult males of many primate species often associate permanently with the group. Label the diagram below with appropriate short summaries to describe the general physical characteristics of all primates.

The primate pictured is a **white-fronted capuchin monkey** (*Cebus albifrons*) from northern South America. These monkeys inhabit the mid-canopy deciduous, gallery forests.

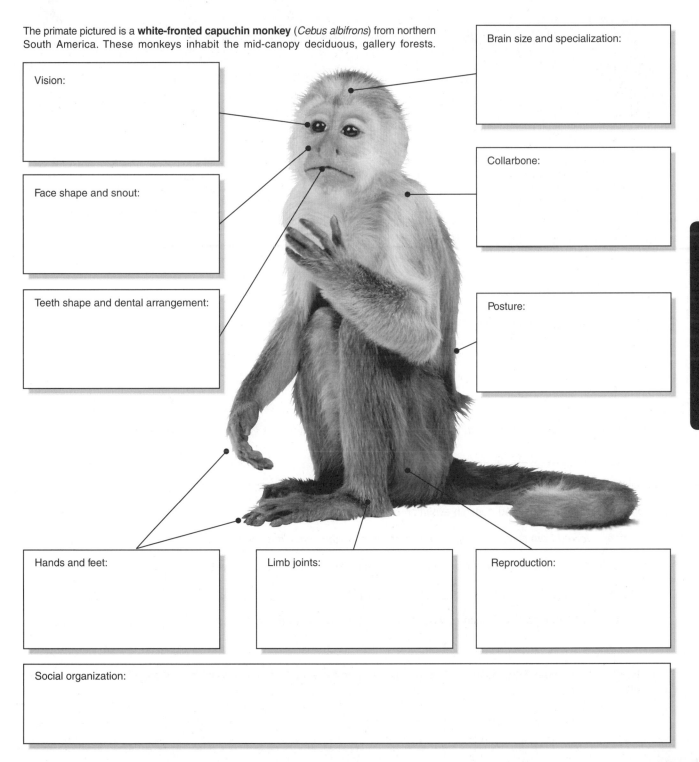

Vision:

Face shape and snout:

Teeth shape and dental arrangement:

Brain size and specialization:

Collarbone:

Posture:

Hands and feet:

Limb joints:

Reproduction:

Social organization:

Human Evolution

Web links: Our Family Tree

A 2

Hominin Evolution

The diagram below shows a provisional 'consensus' view of the family tree for the hominins (the group that includes the modern humans and pre-humans). There is much controversy over the interpretation of fossil data from the period 4-2 million years ago (mya). Some **paleoanthropologists** (scientists who study fossil hominin remains) believe that more branches existed than are shown here, with a number of adaptive radiations occurring over

this period. It is almost certain that the early Australopithecines evolved into *Homo habilis*, which was ancestral to modern humans, by about 2 mya. A divergent branch, genus *Paranthropus*, coexisted with early *Homo*, but eventually became extinct about one million years ago. The diagram below does not attempt to show species relationships. A number of important fossils dated 5-7 mya have been discovered recently.

In 2001, the 6-7 my old remains of a nearly complete skull with gorilla-like features was unearthed in Chad. Nicknamed "Toumai" and assigned to a new genus, **Sahelanthropus tchadensis**, scientists debate whether the skull's features place it in the human family tree, or whether it represents the remains of a proto-gorilla.

The 6 my old remains of five chimpanzee-sized **Orrorin tugenensis** specimens were unearthed at Baringa in Kenya in 2000. The teeth are very humanlike and a perfectly preserved thigh bone clearly shows features associated with walking upright (bipedalism).

Ardipithecus ramidus was an ape with some humanlike features. Two subspecies have been identified: *A. r. ramidus* (4.4 my old) and the older *A. r. kadabba* (5.8 my old). Fossils suggest that it was at least partially bipedal with teeth that were also more humanlike.

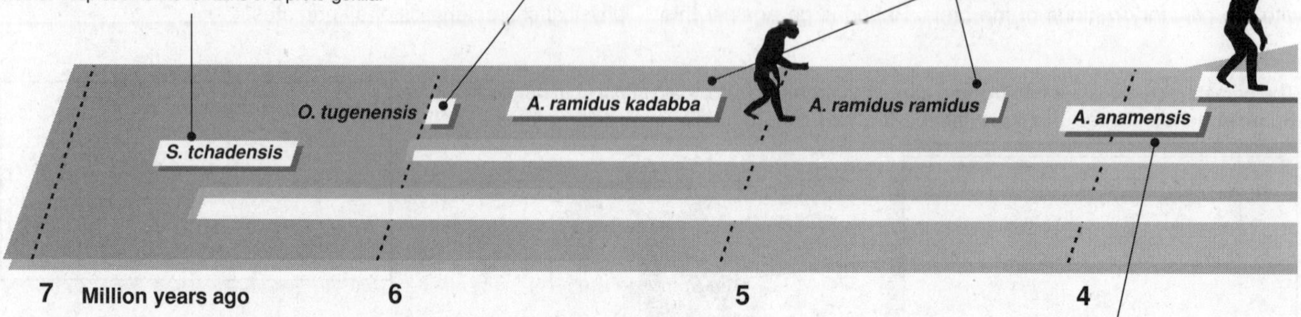

| S. tchadensis | O. tugenensis | A. ramidus kadabba | A. ramidus ramidus | A. anamensis |

| 7 | 6 | 5 | 4 |
Million years ago

New DNA and biochemical evidence suggests that the **last common ancestor** of hominins and apes occurred between 5 and 10 million years ago. The last common ancestor should have a combination of features reminiscent of both humans and apes.

There is a large gap in the fossil record that has until recently been very deficient in early hominin remains. The 1995 discovery of hominin fossils in Kenya, dated about 4 million years old have been named **Australopithecus anamensis**.

1. Explain what distinguishes **hominins** from **hominids** and **hominoids**: _____

_____

_____

2. (a) Describe the key identifying features of the (gracile) **australopithecines**: _____

_____

(b) Identify the species that are normally assigned to this group: _____

_____

3. (a) Identify the species considered to be the common ancestor to later australopithecines and also to genus *Homo*:

_____

(b) State the date range for this hominin: _____

4. People who do not understand hominin evolution often argue that:

"*If humans evolved from chimpanzees, then today's chimpanzees should be continuing to evolve into humans everyday*"

(a) State the date range paleoanthropologists believe hominins and chimpanzees last shared a common ancestor:

_____

(b) Describe two sources of evidence by which researchers have determined this date: _____

_____

(c) Rewrite the statement quoted above to correctly describe the evolutionary relationship between modern chimpanzees and humans:

_____

_____

Related activities: The Emerging View
Web links: Becoming Human

Unassigned fossil remains dated at 1.8 million years old at **Dmanisi**, in the former Soviet republic of Georgia, suggest an unexpectedly early hominid exodus from Africa.

Homo erectus is a long lived species thought to be the first to venture out of Africa. The recently discovered small hominid *H. floresiensis* appears to have been an offshoot of *H. erectus*, evolving in isolation on the island of Flores in Indonesia.

Modern humans may have appeared more than 160 000 years ago with recently discovered sub-species, *H. sapiens idaltu*. It now seems certain that the **Neanderthals** were not the direct ancestors of modern humans. Recent comparison of DNA suggest that Neanderthals split from the human lineage as long as 600 000 years ago.

Homo habilis species may be too variable to be considered a single species and should be split into two. The additional and older species is **Homo rudolfensis** (1470 skull). Only one of these hominids may have been our direct ancestor.

Australopithecus afarensis is thought to be the common ancestor to both Australopithecines and the genus *Homo*.

H. habilis

H. ergaster

H. neanderthalensis

H. sapiens

H. floresiensis

A. garhi

H. rudolfensis

H. erectus

H. antecessor

H. heidelbergensis

A. africanus

A. bahrelgazali

P. robustus

P. boisei

A. afarensis

K. platyops

Chimpanzees

Gorillas

3   2   1   **Million years ago 0**

Kenyanthropus platyops, a 3.5 my old hominin, coexisted with *A. afarensis*.

Australopithecus bahrelghazali was discovered in Chad in 1995, some 2400 km west of the East African Rift, greatly extending the known geographic range of early hominins.

The **megadonts** (genus *Paranthropus*) are large toothed vegetarians that disappear from the fossil record at about 1.5 million years ago. The cause of this extinction is not known but it may have been the result of competition with more advanced humans or changes in their habitat.

5. (a) Describe what a **megadont** is: _____

   (b) Identify two species belonging to this group: _____

   (c) Suggest why they may have become extinct: _____

   _____

6. Using the diagram above determine:

   (a) The total number of hominin species (i.e. from 6 mya to the present day): _____

   (b) The number of hominin species that existed between 3 and 2 million years ago: _____

7. The recent discovery of the oldest hominin has yielded important information about that stage in human evolution.

   (a) Identify the oldest, clearly described hominin fossil: _____

   (b) Describe two features of this species that suggest that it was not just an ancient chimpanzee: _____

   _____

   _____

8. Explain why it is most unlikely that the Neanderthals were ancestors to modern humans: _____

   _____

   _____

   _____

9. Explain why hominin fossils older than about 4.5 million years have been difficult to find: _____

   _____

   _____

Distinguishing Features of Hominins

The data below provides you with lists of features that distinguish the many hominin species from each other. In your reading, the 'known dates' provided may vary from those given below, mainly due to varying interpretations on the dating of sites by different researchers. Some early hominin species, including various australopithecines and *Kenyanthropus*, are not listed.

Distinguishing Features of Early Human Species

	Homo habilis (small)	Homo habilis (large)	Homo erectus	Archaic Homo sapiens	Homo neanderthalensis	Early Homo sapiens
Other name	None	*Homo rudolfensis*	*Homo ergaster* for older African forms	*Homo heidelbergensis*	The Neanderthals	Early anatomically modern humans
Known date (years ago)	2 – 1.6 million	2.4 – 1.6 million	1.8 – 0.3 million	400 000 - 100 000	150 000 - 30 000	160 000 - 60 000
Brain size	500-650 cc	600-800 cc	750-1250 cc	1100-1400 cc	1200-1750 cc	1200-1700 cc
Height	1.0 m	*c.* 1.5 m	1.3 - 1.5 m	?	1.5-1.7 m	1.6-1.85 m
Physique	Relatively long arms	Robust but 'human' skeleton	Robust but 'human' skeleton	Robust but 'human' skeleton	Robust but 'human' skeleton, adapted for cold	Modern skeleton possibly adapted for warmth
Skull shape	Small face with developed nose	Larger, flatter face	Flat, thick skull with sagittal 'keel' and large brow ridge	Higher cranium, face less protruding	Reduced brow ridge, midface projection, long low skull	Small or no brow ridge, shorter and higher skull
Teeth and jaws	Smaller, narrow molars; thinner jaw	Large narrow molars; robust jaw	Smaller teeth than *H. habilis*, robust jaw in larger individuals	Similar to *H. erectus* but smaller teeth	Similar to Archaic *H. sapiens*; except for incisors, smaller teeth	Teeth may be smaller; shorter jaws than Neanderthals; chin developed
Geographical distribution	Eastern, and possibly Southern Africa	Eastern Africa possibly? western Asia (Rep. Georgia)	Africa, Asia, Indonesia, and possibly Europe	Africa, Asia and Europe	Europe and western Asia	Africa and western Asia

Distinguishing Features of Early Hominins

	Orrorin tugenensis	Ardipithecus ramidus	Australopithecus anamensis	Australopithecus afarensis	Australopithecus africanus	Paranthropus robustus
Other name	"Millennium Man"	Two subspecies: *ramidus & kadabba*	None	None	None	*Australopithecus robustus*
Known date (years ago)	6.0 million	4.4 – 5.8 million	4.2 – 3.9 million	3.9 – 2.5 million	~3.0 – 2.3 million	2.2 – 1.5 million
Brain size	? cc	? cc	? cc	400 – 500 cc	400 – 500 cc	530 cc
Height	? m	*c.* 1.22 m	? m	1.07 – 1.52 m	1.1 – 1.4 m	1.1 – 1.3 m
Physique	Possibly bipedal forest dweller. Little else known	Possibly bipedal forest dweller. Little else known	Partial leg bones strongly suggest bipedalism; humerus extremely humanlike	Light build. Some apelike features: relatively long arms, curved fingers/toes, sexual dimorphism	Light build. Probably long arms, more 'human' features, probably less sexual dimorphism	Heavy build. Relatively long arms. Moderate sexual dimorphism
Skull shape	Not yet described	Foramen magnum more forward than apes	Primitive features in the skull, possibly apelike	Apelike face, low forehead, bony brow ridge, flat nose, no chin	Brow ridges less prominent; higher forehead and shorter face	Long, broad, flat face; crest on top of skull; moderate facial buttressing
Teeth and jaws	Not yet described	Teeth are intermediate between those of *A. afarensis* and earlier apes. Smaller, narrow molars; thinner jaw	Very similar to those of older fossil apes, but canines vertical; teeth have thicker tooth enamel like in humans	Human-like teeth, canines smaller than apes, larger than humans. Jaw shape half way between an ape's and human.	Teeth and jaws much larger than in humans; tooth row fully parabolic like humans; canine teeth further reduced	Very thick jaws; small incisors and canines; large molar-like premolars; very large molars
Geographical distribution	Eastern Africa	Eastern Africa	Eastern Africa	Eastern Africa	Southern Africa	Southern Africa

The Emerging View

The view of 'evolutionary tree' illustrated in the *Hominin Evolution* is simplified to make it easier to understand where the various hominin groups lie in relationship to each other. There has been a tendency over the last 40 years to try to fit the assembled fossil evidence into a **linear progression** view of human evolution (next page). In the late 1980s and early 1990s, a large number of new hominin fossils were discovered and some of the earlier finds were also reassessed.

This led to an acknowledgement of the **bushier** nature of the human evolutionary tree. Recently this revised view has been further refined to harmonize the view of human evolution with the evidence gathered on the better understood evolution of other mammals. Human evolution can now be thought of as a succession of **adaptive radiations**, some of which were 'sidelines' to the modern human lineage and all but one species (our own) becoming **extinct**.

Archaic and Modern Humans

Rapid advances in brain size are associated with a suite of new behaviors during this period. Anatomically modern humans emerge from one of the many regional variants and rapidly spread through much of the Old World.

★ The species marked with an asterisk (★) were all unknown a decade or so ago (and may be missing from many textbooks on the subject). There are likely to be many as yet 'undiscovered' species in the fossil record between 7 and 4 million years ago.

Paranthropines

These early hominins represent a group specialized for eating a bulky, low-grade vegetarian diet. They developed large cheek teeth, powerful chewing muscles and a generally **robust** skull (large crests for muscle attachment, heavily buttressed face).

Erectines

Big changes in the post-cranial skeleton with body height achieving modern proportions. Marked behavioral changes are matched by increasing brain volume, with sophisticated tool manufacture and use employed to kill and process small sized game. It is still unclear whether *H. floresiensis* belonged to this group

Habilines

This group shows the first signs of brain enlargement, more meat in the diet as well as the first recognizable stone tool culture. The post-cranial (below the head) skeleton remains small and slight much like that of the australopithecines.

Australopithecines

The earliest of these hominins were among the first apes to achieve bipedalism. They possessed a **gracile** body form and were probably opportunistic omnivores, scavenging meat from carcasses and feeding off a wide range of resources.

Very Early Hominins

Essentially chimpanzee-like animals that have begun to show some human characteristics in their locomotion (bipedalism) and in the shape and arrangement of their teeth. The oldest specimens were only recently discovered; *Orrorin tugenensis* in 2000, *Sahelanthropus tchadensis* in 2001 (although some scientists have suggested that the latter may be a gorilla ancestor).

Homo sapiens

Homo neanderthalensis

Homo floresiensis ★

Homo erectus

Homo sapiens idaltu ★

Homo heidelbergensis

Homo antecessor ★

Homo ergaster

Homo habilis

Homo rudolfensis

Australopithecus africanus

Australopithecus garhi ★

Australopithecus afarensis

Paranthropus robustus

Paranthropus boisei

Paranthropus aethiopicus

Australopithecus bahrelghazali ★

Kenyanthropus platyops ★

Australopithecus anamensis ★

Ardipithecus ramidus ramidus ★

Ardipithecus ramidus kadabba ★

Orrorin tugenensis ★

Sahelanthropus tchadensis ★

Time (millions of years ago)

Human Evolution

Related activities: Hominin Evolution
Web links: Human Skull Identification

RDA 2

A 1960s view of human evolution

The illustration below was in common usage in the popular press 30 years ago to represent the **linear progression** from a primitive apelike ancestor to modern humans. It is still used as a visual metaphor for the idea of evolution in the world of advertising.

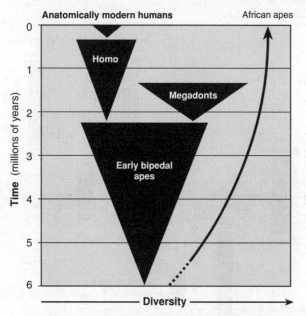

Evolving lineage with the accumulation of gradual genetic changes under the influence of natural selection

Predictions according to the linear progression model

● The fossil record should consistently show smooth intergradations from one species to the next.

Anatomically modern humans

Time (millions of years) — 0 to 6

Homo

Megadonts

Early bipedal apes

African apes

Diversity

The actual evidence observed

● Few smooth intergradations from one species to the next.

● Species tend to appear suddenly in the fossil record.

● The species linger for varying but often very extended periods of time in the fossil record.

● The species disappear as suddenly as they arrived.

● They are replaced by other species which might or might not be closely related to them.

Source: Robert Foley, (1995) *Humans Before Humanity*, Blackwell Publishers

The current view of human evolution

The diagram on the left depicts human evolution as a series of adaptive radiations. The first radiation is that of the **early bipedal apes**, the australopithecines. The second radiation involves the genus *Paranthropus*, a group of species that exploited a coarse, low-grade vegetable food source (nuts, root tubers and seeds) resulting in **megadontic** adaptations (very large teeth). The third radiation is genus *Homo*, with the **habilines** and **erectines** developing a larger brain, diversifying and dispersing from Africa to other parts of the Old World. The last radiation does not involve any major evolutionary divergence, but reflects the dispersal of **modern humans** with considerable geographic separation.

Source: Ian Tattersall, (1995) *The Fossil Trail*, Oxford University Press

1. Explain why the 1960s **linear progression** view of human evolution is not an acceptable scientific model:

_____

_____

_____

2. Explain whether the *emerging view* (on the previous page) and the data above support the **punctuated equilibrium** or **gradualism** models of evolutionary development and the origin of new species:

_____

_____

3. Describe the four main **adaptive radiations** that have occurred during hominin evolution over the last 4 million years:

(a) _____

(b) _____

(c) _____

(d) _____

The Origin of Modern Humans

There is great debate over the origins of "anatomically modern" humans, i.e. the emergence of *Homo sapiens*. The two main contesting theories are the **multiregional** and **replacement** hypotheses, with the **assimilation** model (not shown) being a compromise between the other two. The "moderns" lack some of the features characteristic of earlier, archaic hominins, such as the protruding snout and heavy brow ridges. The modern skulls have an essentially flat face, are globular (rather than elongated), and have a more nearly vertical forehead. The face is narrower and smaller, and the jaw has a protruding chin. The rest of the skeleton is less robust.

Multiregional Hypothesis

Advocates: Milford Wolpoff, University of Michigan
Alan Thorne, Australian National University

Based largely on the fossil evidence and the anatomical characteristics of modern populations, 'multiregional evolution' traces all modern populations back at least 1 million years to when early humans (*Homo erectus*) first left Africa. Modern *Homo sapiens* emerged gradually throughout the world, and as the populations dispersed, they remained in 'genetic contact'. This gene flow between neighboring populations ensured that the general 'modern human blueprint' was adopted by all. This limited gene flow still allowed for slight anatomical differences to be retained or develop in the regional populations. Wolpoff and Thorne who are advocates of this theory maintain that the mitochondrial DNA data can be interpreted in a way that supports the multi-regional model.

See *Scientific American* SPECIAL ISSUE: New Look at Human Evolution, Vol. 13(2), 2003, pp. 46-61, for two excellent articles on each of these models.

Replacement Hypothesis

Advocates: Christopher Stringer, Natural History Museum in London
The late Alan C. Wilson

Also known as the "Out of Africa Hypothesis" and "Eve Hypothesis". This model keeps *Homo sapiens* as a separate species and states that modern humans evolved from archaics in only one location, Africa, and then spread, replacing the archaic populations when they came in contact. The extinction of these regional archaic populations occurred because the modern humans were better adapted. In support of this theory, the late Allan C. Wilson and colleagues carried out genetic studies on modern endemic human populations. They concluded that the evolutionary record of mitochondrial DNA could be traced back to a single female who lived in Africa some 200 000 years ago. This woman, real or hypothetical, has been dubbed 'Eve' by Wilson and his team. By implication, this theory maintains that all modern descendants contain mitochondrial DNA that can be traced directly back to Eve.

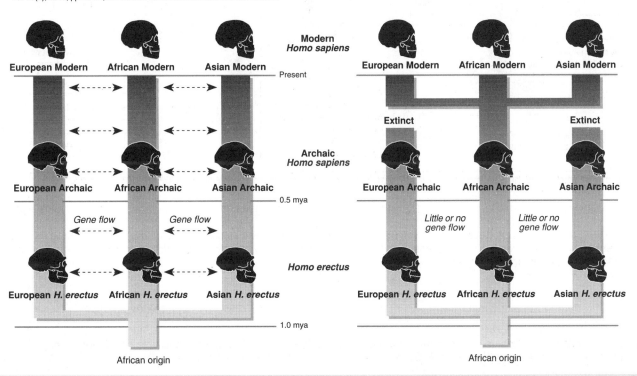

Human Evolution

Predictions made by this model

1. Fossils that show the change from one stage to the next in all geographic regions (transitional forms).

2. Modern traits should appear in the fossil record somewhat simultaneously all over the Old World range of Archaic *Homo sapiens*.

3. Today's modern "racial" traits characteristic of a particular region can be traced back to ancient forms in that region.

4. The human species today should have a high degree of genetic diversity since it is an old species with distinct populations that have had a lot of time to accumulate genetic differences.

5. The amount of genetic variation within each modern human group is about the same since they have all been evolving together.

Source: Michael A. Park, Biological Anthropology, Mayfield Publishing, 1996

Predictions made by this model

1. Transitional forms would be found in only one place (in this case Africa) which is the area of origin for modern humans.

2. Modern traits should appear first in one location (Africa) and then later elsewhere as the modern population spread to other parts of the Old World.

3. Modern and archaic populations should overlap in time outside the area that moderns originated (the process of replacement would not be instantaneous).

4. Humans today should have relatively little genetic diversity since the species is young.

5. Today's modern populations should differ in the amount of genetic variation, the most diversity being found in the region where moderns first evolved (this would have been the oldest group and therefore the one that had the most time for genetic variation to accumulate).

The map below shows a probable origin and dispersal of modern humans throughout the world. An African origin is almost certain, with south eastern Africa being the most likely region. The dispersal was affected at crucial stages by the presence or absence of 'land bridges' formed during the drop in sea level that occurs with the onset of ice ages. The late development of boating and rafting technology slowed dispersal into Australia and the Pacific. New Zealand was one of the last places on Earth to be populated. (On the map, ya = years ago).

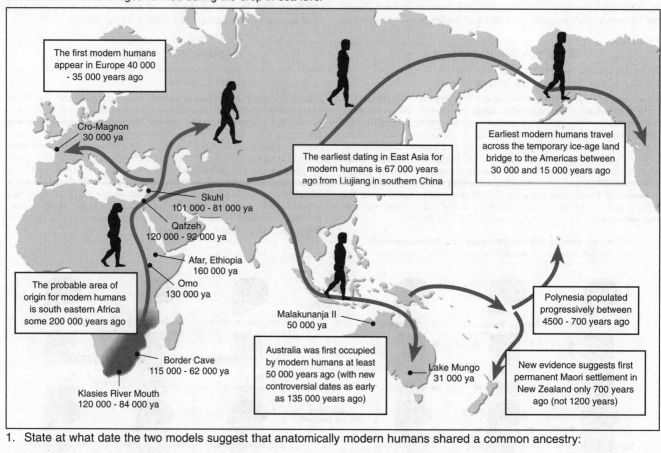

The first modern humans appear in Europe 40 000 - 35 000 years ago

Cro-Magnon
30 000 ya

Skuhl
101 000 - 81 000 ya

Qafzeh
120 000 - 92 000 ya

Afar, Ethiopia
160 000 ya

Omo
130 000 ya

The probable area of origin for modern humans is south eastern Africa some 200 000 years ago

Border Cave
115 000 - 62 000 ya

Klasies River Mouth
120 000 - 84 000 ya

The earliest dating in East Asia for modern humans is 67 000 years ago from Liujiang in southern China

Earliest modern humans travel across the temporary ice-age land bridge to the Americas between 30 000 and 15 000 years ago

Malakunanja II
50 000 ya

Australia was first occupied by modern humans at least 50 000 years ago (with new controversial dates as early as 135 000 years ago)

Lake Mungo
31 000 ya

Polynesia populated progressively between 4500 - 700 years ago

New evidence suggests first permanent Maori settlement in New Zealand only 700 years ago (not 1200 years)

1. State at what date the two models suggest that anatomically modern humans shared a common ancestry:

   (a) Replacement model: _____ years ago   (b) Multiregional model: _____ years ago

2. In 1992, paleoanthropologists (*Nature*, Vol. 357, page 404) recovered the remains of two *Homo erectus* skulls in China, that have modern faces but still possess a cranium typical of *Homo erectus*. Identify which of the two models this new evidence supports and why:

   _____

   _____

3. Mitochondrial DNA was used to compare the genetic relatedness of modern human endemic populations (i.e. native populations from around the world). Explain why it was used instead of DNA from the nucleus:

   _____

   _____

4. Explain the significance of the **gene flow** between early populations of humans in the multiregional model:

   _____

   _____

5. In the 'Out of Africa' model, modern humans move out of Africa to populate the rest of the world. Describe the fate of the other human populations already inhabiting these regions, according to this theory:

   _____

   _____

6. Discuss the implications of an early (135 000 ya) arrival of modern humans into Australia: _____

   _____

Adaptations for Bipedalism

Important modifications in the skeleton are associated with the move to bipedal locomotion in early hominins. The skeleton on the next page is an example of an early bipedal hominin. It is a reconstruction of 'Lucy' (*Australopithecus afarensis*) dated at about 3 million years ago. While Lucy still possessed some ape-like characteristics, such as curved toes, she was a fully-bipedal hominin with all the modern adaptations associated with modern human walking. Lucy was a small individual, only 1.1 meters tall, about the height of a 5-6 year old child. Although there is no doubt that Lucy was habitually bipedal, a number of skeletal features suggest that tree climbing was still an important part of this hominin's niche. Such activities may have been associated with escape from predators, obtaining a secure sleeping place, and foraging for foods found in trees. The features indicating a link with **arboreal** locomotion are indicated on the gorilla skeleton below. *A. afarensis* forms an important link between the quadrupedal locomotion of apes and bipedalism in hominins.

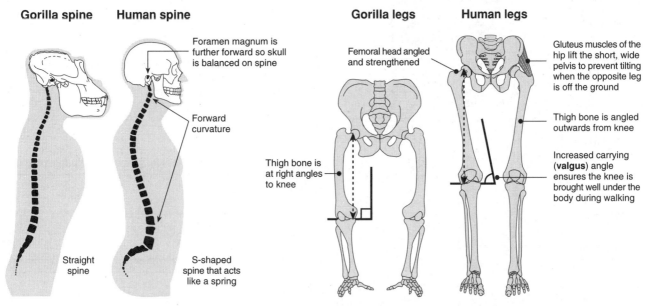

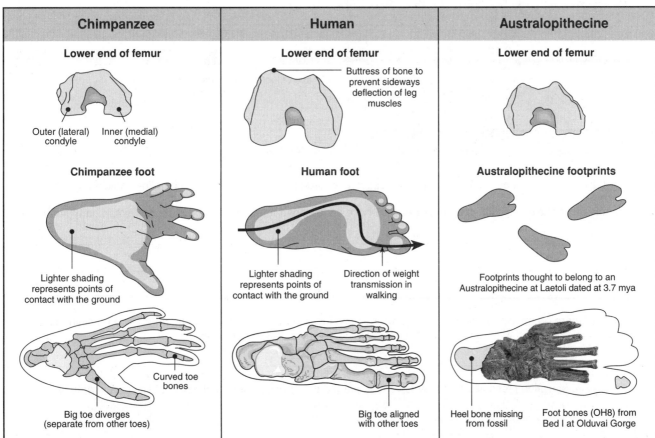

1. Referring to the diagram above, describe whether each of the **australopithecine fossils** compare more closely to the *chimpanzee* or *human* examples (i.e. to which do they bear the closest resemblance):

(a) Lower end of femur: _____

(b) Foot prints: _____

(c) Foot skeleton: _____

Web links: Bipedalism and Nakedness, Compare the Skeletons

RA 3

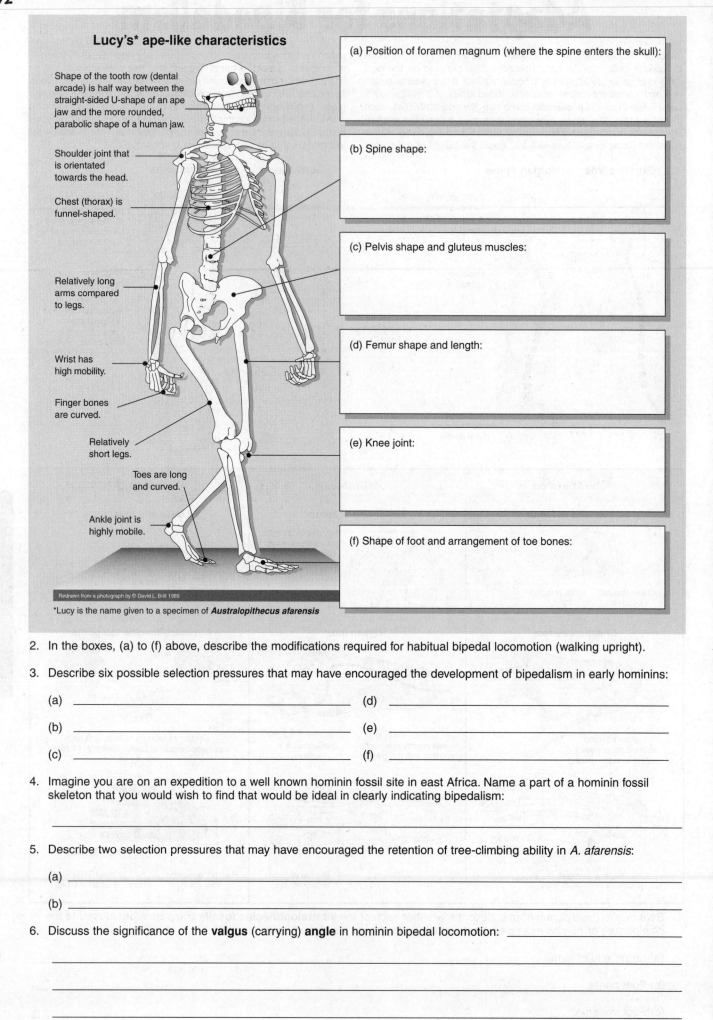

Lucy's* ape-like characteristics

Shape of the tooth row (dental arcade) is half way between the straight-sided U-shape of an ape jaw and the more rounded, parabolic shape of a human jaw.

Shoulder joint that is orientated towards the head.

Chest (thorax) is funnel-shaped.

Relatively long arms compared to legs.

Wrist has high mobility.

Finger bones are curved.

Relatively short legs.

Toes are long and curved.

Ankle joint is highly mobile.

Redrawn from a photograph by © David L. Brill 1985

*Lucy is the name given to a specimen of **Australopithecus afarensis**

(a) Position of foramen magnum (where the spine enters the skull):

(b) Spine shape:

(c) Pelvis shape and gluteus muscles:

(d) Femur shape and length:

(e) Knee joint:

(f) Shape of foot and arrangement of toe bones:

2. In the boxes, (a) to (f) above, describe the modifications required for habitual bipedal locomotion (walking upright).

3. Describe six possible selection pressures that may have encouraged the development of bipedalism in early hominins:

(a) _____   (d) _____

(b) _____   (e) _____

(c) _____   (f) _____

4. Imagine you are on an expedition to a well known hominin fossil site in east Africa. Name a part of a hominin fossil skeleton that you would wish to find that would be ideal in clearly indicating bipedalism:

_____

5. Describe two selection pressures that may have encouraged the retention of tree-climbing ability in A. afarensis:

(a) _____

(b) _____

6. Discuss the significance of the **valgus** (carrying) **angle** in hominin bipedal locomotion: _____

_____

_____

_____

The Development of Intelligence

The human brain is an extraordinary organ and is responsible for our unique human behavioral qualities. Although it makes up just 2% of our body weight, it demands about 20% of the body's metabolic energy at rest. This makes the brain an expensive organ to maintain. The selection pressures for increased brain size must have been considerable for additional energy to be made available. The normal human adult brain averages around 1330 cc, but ranges in size between 1000 and 2000 cc. The modern brain contains as many as 10 000 million nerve cells, each of which has thousands of synaptic connections with other nerve cells. But intelligence is not just a function of **brain size**. There are large mammals, such as elephants and whales, with brain volumes greater than ourselves and yet they are not considered to be as intelligent. It appears that what is more important is the brain size relative to body size. Modern humans have a brain volume three times larger than that predicted for an average monkey or ape with our body size. Another important factor is the way in which the brain is organized. Two areas of the brain have become highly developed in modern humans: **Broca's area** concerned with speech and **Wernicke's area** concerned with comprehension of language.

Growth in Brain size in Humans and Chimpanzees

In most primates, including chimpanzees, brain growth, relative to body size, slows markedly after birth while body growth continues. In human infants, the slowing of brain growth does not occur until more than a year after birth, which results in larger brain masses for humans than for chimpanzees at any given age (or body weight).

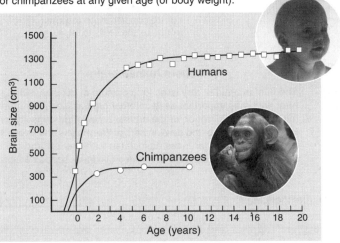

Brain Volume for Hominin Species

This table provides a generalized summary of the changes in estimated brain volume recorded from the fossil remains of hominins. The dates for each species are generally the middle of their time range for long-lived species or at the beginning of their time range for short-lived species.

Hominin species	Years ago (mya)	Average brain Volume (cm³)
Australopithecus afarensis	3.5	440
Australopithecus africanus	2.5	450
Paranthropus robustus	2.0	520
Paranthropus boisei	1.5	515
Homo rudolfensis	2.0	700
Homo habilis	1.8	575
Homo ergaster	1.8	800
Homo erectus	0.5	1100
Homo heidelbergensis	0.2	1250
Homo neanderthalensis	0.05	1550
Homo floresiensis	0.095*	380
Early *Homo sapiens*	0.08	1450

* *H. floresiensis* may have lived as recently as 13 000 ya

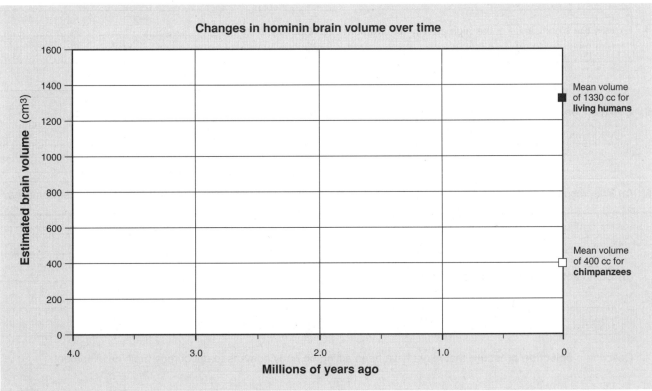

Changes in hominin brain volume over time

Mean volume of 1330 cc for **living humans**

Mean volume of 400 cc for **chimpanzees**

Human Evolution

1. Plot the data in the table on the estimated *Brain Volume for Hominin Species* (above) onto the graph provided.

2. There were two 'bursts' (sudden increases) of brain expansion during human evolution. **Indicate on the graph** you have plotted where you think these two events occurred.

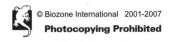

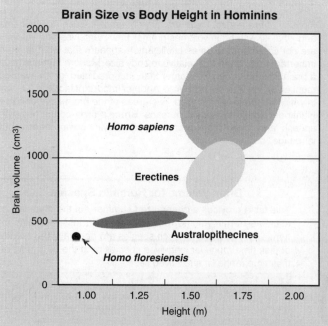

Brain Size vs Body Height in Hominins

Homo sapiens

Erectines

Australopithecines

Homo floresiensis

Brain size can be correlated with body height in hominins. Three distinct clusters emerge, indicating three phases of evolutionary development. *Homo floresiensis*, found on the Indonesian island of Flores, clearly falls outside these clusters. Its brain size to body size ratio is similar to that of the Australopithecines, but key aspects of its morphology, such as its small canine teeth and organization of the brain, identify it as *Homo*. In addition, the Flores finds were associated with relatively advanced stone tools.

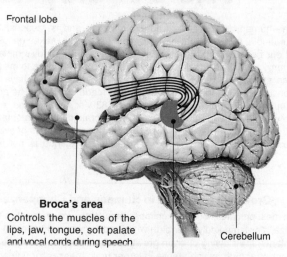

Frontal lobe

Broca's area
Controls the muscles of the lips, jaw, tongue, soft palate and vocal cords during speech

Cerebellum

Wernicke's area
The area of the brain concerned with the comprehension of spoken words, i.e. the ability to listen.

Modern human brain

The human brain is very large for a primate of our size, but this may not be as important as its internal organization. The most important specialization of the human brain is the capacity for language: a result of the development of **Wernicke's** and **Broca's areas**. Specific differences associated with the left and right hemispheres of the brain are associated with these specializations.

3. Explain why brain volume alone is not a reliable indicator of intelligence: _____

_____

_____

4. Explain the significance of the high energy requirement of a relatively large brain: _____

_____

_____

5. Comment on the significance of the brain/body size growth curve in humans compared with other primates:

_____

_____

6. (a) With respect to stature and brain size, comment on the position of *Homo floresiensis* with respect to other hominins:

_____

_____

(b) Comment on the significance of the Flores finds: _____

_____

_____

7. Describe a **selection pressure** that might have been acting on early humans to encourage brain development:

_____

_____

_____

Cultural Evolution

Natural selection acting on the expression of genes brought about considerable transformations in the anatomy of early humans. In addition, it was possible for ideas and behaviors that were learned to be passed on to offspring. This non-genetic means of adaptation, called **cultural evolution**, further enhanced the success of early humans.

Resulting physical features

The physical features that developed in response to selection pressures of the environment include:

Head balanced on the top of the backbone, instead of held up by large neck muscles. Large brain capable of learning, planning and passing on ideas. Very keen eyesight, capable of judging distances with eyes located high above the ground. Other senses are less well developed. Light but strong jaw, with teeth suitable for varied foods. Backbone slightly curved, allowing upright standing on two legs without getting tired, thus freeing hands, and giving eyes good all round vision. Hands able to grasp and manipulate objects in a very sensitive way. Legs that allowed efficient walking and running on two legs. Flexible ankle, but rigid and arched foot, allowing efficient walking on hard ground.

Environmental forces

Over many millions of years, the evolution of human ancestors has been directed by the forces of natural selection. Environmental forces such as climatic change causing alterations in habitat and food supply, as well as fierce predators, acted on the gene pool.

Climatic change

The climate became drier and the forests which were the homes of the earlier primates gradually disappeared. This not only reduced shelter but also meant that traditional food sources became scarce or disappeared. New food resources had to be experimented with.

Fierce predators

Many large and fierce predators made a ground dwelling lifestyle dangerous. Early humans would have to protect themselves from attack using smart behavioral solutions.

Adopted niche

An opportunist/scavenger that was able to live reasonably successfully on the ground. Able to exploit a number of varied habitats, early humans utilized a range of food resources.

Cultural forces

Because of the unique combination of brain and specialized physical features mentioned above, early humans very gradually began to direct the course of their own evolution. They began to control their environment; to use it to alter their way of life. At first they did this in small ways, and with little effect on other living things. The result was the development of efficient hunters living in organized groups. Their genes had been almost unchanged, but they now lived more comfortably, with a better survival rate, and more time to plan ahead.

Tool making
Tools made by chipping stones, or shaping bones or wood were used in a wide variety of ways. In some cases, the use of tools replaced the need to develop physical features.

Fire making
Fire is a powerful tool. It provided a means of keeping warm in cold periods, deterring predators from a camp site, and driving animals during a hunt. It was also used to cook, allowing difficult to digest food to be eaten more easily.

Shelter and clothing
The earliest shelters were probably natural ones, such as caves, overhangs and large trees. Creating artificial shelters allowed flexibility in where they were located. Clothing enhanced their ability to withstand cold.

Cooperative hunting
Working in organized groups requiring considerable coordination, early humans were able to tackle large game that would be impossible for a solitary hunter.

1. Explain what is meant by **cultural evolution**: _____

_____

_____

Human Evolution

Related activities: Artificial Selection, The Domestication of Wheat
Web links: Neanderthals: Dig and Deduce

RA 2

Development of Agriculture

People learned to plant and look after food plants, especially grains, and to domesticate animals. In the Middle East, about 8000 BC they learned to grow wheat, while in Mexico, about 500 BC they began to grow maize.

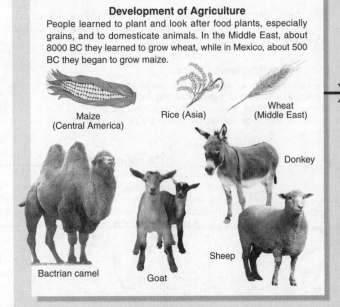

Maize
(Central America)

Rice (Asia)

Wheat
(Middle East)

Donkey

Bactrian camel

Goat

Sheep

Development of Stable Settlements

Communities of successful grain cultivators grew up, living in permanent, stable settlements of quite large size. Such people developed qualities such as patience, industry and a sense of property, and prepared the way for the next step.

Development of Cities

As communities became larger, trade and commerce began to develop. Large cities grew up where markets and trading systems developed. These were places where people could develop special skills such as pottery and metal work. It also resulted in rivalry between states and in wars.

The Present and the Future

Humankind's success has given us the problems of pollution and over-population. Not only can we modify our environment, but because of our knowledge of genetics, we are actually directing the evolution of other living things by selective breeding. It even seems likely that we may soon be able to direct our own evolution by actually altering genes. In fact we are reaching a stage where we have so much power to alter the environment that we need to think and act very carefully.

The Knowledge Explosion

The sharing of ideas, and more free time for some in the cities resulted in a great speeding up of cultural evolution. In the last 200 years there has been a very rapid development of science and technology. Humankind developed the power to dominate the environment completely. In particular, medical science has largely solved the problems of infectious disease, and technology has allowed us to produce material wealth at a staggering rate.

The move from opportunist scavenger to hunter-gatherer was a major stage in the cultural evolution of humans. It was taken in a series of small steps, over a very long time (perhaps a million years). A few human societies, such as the Australian aborigines last century, were still at this stage until very recently.

2. Describe two probable effects of a drying climate on the selection pressures directing the evolution of early hominids:

_____

_____

_____

3. Explain how each of the cultural developments listed below enhanced the survival ability of early humans:

(a) Manufacture of bone and stone tools: _____

_____

(b) Shelters and clothing: _____

_____

(c) Use of fire: _____

_____

(d) Cooperative hunting: _____

_____

(e) Development of agriculture: _____

_____

(f) Commerce and communication: _____

_____

Diet and Animal Nutrition

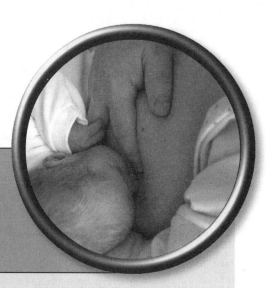

IB SL
Complete:
1, 11-12, 15, 19, 21, 23
Extension: 2-3

IB HL
Complete:
1, 11-12, 15, 19, 21, 23
Extension: 2-3

IB Options
Complete:
Option A: 29-36
Option H: HL: 13-14, 16-18, 20, 22, 24-28

AP Biology
Complete:
1-28
Some numbers extension as appropriate

Learning Objectives

☐ 1. Compile your own glossary from the **KEY WORDS** displayed in **bold type** in the learning objectives below.

Modes of Nutrition *(page 159)*

☐ 2. Distinguish between the different modes of nutrition: **autotrophic**, chemoheterotrophic (=**heterotrophic**). Identify the source of energy and carbon in each case. Define **nutrient** and describe their general role.

Heterotrophic Nutrition *(pages 159-174 and the TRC: Mammalian Dentition)*

☐ 3. Explain why animals need to feed. Describe the three principal modes of **heterotrophic nutrition**: **parasitic**, **saprophytic** (=**saprobiontic**), **holozoic**.

☐ 4. Describe **saprophytic nutrition** as illustrated by the bread mold *Rhizopus*. Identify the structural adaptations of the fungus, the type of food utilized, nutrients and other growth requirements, and the method by which the food is digested and absorbed.

☐ 5. Describe the **parasitic nutrition** of a typical cestode **parasite** as illustrated by the pork tapeworm *Taenia solium*. Identify the structural adaptations of the parasite, the type of food utilized, nutrients and other growth requirements, and the method by which the food is digested and absorbed.

☐ 6. Explain what is meant by **mutualistic nutrition** as illustrated by the nutritional relationship between:
  • Nitrogen-fixing bacterium *Rhizobium* and members of the legume family.
  • Cellulose digesting bacteria and ruminants. Identify the location of the bacteria in the ruminant gut.

☐ 7. Recognize **holozoic nutrition** as the most common nutritional mode amongst animals. Describe structural and functional diversity in the guts and feeding appendages of animals. You may wish to compare phyla, or make comparisons within the same order.

☐ 8. Classify holozoic animals according to the type of food eaten: e.g. **carnivore**, **omnivore**, **herbivore**, and according to the form of the food they take in e.g. large or small particles, or fluid.

☐ 9. Recognize diversity in **feeding methods** amongst holozoic animals by describing the structures and processes involved in fluid feeding, filter feeding, deposit feeding, cropping, and bulk feeding.

☐ 10. Identify and describe the adaptations of mammalian **herbivores** and **carnivores**, as illustrated by a named **ruminant** and a named carnivore. Include reference to:
  • Gut length and the relative capacity of gut regions.
  • The structure of the stomach (simple vs complex).
  • The digestive enzymes present and the role of microbial digestion in nutrition and protein intake.
  • The type and arrangement of teeth (the dentition).

☐ 11. Explain why the **digestion** of large food molecules is essential. Recognize the stages involved in processing food: **ingestion**, **digestion**, **absorption**, and **egestion**. Identify the location of these processes in a generalized **alimentary canal** (**gut**).

Digestion and Absorption in Humans

Enzymes and digestion *(pages 29, 173-176, 179)*

☐ 12. Explain the need for **enzymes** in digestion. Identify broad categories of digestive enzymes.

☐ 13. Identify the digestive glands in humans and their secretions. Describe the composition of **saliva**, **gastric juice**, and **pancreatic juice**. Explain the role of these in providing the optimum pH for enzyme activity.

☐ 14. Draw and explain the structural features of **exocrine glands** as seen using electron microscopy.

☐ 15. Describe the sites of production (source), **substrate**, products (of digestion) and optimum pH conditions for (at least) one **amylase**, **protease**, and **lipase** enzyme.

☐ 16. Explain why protein-digesting enzymes (e.g. pepsin and trypsin) are secreted as inactive precursors. State how they are activated at their site of action.

☐ 17. Discuss the roles of gastric acid and the bacterium *Helicobacter pylori* in the development of ulcers and cancer in the stomach.

☐ 18. Identify examples of membrane-bound enzymes in the epithelium of the small intestine and outline their role. Explain why cellulose is not digested in the human gut.

☐ 19. Draw and label a diagram of the digestive system (e.g. in humans). Identify mouth, esophagus, stomach, liver, small and large intestine, anus, pancreas, and gall bladder. Outline the function of the **stomach**, **small intestine**, and **large intestine**.

☐ 20. Describe the composition and secretion of **bile**. Explain the problem of lipid digestion in a hydrophilic medium and the role of bile in overcoming this problem.

Absorption and transport *(pages 172-178, 180)*

☐ 21. Distinguish between **absorption** and **assimilation**. Identify where each of the following is absorbed: water, small molecules (alcohol, glucose), breakdown products of carbohydrate, protein, and fat digestion.

☐ 22. Draw a portion of the **ileum** in transverse section as seen using light microscopy. Your diagram should show the basic features including the **mucosa** and layers of **longitudinal** and **circular muscle**.

☐ 23. Describe the structure of a villus (including blood and lymph vessels). In general terms, describe how the structure is related to its role in absorption.

☐ 24. Explain the structural features of an epithelial cell of a villus as seen using electron microscopy. Include reference to the following: **microvilli**, **mitochondria**, **pinocytotic vesicles**, and **tight junctions**.

25. Describe the mechanisms by which nutrients are absorbed in the ileum, including the roles of **diffusion**, **facilitated diffusion**, and **active transport** (including **endocytosis**). Appreciate the role of micelles and chylomicrons in lipid absorption and transport.

26. List the materials that are not absorbed and are **egested** and, if required, explain why they remain undigested. Explain the role of the large intestine and rectum in feces formation and egestion.

27. Outline the control of digestive secretion by nerves and hormones, using gastric secretion as an example.

Functions of the Liver *(pages 179, 261-262)*

28. Describe the structure and function of the liver including its role in:
    (a) Regulating nutrient levels in the blood.
    (b) Storage of nutrients.
    (c) Synthesis of plasma proteins and cholesterol.
    (d) Detoxification, e.g. of alcohol.
    (e) Breakdown of hemoglobin.

The Human Diet *(pages 41-42, 178, 181-186, 246)*

29. Give a definition of the term **nutrient**. List the nutrients essential in the human **diet**, and outline their role. Recognize the basis of a **balanced diet** and recognize the role of adequate nutrition in health.

30. Understand aspects of the nutritional requirements in humans with reference to the following:
    (a) The difference between vitamins and minerals, and the role of these in a balanced diet.
    (b) Protein intake and the consequences of **protein deficiency malnutrition**.
    (c) The causes and effects of phenylketonuria (PKU) and the role of diet in managing this disorder.
    (d) The health consequences of diets rich in different types of fatty acids (including monounsaturates).
    (e) The recommended daily intake of **vitamin C** (ascorbic acid) and the consequences of insufficient and excessive intake.

(f) Requirement for calciferol (**vitamin D**), including the consequences of insufficient intake.

(g) The benefits of artificial supplementation as a means of preventing malnutrition using **iodine** supplementation as an example.

(h) The importance of **fiber** as a component of a balanced diet.

(i) The role of other vitamins and minerals (as required), e.g. vitamin A, zinc, calcium, and iron, including disorders arising from deficiencies.

31. Compare the energy content of carbohydrate, fat, and protein. Appreciate how energy needs may vary according to age, gender, **activity** level and **basal metabolic rate**, and condition (e.g. **lean body mass**).

32. Outline the role of the appetite control center in the brain in regulating food intake.

33. Explain how **body mass index** (BMI) is used as a measure of healthy weight and calculate BMI for people of different height and weight.

34. Explain the possible health consequences of diets rich in excessive nutrients (e.g. lipid). Explain what is meant by **malnutrition** and distinguish it from starvation. Appreciate that malnutrition can be caused by any of a number of social, economic, cultural, or environmental factors, alone or in combination. With reference to this:
    (a) Outline the possible reasons for increasing rates of clinical **obesity** in some countries.
    (b) Outline the causes and symptoms of **type II diabetes mellitus** and explain how the disease can be managed through dietary modification.
    (c) Evaluate the evidence for the suggested benefits of reducing dietary **cholesterol**.
    (c) Outline the consequences of anorexia nervosa.

35. Discuss the ethical issues surrounding the eating of animal products, including meat, honey, eggs, and dairy products, including the rationale for the vegetarian or vegan choice.

36. Discuss the benefits of **breast-feeding**, including a evaluation of the difference in composition between human breast milk and artificial (formula) milk.

See the 'Textbook Reference Grid' on pages 8-9 for textbook page references relating to material in this topic.

Supplementary Texts

See pages 5-6 for additional details of this text:

■ Clegg, C.J., 1998. **Mammals: Structure and Function** (John Murray), pp. 12-23.

■ Fullick, A., 2000. **Human Health and Disease** (Heinemann), pp. 55-68.

■ Helms, D.R. *et al.*, 1998. **Biology in the Laboratory** (W.H. Freeman), #35, #40

■ Morton, D. & J.W. Perry, 1998. **Photo Atlas for Anatomy and Physiology** (W.H. Freeman).

See page 6 for details of publishers of periodicals:

STUDENT'S REFERENCE

■ **Why are we so Fat?** National Geographic, 206(2), Aug. 2004, pp. 46-61. *Obesity in America and around the world, including a summary of health problems associated with obesity.*

■ **The Happy Fat** New Scientist, 24 Aug. 2002, pp. 34-37. *The right amount of the right type of fat in the diet is important in mood stability.*

■ **The Good, the Fad and the Unhealthy** New Scientist, 27 Sept. 2006, pp. 42-49. *The facts, the myths and the downright lies of nutrition.*

■ **Minerals and Bioavailability** Biol. Sci. Rev., 12 (5) May 2000, pp. 38-40. *The role of minerals in the diet, including reference to their bioavailability.*

■ **The Pancreas and Pancreatitis** Biol. Sci. Rev., 13(5) May 2001, pp. 2-6. *The structure and role of the pancreas, including acinar cell secretion.*

■ **The Biology of Milk** Biol. Sci. Rev., 16(3) Feb. 2004, pp. 2-6. *The production and composition of milk, its role in mammalian biology, and the physiological processes controlling its release.*

TEACHER'S REFERENCE

■ **Obesity: An Overblown Epidemic?** Scientific American, June 2005, pp. 48-55. *Arguments for and against the conventional wisdom linking obesity to poorer health and disease.*

■ **Lactose Intolerance** Biol. Sci. Rev., 17(3), Feb. 2005, pp. 28-31. *The nature of lactose intolerance: a physiological response following a genetically programed loss of the enzyme lactase.*

■ **Cut the Carbs** New Scientist, 18 March 2000, pp. 26-31. *An analysis of human dietary fads, and a synopsis of nutritional guidelines. A comparison of carnivore and herbivore guts is included.*

■ **Rebuilding the Food Pyramid** Scientific American, Jan. 2003, pp. 52-59. *A major revision of older nutritional guidelines. A critique of dietary information and an analysis of what we should be eating now (a good topic for debate).*

■ **A Pastry a Day** New Scientist, 26 Nov. 2005, pp. 39-41. *Questioning the accuracy of BMI and whether being overweight per se is a health risk.*

See pages 10-11 for details of how to access **Bio Links** from our web site: **www.thebiozone.com** From Bio Links, access sites under the topics:
ANIMAL BIOLOGY: • Comparative vertebrate anatomy lecture notes ... *and others* > **Nutrition:** • Human anatomy online - Digestive system • Large intestine: Introduction and index • Nutrient requirements • Constituents of human milk • The pancreas • Your digestive system and how it works ... *and others*

BIODIVERSITY > **Taxonomy and Classification** • Will's skull page

HEALTH AND DISEASE > **Human Health Issues:** • British Nutrition Foundation • Eat well, eat safe • National eating Disorder Association • What shape is your pyramid • Food science central • Food additives guide ... *and others*

Presentation MEDIA to support this topic:

HEALTH & DISEASE:
• **Non-infectious Disease**

Modes of Nutrition

The way in which living organisms obtain their source of energy and carbon is termed their nutritional mode. There is a great diversity in nutritional modes amongst different phyla, with the prokaryotes (bacteria) showing the greatest variety in terms of the range of organic and inorganic compounds used as energy sources. The diagram below illustrates the classification of nutritional modes in living organisms. The diagram simplifies the real situation and concentrates on the diversity within eukaryotic groups. Aspects of nutrition in a typical saprophyte and a specialized mammalian parasite are described later in this topic.

Nutritional Patterns in Organisms

Living organisms can be classified according to their source of energy and carbon. According to their **energy source**, organisms are classified as either **phototrophs** (using light as their main energy source) or **chemotrophs** (using inorganic or organic compounds for energy). As a **carbon source**, autotrophs (*self-feeders*) use carbon dioxide, and **heterotrophs** (*feeders on others*) need an organic carbon source. Most organisms are either photoautotrophs, chemoautotrophs, or chemoheterotrophs. Prokaryotes show a huge variety of nutritional modes. Many are photo- or chemoautotrophs (chemosynthetic) but a large number are chemoheterotrophs (as are animals and fungi). For many, the energy and carbon source is glucose.

Heterotrophic Nutrition (Chemoheterotrophs*)

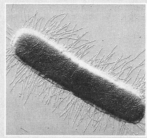

Most of the bacteria with which we are familiar are chemoheterotrophs.

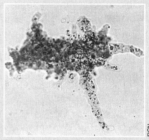

Protozoans, such as *Amoeba*, engulf food particles by phagocytosis.

* A few bacterial groups are photoheterotrophic.

Autotrophic Nutrition

Photoautotrophs: Photosynthetic bacteria, cyanobacteria, algae, plants.

Chemoautotrophs: Sulfur, iron, hydrogen, and nitrifying bacteria.

Fungi may be saprophytic (see below), parasitic, or mutualistic.

Feeding provides animals with a carbon and energy source: glucose.

Nutritional Modes of Heterotrophs

Heterotrophic organisms feed on organic material in order to obtain the energy and nutrients they require. They depend either directly on other organisms (dead or alive), or their by-products (e.g. feces, cell walls, or food stores). There are three principal modes of heterotrophic nutrition: saprophytic (saprotrophic), parasitic, and holozoic. Within the animal phyla, holozoic nutrition is the most common nutritional mode.

Most fungi and many bacteria are saprophytes (also called saprotrophs). They are decomposer organisms feeding off dead or decaying matter.

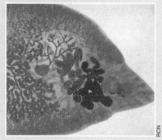

Parasites, e.g. flukes, live on or within their host for much or all of their life. Bacteria, fungi, protists, and animals all have parasitic representatives.

Holozoic means to feed on solid organic material from the bodies of other organisms. It is the main feeding mode of animals, although a few specialized plants may obtain some nutrients this way. Holozoic animals are classified according to the form of the food they take in: small or large particles, or fluid.

1. Discuss the differences in nutritional mode between photoautotrophs, chemoautotrophs, and chemoheterotrophs:

_____

_____

_____

_____

_____

2. Explain how saprotrophs differ from parasites: _____

_____

Diet and Animal Nutrition

Related activities: Plants as Producers, Saprophytic Nutrition, Parasitic Nutrition

A 2

Saprophytic Nutrition

All fungi lack chlorophyll and are **heterotrophic**, absorbing nutrients by direct absorption from the substrate. Many are **saprophytic** (also called saprotrophic or saprobiontic), feeding on dead organic matter, although some are parasitic or live in a relationship with another organism (mutualistic). Parasitic fungi are common plant pathogens, invading plant tissues through stomata, wounds, or by penetrating the epidermis. Mutualistic fungi are very important: they form lichens in association with algae or cyanobacteria, and the mutualistic mycorrhizal associations between fungi and plant roots are essential to the health of many forest plants. Saprophytic fungi, together with bacteria, are the major decomposers of the biosphere. They contribute to decay and therefore to nutrient recycling. Like all fungi, the body is composed of rapidly growing filaments called **hyphae**, which are **usually** divided by incomplete compartments called **septa**. The hyphae together form a large mass called a **mycelium** (the feeding body of the fungus). The familiar mushroom-like structures that we see are the above-ground reproductive bodies that arise from the main mycelium. The nutrition of a typical saprophyte, *Rhizopus*, is outlined below.

Bread Mold (*Rhizopus*)

Saprophytes grow best in dark, moist environments, but are found wherever organic material is available. *Rhizopus* is a common fungus, found on damp, stale bread and rotting fruit. Unlike many fungi, *Rhizopus* has hyphae that are undivided by septa.

Sporangium (fruiting body)

Stolons: hyphae growing horizontally on the substrate

Hyphal tip enlarged right

Rhizoids: hyphae that anchor stolons to the substrate

The entire tangled aggregation of hyphae is termed the **mycelium**

Rhizopus mycelium

Saprophytic Nutrition in Bread Mold (*Rhizopus*)

Nutrients required by most saprophytes

An organic carbon source, e.g. starch, cellulose, glucose.

A source of nitrogen

Growth factors such as vitamins

Some ions, e.g. magnesium, phosphorus, trace elements

Hypha

Transport

Cell wall

Products absorbed

Enzymatic digestion

Excess nutrients are stored as glycogen within **vacuoles** in the mycelium.

Sugars
Fatty acids
Glycerol
Amino acids

Digestion occurs outside the fungal body. The small molecules are then absorbed by the hyphae across the chitinous cell wall and the plasma membrane and are transported to all parts of the fungus.

Enzymes secreted from the hyphal tip digest the complex carbohydrate, proteins, and fats in the substrate.

The environmental requirements of fungi are met by the substrate on which they are growing:

■ Temperature between 5° and 25°C
■ Water (the fungal body is about 90% water)
■ Oxygen (very few fungi are anaerobic)
■ Neutral to slightly acid pH (pH 5.6-7) .

1. (a) Clearly describe the structure of the feeding body of a saprophytic fungus: _____

_____

(b) Explain why a moist environment is essential for fungal growth: _____

2. Identify four nutrients required by a saprophytic fungus:

(a) _____ (c) _____

(b) _____ (d) _____

3. State where these nutrients come from: _____

_____

4. Describe the way in which a saprophytic fungus obtains its nutrients: _____

_____

_____

5. Contrast digestion and absorption in a saprophytic fungus and a holozoic animal: _____

_____

_____

Related activities: The Human Digestive Tract

Parasitic Nutrition

Parasitism is the most common of all symbiotic relationships. Here the host is always harmed by the presence of the parasite but is usually not killed. The main benefit derived by the parasite is obtaining nutrition, but there may be secondary advantages, such as protection. Many animal groups have members that have adopted a **parasitic** lifestyle, although parasites occur more commonly in particular taxa. Insects, some annelids (e.g. leeches), and flatworms have many parasitic representatives, and two classes of flatworms are entirely parasitic. Animal parasites are highly specialized carnivores, feeding off the body fluids or skin of host species. Parasites that attach to the outside of a host are called **ectoparasites** and have mouthparts specialized for piercing and sucking blood or tissue fluids. Those that live within the body of the host are called **endoparasites**. They may obtain nutrients by sucking or absorb simple food compounds directly from the host, as in the case of the pork tapeworm shown below. All 3400 or so species of tapeworm are endoparasites and the majority are adapted for living in the guts of vertebrates. In all species, a primary host and one or more intermediate hosts are required to complete the life cycle.

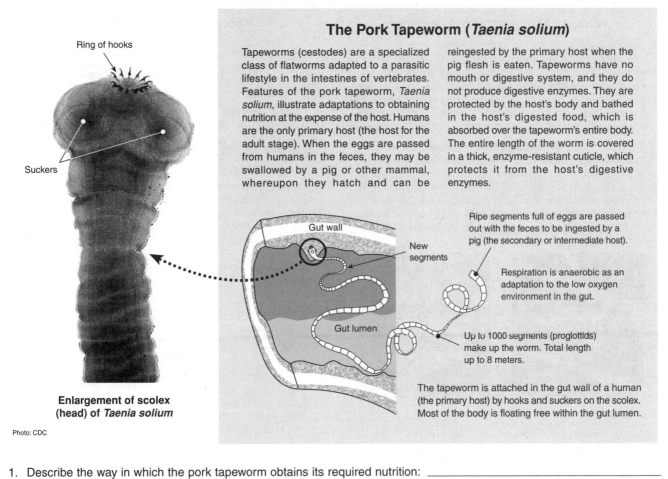

Ring of hooks

Suckers

Enlargement of scolex (head) of *Taenia solium*

Photo: CDC

The Pork Tapeworm (*Taenia solium*)

Tapeworms (cestodes) are a specialized class of flatworms adapted to a parasitic lifestyle in the intestines of vertebrates. Features of the pork tapeworm, *Taenia solium*, illustrate adaptations to obtaining nutrition at the expense of the host. Humans are the only primary host (the host for the adult stage). When the eggs are passed from humans in the feces, they may be swallowed by a pig or other mammal, whereupon they hatch and can be reingested by the primary host when the pig flesh is eaten. Tapeworms have no mouth or digestive system, and they do not produce digestive enzymes. They are protected by the host's body and bathed in the host's digested food, which is absorbed over the tapeworm's entire body. The entire length of the worm is covered in a thick, enzyme-resistant cuticle, which protects it from the host's digestive enzymes.

Gut wall

New segments

Gut lumen

Ripe segments full of eggs are passed out with the feces to be ingested by a pig (the secondary or intermediate host).

Respiration is anaerobic as an adaptation to the low oxygen environment in the gut.

Up to 1000 segments (proglottids) make up the worm. Total length up to 8 meters.

The tapeworm is attached in the gut wall of a human (the primary host) by hooks and suckers on the scolex. Most of the body is floating free within the gut lumen.

1. Describe the way in which the pork tapeworm obtains its required nutrition: _____

_____

2. Briefly describe four adaptations of the pork tapeworm for its parasitic lifestyle (include two nutritional adaptations):

(a) _____

(b) _____

(c) _____

(d) _____

3. (a) Explain what is meant by a primary host: _____

(b) Explain what is meant by an intermediate host: _____

(c) Name the primary host for the pork tapeworm: _____

(d) Name an intermediate host for the pork tapeworm: _____

4. Identify a similarity between the nutrition of a tapeworm and the nutrition of a saprophytic fungus (see previous page):

_____

5. Name another animal parasite and give its primary host: _____

Related activities: Saprophytic Nutrition

RA 2

Diet and Animal Nutrition

Mutualistic Nutrition

Although nitrogen is an abundant element, making up about 80% of the Earth's atmosphere, biologically available nitrogen compounds are relatively scarce. Atmospheric nitrogen (N_2) is stable, and a lot of energy is required to break the dinitrogen bond and form organic compounds. However, many prokaryotes are able to do this, and plants that can use bacteria to fix nitrogen have a great nutritional advantage. Much of the nitrogen available to plants is supplied by nitrogen-fixing bacteria. These bacteria reduce atmospheric nitrogen to ammonium ions, combining them with organic acids to produce amino acids. The amino acids provide a nitrogen supply to plants. Nitrogen fixation in plants occurs within **root nodules**: unique associations or **symbioses** between plants and nitrogen fixing bacteria. The presence of nodules allows plants to grow successfully even when soil nitrate is low. When the plant dies, the nitrogen is returned to the soil through decomposition. For this reason, nitrogen fixing plants (particularly legumes) are important in soil management, and promote natural soil fertility when used in crop rotations.

Nitrogen Fixation in Root Nodules

Root nodules are a root **symbiosis** between a higher plant and a bacterium. The bacteria fix atmospheric nitrogen and are extremely important to the nutrition of many plants, including the economically important legume family. Root nodules are extensions of the root tissue caused by entry of a bacterium. In legumes, this bacterium is *Rhizobium*. Other bacterial genera are involved in the root nodule symbioses in non-legume species.

The bacteria in these symbioses live in the nodule where they fix atmospheric nitrogen and provide the plant with most, or all, of its nitrogen requirements. In return, they have access to a rich supply of carbohydrate. The fixation of atmospheric nitrogen to ammonia occurs within the nodule, using the enzyme **nitrogenase**. Nitrogenase is inhibited by oxygen and the nodule provides a low O_2 environment in which fixation can occur.

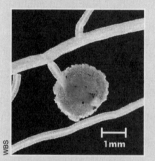 

1mm

WBS

Two examples of legume nodules caused by *Rhizobium*. The photographs above show the size of a single nodule (left), and the nodules forming clusters around the roots of *Acacia* (right).

Root Nodules in Legumes

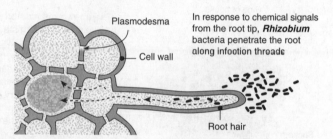

Plasmodesma

Cell wall

In response to chemical signals from the root tip, *Rhizobium* bacteria penetrate the root along infection threads

Root hair

After infecting a root, the bacteria produce a hormone-like chemical, which induces the formation of the enlarged nodule. *Rhizobium* bacteria are free living in the soil, but adopt a large bacteroid morphology when they invade a root and induce nodule formation.

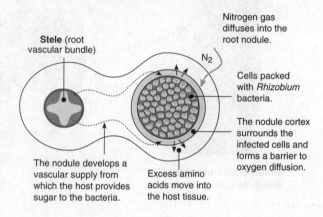

Stele (root vascular bundle)

Nitrogen gas diffuses into the root nodule.

N_2

Cells packed with *Rhizobium* bacteria.

The nodule cortex surrounds the infected cells and forms a barrier to oxygen diffusion.

The nodule develops a vascular supply from which the host provides sugar to the bacteria.

Excess amino acids move into the host tissue.

1. Explain the term **symbiosis** in relation to plants and nitrogen fixing bacteria: _____

_____

2. Root nodules are a mutualistic relationship between a bacterium and a plant. Explain the benefits of the relationship to:

   (a) The plant: _____

   _____

   (b) The bacterium: _____

   _____

3. Identify the bacterial genus involved in root nodule formation in legumes: _____

4. Explain the purpose of the following features of a root nodule:

   (a) The nodule cortex: _____

   (b) The vascular supply to the nodule: _____

5. Identify two examples of leguminous plants: _____

6. Identify the stimulus for the formation of the enlarged nodule: _____

_____

Related activities: Uptake in the Root

Methods of Feeding

Animals show great variety in their diets and their methods of obtaining food. Animals may feed on solid or fluid food and may suck, bite, lap, or swallow it whole. The adaptations of mouthparts and other feeding appendages reflects both the diet and the way in which they obtain their food. Different modes of feeding among animals are illustrated below.

Fluid feeding

Fly

Spider

Fluid feeders suck or lap up fluids such as blood, plant sap, or nectar. Many insects (flies, moths, butterflies, aphids), annelids, arachnids and some mammals exploit these food sources. Fluid feeders have mouthparts and guts that enable them to obtain and process a liquid diet. Many have piercing or tubular mouthparts to obtain fluids directly. Others, like spiders, secrete enzymes into the captured prey and then suck up their liquefied remains.

Filter feeding

Sponges and feather stars

Tubeworms

An extraordinary range of animals from simple sponges to large marine vertebrates, like the baleen whales, feed by filtering suspended particles out of the water. Special cells lining the body of sponges create water currents and engulf the food particles that are brought in. Many filter feeding annelids, echinoderms, and molluscs, e.g. tubeworms and feather stars, rely on mucus and cilia to trap food particles and move them to the mouth.

Bulk feeding and cropping

Lions

Chewing insect

A great number of animals feed on large food masses which may be caught (actively or otherwise) and ingested whole or in pieces. Examples include snakes and most mammalian predators. Most have fangs for holding prey and/or teeth for cutting flesh. Other animals are grazing or cropping herbivores (e.g. many insects and mammalian herbivores), cutting off pieces of vegetation and using their mouthparts to chew the vegetation into pieces.

Sieve and deposit feeding

Humpback whales

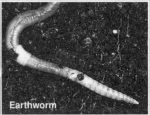
Earthworm

Humpback and other baleen whales use comblike plates suspended from the upper jaw to sieve shrimps and fish from large volumes of water. Food is trapped against the plates when the mouth closes and water is forced out. Earthworms are nonselective deposit feeders, moving through the soil using a powerful muscular pharynx to suck in a mix of organic and inorganic material. The undigested residue is egested as castings at the soil surface.

1. Describe one **structural** adaptation for obtaining food in the following animals:

    (a) A blood sucking mosquito: _____

    (b) A filter feeding whale: _____

    (c) A mammalian predatory carnivore: _____

    (d) A leaf chewing grasshopper: _____

    (e) An ambush predator, such as a python: _____

    (f) A filter feeding marine invertebrate: _____

    (g) *Hydra*: _____

2. Describe one **behavioral** adaptation for obtaining food in the following animals:

    (a) A blood sucking mosquito: _____

    (b) A filter feeding whale: _____

    (c) A mammalian predator: _____

    (d) Chimpanzees hunting for monkeys: _____

    (e) An ambush predator, such as a python: _____

    (f) A filter feeding marine invertebrate: _____

    (g) Scavenging bird (gull or vulture): _____

Related activities: Adaptations and Fitness, Insect Mouthparts

A 2

Diet and Animal Nutrition

Food Vacuoles and Simple Guts

The simplest form of digestion occurs inside cells (**intracellularly**) within food vacuoles. This process is relatively slow and digestion is exclusively intracellular only in protozoa and sponges. In animals with simple, sac-like guts, digestion begins **extracellularly** (with secretion of enzymes to the outside or into the digestive cavity) and is completed intracellularly.

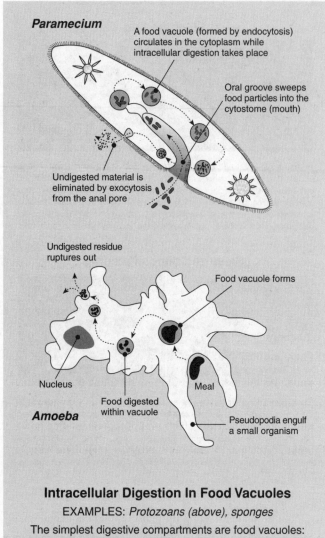

Paramecium

A food vacuole (formed by endocytosis) circulates in the cytoplasm while intracellular digestion takes place

Oral groove sweeps food particles into the cytostome (mouth)

Undigested material is eliminated by exocytosis from the anal pore

Undigested residue ruptures out

Food vacuole forms

Nucleus

Meal

Amoeba

Food digested within vacuole

Pseudopodia engulf a small organism

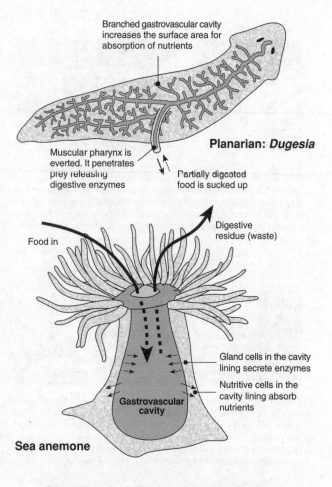

Branched gastrovascular cavity increases the surface area for absorption of nutrients

Planarian: *Dugesia*

Muscular pharynx is everted. It penetrates prey releasing digestive enzymes

Partially digested food is sucked up

Food in

Digestive residue (waste)

Gland cells in the cavity lining secrete enzymes

Nutritive cells in the cavity lining absorb nutrients

Gastrovascular cavity

Sea anemone

Intracellular Digestion In Food Vacuoles

EXAMPLES: *Protozoans (above), sponges*

The simplest digestive compartments are food vacuoles: organelles where a single cell can digest its food without the digestive enzymes mixing with the cell's own cytoplasm. Sponges and protozoans (e.g. *Paramecium* and *Amoeba*) digest food in this way. *Paramecium* sweeps food into a food groove, from where vacuoles form. *Amoeba* engulf food using cytoplasmic extensions called pseudopodia. Digestion is intracellular, occurring within the cell itself.

Digestion In A Gastrovascular Cavity

EXAMPLES: *Cnidarians, flatworms (above)*

Some of the simplest animals have a digestive sac or gastrovascular cavity with a single opening through which food enters and digested waste passes out. In organisms with this system, digestion is both extra- and intracellular. Digestion begins (using secreted enzymes) either in the cavity (in cnidarians) or outside it (flatworms). In both these groups, the digestion process is completed intracellularly within the vacuoles in cells.

1. Describe two ways in which simple saclike gastrovascular cavities differ from tubelike guts:

   (a) _____

   (b) _____

2. (a) Distinguish between intracellular and extracellular digestion: _____

   _____

   (b) Explain why intracellular digestion is not suitable as the only means of digestion for most animals: _____

   _____

3. State the main difference between extracellular digestion in sea anemones and *Dugesia*: _____

   _____

Related activities: Diversity in Tube Guts, Adaptations for Absorption

Diversity in Tube Guts

Tube-like digestive tracts (guts) run through the body from the mouth to the anus. The gut can be divided into regions where different stages in the processing of food occur along its length. Tube guts are relatively uniform in their general structure: there are regions for storing, digesting, absorbing and eliminating the food. However the different specializations that occur in each gut region will depend both on the diet and the method of ingestion (prechewed, liquid, unchewed). Some variations on the structure and regional specializations of tube guts are shown below.

Digestion in Complete Tube Guts

EXAMPLES: *Most animals: nematodes, annelids, molluscs, arthropods, echinoderms, chordates*

In contrast to the sac-like cavities of cnidarians and flatworms, most animals have digestive tubes running between two openings: a **mouth** and an **anus**. The food moves along the tube in one direction so the gut can be organized into specialized regions that carry out digestion and absorption of nutrients in a stepwise fashion. Usually, food ingested at the mouth and pharynx passes through an esophagus to a crop, gizzard or stomach. In the intestine, digestive enzymes break down the food molecules and nutrients are absorbed across the epithelium of the gut wall. Undigested wastes are passed out (egested) through the anus. The degree of specialization within tube guts varies depending on the animal and the type of diet. Four examples of regional specialization to suit different diets are illustrated.

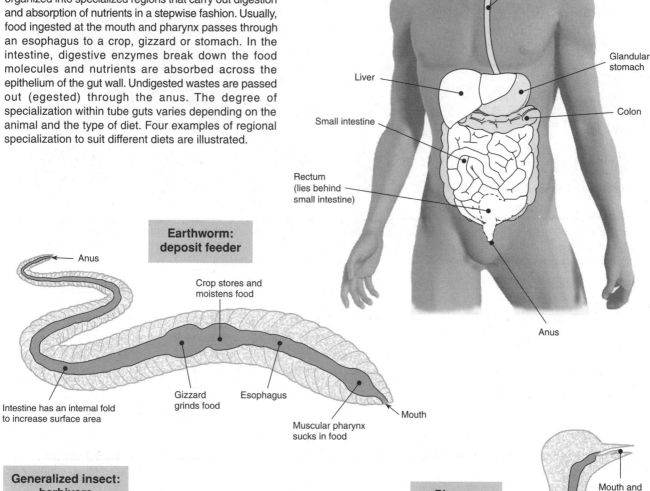

Human: mammalian omnivore

- Mouth, tongue and teeth
- Salivary gland
- Throat (pharynx)
- Salivary glands
- Esophagus
- Liver
- Glandular stomach
- Small intestine
- Colon
- Rectum (lies behind small intestine)
- Anus

Earthworm: deposit feeder

- Anus
- Crop stores and moistens food
- Intestine has an internal fold to increase surface area
- Gizzard grinds food
- Esophagus
- Muscular pharynx sucks in food
- Mouth

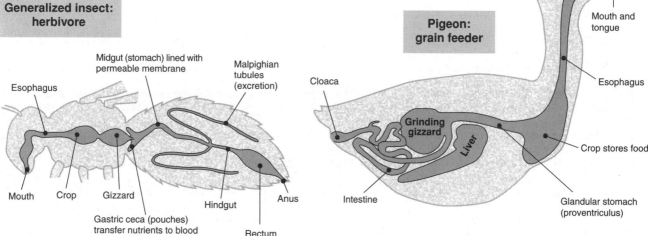

Generalized insect: herbivore

- Esophagus
- Midgut (stomach) lined with permeable membrane
- Malpighian tubules (excretion)
- Mouth
- Crop
- Gizzard
- Gastric ceca (pouches) transfer nutrients to blood
- Hindgut
- Rectum
- Anus

Pigeon: grain feeder

- Mouth and tongue
- Cloaca
- Grinding gizzard
- Liver
- Esophagus
- Crop stores food
- Intestine
- Glandular stomach (proventriculus)

Diet and Animal Nutrition

Related activities: Mammalian Guts, The Human Digestive Tract, Adaptations for Absorption

A 2

Recognizing Digestive Organs in a Dissection

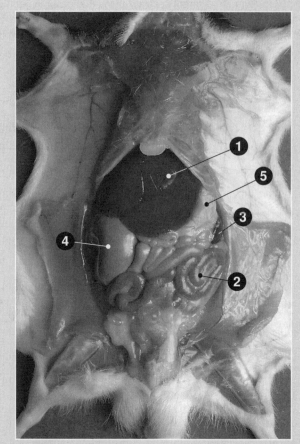

A: Rat abdominal organs *in situ*

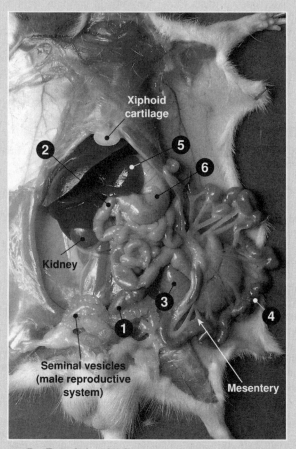

B: Rat abdominal organs *partially dissected*

In your studies of anatomy, you may be required to complete an actual, or virtual, dissection. The photographs (A and B) above show dissection of the body cavity of a laboratory white rat. **A** shows the organs *in situ*, as they appear undisturbed in the abdomen. **B** shows the organs after they have been partially dissected out. The numbers indicate structures to be labeled.

A. 1 _____   B. 1 _____

   2 _____   2 _____

   3 _____   3 _____

   4 _____   4 _____

   5 _____   5 _____

                                            6 _____

1. Some structures have a similar function in different animals. State the general function of the following gut structures:

   (a) Gizzard: _____

   (b) Stomach or crop: _____

   (c) Intestine (midgut in insects): _____

2. (a) In the dissections of the rat (above), label each of the structures indicated in the spaces provided (photo A: 1-5, photo B: 1-6). Some structures are the same, but the same numbers do not necessarily indicate the same structure.

   (b) Of the various guts pictured opposite, which one does the rat gut most closely resemble: _____

   (c) Explain your answer to (b) in terms of the structures present and absent: _____

   _____

   _____

   (d) State one reason why you might expect this similarity: _____

Insect Mouthparts

Insect mouthparts consist of the labrum and three sets of modified, paired appendages known as the mandibles, maxillae, and labium. They are variously adapted to tackle different diets and, in some cases, this has involved loss or fusion of some of the paired appendages. In chewing insects, the **labrum** forms an upper lip and helps pull food into the mouth. The **mandibles** form the first pair of mouthparts and are used as jaws to chew, cut, and tear food, and may also be used to carry things, fight (see right), or to mold wax. The **maxillae** form the second pair of mouthparts and are used for food sensing and handling. The **labium** is a single structure formed from a fused pair of mouthparts. It acts as a lower lip to close the mouth. Both the maxillae and the labium may have finger-like extensions called **palps**. The particular form of the mouthparts depends on the diet, and sometimes on the life stage. In many insects, metamorphosis from the larval to adult stage involves a structural and functional change in the mouthparts associated with a change in diet.

The ferocious-looking mandibles on this stag beetle are not for feeding, but are used for ritualized combat with other stag beetles.

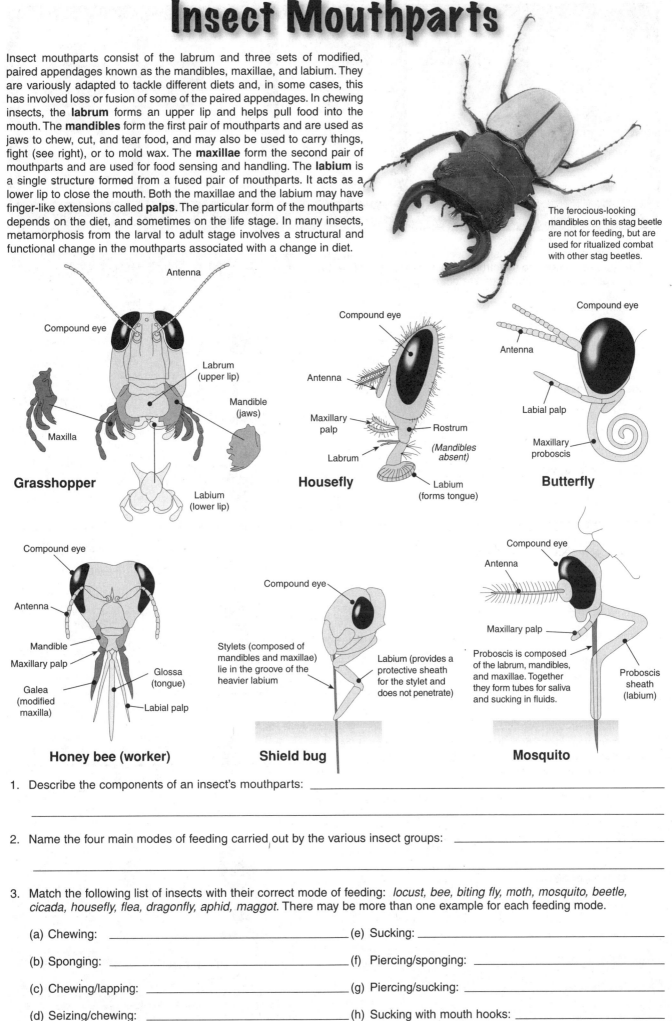

Grasshopper

Housefly

Butterfly

Honey bee (worker)

Shield bug

Mosquito

1. Describe the components of an insect's mouthparts: _____

   _____

2. Name the four main modes of feeding carried out by the various insect groups: _____

   _____

3. Match the following list of insects with their correct mode of feeding: *locust, bee, biting fly, moth, mosquito, beetle, cicada, housefly, flea, dragonfly, aphid, maggot.* There may be more than one example for each feeding mode.

   (a) Chewing: _____   (e) Sucking: _____

   (b) Sponging: _____   (f) Piercing/sponging: _____

   (c) Chewing/lapping: _____   (g) Piercing/sucking: _____

   (d) Seizing/chewing: _____   (h) Sucking with mouth hooks: _____

Related activities: Digesting Different Diets

RA 2

Diet and Animal Nutrition

168

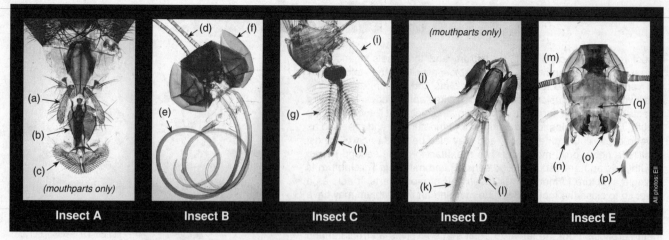

Insect A   Insect B   Insect C   Insect D   Insect E

4. For each of the photographs of insects above (**A - E**), identify the **type of insect** and the structures labeled (a)-(q). Note that some of the labeled structures are not mouthparts:

Identity of **insect A**: _____

    (a) _____ (c) _____

    (b) _____

Identity of **insect B**: _____

    (d) _____ (f) _____

    (e) _____

Identity of **insect C**: _____

    (g) _____ (i) _____

    (h) _____

Identity of **insect D**: _____

    (j) _____ (l) _____

    (k) _____

Identity of **insect E**: _____

    (m) _____ (p) _____

    (n) _____ (q) _____

    (o) _____

5. The diagrams on the right illustrate the arrangement of the mouthparts for various insects. Use highlighter pens to create a color key and color in each type of mouthpart.

6. Many insects undergo metamorphosis at certain stages in their life cycle. Butterflies start their active life as caterpillars, after which they pass through a pupal stage, to finally emerge as butterflies. Comment on the diets and changes to the mouthparts of caterpillars and their adult forms (butterflies):

(a) Caterpillar diet: _____

    Mouthparts: _____

    _____

(b) Butterfly diet: _____

    Mouthparts: _____

    _____

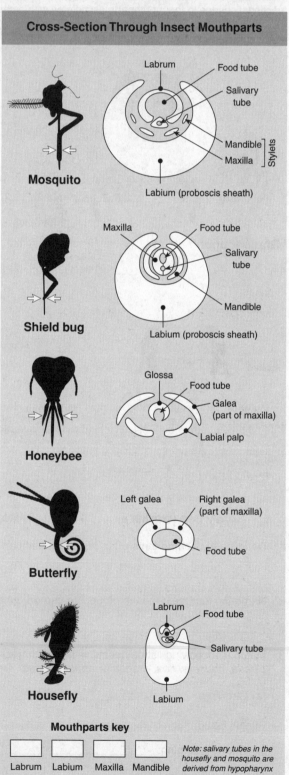

Cross-Section Through Insect Mouthparts

Mosquito — Labrum, Food tube, Salivary tube, Mandible, Maxilla (Stylets), Labium (proboscis sheath)

Shield bug — Maxilla, Food tube, Salivary tube, Mandible, Labium (proboscis sheath)

Honeybee — Glossa, Food tube, Galea (part of maxilla), Labial palp

Butterfly — Left galea, Right galea (part of maxilla), Food tube

Housefly — Labrum, Food tube, Salivary tube, Labium

Mouthparts key

Labrum   Labium   Maxilla   Mandible

Note: salivary tubes in the housefly and mosquito are derived from hypopharynx

Mammalian Guts

Among animals, bulky, high fiber diets are harder to digest than diets containing very little plant material. Herbivores therefore tend to have longer guts with larger chambers than carnivores. Grazing mammals are dependent on symbiotic microorganisms to digest plant cellulose for them. This microbial activity may take place in the stomach (foregut fermentation) or the colon and cecum (hindgut fermentation). Some grazers are ruminants; regurgitating and rechewing partially digested food, which is then reswallowed. The diagrams below compare gut structure in representative mammals. Further detail of the adaptations of carnivores and ruminant herbivores is provided on the next page.

Omnivore
Human: *Homo sapiens*

Omnivorous diets can vary enormously and the specific structure of the gut varies accordingly. Some contain a lot of plant material, with animal flesh eaten occasionally. Pigs, bears, and some primates such as chimpanzees, are omnivores of this sort. Other omnivores forage for animal and vegetable foods about equally. The food predominating in the diet at any time will depend on seasonal availability and preference.

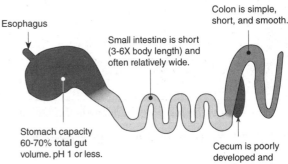

Small intestine is of medium length (10-11X body length in humans, but shorter in some other omnivores).

Colon is relatively long. The degree of pouching is related to fiber content of the diet. Usually some fermentation by gut bacteria occurs here.

Esophagus

Cecum: usually poorly developed

Stomach capacity in humans is 20-30% of total gut volume, but greater in some other omnivores. pH 2.

Appendix

Carnivore
Dog: *Canis familiaris*

The guts of carnivores are adapted for processing animal flesh. The viscera (gut and internal organs) of killed or scavenged animals are eaten as well as the muscle, and provide valuable nutrients. Regions for microbial fermentation are poorly developed or absent. Some animals evolved as carnivores, but have since become secondarily adapted to a more omnivorous diet (bears) or a highly specialized herbivorous diet (pandas). Their guts retain the basic features of a carnivore's gut.

Esophagus

Colon is simple, short, and smooth.

Small intestine is short (3-6X body length) and often relatively wide.

Stomach capacity 60-70% total gut volume. pH 1 or less.

Cecum is poorly developed and may be absent.

Herbivore: foregut digestion
Cattle: *Bos taurus*

Cattle, sheep, deer, and goats are ruminants. The stomach is divided into a series of large chambers, including a rumen, which contains bacteria and ciliates that digest the plant material in the diet. The division of the stomach into chambers means that the passage of food is slowed and there is time for the microorganisms to act on the plant cellulose. Volatile fatty acids released by the microbes provide energy, and digestion of the microbes themselves provides the ruminant with protein.

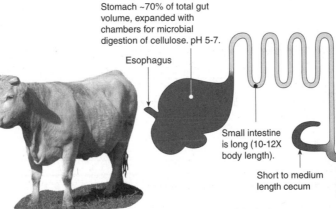

Stomach ~70% of total gut volume, expanded with chambers for microbial digestion of cellulose. pH 5-7.

Esophagus

Small intestine is long (10-12X body length).

Short to medium length cecum

Colon of medium length. Fermentation not as important here.

Herbivore: hindgut digestion
Rabbit: *Oryctolagus cuniculus*

Rabbits are specialized herbivores. The cecum is expanded into a very large chamber for digestion of cellulose. At the junction between the ileum and the colon, indigestible fiber is pushed into the colon where it forms hard feces. Digestible matter passes into the cecum where anaerobic bacteria ferment the material and more absorption takes place. Vitamins and microbial proteins from this fermentation are formed into soft fecal pellets, which pass to the anus and are reingested (coprophagy).

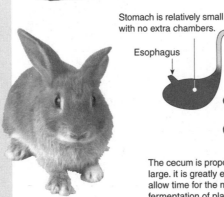

Stomach is relatively small with no extra chambers.

Small intestine is shorter than in foregut fermenters

Esophagus

The cecum is proportionally very large. it is greatly expanded to allow time for the microbial fermentation of plant matter.

The colon is very long and pouched. The special fecal pellets resulting from cecal fermentation are reingested directly from the anus.

Diet and Animal Nutrition

Related activities: Diversity in Tube Guts, Digesting Different Diets

A 2

Ruminant herbivore: Cattle (*Bos taurus*)

Ruminants are specialized herbivores with teeth adapted for chewing and grinding. Their nutrition is dependent on their mutualistic relationship with their microbial gut flora (bacteria and ciliates), which digest plant material and provide the ruminant with energy and protein. In return, the rumen provides the microbes with a warm, oxygen free, nutrient rich environment.

Carnivore: Lion (*Panthera leo*)

The teeth and guts of carnivores are superbly adapted for eating animal flesh. The canine and incisor teeth are specialized to bite down and cut, while the carnassials are enlarged, lengthened, and positioned to act as shears to slice through flesh. As meat is easier to digest than cellulose, the guts of carnivores are comparatively more uniform and shorter than those of herbivores.

Dental adaptations

Flow of food in the stomach

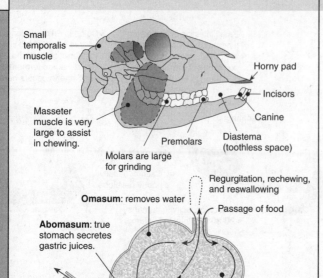

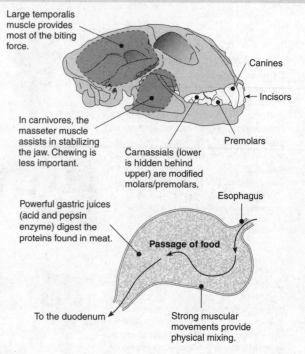

1. For each of the following, summarize the **structural** differences between the guts of a carnivore and a named herbivore:

   (a) Size of stomach (relative to body size): _____

   _____

   (b) Relative length of small intestine: _____

   _____

   (c) Development of hind gut (cecum and colon): _____

   _____

2. (a) Explain the role of microbial fermentation in the nutrition of foregut fermenting herbivores: _____

   _____

   _____

   (b) Describe a herbivorous diet that is less reliant on microbial fermentation: _____

3. Contrast the pH of the stomach contents in carnivores, omnivores, and herbivores, and explain the differences:

   _____

   _____

   _____

4. Identify and explain a structural difference between carnivores and ruminant herbivores with respect to:

   (a) The teeth: _____

   _____

   (b) The jaw musculature: _____

   _____

Digesting Different Diets

During digestion, food is changed by physical and chemical means from its original state until its constituents are released as small, simple molecules that can be absorbed and assimilated. The content of animal diets is tremendously variable and the ways in which animals have evolved to process their food is similarly varied. Some foods, like egg and honey, are pure, concentrated nutriment. Other diets are of high nutritional value, but contain large volumes of water (e.g. blood) or are bulky and take a long time to digest (whole prey items). Other diets are not only bulky, but are also of low nutritional value (e.g. vegetation). Some adaptations for dealing with particular, specialized diets are explained below.

Animal	Diet and Problems	Adaptations to Diet

Mosquito

Others: leeches, spiders, ticks

High fluid diet: blood

Blood is a high protein, low bulk, fluid. The problems associated with processing it are:

- Preventing coagulation of blood and blockage of mouthparts during ingestion.
- Storage of a large quantity of fluid.
- Slowing passage of low bulk food through the gut so that it can be digested.

Powerful **anticoagulants** are injected using the piercing mouthparts. These keep the blood flowing.

A greatly **enlarged crop** stores the blood, releasing it slowly in smaller amounts into the stomach (midgut).

The **stomach is divided** into three sequential regions that absorb water to concentrate the blood, secrete protease enzymes for digestion, and absorb nutrients.

Bumble bee

Others: honeybees, aphids, butterflies

High fluid diet: plant sap and nectar

Plant sap is high volume sugary fluid. The problems associated with processing it are:

- Eliminating large volumes of water and obtaining sufficient protein and vitamins.
- Storage of a large quantity of fluid.
- Dilution of enzymes by the large volumes.
- In some cases, excessive sugar intake.

The **stomach is greatly dilated** and divided into three regions. The first and last parts are greatly coiled and actively remove water.

The **mid region** of the stomach is **specialized** for secretion of carbohydrase enzymes and absorption. It receives the sap only after most of the water is removed.

Unabsorbed sugars can be passed out of the hindgut in copious amounts known as "honeydew". This allows them to absorb enough food to meet protein needs.

Sheep

Others: All ruminants: e.g. cows

Bulky, high cellulose diet: grass

Plant material contains large amounts of cellulose. Problems with this diet include:

- Ingesting enough to meet protein and vitamin needs. Digesting the cellulose.
- Storing large volumes of bulky material.
- Coping with large amounts of gas produced by fermenting plant material.

Stomach is greatly expanded into several, large storage and fermentation chambers (e.g. the rumen) containing microorganisms (bacteria and ciliate Protozoa).

The **gut symbionts digest the cellulose**, producing volatile fatty acids, which are absorbed directly from the chambers and provide energy and nutrients. Digestion of the microorganisms themselves provides protein.

Some material is regurgitated and rechewed. Smaller particles pass onto the absorptive region of the stomach.

Koala

Toxic plants: *Eucalyptus* leaves

Problems with this diet are:

- The leaves contain toxins in the oils, waxes and resins, e.g. hydrocyanic acid.
- It is low in energy and quality (low protein).
- The diet is bulky and high volume.

Note: some insects e.g. monarch butterflies, eat toxic plants and use the toxins for defense

The **cecum** of the hindgut is **greatly expanded** to form a fermentation chamber containing microorganisms which digest the cellulose of the plant material.

They meet their protein needs by eating **large volumes**.

Koalas are able to **detoxify eucalypt poisons** by forming nontoxic compounds in the liver, which are then excreted.

Koalas are **fastidious** feeders and select only certain age leaves of certain species.

---

1. Describe one common feature of the guts of fluid feeders: _____

_____

2. Explain why it is so important for fluid feeders to reduce the volume of their ingested food by absorbing water:

_____

_____

3. Discuss the advantages and disadvantages of a diet consisting of a toxic plant: _____

_____

_____

4. (a) Explain how ruminant herbivores supplement the protein content of their diet: _____

_____

(b) Explain why koalas are less able to do this: _____

_____

Related activities: Methods of Feeding, Mammalian Guts

RA 2

Diet and Animal Nutrition

Adaptations for Absorption

In most animal phyla, the small products of enzymic digestion are absorbed through a gut lining. Absorption of the simple components of food (e.g. simple sugars, amino acids, fatty acids and glycerol) must take place before the nutrients can be assimilated (taken up by all the body's cells). In animals with a tubular gut, it is an advantage to maximize the uptake of nutrients from the intestine as the digested food passes through. There is great diversity amongst the invertebrate phyla in the way in which absorption is facilitated. In cnidarians, specialized cells lining the gut ingest food particles directly by phagocytosis. In other phyla, the inner surface area of the gut is increased by infolding so that the area over which nutrient uptake can occur is very large. This is the case in vertebrates also, as shown for mammals in the activity *Stomach and Small Intestine*.

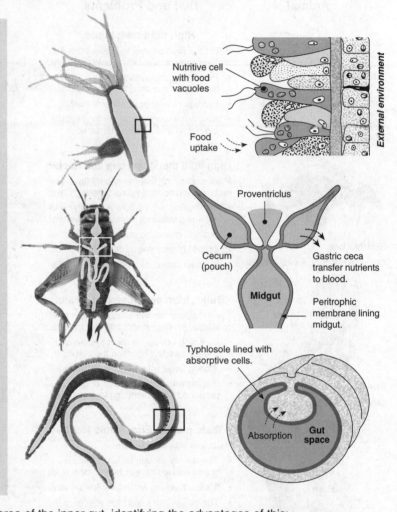

Cnidarian gastrovascular cavity

EXAMPLE: *Hydra*

In *Hydra*, specialized cells line the gastrovascular cavity. Some of these secrete enzymes into the cavity to begin digestion. Special nutritive cells (illustrated) take in the partly digested fragments by phagocytosis, to form food vacuoles where digestion is completed. These cells have beating hair-like flagella that create currents and improve the delivery of food to the cells.

Insect gastric ceca

EXAMPLE: Grasshopper or locust

In insects of the grasshopper family (and others), the gastric ceca (*sing.* cecum) are midgut pouches just behind the proventriculus. The ceca improve absorption by transferring nutrients into the blood. Secretion of enzymes and absorption of nutrients occurs in the midgut. Unlike the fore- and hindgut (which are lined with chitin), the midgut is lined with a permeable peritrophic membrane which allows nutrient absorption.

Annelid typhlosole

EXAMPLE: *Lumbricus* (earthworm)

In earthworms, the entire length of the small intestine is folded into a structure called the typhlosole. Secretion of enzymes, digestion and absorption all occur in the intestine and the typhlosole increases the amount of surface area for absorption of nutrients. Not all annelids have a typhlosole, although many have similar foldings to increase surface area.

1. Discuss adaptations for increasing the surface area of the inner gut, identifying the advantages of this:

_____

_____

_____

_____

_____

2. Refer to the activity *Stomach and Small Intestine* and answer the following:

(a) Identify the features and structures in the mammalian gut that increase surface area: _____

_____

(b) Explain how the transport of nutrients from the gut is facilitated: _____

_____

(c) Compare the degree of infolding with that generally found in invertebrates and suggest a reason for the difference:

_____

_____

Related activities: Food Vacuoles and Simple Guts, Stomach and Small Intestine

The Human Digestive Tract

It is estimated that an adult consumes about 20 000 kg of food between the ages of 18 and 38 years; about a metric tonne a year. Although babies grow rapidly from birth, growth is not the most significant reason for our ongoing eating. Our bodies require a constant source of energy for the vast number of biochemical reactions that constitute **metabolism**. Food provides the source of this energy. Tube-like digestive tracts (guts) run through the body from the mouth to the anus. The digestive tract prepares the food we eat for use by the body's cells through five basic activities: eating (ingestion), movement (of food through the gut), digestion (physical and chemical breakdown), absorption, and elimination. However the different specializations that occur in each region will depend both on the diet and the method of ingestion (prechewed, liquid, unchewed).

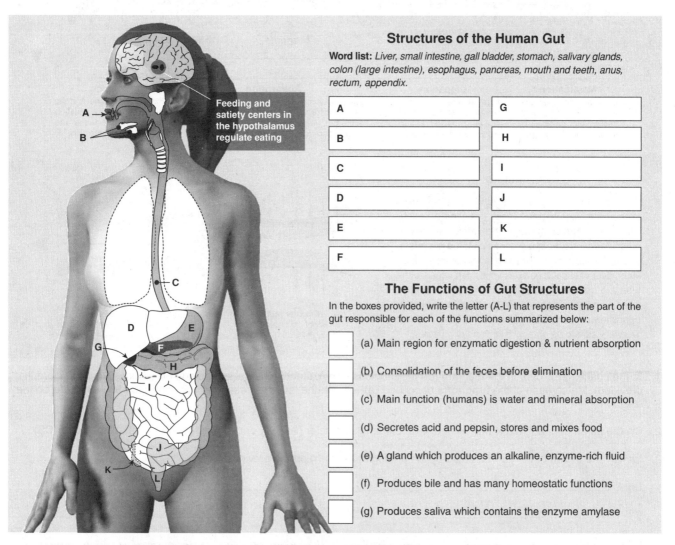

Feeding and satiety centers in the hypothalamus regulate eating

Structures of the Human Gut

Word list: *Liver, small intestine, gall bladder, stomach, salivary glands, colon (large intestine), esophagus, pancreas, mouth and teeth, anus, rectum, appendix.*

A		G	
B		H	
C		I	
D		J	
E		K	
F		L	

The Functions of Gut Structures

In the boxes provided, write the letter (A-L) that represents the part of the gut responsible for each of the functions summarized below:

- (a) Main region for enzymatic digestion & nutrient absorption
- (b) Consolidation of the feces before elimination
- (c) Main function (humans) is water and mineral absorption
- (d) Secretes acid and pepsin, stores and mixes food
- (e) A gland which produces an alkaline, enzyme-rich fluid
- (f) Produces bile and has many homeostatic functions
- (g) Produces saliva which contains the enzyme amylase

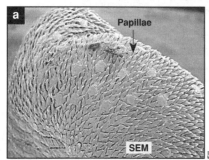

a Papillae

SEM

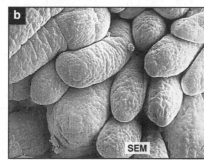

b

SEM

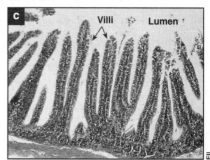

c Villi Lumen

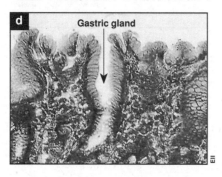

d Gastric gland

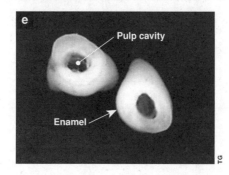

e Pulp cavity

Enamel

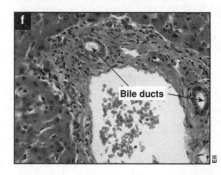

f Bile ducts

Diet and Animal Nutrition

Related activities: Diversity in Tube Guts, Mammalian Guts
Web links: Digestion Animation

RA 2

Processes in a Tube Gut

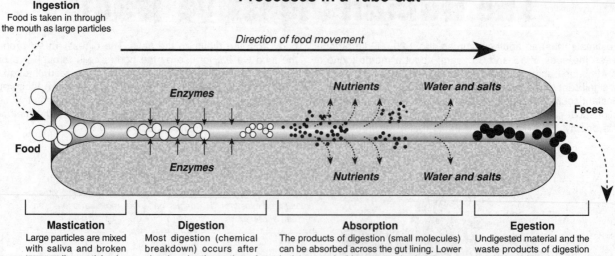

Ingestion
Food is taken in through the mouth as large particles

Direction of food movement

Enzymes

Nutrients   *Water and salts*

Feces

Food

Enzymes

Nutrients   *Water and salts*

Mastication
Large particles are mixed with saliva and broken into smaller particles by mastication (chewing).

Digestion
Most digestion (chemical breakdown) occurs after chewing, by the action of enzymes acting on the food.

Absorption
The products of digestion (small molecules) can be absorbed across the gut lining. Lower in the gut, valuable water and salts are also reabsorbed from the slurry passing through.

Egestion
Undigested material and the waste products of digestion are formed into feces and eliminated by defecation.

Peristalsis

When food is processed in a tube gut it is usually formed into small lumps (each is called a bolus). These are moved through the gut by waves of muscular contraction; a process called **peristalsis**. The wall of a gut tube has two layers of muscle: an inner layer of circular muscles which can squeeze the tube to a narrower diameter, and longitudinal muscles which can contract to shorten the tube. They work in opposite ways; one contracts while the other relaxes. They are said to be antagonistic pairs of muscles.

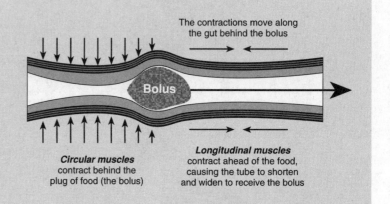

The contractions move along the gut behind the bolus

Bolus

Circular muscles
contract behind the plug of food (the bolus)

Longitudinal muscles
contract ahead of the food, causing the tube to shorten and widen to receive the bolus

1. In the spaces provided on the diagram (on the previous page), identify the parts labeled **A-L** (choose from the word list provided). Match each of the **functions** described (a)-(g) with the letter representing the corresponding structure on the diagram.

2. On the same diagram, mark with lines and labels: anal sphincter (**AS**), pyloric sphincter (**PS**), cardiac sphincter (**CS**).

3. Identify the region of the gut illustrated by the photographs (**a**)-(**f**) on the previous page:

   (a) _____   (b) _____

   (c) _____   (d) _____

   (e) _____   (f) _____

4. Explain how a **bolus** of food is moved through a tube gut: _____

   _____

   _____

   _____

5. Describe an advantage of having a gut where food moves in only one direction: _____

   _____

6. Identify one factor that would influence the length and specialization in the gut: _____

7. Briefly describe how the following processes are involved in processing food:

   (a) Mastication: _____

   _____

   (b) Absorption: _____

   _____

Stomach and Small Intestine

Digestion in the gut depends on both the physical movement of the food and its enzymatic breakdown into constituent components. Most digestion occurs in the stomach and small intestine. The digestive enzymes involved may be bound to the surfaces of the intestinal epithelial cells or occur as components of the secretions of digestive glands (e.g. pancreas). The structure and functions of the stomach and small intestines, and their enzymic secretions are shown on this and the next page.

The Stomach and Organs of the Small Intestine

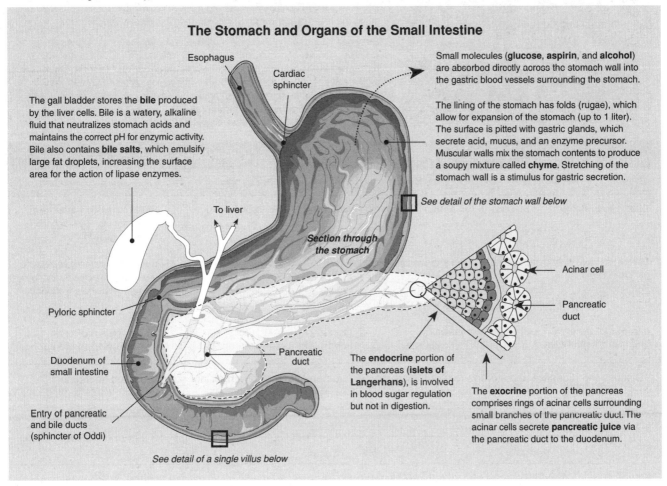

Esophagus

Cardiac sphincter

Small molecules (**glucose**, **aspirin**, and **alcohol**) are absorbed directly across the stomach wall into the gastric blood vessels surrounding the stomach.

The gall bladder stores the **bile** produced by the liver cells. Bile is a watery, alkaline fluid that neutralizes stomach acids and maintains the correct pH for enzymic activity. Bile also contains **bile salts**, which emulsify large fat droplets, increasing the surface area for the action of lipase enzymes.

The lining of the stomach has folds (rugae), which allow for expansion of the stomach (up to 1 liter). The surface is pitted with gastric glands, which secrete acid, mucus, and an enzyme precursor. Muscular walls mix the stomach contents to produce a soupy mixture called **chyme**. Stretching of the stomach wall is a stimulus for gastric secretion.

To liver

See detail of the stomach wall below

Section through the stomach

Acinar cell

Pancreatic duct

Pyloric sphincter

Duodenum of small intestine

Pancreatic duct

The **endocrine** portion of the pancreas (**islets of Langerhans**), is involved in blood sugar regulation but not in digestion.

Entry of pancreatic and bile ducts (sphincter of Oddi)

The **exocrine** portion of the pancreas comprises rings of acinar cells surrounding small branches of the pancreatic duct. The acinar cells secrete **pancreatic juice** via the pancreatic duct to the duodenum.

See detail of a single villus below

Detail of a Single Villus From Intestinal Wall

Epithelial cells on the tip of the villus are brushed off as a result of regular wear and tear.

The intestinal enzymes are bound to surfaces of the epithelial cells

Epithelial cells divide and migrate toward the tip of the villus to replace lost and worn cells.

Crypt of Lieberkühn: tubular exocrine gland that secretes alkaline fluid

Brunner's gland produces mucus which empties into the crypt of Lieberkühn

Goblet cells in the epithelium produce mucus

Columnar epithelium

Capillary network

Lymph vessel

Detail of the Stomach Wall

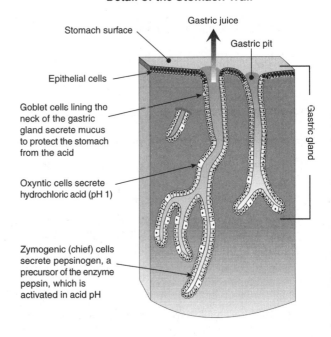

Gastric juice

Stomach surface

Gastric pit

Epithelial cells

Goblet cells lining the neck of the gastric gland secrete mucus to protect the stomach from the acid

Oxyntic cells secrete hydrochloric acid (pH 1)

Zymogenic (chief) cells secrete pepsinogen, a precursor of the enzyme pepsin, which is activated in acid pH

Gastric gland

1. Describe the two important roles of gut movements: _____

_____

_____

Related activities: The Human Digestive Tract, The Large Intestine
Web links: Acid Secretion in the Stomach

A 2

Diet and Animal Nutrition

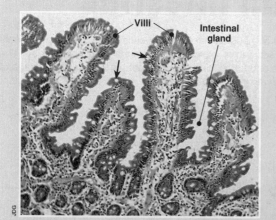

Villi   Intestinal gland

Intestinal villi and microvilli

The photograph (left) shows a section through the ileum with the **intestinal villi** and **intestinal glands** (crypts of Lieberkühn) indicated. The intestinal glands secrete mucus and alkaline fluid. **Epithelial cells** lining the surface of the villi are regularly worn off and replaced by new cells migrating from the base of the intestinal glands. Each epithelial cell has many **microvilli** (microscopic projections called the brush border) which further increase the intestinal surface area.

Enzymes bound to the microvilli surfaces of the epithelial cells (peptidases, maltase, lactase, and sucrase) break down small peptides and carbohydrate molecules into their constituent parts. The breakdown products (monosaccharides, amino acids) are then absorbed into the underlying blood and lymph vessels. **Mucous cells** (white spots arrowed) produce mucus to protect the epithelial cells from enzymatic digestion. The **blood vessels** transport nutrients to the liver. **Lymph vessels** transport the products of fat digestion.

Enzyme secretions of the gut and their role in digestion

Secretion and source	Site of action	Active enzyme	Substrate and products	Control of secretion
Gastric juice: stomach	Stomach	Pepsin	Protein ⟶ peptides	Reflex stimulation, stretching of the stomach wall, and the hormone **gastrin**.
Pancreatic juice: pancreas (exocrine region only)	Duodenum	Pancreatic amylase Trypsin Chymotrypsin Pancreatic lipase	Starch ⟶ maltose Protein ⟶ peptides Protein ⟶ peptides Fats ⟶ fatty acids + glycerol	Control of pancreatic secretions is via release of the hormones **secretin** and **cholecystokinin**.
Intestinal juice and enzymes: small intestine	Small intestine	Maltase Peptidases	Maltose ⟶ glucose Polypeptides ⟶ amino acids	Reflex action and contact with intestinal wall.

2. Discuss the digestive and storage role of the stomach in humans, identifying important structures and secretions:

_____

_____

_____

_____

_____

3. Identify two sites for enzyme secretion in the gut, give an example of an enzyme produced there, and state its role:

   (a) Site: _____ Enzyme: _____

   Enzyme's role: _____

   (b) Site: _____ Enzyme: _____

   Enzyme's role: _____

4. (a) Suggest why the pH of the gut secretions varies at different regions in the gut: _____

   _____

   (b) Explain why it is necessary for protein-digesting enzymes (e.g. trypsin, chymotrypsin, and pepsin) to be secreted in an inactive form and then activated after release:

   _____

   _____

5. Explain why alcohol exerts its effects more rapidly when the stomach is empty (rather than full): _____

   _____

6. Explain the role of sphincter muscles in the digestive tract: _____

   _____

The Large Intestine

After most of the nutrients have been absorbed in the small intestine, the remaining fluid contents pass into the large intestine (appendix, cecum, and colon). The fluid comprises undigested or undigestible food, bacteria, dead cells sloughed off from the gut wall, mucus, bile, ions, and a large amount of water. In humans and other omnivores, the large intestine is concerned mainly with the reabsorption of water and electrolytes. Infection or disease can cause an increase in gut movements, resulting in insufficient reabsorption of water and diarrhea. Sluggish gut movements cause the reabsorption of too much water and the feces become hard and difficult to pass, a condition known as constipation. The semi-solid waste material (feces) passes from the **colon** to the rectum, where it is stored and consolidated before being expelled (egested). Egestion of feces is controlled by the activity of two sphincters in the **anus**, one being under involuntary reflex control.

The Large Intestine

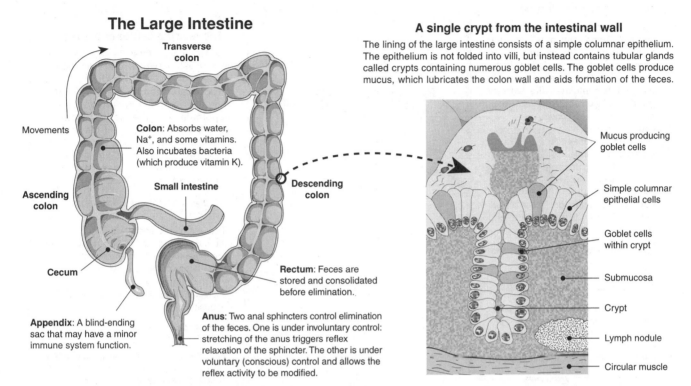

Transverse colon

Movements

Colon: Absorbs water, Na⁺, and some vitamins. Also incubates bacteria (which produce vitamin K).

Small intestine

Descending colon

Ascending colon

Cecum

Appendix: A blind-ending sac that may have a minor immune system function.

Rectum: Feces are stored and consolidated before elimination.

Anus: Two anal sphincters control elimination of the feces. One is under involuntary control: stretching of the anus triggers reflex relaxation of the sphincter. The other is under voluntary (conscious) control and allows the reflex activity to be modified.

A single crypt from the intestinal wall

The lining of the large intestine consists of a simple columnar epithelium. The epithelium is not folded into villi, but instead contains tubular glands called crypts containing numerous goblet cells. The goblet cells produce mucus, which lubricates the colon wall and aids formation of the feces.

Mucus producing goblet cells

Simple columnar epithelial cells

Goblet cells within crypt

Submucosa

Crypt

Lymph nodule

Circular muscle

Appendicitis

Obstruction of the appendix by fecal matter or some other cause can lead to an inflammation called *appendicitis*. Appendicitis usually develops rapidly with little warning over a period of 6-12 hours. The usual symptom is abdominal pain, accompanied by nausea, vomiting and a slight fever. When severe, it can be life threatening. Acute appendicitis is treated by surgical removal of the appendix (**appendectomy**). The entire procedure usually takes about one hour and is performed in one of two ways: through what is called an open operation or through the laparoscopic technique.

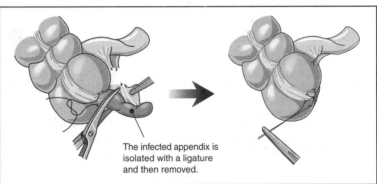

The infected appendix is isolated with a ligature and then removed.

1. Outline the main function of the large intestine: _____

2. Suggest why the lining of the large intestine consists of crypts as opposed to villi like projections: _____

   _____

3. The photograph below shows a cross section through the colon wall. Using the diagram of the single crypt (above right) label the features indicated using the following word list: *circular muscle, submucosa, lymph nodule, epithelial cells*.

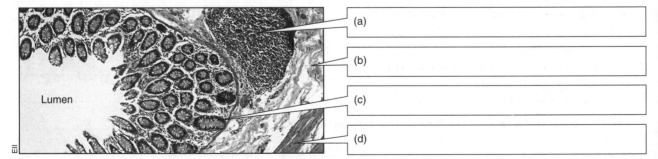

Lumen

(a)

(b)

(c)

(d)

Diet and Animal Nutrition

Related activities: Stomach and Small Intestine

A 2

The Control of Digestion

The majority of digestive juices are secreted only when there is food in the gut and both nervous and hormonal mechanisms are involved in coordinating and regulating this activity appropriately. The digestive system is innervated by branches of the **autonomic nervous system** (sympathetic and parasympathetic stimulation).

Hormonal regulation is achieved through the activity of several hormones: **gastrin**, **secretin**, and **cholecystokinin** (formerly called **pancreozymin**). These are released into the bloodstream in response to nervous or chemical stimuli and influence the activity of gut and associated organs.

Hormonal and Nervous Control of Digestion

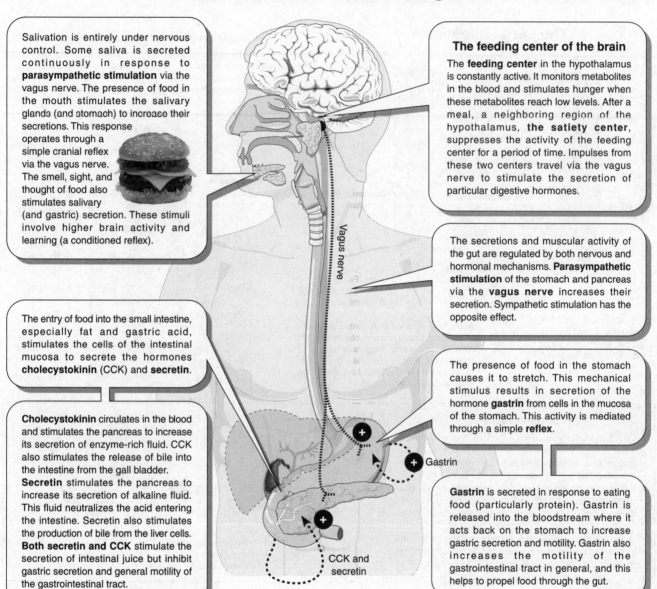

Salivation is entirely under nervous control. Some saliva is secreted continuously in response to **parasympathetic stimulation** via the vagus nerve. The presence of food in the mouth stimulates the salivary glands (and stomach) to increase their secretions. This response operates through a simple cranial reflex via the vagus nerve. The smell, sight, and thought of food also stimulates salivary (and gastric) secretion. These stimuli involve higher brain activity and learning (a conditioned reflex).

The feeding center of the brain
The **feeding center** in the hypothalamus is constantly active. It monitors metabolites in the blood and stimulates hunger when these metabolites reach low levels. After a meal, a neighboring region of the hypothalamus, **the satiety center**, suppresses the activity of the feeding center for a period of time. Impulses from these two centers travel via the vagus nerve to stimulate the secretion of particular digestive hormones.

The secretions and muscular activity of the gut are regulated by both nervous and hormonal mechanisms. **Parasympathetic stimulation** of the stomach and pancreas via the **vagus nerve** increases their secretion. Sympathetic stimulation has the opposite effect.

The entry of food into the small intestine, especially fat and gastric acid, stimulates the cells of the intestinal mucosa to secrete the hormones **cholecystokinin** (CCK) and **secretin**.

The presence of food in the stomach causes it to stretch. This mechanical stimulus results in secretion of the hormone **gastrin** from cells in the mucosa of the stomach. This activity is mediated through a simple **reflex**.

Cholecystokinin circulates in the blood and stimulates the pancreas to increase its secretion of enzyme-rich fluid. CCK also stimulates the release of bile into the intestine from the gall bladder. **Secretin** stimulates the pancreas to increase its secretion of alkaline fluid. This fluid neutralizes the acid entering the intestine. Secretin also stimulates the production of bile from the liver cells. **Both secretin and CCK** stimulate the secretion of intestinal juice but inhibit gastric secretion and general motility of the gastrointestinal tract.

Gastrin is secreted in response to eating food (particularly protein). Gastrin is released into the bloodstream where it acts back on the stomach to increase gastric secretion and motility. Gastrin also increases the motility of the gastrointestinal tract in general, and this helps to propel food through the gut.

Vagus nerve

Gastrin

CCK and secretin

1. Describe the role of each of the following stimuli in the control of digestion, identifying both the response and its effect:

   (a) Presence of food in the mouth: _____

   _____

   (b) Presence of fat and acid in the small intestine: _____

   _____

   (c) Stretching of the stomach by the presence of food: _____

   _____

2. Outline the role of the vagus nerve in regulating digestive activity: _____

   _____

The Role of the Liver

The liver is a large organ, weighing about 1.4 kg, and is well supplied with blood. It carries out several hundred different functions and has a pivotal role in the maintenance of homeostasis. Its role in the digestion of food centers around the production of the alkaline fluid, **bile**, which is secreted at a rate of 0.8-1.0 liter per day. It is also responsible for processing absorbed nutrients, which arrive at the liver via the hepatic portal system. These functions are summarized below.

Digestive Functions of the Liver

The digestive role of the liver is in the production of **bile**. Bile is a yellow, brown, or olive-green alkaline fluid (pH 7.6–8.6), consisting of water and bile salts, cholesterol, lecithin, bile pigments, and several ions. The bile salts are used in the small intestine to break up (**emulsify**) fatty molecules for easier digestion and absorption. The high pH neutralizes the acid entering the small intestine from the stomach. Bile is also partly an excretory product; the breakdown of red blood cells in the liver produces the principal bile pigment, **bilirubin**. Bacteria act on the bile pigments, giving the brownish color to feces. The production and secretion of bile is regulated through nervous and hormonal mechanisms. The hormones (secretin and cholecystokinin) are released into the blood from the intestinal mucosa in response to the presence of food (especially fat) in the small intestine.

Liver Tissue

The liver tissue is made up of many lobules, each one comprising cords of liver cells (hepatocytes), radiating from a central vein (CV), and surrounded by branches of the hepatic artery, hepatic portal vein, and bile ductule. Bile is produced by the individual liver cells, which secrete it into canaliculi that empty into small bile ducts. The hepatocytes also process the nutrients entering the liver via the hepatic portal system.

Internal Gross Structure of the Human Liver

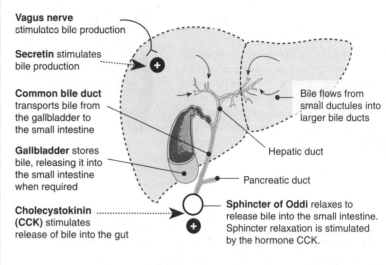

Vagus nerve stimulates bile production

Secretin stimulates bile production

Common bile duct transports bile from the gallbladder to the small intestine

Gallbladder stores bile, releasing it into the small intestine when required

Cholecystokinin (CCK) stimulates release of bile into the gut

Bile flows from small ductules into larger bile ducts

Hepatic duct

Pancreatic duct

Sphincter of Oddi relaxes to release bile into the small intestine. Sphincter relaxation is stimulated by the hormone CCK.

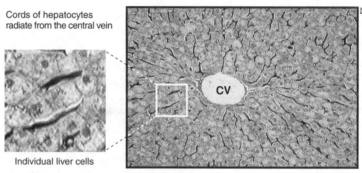

Cords of hepatocytes radiate from the central vein

CV

Individual liver cells

1. The liver produces bile. Describe the two main functions of bile in digestion:

   (a) _____

   (b) _____

2. Describe the two primary functions of the liver related to the processing of digestion products arriving from the gut:

   (a) _____

   (b) _____

3. Explain the role of the gall bladder in digestion: _____

   _____

4. Describe in what way bile is an excretory product as well as a digestive secretion: _____

   _____

   _____

5. Name the two principal hormones controlling the production (secretion) and release of bile, and state the effect of each:

   (a) Hormone 1: _____ Effect: _____

   (b) Hormone 2: _____ Effect: _____

6. State the stimulus for hormonal stimulation of bile secretion: _____

   _____

Diet and Animal Nutrition

Related activities: The Liver's Homeostatic Role, The Control of Digestion

A 2

Absorption and Transport

All the chemical and physical processes of digestion from the mouth to the small intestine are aimed at the breakdown of food molecules into forms that can pass through intestinal lining into the underlying blood and lymph vessels. These breakdown products include monosaccharides, amino acids, fatty acids, glycerol, and glycerides. Passage of these molecules from the gut into the blood or lymph is called **absorption**. After absorption, nutrients are transported directly or indirectly to the liver for storage or processing. Some of the features of nutrient absorption and transport are shown below. For simplicity, all nutrients are shown in the lumen of the intestine, even though some nutrients are digested on the epithelial cell surfaces.

The Hepatic Portal System

The liver obtains oxygenated blood from the hepatic artery, but it also receives deoxygenated blood containing newly absorbed nutrients via the hepatic portal vein. The **hepatic portal system** refers to all the blood flow from the digestive organs that passes through the liver before returning to the heart. Hepatic portal blood is rich in nutrients: the liver monitors and processes this load before the blood passes into general circulation.

Absorption: Most of the simple molecules that are the final products of food breakdown are absorbed by the epithelial cells of the villi into the blood vessels and are transported directly to the liver where they are processed.

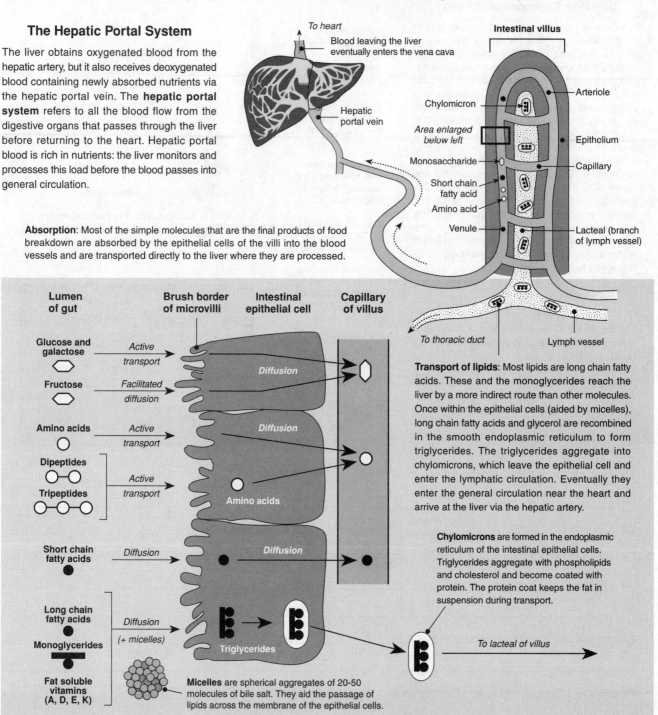

Transport of lipids: Most lipids are long chain fatty acids. These and the monoglycerides reach the liver by a more indirect route than other molecules. Once within the epithelial cells (aided by micelles), long chain fatty acids and glycerol are recombined in the smooth endoplasmic reticulum to form triglycerides. The triglycerides aggregate into chylomicrons, which leave the epithelial cell and enter the lymphatic circulation. Eventually they enter the general circulation near the heart and arrive at the liver via the hepatic artery.

Chylomicrons are formed in the endoplasmic reticulum of the intestinal epithelial cells. Triglycerides aggregate with phospholipids and cholesterol and become coated with protein. The protein coat keeps the fat in suspension during transport.

Micelles are spherical aggregates of 20-50 molecules of bile salt. They aid the passage of lipids across the membrane of the epithelial cells.

1. State the function of the following in fat digestion:

(a) Micelles: _____

(b) Chylomicrons: _____

2. Explain why it is important that venous blood from the gut is transported first to the liver via the hepatic portal circulation:

_____

_____

Related activities: Stomach and Small Intestine, Mammalian Transport, The Liver's Homeostatic Role

A Balanced Diet

Nutrients are required for metabolism, tissue growth and repair, and as an energy source. Good nutrition (provided by a **balanced diet**) is recognized as a key factor in good health. Conversely poor nutrition (malnutrition) may cause ill-health or **deficiency diseases**. A diet refers to the quantity and nature of the food eaten. While not all foods contain all the representative nutrients, we can obtain the required balance of different nutrients by eating a wide variety of foods. In a recent overhaul of previous dietary recommendations, the health benefits of monounsaturated fats (such as olive and canola oils), fish oils, and whole grains have been recognized, and people are being urged to reduce their consumption of highly processed foods and saturated (rather than total) fat. Those on diets that restrict certain food groups (e.g. vegans) must take care to balance their intake of foods to ensure an adequate supply of protein and other nutrients (e.g. iron and B vitamins). Dietary information, including **Recommended Daily Amounts** (RDAs) for energy and nutrients, is provided to consumers through the food labeling. Such information helps individuals to assess their nutrient and energy intake and adjust their diet accordingly.

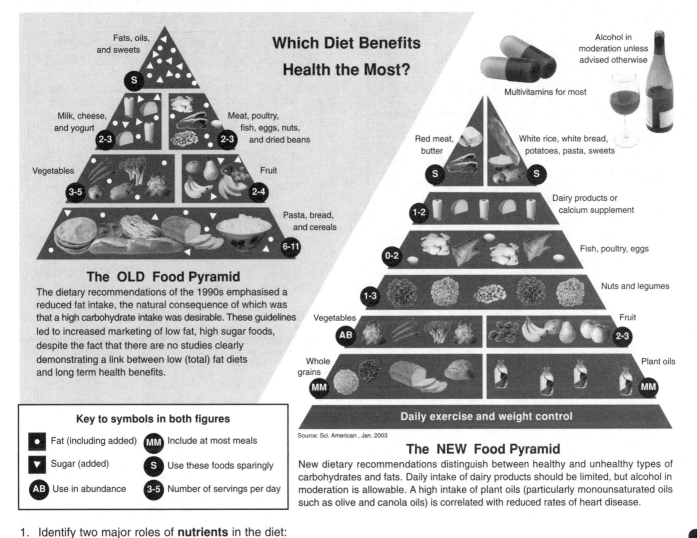

Which Diet Benefits Health the Most?

The OLD Food Pyramid
The dietary recommendations of the 1990s emphasised a reduced fat intake, the natural consequence of which was that a high carbohydrate intake was desirable. These guidelines led to increased marketing of low fat, high sugar foods, despite the fact that there are no studies clearly demonstrating a link between low (total) fat diets and long term health benefits.

Source: Sci. American , Jan. 2003

The NEW Food Pyramid
New dietary recommendations distinguish between healthy and unhealthy types of carbohydrates and fats. Daily intake of dairy products should be limited, but alcohol in moderation is allowable. A high intake of plant oils (particularly monounsaturated oils such as olive and canola oils) is correlated with reduced rates of heart disease.

Key to symbols in both figures

Fat (including added)	MM	Include at most meals	
Sugar (added)	S	Use these foods sparingly	
AB Use in abundance	3-5	Number of servings per day	

1. Identify two major roles of **nutrients** in the diet:

   (a) _____

   (b) _____

2. (a) Compare the two food pyramids (above) and discuss how they differ in their recommendations for good nutrition:

   _____

   _____

   _____

   _____

   _____

   _____

   _____

   _____

Diet and Animal Nutrition

Related activities: Deficiency Diseases, Dietary Disorders
Web links: Metabolic Disorders

DA 2

Labeling Food Products

Nutritional facts labels are used as a guide that consumers can use to determine if a particular food is a good source of a particular nutrient or to compare different brands of a similar type of food.

Calories provide a measure of how much energy is contained per serving.

These nutrients should be limited as they are usually consumed in adequate amounts during the day. Excessive consumption of some of these nutrients can lead to chronic diseases.

Eating enough of these nutrients can improve health and help reduce the risk of some diseases.

For labeling purposes, the US FDA set 2000 calories as the reference amount for calculating %DVs. 5% DV is considered low, whereas greater than 20% is considered high.

BBT's Cheesy Pasta Meal

Nutritional Facts

Serving size 1 cup (228 g)
Servings per container 2

Amount per serving
Calories 250 **Calories from fat** 110

	% Daily Value *
Total Fat 12 g	18%
Saturated Fat 3 g	15%
Cholesterol 30 mg	10%
Sodium 470 mg	20%
Total Carbohydrate 31 g	10%
Dietary Fiber 0 g	0%
Sugars 5 g	
Protein 5 g	
Vitamin A	4%
Vitamin C	2%
Calcium	20%
Iron	4%

Percentage Daily Values are based on a 2000 calorie diet. Your daily values may be higher or lower depending on your calorie needs.

		Calories	2000	2500
Total Fat	Less than		65 g	80 g
Sat Fat	Less than		20 g	25 g
Cholesterol	Less than		300 mg	300 mg
Sodium	Less than		2400 mg	2400 mg
Total Carbo	Less than		300 mg	375 mg
Dietary Fiber	Less than		25 mg	30 mg

Recommended Dietary Allowance (RDA) for selected nutrients

The RDA represents the establishment of a nutritional norm for planning and assessing dietary intake.

RDAs are the levels of intake of essential nutrients considered to be adequate to meet the known needs of practically all healthy people.

RDA figures were first published in 1943 and have been updated and expanded as more data became available and scientists developed a better understanding of nutritional requirements.

The table below shows RDAs (expressed as average daily intake) for selected nutrients for particular groups of the population.

Age range (years)	Protein (g)	Calcium (mg)	Iron (mg)	Folate (µg)	Vit. A (µg)	Vit. C (mg)
Males						
11 - 14	45	1300	12	150	1000	50
15 - 18	59	1300	12	200	1000	60
19 - 24	58	1000	10	200	1000	60
24 +	63	1200	10	200	1000	60
Females						
11 - 14	46	1300	15	150	800	50
15 - 18	44	1300	15	180	800	60
19 - 24	46	1000	15	180	800	60
24 +	50	1200	15	180	800	60
Pregnant*	60	1100	30	400	800	70
Lactating*	65	1200	15	280	1200	90

* RDA based on women 19-54 years.
* RDA for pregnancy is for the 2nd and 3rd trimester.

Source: US FDA

(b) Based on the information on the graph (right), state the evidence that might support the revised recommendations:

_____

_____

_____

_____

_____

_____

Percentage of calories from fat in the traditional diet

Incidence of coronary heart disease per 10 000 men (over a 10 year period)

	38%	40%
	3000	
10%		
500		200

Country	Japan	Eastern Finland	Crete
Type of fat consumed	Low fat	Saturated fat	Monounsaturated fat (olive oil)

3. With reference to the table above left, describe the type of information found on the label of a typical food product:

_____

_____

_____

4. With reference to the table above right, contrast the nutritional requirements of non-pregnant and lactating women:

_____

_____

_____

5. Suggest how **RDAs** can be applied in each of the following situations:

(a) Dietary planning and assessment: _____

_____

(b) Food labeling and consumer information: _____

_____

Deficiency Diseases

Malnutrition is the general term for nutritional disorders resulting from not having enough food (starvation), not enough of the right food (deficiency), or too much food (obesity). Children under five are most at risk from starvation and deficiency diseases because they are growing rapidly and are more susceptible to disease. Malnutrition is a key factor in the deaths of six million children each year, and in developing countries, dietary deficiencies are a major problem. In these countries malnutrition usually presents as **marasmus** or **kwashiorkor** (energy and protein deficiencies).

Specific vitamin and mineral deficiencies (below and opposite) in adults are associated with specific disorders, e.g. **beriberi** (vitamin B₁), **scurvy** (vitamin C), **rickets** (vitamin D), **pellagra** (niacin) or **anemia** (iron). Vitamin deficiencies in childhood result in chronic, lifelong disorders. Deficiency diseases are rare in developed countries. People who do suffer from some form of dietary deficiency are either alcoholics, people with intestinal disorders that prevent proper nutrient uptake, or people with very restricted diets (e.g. vegans).

Vitamin D Deficiency
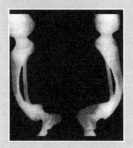
Lack of vitamin D in children produces the disease rickets. In adults a similar disease is called osteomalacia. Suffers typically show skeletal deformities (e.g. bowed legs, left) because inadequate amounts of calcium and phosphorus are incorporated into the bones. Vitamin D is produced by the skin when exposed to sunlight and it is vital for the absorption of calcium from the diet.

Vitamin A Deficiency
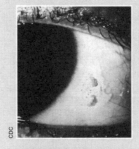
Vitamin A (found in animal livers, eggs, and dairy products) is essential for the production of light-absorbing pigments in the eye and for the formation of cell structures. Symptoms of deficiency include loss of night vision, inflammation of the eye, **keratomalacia** (damage to the cornea), and the appearance of **Bitots spots** – foamy, opaque patches on the white of the eye (refer to photo).

Vitamin C Deficiency
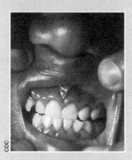
Vitamin C deficiency causes a disease known as scurvy. It is now rare in developed countries because of increased consumption of fresh fruit and vegetables. Inadequate vitamin C intake disturbs the body's normal production of collagen, a protein in connective tissue that holds body structures together. This results in poor wound healing, rupture of small blood vessels (visible bleeding in the skin), swollen gums, and loose teeth.

Vitamin B₁₂ Deficiency
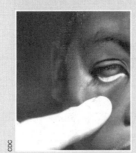
Found primarily in meat, but also in eggs and dairy products. B₁₂ is required for nucleic acid and protein metabolism, and for the maturation of red blood cells. It is essential for proper growth and for the proper nervous system function. B₁₂ deficiency results in **pernicious anaemia**, poor appetite, weight loss, growth failure, tiredness, brain damage, nervousness, muscle twitching, degeneration of the spinal cord, depression, and lack of balance.

Kwashiorkor
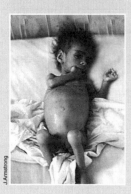
A severe type of protein-energy deficiency in young children (1-3 years old), occurring mainly in poor rural areas in the tropics. Kwashiorkor occurs when a child is suddenly weaned on to a diet that is low in calories, protein, and certain essential micronutrients. The problem is often made worse by a poor appetite due to illnesses such as measles. Children have stunted growth, oedema (accumulation of fluid in the tissues), and are inactive, apathetic and weak. Resistance against infection is lost, which may be fatal.

Marasmus

Marasmus is the most common form of deficiency disease. It is a severe form of protein and energy malnutrition that usually occurs in famine or starvation conditions. Children suffering from marasmus are stunted and extremely emaciated. They have loose folds of skin on the limbs and buttocks, due to the loss of fat and muscle tissue. Unlike kwashiorkor sufferers, marasmus does not cause the bloated and elongated abdomen. However sufferers have no resistance to disease and common infections are typically fatal.

1. Distinguish between **malnutrition** and **starvation**: _____

2. For each of the following vitamins, identify the natural sources of the vitamin, its function, and effect of deficiency:

(a) Vitamin A: _____

Function: _____

Deficiency: _____

(b) Vitamin B₁₂: _____

Function: _____

Deficiency: _____

Common Mineral Deficiencies

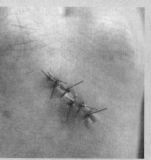

Calcium Deficiency

Calcium is required for enzyme function, formation of bones and teeth, blood clotting, and muscular contraction. Calcium deficiency causes poor bone growth and structure, increasing the tendency of bones to fracture and break. It also results in muscular spasms and poor blood clotting ability.

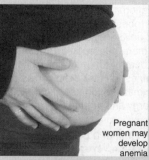

Zinc Deficiency

Zinc is found in red meat, poultry, fish, whole grain cereals and breads, legumes, and nuts. It is important for enzyme activity, production of insulin, making of sperm, and perception of taste. A deficiency in zinc causes growth retardation, a delay in puberty, muscular weakness, dry skin, and a delay in wound healing.

Iron Deficiency

Anemia results from lower than normal levels of hemoglobin in red blood cells. Iron from the diet is required to produce haemoglobin. People most at risk include women during pregnancy and those with an inadequate dietary intake. Symptoms include fatigue, fainting, breathlessness, and heart palpitations.

Pregnant women may develop anemia

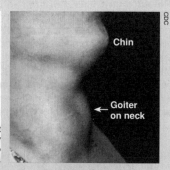

Chin

Goiter on neck

Iodine Deficiency

Iodine is essential for the production of thyroid hormones. These hormones control the rate of metabolism, growth, and development. Shortage of iodine in the diet may lead to **goiter** (thyroid enlargement as shown above). Iodine deficiency is also responsible for some cases of thyroid underactivity (**hypothyroidism**).

(c) Vitamin C: _____

    Function: _____

    Deficiency: _____

(d) Vitamin D: _____

    Function: _____

    Deficiency: _____

3. Suggest why young children, pregnant women, and athletes are among the most susceptible to dietary deficiencies:

_____

_____

_____

4. Explain why a lack of iron leads to the symptoms of anemia (fatigue and breathlessness): _____

_____

_____

5. Using vitamin C as an example, explain how the recommended daily requirements for vitamins are established:

_____

_____

6. Using the example of **iodine**, explain how artificial dietary supplementation can be achieved and discuss its benefits:

_____

_____

7. Using the example of protein deficiency, explain why malnourished people have a poor resistance to disease:

_____

_____

_____

Dietary Disorders

Most forms of malnutrition in western societies are the result of poorly balanced nutrient intakes rather than a lack of food *per se*. Dietary disorders may arise as a result of overeating (**obesity**), insufficient food intake (**anorexia nervosa**), or abnormally erratic eating habits (**bulimia nervosa**). Other health problems typically prevalent in western societies, including **cardiovascular diseases**, have been associated to varying degrees with the consumption of highly processed foods, high in cholesterol and saturated fats. Low fiber intake is a factor in the development of **colon cancer**, while high salt intake may lead to **hypertension**.

Anorexia Nervosa

An eating disorder characterized by an intense fear of being fat, severe weight loss, and a wilful avoidance of food. Clinically, anorexics are below 75% of the weight expected for their height and age. Anorexia most often affects teenage girls and young adult women (approximately 5% of sufferers are male). The exact cause of this form of self-starvation is not known, but research suggests that it is caused when emotional distress interacts with a physiological imbalance in a vulnerable individual. Anorexia is quite distinct from **bulimia**. Bulimics generally binge eat, and then purge their stomachs, rather than avoiding food altogether.

Obesity

Obesity is the most common form of malnutrition in affluent societies. It is a condition where there is too much body fat (not the same as being overweight). In the USA, nearly 25% of all adults are obese. Some genetic and hormonal causes are known, although obesity is a result of energy intake (eating) exceeding the **net energy expenditure**. Dieting is often ineffective for long-term weight loss because once normal eating is resumed the body responds by storing more fat in fat cells. Obesity increases the incidence of hypertension (high blood pressure), stroke, coronary artery disease, and Type II (adult onset) diabetes mellitus.

Health risks associated with anorexia nervosa

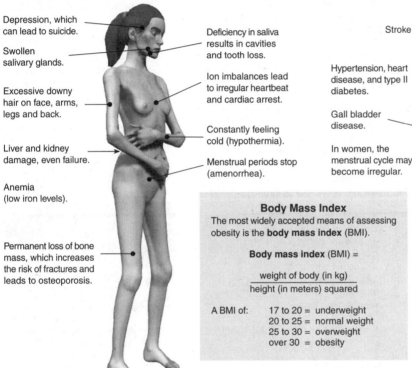

Health risks associated with obesity

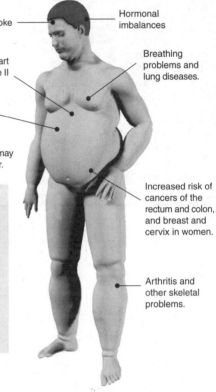

Body Mass Index
The most widely accepted means of assessing obesity is the **body mass index** (BMI).

Body mass index (BMI) =

$$\frac{\text{weight of body (in kg)}}{\text{height (in meters) squared}}$$

A BMI of:
17 to 20 = underweight
20 to 25 = normal weight
25 to 30 = overweight
over 30 = obesity

1. Describe the two basic energy factors that determine how a person's weight will change: _____

2. Using the BMI, calculate the minimum and maximum weight at which a 1.85 m tall man would be considered:

   (a) Overweight: _____   (c) Obese: _____

   (b) Normal weight: _____   (d) Underweight: _____

3. State the possible health consequences of the following aspects of a diet:

   (a) High salt consumption: _____

   (b) Low fiber content: _____

   (c) High cholesterol content: _____

4. Identify the key differences between anorexia nervosa and bulimia nervosa: _____

Related activities: Deficiency Diseases, Diabetes Mellitus

DA 1

Diet and Animal Nutrition

Diabetes Mellitus

Diabetes is a general term for a range of disorders sharing two common symptoms: production of large amounts of urine and excessive thirst. **Diabetes mellitus** is the most common form of diabetes and is characterized by **hyperglycemia** (high blood sugar). **Type 1** is characterised by a complete lack of insulin production and usually begins in childhood, while **type 2** is more typically a disease of older, overweight people whose cells develop a resistance to insulin uptake. Both types are chronic, incurable conditions and are managed differently. Type 1 is treated primarily with insulin injection, whereas type 2 sufferers manage their disease through diet and exercise in an attempt to limit the disease's long term detrimental effects.

Symptoms of Type 2 Diabetes Mellitus

a Symptoms may be mild at first. The body's cells do not respond appropriately to the insulin that is present and blood glucose levels become elevated. Normal blood glucose level is 60-110 mgL^{-1}. In diabetics, fasting blood glucose level is 126 mgL^{-1} or higher.

b Symptoms occur with varying degrees of severity:

► Cells are starved of fuel. This can lead to increased appetite and overeating and may contribute to an existing obesity problem.

► Urine production increases to rid the body of the excess glucose. Glucose is present in the urine and patients are frequently very thirsty.

► The body's inability to use glucose properly leads to muscle weakness and fatigue, irritability, frequent infections, and poor wound healing.

c Uncontrolled elevated blood glucose eventually results in damage to the blood vessels and leads to:

► coronary artery disease
► peripheral vascular disease
► retinal damage, blurred vision and blindness
► kidney damage and renal failure
► persistent ulcers and gangrene

Risk Factors

Obesity: BMI greater than 27. Distribution of weight is also important.

Age: Risk increases with age, although the incidence of type 2 diabetes is increasingly reported in obese children.

Sedentary lifestyle: Inactivity increases risk through its effects on bodyweight.

Family history: There is a strong genetic link for type 2 diabetes. Those with a family history of the disease are at greater risk.

Ethnicity: Certain ethnic groups are at higher risk of developing of type 2 diabetes.

High blood pressure: Up to 60% of people with undiagnosed diabetes have high blood pressure.

High blood lipids: More than 40% of people with diabetes have abnormally high levels of cholesterol and similar lipids in the blood.

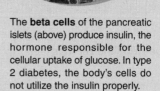

The **beta cells** of the pancreatic islets (above) produce insulin, the hormone responsible for the cellular uptake of glucose. In type 2 diabetes, the body's cells do not utilize the insulin properly.

Treating Type 2 Diabetes

Diabetes is not curable but can be managed to minimize the health effects:

► Regularly check blood glucose level

► Manage diet to reduce fluctuations in blood glucose level

► Take regular exercise

► Reduce weight

► Reduce blood pressure

► Reduce or stop smoking

► Take prescribed anti-diabetic drugs

► In time, insulin therapy may be required

Cellular uptake of glucose is impaired and glucose enters the bloodstream instead. Type 2 diabetes is sometimes called **insulin resistance**.

Fat cell

Insulin

1. Distinguish between type 1 and type 2 diabetes, relating the differences to the different methods of treatment:

_____

_____

2. Explain what dietary advice you would give to a person diagnosed with type 2 diabetes: _____

_____

_____

3. Explain why the increase in type 2 diabetes is considered epidemic in the developed world: _____

_____

Related activities: Control of Blood Glucose, Dietary Disorders

Gas Exchange in Animals

IB SL	IB HL	IB Options	AP Biology
Complete: 1-3, 8-9, 12, 14, 16, 18 Extension: 5-7, 15, 17	Complete: 1-3, 8-9, 12, 14, 16, 18 Extension: 5-7, 15, 17	Complete: Option B: SL: 23-26 Option H: HL: 19-23, 26-33	Complete: 1-33 Some numbers extension as appropriate

Learning Objectives

☐ 1. Compile your own glossary from the **KEY WORDS** displayed in **bold type** in the learning objectives below.

The Need for Gas Exchange *(pages 189, 198)*

☐ 2. Recognize that organisms need to exchange materials with their environment: **respiratory gases**, nutrients, and excretory products.

☐ 3. Distinguish between **cellular respiration** and **gas exchange**. Explain how cellular respiration creates a constant demand for **oxygen** and a need to eliminate **carbon dioxide** gas.

☐ 4. Understand that the physical properties of an environment place particular constraints on the type of gas exchange system that can be used. Outline the **physical characteristics** of marine, freshwater, and terrestrial environments. Explain briefly how the structural and physiological features of organisms relate to the environment in which they are found.

☐ 5. Identify the process by which gases are exchanged across gas exchange surfaces. Describe the essential features of gas exchange surfaces. With reference to **Fick's law** explain the significance of these features.

☐ 6. Describe the relationship between an organism's size and its surface area (the **surface area: volume ratio** or **SA:V**). Explain the significance of this relationship to the exchange of gases with the environment.

☐ 7. Recognize that the development of gas exchange systems and **respiratory pigments** in organisms are adaptations to facilitate adequate rates of gas exchange in specific environments.

Gas Exchange in Animals *(pages 190-192 and the TRC: Gas Exchange in Water)*

☐ 8. Recall the essential features of a gas exchange surface. Describe how the gas exchange surfaces of animals are maintained in a functional state.

☐ 9. Explain what is meant by **ventilation** and distinguish it from gas exchange. Explain the necessity for a ventilation system (or mechanism) in animals. With reference to any of the examples below (#10-13), identify the features of animal gas exchange systems.

☐ 10. Gas exchange over the **body surface** with (e.g. annelids) or without (e.g. protists, flatworms) a circulatory system.

☐ 11. **Gills** (fish and aquatic arthropods). Describe the features of the gas exchange system in bony fish. Relate the structure of gills to their suitability as gas exchange organs in water. If required, explain how gases are exchanged between the water and the blood in the gill capillaries, and explain the role of countercurrent exchange in facilitating this exchange. Comment on the oxygen extraction rates achieved by gills (vs the rates achieved by lungs in air). *Material specifically covering the structure and function of gills in fish is provided in an activity on the Teacher Resource CD-ROM.*

☐ 12. **Lungs** (vertebrates other than fish). Using a diagram, describe the general features of the ventilation system in a mammal (e.g. a human). Relate the structure of lungs to their suitability as gas exchange organs in air.

☐ 13. **Tracheal tubes** (e.g. insects). Describe the location and structure of tracheal tubes, including the role of the spiracles. Describe the way in which gases move into and out of the tracheae and the tissues. As extension, describe the various adaptations of aquatic insects to gas exchange. *Additional material covering the adaptations of aquatic insects is provided in an activity on the Teacher Resource CD ROM.*

Gas exchange in humans *(pages 193-196 and the TRC: Review of Lung Structure)*
Humans can be used as a mammalian example.

☐ 14. In more detail than #12 above, describe the structure, location, adaptations, and function of the ventilation system in humans (**trachea**, **bronchi**, **bronchioles**, **lungs**, and **alveoli**).

☐ 15. Describe the distribution of the following tissues and cells in the trachea, bronchi, and bronchioles: **cartilage**, **ciliated epithelium**, **goblet cells**, and **smooth muscle cells**. Describe the function of the cartilage, **cilia**, goblet cells, smooth muscle, and **elastic fibers** in the gas exchange system.

☐ 16. List the features of the alveoli that are adaptations to their functional role in gas exchange, including reference to the total surface area provided, the single epithelial layer, moist lining, and capillary network.

☐ 17. Recognize the relationship between gas exchange surfaces (alveoli) and the blood vessels in the lung tissue. Draw a simple diagram of an **alveolus** (air sac) to illustrate the movement of O_2 and CO_2, into and out of the blood in the surrounding capillary.

☐ 18. Recall the structure of the thorax in humans and describe the mechanism of ventilation (**breathing**). Include reference to the following:

(a) The role of the **diaphragm**, internal and external **intercostal muscles**, and the abdominal muscles in changing the air pressure in the lungs.

(b) The distinction between **inspiration** (inhalation) as an active process and **expiration** (exhalation) as a passive process (during normal, quiet breathing).

(c) The difference between quiet and forced breathing.

(d) The role of **surfactant** in lung function.

(e) The composition of inhaled and exhaled air.

Control of Breathing *(pages 195-197, 307-308 and the TRC: Effects of Training)*

☐ 19. Explain how basic rhythm of breathing is controlled through the activity of the **respiratory center** in the medulla and its output via the **phrenic nerves** and the **intercostal nerves**.

☐ 20. Explain the role of the **stretch receptors** and the **vagus nerve** in ending inspiration during normal breathing. Identify this control as the **inflation reflex**.

☐ 21. Identify influences on the respiratory center and comment on how these reflect changes in the body's demand for oxygen. Include reference to the activity of the **carotid** and **aortic bodies** (chemoreceptors in the carotid arteries and the aorta).

☐ 22. Distinguish between **involuntary** and **voluntary control** of breathing.

☐ 23. Explain how and why **ventilation rate** varies with **exercise**. Your explanation should include reference to the changes in blood composition that occur with exercise and the physiological effects of these changes. Understanding the mechanisms by which ventilation rate is adjusted to meet the demands of exercise requires a basic understanding of the mechanisms controlling breathing (see #19-22).

☐ 24. Explain how ventilation is measured in humans using a **spirometer**. Define the terms: **tidal volume**, **vital capacity**, **residual volume**, **dead space air**.

☐ 25. Explain how the breathing (ventilation) rate and **pulmonary ventilation** (PV) rate are calculated and expressed. Provide some typical values for **breathing rate**, **tidal volume**, and **PV**. Describe how each of these is affected by strenuous exercise.

Gas Transport in Humans *(pages 198-200)*

☐ 26. Describe the general role of respiratory pigments (**myoglobin** and fetal and adult **hemoglobin**) in the transport and delivery of oxygen to the tissues.

☐ 27. Define the term **partial pressure** and understand its significance with respect to gas transport.

☐ 28. Explain the ways in which CO_2 is carried in the blood, including the action and role of the following: carbonic anhydrase, **chloride shift**, plasma proteins as blood buffers, and hydrogen-carbonate (bicarbonate) ions.

☐ 29. Describe the transport of oxygen in relation to the **oxygen-hemoglobin dissociation curve**. Explain the oxygen dissociation curves of adult and fetal **hemoglobin** and **myoglobin** and identify the significance of the differences described.

☐ 30. Describe the effect of pH (CO_2 level) on the oxygen-hemoglobin dissociation curve (the **Bohr effect**) and explain its significance.

Gas Exchange and High Altitude *(page 203)*

☐ 31. Explain the problem of gas exchange at **high altitude**. Describe the short and long term effects of high altitude on human physiology, and explain the way the body **acclimatizes**. Include reference to blood composition (red blood cell number, blood viscosity), density of capillaries, and breathing and heart rates. Comment on the significance of these changes to the maintenance of adequate rates of exchange at altitude.

Respiratory Disorders *(pages 66, 201-202)*

☐ 32. Outline the possible causes of **lung cancer**, including the link between tobacco smoking and lung cancer. Briefly describe the effects of lung cancer on the gas exchange system, identifying detrimental changes to the alveolar epithelium, lung capacity, blood vessel walls, and composition of gases in the lung.

☐ 33. Describe the probable causes of **asthma,** its effects on the gas exchange system, and the physiological basis of the response.

 See the 'Textbook Reference Grid' on pages 8-9 for textbook page references relating to material in this topic.

Supplementary Texts

See pages 5-6 for additional details of this text:

■ Clegg, C.J., 1998. **Mammals: Structure and Function** (John Murray), pp. 24-31.

■ Helms, D.R. *et al.*, 1998. **Biology in the Laboratory** (W.H. Freeman), #35, #39.

■ Morton, D. & J.W. Perry, 1998. **Photo Atlas for Anatomy and Physiology** (W.H. Freeman).

See page 6 for details of publishers of periodicals.

STUDENT'S REFERENCE

■ **Lungs and the Control of Breathing** Bio. Sci. Rev. 14(4) April 2002, pp. 2-5. *The mechanisms, control, and measurement of breathing in humans. This article includes good, clear diagrams and useful summaries of important points.*

■ **Gas Exchange in the Lungs** Bio. Sci. Rev. 16(1) Sept. 2003, pp. 36-38. *The structure and function of the alveoli of the lungs, with an account of respiratory problems and diseases such as respiratory distress syndrome and emphysema.*

■ **Red Blood Cells** Bio. Sci. Rev. 11(2) Nov. 1998, pp. 2-4. *The structure and function of red blood cells, including details of oxygen transport.*

■ **Fetal Hemoglobin** Biol. Sci. Rev., 16(1) Sept. 2003, pp. 15-17. *The complex structure of hemoglobin molecules: the molecule in red blood cells that delivers oxygen to the tissues.*

■ **Humans with Altitude** New Scientist, 2 Nov. 2002, pp. 36-39. *The short term adjustments and (evolutionary) adaptations of those living at altitude.*

■ **Smoking** Biol. Sci. Rev., 10(1) Sept. 1997, pp. 14-16. *Smoking related diseases and the effects of tobacco smoking on human physiology.*

■ **Dust to Dust** New Scientist, 21 Sept. 2002 (Inside Science). *A supplement that concentrates on dust pollution, but also examines the impact of this pollutant on respiratory health.*

■ **Environmental Lung Disease** New Scientist, 23 September 1995 (Inside Science). *An excellent supplement on lung disorders, with good diagrams illustrating lung functioning and gas transport.*

TEACHER'S REFERENCE

■ **Breathless** New Scientist, 8 March 2003, pp. 46-49. *Adaptations for gas exchange in shark species able to withstand anoxia. A better understanding of the mechanisms for this may help with treatment of stoke and heart attack victims.*

■ **Spectrophotometric Properties of Hemoglobin** The Am. Biology Teacher, 59(2), Feb. 1997, pp. 104-107. *Measuring spectral absorption for oxyhemoglobin and carboxyhemoglobin, and the role of hemoglobin as an oxygen transport molecule in the blood.*

■ **The Effect of Hyperventilation on the Ability to Hold one's Breath** The Am. Biology Teacher, 59(4), April, 1997, pp. 229-231. *Investigating the effects of hyperventilation and blood CO_2 and O_2 level on respiratory physiology.*

See pages 10-11 for details of how to access **Bio Links** from our web site: **www.thebiozone.com** From Bio Links, access sites under the topics:

GENERAL BIOLOGY ONLINE RESOURCES > Online Textbooks and Lecture Notes • An on-line biology book • Learn.co.uk *... and others >* **General Online Biology Resources** • Advancing in natural science • Virtual library: Biosciences • Ken's bio-web resources *... and others*

ANIMAL BIOLOGY: • Anatomy and physiology • Human physiology lecture notes *... and others* > **Gas Exchange:** • Gas exchange • Lesson 11: The respiratory system • Respiration in aquatic insects • Respiratory system • Respiratory system: Chpt 41 • Tracheal breathing > **Support and Movement:** • Sports science: Energy • Energy production during physical activity • Energy systems Part I *... and others*

HEALTH AND DISEASE > Non-Infectious Diseases: • Asthma • Chemicals and human health • American Cancer Society *... and others*

Presentation MEDIA to support this topic: **HEALTH & DISEASE:** • **Non-infectious Disease**

Introduction to Gas Exchange

Living cells require energy for the activities of life. Energy is released in cells by the breakdown of sugars and other substances in the metabolic process called **cellular respiration**. As a consequence of this process, gases need to be exchanged between the respiring cells and the environment. In most organisms (with the exception of some bacterial groups) these gases are carbon dioxide (CO_2) and oxygen (O_2). The diagram below illustrates this process for an animal. Plant cells also respire, but their gas exchange budget is different because they also produce O_2 and consume CO_2 in photosynthesis.

The Need for Gas Exchange

Gas exchange is the process by which oxygen is acquired and carbon dioxide is removed. Cellular respiration creates a constant demand for oxygen (O_2) and a need to eliminate carbon dioxide gas (CO_2).

Gas exchange surfaces provide a means for gases to enter and leave the body. Some organisms use the body surface as the sole gas exchange surface, but many have specialized gas exchange structures (e.g. lungs, gills, or stomata). Amphibians use the body surface and simple lungs to provide for their gas exchange requirements.

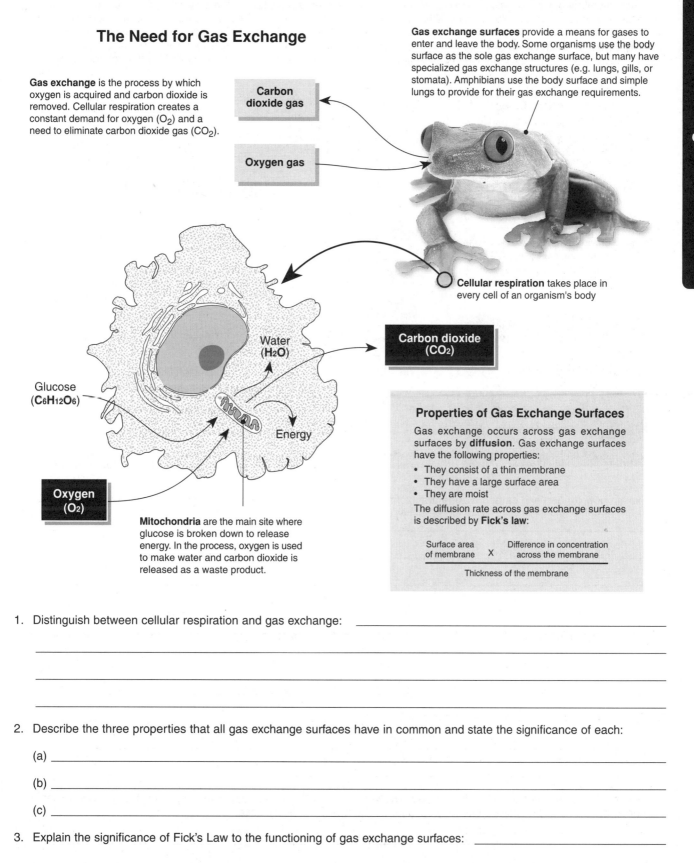

Carbon dioxide gas

Oxygen gas

Cellular respiration takes place in every cell of an organism's body

Water (H_2O)

Carbon dioxide (CO_2)

Glucose ($C_6H_{12}O_6$)

Energy

Oxygen (O_2)

Mitochondria are the main site where glucose is broken down to release energy. In the process, oxygen is used to make water and carbon dioxide is released as a waste product.

Properties of Gas Exchange Surfaces

Gas exchange occurs across gas exchange surfaces by **diffusion**. Gas exchange surfaces have the following properties:

- They consist of a thin membrane
- They have a large surface area
- They are moist

The diffusion rate across gas exchange surfaces is described by **Fick's law**:

$$\frac{\text{Surface area of membrane} \quad X \quad \text{Difference in concentration across the membrane}}{\text{Thickness of the membrane}}$$

1. Distinguish between cellular respiration and gas exchange: _____

_____

_____

_____

2. Describe the three properties that all gas exchange surfaces have in common and state the significance of each:

(a) _____

(b) _____

(c) _____

3. Explain the significance of Fick's Law to the functioning of gas exchange surfaces: _____

_____

_____

Related activities: Gas Exchange in Animals, Gas Exchange in Insects

A 1

Gas Exchange in Insects

One advantage of gas exchange for terrestrial animals is that oxygen is proportionately more abundant in air than in water. However, terrestrial life also presents certain problems: body water can be lost easily through any exposed surface that is moist, thin, permeable, and vascular enough to serve as a respiratory membrane. Most insects are small terrestrial animals with a large surface area to volume ratio. Although they are highly susceptible to drying out, they are covered by a hard exoskeleton with a waxy outer layer that minimizes water loss. Tracheal systems are the most common gas exchange organs

of terrestrial arthropods, including insects. Most body segments have paired apertures called spiracles in the lateral body wall through which air enters. Filtering devices in the spiracles prevent small particles from clogging the system, and valves control the degree to which the spiracles are open. In small insects, diffusion is the only mechanism needed to exchange gases, because it occurs so rapidly through the air-filled tubules. Larger, more active insects, such as locusts (below) have a tracheal system which includes air sacs that can be compressed and expanded to assist in moving air through the tubules.

Insect Tracheal Tubes

Insects, and some spiders, transport gases via a system of branching tubes called tracheae or tracheal tubes. The gases move by diffusion across the moist lining directly to and from the tissues. The end of each tube contains a small amount of fluid in which the respiratory gases are dissolved. The fluid is drawn into the muscle tissues during their contraction, and is released back into the tracheole when the muscle rests. Insects ventilate their tracheal system by making rhythmic body movements to help move the air in and out of the tracheae.

Spiracle openings on the abdomen

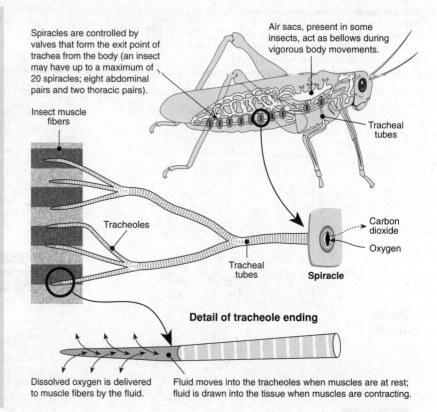

Spiracles are controlled by valves that form the exit point of trachea from the body (an insect may have up to a maximum of 20 spiracles; eight abdominal pairs and two thoracic pairs).

Insect muscle fibers

Air sacs, present in some insects, act as bellows during vigorous body movements.

Tracheal tubes

Tracheoles

Tracheal tubes

Carbon dioxide

Oxygen

Spiracle

Detail of tracheole ending

Dissolved oxygen is delivered to muscle fibers by the fluid.

Fluid moves into the tracheoles when muscles are at rest; fluid is drawn into the tissue when muscles are contracting.

1. Explain how oxygen and carbon dioxide are exchanged between the air and body tissues at the end of insect tracheoles:

_____

_____

_____

_____

2. Valves in the spiracles can regulate the amount of air entering the tracheal system. Suggest a reason for this adaptation:

_____

_____

3. Explain how ventilation is achieved in a terrestrial insect: _____

_____

_____

4. Even though most insects are small, they have evolved an efficient and highly developed gas exchange system that is independent of diffusion across the body surface. Suggest why this is the case:

_____

_____

_____

Activity links: Gas Exchange in Animals

Gas Exchange in Animals

The way in which gas exchange is achieved is influenced by the animal's general body form and by the environment in which the animal lives. Small, aquatic organisms such as sponges, flatworms and cnidarians, require no specialized respiratory structures. Gases are exchanged between the surrounding water (or moist environment) and the body's cells by diffusion directly across the organism's surface. Larger animals require specialized gas exchange systems. The complexity of these is related to the efficiency of gas exchange required, which is determined by the oxygen demands of the organism.

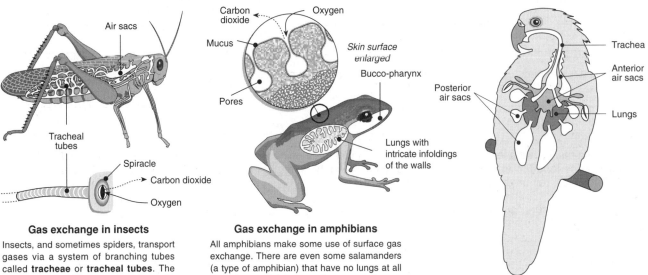

Gas exchange in insects

Insects, and sometimes spiders, transport gases via a system of branching tubes called **tracheae** or **tracheal tubes**. The gases move by diffusion across the moist lining directly to and from the tissues. The end of each tube contains a small amount of fluid which regulates the movement of gases by changing the surface area of air in contact with the cells.

Gas exchange in amphibians

All amphibians make some use of surface gas exchange. There are even some salamanders (a type of amphibian) that have no lungs at all and rely completely on surface gas exchange. This is only possible if the surface is kept moist by secretions from mucous glands. Frogs carry out gas exchange through the skin and in the lungs. At times of inactivity, the skin alone is a sufficient surface with either water or air.

Gas exchange in birds

A bird has air sacs in addition to lungs. The air sacs function in ventilating the lungs, where gas exchange takes place. Together, the anterior and posterior air sacs function as bellows that keep air flowing through the lungs continuously and in one direction.

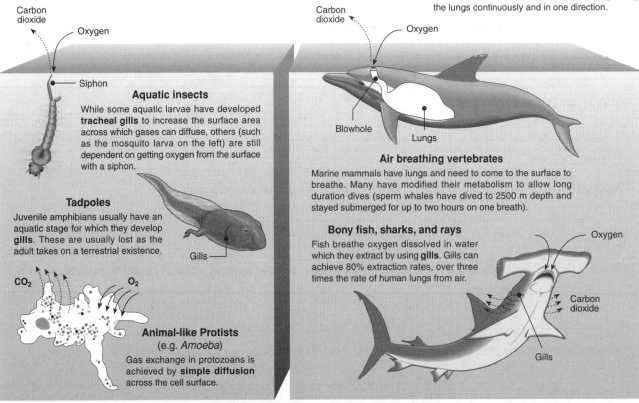

Aquatic insects

While some aquatic larvae have developed **tracheal gills** to increase the surface area across which gases can diffuse, others (such as the mosquito larva on the left) are still dependent on getting oxygen from the surface with a siphon.

Tadpoles

Juvenile amphibians usually have an aquatic stage for which they develop **gills**. These are usually lost as the adult takes on a terrestrial existence.

Animal-like Protists
(e.g. *Amoeba*)

Gas exchange in protozoans is achieved by **simple diffusion** across the cell surface.

Air breathing vertebrates

Marine mammals have lungs and need to come to the surface to breathe. Many have modified their metabolism to allow long duration dives (sperm whales have dived to 2500 m depth and stayed submerged for up to two hours on one breath).

Bony fish, sharks, and rays

Fish breathe oxygen dissolved in water which they extract by using **gills**. Gills can achieve 80% extraction rates, over three times the rate of human lungs from air.

Jellyfish increase their surface area for gas exchange by having ruffles.

Nudibranch snails have elaborate exposed gills to assist gas exchange.

Some salamanders have no lungs and breathe solely through their skin.

Tube worms carry out gas exchange with feathery extensions in the water.

Related activities: Gas Exchange in Insects

RA 2

1. Suggest two reasons for the development of gas exchange structures and systems in animals:

   (a) _____

   (b) _____

2. (a) Explain why the air sacs of birds provide more efficient use of the air taken in with each breath:

   _____

   _____

   (b) Explain why birds require such an efficient method of gas exchange: _____

   _____

   _____

3. Complete the following list as a summary of the main features of the respiratory structures found in animals. Briefly describe the **location in the body** of each system, name the animal group or groups that use each system, and state in which medium (air or water) each system is used:

   (a) **Body surface**: Location in the body: _____

   _____

   Animal groups: _____ Medium: _____

   (b) **Tracheal tubes**: Location in the body: _____

   _____

   Animal groups: _____ Medium: _____

   (c) **Gills**: Location in the body: _____

   _____

   Animal groups: _____ Medium: _____

   (d) **Lungs**: Location in the body: _____

   _____

   Animal groups: _____ Medium: _____

4. Describe two ways in which air breathers manage to keep their gas exchange surfaces moist:

   (a) _____

   (b) _____

5. Explain why organisms with gills are at risk when their water is polluted by large amounts of organic material:

   _____

   _____

6. Using examples, discuss the relationship between an animal's type of gas exchange system and its environment:

   _____

   _____

   _____

   _____

   _____

   _____

   _____

The Human Respiratory System

Lungs are internal sac-like organs found in most amphibians, and all reptiles, birds, and mammals. The paired lungs of mammals are connected to the outside air by way of a system of tubular passageways: the trachea, bronchi, and bronchioles. Ciliated, mucus secreting epithelium lines this system of tubules, trapping and removing dust and pathogens before they reach the gas exchange surfaces. Each lung is divided into a number of lobes, each receiving its own bronchus. Each bronchus divides many times, terminating in the respiratory bronchioles from which arise 2-11 alveolar ducts and numerous **alveoli** (air sacs). These provide a very large surface area (70 m²) for the exchange of respiratory gases by diffusion between the alveoli and the blood in the capillaries. The details of this exchange across the **respiratory membrane** are described on the next page.

Morphology of the Respiratory System

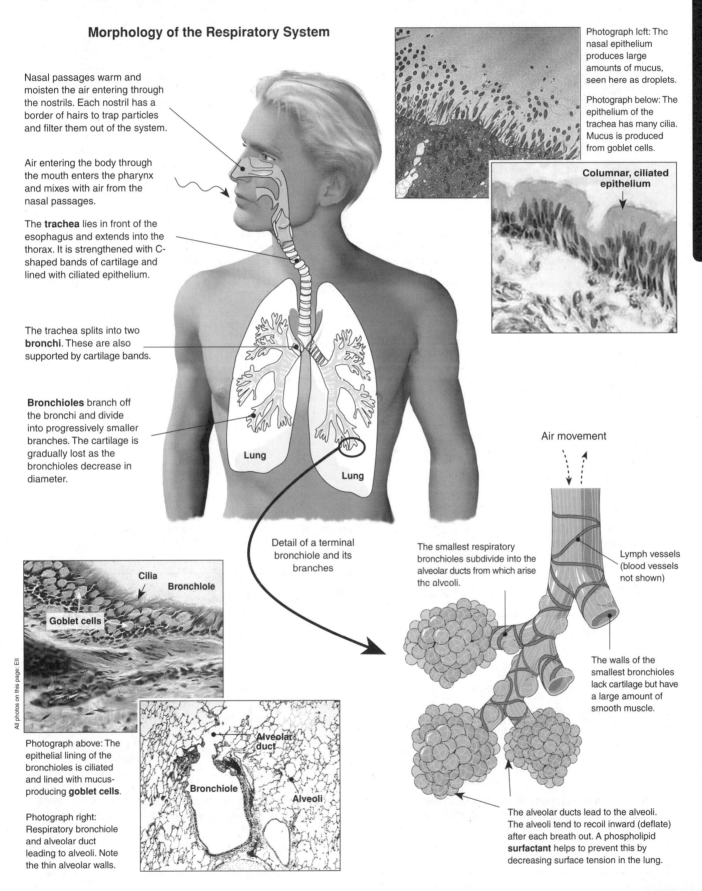

Nasal passages warm and moisten the air entering through the nostrils. Each nostril has a border of hairs to trap particles and filter them out of the system.

Air entering the body through the mouth enters the pharynx and mixes with air from the nasal passages.

The **trachea** lies in front of the esophagus and extends into the thorax. It is strengthened with C-shaped bands of cartilage and lined with ciliated epithelium.

The trachea splits into two **bronchi**. These are also supported by cartilage bands.

Bronchioles branch off the bronchi and divide into progressively smaller branches. The cartilage is gradually lost as the bronchioles decrease in diameter.

Lung

Lung

Photograph left: The nasal epithelium produces large amounts of mucus, seen here as droplets.

Photograph below: The epithelium of the trachea has many cilia. Mucus is produced from goblet cells.

Columnar, ciliated epithelium

Detail of a terminal bronchiole and its branches

Air movement

The smallest respiratory bronchioles subdivide into the alveolar ducts from which arise the alveoli.

Lymph vessels (blood vessels not shown)

The walls of the smallest bronchioles lack cartilage but have a large amount of smooth muscle.

Cilia
Bronchiole

Goblet cells

All photos on this page: EII

Photograph above: The epithelial lining of the bronchioles is ciliated and lined with mucus-producing **goblet cells**.

Photograph right: Respiratory bronchiole and alveolar duct leading to alveoli. Note the thin alveolar walls.

Alveolar duct

Bronchiole

Alveoli

The alveolar ducts lead to the alveoli. The alveoli tend to recoil inward (deflate) after each breath out. A phospholipid **surfactant** helps to prevent this by decreasing surface tension in the lung.

Related activities: Gas Transport in Humans
Web links: Review of Lung Function

RA 2

An Alveolus

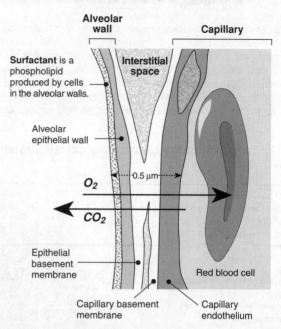

The diagram above illustrates the physical arrangement of the alveoli to the capillaries through which the blood moves. Phagocytic monocytes and macrophages are also present to protect the lung tissue. Elastic connective tissue gives the alveoli their ability to expand and recoil.

The Respiratory Membrane

The **respiratory membrane** is the term for the layered junction between the alveolar epithelial cells, the endothelial cells of the capillary, and their associated basement membranes (thin, collagenous layers that underlie the epithelial tissues). Gases move freely across this membrane.

1. (a) Explain how the basic structure of the human respiratory system provides such a large area for gas exchange:

_____

_____

(b) Identify the general region of the lung where exchange of gases takes place: _____

2. Describe the structure and purpose of the respiratory membrane: _____

_____

_____

3. Describe the role of the surfactant in the alveoli: _____

_____

4. Using the information above and on the previous page, complete the table below summarizing the **histology of the respiratory pathway**. Name each numbered region and use a tick or cross to indicate the presence or absence of particular tissues.

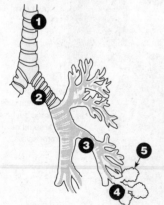

	Region	Cartilage	Ciliated epithelium	Goblet cells (mucus)	Smooth muscle	Connective tissue
1						✓
2						
3		gradually lost				
4	Alveolar duct		✗	✗		
5					very little	

5. Babies born prematurely are often deficient in surfactant. This causes respiratory distress syndrome; a condition where breathing is very difficult. From what you know about the role of surfactant, explain the symptoms of this syndrome:

_____

_____

Breathing in Humans

In mammals, the mechanism of breathing (ventilation) provides a continual supply of fresh air to the lungs and helps to maintain a large diffusion gradient for respiratory gases across the gas exchange surface. Oxygen must be delivered regularly to supply the needs of respiring cells. Similarly, carbon dioxide, which is produced as a result of cellular metabolism, must be quickly eliminated from the body. Adequate lung ventilation is essential to these exchanges. The cardiovascular system participates by transporting respiratory gases to and from the cells of the body. The volume of gases exchanged during breathing varies according to the physiological demands placed on the body (e.g. by exercise). These changes can be measured using spirometry.

Inspiration (inhalation or breathing in)

During quiet breathing, inspiration is achieved by increasing the space (therefore decreasing the pressure) inside the lungs. Air then flows into the lungs to fill the space. Inspiration is always an active process involving muscle contraction.

1a External intercostal muscles contract causing the ribcage to expand and move up

1b Diaphragm contracts and drops downwards

2 Thoracic volume increases, lungs expand, and the pressure inside the lungs decreases

3 Air flows into the lungs in response to the pressure gradient

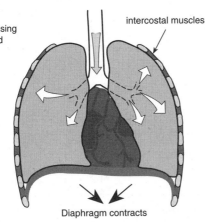

intercostal muscles

Diaphragm contracts

Expiration (exhalation or breathing out)

During quiet breathing, expiration is achieved passively by decreasing the space (thus increasing the pressure) inside the lungs. Air then flows passively out of the lungs to equalize with the air pressure. In active breathing, muscle contraction is involved in bringing about both inspiration and expiration.

1 In **quiet breathing**, external intercostal muscles and diaphragm relax. Elasticity of the lung tissue causes recoil.

In **forced breathing**, the internal intercostals and abdominal muscles also contract to increase the force of the expiration

2 Thoracic volume decreases and the pressure inside the lungs increases

3 Air flows passively out of the lungs in response to the pressure gradient

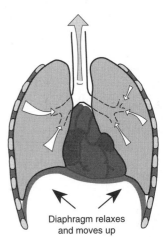

Diaphragm relaxes and moves up

Using spirometry to determine changes in lung volume

The apparatus used to measure the amount of air exchanged during breathing and the rate of breathing is a **spirometer** (also called a respirometer). A simple spirometer consists of a weighted drum, containing oxygen or air, inverted over a chamber of water. A tube connects the air-filled chamber with the subject's mouth, and soda lime in the system absorbs the carbon dioxide breathed out. Breathing results in a trace called a spirogram, from which lung volumes can be measured directly.

During inspiration
Air is removed from the chamber, the drum sinks, and an upward deflection is recorded on the paper on the rotating drum.

During expiration
Air is added to the chamber, the drum rises, and a downward deflection is recorded.

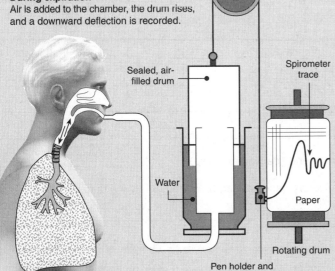

Pulley

Sealed, air-filled drum

Spirometer trace

Water

Paper

Rotating drum

Pen holder and counter balance

Lung Volumes and Capacities

The air in the lungs can be divided into volumes. Lung capacities are combinations of volumes.

Description of volume	Vol (liter)
Tidal volume (TV)	0.5
Volume of air breathed in and out in a single breath	
Inspiratory reserve volume (IRV)	3.3
Volume breathed in by a maximum inspiration at the end of a normal inspiration	
Expiratory reserve volume (ERV)	1.0
Volume breathed out by a maximum effort at the end of a normal expiration	
Residual volume (RV)	1.2
Volume of air remaining in the lungs at the end of a maximum expiration	
Description of capacity	
Inspiratory capacity (IC) = TV + IRV	3.8
Volume breathed in by a maximum inspiration at the end of a normal expiration	
Vital capacity (VC) = IRV + TV + ERV	4.8
Volume breathed in by a maximum inspiration following a maximum expiration	
Total lung capacity (TLC) = VC + RV	6.0
The total volume of the lungs. Only a fraction of TLC is used in normal breathing	

Only about 70% of the air that is inhaled reaches the alveoli. The rest remains in the air spaces of the nose, throat, larynx, trachea and bronchi. This air is unavailable for gas exchange and is called the **dead air volume (dead space air)**.

Related activities: Control of Breathing **Web links**: Effects of Training, Review of Lung Function, Respiratory Basics Learning Activity

DA 2

Measuring Changes in Lung Volume

Changes in lung volume can be measured using spirometry (see opposite). Total adult lung volume varies between 4 and 6 liters (L or dm³) (it is greater in males). The **vital capacity** is somewhat less than this because of the residual volume of air remaining in the lungs even after expiration. The exchange between fresh air and the residual volume is a slow process and the composition of gases in the lungs remains relatively constant (table, right). Once measured, the **tidal volume** can be used to calculate the pulmonary ventilation rate or **PV**: the amount of air exchanged with the environment per minute. During exercise, breathing rate, tidal volume, and PV increase up to a maximum (indicated below).

Respiratory gas	Approximate percentages of O_2 and CO_2		
	Inhaled air	Air in lungs	Exhaled air
O_2	21.0	13.8	16.4
CO_2	0.04	5.5	3.6

Above: The percentages of respiratory gases in air (by volume) during normal breathing. The percentage volume of oxygen in the alveolar air (in the lung) is lower than that in the exhaled air because of the influence of the dead air volume in the airways (air unavailable for gas exchange).

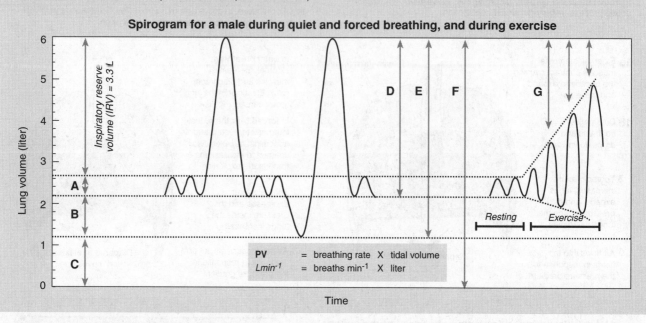

Spirogram for a male during quiet and forced breathing, and during exercise

$$PV \quad Lmin^{-1} = \text{breathing rate} \times \text{tidal volume} = \text{breaths min}^{-1} \times \text{liter}$$

1. (a) Briefly outline the sequence of events involved in quiet breathing: _____

_____

_____

(b) Explain the essential difference between this and the situation during heavy exercise or forced breathing:

_____

_____

2. Using the definitions given previously, identify the volumes and capacities indicated by the letters A-F on the spirogram diagram above. For each, indicate the volume (vol) in liters. The inspiratory reserve volume has been identified for you:

(a) A: _____ Vol: _____   (d) D: _____ Vol: _____

(b) B: _____ Vol: _____   (e) E: _____ Vol: _____

(c) C: _____ Vol: _____   (f) F: _____ Vol: _____

3. Explain what is happening in the sequence indicated by the letter **G**: _____

_____

4. Calculate PV when breathing rate is 15 breaths per minute and tidal volume is 4.0 L: _____

5. The table above gives approximate percentages for respiratory gases during breathing. Study the data and then:

(a) Calculate the difference in CO_2 between inhaled and exhaled air: _____

(b) Explain where this 'extra' CO_2 comes from: _____

(c) Explain why the dead air volume raises the oxygen content of exhaled air above that in the lungs: _____

_____

Control of Breathing

The basic rhythm of breathing is controlled by the **respiratory center**, a cluster of neurons located in the medulla oblongata. This rhythm is adjusted in response to the physical and chemical changes that occur when we carry out different activities. Although the control of breathing is involuntary, we can exert some degree of conscious control over it. The diagram below illustrates these controls.

The Control of Breathing

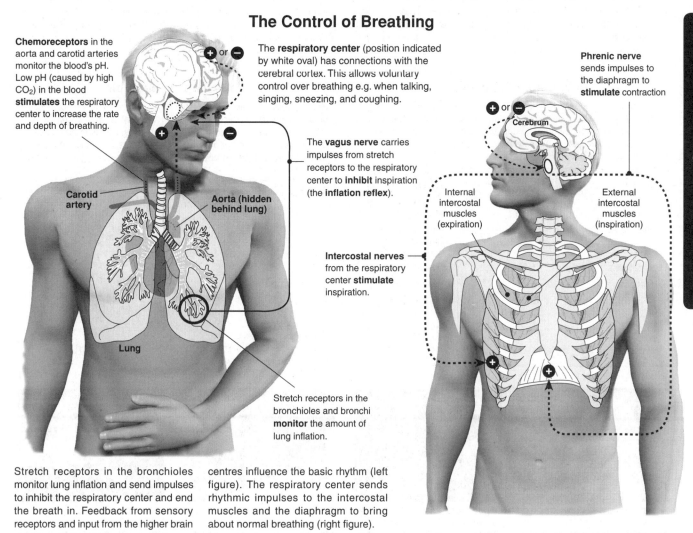

Chemoreceptors in the aorta and carotid arteries monitor the blood's pH. Low pH (caused by high CO_2) in the blood **stimulates** the respiratory center to increase the rate and depth of breathing.

The **respiratory center** (position indicated by white oval) has connections with the cerebral cortex. This allows voluntary control over breathing e.g. when talking, singing, sneezing, and coughing.

Phrenic nerve sends impulses to the diaphragm to **stimulate** contraction

Carotid artery

Aorta (hidden behind lung)

The **vagus nerve** carries impulses from stretch receptors to the respiratory center to **inhibit** inspiration (the **inflation reflex**).

Internal intercostal muscles (expiration)

External intercostal muscles (inspiration)

Cerebrum

Intercostal nerves from the respiratory center **stimulate** inspiration.

Lung

Stretch receptors in the bronchioles and bronchi **monitor** the amount of lung inflation.

Stretch receptors in the bronchioles monitor lung inflation and send impulses to inhibit the respiratory center and end the breath in. Feedback from sensory receptors and input from the higher brain centres influence the basic rhythm (left figure). The respiratory center sends rhythmic impulses to the intercostal muscles and the diaphragm to bring about normal breathing (right figure).

1. Explain how the basic rhythm of breathing is controlled: _____

_____

2. Describe the role of each of the following in the regulation of breathing:

   (a) Phrenic nerve: _____

   (b) Intercostal nerves: _____

   (c) Vagus nerve: _____

   (d) Inflation reflex: _____

3. (a) Describe the effect of low blood pH on the rate and depth of breathing: _____

   _____

   (b) Explain how this effect is mediated: _____

   _____

   (c) Suggest why blood pH is a good mechanism by which to regulate breathing rate: _____

   _____

   _____

Related activities: Gas Transport in Humans
Web links: Review of Lung Function

A 2

Respiratory Pigments

Regardless of the gas exchange system present, the amount of oxygen that can be carried in solution in the blood is small. The efficiency of gas exchange in animals is enhanced by the presence of **respiratory pigments**. All respiratory pigments consist of proteins complexed with iron or copper. They combine reversibly with oxygen and greatly increase the capacity of blood to transport oxygen and deliver it to the tissues. For example, the amount of oxygen dissolved in the plasma in mammals is only about 2 cm³ O₂ per liter. However the amount carried bound to hemoglobin is 100 times this. Hemoglobin is the most widely distributed respiratory pigment and is characteristic of all vertebrates and many invertebrate taxa. Other respiratory pigments include chlorocruorin, hemocyanin, and hemerythrin. Note that the precise structure and carrying capacity of any one particular pigment type varies between taxa (see the range of hemoglobins in the table below).

Respiratory Pigments

Respiratory pigments are colored proteins capable of combining reversibly with oxygen, hence increasing the amount of oxygen that can be carried by the blood. Pigments typical of representative taxa are listed below. Note that the polychaetes are very variable in terms of the pigment possessed.

Taxon	Oxygen capacity (cm³ O₂ per 100 cm³ blood)	Pigment
Oligochaetes	1 - 10	Hemoglobin
Polychaetes	1 - 10	Hemoglobin, chlorocruorin, or hemerythrin
Crustaceans	1 - 6	Hemocyanin
Molluscs	1 - 6	Hemocyanin
Fishes	2 - 4	Hemoglobin
Reptiles	7 - 12	Hemoglobin
Birds	20 - 25	Hemoglobin
Mammals	15 - 30	Hemoglobin

Mammalian Hemoglobin

Hemoglobin is a globular protein consisting of 574 amino acids arranged in four polypeptide sub-units: two identical **beta chains** and two identical **alpha chains**. The four sub-units are held together as a functional unit by bonds. Each sub-unit has an iron-containing heme group at its center and binds one molecule of oxygen.

Chemical formula:
$$C_{3032}H_{4816}O_{872}N_{780}S_8Fe_4$$

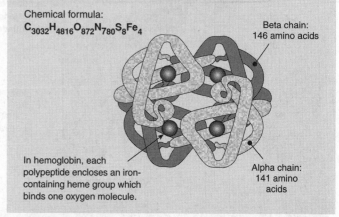

Beta chain: 146 amino acids

In hemoglobin, each polypeptide encloses an iron-containing heme group which binds one oxygen molecule.

Alpha chain: 141 amino acids

Aquatic polychaete fanworms e.g. *Sabella*, possess **chlorocruorin**.

Oligochaete annelids, such as earthworms, have **hemoglobin**.

Aquatic crustaceans e.g. crabs, possess **hemocyanin** pigment.

Vertebrates such as this fish have **hemoglobin** pigment.

Cephalopod molluscs such as *Nautilus* contain **hemocyanin**.

Birds, being vertebrates contain the pigment **hemoglobin**.

Many large active polychaetes, e.g. *Nereis*, contain **hemoglobin**.

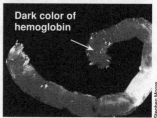

Dark color of hemoglobin

Chironomus is one of only two insect genera to contain a pigment.

1. (a) Explain how respiratory pigments increase the carrying capacity of the blood: _____

_____

 (b) Identify which feature of a respiratory pigment determines its oxygen carrying capacity: _____

_____

2. With reference to hemoglobin, suggest how oxygen carrying capacity is related to metabolic activity: _____

_____

_____

3. Suggest why larger molecular weight respiratory pigments are carried dissolved in the plasma rather than within cells:

_____

Gas Transport in Humans

The transport of respiratory gases around the body is the role of the blood and its respiratory pigments. Oxygen is transported throughout the body chemically bound to the respiratory pigment **hemoglobin** inside the red blood cells. In the muscles, oxygen from hemoglobin is transferred to and retained by **myoglobin**, a molecule that is chemically similar to hemoglobin except that it consists of only one heme-globin unit. Myoglobin has a greater affinity for oxygen than hemoglobin and acts as an oxygen store within muscles, releasing the oxygen during periods of prolonged or extreme muscular activity. If the myoglobin store is exhausted, the muscles are forced into oxygen debt and must respire anaerobically. The waste product of this, lactic acid, accumulates in the muscle and is transported (as lactate) to the liver where it is metabolized under aerobic conditions.

Gas Exchange and Transport

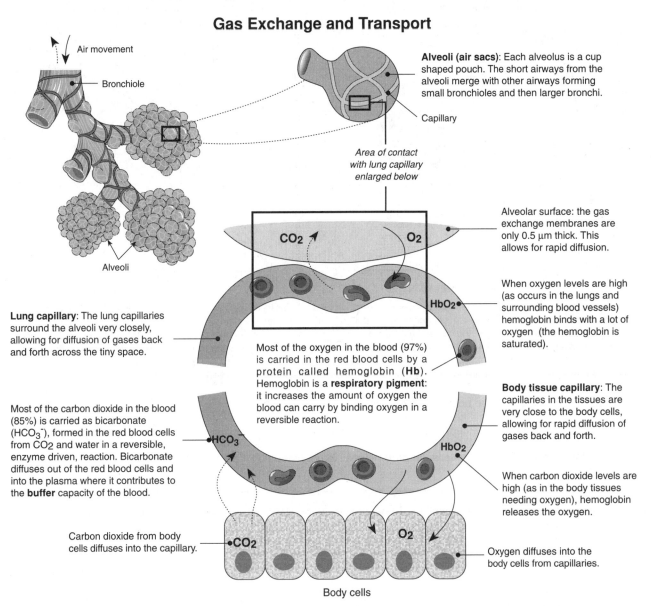

Air movement

Bronchiole

Alveoli (air sacs): Each alveolus is a cup shaped pouch. The short airways from the alveoli merge with other airways forming small bronchioles and then larger bronchi.

Capillary

Alveoli

Area of contact with lung capillary enlarged below

Alveolar surface: the gas exchange membranes are only 0.5 μm thick. This allows for rapid diffusion.

CO_2 O_2

HbO_2

When oxygen levels are high (as occurs in the lungs and surrounding blood vessels) hemoglobin binds with a lot of oxygen (the hemoglobin is saturated).

Lung capillary: The lung capillaries surround the alveoli very closely, allowing for diffusion of gases back and forth across the tiny space.

Most of the oxygen in the blood (97%) is carried in the red blood cells by a protein called hemoglobin (**Hb**). Hemoglobin is a **respiratory pigment**: it increases the amount of oxygen the blood can carry by binding oxygen in a reversible reaction.

Body tissue capillary: The capillaries in the tissues are very close to the body cells, allowing for rapid diffusion of gases back and forth.

Most of the carbon dioxide in the blood (85%) is carried as bicarbonate (HCO_3^-), formed in the red blood cells from CO_2 and water in a reversible, enzyme driven, reaction. Bicarbonate diffuses out of the red blood cells and into the plasma where it contributes to the **buffer** capacity of the blood.

HCO_3^-

HbO_2

When carbon dioxide levels are high (as in the body tissues needing oxygen), hemoglobin releases the oxygen.

Carbon dioxide from body cells diffuses into the capillary.

CO_2 O_2

Oxygen diffuses into the body cells from capillaries.

Body cells

Transport of Carbon Dioxide in the Blood

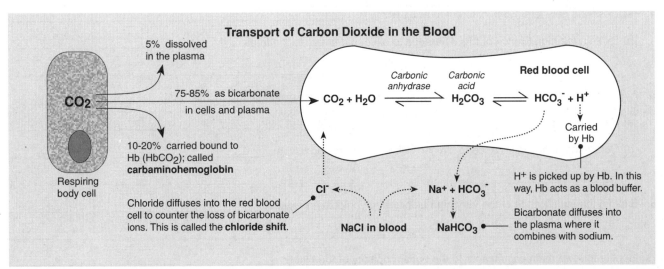

5% dissolved in the plasma

75-85% as bicarbonate in cells and plasma

10-20% carried bound to Hb (HbCO$_2$); called **carbaminohemoglobin**

CO_2

Respiring body cell

Chloride diffuses into the red blood cell to counter the loss of bicarbonate ions. This is called the **chloride shift**.

Carbonic anhydrase   Carbonic acid   **Red blood cell**

$CO_2 + H_2O \rightleftharpoons H_2CO_3 \rightleftharpoons HCO_3^- + H^+$

Carried by Hb

Cl^-

NaCl in blood

$Na^+ + HCO_3^-$

$NaHCO_3$

H^+ is picked up by Hb. In this way, Hb acts as a blood buffer.

Bicarbonate diffuses into the plasma where it combines with sodium.

Related activities: The Human Respiratory System, Respiratory Pigments

A 2

Oxygen does not easily dissolve in blood, but is carried in chemical combination with hemoglobin (Hb) in red blood cells. The most important factor determining how much oxygen is carried by Hb is the level of oxygen in the blood. The greater the oxygen tension, the more oxygen will combine with Hb. This relationship can be illustrated with an oxygen-hemoglobin dissociation curve as shown below (Fig. 1). In the lung capillaries, (high O_2), a lot of oxygen is picked up and bound by Hb. In the tissues, (low O_2), oxygen is released. In skeletal muscle, myoglobin picks up oxygen from hemoglobin and therefore serves as an oxygen store when oxygen tensions begin to fall. The release of oxygen is enhanced by the **Bohr effect** (Fig. 2).

Respiratory Pigments and the Transport of Oxygen

Fig. 1: Dissociation curves for hemoglobin and myoglobin at normal body temperature for fetal and adult human blood.

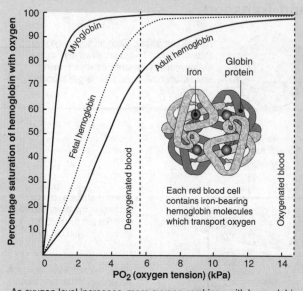

Fig. 2: Oxygen-hemoglobin dissociation curves for human blood at normal body temperature at different blood pH.

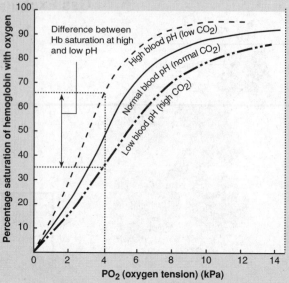

As oxygen level increases, more oxygen combines with hemoglobin (Hb). Hb saturation remains high, even at low oxygen tensions. Fetal Hb has a high affinity for oxygen and carries 20-30% more than maternal Hb. Myoglobin in skeletal muscle has a very high affinity for oxygen and will take up oxygen from hemoglobin in the blood.

As pH increases (lower CO_2), more oxygen combines with Hb. As the blood pH decreases (higher CO_2), Hb binds less oxygen and releases more to the tissues (**the Bohr effect**). The difference between Hb saturation at high and low pH represents the amount of oxygen released to the tissues.

1. (a) Identify two regions in the body where oxygen levels are very high: _____

    (b) Identify two regions where carbon dioxide levels are very high: _____

2. Explain the significance of the **reversible binding** reaction of hemoglobin (Hb) to oxygen: _____
    _____

3. (a) Hemoglobin saturation is affected by the oxygen level in the blood. Describe the nature of this relationship: _____
    _____

    (b) Comment on the significance of this relationship to oxygen delivery to the tissues: _____
    _____

4. (a) Describe how fetal Hb is different to adult Hb: _____

    (b) Explain the significance of this difference to oxygen delivery to the fetus: _____
    _____

5. At low blood pH, less oxygen is bound by hemoglobin and more is released to the tissues:

    (a) Name this effect: _____

    (b) Comment on its significance to oxygen delivery to respiring tissue: _____
    _____

6. Explain the significance of the very high affinity of myoglobin for oxygen: _____
    _____

7. Identify the two main contributors to the buffer capacity of the blood: _____

Diseases Caused by Smoking

Tobacco smoking has only recently been accepted as a major health hazard, despite its practice in Western countries for more than 400 years, and much longer elsewhere. Cigarettes became popular at the end of World War I because they were cheap, convenient, and easier to smoke than pipes and cigars. They remain popular for the further reason that they are more addictive than other forms of tobacco. The milder smoke can be more readily inhaled, allowing **nicotine** (a powerful addictive poison) to be quickly absorbed into the bloodstream. **Lung cancer** is the most widely known and most harmful effect of smoking; 98% of cases are associated with cigarette smoking. Symptoms include chest pain, breathlessness, and coughing up blood. Tobacco smoking is also directly associated with *coronary artery disease, emphysema, chronic bronchitis, peripheral vascular disease,* and *stroke*. The damaging components of cigarette smoke include tar, carbon monoxide, nitrogen dioxide, and nitric oxide. Many of these harmful chemicals occur in greater concentrations in sidestream smoke (**passive smoking**) than in mainstream smoke (inhaled) due to the presence of a filter in the cigarette.

Gas Exchange in Animals

Long term effects of tobacco smoking

Smoking damages the arteries of the brain and may result in a **stroke**.

All forms of tobacco-smoking increase the risk of **mouth cancer**, **lip cancer**, and **cancer of the throat** (pharynx).

Lung cancer is the best known harmful effect of smoking.

In a young man who smokes 20 cigarettes a day, the risk of **coronary artery disease** is increased by about three times over that of a nonsmoker.

Smoking leads to severe constriction of the arteries supplying blood to the extremities and leads to **peripheral vascular disease**.

Short term effects of tobacco smoking

- Reduction in capacity of the lungs.
- Increase in muscle tension and a decrease in steadiness of the hands.
- Raised blood pressure (10-30 points).
- Very sharp rise in carbon monoxide levels in the lungs contributing to breathlessness.
- Increase in pulse rate by up to 20 beats per minute.
- Surface blood vessel constriction drops skin temperature by up to 5°C.
- Dulling of appetite as well as the sense of smell and taste.

How smoking damages the lungs

Non-smoker

Normal alveoli arrangement

Cilia

Thin layer of mucus

Cells lining airways

Smoker

Coalesced alveoli

Smoke particles

Extra mucus produced

Cancerous cell

Smoke particles indirectly destroy the walls of the lung's alveoli.

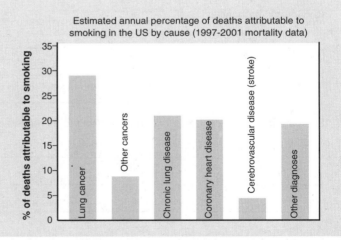

Cavities lined by heavy black tar deposits.

Gross pathology of lung tissue from a patient with emphysema. Tobacco tar deposits can be seen. Tar contains at least 17 known carcinogens.

SMOKING CAUSES LUNG CANCER
Ka mate koe i te kai hikareti
Ministry of Health Warning

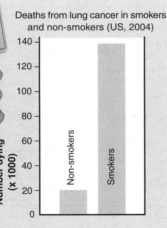

Deaths from lung cancer in smokers and non-smokers (US, 2004)

Estimated annual percentage of deaths attributable to smoking in the US by cause (1997-2001 mortality data)

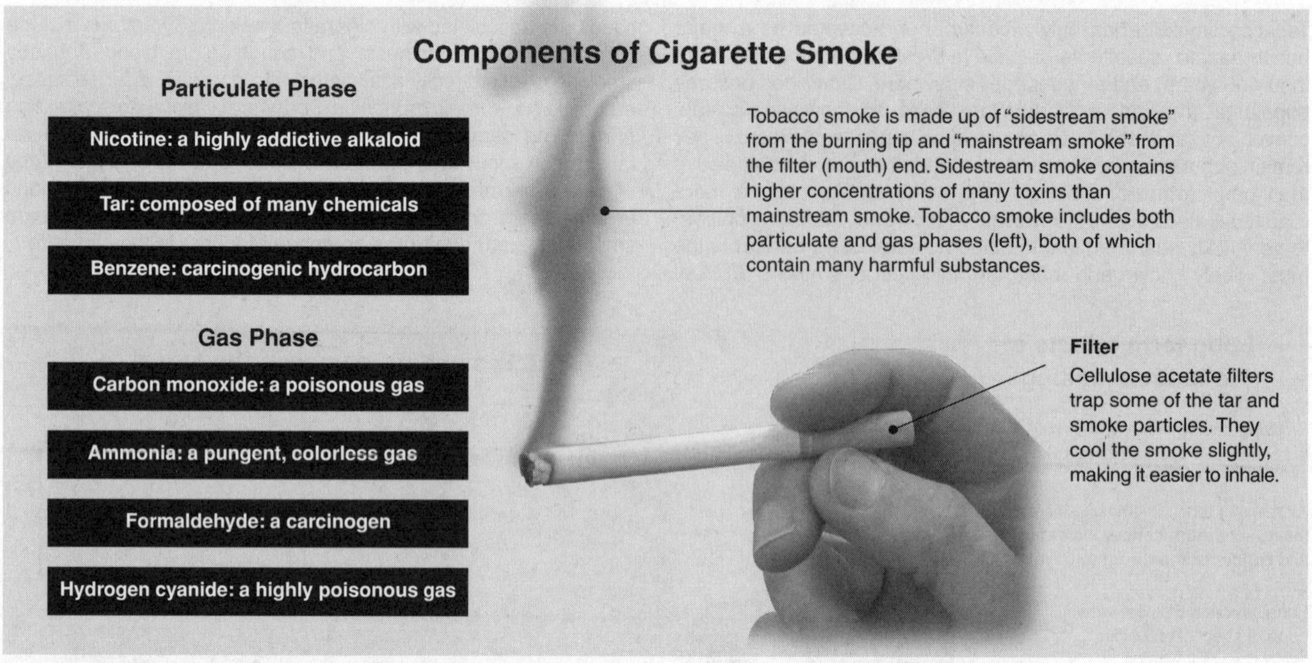

Components of Cigarette Smoke

Particulate Phase

Nicotine: a highly addictive alkaloid

Tar: composed of many chemicals

Benzene: carcinogenic hydrocarbon

Gas Phase

Carbon monoxide: a poisonous gas

Ammonia: a pungent, colorless gas

Formaldehyde: a carcinogen

Hydrogen cyanide: a highly poisonous gas

Tobacco smoke is made up of "sidestream smoke" from the burning tip and "mainstream smoke" from the filter (mouth) end. Sidestream smoke contains higher concentrations of many toxins than mainstream smoke. Tobacco smoke includes both particulate and gas phases (left), both of which contain many harmful substances.

Filter
Cellulose acetate filters trap some of the tar and smoke particles. They cool the smoke slightly, making it easier to inhale.

1. Discuss the physical changes to the lung that result from long-term smoking:

_____

_____

_____

_____

2. Determine the physiological effect of each of the following constituents of tobacco smoke when inhaled:

(a) Tar: _____

_____

(b) Nicotine: _____

_____

(c) Carbon monoxide: _____

_____

3. Describe the symptoms of the following diseases associated with long-term smoking:

(a) Emphysema: _____

_____

(b) Chronic bronchitis: _____

_____

(c) Lung cancer: _____

_____

4. Evaluate the evidence linking cigarette smoking to increased incidence of respiratory and cardiovascular diseases:

_____

_____

_____

_____

The Effects of High Altitude

The air at high altitudes contains less oxygen than the air at sea level. Air pressure decreases with altitude so the pressure (therefore amount) of oxygen in the air also decreases. Sudden exposure to an altitude of 2000 m would make you breathless on exertion and above 7000 m most people would become unconscious. The effects of altitude on physiology are related to this lower oxygen availability. Humans and other animals can make some physiological adjustments to life at altitude; this is called acclimatization. Some of the changes to the cardiovascular and respiratory systems to high altitude are outlined below.

Mountain Sickness

Altitude sickness or mountain sickness is usually a mild illness associated with trekking to altitudes of 5000 meters or so. Common symptoms include headache, insomnia, poor appetite and nausea, vomiting, dizziness, tiredness, coughing and breathlessness. The best way to avoid mountain sickness is to ascend to altitude slowly (no more than 300 m per day above 3000 m). Continuing to ascend with mountain sickness can result in more serious illnesses: accumulation of fluid on the brain (cerebral edema) and accumulation of fluid in the lungs (pulmonary edema). These complications can be fatal if not treated with oxygen and a rapid descent to lower altitude.

Physiological Adjustment to Altitude

Effect	Minutes	Days	Weeks
Increased heart rate	←——————→		
Increased breathing		←————→	
Concentration of blood		←——→	
Increased red blood cell production			←————→
Increased capillary density			←——→

The human body can make adjustments to life at altitude. Some of these changes take place almost immediately: breathing and heart rates increase. Other adjustments may take weeks (see above). These responses are all aimed at improving the rate of supply of oxygen to the body's tissues. When more permanent adjustments to physiology are made (increased blood cells and capillary networks) heart and breathing rates can return to normal.

People who live permanently at high altitude, e.g. Tibetans, Nepalese, and Peruvian Indians, have physiologies adapted (genetically, through evolution) to high altitude. Their blood volumes and red blood cell counts are high, and they can carry heavy loads effortlessly despite a small build. In addition, their metabolism uses oxygen very efficiently.

Llamas, vicunas, and Bactrian camels are well suited to high altitude life. Vicunas and llamas, which live in the Andes, have high blood cell counts and their red blood cells live almost twice as long as those in humans. Their hemoglobin also picks up and offloads oxygen more efficiently than the hemoglobin of most mammals.

1. (a) Describe the general effects of high altitude on the body: _____

_____

   (b) Name the general term given to describe these effects: _____

2. (a) Name one short term physiological adaptation that humans make to high altitude: _____

_____

   (b) Explain how this adaptation helps to increase the amount of oxygen the body receives: _____

_____

3. (a) Describe one longer term adaptation that humans can make to living at high altitude: _____

_____

   (b) Explain how this adaptation helps to increase the amount of oxygen the body receives: _____

_____

Related activities: Adaptations and Fitness

A 2

Animal Transport Systems

IB SL	IB HL	IB Options	AP Biology
Complete:	Complete:	Complete:	Complete:
1-3, 10, 15, 17, 19-20, 23	1-3, 10, 15, 17, 19-20, 23	Option B: SL: 26-29	1-29
Extension: 4, 7, 9	Extension: 4, 7, 9	Option H: HL: 21, 24, 30-32	Some numbers extension as appropriate

Learning Objectives

☐ 1. Compile your own glossary from the **KEY WORDS** displayed in **bold type** in the learning objectives below.

Background and Required Knowledge

☐ 2. Explain the need for **transport systems** in different organisms (e.g. multicellular plants, animals) in relation to size and **surface area to volume ratio**.

☐ 3. Recognize the relationship between the transport systems of larger organisms and their specialized exchange systems.

Animal Transport Systems *(pages 206-208, 218)*

☐ 4. Explain why animals above a certain size require an internal transport system. Describe the components and functions of transport systems in animals, including the **blood vessels**, **heart**, and **blood** (or **hemolymph**).

Open & closed circulatory systems

☐ 5. Giving examples, and using schematic diagrams, describe the basic structure and function of the two types of circulatory system found in animals:

☐ **Open circulatory systems** (arthropods, most molluscs).

☐ **Closed circulatory systems** (vertebrates and some invertebrates, e.g. many annelids, cephalopods).

For each type of system, consider the following:
- The types of blood vessels present and whether or not these are continuous, closed channels.
- How exchanges occur between the blood and tissues and the efficiency of these.
- The basic structure of the heart.
- The relative speed and pressure of fluid circulation.

☐ 6. Giving examples, describe the features of:

☐ Closed, **single circulatory systems**

☐ Closed, **double circulatory systems** in representative classes, e.g. amphibians, reptiles, and mammals.

For each type of system, consider the following:
- Whether or not the blood returns to the heart after being oxygenated at the gas exchange surface.
- Whether the blood flows around the body at relatively low or relatively high pressure.
- How the heart structure influences blood flow and the efficiency of the transport system as a whole.

The human circulatory system

☐ 7. In more detail than in #6, describe the **closed, double circulatory system** of a mammal, identifying: **carotid arteries**, **heart** and associated vessels, **liver** and **kidneys** and associated vessels. Indicate the direction of blood flow and the relative oxygen content of the blood at different points. Distinguish between the **pulmonary circulation** and the **systemic circulation**.

Vessels and Body Fluids *(pages 198-200, 211-217 and see the TRC: Blood Vessels)*

☐ 8. Appreciate that all the **blood vessels** in the closed circulatory of vertebrates are lined with a thin endothelium, and the basic structure of each type of vessel is relatively uniform in all vertebrate classes.

☐ 9. Recognize the structure of **arteries**, **veins**, and **capillaries** using a light microscope.

☐ 10. Explain the relationship between the structure and functional role of **arteries**, **capillaries**, **veins**, and (if required) **arterioles**. Draw labeled diagrams to illustrate the important features of these comparisons.

☐ 11. Explain the importance of **capillaries**. Draw a diagram to show the relative positions of blood vessels in a capillary network and their relationship to the **lymphatic vessels** (in humans). Distinguish between **blood**, **lymph**, **plasma**, and **tissue fluid**.

☐ 12. Describe the formation and roles of **tissue fluid** and **lymph** in humans. You should demonstrate an awareness of the role of pressure differences in forming tissue fluid, but calculations of these are not required.

☐ 13. Outline the transport functions of the lymphatic system, identifying how lymph is returned to the blood circulatory system. Recognize the lymphatic system as a network of vessels that parallels the blood system.

☐ 14. Using examples, describe the role of the **blood** and **hemolymph** in the transport systems of vertebrates and invertebrates respectively. Include reference to the role of circulatory fluids and **respiratory pigments** in transporting respiratory gases.

☐ 15. Describe the nature and/or composition of **blood** in humans, including the role of each of the following:
Non-cellular components: **plasma** (water, mineral ions, blood proteins, hormones, nutrients, urea, vitamins).
Cellular components: **erythrocytes**, **leukocytes** (**lymphocytes**, **monocytes**, **granulocytes**), **platelets**.

☐ 16. Identify the homeostatic roles of blood, and comment on the role of blood in modern medicine. Giving examples, discuss the difficulties involved in producing viable blood substitutes.

☐ 17. Identify the main substances transported by the blood. If required, state how each of the identified substances is transported (e.g. bound, free in plasma etc.) and/or the sites at which exchanges occur.

Heart Structure and Function *(pages 208-210, 219-222 & the TRC: Review of the Human Heart)*

☐ 18. Using schematic diagrams, compare the basic structure of a mammalian heart with the structure of the heart in other vertebrates, e.g. fish, amphibian, reptile, or bird.

☐ 19. Draw a diagram to describe the internal and external gross structure of a mammalian (e.g. human) **heart**.

Identify: **atria, ventricles, atrioventricular valves**, and **semilunar valves**, as well as the major vessels (**aorta, vena cava, pulmonary artery** and **vein**) and the coronary circulation. Relate the differences in the thickness of the heart chambers to their functions.

☐ 20. Describe the action of the heart in terms of collecting blood, pumping blood, and opening and closing valves. Clearly describe the passage of blood through the heart and describe the role of the valves in this.

☐ 21. Explain the events of the **cardiac cycle**, relating stages in the cycle (**atrial systole, ventricular systole**, and **diastole**) to the maintenance of blood flow through the heart. Describe the **heart sounds** and relate these to stages in the cardiac cycle. Analyze data showing pressure and volume changes in the left atrium, left ventricle, and the aorta during the cardiac cycle.

☐ 22. Understand the terms **systolic** and **diastolic blood pressure**. Describe typical values of these in the normal range and in a person with **hypertension**.

☐ 23. Outline the control of heartbeat in terms of the **pacemaker**, nerves, and **adrenaline**. Understand what is meant by the **myogenic** nature of the heartbeat,

☐ 24. In more detail than in #23 above, outline the mechanisms controlling heartbeat, including the role of the **sinoatrial node** (SAN), the **atrioventricular** (AV) **node**, and the conducting fibers in the ventricular walls (**bundle of His**, and the **Purkinje fibers**). Relate the activity of the SAN to the **intrinsic heart rate**.

☐ 25. Describe the extrinsic regulation of **heart rate** through **autonomic nerves** (vagus and cardiac nerves). Identify the role of the **medulla, baroreceptors** (pressure receptors), and **chemoreceptors** in the response of the heart to changing demands.

The Effects of Exercise *(pages 223-224 and the TRC and Web links: Effects of Training)*

☐ 26. Define the terms: **pulse** and **pulse rate** and explain how they relate to heart rate. Explain the significance of resting pulse rate in relation to physical **fitness**.

☐ 27. Investigate the effects of exercise on the body. List measurements that could be made to test fitness.

☐ 28. Explain how **training** affects the cardiovascular system. Explain what is meant by **cardiac output** and state how it is calculated. Explain how **heart rate, stroke volume, venous return**, and cardiac output change with exercise.

☐ 29. Discuss the short and long term physiological effects of **aerobic exercise**, including: appropriate redistribution of blood flow in response to exercise and adaptation of the cardiovascular and musculoskeletal system to regular exercise (effect on resting heart rate, stroke volume, endurance, and general health).

Cardiovascular Diseases *(see the TRC: Cardiovascular Disease)*

☐ 30. Recognize the term **cardiovascular disease** (CVD), as a broad term encompassing a variety of diseases.

☐ 31. Describe the causes and features of **coronary thrombosis** and **atherosclerosis**. Identify the effect of atherosclerosis on blood flow and its relationship to **myocardial infarction** (heart attack).

☐ 32. Describe **risk factors** in the development of CVD, including genetic factors, gender, and lifestyle factors such as cigarette smoking and obesity. Distinguish between controllable and uncontrollable **risk factors**, and give examples of each.

Animal Transport Systems

See the 'Textbook Reference Grid' on pages 8-9 for textbook page references relating to material in this topic.

Supplementary Texts

See pages 5-6 for additional details of these texts:

■ Adds, J. *et al.*, 2004. **Exchange & Transport, Energy & Ecosystems** (NelsonThornes), chpt. 2

■ Clegg, C.J., 1998. **Mammals: Structure and Function** (John Murray), pp. 30-38.

■ Helms, D.R. *et al.*, 1998. **Biology in the Laboratory** (W.H. Freeman), #36, #38.

■ Morton, D. & J.W. Perry, 1998. **Photo Atlas for Anatomy and Physiology** (W.H. Freeman).

See page 6 for details of publishers of periodicals:

STUDENT'S REFERENCE

■ **Venous Disease** Biol. Sci. Rev., 19(3), Feb. 2007, pp. 15-17. *This occurs when damage to the deep veins and their valves puts superficial veins under even more pressure.*

Presentation MEDIA to support this topic:

HEALTH & DISEASE:
• **Non-infectious Disease**

■ **Keeping Pace - Cardiac Muscle and Heartbeat** Biol. Sci. Rev., 19(3), Feb. 2007, pp. 21-24. *Cardiac muscle cells can generate electrical activity like nerve impulses, and these impulses produce a smooth contraction of the muscle.*

■ **Red Blood Cells** Bio. Sci. Rev. 11(2) Nov. 1998, pp. 2-4. *Erythrocyte structure and function, including the details of oxygen transport.*

■ **Fascinating Rhythm** New Scientist, 3 January 1998, pp. 20-25. *Cardiac rhythm and how changes in the rhythm can signify the onset of disease.*

■ **Cunning Plumbing** New Scientist, 6 February 1999, pp. 32-37. *The arteries can actively respond to changes in blood flow, spreading the effects of mechanical stresses to avoid extremes.*

■ **A Fair Exchange** Biol. Sci. Rev., 13(1), Sept. 2000, pp. 2-5. *Formation and reabsorption of tissue fluid (includes disorders of fluid balance).*

■ **Keeping Pace - Cardiac Muscle and Heartbeat** Biol. Sci. Rev., 19(3), Feb. 2007, pp. 21-24. *Cardiac muscle cells can generate electrical activity like nerve impulses, and these impulses produce a smooth contraction of the muscle.*

■ **Blood Pressure** Biol. Sci. Rev., 12(5) May 2000, pp. 9-12. *Blood pressure: its control, measurement, and significance to diagnosis.*

TEACHER'S REFERENCE

■ **The Search for Blood Substitutes** Scientific American, Feb. 1998, pp. 60-65. *Finding a successful blood substitute depends on being able to replicate to the exact properties of blood.*

■ **Defibrillation: The Spark of Life** Scientific American, June 1998, pp. 68-73. *This article explains how an electric shock resets the heart's rhythm after heart failure.*

■ **Measuring How Elastic Arteries Function** The Am. Biology Teacher, 59(8), Oct. 1997, pp. 513-517. *Investigating blood flow through elastic arteries, including: changes in blood pressure, the role of elastin and collagen, and the mechanical properties of arteries.*

■ **Atherosclerosis: The New View** Scientific American, May 2002, pp. 28-37. *The latest views on the pathological development and rupture of plaques in atherosclerosis. An excellent account.*

■ **Breaking Out of the Box** The Am. Biology Teacher, 63(2), Feb. 2001, pp. 101-115. *Investigating cardiovascular activity: a web-based activity on the cardiac cycle.*

■ **On Two Hearts & Other Coronary Reflections** The Am. Biology Teacher, 60(1), Jan. 1998, pp. 66-69. *Heart disease: atherosclerosis and its effects on the health of the circulatory system.*

■ **Modeling Blood Flow in the Aorta** The Am. Biology Teacher, 59(9), Nov. 1997, pp. 586-588. *Modeling blood flow in the aorta as a way to investigate the fluid dynamics of the CVS.*

See pages 10-11 for details of how to access **Bio Links** from our web site: **www.thebiozone.com** From Bio Links, access sites under the topics:

GENERAL BIOLOGY ONLINE RESOURCES > **Online Textbooks and Lecture Notes:** • S-Cool! A level biology revision guide • Learn.co.uk • Mark Rothery's biology web site ... *and others* > **Glossaries:** • Animal anatomy glossary • Glossary of the heart • Kimball's biology glossary

ANIMAL BIOLOGY: • Anatomy and physiology • Human physiology lecture notes ... *and others* > **Circulatory System:** • Animal circulatory systems • How the heart works • NOVA online: Cut to the heart • The circulatory system • The heart: A virtual exploration • The matter of the human heart ... *and others*

HEALTH AND DISEASE > Non-infectious Disease: • American Heart Association • Cardiology compass • Heart disease

---

Internal Transport in Animals

Animal cells require a constant supply of nutrients and oxygen, and continuous removal of wastes. Simple, small organisms (e.g. sponges, cnidarians, flatworms, nematodes) can achieve this through simple diffusion across moist body surfaces without requiring a specialised system (below). Larger, more complex organisms require a circulatory system to transport materials because diffusion is too inefficient and slow to supply all the cells

of the body adequately. The principal components of a circulatory system are blood, a heart, and blood vessels. Circulatory systems transport nutrients, oxygen, carbon dioxide, wastes, and hormones. They also help to maintain fluid balance, regulate body temperature, and may assist in the defence of the body against invading microorganisms. In the diagram below, simple diffusion is compared with transport by a circulatory system.

Transport via Diffusion

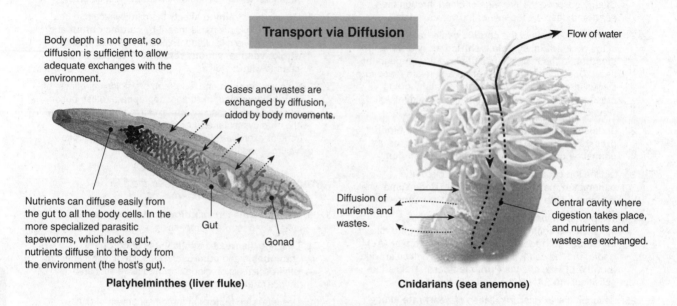

Body depth is not great, so diffusion is sufficient to allow adequate exchanges with the environment.

Gases and wastes are exchanged by diffusion, aided by body movements.

Nutrients can diffuse easily from the gut to all the body cells. In the more specialized parasitic tapeworms, which lack a gut, nutrients diffuse into the body from the environment (the host's gut).

Gut

Gonad

Platyhelminthes (liver fluke)

Flow of water

Diffusion of nutrients and wastes.

Central cavity where digestion takes place, and nutrients and wastes are exchanged.

Cnidarians (sea anemone)

Transport via a Circulatory System

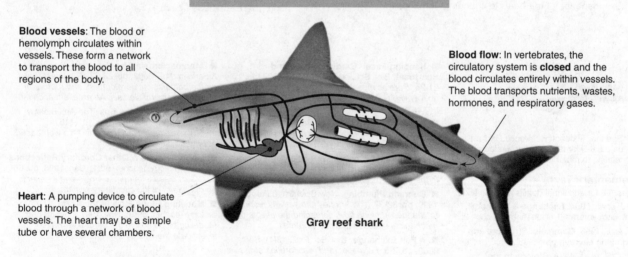

Blood vessels: The blood or hemolymph circulates within vessels. These form a network to transport the blood to all regions of the body.

Blood flow: In vertebrates, the circulatory system is **closed** and the blood circulates entirely within vessels. The blood transports nutrients, wastes, hormones, and respiratory gases.

Heart: A pumping device to circulate blood through a network of blood vessels. The heart may be a simple tube or have several chambers.

Gray reef shark

1. Explain why animals above a certain size require an internal transport system of some kind:

   _____

2. Briefly describe the function of each of the three major components of a circulatory system in an animal:

   (a) Blood vessels: _____

   (b) Heart: _____

   (c) Blood or hemolymph: _____

   _____

3. For simple aquatic organisms, diffusion presents no problem because they are surrounded in a fluid medium. Explain how similar organisms living on land are able to use diffusion to obtain nutrients and dispose of wastes:

   _____

Related activities: Circulatory Systems

Circulatory Systems

Animal cells require a constant supply of nutrients and oxygen, and continuous removal of wastes. Simple, small organisms can achieve this through simple diffusion across moist body surfaces. Larger, more complex organisms require a circulatory system to transport materials because diffusion is too inefficient and slow to supply all the cells of the body adequately. Circulatory systems transport nutrients, oxygen, carbon dioxide, wastes, and hormones. They may also help to maintain fluid balance, regulate body temperature, and assist in defense against invading microorganisms. Two basic types of circulatory systems have evolved in animals. Many invertebrates have an **open circulatory system**, while vertebrates have a **closed circulatory system**. The latter is often called a cardiovascular system because it consists of a heart and a network of tube-like vessels.

Types of Circulatory Systems

Spiders

Insects

Crustaceans

Open Circulation Systems

Arthropods and molluscs (except squid and octopus) have open circulatory systems in which the blood is pumped by a tubular, or sac-like, heart through short vessels into large spaces in the body cavity. The blood bathes the cells before reentering the heart through holes (**ostia**). Muscle action may assist the circulation of the blood.

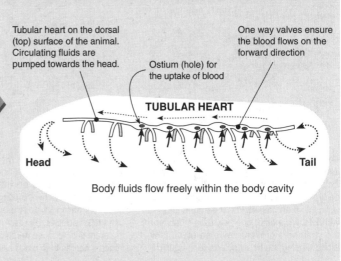

Tubular heart on the dorsal (top) surface of the animal. Circulating fluids are pumped towards the head.

Ostium (hole) for the uptake of blood

One way valves ensure the blood flows on the forward direction

TUBULAR HEART

Head

Tail

Body fluids flow freely within the body cavity

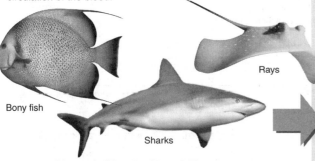

Bony fish

Rays

Sharks

Closed, Single Circuit Systems

In closed circulation systems, the blood is contained within vessels and is returned to the heart after every circulation of the body. Exchanges between the blood and the fluids bathing the cells occur by diffusion across capillaries. In single circuit systems, typical of fish, the blood goes directly from the gills to the body. The blood loses pressure at the gills and flows at low pressure around the body.

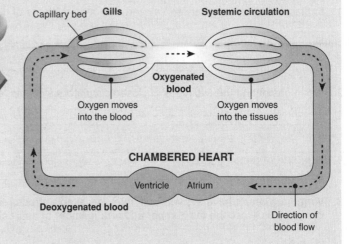

Capillary bed Gills Systemic circulation

Oxygenated blood

Oxygen moves into the blood

Oxygen moves into the tissues

CHAMBERED HEART

Ventricle Atrium

Deoxygenated blood

Direction of blood flow

Reptiles

Birds

Amphibians

Closed, Double Circuit Systems

Double circulation systems occur in all vertebrates other than fish. The blood is pumped through a pulmonary circuit to the lungs, where it is oxygenated. The blood returns to the heart, which pumps the oxygenated blood, through a systemic circuit, to the body. In amphibians and most reptiles, the heart is not completely divided and there is some mixing of oxygenated and deoxygenated blood. In birds and mammals, the heart is fully divided and there is no mixing.

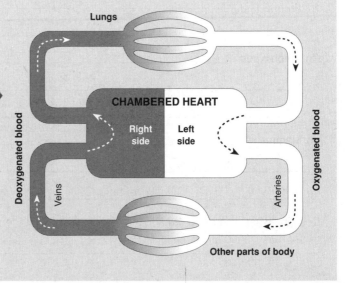

Lungs

CHAMBERED HEART

Deoxygenated blood

Right side

Left side

Oxygenated blood

Veins

Arteries

Other parts of body

Animal Transport Systems

Related activities: Transport in Animals, Mammalian Transport, Vertebrate Hearts

A 1

Fish Heart

Conus arteriosus, Ventricle, Atrium, Sinus venosus, From rest of body

To gills

Ventral aorta, Atrioventricular valves, Sinoatrial valves, From rest of body

The fish heart is linear, with a sequence of three chambers in series (the conus may be included as a fourth chamber). Blood from the body first enters the heart through the sinus venosus, then passes into the atrium and the ventricle. A series of one-way valves between the chambers prevents reverse blood flow. Blood leaving the heart travels to the gills.

Amphibian Heart

To lungs, To rest of body

From rest of body, From lungs

Right atrium, Left atrium

Ventricle (single chamber)

Amphibian hearts are three chambered. The atrium is divided into left and right chambers, but the ventricle lacks an internal dividing wall. Although this allows mixing of oxygenated and deoxygenated blood, the spongy nature of the ventricle reduces mixing. Amphibians are able to tolerate this because much of their oxygen uptake occurs across their moist skin, and not their lungs.

Mammalian Heart

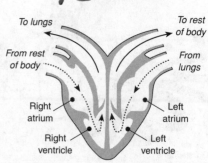

To lungs, To rest of body

From rest of body, From lungs

Right atrium, Left atrium

Right ventricle, Left ventricle

In birds and mammals, the heart is fully partitioned into two halves, resulting in four chambers. Blood circulates through two circuits, with no mixing of the two. Oxygenated blood from the lungs is kept separated from the deoxygenated blood returning from the rest of the body.

1. Explain the difference between closed and open systems of circulation: _____

_____

_____

2. When comparing the two types of closed circulatory systems, explain why a double is more efficient than a single circuit:

_____

_____

_____

3. Vertebrate hearts have evolved from relatively simple structures (as in fish) to more complex organs such as those found in mammals. Describe the number and arrangement of heart chambers in:

(a) Fish: _____

_____

_____

(b) Amphibians: _____

_____

_____

(c) Mammals: _____

_____

_____

4. Describe where the blood flows to after it passes through the gills in a fish: _____

_____

_____

Vertebrate Hearts

The heart is the centre of the cardiovascular system. In humans, it is a hollow, muscular organ, weighing on average 342 grams. Each day it beats over 100 000 times to pump 3780 litres of blood through 100 000 kilometres of blood vessels. The heart lies between the lungs, to the left of the body's midline. It comprises a system of four muscular chambers, which alternately fill and empty of blood, acting as a double pump. The left side pumps blood to the body tissues, while the right side pumps blood to the lungs. The two upper chambers are the atria (right and left). The two lower chambers are the right and left ventricles. Both upper and lower chambers are separated by a partition or **septum**. The coronary arteries branch from the aorta and provide the circulation for the heart muscle itself. It is these arteries that become blocked in many cases of heart disease. The structure of other vertebrate hearts is discussed in the previous activity: *Circulatory Systems*.

Human Heart Structure

(sectioned, anterior view)

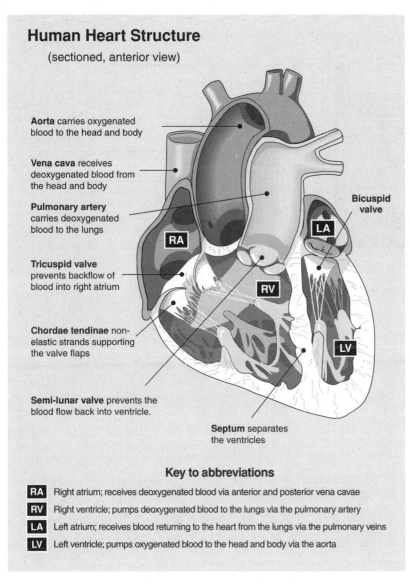

Aorta carries oxygenated blood to the head and body

Vena cava receives deoxygenated blood from the head and body

Pulmonary artery carries deoxygenated blood to the lungs

Bicuspid valve

RA

LA

Tricuspid valve prevents backflow of blood into right atrium

RV

Chordae tendinae non-elastic strands supporting the valve flaps

LV

Semi-lunar valve prevents the blood flow back into ventricle.

Septum separates the ventricles

Key to abbreviations

RA Right atrium; receives deoxygenated blood via anterior and posterior vena cavae

RV Right ventricle; pumps deoxygenated blood to the lungs via the pulmonary artery

LA Left atrium; receives blood returning to the heart from the lungs via the pulmonary veins

LV Left ventricle; pumps oxygenated blood to the head and body via the aorta

Top view of a heart in section, showing valves

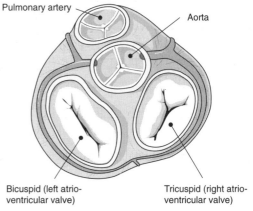

Pulmonary artery

Aorta

Bicuspid (left atrio-ventricular valve)

Tricuspid (right atrio-ventricular valve)

Posterior view of heart

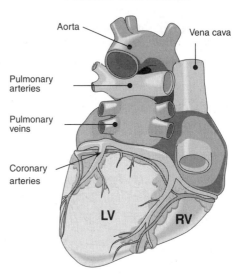

Aorta

Vena cava

Pulmonary arteries

Pulmonary veins

Coronary arteries

LV

RV

Animal Transport Systems

1. Explain the purpose of the valves in the heart: _____

_____

2. Discuss the structure of the heart in at least two vertebrates, relating features of the heart's structure and function to the animal's size, metabolic rate, or environment in each case:

_____

_____

_____

_____

_____

_____

_____

3. In the schematic diagram of the human heart (below), label the four chambers and the main vessels entering and leaving them. The arrows indicate the direction of blood flow. Use large coloured circles to mark the position of each of the four valves.

4. Using the diagram of the human heart (below) as a guide, as well as the diagrams at the top of page 208, construct schematic diagrams for an amphibian and a fish heart:

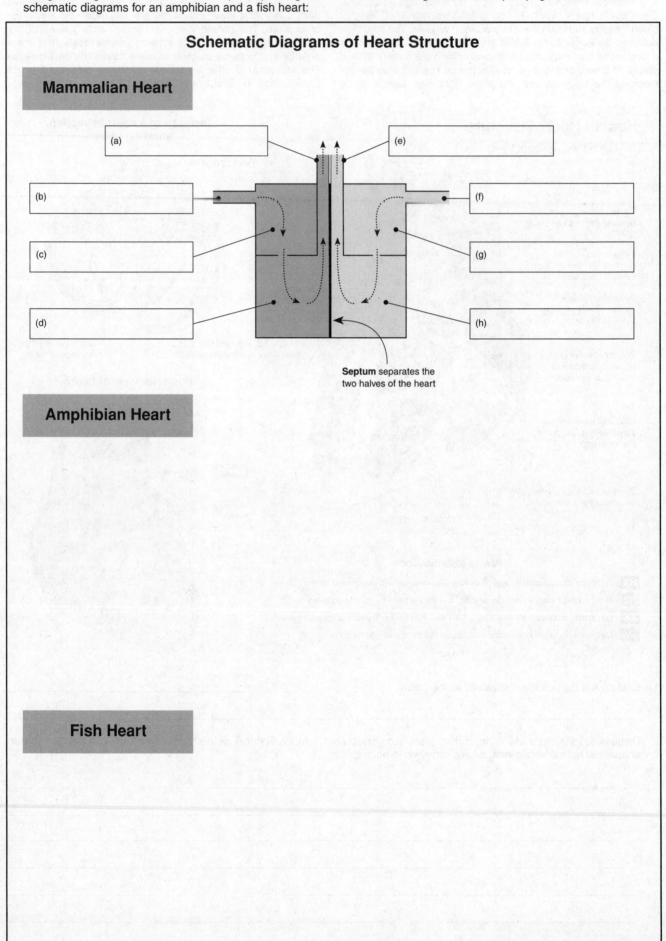

Schematic Diagrams of Heart Structure

Mammalian Heart

(a)

(e)

(b)

(f)

(c)

(g)

(d)

(h)

Septum separates the two halves of the heart

Amphibian Heart

Fish Heart

Arteries

In vertebrates, arteries are the blood vessels that carry blood away from the heart to the capillaries within the tissues. The large arteries that leave the heart divide into medium-sized (distributing) arteries. Within the tissues and organs, these distribution arteries branch to form very small vessels called **arterioles**, which deliver blood to capillaries. Arterioles lack the thick layers of arteries and consist only of an endothelial layer wrapped by a few smooth muscle fibers at intervals along their length. Resistance to blood flow is altered by contraction (**vasoconstriction**) or relaxation (**vasodilation**) of the blood vessel walls, especially in the arterioles. Vasoconstriction increases resistance and leads to an increase in blood pressure whereas vasodilation has the opposite effect. This mechanism is important in regulating the blood flow into tissues.

Arteries

Arteries have an elastic, stretchy structure that gives them the ability to withstand the high pressure of blood being pumped from the heart. At the same time, they help to maintain pressure by having some contractile ability themselves (a feature of the central muscle layer). Arteries nearer the heart have more elastic tissue, giving greater resistance to the higher blood pressures of the blood leaving the left ventricle. Arteries further from the heart have more muscle to help them maintain blood pressure. Between heartbeats, the arteries undergo elastic recoil and contract. This tends to smooth out the flow of blood through the vessel.

Arteries comprise three main regions (right):

1. A thin inner layer of epithelial cells called the **endothelium** lines the artery.

2. A central layer (the **tunica media**) of elastic tissue and smooth muscle that can stretch and contract.

3. An outer connective tissue layer (the **tunica externa**) has a lot of elastic tissue.

Artery Structure

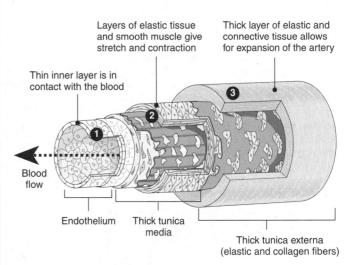

Thin inner layer is in contact with the blood

Layers of elastic tissue and smooth muscle give stretch and contraction

Thick layer of elastic and connective tissue allows for expansion of the artery

Blood flow

Endothelium

Thick tunica media

Thick tunica externa (elastic and collagen fibers)

Cross section through a large artery

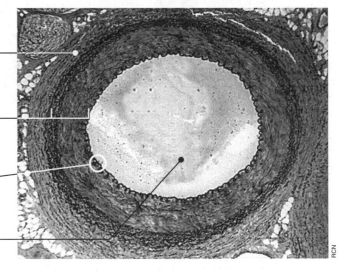

(a)

(b)

(c)

(d)

RCN

1. Using the diagram to help you, label the photograph of the cross section through an artery (above).

2. (a) Explain why the walls of arteries need to be thick with a lot of elastic tissue: _____

   _____

   (b) Explain why arterioles lack this elastic tissue layer: _____

   _____

3. Explain the purpose of the smooth muscle in the artery walls: _____

   _____

4. (a) Describe the effect of vasodilation on the diameter of an arteriole: _____

   (b) Describe the effect of vasodilation on blood pressure: _____

Related activities: Heart Function
Web links: Review of Blood Vessels

A 1

Animal Transport Systems

Veins

Veins are the blood vessels that return blood to the heart from the tissues. The smallest veins (**venules**) return blood from the capillary beds to the larger veins. Veins and their branches contain about 59% of the blood in the body. The structural differences between veins and arteries are mainly associated with differences in the relative thickness of the vessel layers and the diameter of the lumen. These, in turn, are related to the vessel's functional role.

Veins

When several capillaries unite, they form small veins called **venules**. The venules collect the blood from capillaries and drain it into **veins**. Veins are made up of essentially the same three layers as arteries but they have less elastic and muscle tissue and a larger **lumen**. The venules closest to the capillaries consist of an **endothelium** and a tunica externa of connective tissue. As the venules approach the veins, they also contain the tunica media characteristic of veins (right). Although veins are less elastic than arteries, they can still expand enough to adapt to changes in the pressure and volume of the blood passing through them. Blood flowing in the veins has lost a lot of pressure because it has passed through the narrow capillary vessels. The low pressure in veins means that many veins, especially those in the limbs, need to have valves to prevent backflow of the blood as it returns to the heart.

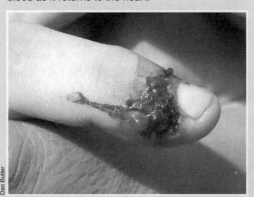

If a vein is cut, as is shown in this severe finger wound, the blood oozes out slowly in an even flow, and usually clots quickly as it leaves. In contrast, arterial blood spurts rapidly and requires pressure to staunch the flow.

Vein Structure

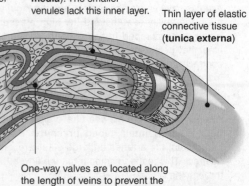

Inner thin layer of simple squamous epithelium lines the vein (**endothelium** or **tunica intima**).

Central thin layer of elastic and muscle tissue (**tunica media**). The smaller venules lack this inner layer.

Thin layer of elastic connective tissue (**tunica externa**)

Blood flow

One-way valves are located along the length of veins to prevent the blood from flowing backwards.

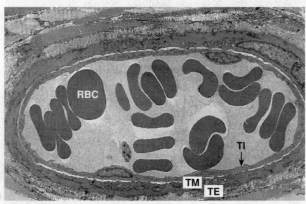

Above: TEM of a vein showing red blood cells (RBC) in the lumen, and the tunica intima (TI), tunica media (TM), and tunica externa (TE).

1. Contrast the structure of veins and arteries for each of the following properties:

   (a) Thickness of muscle and elastic tissue: _____

   _____

   (b) Size of the lumen (inside of the vessel): _____

   _____

2. With respect to their functional roles, give a reason for the difference you have described above: _____

   _____

   _____

3. Explain the role of the valves in assisting the veins to return blood back to the heart: _____

   _____

4. Blood oozes from a venous wound, rather than spurting as it does from an arterial wound. Account for this difference:

   _____

   _____

   _____

Related activities: Arteries
Web links: Review of Blood Vessels

Capillaries and Tissue Fluid

In vertebrates, capillaries are very small vessels that connect arterial and venous circulation and allow efficient exchange of nutrients and wastes between the blood and tissues. Capillaries form networks or beds and are abundant where metabolic rates are high. Fluid that leaks out of the capillaries has an essential role in bathing the tissues. The movement of fluid into and out of capillaries depends on the balance between the blood (hydrostatic) pressure (HP) and the solute potential (ψs) at each end of a capillary bed. Not all the fluid is returned to the capillaries and this extra fluid must be returned to the general circulation. This is the role of the **lymphatic system**; a system of vessels that parallels the system of arteries and veins. The lymphatic system also has a role in internal defense, and in transporting lipids absorbed from the digestive tract. Note: A version of this activity (without reference to solute potential terminology), is available on the web and the Teacher Resource CD-ROM.

Exchanges in Capillaries

Blood passes from the arterioles into capillaries: small blood vessels with a diameter of just 4-10 µm. Red blood cells are 7-8 µm and only just squeeze through. The only tissue present is an **endothelium** of squamous epithelial cells. Capillaries form networks of vessels that penetrate all parts of the body. They are so numerous that no cell is more than 25 µm from any capillary. It is in the capillaries that the exchange of materials between the body cells and the blood takes place. Blood pressure causes fluid to leak from capillaries through small gaps where the endothelial cells join. This fluid bathes the tissues, supplying nutrients and oxygen, and removing wastes (right). The density of capillaries in a tissue is an indication of that tissue's metabolic activity. For example, cardiac muscle relies heavily on oxidative metabolism. It has a high demand for blood flow and is well supplied with capillaries. Smooth muscle is far less active than cardiac muscle, relies more on anaerobic metabolism, and does not require such an extensive blood supply.

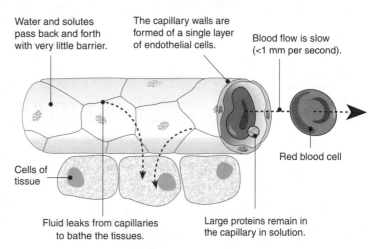

Water and solutes pass back and forth with very little barrier.

The capillary walls are formed of a single layer of endothelial cells.

Blood flow is slow (<1 mm per second).

Red blood cell

Cells of tissue

Fluid leaks from capillaries to bathe the tissues.

Large proteins remain in the capillary in solution.

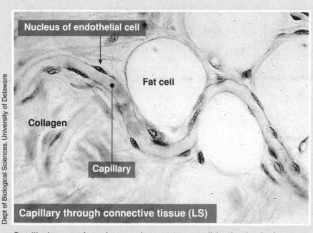

Nucleus of endothelial cell

Fat cell

Collagen

Capillary

Dept of Biological Sciences. University of Delaware

Capillary through connective tissue (LS)

Capillaries are found near almost every cell in the body. In many places, the capillaries form extensive branching networks. In most tissues, blood normally flows through only a small portion of a capillary network when the metabolic demands of the tissue are low. When the tissue becomes active, the entire capillary network fills with blood.

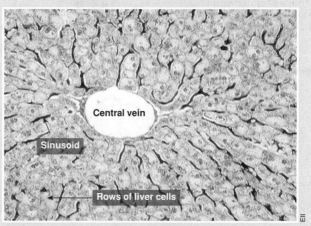

Central vein

Sinusoid

Rows of liver cells

Microscopic blood vessels in some dense organs, such as the liver (above), are called **sinusoids**. They are wider than capillaries and follow a more convoluted path through the tissue. Instead of the usual endothelial lining, they are lined with phagocytic cells. Like capillaries, sinusoids transport blood from arterioles to venules.

Animal Transport Systems

1. Describe the structure of a capillary, contrasting it with the structure of a vein and an artery:

2. Sinusoids provide a functional replacement for capillaries in some organs:

(a) Describe how sinusoids differ structurally from capillaries:

(b) Describe in what way capillaries and sinusoids are similar:

Related activities: The Lymphatic System, Arteries, Veins
Web links: Review of Blood Vessels, Capillaries and Tissue Fluid

RA 2

213

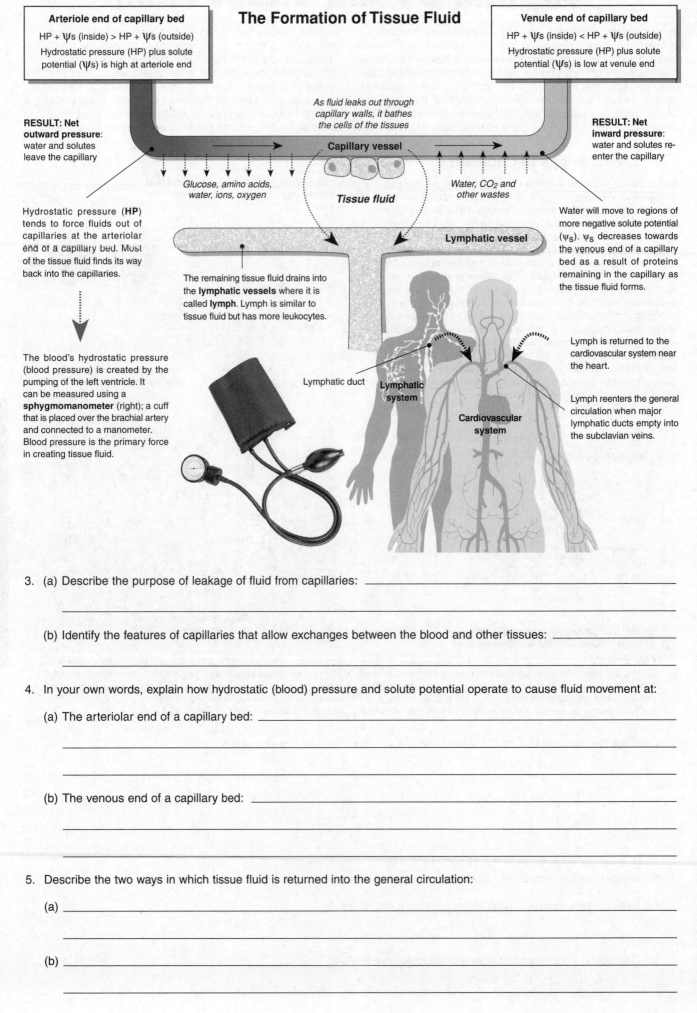

The Formation of Tissue Fluid

Arteriole end of capillary bed

HP + Ψs (inside) > HP + Ψs (outside)

Hydrostatic pressure (HP) plus solute potential (Ψs) is high at arteriole end

Venule end of capillary bed

HP + Ψs (inside) < HP + Ψs (outside)

Hydrostatic pressure (HP) plus solute potential (Ψs) is low at venule end

As fluid leaks out through capillary walls, it bathes the cells of the tissues

RESULT: Net outward pressure: water and solutes leave the capillary

RESULT: Net inward pressure: water and solutes re-enter the capillary

Capillary vessel

Glucose, amino acids, water, ions, oxygen

Water, CO₂ and other wastes

Tissue fluid

Hydrostatic pressure (**HP**) tends to force fluids out of capillaries at the arteriolar end of a capillary bed. Most of the tissue fluid finds its way back into the capillaries.

Water will move to regions of more negative solute potential (ψ_S). ψ_S decreases towards the venous end of a capillary bed as a result of proteins remaining in the capillary as the tissue fluid forms.

Lymphatic vessel

The remaining tissue fluid drains into the **lymphatic vessels** where it is called **lymph**. Lymph is similar to tissue fluid but has more leukocytes.

The blood's hydrostatic pressure (blood pressure) is created by the pumping of the left ventricle. It can be measured using a **sphygmomanometer** (right); a cuff that is placed over the brachial artery and connected to a manometer. Blood pressure is the primary force in creating tissue fluid.

Lymphatic duct

Lymphatic system

Cardiovascular system

Lymph is returned to the cardiovascular system near the heart.

Lymph reenters the general circulation when major lymphatic ducts empty into the subclavian veins.

3. (a) Describe the purpose of leakage of fluid from capillaries: _____

_____

(b) Identify the features of capillaries that allow exchanges between the blood and other tissues: _____

_____

4. In your own words, explain how hydrostatic (blood) pressure and solute potential operate to cause fluid movement at:

(a) The arteriolar end of a capillary bed: _____

_____

_____

(b) The venous end of a capillary bed: _____

_____

_____

5. Describe the two ways in which tissue fluid is returned into the general circulation:

(a) _____

_____

(b) _____

_____

Blood

Blood makes up about 8% of body weight. Blood is a complex liquid tissue comprising cellular components suspended in plasma. If a blood sample is taken, the cells can be separated from the plasma by centrifugation. The cells (formed elements) settle as a dense red pellet below the transparent, straw-colored plasma. Blood performs many functions: it transports nutrients, respiratory gases, hormones, and wastes; it has a role in thermoregulation through the distribution of heat; it defends against infection; and its ability to clot protects against blood loss. The examination of blood is also useful in diagnosing disease. The cellular components of blood are normally present in particular specified ratios. A change in the morphology, type, or proportion of different blood cells can therefore be used to indicate a specific disorder or infection (see the next page).

Non-Cellular Blood Components

The non-cellular blood components form the plasma. Plasma is a watery matrix of ions and proteins and makes up 50-60% of the total blood volume.

Water
The main constituent of blood and lymph.
Role: Transports dissolved substances. Provides body cells with water. Distributes heat and has a central role in thermoregulation. Regulation of water content helps to regulate blood pressure and volume.

Mineral ions
Sodium, bicarbonate, magnesium, potassium, calcium, chloride.
Role: Osmotic balance, pH buffering, and regulation of membrane permeability. They also have a variety of other functions, e.g. Ca^{2+} is involved in blood clotting.

Plasma proteins
7-9% of the plasma volume.
Serum albumin
Role: Osmotic balance and pH buffering, Ca^{2+} transport.
Fibrinogen and prothrombin
Role: Take part in blood clotting.
Immunoglobulins
Role: Antibodies involved in the immune response.
α-globulins
Role: Bind/transport hormones, lipids, fat soluble vitamins.
β-globulins
Role: Bind/transport iron, cholesterol, fat soluble vitamins.
Enzymes
Role: Take part in and regulate metabolic activities.

Substances transported by non-cellular components
Products of digestion
Examples: sugars, fatty acids, glycerol, and amino acids.
Excretory products
Example: urea
Hormones and vitamins
Examples: insulin, sex hormones, vitamins A and B_{12}.
Importance: These substances occur at varying levels in the blood. They are transported to and from the cells dissolved in the plasma or bound to plasma proteins.

Cellular Blood Components

The cellular components of the blood (also called the formed elements) float in the plasma and make up 40-50% of the total blood volume.

Erythrocytes (red blood cells or RBCs)
5-6 million per mm^3 blood; 38-48% of total blood volume.
Role: RBCs transport oxygen (O_2) and a small amount of carbon dioxide (CO_2). The oxygen is carried bound to hemoglobin (Hb) in the cells. Each Hb molecule can bind four molecules of oxygen.

7-8 µm

2 µm

Platelets
Small, membrane bound cell fragments derived from bone marrow cells; about 1/4 the size of RBCs.
0.25 million per mm^3 blood.
Role: To start the blood clotting process.

Leukocytes (white blood cells)
5-10 000 per mm^3 blood
2-3% of total blood volume.
Role: Involved in internal defense. There are several types of white blood cells (see below).

Lymphocytes
T and B cells.
24% of the white cell count.
Role: Antibody production and cell mediated immunity.

Neutrophils
Phagocytes.
70% of the white cell count.
Role: Engulf foreign material.

Eosinophils
Rare leukocytes; normally 1.5% of the white cell count.
Role: Mediate allergic responses such as hayfever and asthma.

Basophils
Rare leukocytes; normally 0.5% of the white cell count.
Role: Produce heparin (an anti-clotting protein), and histamine. Involved in inflammation.

Animal Transport Systems

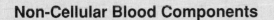

Related activities: Gas Transport in Humans, The Body's Defenses, Thermoregulation in Humans, Blood Clotting & Defense

A 2

The Examination of Blood

Different types of microscopy give different information about blood. A SEM (right) shows the detailed external morphology of the blood cells. A fixed smear of a blood sample viewed with a light microscope (far right) can be used to identify the different blood cell types present, and their ratio to each other. Determining the types and proportions of different white blood cells in blood is called a **differential white blood cell count**. Elevated counts of particular cell types indicate allergy or infection.

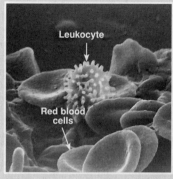

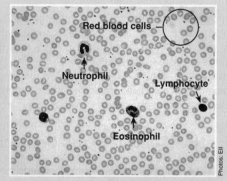

SEM of red blood cells and a leukocytes. **Light microscope** view of a fixed blood smear.

1. For each of the following blood functions, identify the component (or components) of the blood responsible and state how the function is carried out (the mode of action). The first one is done for you:

   (a) **Temperature regulation.** *Blood component:* Water component of the plasma

   Mode of action: Water absorbs heat and dissipates it from sites of production (e.g. organs)

   (b) **Protection against disease.** *Blood component:* _____

   Mode of action: _____

   (c) **Communication between cells, tissues, and organs.** *Blood component:* _____

   Mode of action: _____

   (d) **Oxygen transport.** *Blood component:* _____

   Mode of action: _____

   (e) **CO$_2$ transport.** *Blood components:* _____

   Mode of action: _____

   (f) **Buffer against pH changes.** *Blood components:* _____

   Mode of action: _____

   (g) **Nutrient supply.** *Blood component:* _____

   Mode of action: _____

   (h) **Tissue repair.** *Blood components:* _____

   Mode of action: _____

   (i) **Transport of hormones, lipids, and fat soluble vitamins.** *Blood component:* _____

   Mode of action: _____

2. Identify a feature that distinguishes red and white blood cells: _____

3. Explain two physiological advantages of red blood cell structure (lacking nucleus and mitochondria):

   (a) _____

   (b) _____

4. Suggest what each of the following results from a differential white blood cell count would suggest:

   (a) Elevated levels of eosinophils (above the normal range): _____

   (b) Elevated levels of neutrophils (above the normal range): _____

   (c) Elevated levels of basophils (above the normal range): _____

   (d) Elevated levels of lymphocytes (above the normal range): _____

The Search for Blood Substitutes

Blood's essential homeostatic role is evident when considering the problems encountered when large volumes of blood are lost. Transfusion of whole blood (see photograph below) or plasma is an essential part of many medical procedures, e.g. after trauma or surgery, or as a regular part of the treatment for some disorders (e.g. thalassemia). This makes blood a valuable commodity. A blood supply relies on blood donations, but as the demand for blood increases, the availability of donors continues to decline. This decline is partly due to more stringent screening of donors for diseases such as HIV/AIDS, hepatitis, and variant CJD. The inadequacy of blood supplies has made the search for a safe, effective blood substitute the focus of much research. Despite some possibilities, no currently available substitute reproduces all of blood's many homeostatic functions.

Essential criteria for a successful blood substitute

❏ The substitute should be non-toxic and free from diseases.

❏ It should work for all blood types.

❏ It should not cause an immune response.

❏ It should remain in circulation until the blood volume is restored and then it should be safely excreted.

❏ It must be easily transported and suitable for storage under normal refrigeration.

❏ It should have a long shelf life.

❏ It should perform some or all of blood tasks.

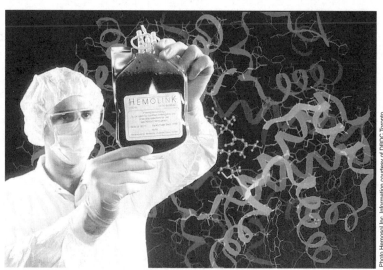

Photo Hemosol Inc. Information courtesy of DRDC Toronto

A shortfall in blood supplies, greater demand, and public fear of contaminated blood, have increased the need for a safe, effective blood substitute. Such a substitute must fulfil strict criteria (above).

A researcher displays a hemoglobin based artificial blood product, developed by Defense R&D Canada, Toronto and now produced under license by Hemosol Inc. Human testing and marketing has now progressed successfully into advanced trials. A human hemoglobin molecule is pictured in the background. Photo with permission from Hemosol inc.

Animal Transport Systems

Chemical based

These rely on synthetic oxygen-carrying compounds called **perfluorocarbons** (PFCs). PFCs are able to dissolve large quantities of gases. They do not dissolve freely in the plasma, so they must be emulsified with an agent that enables them to be dispersed in the blood.

Advantages: PFCs can transport a lot of oxygen, and transfer gases quickly.

Disadvantages: May result in oxygen accumulation in the tissues, which can lead to damage.

Examples: Oxygent™: Produced in commercial quantities using PFC emulsion technology; Perflubon (a PFC), water, a surfactant, and salts, homogenized into a stable, biologically compatible emulsion.

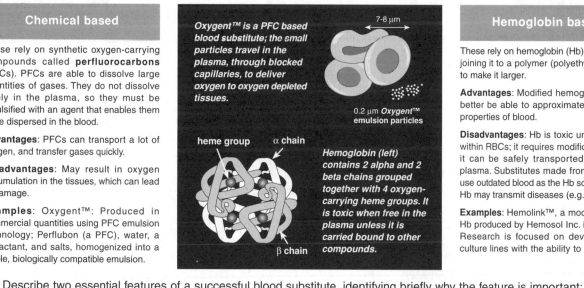

Oxygent™ is a PFC based blood substitute; the small particles travel in the plasma, through blocked capillaries, to deliver oxygen to oxygen depleted tissues.

7-8 μm

0.2 μm Oxygent™ emulsion particles

heme group   α chain

Hemoglobin (left) contains 2 alpha and 2 beta chains grouped together with 4 oxygen-carrying heme groups. It is toxic when free in the plasma unless it is carried bound to other compounds.

β chain

Hemoglobin based

These rely on hemoglobin (Hb), modified by joining it to a polymer (polyethylene glycol) to make it larger.

Advantages: Modified hemoglobin should better be able to approximate the various properties of blood.

Disadvantages: Hb is toxic unless carried within RBCs; it requires modification before it can be safely transported free in the plasma. Substitutes made from human Hb use outdated blood as the Hb source. Bovine Hb may transmit diseases (e.g. BSE).

Examples: Hemolink™, a modified human Hb produced by Hemosol Inc. in California. Research is focused on developing cell culture lines with the ability to produce Hb.

1. Describe two essential features of a successful blood substitute, identifying briefly why the feature is important:

   (a) _____

   (b) _____

2. Identify the two classes of artificial blood substitutes: _____

3. Discuss the advantages and risks associated with the use of blood substitutes: _____

   _____

   _____

   _____

   _____

   _____

Mammalian Transport

The blood vessels of the circulatory system form a vast network of tubes that carry blood away from the heart, transport it to the tissues of the body, and then return it to the heart. The arteries, arterioles, capillaries, venules, and veins are organized into specific routes to circulate the blood throughout the body. The figure below shows a number of the basic **circulatory routes** through which the blood travels. Mammals have a **double** **circulatory system**: a **pulmonary system** (or circulation), which carries blood between the heart and lungs, and a **systemic system** (circulation), which carries blood between the heart and the rest of the body. The systemic circulation has many subdivisions. Two important subdivisions are the coronary (cardiac) circulation, which supplies the heart muscle, and the **hepatic portal circulation**, which runs from the gut to the liver.

Schematic Overview of the Human Circulatory System

Deoxygenated blood (colored gray below) travels to the right side of the heart via the vena cavae. The heart pumps the deoxygenated blood to the lungs where it releases carbon dioxide and receives oxygen. The oxygenated blood (colored white below) travels via the pulmonary vein back to the heart from where it is pumped to all parts of the body. The **venous system** (figure, left) returns blood from the capillaries to the heart. The **arterial system** (figure right) carries blood from the heart to the capillaries. **Portal systems** carry blood between two capillary beds.

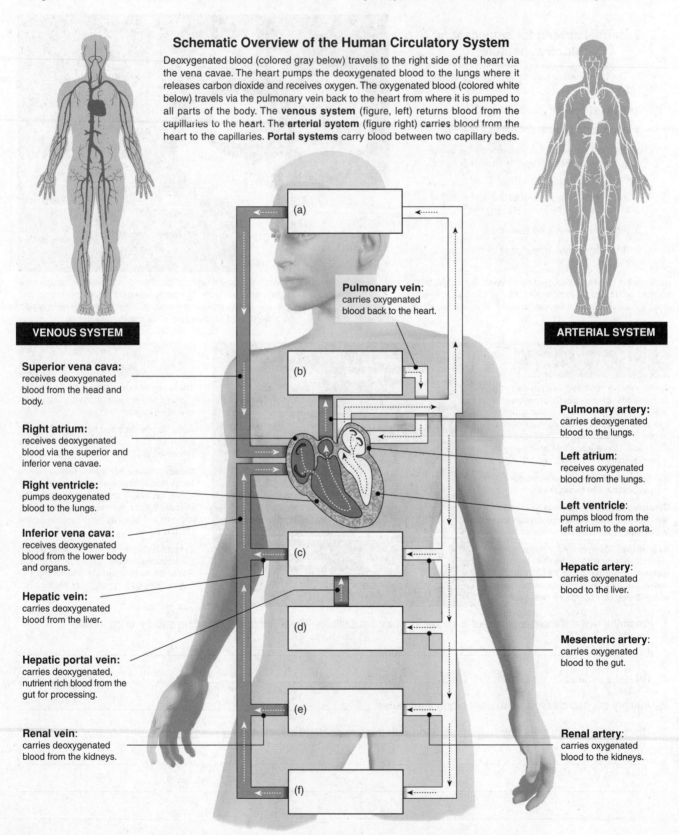

VENOUS SYSTEM

Superior vena cava: receives deoxygenated blood from the head and body.

Right atrium: receives deoxygenated blood via the superior and inferior vena cavae.

Right ventricle: pumps deoxygenated blood to the lungs.

Inferior vena cava: receives deoxygenated blood from the lower body and organs.

Hepatic vein: carries deoxygenated blood from the liver.

Hepatic portal vein: carries deoxygenated, nutrient rich blood from the gut for processing.

Renal vein: carries deoxygenated blood from the kidneys.

Pulmonary vein: carries oxygenated blood back to the heart.

ARTERIAL SYSTEM

Pulmonary artery: carries deoxygenated blood to the lungs.

Left atrium: receives oxygenated blood from the lungs.

Left ventricle: pumps blood from the left atrium to the aorta.

Hepatic artery: carries oxygenated blood to the liver.

Mesenteric artery: carries oxygenated blood to the gut.

Renal artery: carries oxygenated blood to the kidneys.

1. Complete the diagram above by labeling the boxes with the organs or structures they represent.

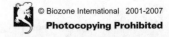
A 1   **Related activities:** Circulatory Systems

Heart Function

The **cardiac cycle** refers to the sequence of events of a heartbeat The pumping of the heart consists of alternate contractions (**systole**) and relaxations (**diastole**). During a complete cycle, each chamber undergoes a systole and a diastole. For a heart beating at 75 beats per minute, one cardiac cycle lasts about 0.8 seconds. Pressure changes within the heart's chambers generated by the cycle of contraction and relaxation are responsible for blood movement and cause the heart valves to open and close, preventing the backflow of blood. The noise of the blood when the valves open and close produces the heartbeat sound (**lubb-dupp**).

The Cardiac Cycle

The **pulse** results from the rhythmic expansion of the arteries as the blood spurts from the left ventricle. Pulse rate therefore corresponds to heart rate.

Stage 1: Atrial systole and ventricular filling The ventricles relax and blood flows into them from the atria. Note that 70% of the blood from the atria flows passively into the ventricles. It is during the last third of ventricular filling that the atria contract.

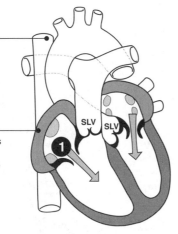

Heart during ventricular filling

Stage 2: Ventricular systole The atria relax, the ventricles contract, and blood is pumped from the ventricles into the aorta and the pulmonary artery. The start of ventricular contraction coincides with the first heart sound.

Stage 3: (not shown) There is a short period of atrial and ventricular relaxation (diastole). Semilunar valves (**SLV**) close to prevent backflow into the ventricles (see diagram, left). The cycle begins again.

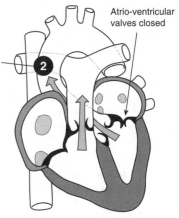

Atrio-ventricular valves closed

Heart during ventricular contraction

The Cardiac Cycle and the ECG

The electrical impulses transmitted through the heart generate electrical currents that can be detected by placing metal electrodes on the body's surface. They can be recorded on a heart monitor as a trace, called an **electrocardiogram** or ECG. The ECG pattern is the result of the different impulses produced at each phase of the **cardiac cycle**. A normal ECG (below) shows a regular repeating pattern of electrical pulses. Each wave of electrical activity brings about a corresponding contraction in the part of the heart receiving the electrical impulse. Each part of the ECG is given a letter according to an international code (below). An ECG provides a useful method of monitoring changes in heart rate and activity and detection of heart disorders.

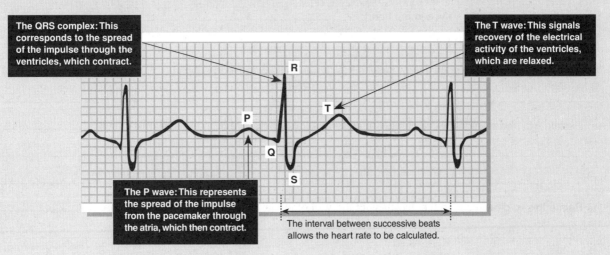

The QRS complex: This corresponds to the spread of the impulse through the ventricles, which contract.

The T wave: This signals recovery of the electrical activity of the ventricles, which are relaxed.

The P wave: This represents the spread of the impulse from the pacemaker through the atria, which then contract.

The interval between successive beats allows the heart rate to be calculated.

Animal Transport Systems

1. Identify each of the following phases of an ECG by its international code:

   (a) Excitation of the ventricles and ventricular systole: _____

   (b) Electrical recovery of the ventricles and ventricular diastole: _____

   (c) Excitation of the atria and atrial systole: _____

2. Suggest the physiological reason for the period of electrical recovery experienced each cycle (the T wave):

   _____

   _____

   _____

Related activities: Vertebrate Hearts, Arteries, Veins, Capillaries & Tissue Fluid
Web links: Review of the Human Heart, Electrocardiogram

RA 2

Pressure Changes and the Asymmetry of the Heart

aorta, 100 mg Hg

The heart is not a symmetrical organ. The left ventricle and its associated arteries are thicker and more muscular than the corresponding structures on the right side. This asymmetry is related to the necessary pressure differences between the pulmonary (lung) and systemic (body) circulations (not to the distance over which the blood is pumped per se). The graph below shows changes blood pressure in each of the major blood vessel types in the systemic and pulmonary circuits (the horizontal distance not to scale). The pulmonary circuit must operate at a much lower pressure than the systemic circuit to prevent fluid from accumulating in the alveoli of the lungs. The left side of the heart must develop enough "spare" pressure to enable increased blood flow to the muscles of the body and maintain kidney filtration rates without decreasing the blood supply to the brain.

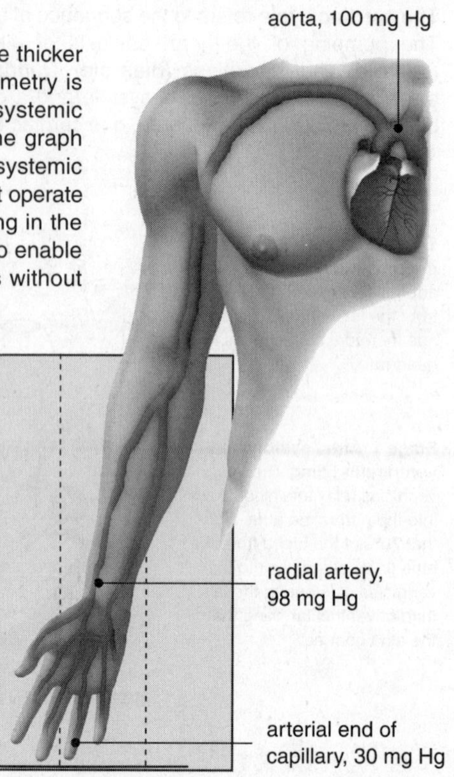

Blood pressure during contraction (systole)

Blood pressure during contraction (diastole)

The greatest fall in pressure occurs when the blood moves into the capillaries, even though the distance through the capillaries represents only a tiny proportion of the total distance traveled.

radial artery, 98 mg Hg

arterial end of capillary, 30 mg Hg

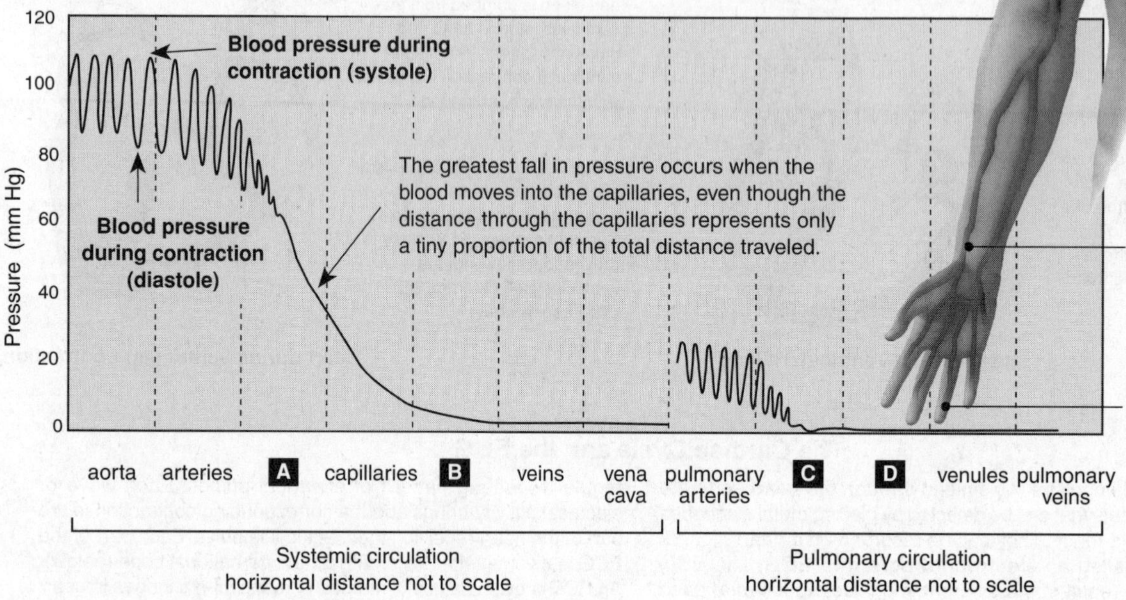

Pressure (mm Hg)

aorta   arteries   **A**   capillaries   **B**   veins   vena cava   pulmonary arteries   **C**   **D**   venules   pulmonary veins

Systemic circulation
horizontal distance not to scale

Pulmonary circulation
horizontal distance not to scale

2. Explain the purpose of the valves in the heart: _____

_____

3. The heart is full of blood. Suggest why, despite this, it needs its own blood supply: _____

_____

4. (a) Explain why the pulmonary circuit must operate at a lower pressure than the systemic circuit: _____

_____

_____

(b) Relate this to differences in the thickness of the wall of the left and right ventricles of the heart: _____

_____

_____

5. Identify the vessels corresponding to the letters **A-D** on the graph above:

A: _____ B: _____ C: _____ D: _____

6. (a) Find out what is meant by the **pulse pressure** and explain how it is calculated: _____

_____

(b) Predict what happens to the pulse pressure between the aorta and the capillaries: _____

_____

7. Explain what you are recording when you take a **pulse**: _____

_____

Control of Heart Activity

When removed from the body the cardiac muscle continues to beat. Therefore, the origin of the heartbeat is **myogenic**: the contractions arise as an intrinsic property of the cardiac muscle itself. The heartbeat is regulated by a special conduction system consisting of the pacemaker (**sinoatrial node**) and specialized conduction fibers called **Purkinje fibers**. The pacemaker sets a basic rhythm for the heart, but this rate is influenced by the cardiovascular control center in the medulla in response to sensory information from pressure receptors in the walls of the heart and blood vessels, and by higher brain functions. Changing the rate and force of heart contraction is the main mechanism for controlling cardiac output in order to meet changing demands.

Generation of the Heartbeat

The basic rhythmic heartbeat is **myogenic**. The nodal cells (SAN and atrioventricular node) spontaneously generate rhythmic action potentials without neural stimulation. The normal resting rate of self-excitation of the SAN is about 50 beats per minute.

The amount of blood ejected from the left ventricle per minute is called the **cardiac output**. It is determined by the **stroke volume** (the volume of blood ejected with each contraction) and the **heart rate** (number of heart beats per minute).

Cardiac output
= stroke volume x heart rate

Cardiac muscle responds to stretching by contracting more strongly. The greater the blood volume entering the ventricle, the greater the force of contraction. This relationship is known as **Starling's Law.**

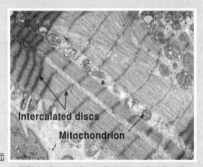

A TEM photo of cardiac muscle showing branched fibers (muscle cells). Each muscle fiber has one or two nuclei and many large mitochondria. **Intercalated discs** are specialized electrical junctions that separate the cells and allow the rapid spread of impulses through the heart muscle.

Sinoatrial node (SAN) is also called the **pacemaker**. It is a mass of specialized muscle cells near the opening of the superior vena cava. The pacemaker initiates the cardiac cycle, spontaneously generating action potentials that cause the atria to contract. The SAN sets the basic pace of the heart rate, although this rate is influenced by hormones and impulses from the autonomic nervous system.

Atrioventricular node (AVN) at the base of the atrium briefly delays the impulse to allow time for the atrial contraction to finish before the ventricles contract.

Bundle of His (atrioventricular bundle) containing Purkinje tissue. A tract of conducting fibers that distribute the action potentials over the ventricles causing ventricular contraction.

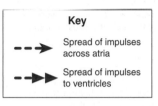

Key

- ‑ ‑ ► Spread of impulses across atria
- ‑ ‑ ►► Spread of impulses to ventricles

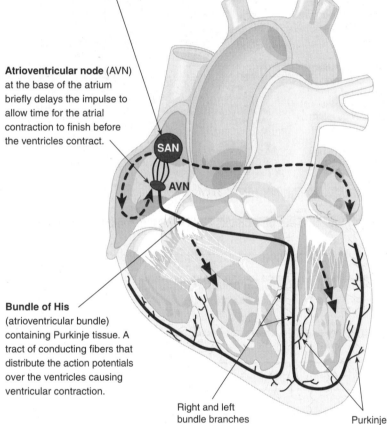

Right and left bundle branches

Purkinje fibers

Animal Transport Systems

1. Identify the role of each of the following in heart activity:

   (a) The sinoatrial node: _____

   (b) The atrioventricular node: _____

   (c) The bundle of His: _____

2. Explain the significance of the delay in impulse conduction at the AVN: _____

   _____

3. (a) Calculate the **cardiac output** when stroke volume is 70 cm^3 and the heart rate is 70 beats per minute:

   _____

   (b) Trained endurance athletes have a very high cardiac output. Suggest how this is achieved: _____

   _____

Autonomic Nervous System
Control of Heartbeat

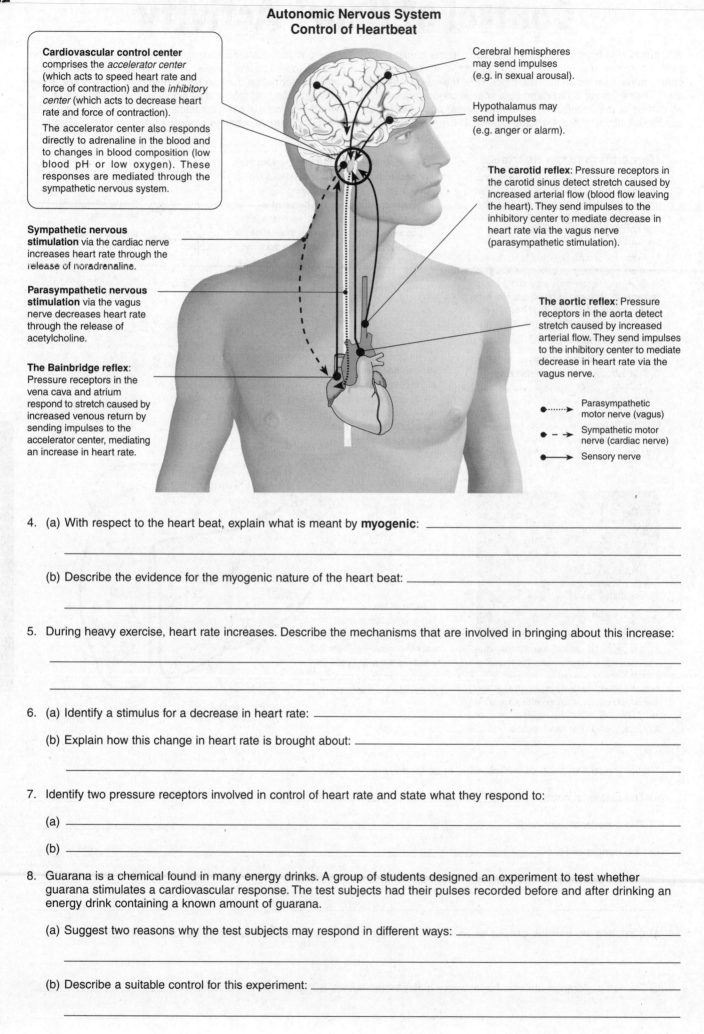

Cardiovascular control center comprises the *accelerator center* (which acts to speed heart rate and force of contraction) and the *inhibitory center* (which acts to decrease heart rate and force of contraction).

The accelerator center also responds directly to adrenaline in the blood and to changes in blood composition (low blood pH or low oxygen). These responses are mediated through the sympathetic nervous system.

Sympathetic nervous stimulation via the cardiac nerve increases heart rate through the release of noradrenaline.

Parasympathetic nervous stimulation via the vagus nerve decreases heart rate through the release of acetylcholine.

The Bainbridge reflex: Pressure receptors in the vena cava and atrium respond to stretch caused by increased venous return by sending impulses to the accelerator center, mediating an increase in heart rate.

Cerebral hemispheres may send impulses (e.g. in sexual arousal).

Hypothalamus may send impulses (e.g. anger or alarm).

The carotid reflex: Pressure receptors in the carotid sinus detect stretch caused by increased arterial flow (blood flow leaving the heart). They send impulses to the inhibitory center to mediate decrease in heart rate via the vagus nerve (parasympathetic stimulation).

The aortic reflex: Pressure receptors in the aorta detect stretch caused by increased arterial flow. They send impulses to the inhibitory center to mediate decrease in heart rate via the vagus nerve.

····▸ Parasympathetic motor nerve (vagus)

·-▸ Sympathetic motor nerve (cardiac nerve)

──▸ Sensory nerve

4. (a) With respect to the heart beat, explain what is meant by **myogenic**: _____

_____

(b) Describe the evidence for the myogenic nature of the heart beat: _____

_____

5. During heavy exercise, heart rate increases. Describe the mechanisms that are involved in bringing about this increase:

_____

_____

6. (a) Identify a stimulus for a decrease in heart rate: _____

(b) Explain how this change in heart rate is brought about: _____

_____

7. Identify two pressure receptors involved in control of heart rate and state what they respond to:

(a) _____

(b) _____

8. Guarana is a chemical found in many energy drinks. A group of students designed an experiment to test whether guarana stimulates a cardiovascular response. The test subjects had their pulses recorded before and after drinking an energy drink containing a known amount of guarana.

(a) Suggest two reasons why the test subjects may respond in different ways: _____

_____

(b) Describe a suitable control for this experiment: _____

_____

Exercise and Blood Flow

Exercise promotes health by improving the rate of blood flow back to the heart (venous return). This is achieved by strengthening all types of muscle and by increasing the efficiency of the heart.

During exercise blood flow to different parts of the body changes in order to cope with the extra demands of the muscles, the heart and the lungs.

1. The following table gives data for the **rate** of blood flow to various parts of the body at rest and during strenuous exercise. **Calculate** the **percentage** of the total blood flow that each organ or tissue receives under each regime of activity.

Organ or tissue	At rest		Strenuous exercise	
	cm^3 min^{-1}	% of total	cm^3 min^{-1}	% of total
Brain	700	14	750	4.2
Heart	200		750	
Lung tissue	100		200	
Kidneys	1100		600	
Liver	1350		600	
Skeletal muscles	750		12 500	
Bone	250		250	
Skin	300		1900	
Thyroid gland	50		50	
Adrenal glands	25		25	
Other tissue	175		175	
TOTAL	5000	**100**	17 800	**100**

2. Explain how the body increases the rate of blood flow during exercise: _____

_____

_____

3. (a) State approximately how many times the total rate of blood flow increases between rest and exercise: _____

(b) Explain why the increase is necessary: _____

_____

_____

4. (a) Identify which organs or tissues show no change in the rate of blood flow with exercise: _____

_____

(b) Explain why this is the case: _____

_____

_____

_____

5. (a) Identify the organs or tissues that show the most change in the rate of blood flow with exercise: _____

_____

(b) Explain why this is the case: _____

_____

_____

_____

Animal Transport Systems

Related activities: Energy and Exercise
Web links: Effects of Training

DA 2

Endurance refers to the ability of the muscles and the cardiovascular and respiratory systems to carry out exercise. Muscular endurance allows sprinters to run fast for a short time or body builders and weight lifters to lift an immense weight and hold it for a few seconds. Cardiovascular and respiratory endurance refer to the body as a whole: the ability to endure a high level of activity over a prolonged period. This type of endurance is seen in marathon runners, and long distance swimmers and cyclists. Different sports ("short burst sports" compared with endurance type sports) require different training methods and the physiologies (muscle bulk and cardiovascular fitness) of the athletes can be quite different.

The human heart and circulatory system make a number of adjustments in response to aerobic or endurance training. These include:

- **Heart size**: Increases. The left ventricle wall becomes thicker and its chamber bigger.

- **Heart rate**: Heart rate (at rest and during exercise) decreases markedly from non-trained people.

- **Recovery**: Recovery after exercise (of breathing and heart rate) is faster in trained athletes.

- **Stroke volume**: The volume of blood pumped with each heart beat increases with endurance training.

- **Blood volume**: Endurance training increases blood volume (the amount of blood in the body).

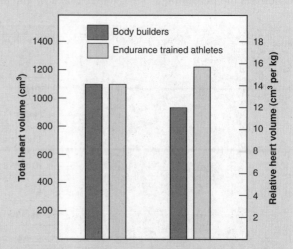

Difference in heart size of highly trained body builders and endurance athletes. Total heart volume is compared to heart volume as related to body weight. Average weights as follows: Body builders = 90.1 kg. Endurance athletes = 68.7 kg.

Weightlifters have good muscular endurance; they lift extremely heavy weights and hold them for a short time. Typical sports with high muscular endurance but lower cardiovascular endurance are sprinting, weight lifting, body building, boxing and wrestling.

Distance runners have very good cardiovascular and respiratory endurance; they sustain high intensity exercise for a long time. Typical sports needing cardiovascular endurance are distance running, cycling, and swimming (triathletes combine all three).

6. Suggest a reason why heart size increases with endurance activity: _____

_____

7. In the graph above right, explain why the relative heart volume of endurance athletes is greater than that of body builders, even though their total heart volumes are the same:

_____

8. Heart stroke volume increases with endurance training. Explain how this increases the efficiency of the heart as a pump:

_____

9. Resting heart rates are much lower in trained athletes compared with non-active people. Explain the health benefits of a lower resting heart rate:

_____

_____

Reproduction and Development

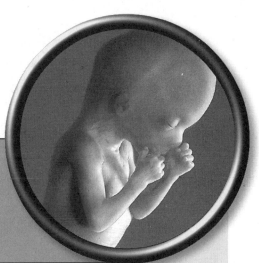

IB SL
Complete:
1, 12, 20-22, 35
Extension: 2, 36

IB HL
Complete:
1, 5, 8, 12-32, 35
Extension: 2, 36

IB Options
Not applicable
to options

AP Biology
Complete:
1-22, 23 or 24, 25-36
Some numbers
extension as
appropriate

Learning Objectives

☐ 1. Compile your own glossary from the **KEY WORDS** displayed in **bold type** in the learning objectives below.

Principles of Reproduction *(pages 227-230)*

☐ 2. Explain the need for **reproduction** and identify the risks, benefits, and energetic costs associated with it.

☐ 3. Distinguish between **sexual** and **asexual reproduction**. Discuss the consequences and advantages of each. Understand that **haploid** and **diploid** phases occur in the life cycles of sexually reproducing organisms. Giving examples, briefly describe features of the following types of reproduction: **budding**, **fragmentation**, **parthenogenesis**, **hermaphroditism**, and reproduction involving two **separate sexes**.

☐ 4. Explain the role of **gamete formation** and **fertilization** in **sexual reproduction**. Describe differences between male gametes (**sperm**) and female gametes (**eggs**) in terms of size, the number produced, and motility.

☐ 5. Recall the role of **meiosis** in producing gametes, identifying the significance of the reduction division. Explain how **fertilization** restores the diploid chromosome number in the zygote. Interpret **life cycles** of organisms in terms of **mitosis, meiosis, fertilization,** and **chromosome number**.

Sexual Reproduction in Animals

Reproductive patterns *(pages 229-232, 326-328)*

☐ 6. Distinguish between **internal** and **external fertilization** and describe the features associated with each. Describe the advantages and disadvantages of each method. Identify animals with each type of strategy.

☐ 7. Relate the evolution of vertebrate reproductive systems to the move to being land-living. Identify reproductive strategies in amphibians that reflect their partial adaptation to terrestrial lifestyles.

☐ 8. With respect to internal fertilization, define the term **copulation** and distinguish it from **fertilization**. Identify the structures that have developed in males and females to enable internal fertilization.

☐ 9. Using examples, distinguish between **internal** and **external development** of the **embryo** and describe the features associated with each method. Describe the advantages and disadvantages of each strategy. Explain the terms **oviparous** and **viviparous**, and give examples of animals with each type of reproduction.

☐ 10. Describe diversity seen in the reproductive structures and strategies of animals (including **courtship, mating,** and **parental care** behaviors). Useful comparisons can be made between amphibians, birds, and mammals, and between vertebrates and invertebrates.

☐ 11. Describe the structure of the reproductive system in at least two animals. Identify the location and function of: **gonad** (**testis, ovary**), **oviduct, penis** (if present), **vagina** (if present), **uterus** (if present). Identify any associated structures that have a role in reproduction.

Reproduction in Humans

Reproductive organs *(pages 233, 239-240)*

☐ 12. Using a labeled diagram, describe the structure and function of adult male and female reproductive systems in humans. Note the relative positions of the organs but do not include any histological details.

☐ 13. Draw the structure of **testis** tissue as seen using a light microscope. Include reference to **seminiferous tubules**, blood capillaries, and **interstitial cells**. Draw a seminiferous tubule with adjacent interstitial cells in XS. Indicate the **Sertoli cells** and developing sperm.

☐ 14. Outline the processes involved in **spermatogenesis** and their location. Include reference to mitosis, cell growth, meiosis, and cell differentiation. Outline the role of follicle stimulating hormone (**FSH**), luteinizing hormone (**LH**), and **testosterone** in spermatogenesis.

☐ 15. Draw the structure of the ovary as seen using a light microscope. Include reference to the following: **primary oocytes, zona pellucida, Graafian follicles**.

☐ 16. Outline the processes involved in **oogenesis**, including reference to mitosis, cell growth, meiosis, the unequal division of the cytoplasm, and the degeneration of the **polar bodies**. If required, outline the role of **hormones** in **gametogenesis** in females.

☐ 17. Compare spermatogenesis and oogenesis with respect to the number of gametes formed and the timing of the gamete formation and release.

☐ 18. Draw the structure of mature **sperm** and **egg**, relating specific features to their functional role.

☐ 19. Outline the role of the **epididymis, seminal vesicle,** and **prostate gland** in the production of **semen**.

The menstrual cycle *(pages 234-235)*

☐ 20. Explain the main features of the human **menstrual cycle** including the development of the ovarian **follicles** and **corpora lutea**, the cyclical changes to the **uterine endometrium**, and **menstruation**.

☐ 21. Relate the changes in the menstrual cycle to the changes in the hormones regulating the cycle: **progesterone, estrogen, FSH,** and **LH**. Emphasize the role of **feedback control** in the menstrual cycle.

Human development *(pages 241-247 & the TRC)*

☐ 22. Explain what is meant by **puberty** and describe the physical changes associated with it. Identify **primary** and **secondary sexual characteristics** in males and females and the explain the role of **sex hormones** (**testosterone** and **estrogen**) in human development.

☐ 23. Recall the difference between copulation and **fertilization**. Appreciate how fertilization in humans is dependent on the timing of gamete transfer. In general terms, describe the events in fertilization.

☐ 24. In more detail than #23, describe fertilization, including reference to the timing and significance of the **acrosome reaction**, **penetration** of the egg membrane by the sperm, and the **cortical reaction**.

☐ 25. Describe early embryonic development up to the **implantation** of the **blastocyst** (including **cleavage**).

☐ 26. Describe the main events in **embryonic development** between implantation and 5-8 weeks. Include reference to the early development of both the nervous and circulatory systems.

☐ 27. Explain the role of **human chorionic gonadotropin** (also called human chorionic gonadotrophin or HCG) in early pregnancy. Identify the source of this hormone.

☐ 28. Draw a diagram of the uterus during **pregnancy** and identify the following: **uterus, placenta, umbilical cord, embryonic membranes, amniotic fluid, fetus**. Recognize pregnancy as the period of **gestation**.

☐ 29. Describe the role of the amniotic sac and amniotic fluid in supporting and protecting the fetus. Appreciate the role of **placenta** in the exchange of materials between the maternal and fetal blood.

☐ 30. Describe the structure and function of the **placenta**. Explain how the placenta is maintained during **pregnancy** and describe its functions in relation to the development of the embryo.

☐ 31. Outline the process of **birth** (parturition) and its control, including the role of **oxytocin** and **progesterone**. Recognize the role of **positive feedback** in birth.

☐ 32. Explain what is meant by **lactation** and explain its importance to early nutrition. Describe the function and regulation of **prolactin** and **oxytocin** in lactation.

☐ 33. Explain the biological basis of **aging** and discuss the physiological changes that occur as a result of it. Include reference to **menopause** and degenerative diseases such as **osteoporosis** and Alzheimer's disease. This material is provided in the activity '*Aging*' on the Teacher Resource CD-ROM.

Reproductive Technology *(pages 236-238)*

☐ 34. Explain what is meant by **contraception**. Describe four methods of contraception, including at least one method from each of the following: **mechanical, chemical,** and **behavioral**. Discuss the ethics of **family planning** and contraception.

☐ 35. Outline the process of **in vitro fertilization** (IVF). Explain when this technique is used and discuss the ethical issues associated with it.

☐ 36. Describe the procedures involved in some other reproductive technologies available to enhance human fertility, including **gamete intrafallopian transfer** (GIFT) and **artificial insemination** (AI).

See the 'Textbook Reference Grid' on pages 8-9 for textbook page references relating to material in this topic.

Supplementary Texts

See pages 5-6 for additional details of these texts:

■ Clegg, C.J., 1998. **Mammals: Structure and Function** (John Murray), pp. 78-86.

■ Helms, D.R. *et al.*, 1998. **Biology in the Laboratory** (W.H. Freeman), #36, #40.

■ Morton, D. & J.W. Perry, 1998. **Photo Atlas for Anatomy and Physiology** (W.H. Freeman).

■ Murray, P. & N. Owens, 2001. **Behavior and Populations** (Collins), pp. 28-61.

See page 6 for details of publishers of periodicals:

STUDENT'S REFERENCE

■ **Animal Attraction** National Geographic, July 2003, pp. 28-55. *An engaging and expansive account of mating in the animal world.*

■ **The Trouble with Sex** New Scientist, 6 Dec. 2003, pp. 44-47. *Sex must confer an advantage because it is so common. Recent experiments point to the unpredictability of the environment being an important consideration.*

■ **Why we don't Lay Eggs** New Scientist, 12 June 1999, pp. 26-31. *Mammalian reproduction: the role of the placenta, the evolution of live birth, and mammalian exceptions to the usual pattern.*

■ **Future Child** New Scientist, 21 Oct. 2006, pp. 41-54. *A series of articles looking at the future of reproduction and reproductive technology. Includes the possibility of IVF or IVM as the norm for reproducing and creating sex cells from stem cells.*

■ **The Biology of Milk** Biol. Sci. Rev., 16(3) Feb. 2004, pp. 2-6. *The production and composition of milk, its role in mammalian biology, and the physiological processes controlling its release.*

■ **Spermatogenesis** Biol. Sci. Rev., 15(4) April 2003, pp. 10-14. *The process and control of sperm production in humans, with a discussion of the possible reasons for male infertility.*

■ **The Great Escape** New Scientist, 15 Sept. 2001, (Inside Science). *How the fetus is accepted by the mother's immune system during pregnancy.*

■ **Measuring Female Hormones in Saliva** Biol. Sci. Rev., 13(3) Jan. 2001, pp. 37-39. *The female reproductive system, and the complex hormonal control of the female menstrual cycle.*

■ **Adolescence - Hormones Rule OK?** Biol. Sci. Rev., 19(3) Feb. 2007, pp. 2-6. *The hormonal changes bringing about reproductive maturity.*

■ **The Placenta** Biol. Sci. Rev., 12 (4) March 2000, pp. 2-5. *The structure and function of the human placenta (includes prenatal diagnoses).*

■ **Menopause - Design Fault, or By Design** Biol. Sci. Rev., 14(1) Sept. 2001, pp. 2-6. *An excellent synopsis of the basic biology of menopause.*

■ **Aging** National Geographic, 192(5), Nov. 1997, pp. 2-31. *An account of the physiological aspects of aging as well as the social issues of elderly care.*

■ **Turning Back the Years** New Scientist, 14 Jan. 2006, pp. 42-45. *Putting patients on the brink of death into a state of suspended animation, giving surgeons time to perform life-saving operations.*

■ **How to Live to be 100... and Enjoy it** New Scientist, 3 June 2006, pp. 35-45. *Nine things that seem to lead to a longer happier life and why.*

■ **Age - Old Story** New Scientist, 23 Jan. 1999, (Inside Science). *The processes involved in aging. An accessible, easy-to-read, but thorough account.*

TEACHER'S REFERENCE

■ **Pregnancy Tests** Scientific American, Nov. 2000, pp. 92-93. *Pregnancy tests: how they work and the role of HCG in signalling pregnancy.*

■ **The Evolution of Human Birth** Sci. American, Nov. 2001, pp. 60-65. *An examination of the unique aspects of human reproduction and how they arose.*

■ **Modeling Radial Holoblastic Cleavage** The Am. Biology Teacher, May 2000, pp. 362-364.

Making 3D models to help students understand the concepts behind embryological processes.

■ **Boy or Girl** New Scientist, 14 Sept. 2002, pp. 42-45. *Conception and the determination of offspring gender: not a matter of chance alone.*

■ **The Timing of Birth** Scientific American, March 1999, pp. 50-57. *A hormone found in the human placenta influences the timing of delivery.*

■ **Let me Out** New Scientist, 10 Jan. 1998, pp. 24-29. *Fetus and mother are in conflict and it is the fetus that determines the timing of birth.*

■ **Male Contraception** Biol. Sci. Rev., 13(2) Nov. 2000, pp. 6-9. *A new contraceptive technology involves the inhibition of spermatogenesis in males.*

See pages 10-11 for details of how to access **Bio Links** from our web site: **www.thebiozone.com** From Bio Links, access sites under the topics:

GENERAL BIOLOGY ONLINE RESOURCES > Online Textbooks and Lecture Notes: • An on-line biology book • Learn.co.uk ... *and others*

ANIMAL BEHAVIOR: • How females choose their mates • Sexual selection ... *and others*

ANIMAL BIOLOGY: • Anatomy and physiology • Human physiology lecture notes ... *and others* > **Reproduction and Development:** • Anatomical travelogue • Developmental biology • Dynamic development • Embryo images online • Learn. co.uk: Reproduction • Menstrual cycle and pregnancy • Fertility UK: Physiology • Hormones of the reproductive system ... *and others*

BIOTECHNOLOGY > Applications in Biotechnology > Reproductive Biotechnology: • Assisted reproductive technologies • Atlanta Reproductive Health Center ... *and others*

Asexual Reproduction

In most forms of asexual reproduction, the parent splits, fragments, or buds to produce offspring identical to itself. Parthenogenesis is a special type of asexual reproduction where unfertilized eggs give rise to clones. Asexually reproducing organisms do not need to find a mate, so the energy that might otherwise be used for sexual activity can be used for other things. Asexual reproduction is rapid, but all the offspring are genetically identical. If conditions change there is little ability to adapt.

Binary Fission

Binary fission is a method of asexual reproduction that occurs in prokaryotes (bacteria and cyanobacteria) and protists (e.g. **Amoeba** and **Paramecium**). Binary fission occurs by division of a parent body into two, more or less equal, parts. The cell's DNA is replicated, followed by division of the nucleoplasm (in prokaryotes) or the cytoplasm (protists). The series (right) shows stages in the process of binary fission in *Amoeba*. The photograph below this series shows binary fission in *Paramecium*. The nucleus has divided and the cytoplasm is dividing. The arrows indicate where a constriction is developing in the cell.

Note that some life cycle stages of parasitic protozoans, such as the malarial parasite *Plasmodium*, undergo **multiple fission**. The nucleus divides repeatedly before the final division of the cytoplasm to produce many new cells. Repeated cycles of multiple fission produce large numbers of offspring very rapidly.

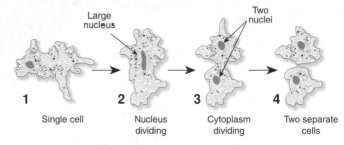

Amoeba undergoing fission

1 — Single cell
2 — Nucleus dividing
3 — Cytoplasm dividing
4 — Two separate cells

Large nucleus · Two nuclei

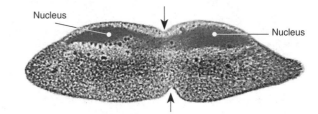

Nucleus — Nucleus

Paramecium (photo RCN)

Budding and Fragmentation

Sponges and most cnidarians (e.g. *Hydra*) can reproduce by **budding**. A small part of the parent body separates from the rest and develops into a new individual. This new individual may remain attached as part of the colony, or the budding offspring may constrict at its point of attachment (arrowed on the photograph) and eventually be released as an independent organism.

The photo (right) shows *Hydra* budding. The new individual is forming on the right of the animal. Cnidarians also undergo **fragmentation**. In this natural process, the organism spontaneously divides into fragments which then regenerate. Fragmentation also occurs in sponges and flatworms (platyhelminthes).

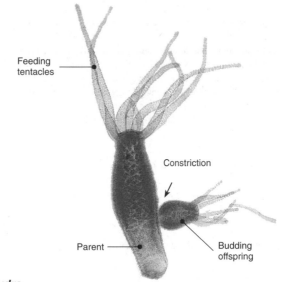

Feeding tentacles

Constriction

Parent — Budding offspring

Hydra (photo EII)

1. Name the reproductive process occurring in the photograph of *Paramecium* above: _____

2. Name the reproductive process occurring in *Hydra*: _____

3. (a) Suggest why multiple fission produces offspring more rapidly than does simple binary fission: _____

   _____

   _____

   _____

   (b) Explain the advantage of multiple fission to an intracellular parasite such as *Plasmodium*: _____

   _____

   _____

Reproduction and Development

Related activities: Malaria

A 1

Alternating Asexual and Sexual Cycles of Reproduction

Some organisms combine several cycles of asexual reproduction by **parthenogenesis** (below, left) with periods when they reproduce sexually (producing gametes by meiosis which combine in fertilization). The parthenogenetic phase enables the rapid reproduction of a well adapted clone. The sexual phase is induced when the environment becomes unfavorable for the clone. The new generation, produced by sexual reproduction, may include some individuals that are better adapted to a new set of environmental conditions.

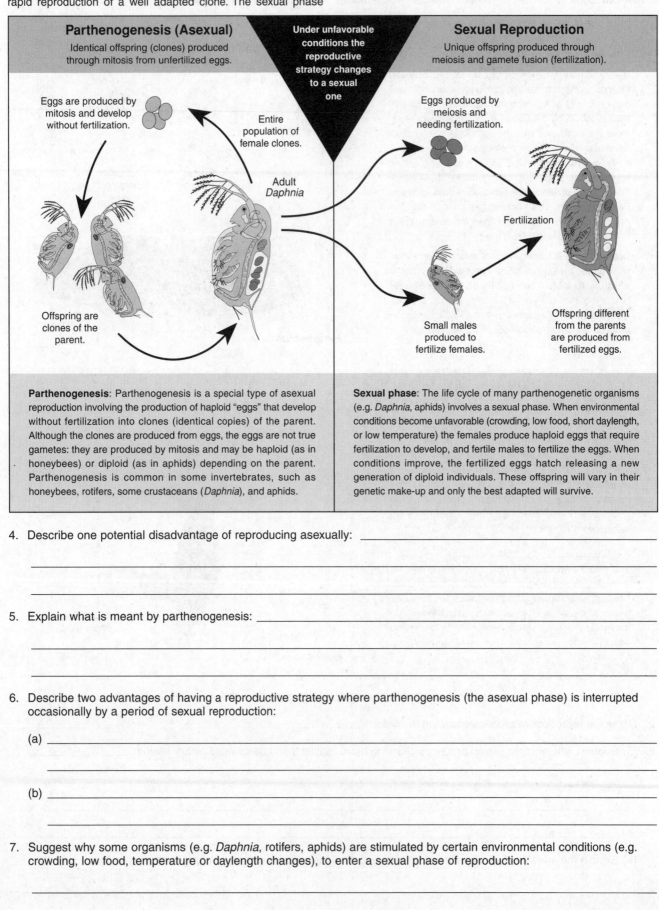

Parthenogenesis (Asexual)
Identical offspring (clones) produced through mitosis from unfertilized eggs.

Under unfavorable conditions the reproductive strategy changes to a sexual one

Sexual Reproduction
Unique offspring produced through meiosis and gamete fusion (fertilization).

Eggs are produced by mitosis and develop without fertilization.

Entire population of female clones.

Adult *Daphnia*

Offspring are clones of the parent.

Eggs produced by meiosis and needing fertilization.

Fertilization

Small males produced to fertilize females.

Offspring different from the parents are produced from fertilized eggs.

Parthenogenesis: Parthenogenesis is a special type of asexual reproduction involving the production of haploid "eggs" that develop without fertilization into clones (identical copies) of the parent. Although the clones are produced from eggs, the eggs are not true gametes: they are produced by mitosis and may be haploid (as in honeybees) or diploid (as in aphids) depending on the parent. Parthenogenesis is common in some invertebrates, such as honeybees, rotifers, some crustaceans (*Daphnia*), and aphids.

Sexual phase: The life cycle of many parthenogenetic organisms (e.g. *Daphnia*, aphids) involves a sexual phase. When environmental conditions become unfavorable (crowding, low food, short daylength, or low temperature) the females produce haploid eggs that require fertilization to develop, and fertile males to fertilize the eggs. When conditions improve, the fertilized eggs hatch releasing a new generation of diploid individuals. These offspring will vary in their genetic make-up and only the best adapted will survive.

4. Describe one potential disadvantage of reproducing asexually: _____

_____

_____

5. Explain what is meant by parthenogenesis: _____

_____

_____

6. Describe two advantages of having a reproductive strategy where parthenogenesis (the asexual phase) is interrupted occasionally by a period of sexual reproduction:

(a) _____

_____

(b) _____

_____

7. Suggest why some organisms (e.g. *Daphnia*, rotifers, aphids) are stimulated by certain environmental conditions (e.g. crowding, low food, temperature or daylength changes), to enter a sexual phase of reproduction:

_____

_____

Animal Sexual Reproduction

All types of sexual reproduction involve the production of **gametes** (sex cells), produced by special sex organs called **gonads**. Female gametes (**eggs**) and male gametes (**sperm**) come together in **fertilization**. Animal sexual reproduction follows one of three main patterns, determined by the location of fertilization and embryonic development. These patterns are: external fertilization and development; internal fertilization followed by external development; internal fertilization and development. **External fertilization** is found in many aquatic invertebrates and most fish, where eggs and sperm are released into the surrounding water. Male and female parents usually release their gametes (spawn) at the same time and place in

order to increase the chances of successful fertilization. In other invertebrates, reptiles, sharks, birds, and mammals, sperm are transferred from the male to inside the female's genital tract during the act of **copulation**. This **internal fertilization** increases the chance that the gametes will meet successfully. In birds and most reptiles, one adaptation to life on land has been the evolution of the **amniote egg**: a structure that enables the embryo to complete its development outside the parent surrounded by a protective shell and nourished by a yolk sac. The pattern of internal development in mammals provides the most advantages for the embryo in terms of nourishment and protection during development.

Achieving Fertilization: The Mating Game

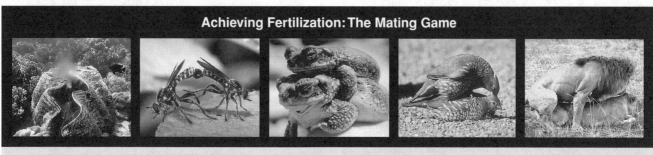

Many marine invertebrates release gametes into the sea. Fertilization and development are external to the parent. *Example: giant clam*

Insects often have elaborate courtship rituals. Fertilization is internal, but the eggs are laid and develop externally. *Example: dipteran flies*

In amphibians, a prolonged coupling, called amplexus, precedes gamete release and external fertilization. *Example: frogs*

In birds and reptiles gamete fertilization is internal but the eggs are laid (usually in nests) and develop externally. *Example: quail*

Mammals exhibit internal fertilization, a long period of internal development, and often prolonged parental care. *Example: African lions*

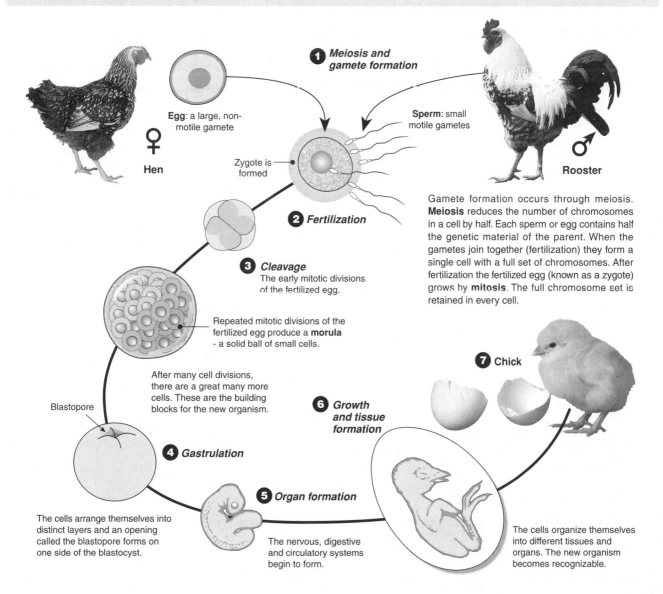

1 *Meiosis and gamete formation*

Egg: a large, non-motile gamete

♀ **Hen**

Sperm: small motile gametes

♂ **Rooster**

Zygote is formed

2 *Fertilization*

3 *Cleavage*
The early mitotic divisions of the fertilized egg.

Repeated mitotic divisions of the fertilized egg produce a **morula** - a solid ball of small cells.

After many cell divisions, there are a great many more cells. These are the building blocks for the new organism.

Blastopore

4 *Gastrulation*

The cells arrange themselves into distinct layers and an opening called the blastopore forms on one side of the blastocyst.

5 *Organ formation*

The nervous, digestive and circulatory systems begin to form.

6 *Growth and tissue formation*

7 Chick

The cells organize themselves into different tissues and organs. The new organism becomes recognizable.

Gamete formation occurs through meiosis. **Meiosis** reduces the number of chromosomes in a cell by half. Each sperm or egg contains half the genetic material of the parent. When the gametes join together (fertilization) they form a single cell with a full set of chromosomes. After fertilization the fertilized egg (known as a zygote) grows by **mitosis**. The full chromosome set is retained in every cell.

Reproduction and Development

Related activities: Animal Reproductive Structures, Parental Care

A 2

Hermaphroditism

Most animals have separate sexes (individuals are either male or female). However, in some animals both sperm and eggs can be produced in the same individual. Such animals are known as **hermaphrodites**. In earthworms (below), flatworms, and some molluscs (e.g. land snails), both male and female organs are active in the same animal and there is typically a reciprocal transfer of sperm (each receives sperm from the other during copulation). In this type of hermaphroditism, there is no self fertilization: a mate is necessary for any fertilization to occur. However, some specialized hermaphroditic animals, such as parasitic tapeworms, are capable of self-fertilization.

The photo above shows two earthworms in a mating clasp. Each worm places its reproductive region (the clitellum) against the reproductive region of the other worm, and sperm is exchanged.

Courtship and mating in the snail *Cantareus aspersus* (formerly *Helix aspersa*, above). During an elaborate courtship (A), calcareous darts are fired from the genital opening (behind the tentacle) into the body of the partner. Mating (B) involves reciprocal transfer of sperm via a penis (P).

1. Describe one advantage of sexual reproduction: _____

   _____

2. Describe one potential disadvantage of sexual reproduction: _____

   _____

3. Compare and contrast the key differences between male and female gametes in relation to:

   (a) The size of gametes: _____

   (b) Number of gametes produced: _____

   (c) Motility of gametes: _____

4. Distinguish between **internal** fertilization and **external** fertilization, identifying advantages of each strategy:

   _____

   _____

   _____

   _____

5. (a) Name an animal group with internal fertilization but external development: _____

   (b) Name an animal group with internal fertilization and internal development: _____

   (c) Describe one benefit and one cost involved in providing for internal development of an embryo:

   Benefit: _____

   Cost: _____

6. Explain why each new individual produced from the fusion of the two gametes is unique: _____

   _____

Animal Reproductive Strategies

To reproduce sexually, animals must have systems to ensure that gametes meet and fertilization takes place. There is a huge range in the complexity of reproductive structures in animals: the least complex do not even have distinct gonads, whereas the most complex comprise numerous ducts, glands, and accessory structures to produce the gametes and protect the eggs and developing embryos. Diverse systems for reproduction have evolved amongst the invertebrates; some of the most complex are found in parasitic flatworms. Insects, which have separate sexes and highly developed reproductive systems, are illustrated in detail here. Insects frequently also have elaborate courtship and mating behaviors associated with successful transfer of gametes. Amongst the vertebrates, the basic structures of the reproductive system are relatively uniform, but there is huge variation in the strategies shown by different vertebrate groups. Biologists distinguish **oviparous** (egg laying) animals from, **viviparous** (live bearing) animals. A small number of vertebrates are also **ovoviviparous**: the young are born live but their nutrition inside the mother is derived from stores within the egg. This strategy is typical of non-mammal species that bear live young. Here the contrast is made between the reproductive strategies of amphibians, which rely heavily on water for their reproduction, and the strategy of birds, in which the evolution of a shelled egg has freed them from their reproductive dependence on water.

Reproductive Strategies of Frogs

In most frogs and toads, fertilization is external. This is achieved when the male clasps the female. Called **amplexus**, this clasping may last several hours or even days until the female lays her eggs. Not all frogs lay eggs in water. Some frogs have adopted novel behavior and physiological strategies to avoid their eggs becoming an easy meal. The examples here (right and below) illustrate the variety of solutions developed by different frog species.

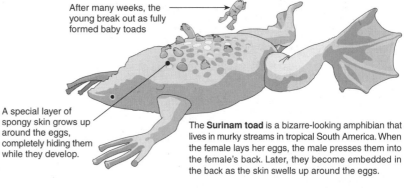

After many weeks, the young break out as fully formed baby toads

A special layer of spongy skin grows up around the eggs, completely hiding them while they develop.

The **Surinam toad** is a bizarre-looking amphibian that lives in murky streams in tropical South America. When the female lays her eggs, the male presses them into the female's back. Later, they become embedded in the back as the skin swells up around the eggs.

 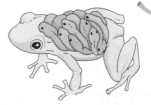  

Male

Some frogs lay their eggs in a nest of foam either on land (attached to leaves) or floating on water. The foam not only hides the eggs from predators, but it keeps them moist and prevents them from drying out.

Some species of small frogs in both South America and Africa lay eggs that hatch into tadpoles on land. The tadpoles stick to the back of one of the parents with mouthparts modified to function as suckers. The parent carries the tadpoles to water.

Some frog species lay eggs on leaves or branches overhanging the water. In some of these species one of the parents remains with the eggs until they hatch. The tadpoles that emerge from the eggs drop into the water below to complete their development.

When a female midwife toad lays her string of eggs, the male winds them around his back legs. He carries the eggs for about a month, visiting puddles to keep them moist. When the eggs are ready to hatch he places them in a suitable pool.

The Structure and Physiology of a Bird's Egg

Both reptiles and birds (which evolved from reptilian ancestors) developed watertight shelled eggs, called **cleidoic eggs**. The egg is supplied with all the necessary food material as well as fats that yield water when metabolized. The shell enclosing the egg provides protection and reduces water loss, yet permits gas exchange. Waste materials from the developing chick embryo are stored in the egg.

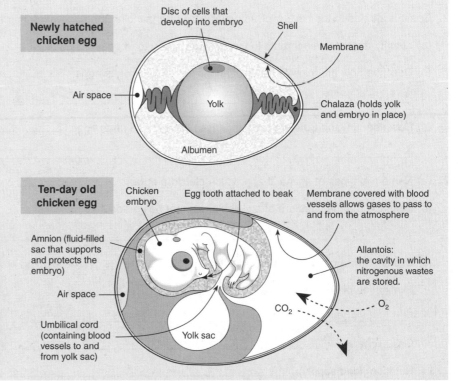

Newly hatched chicken egg

Disc of cells that develop into embryo

Shell

Membrane

Air space

Yolk

Chalaza (holds yolk and embryo in place)

Albumen

Ten-day old chicken egg

Chicken embryo

Egg tooth attached to beak

Membrane covered with blood vessels allows gases to pass to and from the atmosphere

Amnion (fluid-filled sac that supports and protects the embryo)

Allantois: the cavity in which nitrogenous wastes are stored.

Air space

CO_2

O_2

Umbilical cord (containing blood vessels to and from yolk sac)

Yolk sac

Related activities: Animal Sexual Reproduction, Breeding Behavior

RA 2

Reproduction and Development

Reproductive Strategies of Insects

Insects reproduce sexually, mainly by internal fertilization followed by the production of yolk-filled eggs. A single pair of gonads is located in the abdomen. Most insects transfer sperm within small packets called **spermatophores**. Claspers at the end of the male's abdomen hold the female's abdomen during copulation. The terminal segments of the female's abdomen may form an **ovipositor**, often extendable or needle-like, with which they lay their eggs. Depending on the insect species, eggs may be buried in soil, animal dung, or rotting carcasses, injected into plant tissue or living hosts, or cemented to twigs or leaves.

Mating in Damselflies

Species in the order Odonata (damselflies and dragonflies) are unique amongst the insects in that the male copulatory apparatus is situated on abdominal segments close to its thorax. However, the testes are located at the end of its abdomen so that, prior to mating, the male has to bend the abdomen round to transfer semen from the testes to the penis. The location of the male genitals also accounts for the unique "wheel position" adopted by members of this order (below).

Insect reproductive organs

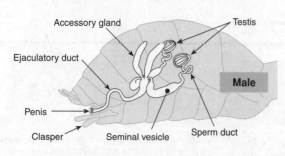

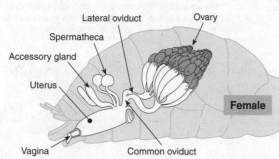

The male damselfly grips onto a twig with its front legs during mating while holding the female behind the head with clasping organs at the end of its abdomen.

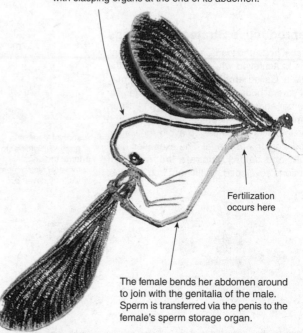

Fertilization occurs here

The female bends her abdomen around to join with the genitalia of the male. Sperm is transferred via the penis to the female's sperm storage organ.

1. Giving examples, distinguish between **oviparous** and **viviparous** vertebrates: _____

_____

_____

2. Some frogs and toads have evolved novel ways of enhancing the survival of their eggs.

   (a) Identify the two main threats to the survival of frog/toad eggs: _____

   (b) Describe how the midwife toad enhances the survival of its eggs: _____

   _____

   (c) Describe how the Surinam toad enhances the survival of its eggs: _____

   _____

3. (a) Name two types of animal that produce **cleidoic eggs**: _____

   (b) Describe the main feature of a cleidoic egg that has made it so successful: _____

   _____

   (c) Explain how a cleidoic egg provides for the following needs of a developing embryo:

   Elimination of wastes: _____

   _____

   Gas exchange: _____

   Nutrition (food supply): _____

Female Reproductive System

The female reproductive system in mammals produces eggs, receives the penis and sperm during sexual intercourse, and houses and nourishes the young. Female reproductive systems in mammals are similar in their basic structure (uterus, ovaries etc.) but the shape of the uterus and the form of the placenta during pregnancy vary. The human system is described below.

Oogenesis

Oogenesis is the process by which mature ova (egg cells) are produced by the ovary. Oogonia are formed in the female embryo and undergo repeated mitotic divisions to form the primary oocyte. These remain in prophase of meiosis I throughout childhood. At this stage, all the eggs a female will ever have are present, but they remain in this resting phase until puberty. At puberty, meiosis resumes. Eggs are released, arrested in metaphase of meiosis II. This second division is only completed upon fertilization.

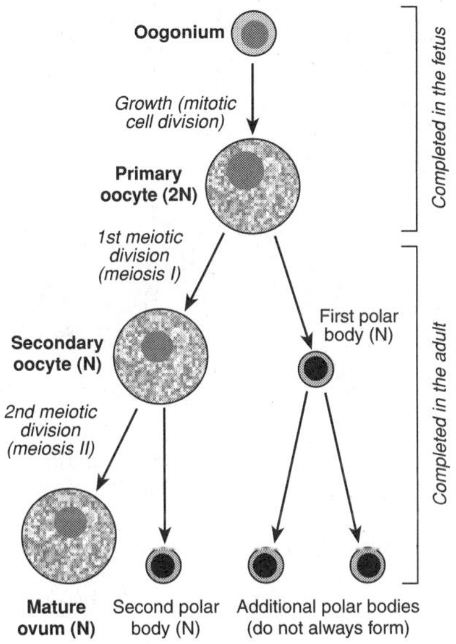

Oogonium

Growth (mitotic cell division)

Primary oocyte (2N)

1st meiotic division (meiosis I)

Secondary oocyte (N)

First polar body (N)

2nd meiotic division (meiosis II)

Mature ovum (N) · Second polar body (N) · Additional polar bodies (do not always form)

Completed in the fetus

Completed in the adult

The Female Reproductive System

(a) (b) (c)

Spine

Colon

(d)

Bladder

(e)

Pubis

Anus

(f)

Urethra · Labia

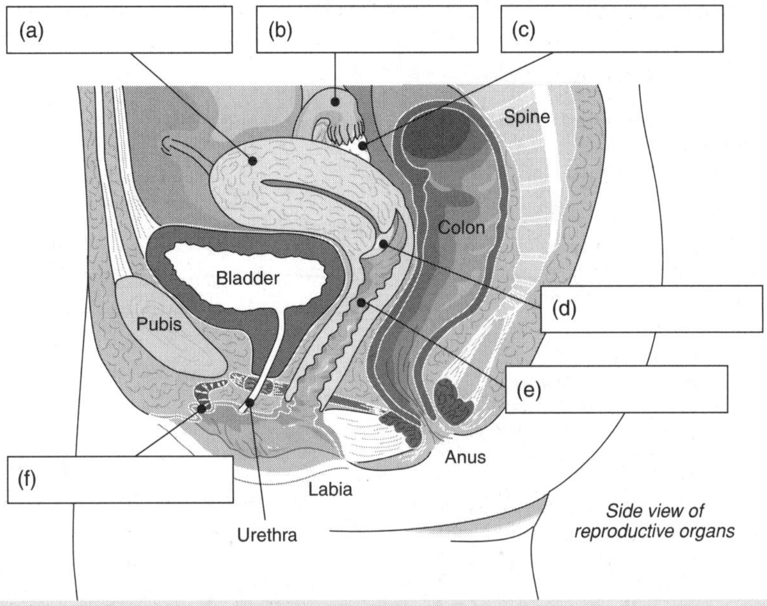

Side view of reproductive organs

Ovulation and Implantation

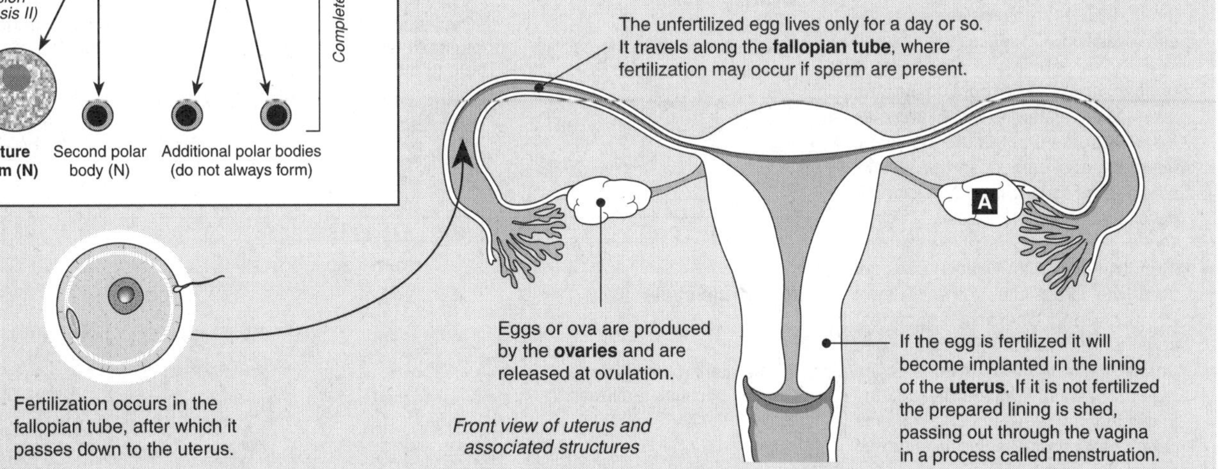

The unfertilized egg lives only for a day or so. It travels along the **fallopian tube**, where fertilization may occur if sperm are present.

Eggs or ova are produced by the **ovaries** and are released at ovulation.

If the egg is fertilized it will become implanted in the lining of the **uterus**. If it is not fertilized the prepared lining is shed, passing out through the vagina in a process called menstruation.

Fertilization occurs in the fallopian tube, after which it passes down to the uterus.

Front view of uterus and associated structures

A

1. The female human reproductive system and associated structures are illustrated above. Using the word list, identify the labeled parts. **Word list**: *ovary, uterus (womb), vagina, fallopian tube (oviduct), cervix, clitoris.*

2. In a few words or a short sentence, state the function of each of the structures labeled (a) - (d) in the above diagram:

   (a) _____

   (b) _____

   (c) _____

   (d) _____

3. (a) Name the organ labeled (**A**) in the diagram: _____

   (b) Name the event associated with this organ that occurs every month: _____

   (c) Name the process by which mature ova are produced: _____

4. (a) Name the stage in meiosis at which the oocyte is released from the ovary: _____

   (b) State when in the reproductive process meiosis II is completed: _____

Activity links: The Menstrual Cycle · RA 2

Reproduction and Development

The Menstrual Cycle

In non-primate mammals the reproductive cycle is characterized by a **breeding season** and an **estrous cycle** (a period of greater sexual receptivity during which ovulation occurs). In contrast, humans and other primates are sexually receptive throughout the year and may mate at any time. Like all placental mammals, their uterine lining thickens in preparation for pregnancy. However, unlike other mammals, primates shed this lining as a discharge through the vagina if fertilization does not occur. This event, called **menstruation**, characterizes the human reproductive or **menstrual cycle**. In human females, the menstrual cycle starts from the first day of bleeding and lasts for about 28 days. It involves a predictable series of changes that occur in response to hormones. The cycle is divided into three phases (see below), defined by the events in each phase.

The Menstrual Cycle

Luteinizing hormone (LH) and follicle stimulating hormone (FSH): These hormones from the anterior pituitary have numerous effects. FSH stimulates the development of the ovarian follicles resulting in the release of estrogen. Estrogen levels peak, stimulating a surge in LH and triggering ovulation.

Hormone levels: Of the follicles that begin developing in response to FSH, usually only one (the Graafian follicle) becomes dominant. In the first half of the cycle, estrogen is secreted by this developing Graafian follicle. Later, the Graafian follicle develops into the corpus luteum (below right) which secretes large amounts of progesterone (and smaller amounts of estrogen).

The corpus luteum: The Graafian follicle continues to grow and then (around day 14) ruptures to release the egg (ovulation). LH causes the ruptured follicle to develop into a corpus luteum (yellow body). The corpus luteum secretes progesterone which promotes full development of the uterine lining, maintains the embryo in the first 12 weeks of pregnancy, and inhibits the development of more follicles.

Menstruation: If fertilization does not occur, the corpus luteum breaks down. Progesterone secretion declines, causing the uterine lining to be shed (menstruation). If fertilization occurs, high progesterone levels maintain the thickened uterine lining. The placenta develops and nourishes the embryo completely by 12 weeks.

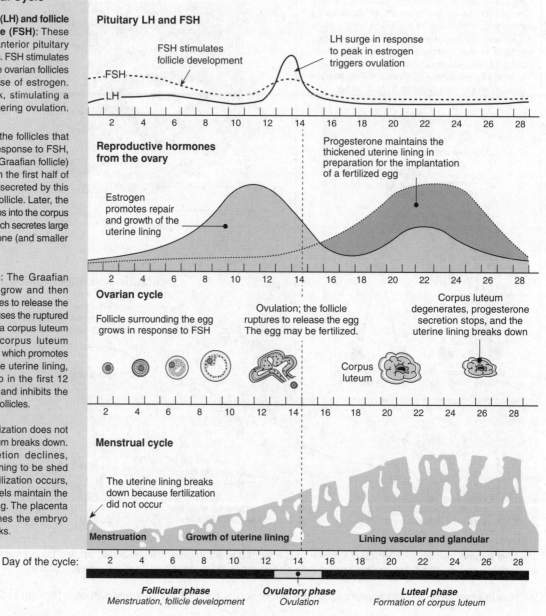

1. Name the hormone responsible for:

   (a) Follicle growth: _____ (b) Ovulation: _____

2. Each month, several ovarian follicles begin development, but only one (the Graafian follicle) develops fully:

   (a) Name the hormone secreted by the developing follicle: _____

   (b) State the role of this hormone during the follicular phase: _____

   (c) Suggest what happens to the follicles that do not continue developing: _____

3. (a) Identify the principal hormone secreted by the corpus luteum: _____

   (b) State the purpose of this hormone: _____

4. State the hormonal trigger for menstruation: _____

A 2

Related activities: Control of the Menstrual Cycle
Web links: The Menstrual Cycle Animation

Control of the Menstrual Cycle

The female menstrual cycle is regulated by the interplay of several reproductive hormones. The main control centers for this regulation are the **hypothalamus** and the **anterior pituitary gland**. The hypothalamus secretes GnRH (gonadotrophin releasing hormone), a hormone that is essential for normal gonad function in males and females. GnRH is transported in blood vessels to the anterior pituitary where it brings about the release of two hormones: follicle stimulating hormone (FSH) and luteinizing hormone (LH). It is these two hormones that induce the cyclical changes in the ovary and uterus. Regulation of blood hormone levels during the menstrual cycle is achieved through **negative feedback** mechanisms. The exception to this is the mid cycle surge in LH (see previous page) which is induced by the rapid increase in estrogen secreted by the developing follicle.

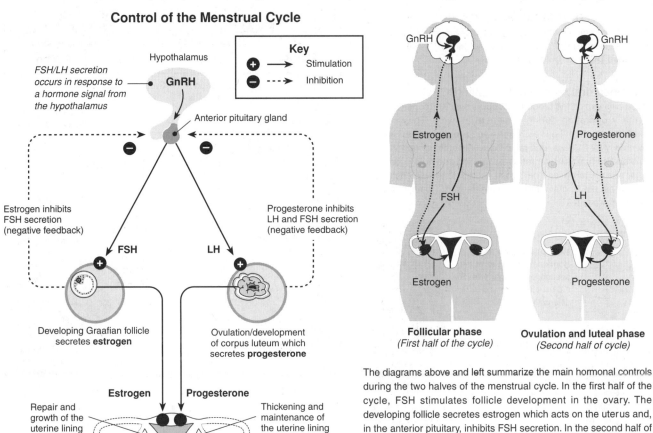

Control of the Menstrual Cycle

Follicular phase
(First half of the cycle)

Ovulation and luteal phase
(Second half of cycle)

The diagrams above and left summarize the main hormonal controls during the two halves of the menstrual cycle. In the first half of the cycle, FSH stimulates follicle development in the ovary. The developing follicle secretes estrogen which acts on the uterus and, in the anterior pituitary, inhibits FSH secretion. In the second half of the cycle, LH induces ovulation and development of the corpus luteum. The corpus luteum secretes progesterone which acts on the uterus and also inhibits further secretion of LH (and also FSH).

1. Using the information above and on the previous page, complete the table below summarizing the role of hormones in the control of the menstrual cycle. To help you, some of the table has been completed:

Hormone	Site of secretion	Main effects and site of action during the menstrual cycle
GnRH		
		Stimulates the growth of ovarian follicles
LH		
		At high level, stimulates LH surge. Promotes growth and repair of the uterine lining.
Progesterone		

2. Briefly explain the role of negative feedback in the control of hormone levels in the menstrual cycle:

_____

_____

3. **FSH** and **LH** (called ICSH or interstitial cell stimulating hormone in males) also play a central role in male reproduction. Refer to the activity *Male Reproductive System* and state how these two hormones are involved **in male reproduction**:

_____

Related activities: The Menstrual Cycle, Male Reproductive System, Sexual Development

A 2

Reproduction and Development

Contraception

Humans have many ways in which to manage their own reproduction. They may choose to prevent or assist fertilization of an egg by a sperm (conception). **Contraception** refers to the use of methods or devices that prevent conception. There are many contraceptive methods available including physical barriers (such as condoms) that prevent egg and sperm ever meeting. The most effective methods (excluding sterilization) involve chemical interference in the normal female cycle so that egg production is inhibited. This is done by way of **oral contraceptives** (below, left) or hormonal implants. If taken properly, oral contraceptives are almost 100% effective at preventing pregnancy. The placement of their action in the normal cycle of reproduction (from gametogenesis to pregnancy) is illustrated below. Other contraceptive methods are included for comparison.

Hormonal Contraception

The most common method by which to prevent conception using hormones is by using an oral contraceptive pill (OCP). These may be **combined OCPs**, or low dose mini pills.

Combined oral contraceptive pills (OCPs)

These pills exploit the feedback controls over hormone secretion normally operating during a menstrual cycle. They contain combinations of synthetic **estrogens** and **progesterone**. They are taken daily for 21 days, and raise the levels of these hormones in the blood so that FSH secretion is inhibited and no ova develop. Sugar pills are taken for 7 days; long enough to allow menstruation to occur but not long enough for ova to develop. Combined OCPs can be of two types:

Monophasic pills (left): Hormones (**H**) are all at one dosage level. Sugar pills (**S**) are usually larger and differently colored.

Triphasic pills (right): The hormone dosage increases in stages (**1,2,3**), mimicking the natural changes in a menstrual cycle.

Mini-pill (progesterone only)

The mini-pill contains 28 days of low dose progesterone; generally too low to prevent ovulation. The pill works by thickening the cervical mucus and preventing endometrial thickening. The mini-pill is less reliable than combined pills and must be taken at a regular time each day. However, it is safer for older women and those who are breastfeeding.

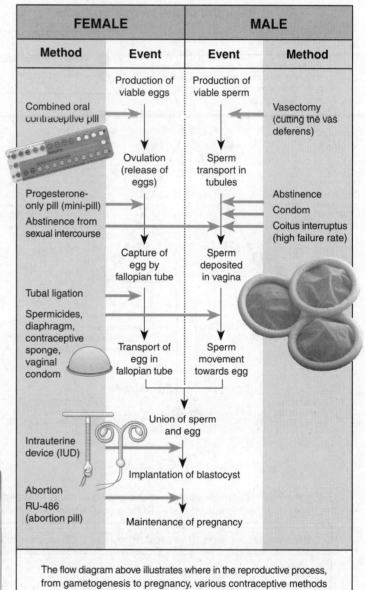

FEMALE		MALE	
Method	**Event**	**Event**	**Method**
	Production of viable eggs	Production of viable sperm	
Combined oral contraceptive pill			Vasectomy (cutting the vas deferens)
	Ovulation (release of eggs)	Sperm transport in tubules	
Progesterone-only pill (mini-pill)			Abstinence
Abstinence from sexual intercourse			Condom
			Coitus interruptus (high failure rate)
	Capture of egg by fallopian tube	Sperm deposited in vagina	
Tubal ligation			
Spermicides, diaphragm, contraceptive sponge, vaginal condom	Transport of egg in fallopian tube	Sperm movement towards egg	
	Union of sperm and egg		
Intrauterine device (IUD)			
	Implantation of blastocyst		
Abortion RU-486 (abortion pill)			
	Maintenance of pregnancy		

The flow diagram above illustrates where in the reproductive process, from gametogenesis to pregnancy, various contraceptive methods operate. Note the early action of hormonal contraceptives.

1. Explain briefly how the **combined oral contraceptive pill** acts as a contraceptive: _____

_____

_____

2. Contrast the mode of action of OCPs with that of the mini-pill, giving reasons for the differences: _____

_____

_____

3. Suggest why oral contraceptives offer such effective control over conception: _____

_____

_____

Treating Female Infertility

Failure to ovulate is one of the most common causes of female infertility. In most cases, the cause is hormonal, although sometimes the ovaries may be damaged or not functioning normally. Female infertility may also arise through damage to the fallopian tubes as a result of infection or scarring. These cases are usually treated with hormones, followed by IVF (see below and the next page). Most treatments for female infertility involve the use of synthetic female hormones, which stimulate ovulation, boost egg production, and induce egg release.

Treating Female Infertility

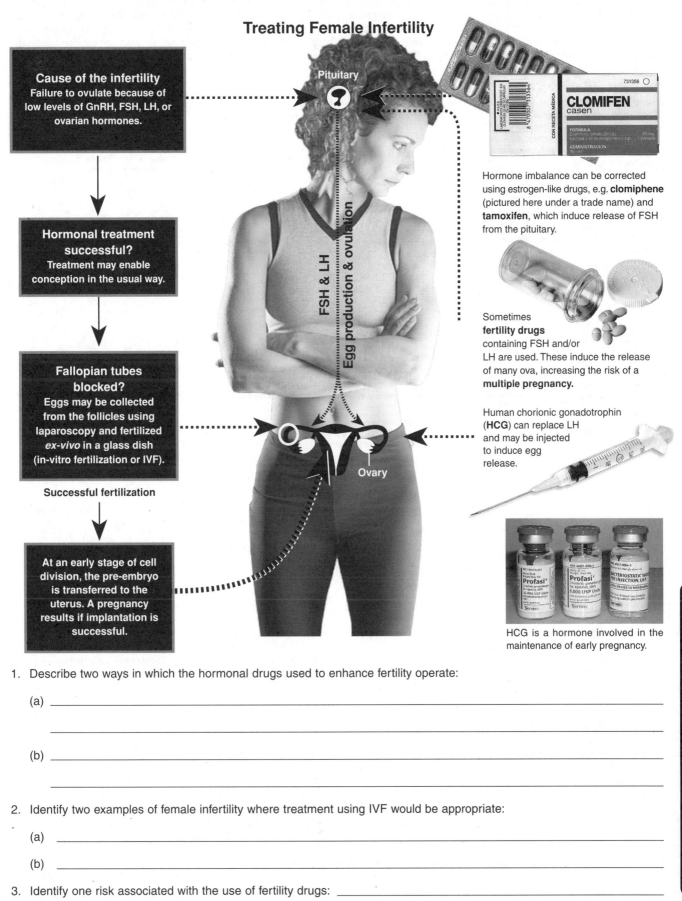

Cause of the infertility
Failure to ovulate because of low levels of GnRH, FSH, LH, or ovarian hormones.

Hormonal treatment successful?
Treatment may enable conception in the usual way.

Fallopian tubes blocked?
Eggs may be collected from the follicles using laparoscopy and fertilized *ex-vivo* in a glass dish (in-vitro fertilization or IVF).

Successful fertilization

At an early stage of cell division, the pre-embryo is transferred to the uterus. A pregnancy results if implantation is successful.

Pituitary

FSH & LH

Egg production & ovulation

Ovary

Hormone imbalance can be corrected using estrogen-like drugs, e.g. **clomiphene** (pictured here under a trade name) and **tamoxifen**, which induce release of FSH from the pituitary.

Sometimes **fertility drugs** containing FSH and/or LH are used. These induce the release of many ova, increasing the risk of a **multiple pregnancy.**

Human chorionic gonadotrophin (**HCG**) can replace LH and may be injected to induce egg release.

HCG is a hormone involved in the maintenance of early pregnancy.

1. Describe two ways in which the hormonal drugs used to enhance fertility operate:

   (a) _____

   _____

   (b) _____

   _____

2. Identify two examples of female infertility where treatment using IVF would be appropriate:

   (a) _____

   (b) _____

3. Identify one risk associated with the use of fertility drugs: _____

Related activities: Human Reproductive Technology

A 2

Reproduction and Development

Human Reproductive Technology

Infertility may result from a disturbance of any of the factors involved in fertilization or embryonic development. Female infertility may be due to a failure to ovulate, requiring stimulation of the ovary, with or without hormone therapy. For couples with one or both partners incapable of providing suitable gametes, it may be possible for them to receive eggs and/or sperm from donors. **Artificial insemination** (AI) may be used to introduce selected sperm from the male partner or from a donor. **In vitro fertilization** (IVF) may be used for patients with irreparable damage to the fallopian tubes. The **gamete intrafallopian**

transfer (GIFT) technique is now widely accepted as a form of treatment for patients with one or more functioning fallopian tubes. **Surrogate mothers** may be used to 'incubate' the fetus in cases where the woman is incapable of sustaining a pregnancy. **Fertility drugs** may be used to treat ovulation failure, as well as to induce the production of many eggs for use in IVF or GIFT. Such drugs stimulate the pituitary gland and may induce the simultaneous release of numerous eggs; an event called *superovulation*. If each egg is allowed to be fertilized, the resulting embryos may then be frozen after 24-72 hours culture.

Causes of Infertility

Infertility is a common problem (as many as one in six couples require help from a specialist). The cause of the infertility may be inherited, due to damage caused by an infectious disease, or psychological.

Causes of male infertility:
- *Penis:* Fails to achieve or maintain erection; abnormal ejaculation.
- *Testes:* Too few sperm produced or sperm are abnormally shaped, have impaired motility, or too short lived.
- *Vas deferens:* Blockage or structural abnormality may impede passage of sperm.

Causes of female infertility:
- *Fallopian tubes:* Blockage may prevent sperm from reaching egg; one or both tubes may be damaged (disease) or absent (congenital).
- *Ovaries:* Eggs may fail to mature or may not be released.
- *Uterus:* Abnormality or disorder may prevent implantation of the egg.
- *Cervix:* Antibodies in cervical mucus may damage or destroy the sperm.

In Vitro Fertilization (IVF)

The woman is given hormone therapy (fertility drugs) causing a number of eggs to mature at the same time (superovulation).

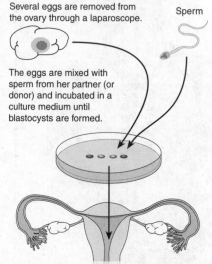

Several eggs are removed from the ovary through a laparoscope.

Sperm

The eggs are mixed with sperm from her partner (or donor) and incubated in a culture medium until blastocysts are formed.

The blastocyst(s) is then implanted in the mother's uterus and the pregnancy is allowed to continue normally.

Gamete Intrafallopian Transfer (GIFT)

A procedure for assisting conception, suitable only for women with healthy fallopian tubes.

Using a needle for aspiration, under laparoscopic or ultrasound guidance, the eggs are removed from the ovary.

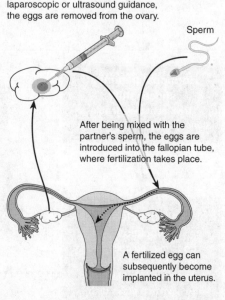

Sperm

After being mixed with the partner's sperm, the eggs are introduced into the fallopian tube, where fertilization takes place.

A fertilized egg can subsequently become implanted in the uterus.

Biological Origins of Gamete Donations

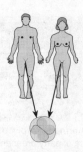

Both partners provide gametes for IVF or GIFT (they donate their own gametes).

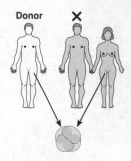

Male partner unable to provide sperm; sperm from male donor.

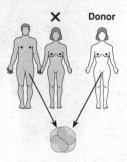

Female partner unable to provide eggs; egg from female donor.

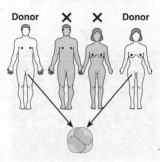

Both partners unable to provide gametes; sperm and egg obtained from donors.

1. Identify three causes of infertility for men: _____

2. Identify three causes of infertility for women: _____

3. Describe the key stages of **IVF**: _____

_____

_____

4. Identify the fundamental way in which **GIFT** differs from IVF: _____

_____

Male Reproductive System

The reproductive role of the male is to produce the sperm and deliver them to the female. When a sperm combines with an egg, it contributes half the genetic material of the offspring and, in humans and other mammals, determines its sex. The reproductive structures in human males (shown below) are in many ways typical of other mammals.

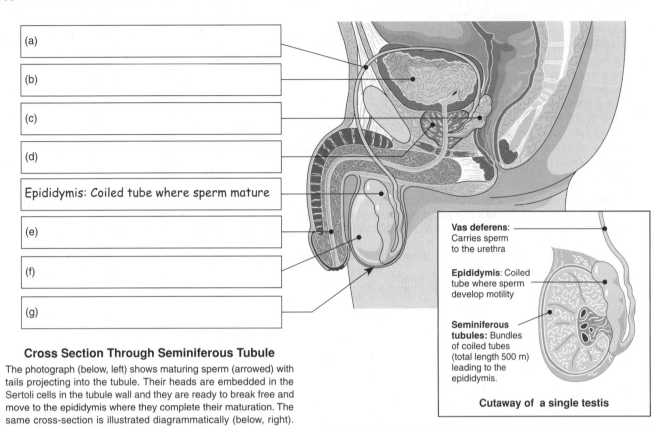

(a)

(b)

(c)

(d)

Epididymis: Coiled tube where sperm mature

(e)

(f)

(g)

Vas deferens: Carries sperm to the urethra

Epididymis: Coiled tube where sperm develop motility

Seminiferous tubules: Bundles of coiled tubes (total length 500 m) leading to the epididymis.

Cutaway of a single testis

Cross Section Through Seminiferous Tubule

The photograph (below, left) shows maturing sperm (arrowed) with tails projecting into the tubule. Their heads are embedded in the Sertoli cells in the tubule wall and they are ready to break free and move to the epididymis where they complete their maturation. The same cross-section is illustrated diagrammatically (below, right).

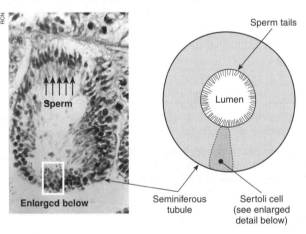

Sperm

Enlarged below

Sperm tails

Lumen

Seminiferous tubule

Sertoli cell (see enlarged detail below)

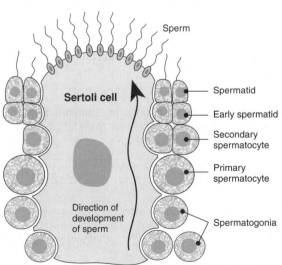

Sperm

Sertoli cell

Spermatid

Early spermatid

Secondary spermatocyte

Primary spermatocyte

Spermatogonia

Direction of development of sperm

Spermatogenesis

Spermatogenesis is the process by which mature spermatozoa (sperm) are produced in the testis. In humans, they are produced at the rate of about 120 million per day. Spermatogenesis is regulated by the hormones **FSH** (from the anterior pituitary) and testosterone (secreted from the testes in response to **ICSH** (LH) from the anterior pituitary). Spermatogonia, in the outer layer of the seminiferous tubules, multiply throughout reproductive life. Some of them divide by meiosis into spermatocytes, which produce spermatids. These are transformed into mature sperm by the process of spermiogenesis in the seminiferous tubules of the testis. Full sperm motility is achieved in the epididymis.

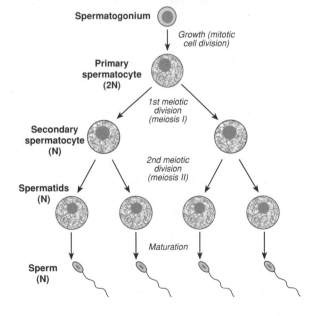

Spermatogonium

Growth (mitotic cell division)

Primary spermatocyte (2N)

1st meiotic division (meiosis I)

Secondary spermatocyte (N)

2nd meiotic division (meiosis II)

Spermatids (N)

Maturation

Sperm (N)

Reproduction and Development

RA 3

Sperm Structure

Mature spermatozoa (sperm) are produced by a process called spermatogenesis in the testes (see description of the process on the previous page). Meiotic division of spermatocytes produces spermatids which then differentiate into mature sperm. Sperm are quite simple in structure because their sole purpose is to swim to the egg and donate their genetic material. They are composed of three regions: headpiece, midpiece, and tail. Sperm do not live long (only about 48 hours), but they swim quickly and there are so many of them (millions per ejaculation) that some are able to reach the egg to fertilize it.

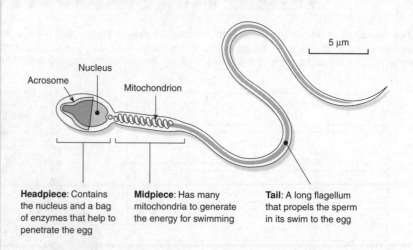

5 µm

Acrosome Nucleus Mitochondrion

Headpiece: Contains the nucleus and a bag of enzymes that help to penetrate the egg

Midpiece: Has many mitochondria to generate the energy for swimming

Tail: A long flagellum that propels the sperm in its swim to the egg

1. The male human reproductive system and associated structures are shown on the previous page. Using the following word list identify the labeled parts (write your answers in the spaces provided on the diagram).
   Word list: *bladder, scrotal sac, sperm duct (vas deferens), seminal vesicle, testis, urethra, prostate gland*

2. In a short sentence, state the function of each of the structures labeled (a)-(g) in the diagram on the previous page:

   (a) _____

   (b) _____

   (c) _____

   (d) _____

   (e) _____

   (f) _____

   (g) _____

3. (a) Name the process by which mature sperm are formed: _____

   (b) Name the hormones regulating this process: _____

   (c) State where most of this process occurs: _____

   (d) State where the process is completed: _____

4. The secretions of the prostate gland (which make up a large proportion of the seminal fluid produced in an ejaculation) are of alkaline pH, while the secretions of the vagina are normally slightly acidic. With this information, explain the role the prostate gland secretions have in maintaining the viability of sperm deposited in the vagina.

   _____

   _____

5. Each ejaculation of a healthy, fertile male contains 100-400 million sperm. Suggest why so many sperm are needed:

   _____

   _____

6. Recently, concern has been expressed about the level of synthetic estrogen-like chemicals in the environment. Explain the reason for this concern and discuss evidence in support of the claim that these chemicals lower male fertility:

   _____

   _____

   _____

   _____

Fertilization and Early Growth

When an egg cell is released from the ovary it is arrested in metaphase of meiosis II and is termed a secondary oocyte. **Fertilization** occurs when a sperm penetrates an egg cell at this stage and the sperm and egg nuclei unite to form the zygote. Fertilization is always regarded as time 0 in a period of gestation (pregnancy) and has five distinct stages (below). After fertilization, the zygote begins its **development** i.e. its growth and differentiation into a multicellular organism (see next page).

Fertilization (Time 0)

The stages in fertilization are represented below in a numbered sequence (1-5)

1. Capacitation
The surface of the sperm cell undergoes changes that are essential to enabling the acrosome reaction and sperm entry.

2. The Acrosome Reaction
Enzymes from the acrosome (an enzyme-filled bag at the tip of the sperm) are released and digest a pathway through the follicle cells (not shown) and the jelly-like zona pellucida surrounding the egg cell (secondary oocyte).

3. Fusion of Sperm Head
The plasma membranes of the sperm and egg fuse, and the nucleus of the sperm enters the egg cytoplasm. Fusion causes a sudden membrane depolarization that acts as a "fast block" to further sperm entry. The fusion of the two plasma membranes also triggers the completion of meiosis II in the egg cell and induces the cortical reaction (below).

4. The Cortical Reaction
The fusion of the two plasma membranes induces a permanent change in the egg surface that prevents further sperm entry. Cortical granules in the egg cytoplasm release their contents into the space between the plasma membrane and the vitelline layer. Substances released from the granules raise and harden the vitelline layer to form a slow (permanent) block to further sperm entry.

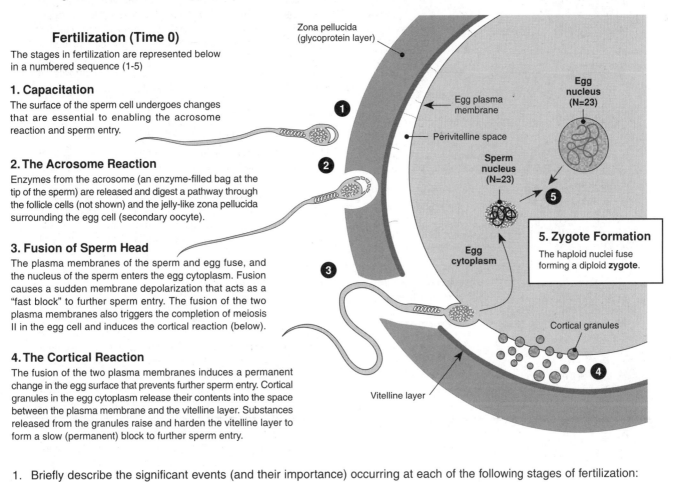

Zona pellucida (glycoprotein layer)

Egg plasma membrane

Perivitelline space

Egg nucleus (N=23)

Sperm nucleus (N=23)

Egg cytoplasm

5. Zygote Formation
The haploid nuclei fuse forming a diploid **zygote**.

Cortical granules

Vitelline layer

1. Briefly describe the significant events (and their importance) occurring at each of the following stages of fertilization:

(a) Capacitation: _____

_____

(b) The acrosome reaction: _____

_____

(c) Fusion of egg and sperm plasma membranes: _____

_____

(d) The cortical reaction: _____

_____

(e) Fusion of egg and sperm nuclei: _____

_____

2. Explain the significance of the blocks that prevent entry of more than one sperm into the egg (polyspermy):

_____

_____

3. (a) Explain why the egg cell, when released from the ovary, is termed a secondary oocyte: _____

_____

(b) State at which stage, its meiotic division is completed: _____

Related activities: Female Reproductive System
Web links: Fertilization

A 2

Reproduction and Development

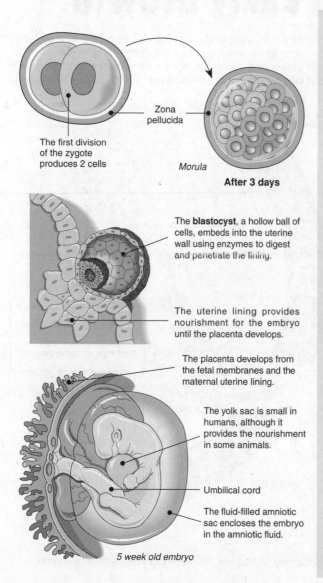

Zona pellucida

The first division of the zygote produces 2 cells

Morula

After 3 days

The **blastocyst**, a hollow ball of cells, embeds into the uterine wall using enzymes to digest and penetrate the lining.

The uterine lining provides nourishment for the embryo until the placenta develops.

The placenta develops from the fetal membranes and the maternal uterine lining.

The yolk sac is small in humans, although it provides the nourishment in some animals.

Umbilical cord

The fluid-filled amniotic sac encloses the embryo in the amniotic fluid.

5 week old embryo

Early Growth and Development

Cleavage and Development of the Morula

Immediately after fertilization, rapid cell division takes place. These early cell divisions are called **cleavage** and they increase the number of cells, but not the size of the zygote. The first cleavage is completed after 36 hours, and each succeeding division takes less time. After 3 days, successive cleavages have produced a solid mass of cells called the **morula**, (left) which is still about the same size as the original zygote.

Implantation of the Blastocyst (after 6-8 days)

After several days in the uterus, the morula develops into the blastocyst. It makes contact with the uterine lining and pushes deeply into it, ensuring a close maternal-fetal contact. Blood vessels provide early nourishment as they are opened up by enzymes secreted by the blastocyst. The embryo produces **HCG** (human chorionic gonadotropin), which prevents degeneration of the corpus luteum and signals that the woman is pregnant.

Embryo at 5-8 Weeks

Five weeks after fertilization, the embryo is only 4-5 mm long, but already the central nervous system has developed and the heart is beating. The embryonic membranes have formed; the amnion encloses the embryo in a fluid-filled space, and the allanto-chorion forms the fetal portion of the placenta. From two months the embryo is called a fetus. It is still small (30-40 mm long), but the limbs are well formed and the bones are beginning to harden. The face has a flat, rather featureless appearance with the eyes far apart. Fetal movements have begun and brain development proceeds rapidly. The placenta is well developed, although not fully functional until 12 weeks. The umbilical cord, containing the fetal umbilical arteries and vein, connects fetus and mother.

4. State what contribution the sperm and egg cell make to each of the following:

(a) The nucleus of the zygote: Sperm contribution: _____   Egg contribution: _____

(b) The cytoplasm of the zygote: Sperm contribution: _____   Egg contribution: _____

5. Explain what is meant by cleavage and comment on its significance to the early development of the embryo:

_____

_____

6. (a) Explain the importance of implantation to the early nourishment of the embryo: _____

_____

(b) Identify the fetal tissues that contribute to the formation of the placenta: _____

(c) Suggest a purpose of the amniotic sac and comment on its importance to the developing embryo: _____

_____

(d) Suggest why the heart is one of the very first structures to develop in the embryo: _____

_____

7. State why the fetus is particularly prone to damage from drugs towards the end of the first trimester (2-3 months):

_____

_____

The Placenta

As soon as an embryo embeds in the uterine wall it begins to obtain nutrients from its mother and increase in size. At two months, when the major structures of the adult are established, it is called a fetus. It is entirely dependent on its mother for nutrients, oxygen, and elimination of wastes. The placenta is the specialized organ that performs this role, enabling exchange between fetal and maternal tissues, and allowing a prolonged period of fetal growth and development within the protection of the uterus. The placenta also has an endocrine role, producing hormones that enable the pregnancy to be maintained.

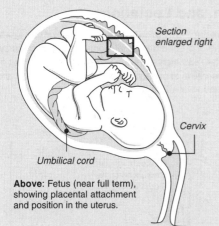

Section enlarged right

Cervix

Umbilical cord

Above: Fetus (near full term), showing placental attachment and position in the uterus.

Below: Photograph shows a 14 week old fetus. Limbs are fully formed, many bones are beginning to ossify, and joints begin to form. Facial features are becoming more fully formed.

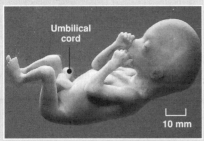

Umbilical cord

10 mm

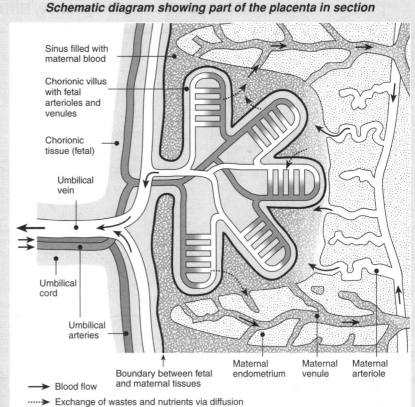

Schematic diagram showing part of the placenta in section

Sinus filled with maternal blood

Chorionic villus with fetal arterioles and venules

Chorionic tissue (fetal)

Umbilical vein

Umbilical cord

Umbilical arteries

Boundary between fetal and maternal tissues

Maternal endometrium

Maternal venule

Maternal arteriole

→ Blood flow

·····► Exchange of wastes and nutrients via diffusion

The placenta is a disc-like organ, about the size of a dinner plate and weighing about 1 kg. It develops when fingerlike projections of the fetal chorion (the chorionic villi) grow into the endometrium of the uterus. The villi contain the numerous capillaries connecting the fetal arteries and vein. They continue invading the maternal tissue until they are bathed in the maternal blood sinuses. The maternal and fetal blood vessels are in such close proximity that oxygen and nutrients can diffuse from the maternal blood into the capillaries of the villi. From the villi, the nutrients circulate in the umbilical vein, returning to the fetal heart. Carbon dioxide and other wastes leave the fetus through the umbilical arteries, pass into the capillaries of the villi, and diffuse into the maternal blood. Note that fetal blood and maternal blood do not mix: the exchanges occur via diffusion through thin walled capillaries.

1. In simple terms, describe the basic structure of the human placenta: _____

_____

_____

_____

2. The umbilical cord contains the fetal arteries and vein. Describe the status of the blood in each type of fetal vessel:

   (a) Fetal arteries: Oxygenated and containing nutrients / Deoxygenated and containing nitrogenous wastes (delete one)

   (b) Fetal vein: Oxygenated and containing nutrients / Deoxygenated and containing nitrogenous wastes (delete one)

3. Teratogens are substances that may cause malformations in embryonic development (e.g. nicotine, alcohol):

   (a) Give a general explanation why substances ingested by the mother have the potential to be harmful to the fetus:

   _____

   (b) Explain why cigarette smoking is so harmful to fetal development: _____

   _____

Related activities: Fertilization and Early Growth

A 2

Reproduction and Development

The Hormones of Pregnancy

Human reproductive physiology occurs in a cycle (the menstrual cycle) which follows a set pattern and is regulated by the interplay of several hormones. Control of hormone release is brought about through feedback mechanisms: the levels of the female reproductive hormones, estrogen and progesterone, regulate the secretion of the pituitary hormones that control the ovarian cycle (see earlier pages). Pregnancy interrupts this cycle and maintains the corpus luteum and the placenta as endocrine organs with the specific role of maintaining the developing fetus for the period of its development. During the last month of pregnancy the peptide hormone oxytocin induces the uterine contraction that will expel the baby from the uterus.

Hormonal Changes During Pregnancy, Birth, and Lactation

During the first 12-16 weeks pregnancy, the corpus luteum secretes enough progesterone to maintain the uterine lining and sustain the developing embryo. After this, the placenta takes over as the primary endocrine organ of pregnancy. **Progesterone** and **estrogen** from the placenta maintain the uterine lining, inhibit the development of further ova (eggs), and prepare the breast tissue for **lactation** (milk production). At the end of pregnancy, the placenta loses competency, progesterone levels fall, and high estrogen levels trigger the onset of labor. After birth, the secretion of prolactin increases. Prolactin maintains lactation during the period of infant nursing.

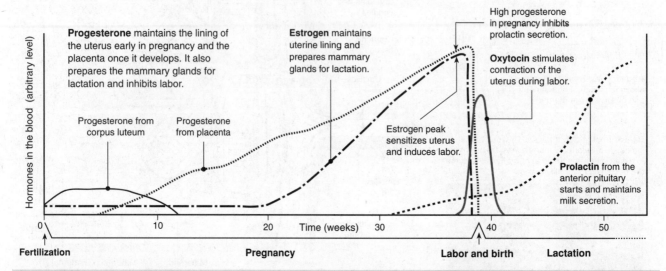

1. (a) Explain why the corpus luteum is the main source of progesterone in early pregnancy:

    _____

    (b) Name the hormones responsible for maintaining pregnancy: _____

2. (a) Name two hormones involved in labor (onset of the birth process): _____

    (b) Describe two physiological factors in initiating labor: _____

    _____

3. Explain why prolactin secretion increases markedly after birth: _____

    _____

Hormones in Pregnancy

HCG (Human chorionic gonadotropin)
- Secreted by the developing embryo
- Maintains corpus luteum

Progesterone
- Maintains endometrium
- Inhibits uterine contraction

Estrogens
- Maintain endometrium
- Prepare mammary glands for lactation
- Very high levels increase the sensitivity of the uterus to oxytocin

Human placental lactogen (HPL)
- Stimulates breast growth & development

Relaxin
- Produced by the placenta towards the end of the pregnancy
- Relaxes pubic symphysis at birth
- Helps dilate cervix at birth

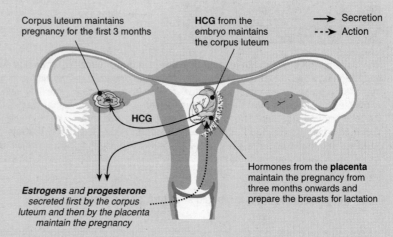

Note that increasingly through pregnancy the placenta also secretes HCS (human chorionic somatotropin) which has general effects on maternal metabolism to the benefit of fetal growth.

Related activities: The Menstrual Cycle, Control of the Menstrual Cycle, Birth and Lactation

Birth and Lactation

A human pregnancy (the period of **gestation**) lasts, on average, about 38 weeks after fertilization. It ends in labor, the birth of the baby, and expulsion of the placenta. During pregnancy, progesterone maintains the placenta and inhibits contraction of the uterus. At the end of a pregnancy, increasing estrogen levels overcome the influence of progesterone and labor begins. Prostaglandins, factors released from the placenta, and the physiological state of the baby itself are also involved in

triggering the actual timing of labor onset. Labor itself comprises three stages (below), and ends with the delivery of the placenta. After birth, the mother provides nutrition for the infant through **lactation**: the production and release of milk from mammary glands. Breast milk provides infants with a complete, easily digested food for the first 4-6 months of life. All breast milk contains maternal antibodies, which give the infant protection against infection while its own immune system develops.

Birth and the Stages of Labor

Stage 1: Dilation

Duration: 2-20 hours

The time between the onset of labor and complete opening (dilation) of the cervix. The amniotic sac may rupture at this stage, releasing its fluid. The hormone **oxytocin** stimulates the uterine contractions necessary to dilate the cervix and expel the baby. It is these uterine contractions that give the pain of labor, most of which is associated with this first stage.

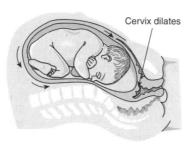

Cervix dilates

Stage 2: Expulsion

Duration: 2-100 minutes

The time from full dilation of the cervix to delivery. Strong, rhythmic contractions of the uterus pass in waves (arrows), and push the baby to the end of the vagina, where the head appears.

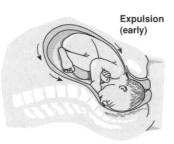

Expulsion (early)

As labor progresses, the time between each contraction shortens. Once the head is delivered, the rest of the body usually follows very rapidly. Delivery completes stage 2.

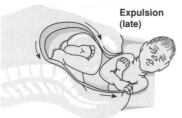

Expulsion (late)

Stage 3: Delivery of placenta

Time: 5-45 minutes after delivery

The third or **placental stage**, refers to the expulsion of the placenta from the uterus. After the placenta is delivered, the placental blood vessels constrict to stop bleeding.

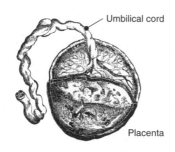

Umbilical cord

Placenta

Delivery of the Baby: The End of Stage 2

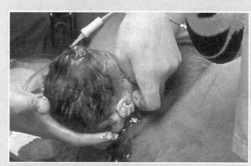

Delivery of the head. This baby is face forward. The more usual position for delivery is face to the back of the mother.

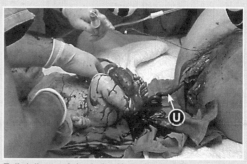

Full delivery of the baby. Note the umbilical cord (U), which supplies oxygen until the baby's breathing begins.

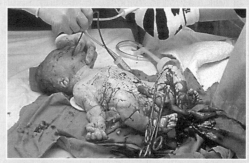

Post-birth check of the baby. The baby is still attached to the placenta and the airways are being cleared of mucus.

1. Name the three stages of birth, and briefly state the main events occurring in each stage:

   (a) Stage 1: _____

   (b) Stage 2: _____

   (c) Stage 3: _____

2. (a) Name the hormone responsible for triggering the onset of labor: _____

   (b) Describe two other factors that might influence the timing of labor onset: _____

   _____

   _____

Related activities: The Hormones of Pregnancy

A 2

Reproduction and Development

Lactation and its Control

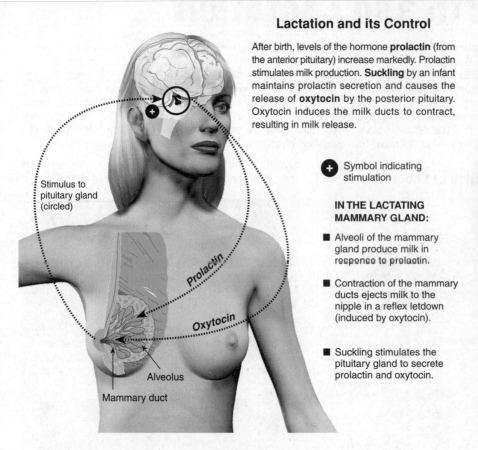

Stimulus to pituitary gland (circled)

Prolactin

Oxytocin

Alveolus

Mammary duct

After birth, levels of the hormone **prolactin** (from the anterior pituitary) increase markedly. Prolactin stimulates milk production. **Suckling** by an infant maintains prolactin secretion and causes the release of **oxytocin** by the posterior pituitary. Oxytocin induces the milk ducts to contract, resulting in milk release.

⊕ Symbol indicating stimulation

IN THE LACTATING MAMMARY GLAND:

■ Alveoli of the mammary gland produce milk in response to prolactin.

■ Contraction of the mammary ducts ejects milk to the nipple in a reflex letdown (induced by oxytocin).

■ Suckling stimulates the pituitary gland to secrete prolactin and oxytocin.

It is essential to establish breast feeding soon after birth, as this is when infants exhibit the strong reflexes that enable them to learn to suckle effectively. The first formed milk, colostrum, has very little sugar, virtually no fat, and is rich in maternal antibodies. Breast milk that is produced later has a higher fat content, and its composition varies as the nutritional needs of the infant change during growth.

3. Explain why the umbilical cord continues to supply blood to the baby for a short time after delivery: _____

_____

4. For each of the following processes, state the primary controlling hormone and its site of production:

(a) Uterine contraction during labor: Hormone: _____   Site of production: _____

(b) Production of milk: Hormone: _____   Site of production: _____

(c) Milk ejection in response to suckling: Hormone: _____   Site of production: _____

5. State which hormone inhibits prolactin secretion during pregnancy: _____

6. Describe two benefits of breast feeding to the health of the infant:

(a) _____

(b) _____

7. (a) Describe the nutritional differences between the first formed milk (colostrum) and the milk that is produced later:

_____

_____

(b) Suggest a reason for these differences: _____

_____

8. Explain why the nutritional composition of breast milk might change during a six-month period of breast feeding:

_____

9. Infants exhibit marked growth spurts at six weeks and three months of age. At these times, their caloric (energy intake) requirements also increase sharply. With reference to what you know about the control of lactation, suggest how a breast-feeding mother could continue to provide for the increased energy requirements of her infant:

_____

_____

Sexual Development

Like many animals, humans differentiate into the male or female sex by the action of a combination of different hormones. The hormones testosterone (in males), and estrogen and progesterone (in females), are responsible for puberty (the onset of sexual maturity), the maintenance of gender differences, and the production of gametes. In females, estrogen and progesterone also regulate the menstrual cycle, and ensure the maintenance of pregnancy and nourishment of young.

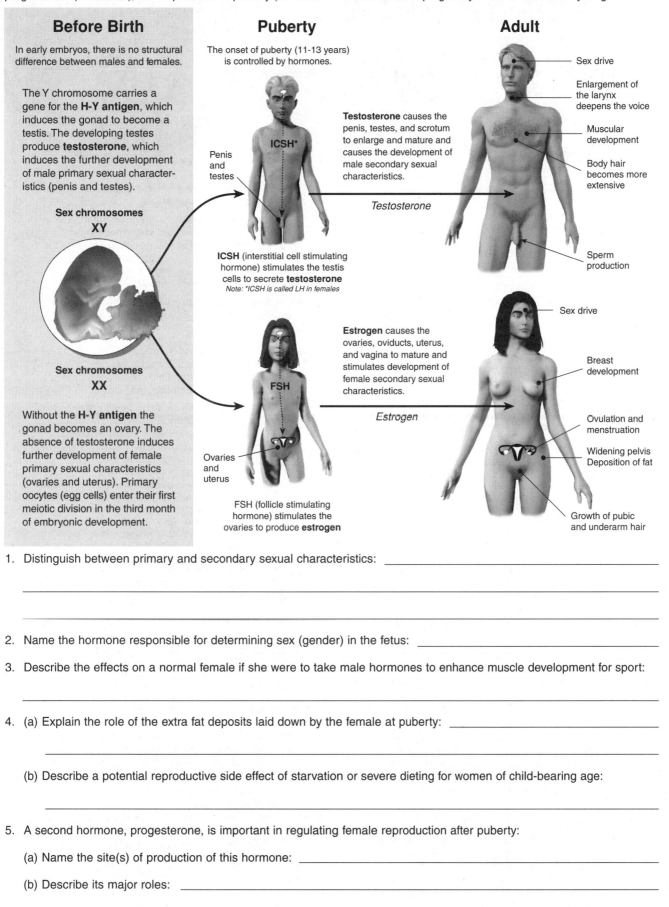

Before Birth

In early embryos, there is no structural difference between males and females.

The Y chromosome carries a gene for the **H-Y antigen**, which induces the gonad to become a testis. The developing testes produce **testosterone**, which induces the further development of male primary sexual characteristics (penis and testes).

**Sex chromosomes
XY**

**Sex chromosomes
XX**

Without the **H-Y antigen** the gonad becomes an ovary. The absence of testosterone induces further development of female primary sexual characteristics (ovaries and uterus). Primary oocytes (egg cells) enter their first meiotic division in the third month of embryonic development.

Puberty

The onset of puberty (11-13 years) is controlled by hormones.

ICSH*

Penis and testes

ICSH (interstitial cell stimulating hormone) stimulates the testis cells to secrete testosterone
Note: *ICSH is called LH in females

Testosterone causes the penis, testes, and scrotum to enlarge and mature and causes the development of male secondary sexual characteristics.

Testosterone

FSH

Ovaries and uterus

FSH (follicle stimulating hormone) stimulates the ovaries to produce estrogen

Estrogen causes the ovaries, oviducts, uterus, and vagina to mature and stimulates development of female secondary sexual characteristics.

Estrogen

Adult

Sex drive

Enlargement of the larynx deepens the voice

Muscular development

Body hair becomes more extensive

Sperm production

Sex drive

Breast development

Ovulation and menstruation

Widening pelvis Deposition of fat

Growth of pubic and underarm hair

1. Distinguish between primary and secondary sexual characteristics: _____

_____

_____

2. Name the hormone responsible for determining sex (gender) in the fetus: _____

3. Describe the effects on a normal female if she were to take male hormones to enhance muscle development for sport:

_____

4. (a) Explain the role of the extra fat deposits laid down by the female at puberty: _____

_____

   (b) Describe a potential reproductive side effect of starvation or severe dieting for women of child-bearing age:

_____

5. A second hormone, progesterone, is important in regulating female reproduction after puberty:

   (a) Name the site(s) of production of this hormone: _____

   (b) Describe its major roles: _____

_____

Related activities: Control of the Menstrual Cycle,
The Hormones of Pregnancy

RA 1

Reproduction and Development

Homeostasis and Excretion

IB SL

Complete:
1-5, 7, 11, 14-15
Extension: 6, 8

IB HL

Complete:
1-5, 7, 11, 14-15,
22, 30, 32-34
Extension: 6, 8

IB Options

Not applicable to
options

AP Biology

Complete:
1-37
*Some numbers
extension as
appropriate*

Learning Objectives

☐ 1. Compile your own glossary from the **KEY WORDS** displayed in **bold type** in the learning objectives below.

Principles of Homeostasis *(pages 250-252, & the TRC: Living in Zero Gravity, Adaptations for Diving)*

☐ 2. Understand the role of **homeostasis** in providing independence from the fluctuating external environment. Identify factors that require regulation in order for an organism to maintain a steady state.

☐ 3. Explain, using examples, the principle of **negative feedback**, identifying how it stabilizes systems against excessive change. Explain the role of **receptors**, **effectors**, and negative feedback in homeostasis.

☐ 4. Appreciate the interdependence and general roles of the two regulatory systems (hormonal and nervous) with which mammals achieve homeostasis.

Nervous regulation *(page 253)*

☐ 5. Outline the general structure of the **nervous system**, relating the structure to the way in which animals receive **stimuli** and generate a **response**.

☐ 6. Appreciate the importance of negative feedback in nervous systems. Contrast the speed of nervous and endocrine responses.

Hormonal regulation *(pages 254-260)*

☐ 7. Understand what is meant by the terms: **endocrine gland**, **hormone**, and **target tissue**. Describe the general organization of the **endocrine system** and appreciate its role in the maintenance of homeostasis.

☐ 8. Explain how hormones act and why they have wide-ranging physiological effects. Explain the role of feedback mechanisms in regulating hormone levels.

☐ 9. Describe the role of the **hypothalamus** and **pituitary gland** in homeostasis. Distinguish between the anterior and posterior pituitary and identify the position and role of the portal vein and **neurosecretory cells**.

☐ 10. Describe the types of **cell signaling** and identify the involvement of signaling molecules in a **signal transduction** pathway. Identify an example of each of the following: **steroid hormone**, **peptide hormone**, and **tyrosine derivative**. Distinguish between the mode of action of steroid and peptide hormones.

Case Studies in Homeostasis

Control of body temperature *(pages 265-269)*

☐ 11. Explain how body temperature is regulated in a mammal. Include reference to the role of:
(a) **Hypothalamus** (heat gain and heat loss centres).
(b) **Autonomic nervous system** and **involuntary activity** such as shivering.
(c) **Thermoreceptors** in the skin (hot/cold receptors).

(d) **Voluntary activity** such as changes in behavior to seek shade or take exercise.

☐ 12. Contrast the mechanisms for **thermoregulation** in an ectotherm (e.g. a reptile) and in an endothermic homeotherm (e.g. a placental mammal). Describe the mechanisms involved in heat production, conservation, and loss, and identify the degree of tolerance to fluctuations in body temperature.

☐ 13. Describe a **countercurrent heat exchange** system and explain its role in regulating heat balance in a named aquatic or terrestrial vertebrate.

Control of blood glucose *(page 263)*

☐ 14. Understand the factors that lead to variation in blood glucose levels. Understand the normal range over which blood glucose levels fluctuate.

☐ 15. Describe the general structure of the pancreas and outline its role as an **endocrine organ**. Explain how the regulation of **blood glucose** level is achieved in humans, including reference to the role of the following:
(a) Negative feedback mechanisms.
(b) The hormones **insulin** and **glucagon**.
(c) The role of the liver in glucose-glycogen conversions.
(d) The difference between type 1 and type 2 diabetes

The effects of exercise *(page 264)*

☐ 16. Describe how homeostasis is maintained during **exercise** and the response of the body to **training**.

Control of thyroxine secretion *(pages 257-258)*

☐ 17. Explain the control of thyroxine secretion by negative feedback. Include reference to the secretion of **TRH** (thyrotropin-releasing hormone), transport to the **anterior pituitary** in the portal vein, secretion of **TSH** (thyroid stimulating hormone), and secretion of thyroxine. Appreciate the general metabolic effects of thyroid hormones. Describe the influence of thyroxine level, TSH level, and body temperature on the hypothalamus and the regulation of TRH secretion.

The homeostatic role of the liver *(pages 261-262)*

☐ 18. Describe the role of the liver in regulating nutrient levels in the blood and in nutrient storage, including:
(a) **Carbohydrate metabolism**: production of glucose from amino acids and storage of glucose.
(b) Protein metabolism, including **deamination**, **transamination**, and the formation of **plasma proteins** and **urea**.
(c) **Fat metabolism**, including the use of fats in respiration, the synthesis of triglycerides and **cholesterol**, and the transport of lipids.
(d) Storage of iron, retinol, and calciferol.
(e) Breakdown of red blood cells and hemoglobin.

☐ 19. Outline the circulation of the blood through the liver tissue. Include the flow through the **hepatic artery**, **hepatic portal vein**, **sinusoids**, and **hepatic vein**.

☐ 20. Outline the general structure and histology of the liver. Identify the following: **liver lobule**, hepatocytes, portal triad, **Kupffer cells**, **sinusoids**, and central vein.

☐ 21. Describe the process of bile secretion, including reference to the composition of bile, the roles of the bile canaliculi, the gall bladder, and the bile duct.

Excretion & Osmoregulation (pages 270-276 & the TRC: Vertebrate Excretion, Excretion in Plants)

☐ 22. Define the terms **excretion** and **osmoregulation**. Appreciate why organisms must regulate water balance and dispose of metabolic waste products.

☐ 23. Identify the major **nitrogenous waste products** excreted by animals (e.g. mammals, birds, and fish) and identify their origin. Appreciate how the excretory product is related to life history and environment.

☐ 24. Appreciate why plants do not face the same excretion problems as animals. Know that oxygen is excreted by plants when production exceeds demand.

☐ 25. Describe diversity in the principal organs of excretion and osmoregulation found in animals. Include reference to the basic structure and role of any of:
(a) **Protonephridia** (flatworms) or **nephridia** (annelids).
(b) **Malpighian tubules** (insects).
(c) **Gills** (fish).
(d) **Kidneys** (all vertebrates).

☐ 26. Identify the non-nitrogenous excretory products in mammals. Name the organs involved in their disposal.

☐ 27. Describe the different homeostatic problems associated with living in salt and fresh water. Describe, with examples, the mechanisms by which animals in fresh and salt water regulate their water and ion balance.

☐ 28. Describe the control of water budget in a desert rodent with reference to structure, physiology and behavior.

☐ 29. Compare the water budget of a desert rodent and a mammal that is not desert adapted, such as a human. Discuss reasons for the differences.

☐ 30. On a diagram, identify the main structures of the mammalian urinary system: **kidneys**, **ureters**, **renal blood vessels**, bladder, urethra (cross ref. with #25(d)).

☐ 31. Describe the gross structure of the mammalian kidney to include the **cortex**, **medulla**, and **renal pelvis**.

The Physiology of Excretion (pages 277-280)

☐ 32. Using a labeled diagram, describe the structure and arrangement of a nephron and its associated blood vessels. Include reference to the structure of the **glomerulus**, and the location of the **convoluted tubules** and **collecting duct**.

☐ 33. Explain concisely how the kidney nephron produces urine. Include reference to:
(a) **Ultrafiltration** in the **glomerulus**, with reference to the role of blood pressure and the ultrastructure of the glomerulus and renal capsule.
(b) The **selective reabsorption** of water and solutes (e.g. glucose) in the **proximal convoluted tubule**.
(c) The roles of the **loop of Henlé**, **medulla**, **collecting duct**, and ADH (anti-diuretic hormone) in the formation of urine and maintenance of water balance. Identify the role of the ionic gradient in the kidney in producing a concentrated urine.

☐ 34. Compare the composition of blood in the renal artery and renal vein, and compare the composition of glomerular filtrate and urine. Account for the differences.

☐ 35. Explain the control of **ADH** secretion. Include the role of hypothalamic **osmoreceptors**, synthesis of ADH by **neurosecretion** and its release from the **posterior pituitary**, the action of ADH on the kidney, and the role of **negative feedback** in regulating ADH output.

☐ 36. Recognize the role of **aldosterone** in promoting sodium reabsorption in the kidney.

☐ 37. Outline the principles involved in **kidney dialysis**. Outline the structure and action of kidney dialysis machines. Appreciate the role of kidney dialysis in the maintenance of homeostasis in cases of kidney failure.

Textbooks

See the 'Textbook Reference Grid' on pages 8-9 for textbook page references relating to material in this topic.

Supplementary Texts

See pages 5-6 for additional details of this text:

■ Clegg, C.J., 1998. **Mammals: Structure and Function** (John Murray), pp. 42-57, 70-71.

■ Helms, D.R. *et al.*, 1998. **Biology in the Laboratory** (W.H. Freeman), #36.

■ Morton, D. & J.W. Perry, 1998. **Photo Atlas for Anatomy and Physiology** (W.H. Freeman).

Periodicals

See page 6 for details of publishers of periodicals:

STUDENT'S REFERENCE

■ **Diabetes** Biol. Sci. Rev., 15(2), Nov. 2002, pp. 30-35. *The homeostatic imbalance that results in diabetes. The role of the pancreas in the hormonal regulation of blood glucose is discussed.*

■ **Glucose Center Stage** Biol. Sci. Rev., 19(2), Nov. 2006, pp. 14-17. *The homeostatic control of blood glucose.*

■ **Homeostasis** Biol. Sci. Rev., 12(5) May 2000, pp. 2-5. *Homeostasis: what it is, the role of negative feedback and the ANS, and the adaptations of organisms for homeostasis in extreme environments (excellent).*

■ **Hormonal Manipulation by Athletes** Biol. Sci. Rev., 15(2) Nov. 2002, pp. 2-5. *The misuse of steroid hormones by athletes: the actions of the hormones (their anabolic effects) and how they are involved in the body's response to exercise.*

■ **Temperature Regulation** Biol. Sci. Rev., 17(2) Nov. 2004, pp. 2-7. *An account of thermoregulation in animals which includes a discussion of how animals cope with extremes of temperature.*

■ **Metabolic Powerhouse** New Scientist, 11 Nov. 2000 (Inside Science). *The myriad roles of the liver in metabolic processes, including discussion of amino acid and glucose metabolism.*

■ **Urea: A Product of Excess Dietary Protein** Biol. Sci. Rev., 17(4) April 2005, pp. 6-8. *An account of how and why urea is formed; nitrogen balance, and urea and the nitrogen cycle.*

■ **The Liver in Health and Disease** Biol. Sci. Rev., 14(2) Nov. 2001, pp. 14-20. *The various roles of the liver, a major homeostatic organ.*

■ **The Kidney** Biol. Sci. Rev., 16(2) Nov. 2003, pp. 2-6. *The structure of the kidneys, and their essential role in regulating extracellular fluid volume, blood pressure, acid-base balance, and metabolic waste products such as urea.* .

■ **Thyroxine** Biol. Sci. Rev., 12(2) Nov. 1999, pp. 19-21. *A good account of the structure of the thyroid, the physiological roles of its hormones, and their regulation through negative feedback.*

■ **Growth Hormone** Biol. Sci. Rev., 12 (4) March 2000, pp. 26-28. *The consequences of growth hormone deficiencies in humans.*

TEACHER'S REFERENCE

■ **Are Your Cells Pregnant?** The Am. Biology Teacher, 63(7), Sept. 2001, pp. 514-517. *An experiment to investigate the principles of hormone release from endocrine cells.*

■ **A Simple Temperature Gradient Apparatus to Determine Thermal Preference in Daphnia** The Am. Biology Teacher, 64(9), Nov. 2002, pp. 679-681. *In this simple experiment, students use a thermal gradient to investigate thermoregulatory behavior and thermal preference in an ectotherm.*

See pages 10-11 for details of how to access **Bio Links** from our web site: **www.thebiozone.com** From Bio Links, access sites under the topics:

ANIMAL BIOLOGY: • Anatomy and physiology • Comparative vertebrate anatomy lecture notes • Human physiology lecture notes > **Excretion**: • Comparative physiology of vertebrate kidneys • Excretory system • The kidney • Urinary system > **Homeostasis**: • Ask the experts: What is homeostasis? • Homeostasis • Homeostasis: general principles • Physiological homeostasis

Presentation MEDIA to support this topic:

HEALTH & DISEASE:
• **Non-Infectious Disease**

Principles of Homeostasis

Homeostasis is the condition where the body's internal environment remains relatively constant, despite external fluctuations. Homeostasis of the internal environment is an essential feature of complex animals and it is the job of the body's **organ systems** to maintain it, even as they make necessary exchanges with the environment. Homeostatic control systems have three functional components: a receptor to detect change, a control centre, and an effector to direct an appropriate response. In negative feedback systems, movement away from an ideal state triggers a mechanism to counteract further change in that direction. Using feedback systems, the body counteracts disturbances and restores the steady state.

Organ systems maintain a constant internal environment that provides for the needs of all the body's cells, making it possible for animals to move through different and often highly variable external environments. This representation of a mammal shows how organ systems permit exchanges with the environment. The exchange surfaces of organ systems are usually internal, but may be connected to the environment via openings on the body surface.

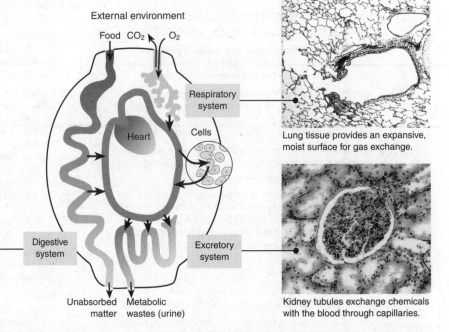

External environment

Food CO₂   O₂

Respiratory system

Heart

Cells

Digestive system

Excretory system

Unabsorbed matter   Metabolic wastes (urine)

Lung tissue provides an expansive, moist surface for gas exchange.

Kidney tubules exchange chemicals with the blood through capillaries.

The finger-like villi of the small intestine greatly expand the surface area for nutrient absorption.

Negative Feedback and Control Systems

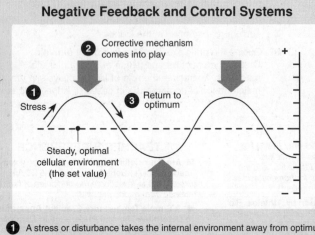

2 Corrective mechanism comes into play

1 Stress

3 Return to optimum

Steady, optimal cellular environment (the set value)

Brain or spinal cord coordinates response

Signal sent

Sensory receptor

Muscle (or gland)

Changed conditions provide feedback to receptor

Receptor detects change in conditions

Effectors respond to change conditions

1 A stress or disturbance takes the internal environment away from optimum

2 Stress is detected by receptors and corrective mechanisms are activated

3 The corrective mechanisms act to restore conditions back to the set value

Negative feedback acts to eliminate any deviation from preferred conditions. It is part of almost all the control systems in living things. The diagram (above left) shows how a stress or disturbance is counteracted by corrective mechanisms that act to restore conditions back to an optimum value. The diagram (above right) illustrates this principle for a biological system.

1. Identify the three main components of a regulatory control system in the human body: _____

_____

2. Explain how animals use feedback mechanisms to maintain a steady state despite their constant exchanges with a variable environment:

_____

_____

_____

Related activities: Maintaining Homeostasis

Maintaining Homeostasis

The various organ systems of the body act to maintain homeostasis through a combination of hormonal and nervous mechanisms. In everyday life, the body must regulate respiratory gases, protect itself against agents of disease (pathogens), maintain fluid and salt balance, regulate energy and nutrient supply, and maintain a constant body temperature. All these must be coordinated and appropriate responses made to incoming stimuli. In addition, the body must be able to repair itself when injured and be capable of reproducing (leaving offspring).

Regulating Respiratory Gases

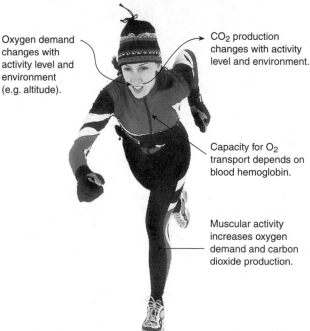

Oxygen demand changes with activity level and environment (e.g. altitude).

CO₂ production changes with activity level and environment.

Capacity for O₂ transport depends on blood hemoglobin.

Muscular activity increases oxygen demand and carbon dioxide production.

Oxygen must be delivered to all cells and carbon dioxide (a waste product of cellular respiration) must be removed. Breathing (inhalation and exhalation) brings in oxygen and expels CO₂. The rate of breathing is varied according to the oxygen requirement. Both gases are transported around the body in the blood; the oxygen mostly bound to hemoglobin.

Coping with Pathogens

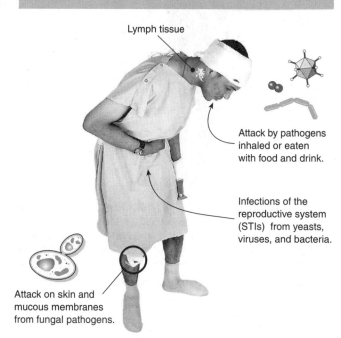

Lymph tissue

Attack by pathogens inhaled or eaten with food and drink.

Infections of the reproductive system (STIs) from yeasts, viruses, and bacteria.

Attack on skin and mucous membranes from fungal pathogens.

All of us are under constant attack from pathogens (disease causing organisms). The body has a number of mechanisms that help to prevent the entry of pathogens and limit the damage they cause if they do enter the body. The skin, the digestive system and the immune system are all involved in limiting damage.

Maintaining Nutrient Supply

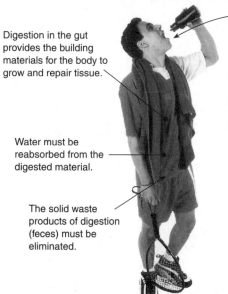

Digestion in the gut provides the building materials for the body to grow and repair tissue.

Food and drink provides energy and nutrients, but supply is pulsed at mealtimes with little in between.

Water must be reabsorbed from the digested material.

The solid waste products of digestion (feces) must be eliminated.

Food and drink must be taken in to maintain the body's energy supplies. Steady levels of energy (as glucose) is available to cells through hormonal regulation of blood sugar levels. Insulin, released by the endocrine cells of the pancreas, causes cells to take up glucose after a meal. Glucagon causes the release of glucose from the liver.

Repairing Injuries

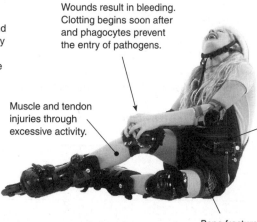

Wounds result in bleeding. Clotting begins soon after and phagocytes prevent the entry of pathogens.

Muscle and tendon injuries through excessive activity.

Hernias can be caused by strain as in heavy lifting.

Bone fractures caused by falls and blows.

Damage to body tissues triggers the inflammatory response. There is pain, swelling, redness, and heat. Phagocytes and other white blood cells move to the injury site. The inflammatory response is started (and ended) by chemical signals (e.g. from histamine and prostaglandins) released when tissue is damaged.

Related activities: The Body's Defenses, Nervous & Hormonal Regulatory Systems, Control of Kidney Function, Exercise & Blood Flow

RA 2

Maintaining Fluid and Ion Balance

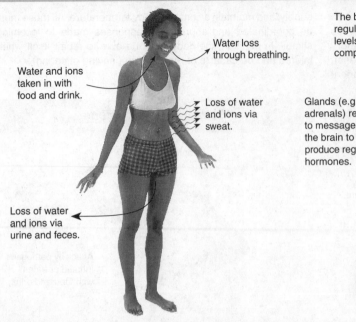

Water loss through breathing.

Water and ions taken in with food and drink.

Loss of water and ions via sweat.

Loss of water and ions via urine and feces.

Coordinating Responses

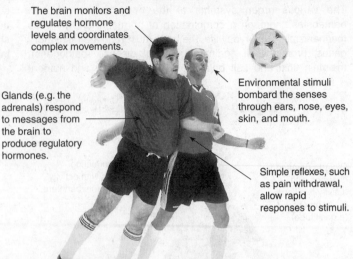

The brain monitors and regulates hormone levels and coordinates complex movements.

Glands (e.g. the adrenals) respond to messages from the brain to produce regulatory hormones.

Environmental stimuli bombard the senses through ears, nose, eyes, skin, and mouth.

Simple reflexes, such as pain withdrawal, allow rapid responses to stimuli.

The levels of water and ions in the body are maintained mainly by the kidneys, although the skin is also important. Osmoreceptors monitor the fluid and ion levels of the blood and bring about the release of regulatory hormones; the kidneys regulate reabsorption of water and sodium from blood in response to levels of the hormones ADH and aldosterone.

The body is constantly bombarded by stimuli from the environment. The brain sorts these stimuli into those that require a response and those that do not. Responses are coordinated via nervous or hormonal controls. Simple nervous responses (reflexes) act quickly. Hormonal responses take longer to produce a response and the response is more prolonged.

1. Describe two mechanisms that operate to restore homeostasis after infection by a pathogen:

(a) _____

_____

_____

(b) _____

_____

_____

2. Describe two mechanisms by which responses to stimuli are brought about and coordinated:

(a) _____

_____

(b) _____

_____

3. Explain two ways in which water and ion balance are maintained. Name the organ(s) and any hormones involved:

(a) _____

_____

(b) _____

_____

4. Explain two ways in which the body regulates its respiratory gases during exercise:

(a) _____

_____

(b) _____

_____

Nervous Regulatory Systems

An essential feature of living organisms is their ability to coordinate their activities. In multicellular animals, such as mammals, detecting and responding to environmental change, and regulating the internal environment (homeostasis) is brought about by two coordinating systems: the nervous and endocrine systems. Although structurally these two systems are quite different, they frequently interact to coordinate behavior and physiology. The nervous system contains cells called neurons (or nerve cells). Neurons are specialized to transmit information in the form of electrochemical impulses (action potentials). The nervous system is a signalling network with branches carrying information directly to and from specific target tissues. Impulses can be transmitted over considerable distances and the response is very precise and rapid. Whilst it is extraordinarily complex, comprising millions of neural connections, its basic plan (below) is quite simple. Further detail on nervous system structure and function is provided in the topic: *Nerves, Muscles, and Movement.*

Coordination by the Nervous System

The vertebrate nervous system consists of the central nervous system (brain and spinal cord), and the nerves and receptors outside it (peripheral nervous system). Sensory input to receptors comes via stimuli. Information about the effect of a response is provided by feedback mechanisms so that the system can be readjusted. The basic organization of the nervous system can be simplified into a few key components: the sensory receptors, a central nervous system processing point, and the effectors which bring about the response (below):

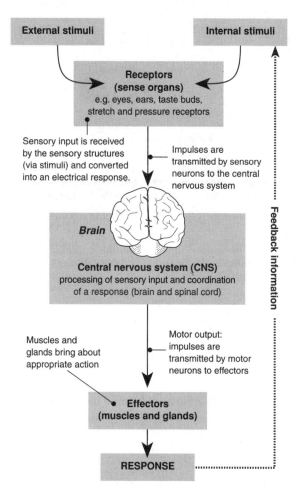

External stimuli

Internal stimuli

Receptors (sense organs)
e.g. eyes, ears, taste buds, stretch and pressure receptors

Sensory input is received by the sensory structures (via stimuli) and converted into an electrical response.

Impulses are transmitted by sensory neurons to the central nervous system

Brain

Central nervous system (CNS)
processing of sensory input and coordination of a response (brain and spinal cord)

Muscles and glands bring about appropriate action

Motor output: impulses are transmitted by motor neurons to effectors

Effectors (muscles and glands)

Feedback information

RESPONSE

Motor cortex coordinates appropriate response

Eye perceives the stimulus and sends messages via sensory neurons to the brain

Motor neurons carry the message to effectors (the muscles of hand and arm)

In the example above, the approach of the frisbee is perceived by the eye. The motor cortex of the brain integrates the sensory message. Coordination of hand and body orientation is brought about through motor neurons to the muscles.

Comparison of nervous and hormonal control

	Nervous control	Hormonal control
Communication	Impulses across synapses	Hormones in the blood
Speed	Very rapid (within a few milliseconds)	Relatively slow (over minutes, hours, or longer)
Duration	Short term and reversible	Longer lasting effects
Target pathway	Specific (through nerves) to specific cells	Hormones broadcast to target cells everywhere
Action	Causes glands to secrete or muscles to contract	Causes changes in metabolic activity

1. Identify the three basic components of a nervous system and explain how they function to maintain homeostasis:

_____

_____

_____

2. Describe two differences between nervous control and endocrine (hormonal) control of body systems:

(a) _____

(b) _____

Hormonal Regulatory Systems

The endocrine system regulates the body's processes by releasing chemical messengers (hormones) into the bloodstream. Hormones are potent chemical regulators: they are produced in minute quantities yet can have a large effect on metabolism. The endocrine system comprises endocrine cells (organized into endocrine glands), and the hormones they produce. Unlike exocrine glands (e.g. sweat and salivary glands), endocrine glands are ductless glands, secreting hormones directly into the bloodstream rather than through a duct or tube. Some organs (e.g. the pancreas) have both endocrine and exocrine regions, but these are structurally and functionally distinct. The basis of hormonal control and the role of negative feedback mechanisms in regulating hormone levels are described below.

The Mechanism of Hormone Action

Endocrine cells produce hormones (chemical messengers) and secrete them into the bloodstream where they are distributed throughout the body. Although hormones are broadcast throughout the body, they affect only specific target cells. These target cells have receptors on the plasma membrane which recognize and bind the hormone (see inset, below right). The binding of hormone and receptor triggers the response in the target cell. Cells are unresponsive to a hormone if they do not have the appropriate receptors.

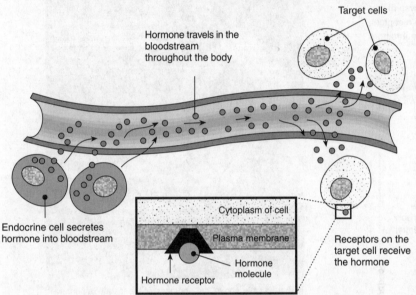

Hormone travels in the bloodstream throughout the body

Target cells

Endocrine cell secretes hormone into bloodstream

Cytoplasm of cell

Plasma membrane

Hormone molecule

Hormone receptor

Receptors on the target cell receive the hormone

Antagonistic Hormones

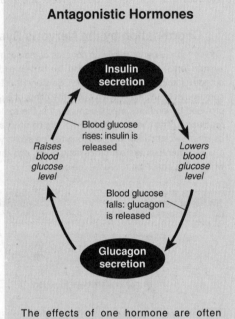

Insulin secretion

Blood glucose rises: insulin is released

Raises blood glucose level

Lowers blood glucose level

Blood glucose falls: glucagon is released

Glucagon secretion

The effects of one hormone are often counteracted by an opposing hormone. Feedback mechanisms adjust the balance of the two hormones to maintain a physiological function. Example: insulin decreases blood glucose and glucagon raises it.

---

1. (a) Explain what is meant by **antagonistic hormones** and describe an example of how two such hormones operate:

   _____

   _____

   Example: _____

   _____

   (b) Explain the role of feedback mechanisms in adjusting hormone levels (explain using an example if this is helpful):

   _____

   _____

   _____

2. Explain how a hormone can bring about a response in target cells even though all cells may receive the hormone:

   _____

   _____

3. Explain why hormonal control differs from nervous system control with respect to the following:

   (a) The speed of hormonal responses is slower: _____

   _____

   (b) Hormonal responses are generally longer lasting: _____

   _____

The Endocrine System

Homeostasis is achieved through the activity of the nervous and endocrine systems, which interact in the regulation of the body's activities. The nervous system is capable of rapid responses to stimuli. Slower responses, and long term adjustments of the body (growth, reproduction, and adaptation to stress), are achieved through endocrine control. The endocrine system comprises **endocrine glands** and their **hormones**. Endocrine glands are ductless glands that are distributed throughout the body. Under appropriate stimulation (see below), they secrete **hormones**: chemical messengers that are carried in the blood to **target** cells, where they have a specific metabolic effect. After exerting their effect, hormones are broken down and excreted from the body. Although a hormone circulates in the blood, only the targets will respond. Hormones may be amino acids, peptides, proteins (often modified), fatty acids, or steroids. Some basic features of the human endocrine system are explained below and the next page.

Hypothalamus
Coordinates nervous and endocrine systems. Secretes releasing hormones, which regulate the hormones of the anterior pituitary. Produces oxytocin and ADH, which are released from the posterior pituitary.

Parathyroid glands
On the surface of the thyroid, they secrete PTH (parathyroid hormone), which regulates blood calcium levels and promotes the release of calcium from bone. High levels of calcium in the blood inhibit PTH secretion.

Pancreas
Specialized α and B endocrine cells in the pancreas produce glucagon and insulin. Together, these control blood sugar levels.

Ovaries (in females)
At puberty the ovaries increase their production of estrogen and progesterone. These hormones control and maintain female characteristics (breast development and pelvic widening), stimulate the menstrual cycle, maintain pregnancy, and prepare the mammary glands for lactation.

Pituitary gland
The pituitary is located below the hypothalamus. It secretes at least nine hormones that regulate the activities of other endocrine glands.

Thyroid gland
Secretes thyroxine, an iodine containing hormone needed for normal growth and development. Thyroxine stimulates metabolism and growth via protein synthesis.

Adrenal glands (above kidneys)
The adrenal medulla produces adrenalin and noradrenalin; responsible for the fight or flight response. The adrenal cortex produces various steroid hormones, including aldosterone (sodium regulation) and cortisol (response to stress).

Testes (in males)
At puberty (the onset of sexual maturity) the testes of males produce testosterone in greater amounts. Testosterone hormone controls and maintains "maleness" (muscular development and deeper voice), and promotes sperm production.

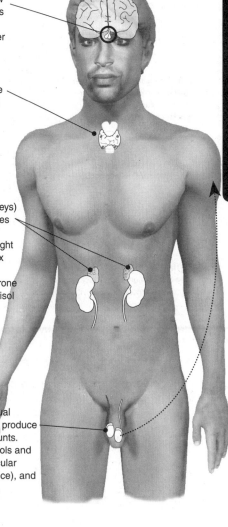

1. Distinguish between a neurotransmitter and a hormone: _____

_____

_____

2. Explain why it is an advantage for hormones to be carried in the blood: _____

_____

_____

3. The dotted arrows in the diagram above indicate the development of secondary sexual characteristics. Identify the male and female hormones involved in the development of these characteristics and state their role:

(a) Male: _____

_____

(b) Female: _____

_____

Related activities: The Pituitary
Web links: Drag and Drop Hormone Match

RA 3

The Role of the Hypothalamus

The hypothalamus contains **neurosecretory cells**, specialized secretory neurons, which are both nerve cells and endocrine cells. They produce hormones (usually peptides) in the cell body, which are packaged into droplets and transported along the axon. At the axon terminal, the **neurohormone** is released into the blood in response to nerve impulses.

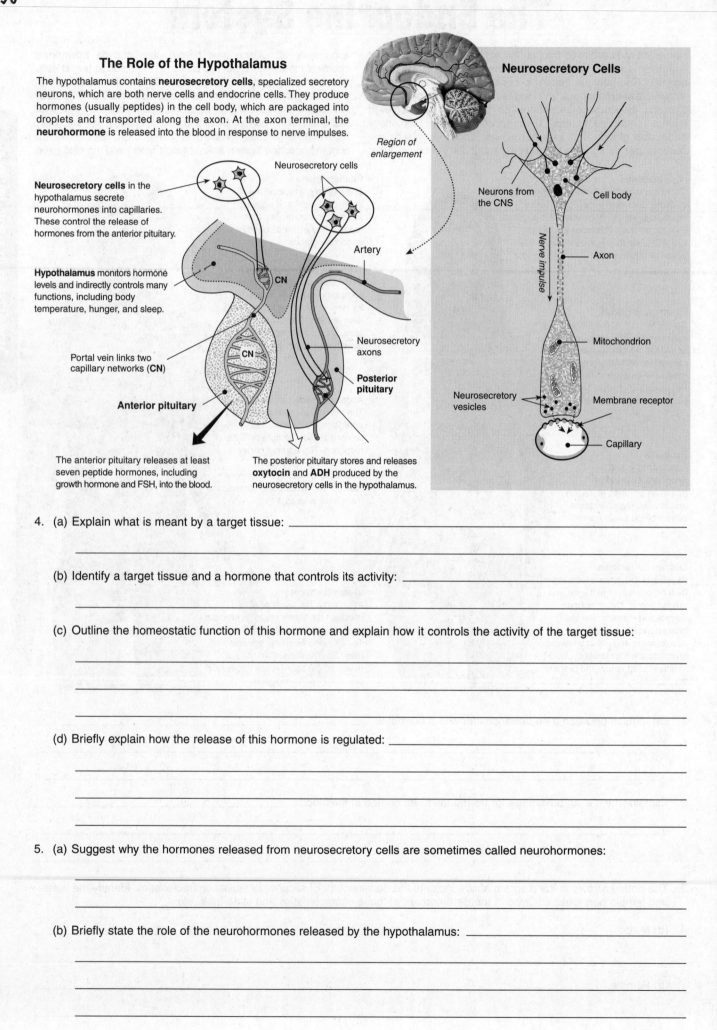

Region of enlargement

Neurosecretory Cells

Neurons from the CNS

Cell body

Nerve impulse

Axon

Mitochondrion

Neurosecretory vesicles

Membrane receptor

Capillary

Neurosecretory cells

Neurosecretory cells in the hypothalamus secrete neurohormones into capillaries. These control the release of hormones from the anterior pituitary.

Hypothalamus monitors hormone levels and indirectly controls many functions, including body temperature, hunger, and sleep.

Portal vein links two capillary networks (**CN**)

Anterior pituitary

Artery

Neurosecretory axons

Posterior pituitary

CN

CN

The anterior pituitary releases at least seven peptide hormones, including growth hormone and FSH, into the blood.

The posterior pituitary stores and releases **oxytocin** and **ADH** produced by the neurosecretory cells in the hypothalamus.

4. (a) Explain what is meant by a target tissue: _____

_____

(b) Identify a target tissue and a hormone that controls its activity: _____

_____

(c) Outline the homeostatic function of this hormone and explain how it controls the activity of the target tissue:

_____

_____

_____

(d) Briefly explain how the release of this hormone is regulated: _____

_____

_____

_____

5. (a) Suggest why the hormones released from neurosecretory cells are sometimes called neurohormones:

_____

_____

(b) Briefly state the role of the neurohormones released by the hypothalamus: _____

_____

_____

_____

The Pituitary

The **hypothalamus** is located at the base of the brain, just above the pituitary gland. Information comes to the hypothalamus through sensory pathways from the sense organs. On the basis of this information, the hypothalamus controls and integrates many basic physiological activities (e.g. temperature regulation, food and fluid intake, and sleep), including the reflex activity of the **autonomic nervous system**. The pituitary gland comprises two regions: the **posterior pituitary** and the **anterior pituitary**.

The **posterior pituitary** is neural (nervous) in origin and is essentially an extension of the hypothalamus. Its neurosecretory cells release oxytocin and ADH directly into the bloodstream in response to nerve impulses. The **anterior pituitary** is connected to the hypothalamus by blood vessels and receives releasing and inhibiting factors from the hypothlamus via a capillary network. These releasing factors regulate the secretion of the anterior pituitary's hormones.

ANTERIOR PITUITARY

The anterior pituitary releases at least seven **peptide hormones** (below) into the blood from simple secretory cells. The release of these hormones is regulated by releasing and inhibiting factors from the hypothalamus.

POSTERIOR PITUITARY

The posterior pituitary develops as an extension of the hypothalamus. The release of its two hormones, oxytocin and antidiuretic hormone, occurs directly as a result of nervous input to the hypothalamus.

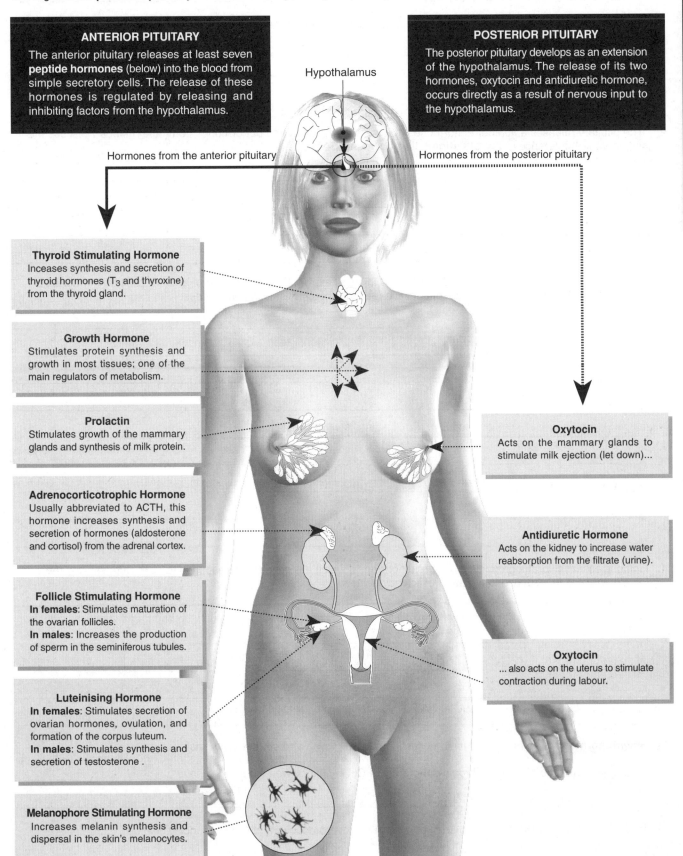

Hypothalamus

Hormones from the anterior pituitary

Hormones from the posterior pituitary

Thyroid Stimulating Hormone
Inceases synthesis and secretion of thyroid hormones (T_3 and thyroxine) from the thyroid gland.

Growth Hormone
Stimulates protein synthesis and growth in most tissues; one of the main regulators of metabolism.

Prolactin
Stimulates growth of the mammary glands and synthesis of milk protein.

Adrenocorticotrophic Hormone
Usually abbreviated to ACTH, this hormone increases synthesis and secretion of hormones (aldosterone and cortisol) from the adrenal cortex.

Follicle Stimulating Hormone
In females: Stimulates maturation of the ovarian follicles.
In males: Increases the production of sperm in the seminiferous tubules.

Luteinising Hormone
In females: Stimulates secretion of ovarian hormones, ovulation, and formation of the corpus luteum.
In males: Stimulates synthesis and secretion of testosterone .

Melanophore Stimulating Hormone
Increases melanin synthesis and dispersal in the skin's melanocytes.

Oxytocin
Acts on the mammary glands to stimulate milk ejection (let down)...

Antidiuretic Hormone
Acts on the kidney to increase water reabsorption from the filtrate (urine).

Oxytocin
... also acts on the uterus to stimulate contraction during labour.

Related activities: The Endocrine System

RA 2

1. (a) Explain how the anterior and posterior pituitary differ with respect to their relationship to the hypothalamus:

_____

_____

_____

_____

(b) Explain how these differences relate to the nature of the hormonal secretions for each region: _____

_____

_____

_____

2. "The pituitary releases a number of hormones that regulate the secretion of hormones from other glands". Discuss this statement with reference to **thyroid stimulating hormone** (TSH):

_____

_____

_____

_____

3. Using the example of TSH and its target tissue (the thyroid), explain how the release of anterior pituitary hormones is regulated. Include reference to the role of negative feedback mechanisms in this process:

_____

_____

_____

_____

_____

_____

_____

_____

_____

4. Iodine is essential for the production of thyroid hormones, which are secreted in response to TSH. Suggest why the thyroid enlarges in response to a dietary deficiency of iodine:

_____

_____

_____

_____

5. **Growth hormone** (GH) has wide ranging effects on tissue growth and protein synthesis.

(a) Suggest what the effect of a chronic **deficiency** of GH in infancy would be: _____

_____

(b) Suggest what the effect of a chronic **hypersecretion** (overproduction) of GH in infancy would be: _____

_____

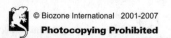

Cell Signaling

Cells use **signals** (chemical messengers) to gather information about, and respond to, changes in their cellular environment and for communication between cells. The signaling and response process is called the **signal transduction pathway**, and often involves a number of enzymes and molecules in a **signal cascade** which causes a large response in the target cell. Cell signaling pathways are categorized primarily on the distance over which the signal molecule travels to reach its target cell, and generally fall into three categories. The **endocrine** pathway involves the transport of hormones over large distances through the circulatory system. During **paracrine** signaling, the signal travels an intermediate distance to act upon neighboring cells. **Autocrine** signaling involves a cell producing and reacting to its own signal. These three pathways are illustrated below.

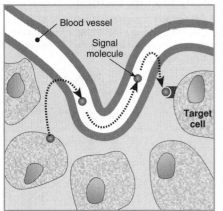

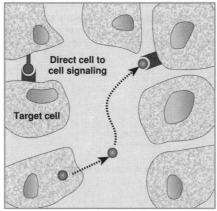

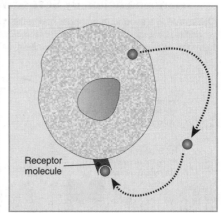

Endocrine signaling: Hormone signals are released by ductless endocrine glands and carried long distances through the body by the circulatory system to the target cells. Examples include sex hormones, growth factors and neurohormones such as dopamine.

Paracrine signaling: Signals released from a cell act upon target cells within the immediate vicinity. The chemical messenger can be transferred through the extracellular fluid (e.g. at synapses) or directly between cells, which is important during embryonic development.

Autocrine signaling: Cells produce and react to their own signals. In vertebrates, when a foreign antibody enters the body, some T-lymphocytes produce a growth factor to stimulate their own production. The increased number of T-lymphocytes helps to fight the infection.

Signaling Receptors and Signaling Molecules

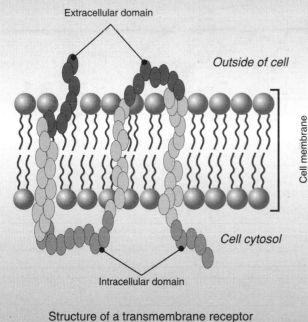

Structure of a transmembrane receptor

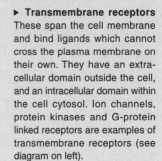

Examples of cell signaling molecules

The binding sites of cell receptors are very specific; they only bind certain **ligands** (signal molecules). This stops them from reacting to every signal bombarding the cell. Receptors fall into two main categories :

▶ **Cytoplasmic receptors**
Cytoplasmic receptors, located within the cell cytoplasm, bind ligands which are able to cross the plasma membrane unaided.

▶ **Transmembrane receptors**
These span the cell membrane and bind ligands which cannot cross the plasma membrane on their own. They have an extracellular domain outside the cell, and an intracellular domain within the cell cytosol. Ion channels, protein kinases and G-protein linked receptors are examples of transmembrane receptors (see diagram on left).

1. Briefly describe the three types of cell signaling:

   (a) _____

   (b) _____

   (c) _____

2. Identify the components that all three cell signaling types have in common: _____

_____

_____

Related activities: Hormonal Regulatory Systems, Signal Transduction

A 2

Signal Transduction

Once a hormone signal is released, it is carried in the blood to target cells that respond specifically to that hormone. Water soluble hormones are carried free in the blood, whilst steroid and thyroid hormones are carried bound to plasma proteins. Target cells possess receptors that bind the hormone and initiate a cascade of reactions ending in an alteration of function in the target cell (e.g. secretion,

change in membrane permeability, protein synthesis, or enzyme activation). Hormones may bind by interacting with transmembrane receptors and activating a second messenger, or they may interact directly with intracellular cytoplasmic receptors. Once the target cell responds, the response is recognized by the hormone-producing cell through a feedback signal and the hormone is degraded.

Hormone Action By Second Messenger

Cyclic AMP is a **second messenger** linking the hormone to the cellular response. Cellular concentration of CAMP increases markedly once a hormone binds and the cascade of enzyme-driven reactions is initiated.

Gene Activation by Steroids

Steroid hormones alter cell function through direct activation of genes. Once inside the target cell, they bind to intracellular receptor sites, creating hormone-receptor complexes that activate specific genes.

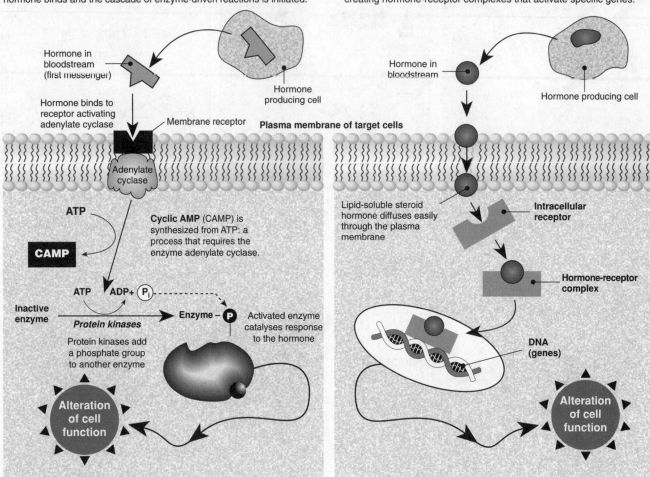

1. Describe the two mechanisms by which a hormone can bring about a cellular response:

(a) _____

_____

(b) _____

_____

2. State in what way these two mechanisms are alike: _____

_____

3. Explain how a very small amount of hormone is able to exert a disproportionately large effect on a target cell:

_____

_____

4. Explain how the binding of a hormone to a target cell can be likened to an enzyme-substrate reaction: _____

_____

_____

Related activities: Hormonal Regulatory Systems, Cell Signaling
Web links: First and Second Messenger System

The Liver's Homeostatic Role

The liver, located just below the diaphragm and making up 3-5% of body weight, is the largest homeostatic organ. It performs a vast number of functions including production of bile, storage and processing of nutrients, and detoxification of poisons and metabolic wastes. The liver has a **unique double blood supply** and up to 20% of the total blood volume flows through it at any one time.

This rich vascularization makes it the central organ for regulating activities associated with the blood and circulatory system. In spite of the complexity of its function, the liver tissue and the liver cells themselves are structurally relatively simple. Features of liver structure and function are outlined below. The histology of the liver in relation to its role is described on the next page.

Homeostatic Functions of the Liver

The liver is one of the largest and most complex organs in the body. It has a central role as an organ of homeostasis and performs many functions, particularly in relation to the regulation of blood composition. General functions of the liver are outlined below. Briefly summarized, the liver:

1. Secretes bile, important in emulsifying fats in digestion.
2. Metabolizes amino acids, fats, and carbohydrates (below).
3. Synthesizes glucose from non-carbohydrate sources when glycogen stores are exhausted (gluconeogenesis).
4. Stores iron, copper, and some vitamins (A, D, E, K, B_{12}).
5. Converts unwanted amino acids to urea (urea cycle).
6. Manufactures heparin and plasma proteins (e.g. albumin).
7. Detoxifies poisons or turns them into less harmful forms.
8. Some liver cells phagocytose worn-out blood cells.
9. Synthesizes cholesterol from acetyl coenzyme A.

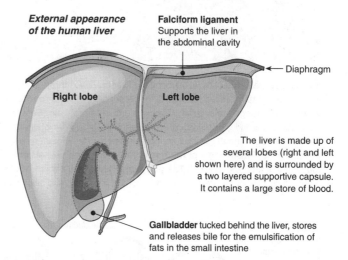

External appearance of the human liver

Falciform ligament Supports the liver in the abdominal cavity

Diaphragm

Right lobe

Left lobe

The liver is made up of several lobes (right and left shown here) and is surrounded by a two layered supportive capsule. It contains a large store of blood.

Gallbladder tucked behind the liver, stores and releases bile for the emulsification of fats in the small intestine

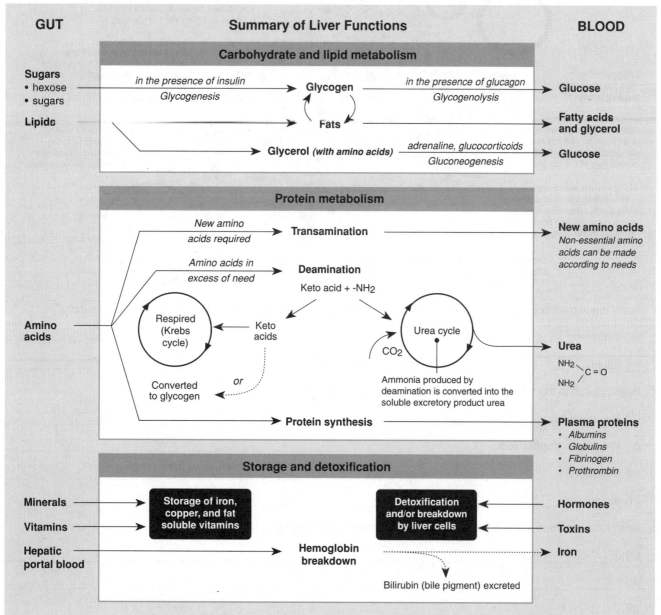

Summary of Liver Functions

GUT

BLOOD

Carbohydrate and lipid metabolism

Sugars
• hexose
• sugars

in the presence of insulin
Glycogenesis

Glycogen

in the presence of glucagon
Glycogenolysis

Glucose

Lipids

Fats

Fatty acids and glycerol

Glycerol (with amino acids)

adrenaline, glucocorticoids
Gluconeogenesis

Glucose

Protein metabolism

New amino acids required

Transamination

New amino acids
Non-essential amino acids can be made according to needs

Amino acids in excess of need

Deamination

Keto acid + $-NH_2$

Amino acids

Respired (Krebs cycle)

Keto acids

Urea cycle

CO_2

Converted to glycogen

or

Ammonia produced by deamination is converted into the soluble excretory product urea

Urea

$$NH_2 - C = O$$
$$NH_2$$

Protein synthesis

Plasma proteins
• Albumins
• Globulins
• Fibrinogen
• Prothrombin

Storage and detoxification

Minerals

Storage of iron, copper, and fat soluble vitamins

Detoxification and/or breakdown by liver cells

Hormones

Vitamins

Toxins

Hepatic portal blood

Hemoglobin breakdown

Iron

Bilirubin (bile pigment) excreted

Related activities: The Role of the Liver

RA 2

The Internal Structure of the Liver

Radiating cords of hepatocytes

CV

Schematic illustration of the arrangement of lobules and portal tracts in liver tissue

Bile ductule

Branch of hepatic portal vein

Branch of hepatic artery

Portal tract (triad)

Bile flow

Blood flows towards the central vein

Central vein

CV

Fibrous connective tissue capsule surrounds lobules

Lobule

The connective tissue capsule covering the liver branches through the tissue, dividing it into functional units called **lobules**. A lobule consists of rows (**cords**) of **hepatocytes** (liver cells) arranged in a radial pattern around a central vein. Between the cords are blood spaces called **sinusoids** and small channels through which the bile flows (the **bile canaliculi**). Between the lobules are branches of the hepatic artery, hepatic portal vein, and bile duct. These form a **portal tract** (triad). Lymphatic vessels and nerves are also found in this area (not shown). **The photograph above** shows most of a liver lobule in a human, illustrating the central vein, the cords of liver cells, and sinusoids (dark spaces).

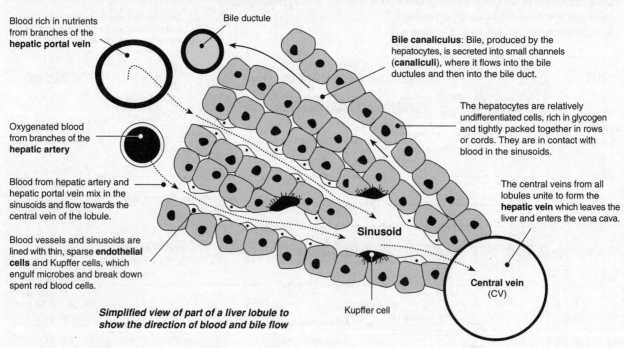

Blood rich in nutrients from branches of the **hepatic portal vein**

Bile ductule

Bile canaliculus: Bile, produced by the hepatocytes, is secreted into small channels (**canaliculi**), where it flows into the bile ductules and then into the bile duct.

The hepatocytes are relatively undifferentiated cells, rich in glycogen and tightly packed together in rows or cords. They are in contact with blood in the sinusoids.

Oxygenated blood from branches of the **hepatic artery**

Blood from hepatic artery and hepatic portal vein mix in the sinusoids and flow towards the central vein of the lobule.

Blood vessels and sinusoids are lined with thin, sparse **endothelial cells** and Kupffer cells, which engulf microbes and break down spent red blood cells.

The central veins from all lobules unite to form the **hepatic vein** which leaves the liver and enters the vena cava.

Sinusoid

Central vein (CV)

Kupffer cell

Simplified view of part of a liver lobule to show the direction of blood and bile flow

1. State the two sources of blood supply to the liver, describing the primary physiological purpose of each supply:

   (a) Supply 1: _____ Purpose: _____

   (b) Supply 2: _____ Purpose: _____

2. Briefly describe the role of the following structures in liver tissue:

   (a) Bile canaliculi: _____

   (b) Phagocytic Kupffer cells: _____

   (c) Central vein: _____

   (d) Sinusoids: _____

3. Briefly explain three important aspects of **either** protein metabolism **or** carbohydrate metabolism in the liver:

   (a) _____

   (b) _____

   (c) _____

Control of Blood Glucose

The endocrine portion of the **pancreas** produces the hormones that regulate blood glucose. Two hormones, insulin and glucagon, maintain blood glucose at a steady state through **negative feedback**. Insulin promotes a decrease in blood glucose synthesizing glycogen and promoting cellular uptake of glucose. Glucagon promotes an increase in blood glucose through the breakdown of glycogen and the synthesis of glucose from amino acids. When normal blood glucose levels are restored, negative feedback stops hormone secretion. Regulating blood glucose to within narrow limits allows energy to be available to cells as needed. Extra energy is stored, as glycogen or fat, and is mobilized to meet energy needs as required. The liver is pivotal in these carbohydrate conversions. One of the consequences of a disruption to this system is the disease **diabetes mellitus**. In type 1 diabetes, the insulin producing β cells of the pancreatic tissue are destroyed as a result of autoimmune activity and insulin is not produced. In type 2 diabetes, the pancreatic cells produce insulin, but the body's cells cease responding its message.

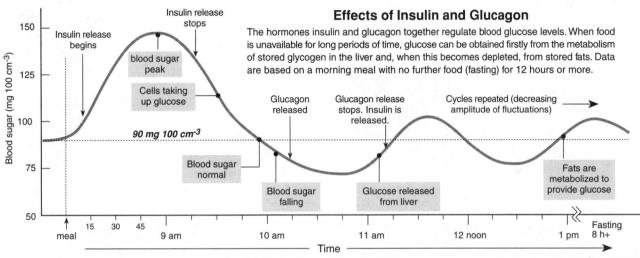

Effects of Insulin and Glucagon

The hormones insulin and glucagon together regulate blood glucose levels. When food is unavailable for long periods of time, glucose can be obtained firstly from the metabolism of stored glycogen in the liver and, when this becomes depleted, from stored fats. Data are based on a morning meal with no further food (fasting) for 12 hours or more.

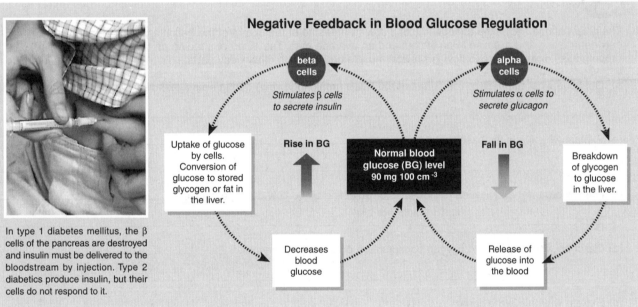

Negative Feedback in Blood Glucose Regulation

In type 1 diabetes mellitus, the β cells of the pancreas are destroyed and insulin must be delivered to the bloodstream by injection. Type 2 diabetics produce insulin, but their cells do not respond to it.

1. (a) Identify the stimulus for the release of insulin: _____

   (b) Identify the stimulus for the release of glucagon: _____

   (c) Explain how glucagon brings about an increase in blood glucose level: _____

   _____

   (d) Explain how insulin brings about a decrease in blood glucose level: _____

   _____

2. Outline the role of negative feedback in the control of blood glucose: _____

   _____

3. Explain why fats are metabolized after a long period without food: _____

   _____

Related activities: The Liver's Homeostatic Role, Stomach and Small Intestine, Diabetes Mellitus   **Web links**: Type 1 Diabetes

A 2

Homeostasis During Exercise

Physical exercise places greater demands on the abilities of the body to maintain a steady state. Extra heat generated during exercise must be dissipated, oxygen demands increase, and there are more waste products produced. The body has an immediate response to exercise but also, over time, responds to the stress of repeated exercise (**training**) by adapting and improving its capacity for exercise and the efficiency with which it performs. This concept is illustrated below. Training causes tissue damage and depletes energy stores, but the body responds by repairing the damage, replenishing energy stores, and adjusting its responses in order to minimise the impact of exercise in the future. The maintenance of homeostasis during exercise is principally the job of the circulatory and respiratory systems, although the skin, kidneys, and liver are also important.

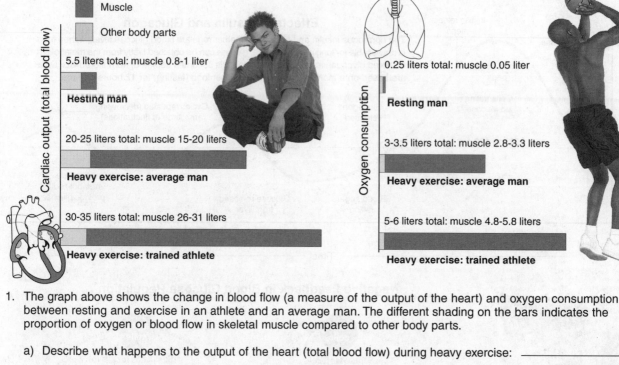

Muscle
Other body parts

Cardiac output (total blood flow)

5.5 liters total: muscle 0.8-1 liter
Resting man

20-25 liters total: muscle 15-20 liters
Heavy exercise: average man

30-35 liters total: muscle 26-31 liters
Heavy exercise: trained athlete

Oxygen consumption

0.25 liters total: muscle 0.05 liter
Resting man

3-3.5 liters total: muscle 2.8-3.3 liters
Heavy exercise: average man

5-6 liters total: muscle 4.8-5.8 liters
Heavy exercise: trained athlete

1. The graph above shows the change in blood flow (a measure of the output of the heart) and oxygen consumption between resting and exercise in an athlete and an average man. The different shading on the bars indicates the proportion of oxygen or blood flow in skeletal muscle compared to other body parts.

    a) Describe what happens to the output of the heart (total blood flow) during heavy exercise: _____
    _____

    (b) Explain why this is the case: _____
    _____

    (c) List the organ(s) and tissues responsible for adjusting blood flow during exercise: _____

2. (a) Describe what happens to oxygen consumption during heavy exercise: _____
    _____

    (b) Explain why this is the case: _____
    _____

    (c) Explain the change in the proportion of oxygen consumed by the muscles during exercise: _____
    _____
    _____

3. Explain the difference in oxygen consumption and blood flow between a trained athlete and an average man:
    _____
    _____
    _____
    _____

Related activities: Exercise and Blood Flow

Mechanisms of Thermoregulation

The process of controlling body temperature is called thermoregulation. For many years, animals were classified as either homeotherms or homoiotherms (= constant body temperature) or poikilotherms (= variable body temperature). Unfortunately, these terms are not particularly accurate for many animals; for example, some mammals (typical homeotherms), may have unstable body temperatures. A more recent, thermal classification of animals is based on the source of the body heat: whether it is largely from the environment (ectothermic) or from metabolic activity (endothermic). This classification can be more accurately applied to most animals but, in reality, many animals still fall somewhere between the two extremes.

How Body Temperature Varies

Aquatic invertebrates like jellyfish are true poikilotherms: their temperature is the same as the environment.	Tuna and some of the larger sharks can maintain body temperatures up to 14°C above the water temperature.	Hibernating rodents and bats let their body temperature drop to well below what is typical for most mammals.	Most birds and mammals maintain a body temperature that varies less than 2°C: they are true homeotherms.

Increasingly homeothermic →

Poikilothermic

Body temperature varies with the environmental temperature. Traditionally includes all animals other than birds and mammals, but many reptiles, some large insects and some large fish are not true poikilotherms because they may maintain body temperatures that are different from the surrounding environment.

Homeothermic

Body temperature remains almost constant despite environmental fluctuations. Traditionally includes birds and mammals, which typically maintain body temperatures close to 37-38°C. Many reptiles are partially homeothermic and achieve often quite constant body temperatures through behavioral mechanisms.

Source of Body Heat

With a few exceptions, most fish are fully ectothermic. Unlike many reptiles they do not usually thermoregulate.	Snakes use heat energy from the environment to increase their body temperature for activity.	Some large insects like bumblebees may raise their temperature for short periods through muscular activity.	Mammals (and birds) achieve high body temperatures through metabolic activity and reduction of heat losses.

Increasingly endothermic →

Ectothermic

Ectotherms depend on the environment for their heat energy. The term ectotherm is often equated with poikilotherm, although they are not the same. Poikilotherms are also ectotherms but many ectotherms may regulate body temperature (often within narrow limits) by changing their behavior (e.g. snakes and lizards).

Endothermic

Endotherms rely largely on metabolic activity for their heat energy. Since they usually maintain a constant body temperature, most endotherms are also homeotherms. As well as birds and mammals, some fast swimming fish, like tuna, and some large insects may also use muscular activity to maintain a high body temperature.

Daily temperature variations in ectotherms and endotherms

Ectotherm: Diurnal lizard (top right)
Body temperature is regulated by behavior so that it does not rise above 40°C. Basking increases heat uptake from the sun. Activity occurs when body temperature is high. Underground burrows are used for retreat.

Endotherm: Human (bottom right)
Body temperature fluctuates within narrow limits over a 24 hour period. Exercise and eating increase body temperature for a short time. Body temperature falls during rest and is partly controlled by an internal rhythm.

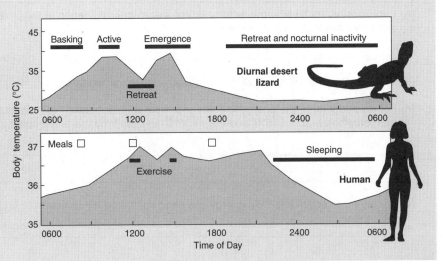

Related activities: Thermoregulation in Mammals

RDA 2

1. (a) Explain what is meant by a homeothermic endotherm: _____

   _____

   (b) Explain why the term "poikilotherm" is not a good term for classifying many terrestrial lizards and snakes:

   _____

   _____

   _____

2. Ectotherms will often maintain high, relatively constant body temperatures for periods in spite of environmental fluctuations, yet they also tolerate marked declines in body temperature to levels lower than are tolerated by endotherms.
   (a) Describe the advantages of letting body temperature fluctuate with the environment (particularly at low temperature):

   _____

   _____

   (b) Suggest why ectothermy is regarded as an adaptation to low or variable food supplies: _____

   _____

   _____

3. Some endotherms do not always maintain a high body temperature. Some, such as small rodents, allow their body temperatures to fall during hibernation. Explain the advantage of this behavior:

   _____

   _____

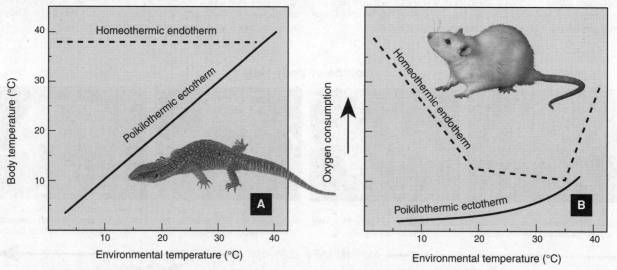

4. The two graphs above illustrate the differences in temperature regulation between a homeothermic endotherm and a poikilothermic ectotherm (such as a fish). Graph A shows change in body temperature with environmental temperature. Graph B shows change in oxygen consumption with environmental temperature. Use the graphs to answer the following:
   (a) Explain how ectotherms and endotherms differ in their response to changes in environmental temperature (graph **A**):

   _____

   (b) Explain why a poikilothermic ectotherm (no behavioral regulation of temperature) would be limited to environments where temperatures were below about 40°C:

   _____

   (c) In graph **B**, state the optimum temperature range for an endotherm: _____

   (d) For an endotherm, the energetic costs of temperature regulation (as measured by oxygen consumption) increase markedly below about 15°C and above 35°C. Explain why this is the case:

   _____

   _____

   _____

   (e) For an ectotherm (Graph B), energy costs increase steadily as environmental temperature increases. Explain why:

   _____

   _____

Thermoregulation in Mammals

For a body to maintain a constant temperature heat losses must equal heat gains. Heat exchanges with the environment occur via three mechanisms: **conduction** (direct heat transfer), **radiation** (indirect heat transfer), and **evaporation**. The importance of each of these depends on environment. For example, there is no evaporative loss in water, but such losses in air can be very high. Coverage of temperature regulation in humans, including the role of the skin, can be found in the next activity.

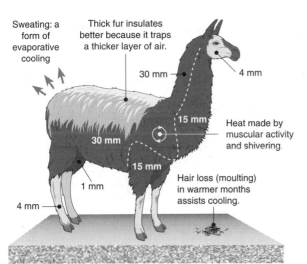

Seals, whales and dolphins have heavily insulated surfaces of fat or blubber (up to 60% of body thickness). Blood is diverted to the outside of the blubber in warm water or if heat needs to be lost.

Large body size reduces heat loss by lowering the surface area to volume ratio.

In all animals, metabolic activity generates heat.

Heat loss from flippers and tail flukes is minimised by the use of **countercurrent heat exchangers** (see top of next page for a full explanation)

Sweating: a form of evaporative cooling

Thick fur insulates better because it traps a thicker layer of air.

30 mm
4 mm
15 mm
30 mm
15 mm
1 mm
4 mm

Heat made by muscular activity and shivering.

Hair loss (moulting) in warmer months assists cooling.

For most mammals, the thickness of the fur or hair varies around the body (as indicated above). Thermoregulation is assisted by adopting body positions that expose or cover areas of thin fur (the figures above are for the llama-like guanaco).

Environmental temperature ranges

°C
100
70
50
20
0
-20
-50
-70

Sea and freshwater

Air temperature on land

Water has a great capacity to transfer heat away from organisms; its cooling power can be more than 50 times greater than that of air. For most aquatic animals (with the exception of aquatic birds and mammals and a few fish) heat retention is impossible. Instead, they carry out their metabolic activities at the ambient temperature. For most marine organisms this does not fluctuate much.

Temperature regulation mechanisms in water

- Low metabolic activity
- Heat generation from metabolic activity
- Insulation layer of blubber
- Changes in circulation patterns when swimming
- Large body size
- Heat exchange systems in limbs or high activity muscle

Temperature regulation mechanisms in air

- Behaviour or habitat choice
- Heat generation from metabolic activity
- Insulation (fat, fur, feathers)
- Changes in blood flow
- Large body size
- Sweating and panting
- Tolerance of fluctuation in body temperature

Animals adapted to temperature extremes (hot or cold) can often tolerate large fluctuations in their body temperature before they become stressed. In camels, the body temperature may fluctuate up to 7°C (34°C to 41°C) over a 24 hour period.

Homeostasis and Excretion

Dog

Panting to lose accumulated heat is important in dogs, which have sweat glands only on the pads of their feet.

Brown bear

Thick hair, fur or wool traps air in a layer next to the skin. This insulating air layer reduces heat loss and slows heat gain.

Elephant seal

Thick blubber and large body size in seals and other marine mammals provide an effective insulation.

Musk oxen

Mammals and birds in cold climates, like the musk oxen above, cluster together to retain body heat.

1. Explain how water differs from air in the way in which it transmits heat away from the body of an organism:

_____

_____

2. Describe two ways in which a mammal (a endothermic homeotherm) maintains its internal body temperature in water:

(a) _____

(b) _____

Related activities: Mechanisms of Thermoregulation, Thermoregulation in Humans, Adaptations and Fitness

RA 2

Countercurrent Heat Exchange Systems

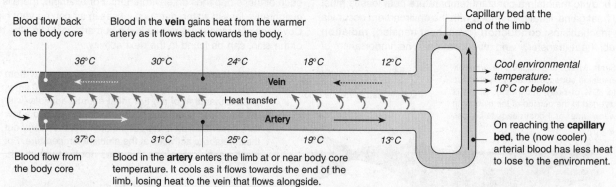

Blood flow back to the body core

Blood in the **vein** gains heat from the warmer artery as it flows back towards the body.

36°C   30°C   24°C   18°C   12°C

Vein

Heat transfer

Artery

37°C   31°C   25°C   19°C   13°C

Blood flow from the body core

Blood in the **artery** enters the limb at or near body core temperature. It cools as it flows towards the end of the limb, losing heat to the vein that flows alongside.

Capillary bed at the end of the limb

Cool environmental temperature: 10°C or below

On reaching the **capillary bed**, the (now cooler) arterial blood has less heat to lose to the environment.

Countercurrent heat exchange systems occur in both aquatic and terrestrial animals as an adaptation to maintaining a stable core temperature. The diagram illustrates the general principle of countercurrent heat exchangers: heat is exchanged between incoming and outgoing blood. In the flippers and fins of whales and dolphins, and the legs of aquatic birds, they minimize heat loss. In some terrestrial animals adapted to hot climates, the countercurrent exchange mechanism works in the opposite way to prevent the head from overheating: venous blood cools the arterial blood before it supplies the brain.

3. (a) Explain how a large body size assists in maintaining body temperature in both aquatic and terrestrial mammals:

_____

(b) Describe a way in which small terrestrial mammals compensate for more rapid heat loss from a high surface area:

_____

_____

4. (a) Explain how thick hair or fur assists in the regulation of body temperature in mammals: _____

_____

_____

(b) Explain why fur/hair thickness varies over different regions of a mammal's body: _____

_____

(c) Explain how you would expect fur thickness to vary between related mammal species at high and low altitude:

_____

(d) Explain how marine mammals compensate for lack of thick hair or fur: _____

_____

5. Giving an example, explain how countercurrent heat exchange systems assist in temperature regulation in mammals:

_____

_____

_____

6. (a) Describe the role that group behavior plays in temperature regulation in some mammals: _____

_____

(b) Name an animal, other than musk oxen, that uses this behavior: _____

(c) Describe another behavior, not reliant on a group, that is important in thermoregulation. For the behavior, suggest when and where it would occur, and comment on its adaptive value:

_____

_____

_____

Thermoregulation in Humans

In humans and other placental mammals, the temperature regulation centre of the body is in the **hypothalamus**. In humans, it has a 'set point' temperature of 36.7°C. The hypothalamus responds directly to changes in core temperature and to nerve impulses from receptors in the skin. It then coordinates appropriate nervous and hormonal responses to counteract the changes and restore normal body temperature. Like a thermostat, the hypothalamus detects a return to normal temperature and the corrective mechanisms are switched off (negative feedback). Toxins produced by pathogens, or substances released from some white blood cells, cause the set point to be set to a higher temperature. This results in fever and is an important defense mechanism in the case of infection.

Counteracting Heat Loss

Heat promoting center* in the hypothalamus monitors fall in skin or core temperature below 35.8°C and coordinates responses that generate and conserve heat. These responses are mediated primarily through the **sympathetic nerves** of the autonomic nervous system.

Thyroxine (together with adrenaline) **increases metabolic rate**.

Under conditions of *extreme* cold, adrenaline and thyroxine increase the energy releasing activity of the liver. Under normal conditions, the liver is thermally neutral.

Muscular activity (including *shivering*) produces internal heat.

Erector muscles of hairs contract to raise hairs and increase insulating layer of air. Blood flow to skin decreases (**vasoconstriction**).

Factors causing heat loss
- Wind chill factor accelerates heat loss through conduction.
- Heat loss due to temperature difference between the body and the environment.
- The rate of heat loss from the body is increased by being wet, by inactivity, dehydration, inadequate clothing, or shock.

Factors causing heat gain
- Gain of heat directly from the environment through radiation and conduction.
- Excessive fat deposits make it harder to lose the heat that is generated through activity.
- Heavy exercise, especially with excessive clothing.

*NOTE: The heat promoting center is also called the "cold centre" and the heat losing center is also called the "hot centre". We have used the terminology descriptive of the activities promoted by the center in each case.

Counteracting Heat Gain

Heat losing center* in the hypothalamus monitors any rise in skin or core temperature above 37.5°C and coordinates responses that increase heat loss. These responses are mediated primarily through the **parasympathetic nerves** of the autonomic nervous system.

Sweating increases. Sweat cools by evaporation.

Muscle tone and **metabolic rate** are decreased. These mechanisms reduce the body's heat output.

Blood flow to skin (**vasodilation**) increases. This increases heat loss.

Erector muscles of hairs relax to flatten hairs and decrease insulating air layer.

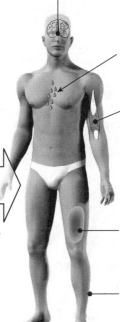

The Skin and Thermoregulation

Thermoreceptors in the dermis (probably free nerve endings) detect changes in skin temperature outside the normal range and send nerve impulses to the hypothalamus, which mediates a response. Thermoreceptors are of two types: **hot thermoreceptors** detect a rise in skin temperature above 37.5°C while the **cold thermoreceptors** detect a fall below 35.8°C. Temperature regulation by the skin involves **negative feedback** because the output is fed back to the skin receptors and becomes part of a new stimulus-response cycle.

Note that the thermoreceptors detect the temperature change, but the hair erector muscles and blood vessels are the **effectors** for mediating a response.

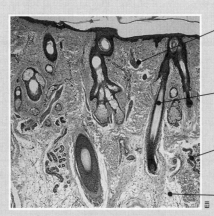

Cross section through the skin of the scalp.

Blood vessels in the dermis dilate (vasodilation) or constrict (vasoconstriction) to respectively promote or restrict heat loss.

Hairs raised or lowered to increase or decrease the thickness of the insulating air layer between the skin and the environment.

Sweat glands produce sweat in response to parasympathetic stimulation from the hypothalamus. Sweat cools through evaporation.

Fat in the subdermal layers insulates the organs against heat loss.

1. State two mechanisms by which body temperature could be reduced after intensive activity (e.g. hard exercise):

   (a) _____ (b) _____

2. Briefly state the role of the following in regulating internal body temperature:

   (a) The hypothalamus: _____

   (b) The skin: _____

   (c) Nervous input to effectors: _____

   (d) Hormones: _____

Related activities: Thermoregulation in Mammals, Fever

Nitrogenous Wastes in Animals

Waste materials are generated by the metabolic activity of cells. If allowed to accumulate, they would reach toxic concentrations and so must be continually removed. Excretion is the process of removing waste products and other toxins from the body. Waste products include carbon dioxide and water, and the nitrogenous (nitrogen containing) wastes that result from the breakdown of amino acids and nucleic acids. The simplest breakdown product of nitrogen containing compounds is ammonia, a small molecule that cannot be retained for long in the body because of its high

toxicity. Most aquatic animals excrete ammonia immediately into the water where it is washed away. Other animals convert the ammonia to a less toxic form that can remain in the body for a short time before being excreted via special excretory organs. The form of the excretory product in terrestrial animals (urea or uric acid) depends on the type of organism and its life history. Terrestrial animals that lay eggs produce uric acid rather than urea, because it is non-toxic and very insoluble. It remains as an inert solid mass in the egg until hatching.

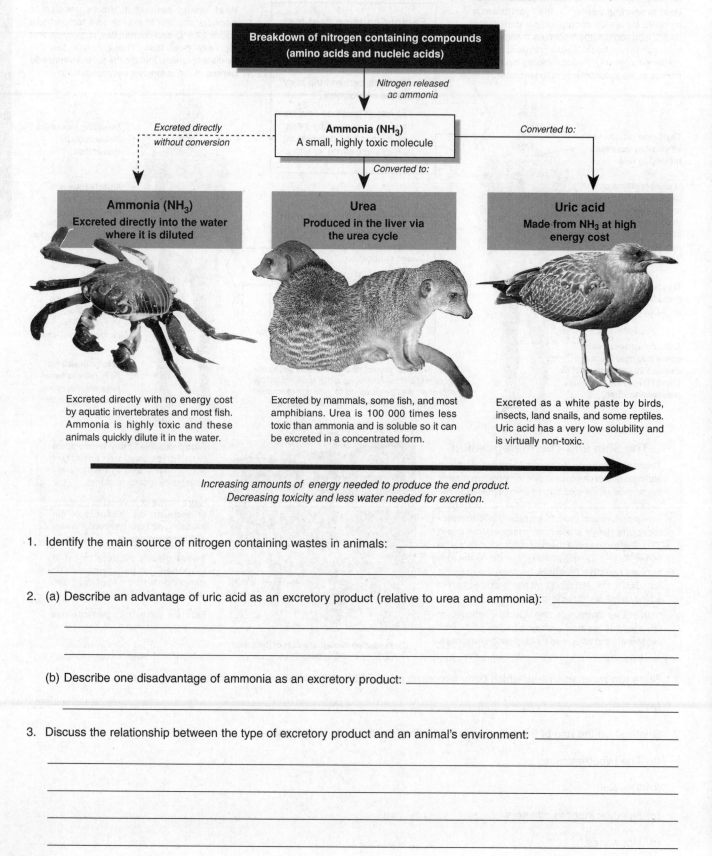

Breakdown of nitrogen containing compounds (amino acids and nucleic acids)

Nitrogen released as ammonia

Ammonia (NH₃)
A small, highly toxic molecule

Excreted directly without conversion

Converted to:

Converted to:

Ammonia (NH₃)
Excreted directly into the water where it is diluted

Urea
Produced in the liver via the urea cycle

Uric acid
Made from NH₃ at high energy cost

Excreted directly with no energy cost by aquatic invertebrates and most fish. Ammonia is highly toxic and these animals quickly dilute it in the water.

Excreted by mammals, some fish, and most amphibians. Urea is 100 000 times less toxic than ammonia and is soluble so it can be excreted in a concentrated form.

Excreted as a white paste by birds, insects, land snails, and some reptiles. Uric acid has a very low solubility and is virtually non-toxic.

Increasing amounts of energy needed to produce the end product.
Decreasing toxicity and less water needed for excretion.

1. Identify the main source of nitrogen containing wastes in animals: _____

_____

2. (a) Describe an advantage of uric acid as an excretory product (relative to urea and ammonia): _____

_____

_____

(b) Describe one disadvantage of ammonia as an excretory product: _____

_____

3. Discuss the relationship between the type of excretory product and an animal's environment: _____

_____

_____

_____

_____

Waste Products in Humans

In humans and other mammals, a number of organs are involved in the excretion of the waste products of metabolism: mainly the kidneys, lungs, skin, and gut. The liver is a particularly important organ in the initial treatment of waste products, particularly the breakdown of hemoglobin and the formation of urea from ammonia. Excretion should not be confused with the elimination or egestion of undigested and unabsorbed food material from the gut. Note that the breakdown products of hemoglobin (blood pigment) are excreted in bile and pass out with the feces, but they are not the result of digestion.

Homeostasis and Excretion

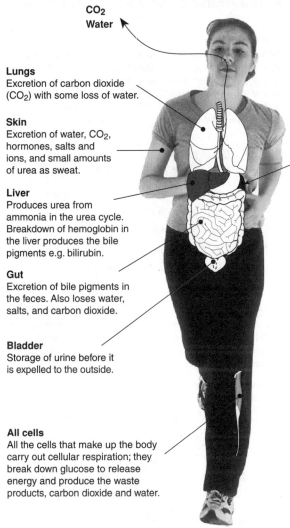

CO₂
Water

Lungs
Excretion of carbon dioxide (CO_2) with some loss of water.

Skin
Excretion of water, CO_2, hormones, salts and ions, and small amounts of urea as sweat.

Liver
Produces urea from ammonia in the urea cycle. Breakdown of hemoglobin in the liver produces the bile pigments e.g. bilirubin.

Gut
Excretion of bile pigments in the feces. Also loses water, salts, and carbon dioxide.

Bladder
Storage of urine before it is expelled to the outside.

All cells
All the cells that make up the body carry out cellular respiration; they break down glucose to release energy and produce the waste products, carbon dioxide and water.

Excretion In Humans

In mammals, the kidney is the main organ of excretion, although the skin, gut, and lungs also play important roles. As well as ridding the body of nitrogenous wastes, the kidney is also able to excrete many unwanted poisons and drugs that are taken in from the environment. Usually these are ingested with food or drink, or inhaled. As long as these are not present in toxic amounts, they can usually be slowly eliminated from the body.

Kidney
Filtration of the blood to remove urea. Unwanted ions, particularly hydrogen (H^+) and potassium (K^+), and some hormones are also excreted by the kidneys. Some poisons and drugs (e.g. penicillin) are also excreted by active secretion into the urine. Water is lost in excreting these substances and extra water may be excreted if necessary.

Substance	Origin*	Organ(s) of excretion
Carbon dioxide		
Water		
Bile pigments		
Urea		
Ions (K+, H+)		
Hormones		
Poisons		
Drugs		

* Origin refers to from where in the body each substance originates

1. In the diagram above, complete the table summarizing the origin of excretory products and the main organ (or organs) of excretion involved for each substance.

2. Explain the role of the liver in excretion, even though it is not an excretory organ itself: _____

_____

_____

3. Tests for pregnancy are sensitive to an excreted substance in the urine. Suggest what type of substance this might be:

_____

4. People sometimes suffer renal (kidney) failure, where the kidneys cease to operate and can no longer produce urine. Given that the kidney rids the body of excessive ions and water, as well as nitrogenous wastes, describe the probable effects of kidney failure. You may wish to discuss this as a group. HINT: Consider the effects of salt and water retention, and the effect of high salt levels on blood pressure and on the heart.

_____

_____

_____

_____

Related activities: Kidney Dialysis

A 3

Water Budget in Mammals

Water loss is a major problem for most mammals. The degree to which urine can be concentrated (and water conserved) depends on the number of nephrons present in the kidney and the length of the loop of Henle. The highest urine concentrations are found in mammals from desert environments, such as kangaroo rats (below). Under normal conditions these animals will not drink water, obtaining most of their water from the metabolic break down of food instead.

Regulation of Water Balance in Humans

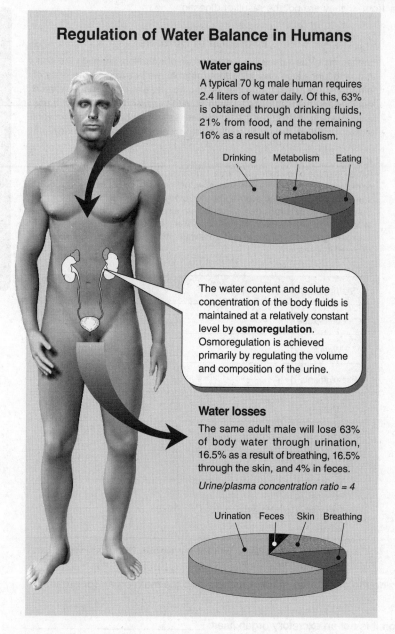

Water gains

A typical 70 kg male human requires 2.4 liters of water daily. Of this, 63% is obtained through drinking fluids, 21% from food, and the remaining 16% as a result of metabolism.

Drinking Metabolism Eating

The water content and solute concentration of the body fluids is maintained at a relatively constant level by **osmoregulation**. Osmoregulation is achieved primarily by regulating the volume and composition of the urine.

Water losses

The same adult male will lose 63% of body water through urination, 16.5% as a result of breathing, 16.5% through the skin, and 4% in feces.

Urine/plasma concentration ratio = 4

Urination Feces Skin Breathing

Adaptations of Arid Adapted Rodents

Most desert-dwelling mammals are adapted to tolerate a low water intake. Arid adapted rodents, such as jerboas and kangaroo rats, conserve water by reducing losses to the environment and obtain the balance of their water needs from the oxidation of dry foods (respiratory metabolism). The table below shows the water balance in a kangaroo rat after eating 100 g of dry pearl barley. Note the high urine to plasma concentration ratio relative to that of humans.

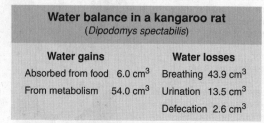

Water balance in a kangaroo rat (*Dipodomys spectabilis*)	
Water gains	**Water losses**
Absorbed from food 6.0 cm^3	Breathing 43.9 cm^3
From metabolism 54.0 cm^3	Urination 13.5 cm^3
	Defecation 2.6 cm^3

Urine/plasma concentration ratio = 17

Adaptations of kangaroo rats

Kangaroo rats, and other arid-adapted rodents, tolerate long periods without drinking, meeting their water requirements from the metabolism of dry foods. They dispose of nitrogenous wastes with very little output of water and they neither sweat nor pant to keep cool.

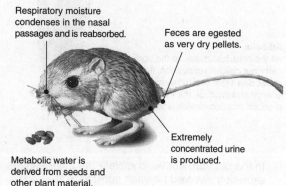

Respiratory moisture condenses in the nasal passages and is reabsorbed.

Feces are egested as very dry pellets.

Extremely concentrated urine is produced.

Metabolic water is derived from seeds and other plant material.

1. Explain why most mammals need to drink regularly: _____

_____

2. Using the tabulated data for the kangaroo rat (above), graph the water gains and losses in the space provided below.

3. Describe three physiological adaptations of desert adapted rodents to low water availability:

(a) _____

(b) _____

(c) _____

Water gains

Water losses

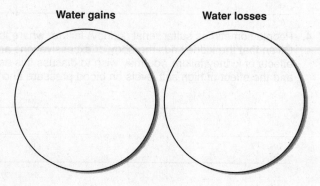

Related activities: Excretion and Osmoregulation

Excretion and Osmoregulation

Many aspects of metabolism, e.g. enzyme activity, membrane transport, and nerve conduction are dependent on particular concentrations of ions and metabolites. To achieve this balance, the salt and water content of the internal environment must be regulated; a process called **osmoregulation**. The mechanisms for obtaining, retaining, and eliminating water and solutes (including excretion of nitrogenous wastes) in marine, freshwater and terrestrial organisms vary considerably. Differences reflect both the constraints of the environment and the evolutionary inheritance of the organism.

Mechanisms against water loss

- Behavior and habitat choice
- Waxy cuticle of insects
- Oily secretion from glands in the skin
- Insulating fur or feathers
- Dry, scaly skin of reptiles

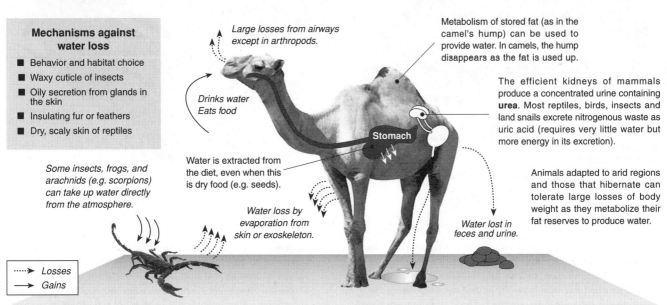

Large losses from airways except in arthropods.

Drinks water
Eats food

Metabolism of stored fat (as in the camel's hump) can be used to provide water. In camels, the hump disappears as the fat is used up.

The efficient kidneys of mammals produce a concentrated urine containing **urea**. Most reptiles, birds, insects and land snails excrete nitrogenous waste as uric acid (requires very little water but more energy in its excretion).

Some insects, frogs, and arachnids (e.g. scorpions) can take up water directly from the atmosphere.

Water is extracted from the diet, even when this is dry food (e.g. seeds).

Stomach

Animals adapted to arid regions and those that hibernate can tolerate large losses of body weight as they metabolize their fat reserves to produce water.

Water loss by evaporation from skin or exoskeleton.

Water lost in feces and urine.

····▶ Losses
——▶ Gains

The primary water balance problem for terrestrial animals is water loss. Water is required for all metabolism, including the metabolism of food and the disposal of waste products. Mammals must **drink water** regularly, although some are able to survive for long periods without drinking by generating water from the metabolism of fats. Mammals have efficient **kidneys** and produce a concentrated urine high in urea. In most land arthropods, water is conserved by limiting losses to the environment. The **chitinous exoskeleton** itself does not reduce water loss much but the waxy cuticle of insects retards water loss very effectively. The respiratory structures of arthropods are chitinous, internal tubes and there is little loss from these. All animals show behavioral adaptations to limiting water loss by seeking out damper environments. This is particularly important for desert animals and for arthropods with little resistance to dehydration.

Tolerance of water loss and burrowing behavior in desert frogs.

Behavioral adaptations, efficient kidneys, and thick fur in kangaroos.

Humidity seeking behavioral adaptations in woodlice.

Chitinous exoskeleton with waxy, waterproof cuticle in insects.

1. (a) Briefly describe four ways in which animals obtain water: _____

_____

(b) Identify three ways in which water is lost: _____

2. Discuss structural and behavioral adaptations for reducing water loss in a named arthropod **or** a named mammal:

_____

_____

_____

_____

_____

_____

_____

Marine Environments

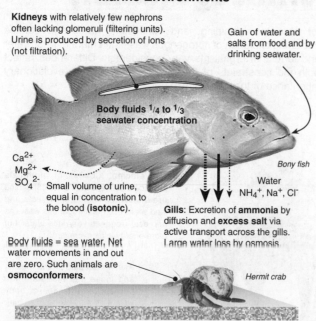

Kidneys with relatively few nephrons often lacking glomeruli (filtering units). Urine is produced by secretion of ions (not filtration).

Gain of water and salts from food and by drinking seawater.

Body fluids ¹/₄ to ¹/₃ seawater concentration

Bony fish

Ca^{2+}
Mg^{2+}
SO_4^{2-}

Small volume of urine, equal in concentration to the blood (**isotonic**).

Water
NH_4^+, Na^+, Cl^-

Gills: Excretion of **ammonia** by diffusion and **excess salt** via active transport across the gills. Large water loss by osmosis.

Body fluids = sea water. Net water movements in and out are zero. Such animals are **osmoconformers**.

Hermit crab

Freshwater Environments

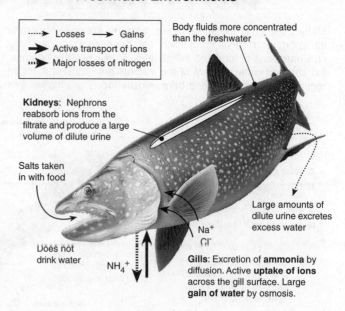

```
·····▷ Losses      ──▶ Gains
──▶ Active transport of ions
··■▶ Major losses of nitrogen
```

Body fluids more concentrated than the freshwater

Kidneys: Nephrons reabsorb ions from the filtrate and produce a large volume of dilute urine

Salts taken in with food

Does not drink water

NH_4^+

Na^+
Cl^-

Large amounts of dilute urine excretes excess water

Gills: Excretion of **ammonia** by diffusion. Active **uptake of ions** across the gill surface. Large **gain of water** by osmosis.

Most marine invertebrates do not regulate salt and water balance; they are **osmoconformers** and their body fluids fluctuate with changes in the environment. Animals, such as fish and marine mammals, that regulate their salt and water fluxes are termed **osmoregulatory**. Bony fish lose water osmotically and counter the loss by drinking salt water and excreting the excess salt. Marine elasmobranchs generate osmotic concentrations in their body fluids similar to seawater by tolerating high urea levels. Excess salt from the diet is excreted via a salt gland in the rectum. Marine mammals produce a urine that is high in both salt and urea. Some intertidal animals tolerate frequent dilutions of normal seawater and may actively take up salts across the gill surfaces to compensate for water gain and salt loss.

Freshwater animals have body fluids that are osmotically more concentrated than the water they live in. Water tends to enter their tissues by osmosis and must be expelled to avoid flooding the body. Simple protozoans use contractile vacuoles to collect the excess water and expel it. Other invertebrates expel water and nitrogenous wastes using simple nephridial organs. Bony fish and aquatic arthropods produce dilute urine (containing ammonia) and actively take up salts across their gills (in aquatic insects these are often non-respiratory, anal gills). The kidneys of **freshwater bony fish** (above) also reabsorb salts from the filtrate through active transport mechanisms. These ion gains are important because some loss of valuable ions occurs constantly as a result of the high urine volume.

Most marine invertebrates, like these sea anemones, are osmoconformers.

Elasmobranchs maintain an osmotic concentration similar to seawater.

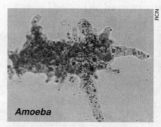

Contractile vacuoles in protozoans collect excess water and expel it.

In aquatic insect larvae, the gills actively take up salts from the water.

3. Describe how freshwater animals can compensate for salt losses that occur when they excrete large amounts of water:

_____

4. (a) Explain what is meant by an **osmoregulator** and give an example: _____

_____ Example: _____

(b) Explain what is meant by an **osmoconformer** and give an example: _____

_____ Example: _____

5. Freshwater and marine bony fish have contrasting excretion and osmoregulation problems. Explain why:

(a) Marine bony fish drink vast quantities of salt water: _____

(b) Freshwater bony fish do not drink water at all: _____

6. Describe the salt and water balance problems faced by migrating fish as they move from a marine environment to freshwater (as happens during spawning runs in salmon):

_____

_____

Invertebrate Excretory Systems

Metabolism produces toxic by-products. The most troublesome of these to eliminate from the body is nitrogenous waste from the metabolism of proteins and nucleic acids. The simplest and most common type of excretory organs, widely distributed in invertebrates, are simple tubes (**protonephridia** and **nephridia**) opening to the outside through a pore. The **malpighian tubules** of insects are highly efficient, removing nitrogenous wastes from the blood, and also functioning in **osmoregulation**. Note that all three forms of nitrogenous waste are represented here: ammonia (flatworms, annelids), urea (annelids), and uric acid (insects).

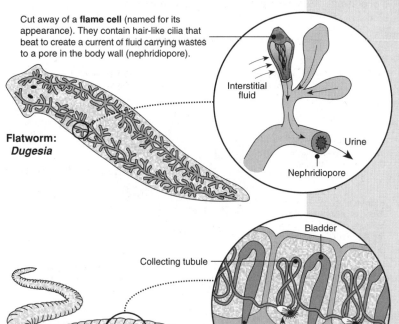

Cut away of a **flame cell** (named for its appearance). They contain hair-like cilia that beat to create a current of fluid carrying wastes to a pore in the body wall (nephridiopore).

Interstitial fluid

Urine

Nephridiopore

Flatworm: *Dugesia*

Platyhelminthes (flatworms)

Excretory system: **protonephridia**

Protonephridia are very simple excretory structures. Each protonephridium comprises a branched tubule ending in a number of blind capillaries called **flame cells**. **Ammonia** is excreted directly into the moist environment. Flatworms do not have a circulatory system or fluid-filled inner body spaces. They use their branching network of flame cells to regulate the composition of the fluid bathing the cells (interstitial fluid). Interstitial fluid enters the flame cell and is propelled along the tubule, away from the blind end, by beating cilia. Tubules merge into ducts that expel the urine through **nephridiopores**.

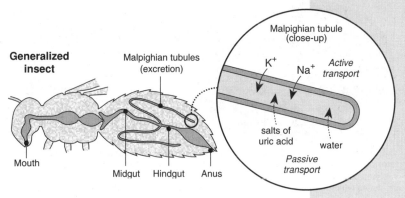

Bladder

Collecting tubule

Nephrostome

Nephridiopore

Earthworm

Annelids (segmented worms)

Excretory system: **nephridia**

In earthworms, each segment has a pair of excretory organs called **nephridia**, which drain the next segment in front. Fluid enters the nephrostome and passes through the collecting tubule. These tubules are surrounded by a capillary network of blood vessels (not shown here) which recover valuable salts from the developing urine. The collecting tubule empties into a storage bladder which expels the dilute urine (a mix of **ammonia** and **urea**) to the outside through the nephridiopore.

Insects

Excretory system: **malpighian tubules**

Generalized insect

Malpighian tubules (excretion)

Mouth

Midgut   Hindgut   Anus

Malpighian tubule (close-up)

K^+ Na^+ Active transport

salts of uric acid   water

Passive transport

Insects have two to several hundred **malpighian tubules** projecting from the junction of the midgut and hindgut. They bathe in the clear fluid (hemolymph) of the insect's body cavity where they actively pump K^+ and Na^+ into the tubule. Water, uric acid salts, and several other substances follow by passive transport. Water and some ions are reabsorbed in the hindgut, while **uric acid** precipitates out as a paste and is passed out of the anus along with the fecal material. The ability to conserve water by excreting solid uric acid has enabled insects to colonize very arid environments.

1. For each of the following, name the organs for excreting nitrogenous waste and state the form of the waste product:

(a) Flatworm: _____ Waste: _____

(b) Insect: _____ Waste: _____

(c) Earthworm: _____ Waste: _____

2. Explain briefly how insects concentrate their nitrogenous waste into a paste: _____

_____

_____

3. For one of the above animals, relate the form of the excretory product to the environment in which the animal lives:

_____

_____

Related activities: Nitrogenous Wastes in Animals

The Urinary System

The mammalian urinary system consists of the kidneys and bladder, and their associated blood vessels and ducts. The kidneys have a plentiful blood supply from the renal artery. The blood plasma is filtered by the kidneys to form urine. Urine is produced continuously, passing along the ureters to the bladder, a hollow muscular organ lined with smooth muscle and stretchable epithelium. Each day the kidneys filter about 180 liters of plasma.

Most of this is reabsorbed, leaving a daily urine output of about 1 liter. By adjusting the composition of the fluid excreted, the kidneys help to maintain the body's internal chemical balance. All vertebrates have kidneys, but their efficiency in producing a concentrated urine varies considerably. Mammalian kidneys are very efficient, producing a urine that is concentrated to varying degrees depending on requirements.

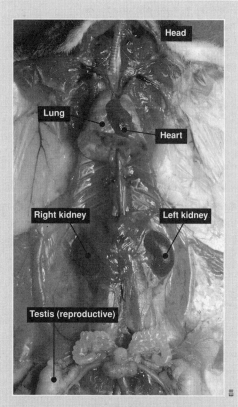

The kidneys of **rats** (above), humans, and other mammals are distinctive, bean shaped organs that lie at the back of the abdominal cavity to either side of the spine. The kidneys lie outside the peritoneum of the abdominal cavity and are partly protected by the lower ribs. Each kidney is surrounded by three layers of tissue. The innermost renal capsule is a smooth fibrous membrane that acts as a barrier against trauma and infection. The two outer layers comprise fatty tissue and fibrous connective tissue. These act to protect the kidney and anchor it firmly in place.

The Human Urinary System

Vena cava returns blood to the heart.

Dorsal aorta supplies oxygenated blood to the body.

Adrenal glands are associated with, but not part of, the urinary system.

Renal vein returns the blood from the kidney to the venous circulation.

Renal artery carries blood from the aorta into the kidney.

Kidney produces urine (blood filtration, the removal of waste products, and the regulation of blood volume).

Ureter carries urine to the bladder.

Bladder (sectioned) stores the urine before it passes out of the body. It can expand to hold about 80% of the daily urine output.

Urethra conducts urine from the bladder to the outside. The urethra is regulated by a voluntary sphincter muscle.

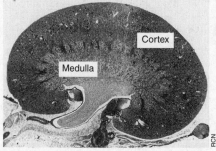

The very precise alignment of the nephrons (the filtering elements of the kidney) and their associated blood vessels gives the kidney tissue a striated appearance, as seen in this cross section.

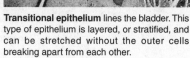

Transitional epithelium lines the bladder. This type of epithelium is layered, or stratified, and can be stretched without the outer cells breaking apart from each other.

1. Identify the components of the urinary system and describe their functions: _____

_____

_____

_____

2. Calculate the percentage of the plasma reabsorbed by the kidneys: _____

3. The kidney receives blood at a higher pressure than other organs. Suggest why this is the case: _____

_____

_____

4. Suggest why the kidneys are surrounded by fatty connective tissue: _____

_____

The Physiology of the Kidney

The functional unit of the kidney, the **nephron**, is a selective filter element, comprising a renal tubule and its associated blood vessels. Filtration, i.e. forcing fluid and dissolved substances through a membrane by pressure, occurs in the first part of the nephron, across the membranes of the capillaries and the glomerular capsule. The passage of water and solutes into the nephron and the formation of the glomerular filtrate depends on the pressure of the blood entering the afferent arteriole (below). If it increases, filtration rate increases; when it falls, glomerular filtration rate also falls. This process is so precisely regulated that, in spite of fluctuations in arteriolar pressure, glomerular filtration rate per day stays constant. After formation of the initial filtrate, the **urine** is modified through secretion and tubular reabsorption according to physiological needs at the time.

Homeostasis and Excretion

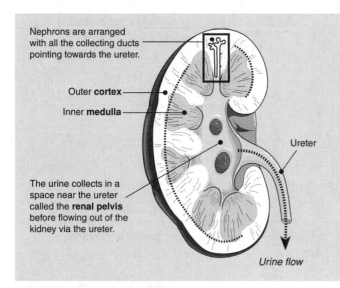

Nephrons are arranged with all the collecting ducts pointing towards the ureter.

Outer **cortex**

Inner **medulla**

Ureter

The urine collects in a space near the ureter called the **renal pelvis** before flowing out of the kidney via the ureter.

Urine flow

Internal Structure of the Human Kidney

Human kidneys are about 100-120 mm long and 25 mm thick. The functional unit of the kidney is the **nephron**. The other parts of the urinary system are primarily passageways and storage areas. The inner tissue of the kidney appears striated (striped), due to alignment of the nephrons and their surrounding blood vessels. It is the precise alignment of the nephrons in the kidney that makes it possible to fit in all the filtering units required. Each kidney contains more than 1 million nephrons. They are **selective filter elements**, which regulate blood composition and pH, and excrete wastes and toxins. The initial urine is formed by **filtration** in the glomerulus. Plasma is filtered through three layers: the capillary wall, and the basement membrane and epithelium of Bowman's capsule. The epithelium comprises very specialized epithelial cells called **podocytes**. The filtrate is modified as it passes through the tubules of the nephron and the final urine passes out the ureter.

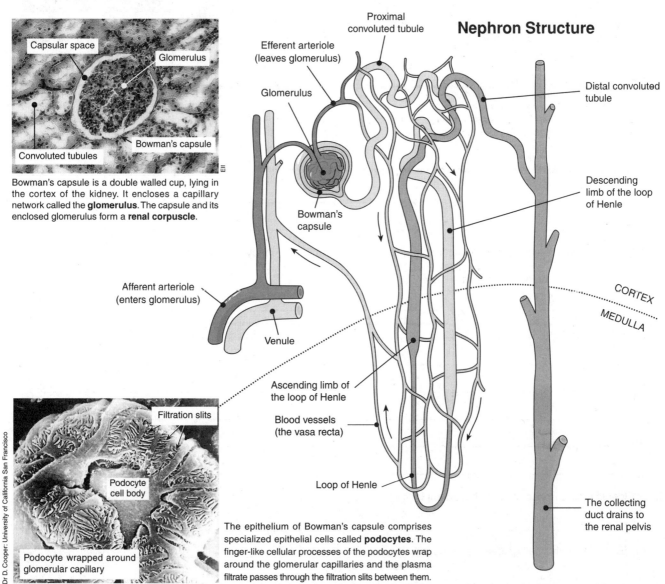

Capsular space

Glomerulus

Convoluted tubules

Bowman's capsule

Bowman's capsule is a double walled cup, lying in the cortex of the kidney. It encloses a capillary network called the **glomerulus**. The capsule and its enclosed glomerulus form a **renal corpuscle**.

Nephron Structure

Proximal convoluted tubule

Efferent arteriole (leaves glomerulus)

Glomerulus

Bowman's capsule

Afferent arteriole (enters glomerulus)

Venule

Ascending limb of the loop of Henle

Blood vessels (the vasa recta)

Loop of Henle

Distal convoluted tubule

Descending limb of the loop of Henle

CORTEX

MEDULLA

The collecting duct drains to the renal pelvis

Filtration slits

Podocyte cell body

Podocyte wrapped around glomerular capillary

Dr D. Cooper: University of California San Francisco

The epithelium of Bowman's capsule comprises specialized epithelial cells called **podocytes**. The finger-like cellular processes of the podocytes wrap around the glomerular capillaries and the plasma filtrate passes through the filtration slits between them.

Related activities: The Urinary System

A 3

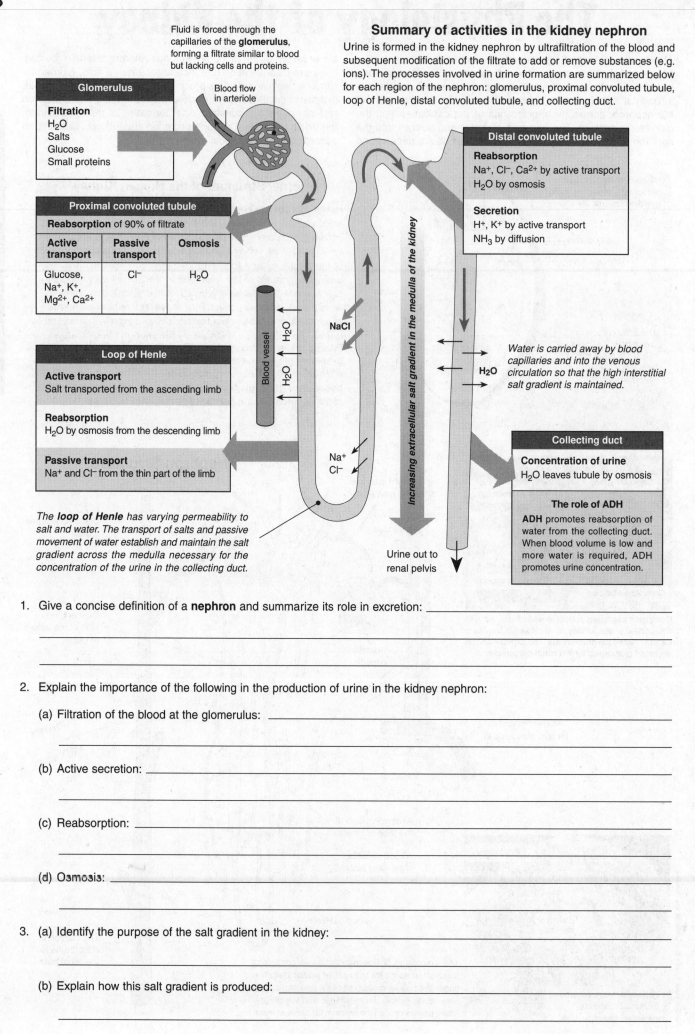

Fluid is forced through the capillaries of the **glomerulus**, forming a filtrate similar to blood but lacking cells and proteins.

Glomerulus

Filtration
H_2O
Salts
Glucose
Small proteins

Blood flow in arteriole

Proximal convoluted tubule

Reabsorption of 90% of filtrate

Active transport	Passive transport	Osmosis
Glucose, Na^+, K^+, Mg^{2+}, Ca^{2+}	Cl^-	H_2O

Loop of Henle

Active transport
Salt transported from the ascending limb

Reabsorption
H_2O by osmosis from the descending limb

Passive transport
Na^+ and Cl^- from the thin part of the limb

The **loop of Henle** has varying permeability to salt and water. The transport of salts and passive movement of water establish and maintain the salt gradient across the medulla necessary for the concentration of the urine in the collecting duct.

Blood vessel

H_2O
H_2O

NaCl

Na^+
Cl^-

Increasing extracellular salt gradient in the medulla of the kidney

Urine out to renal pelvis

H_2O

Summary of activities in the kidney nephron

Urine is formed in the kidney nephron by ultrafiltration of the blood and subsequent modification of the filtrate to add or remove substances (e.g. ions). The processes involved in urine formation are summarized below for each region of the nephron: glomerulus, proximal convoluted tubule, loop of Henle, distal convoluted tubule, and collecting duct.

Distal convoluted tubule

Reabsorption
Na^+, Cl^-, Ca^{2+} by active transport
H_2O by osmosis

Secretion
H^+, K^+ by active transport
NH_3 by diffusion

Water is carried away by blood capillaries and into the venous circulation so that the high interstitial salt gradient is maintained.

Collecting duct

Concentration of urine
H_2O leaves tubule by osmosis

The role of ADH
ADH promotes reabsorption of water from the collecting duct. When blood volume is low and more water is required, ADH promotes urine concentration.

1. Give a concise definition of a **nephron** and summarize its role in excretion: _____

_____

_____

2. Explain the importance of the following in the production of urine in the kidney nephron:

(a) Filtration of the blood at the glomerulus: _____

_____

(b) Active secretion: _____

_____

(c) Reabsorption: _____

_____

(d) Osmosis: _____

_____

3. (a) Identify the purpose of the salt gradient in the kidney: _____

_____

(b) Explain how this salt gradient is produced: _____

_____

Control of Kidney Function

Variations in salt and water intake, and in the environmental conditions to which we are exposed, contribute to fluctuations in blood volume and composition. The primary role of the kidneys is to regulate blood volume and composition (including the removal of nitrogenous wastes), so that homeostasis is maintained. This is achieved through varying the volume and composition of the urine. Two hormones, antidiuretic hormone and aldosterone, are involved in the process.

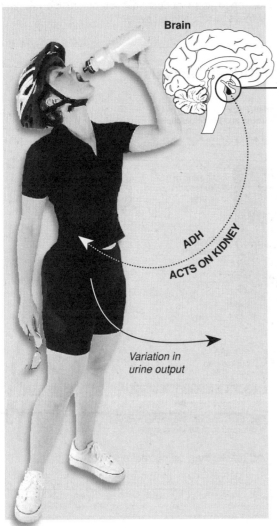

Brain

ADH ACTS ON KIDNEY

Variation in urine output

Control of Blood Volume

Osmoreceptors in the hypothalamus of the brain detect a fall in the concentration of water in the blood. They stimulate **neurosecretory cells in the hypothalamus** to synthesize and secrete the hormone ADH (antidiuretic hormone).

ADH passes from the hypothalamus to the posterior pituitary where it is released into the blood. ADH increases the permeability of the kidney collecting duct to water so that more water is reabsorbed and urine volume decreases.

Factors inhibiting ADH release
- High fluid intake
- High blood volume
- Low blood sodium levels
- Alcohol consumption

ADH levels decrease

Water reabsorption decreases. Urine output increases.

Factors causing ADH release
- Low fluid intake
- Low blood volume
- High blood sodium levels
- Nicotine and morphine

ADH levels increase

Water reabsorption increases. Urine output decreases.

Factors causing release of aldosterone

Low blood volumes also stimulate secretion of aldosterone from the adrenal cortex. This is mediated through a complex pathway involving the hormone renin from the kidney.

Aldosterone

Sodium reabsorption increases, water follows, blood volume restored.

1. (a) *Diabetes insipidus* is a type of diabetes, caused by a lack of ADH. Based on what you know of the role of ADH in kidney function describe the symptoms of this disease:

_____

_____

(b) Suggest how this disorder might be treated: _____

_____

2. Explain why alcohol consumption (especially to excess) causes dehydration and thirst: _____

_____

_____

3. (a) State the effect of aldosterone on the kidney nephron: _____

(b) Explain the net result of this effect: _____

4. Explain how negative feedback mechanisms operate to regulate blood volume and urine output:

_____

_____

_____

Kidney Dialysis

A dialysis machine is a machine designed to remove wastes from the blood. It is used when the kidneys fail, or when blood acidity, urea, or potassium levels increase much above normal. In kidney dialysis, blood flows through a system of tubes composed of partially permeable membranes. Dialysis fluid (dialyzate) has a composition similar to blood except that the concentration of wastes is low. It flows in the opposite direction to the blood on the outside of the dialysis tubes. Consequently, waste products like urea diffuse from the blood into the dialysis fluid, which is constantly replaced. The dialysis fluid flows at a rate of several 100 cm³ per minute over a large surface area. For some people dialysis is an ongoing procedure, but for others dialysis just allows the kidneys to rest and recover.

Principles of Kidney Dialysis

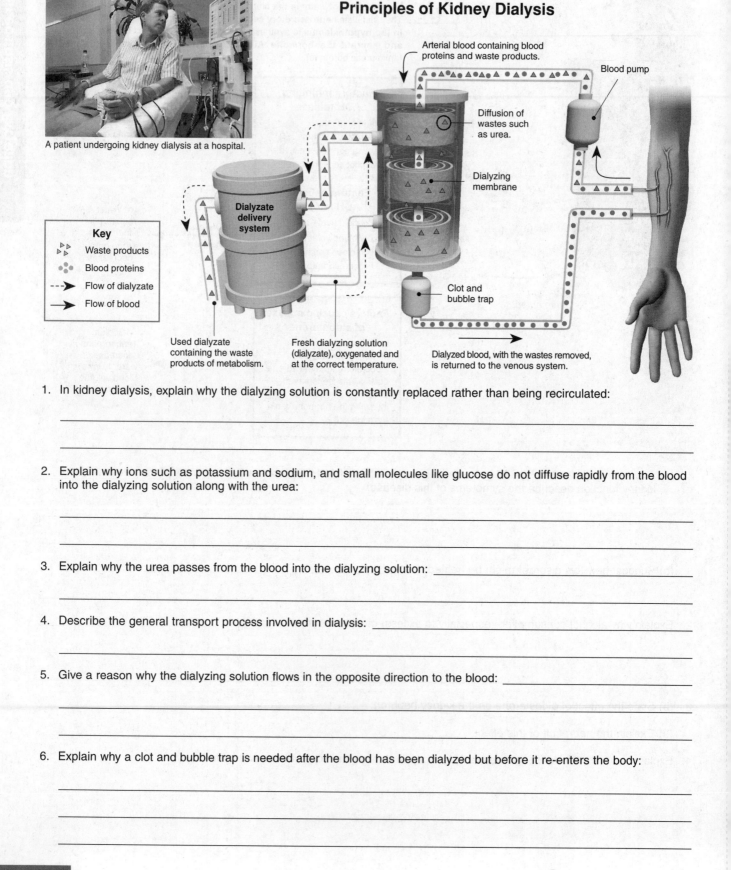

A patient undergoing kidney dialysis at a hospital.

Key
▷▷ Waste products
•° Blood proteins
---→ Flow of dialyzate
——→ Flow of blood

Arterial blood containing blood proteins and waste products.

Blood pump

Diffusion of wastes such as urea.

Dialyzing membrane

Dialyzate delivery system

Clot and bubble trap

Used dialyzate containing the waste products of metabolism.

Fresh dialyzing solution (dialyzate), oxygenated and at the correct temperature.

Dialyzed blood, with the wastes removed, is returned to the venous system.

1. In kidney dialysis, explain why the dialyzing solution is constantly replaced rather than being recirculated:

   _____

   _____

2. Explain why ions such as potassium and sodium, and small molecules like glucose do not diffuse rapidly from the blood into the dialyzing solution along with the urea:

   _____

   _____

3. Explain why the urea passes from the blood into the dialyzing solution: _____

   _____

4. Describe the general transport process involved in dialysis: _____

   _____

5. Give a reason why the dialyzing solution flows in the opposite direction to the blood: _____

   _____

6. Explain why a clot and bubble trap is needed after the blood has been dialyzed but before it re-enters the body:

   _____

   _____

Nerves, Muscles, and Movement

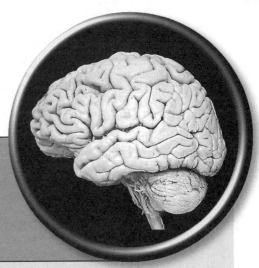

IB SL	IB HL	IB Options	AP Biology
Complete: 1, 4, 10, 12-13, 15-16, 18	Complete: 1, 4, 10, 12-13, 15-16, 18, 27, 29, 32-33	Complete: Option B: SL: 27, 29, 32-34, 36-41 Option E: SL/HL: 11, 19-25 HL: 5-9	Complete: 1-41 Some numbers extension as appropriate

Learning Objectives

☐ 1. Compile your own glossary from the **KEY WORDS** displayed in **bold type** in the learning objectives below.

Nervous Systems *(page 286 and the TRC: Invertebrate Nervous Systems)*

☐ 2. Compare the structure and function of nervous systems in invertebrates, including cnidarians, echinoderms, flatworms, annelids, and arthropods. Describe the trend towards increasing **cephalization** in these taxa and relate it to behavior and sensory development.

☐ 3. Compare the **brain structure** of different vertebrates and relate any differences to the animal's evolutionary history, its environment, and its sensory requirements.

Mammalian Nervous Systems *(pages 284-28)*

☐ 4. Describe the organization of the nervous system, distinguishing between the **central nervous system** (CNS) and the **peripheral nerves** (PNS). State that the nervous system is composed of specialized **neurons** that carry electrical impulses rapidly around the body.

☐ 5. Identify the functional role of the two major divisions of the nervous system (CNS and PNS).

☐ 6. Draw the gross structure of the **brain**, including the **medulla oblongata**, **cerebellum**, **hypothalamus**, **pituitary gland**, and **cerebral hemispheres**. State one function for each of these parts. Describe an example of brain malfunction, e.g. **Alzheimer's disease**.

☐ 7. Recognize the two divisions of the PNS: **sensory division** and **motor division**. Know that the motor division of the PNS is divided into **autonomic** and **somatic nervous systems** and state the role of each.

☐ 8. Recognize the components of the autonomic nervous system (**ANS**): the **sympathetic** and **parasympathetic neurons** (nervous systems). Describe their roles and recognize that they have generally **antagonistic** effects.

☐ 9. Describe the effects of the sympathetic and parasympathetic systems in the control of bladder emptying, pupil diameter, or heart rate and force of contraction. Describe some reflex autonomic activity can be modified by conscious control.

Neuron Structure and Function *(pages 289-294)*

☐ 10. Describe, using diagrams, the structure and function of different types of **neurons**: **motor** (**effector**) and **sensory neurons**, and **relay neurons** (**interneurons**).

☐ 11. Describe the adaptive value a **reflex**. Using an annotated diagram, describe a simple spinal **reflex arc** involving three neurons. Outline examples of reflexes: the **pain withdrawal reflex** and one other spinal reflex, and the pupil reflex and one other **cranial reflex**. Discuss how the pupil reflex is used to test for brain death.

☐ 12. Explain how the **resting potential** of a neuron is established. Include reference to the movement of Na^+ and K^+, the differential permeability of the membrane, and the generation of an **electrochemical gradient**.

☐ 13. Describe the generation of the **nerve impulse** with reference to the change in **membrane permeability** of the nerve leading to **depolarization**.

☐ 14. Describe how an **action potential** is propagated along a myelinated nerve by **saltatory conduction**. Include reference to the **all-or-nothing** nature of the impulse, and role of **myelin** and the **nodes of Ranvier**.

☐ 15. Describe impulse conduction in a **non-myelinated** nerve. Appreciate the difference in speed of conduction between myelinated and non-myelinated fibers.

☐ 16. Identify the role of synapses in the mammalian nervous system. Describe the basic features of a **cholinergic synapse** (as seen using electron microscopy).

☐ 17. With reference to **acetylcholine** and **noradrenaline**, recognize that the synapses of the PNS are classified according the **neurotransmitter** involved.

☐ 18. Explain the principles of synaptic transmission, e.g. at a **cholinergic synapse**. Include reference to the arrival of the **action potential** at the **presynaptic terminal**, the role of Ca^{2+} and **neurotransmitter**, the depolarization of the **post-synaptic neuron**, and subsequent removal of the neurotransmitter. Recognize the **neuromuscular junction** as a specialized cholinergic synapse.

☐ 19. Explain how presynaptic neurons can encourage or inhibit postsynaptic transmission. Appreciate the role of synapses in **unidirectionality** and **integration** through **summation** and **inhibition**.

☐ 20. Describe the effects of neurotransmitters and **psycho-active** drugs on the nervous system and behavior, as illustrated by pain and the action of **endorphins** and **enkephalins**, and Parkinson's and the role of excitatory and inhibitory psychoactive drugs and **dopamine**.

Perception of Stimuli *(pages 283, 295 and the TRC: Sensory Systems, Hearing)*

☐ 21. Describe how senses are used to provide information about the environment. Distinguish between internal and external **stimuli** and give examples of sensory receptors that respond to these, as illustrated by mechanoreceptors, photoreceptors, chemoreceptors, and thermoreceptors. Know that sensory receptors act as **biological transducers**.

Vision *(pages 296-298, and TRC: Visual Defects)*

☐ 22. Using a diagram, describe the basic structure and function of the human **eye**. Include reference to the transmission and refraction of light and the focusing of the image (including **accommodation**).

☐ 23. Annotate a diagram of the **retina**, including identification of the **rods**, **cones**, **bipolar neurons**, **ganglion cells**, and the direction of light movement.

☐ 24. Describe the structure and function of the photo-receptor cells (**rods** and **cones**) in the retina, including the role of the photosensitive pigments, photoreception in bright and dim light, the basis of monochromatic and trichromatic vision, and the neural basis for differences in **sensitivity** and **acuity** between rods and cones.

☐ 25. Outline how visual stimuli are processed in the retina, including reference to generator potentials in the rod or cone cells and action potentials in the **optic nerve**. In as much detail as required, explain the role of the **visual cortex** in processing visual information.

Muscles and Movement *(page 299-304, and the TRC: Animal Symmetry)*

☐ 26. Outline the diversity of **locomotion** in animals as illustrated by: movement in an earthworm, swimming in bony fish, flying in birds, and walking in an arthropod.

☐ 27. Describe the roles of the **nerves**, (skeletal) **muscles**, and **bones** in producing movement or locomotion.

☐ 28. Identify the components of the **musculoskeletal system** and the main regions of the human skeleton. Describe the structure of a **long bone**, including the features conferring strength and shock absorption.

☐ 29. Using an annotated diagram, describe the structure and function of the **elbow joint**, including reference to: **cartilage, synovial fluid, tendons, ligaments,** and named **bones** and **antagonistic muscles**.

☐ 30. Describe the ultrastructure of compact (hard) bone, identifying the periosteum, osteoblasts, **osteocytes,** matrix, lacunae, and **Haversian canals.**

☐ 31. Distinguish between **cardiac muscle, skeletal** (striated) **muscle,** and **smooth muscle,** with reference to their gross structure, physiology, and functional role.

☐ 32. Describe the structure of **skeletal muscle fibers,** as seen with electron microscopy. Identify the **sarcomere** and **myofibrils,** and describe the composition and arrangement of the **(myo)filaments.**

☐ 33. Explain how skeletal muscle contracts. As required, discuss the role of **actin** and **myosin filaments, ATP,** the **sarcoplasmic reticulum,** and **calcium ions.**

☐ 34. Explain the differences in **speed** and **stamina** of **fast twitch** and **slow twitch (tonic) fibers.**

☐ 35. Describe how movement is achieved by **antagonistic muscle action.** Identify the role of reflex inhibition in the movement of antagonistic muscle pairs.

Energy and exercise *(pages 307-309, and TRC & Web links: Muscle Fatigue, Effects of Training)*

☐ 36. Define VO2 and VO2max. Recognize the relationship between fitness and VO2max.

☐ 37. Identify sources of energy for muscle contraction and describe ATP production in muscle during exercise of varying intensity and duration. In terms of energy yield and waste products, compare **aerobic** and **anaerobic** pathways as sources of ATP for muscle contraction,.

☐ 38. Explain **muscle fatigue** and relate it to the increase in **blood lactate,** depletion of carbohydrate supplies, and decreased pH. Explain how these changes provide the stimulus for increased breathing (and heart) rates.

☐ 39. Explain what is meant by **oxygen debt.** Describe the ultimate fate of blood lactate and explain how the oxygen debt is repaid after intense exercise.

☐ 40. Discuss speed and stamina as measures of **fitness.** Discuss the causes, prevention, and treatment of **injuries.** Debate the use of performance enhancing drugs, including anabolic steroids, in sport.

☐ 41. Explain the effects of training on human physiology:
- The effect on the cardiovascular system: blood flow, heart (pulse) rate, **stroke volume, cardiac output.**
- The effect on the respiratory system: breathing rate, **tidal volume,** residual volume, ventilation efficiency.
- The muscles: development of specific fiber types.

See the 'Textbook Reference Grid' on pages 8-9 for textbook page references relating to material in this topic.

Supplementary Texts

See pages 5-6 for additional details of these texts:

■ Adds, J. *et al.* 2003. **Respiration and Coordination** (NelsonThornes), chpt. 2-3 as reqd.

■ Clegg, C.J., 1998. **Mammals: Structure and Function** (John Murray), pp. 58-69, 72-77.

■ Helms, D.R. *et al.,* 1998. **Biology in the Laboratory** (W.H. Freeman), #33, #37, #41.

■ Morton, D. & J.W. Perry, 1998. **Photo Atlas for Anatomy and Physiology** (W.H. Freeman).

See page 6 for details of publishers of periodicals:

STUDENT'S REFERENCE

■ **Skeletal Muscle: Is Bigger Always Better?** Biol. Sci. Rev., 11(2) Nov. 1998, pp. 36-39. *The structure of muscle and physiology of contraction.*

■ **The Autonomic Nervous System** Bio. Sci. Rev. 11(4) March 1999, pp. 30-34. *The structure and function of the autonomic nervous system.*

■ **The Nervous System** (series) New Scientist, 10 June 1989, 11 Nov. 1989, 29 June 1991 (Inside Science). *Nervous system structure and function.*

■ **What's Your Poison** Bio. Sci. Rev. 16(2) Nov. 2003, pp. 33-37. *The action of naturally derived poisons on synaptic transmission. This account includes an account of toxins and their actions.*

■ **A Pacinian Corpuscle** Biol. Sci. Rev., 12(3) Jan. 2000, pp. 33-34. *An account of the structure and operation of a common pressure receptor.*

■ **Before Your Very Eyes** New Scientist 15 March 1997 (Inside Science). *Eye structure, and the perception and processing of visual information.*

■ **Making the Connection** Biol. Sci. Rev.,13(3) Jan. 2001, pp. 10-13. *The central nervous system, neurotransmitters, and synapses.*

■ **Remodelling the Eye** Biol. Sci. Rev., 17(2) Nov. 2004, pp. 9-12. *An account of the structure of the human eye and disorders of vision.*

■ **Neuroscience** Biol. Sci. Rev., 19(1) Sept. 2006, pp. 32-35. *How the brain processes information, brain disorders and the future of neuroscience.*

■ **Color Vision and Color Blindness** Biol. Sci. Rev., 19(3) Feb. 2007, pp. 28-32. *Color is a quality our brains give to light based on the different sensitivities of three types of cones in the retina to different wavelengths of light.*

■ **In the Realm of Your Senses** New Scientist, 31 Jan. 2004, pp. 40-43. *There is a genetic basis to our highly individualized sensory responses.*

TEACHER'S REFERENCE

■ **Electrify Your Mind** New Scientist, 15 April 2006, pp. 34-37. *Transcranial direct current stimulation (tDCS) may make fully functioning brains work even better.*

■ **How Neurons Work: An Analogy & Demonstration Using a Sparkler & a Frying Pan** The Am. Biology Teacher, 68(7), Sept. 2006, pp. 412-417. *Simulating how neurons generate and propagate action potentials.*

■ **Acting Out Muscle Contraction** The Am. Biology Teacher, 65(2), Feb. 2003, pp. 128-132. *An experiment to demonstrate muscle contraction.*

■ **Demonstrating the Stretch Reflex** The Am. Biology Teacher, 62(7), Sept., 2000, pp. 503-507. *Demonstrating muscular coordination and control.*

See pages 10-11 for details of how to access **Bio Links** from our web site: **www.thebiozone.com** From Bio Links, access sites under the topics:

GENERAL BIOLOGY ONLINE RESOURCES > Online Textbooks and Lecture Notes: • S-Cool! A level biology revision guide • Learn.co.uk • Mark Rothery's biology web site ... *and others* **ANIMAL BIOLOGY:** • Comparative vertebrate anatomy lecture notes • Anatomy and physiology • Human physiology lecture notes • WebAnatomy ... *and others* > **Neuroscience:** • Basic neural processes • Cow's eye dissection • Nervous system • Seeing, hearing, smelling the world • The human eye • The effects of LSD on the human brain ... *and others* > **Support & Movement:** • Bone and joint sources • Energy production during physical activity • Exercise physiology • Muscle structure and function • Muscles ... *and others*

Software and video resources for this topic are provided on the Teacher Resource CD-ROM

Detecting Changing States

A **stimulus** is any physical or chemical change in the environment capable of provoking a response in an organism. Animals respond to stimuli in order to survive. This response is adaptive; it acts to maintain the organism's state of homeostasis. Stimuli may be either external (outside the organism) or internal (within its body). Some of the stimuli to which humans and other mammals respond are described below, together with the sense organs that detect and respond to these stimuli. Note that sensory receptors respond only to specific stimuli. The sense organs an animal possesses therefore determine how it perceives the world.

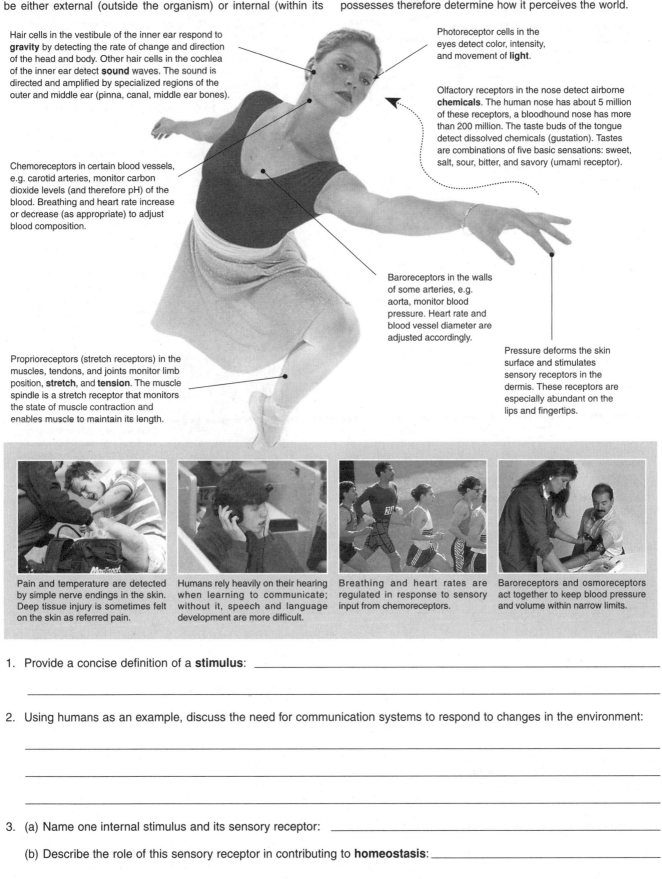

Hair cells in the vestibule of the inner ear respond to **gravity** by detecting the rate of change and direction of the head and body. Other hair cells in the cochlea of the inner ear detect **sound** waves. The sound is directed and amplified by specialized regions of the outer and middle ear (pinna, canal, middle ear bones).

Photoreceptor cells in the eyes detect color, intensity, and movement of **light**.

Olfactory receptors in the nose detect airborne **chemicals**. The human nose has about 5 million of these receptors, a bloodhound nose has more than 200 million. The taste buds of the tongue detect dissolved chemicals (gustation). Tastes are combinations of five basic sensations: sweet, salt, sour, bitter, and savory (umami receptor).

Chemoreceptors in certain blood vessels, e.g. carotid arteries, monitor carbon dioxide levels (and therefore pH) of the blood. Breathing and heart rate increase or decrease (as appropriate) to adjust blood composition.

Baroreceptors in the walls of some arteries, e.g. aorta, monitor blood pressure. Heart rate and blood vessel diameter are adjusted accordingly.

Proprioreceptors (stretch receptors) in the muscles, tendons, and joints monitor limb position, **stretch**, and **tension**. The muscle spindle is a stretch receptor that monitors the state of muscle contraction and enables muscle to maintain its length.

Pressure deforms the skin surface and stimulates sensory receptors in the dermis. These receptors are especially abundant on the lips and fingertips.

Pain and temperature are detected by simple nerve endings in the skin. Deep tissue injury is sometimes felt on the skin as referred pain.

Humans rely heavily on their hearing when learning to communicate; without it, speech and language development are more difficult.

Breathing and heart rates are regulated in response to sensory input from chemoreceptors.

Baroreceptors and osmoreceptors act together to keep blood pressure and volume within narrow limits.

Nerves, Muscles and Movement

1. Provide a concise definition of a **stimulus**: _____

   _____

2. Using humans as an example, discuss the need for communication systems to respond to changes in the environment:

   _____

   _____

   _____

3. (a) Name one internal stimulus and its sensory receptor: _____

   (b) Describe the role of this sensory receptor in contributing to **homeostasis**: _____

   _____

   _____

Related activities: The Basis of Sensory Perception
Web links: Sensory Systems, Hearing

A 2

The Mammalian Nervous System

The **nervous system** is the body's control and communication center. It has three broad functions: detecting stimuli, interpreting them, and initiating appropriate responses. Its basic structure is outlined below. Further detail is provided in the following pages.

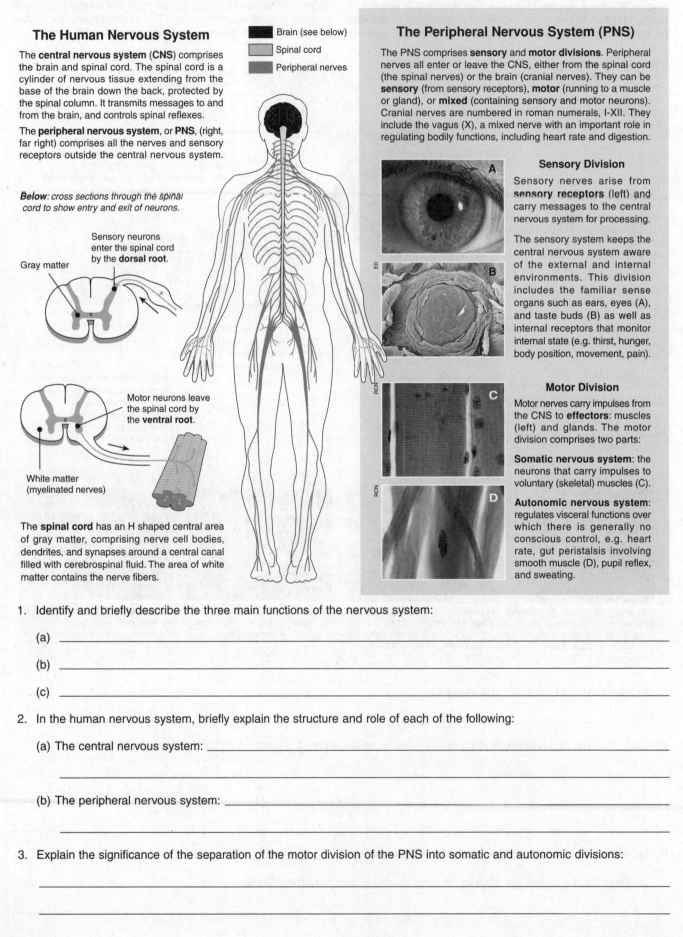

The Human Nervous System

The **central nervous system** (CNS) comprises the brain and spinal cord. The spinal cord is a cylinder of nervous tissue extending from the base of the brain down the back, protected by the spinal column. It transmits messages to and from the brain, and controls spinal reflexes.

The **peripheral nervous system**, or **PNS**, (right, far right) comprises all the nerves and sensory receptors outside the central nervous system.

Below: cross sections through the spinal cord to show entry and exit of neurons.

Gray matter

Sensory neurons enter the spinal cord by the **dorsal root**.

Motor neurons leave the spinal cord by the **ventral root**.

White matter (myelinated nerves)

The **spinal cord** has an H shaped central area of gray matter, comprising nerve cell bodies, dendrites, and synapses around a central canal filled with cerebrospinal fluid. The area of white matter contains the nerve fibers.

Brain (see below)
Spinal cord
Peripheral nerves

The Peripheral Nervous System (PNS)

The PNS comprises **sensory** and **motor divisions**. Peripheral nerves all enter or leave the CNS, either from the spinal cord (the spinal nerves) or the brain (cranial nerves). They can be **sensory** (from sensory receptors), **motor** (running to a muscle or gland), or **mixed** (containing sensory and motor neurons). Cranial nerves are numbered in roman numerals, I-XII. They include the vagus (X), a mixed nerve with an important role in regulating bodily functions, including heart rate and digestion.

Sensory Division

Sensory nerves arise from **sensory receptors** (left) and carry messages to the central nervous system for processing.

The sensory system keeps the central nervous system aware of the external and internal environments. This division includes the familiar sense organs such as ears, eyes (A), and taste buds (B) as well as internal receptors that monitor internal state (e.g. thirst, hunger, body position, movement, pain).

Motor Division

Motor nerves carry impulses from the CNS to **effectors**: muscles (left) and glands. The motor division comprises two parts:

Somatic nervous system: the neurons that carry impulses to voluntary (skeletal) muscles (C).

Autonomic nervous system: regulates visceral functions over which there is generally no conscious control, e.g. heart rate, gut peristalsis involving smooth muscle (D), pupil reflex, and sweating.

1. Identify and briefly describe the three main functions of the nervous system:

    (a) _____

    (b) _____

    (c) _____

2. In the human nervous system, briefly explain the structure and role of each of the following:

    (a) The central nervous system: _____

    _____

    (b) The peripheral nervous system: _____

    _____

3. Explain the significance of the separation of the motor division of the PNS into somatic and autonomic divisions:

    _____

    _____

    _____

Related activities: Nervous Regulatory Systems, The Autonomic Nervous System

The Autonomic Nervous System

The **autonomic nervous system** (ANS) regulates involuntary visceral functions by means of **reflexes**. Although most autonomic nervous system activity is beyond our conscious control, voluntary control over some basic reflexes (such as bladder emptying) can be learned. Most visceral effectors have dual innervation, receiving fibers from both branches of the ANS. These two branches, the **parasympathetic** and **sympathetic** divisions, have broadly opposing actions on the organs they control (excitatory or inhibitory). Nerves in the parasympathetic

division release acetylcholine. This neurotransmitter is rapidly deactivated at the synapse and its effects are short lived and localized. Most sympathetic postganglionic nerves release noradrenaline, which enters the bloodstream and is deactivated slowly. Hence, sympathetic stimulation tends to have more widespread and long lasting effects than parasympathetic stimulation. Aspects of autonomic nervous system structure and function are illustrated below. The arrows indicate nerves to organs or ganglia (concentrations of nerve cell bodies).

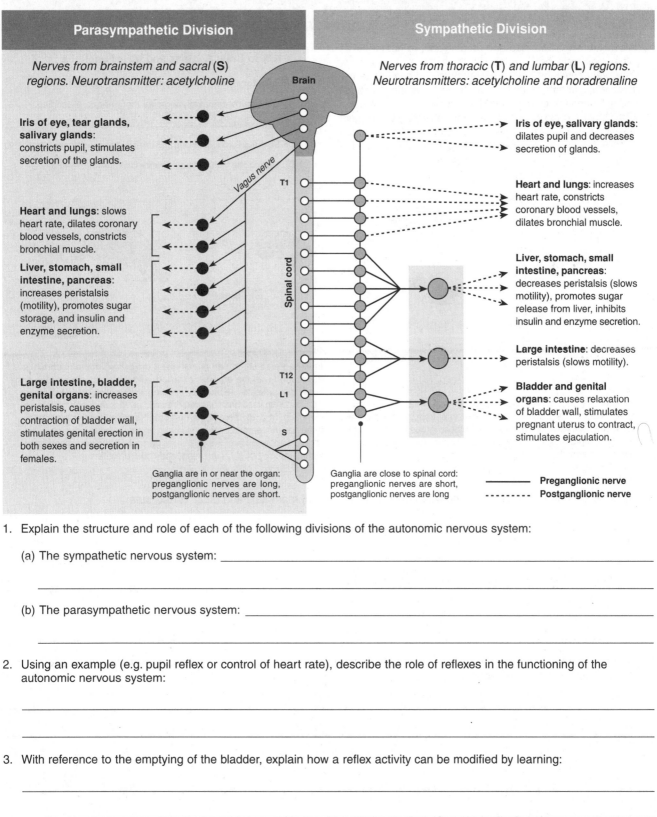

Parasympathetic Division

Nerves from brainstem and sacral (S) regions. Neurotransmitter: acetylcholine

Iris of eye, tear glands, salivary glands: constricts pupil, stimulates secretion of the glands.

Heart and lungs: slows heart rate, dilates coronary blood vessels, constricts bronchial muscle.

Liver, stomach, small intestine, pancreas: increases peristalsis (motility), promotes sugar storage, and insulin and enzyme secretion.

Large intestine, bladder, genital organs: increases peristalsis, causes contraction of bladder wall, stimulates genital erection in both sexes and secretion in females.

Ganglia are in or near the organ: preganglionic nerves are long, postganglionic nerves are short.

Sympathetic Division

Nerves from thoracic (T) and lumbar (L) regions. Neurotransmitters: acetylcholine and noradrenaline

Iris of eye, salivary glands: dilates pupil and decreases secretion of glands.

Heart and lungs: increases heart rate, constricts coronary blood vessels, dilates bronchial muscle.

Liver, stomach, small intestine, pancreas: decreases peristalsis (slows motility), promotes sugar release from liver, inhibits insulin and enzyme secretion.

Large intestine: decreases peristalsis (slows motility).

Bladder and genital organs: causes relaxation of bladder wall, stimulates pregnant uterus to contract, stimulates ejaculation.

Ganglia are close to spinal cord: preganglionic nerves are short, postganglionic nerves are long

⎯⎯⎯⎯ **Preganglionic nerve**
------- **Postganglionic nerve**

Brain · Vagus nerve · Spinal cord · T1 · T12 · L1 · S

Nerves, Muscles and Movement

1. Explain the structure and role of each of the following divisions of the autonomic nervous system:

   (a) The sympathetic nervous system: _____

   _____

   (b) The parasympathetic nervous system: _____

   _____

2. Using an example (e.g. pupil reflex or control of heart rate), describe the role of reflexes in the functioning of the autonomic nervous system:

   _____

   _____

3. With reference to the emptying of the bladder, explain how a reflex activity can be modified by learning:

   _____

   _____

   _____

Related activities: Learned Behavior   **RA 2**

The Vertebrate Brain

The vertebrate brain develops as an expansion of the anterior end of the neural tube in embryos. The forebrain, midbrain, and hindbrain can be seen very early in development, with further differentiation as development continues. The brains of fish and amphibians are relatively unspecialized, with a rudimentary cerebrum and cerebellum. The reptiles show the first real expansion of the cerebrum, with the gray matter external in the cortex. In the birds and mammals, the brain is relatively large, with well developed cerebral and cerebellar regions. In primitive vertebrates, the cerebral regions act primarily as olfactory centers. In higher vertebrates, the cerebrum takes over the many of the functions of other regions of the brain (e.g. the optic lobes), becoming the primary integration center of the brain. The cerebellum also becomes more important as locomotor and other muscular activities increase in complexity. The relative sizes of different regions of vertebrate brains are shown below.

Vertebrate Brains

All vertebrates, from fish and amphibians, to humans and other mammals, have brains with the same basic structure. The brain develops from a hollow tube and comprises the forebrain, midbrain, and hindbrain (which runs into the spinal cord). During the course of vertebrate evolution some parts of the brain (e.g. the medulla) have remained largely unchanged, retaining their primitive functions. Other parts (e.g. the cerebrum of the forebrain) have expanded and taken on new functions.

Key to Brain Regions and their Functions

- **Olfactory bulb**: Receives and processes olfactory signals.
- **Cerebrum**: Behavior, complex thought and reasoning.
- **Cerebellum**: Center for controlling movement and balance.
- **Medulla**: Reflex functions and relay for sensory information.
- **Optic lobe**: Receives and processes visual information.

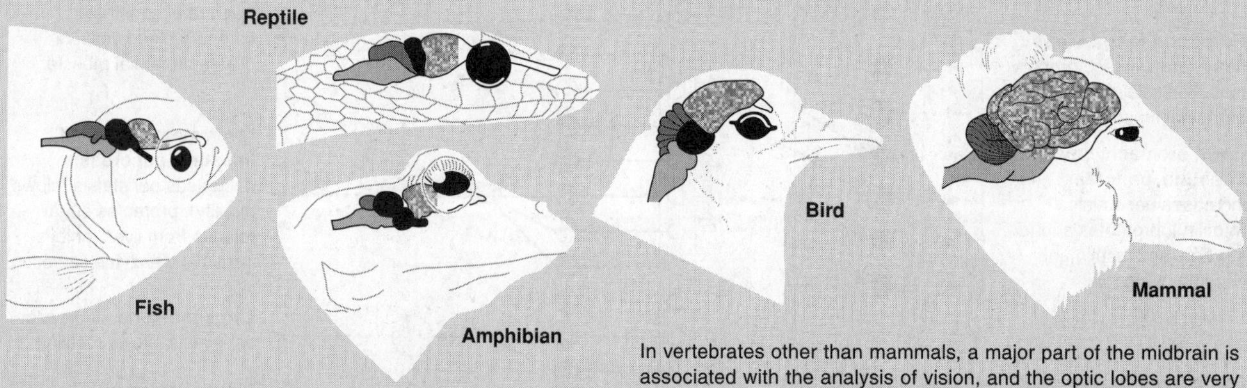

Reptile

Fish

Amphibian

Bird

Mammal

The medulla (part of the hindbrain) in fish, amphibians, and reptiles is prominent. It relays sensory information to or from parts of the brain associated with sensory processing. In these groups both the optic lobe (visual processing) and the centers associated with processing olfactory information (in the thalamus) are also large.

In vertebrates other than mammals, a major part of the midbrain is associated with the analysis of vision, and the optic lobes are very large. In mammals, the analysis of vision is a function of the forebrain. The forebrain itself has changed dramatically in size during vertebrate evolution. In birds most of the cerebrum is associated with complex behavior. In mammals, there has been an progressive increase in the size and importance of the cerebrum; particularly the parts associated with complex thought, reasoning, and communication.

1. (a) Describe one major difference between the brain structure of mammals and other vertebrates:

_____

_____

(b) Suggest what brain structure can tell us about the sensory perception of an animal: _____

_____

_____

2. Discuss the trends in brain development during the course of vertebrate evolution and relate these to changes to changes in lifestyle and behavior:

_____

_____

_____

_____

_____

_____

_____

Related activities: The Human Brain

The Human Brain

The brain is one the largest organs in the body. It is protected by the skull, the meninges (membranous coverings), and the cerebrospinal fluid (CSF). The brain is the control center for the body. It receives a constant flow of information from the senses, but responds only to what is important at the time. Some responses are very simple (e.g. cranial reflexes), whilst others require many levels of processing. The human brain is noted for its large, well developed cerebral region, and the region responsible for complex thought and reasoning. Each cerebral hemisphere is divided into four lobes by deep sulci or fissures. These lobes: temporal, frontal, occipital, and parietal, correspond to the bones of the skull under which they lie.

Primary Structural Regions of the Brain

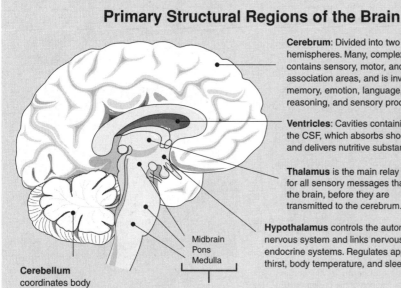

Cerebrum: Divided into two cerebral hemispheres. Many, complex roles. It contains sensory, motor, and association areas, and is involved in memory, emotion, language, reasoning, and sensory processing.

Ventricles: Cavities containing the CSF, which absorbs shocks and delivers nutritive substances.

Thalamus is the main relay center for all sensory messages that enter the brain, before they are transmitted to the cerebrum.

Hypothalamus controls the autonomic nervous system and links nervous and endocrine systems. Regulates appetite, thirst, body temperature, and sleep.

Midbrain
Pons
Medulla

Cerebellum coordinates body movements, posture, and balance.

Brainstem: Relay center for impulses between the rest of the brain and the spinal cord. Controls breathing, heartbeat, and the coughing and vomiting reflexes.

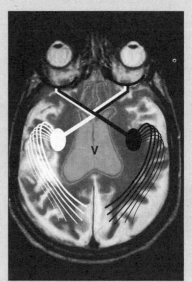

MRI scan of the brain viewed from above. The visual pathway has been superimposed on the image. Note the crossing of sensory neurons to the opposite hemisphere and the fluid filled ventricles (V) in the center.

Sensory and Motor Regions in the Cerebrum

General sensory area receives sensations from receptors in the skin, muscles and viscera. Sensory information from receptors on one side of the body crosses over to the opposite side of the cerebral cortex where conscious sensations are produced. The size of the sensory region for different body parts depends on the number of receptors in that particular body part.

Visual areas within the occipital lobe receive, interpret, and evaluate visual stimuli. In vision, each eye views both sides of the visual field but the brain receives impulses from left and right visual fields separately (see photo caption above). The visual cortex combines the images into a single impression or **perception** of the image.

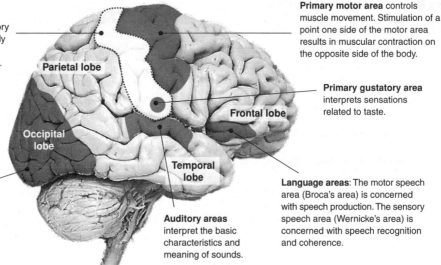

Parietal lobe

Occipital lobe

Temporal lobe

Frontal lobe

Primary motor area controls muscle movement. Stimulation of a point one side of the motor area results in muscular contraction on the opposite side of the body.

Primary gustatory area interprets sensations related to taste.

Language areas: The motor speech area (Broca's area) is concerned with speech production. The sensory speech area (Wernicke's area) is concerned with speech recognition and coherence.

Auditory areas interpret the basic characteristics and meaning of sounds.

1. For each of the following bodily functions, identify the region(s) of the brain involved in its control:

(a) Breathing and heartbeat: _____

(b) Memory and emotion: _____

(c) Posture and balance: _____

(d) Autonomic functions: _____

(e) Visual processing: _____

(f) Body temperature: _____

(g) Language: _____

Related activities: The Development of Intelligence

A 2

Nerves, Muscles and Movement

The Malfunctioning Brain: The Effects of Alzheimer's Disease

Alzheimer's disease is a disabling neurological disorder affecting about 5% of the population over 65. Its causes are largely unknown, its effects are irreversible, and it has no cure. Sufferers of Alzheimer's have trouble remembering recent events and they become confused and forgetful. In the later stages of the disease, people with Alzheimer's become very disorientated, lose past memories, and may become paranoid and moody. Dementia and loss of reason occur at the end stages of the disease.

Cerebral cortex: Conscious thought, reasoning, and language. Alzheimer's sufferers show considerable loss of function from this region.

Hippocampus: A swelling in the floor of the lateral ventricle. It contains complex foldings of the cortical tissue and is involved in the establishment of memory patterns. In Alzheimer's sufferers, it is one of the first regions to show loss of neurons and accumulation of amyloid.

It is not uncommon for Alzheimer's sufferers to wander and become lost and disorientated.

Upper Brain	Lower Brain
Normal	

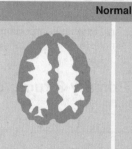 

Early Alzheimer's

 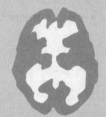

Late Alzheimer's

 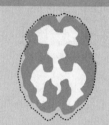

Alzheimer's is associated with accelerated loss of neurons, particularly in regions of the brain that are important for memory and intellectual processing, such as the cerebral cortex and hippocampus. The disease has been linked to abnormal accumulations of protein-rich **amyloid** plaques, which invade the brain tissue and interfere with synaptic transmission. The brain scans above show diminishing brain function in certain areas of the brain in Alzheimer's sufferers. Note, particularly in the two lower scans, how much the brain has shrunk (original size indicated by the dotted line). Light areas indicate brain activity.

(h) Muscular contraction: _____

(i) Sensory processing related to taste: _____

(j) Sensory processing related to sound: _____

2. Describe the likely effect of a loss of function (through injury) to the primary motor area in the left hemisphere:

_____

_____

3. Describe the role of the ventricles of the brain: _____

_____

_____

4. Some loss of neuronal function occurs normally as a result of aging. Identify the features distinguishing Alzheimer's disease from normal age related loss of neuronal function:

_____

_____

_____

Neuron Structure and Function

The nervous and endocrine systems are the body's regulatory and coordinating systems. Homeostasis depends on the ability of the nervous system to detect, interpret, and respond to, internal and external conditions. Sensory receptors relay information to the central nervous system (CNS) where it is interpreted and responses are coordinated. The information is transmitted along nerve cells (**neurons**) as electrical impulses. The speed of impulse conduction depends primarily on the axon diameter and whether or not the axon is myelinated (see below). Within the tolerable physiological range, an increase in temperature also increases the speed of impulse conduction: in cool environments, impulses travel faster in endothermic than in ectothermic vertebrates. Neurons typically consist of a cell body, dendrites, and an axon. Basic types are described below.

The Structure of Neurons

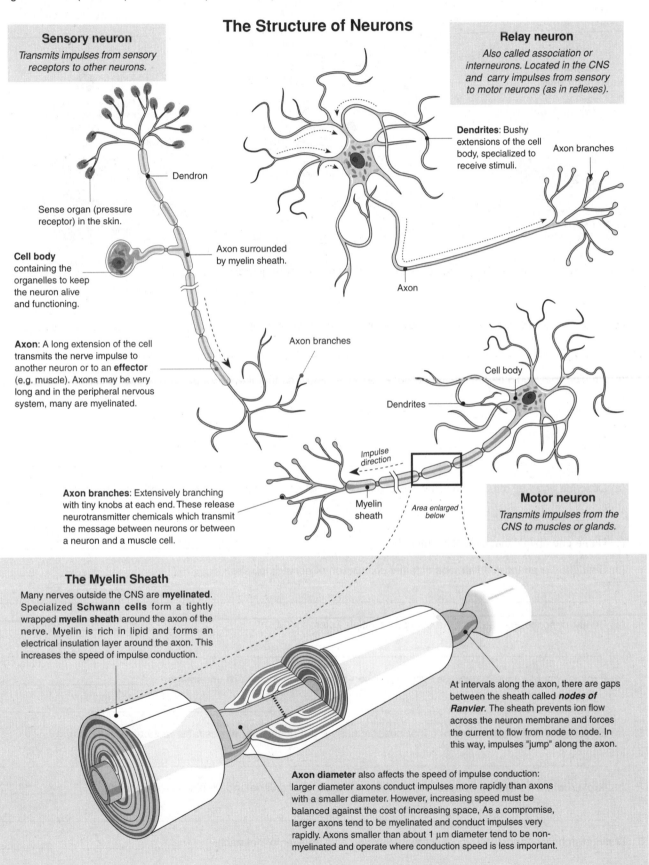

Sensory neuron

Transmits impulses from sensory receptors to other neurons.

Dendron

Sense organ (pressure receptor) in the skin.

Cell body containing the organelles to keep the neuron alive and functioning.

Axon: A long extension of the cell transmits the nerve impulse to another neuron or to an **effector** (e.g. muscle). Axons may be very long and in the peripheral nervous system, many are myelinated.

Axon surrounded by myelin sheath.

Axon branches: Extensively branching with tiny knobs at each end. These release neurotransmitter chemicals which transmit the message between neurons or between a neuron and a muscle cell.

Axon branches

Impulse direction

Myelin sheath

Area enlarged below

Relay neuron

Also called association or interneurons. Located in the CNS and carry impulses from sensory to motor neurons (as in reflexes).

Dendrites: Bushy extensions of the cell body, specialized to receive stimuli.

Axon branches

Axon

Cell body

Dendrites

Motor neuron

Transmits impulses from the CNS to muscles or glands.

The Myelin Sheath

Many nerves outside the CNS are **myelinated**. Specialized **Schwann cells** form a tightly wrapped **myelin sheath** around the axon of the nerve. Myelin is rich in lipid and forms an electrical insulation layer around the axon. This increases the speed of impulse conduction.

At intervals along the axon, there are gaps between the sheath called ***nodes of Ranvier***. The sheath prevents ion flow across the neuron membrane and forces the current to flow from node to node. In this way, impulses "jump" along the axon.

Axon diameter also affects the speed of impulse conduction: larger diameter axons conduct impulses more rapidly than axons with a smaller diameter. However, increasing speed must be balanced against the cost of increasing space, As a compromise, larger axons tend to be myelinated and conduct impulses very rapidly. Axons smaller than about 1 μm diameter tend to be non-myelinated and operate where conduction speed is less important.

Nerves, Muscles and Movement

Related activities: The Mammalian Nervous System, Nervous Regulatory Systems
Web links: Nerve Action Potential

RA 2

A reflex is an automatic response to a stimulus involving a small number of neurons and a central nervous system (CNS) processing point (usually the spinal cord, but sometimes the brain stem). This type of circuit is often called a **reflex arc**. Reflexes permit rapid responses to stimuli. They are classified according to the number of CNS synapses involved; **monosynaptic reflexes** involve only one CNS synapse (e.g. knee jerk), **polysynaptic reflexes** involve two or more (e.g. pain withdrawal reflex). Both are spinal reflexes. The pupil reflex (opening and closure of the pupil) is an example of a cranial reflex.

Pain Withdrawal: A Polysynaptic Reflex Arc

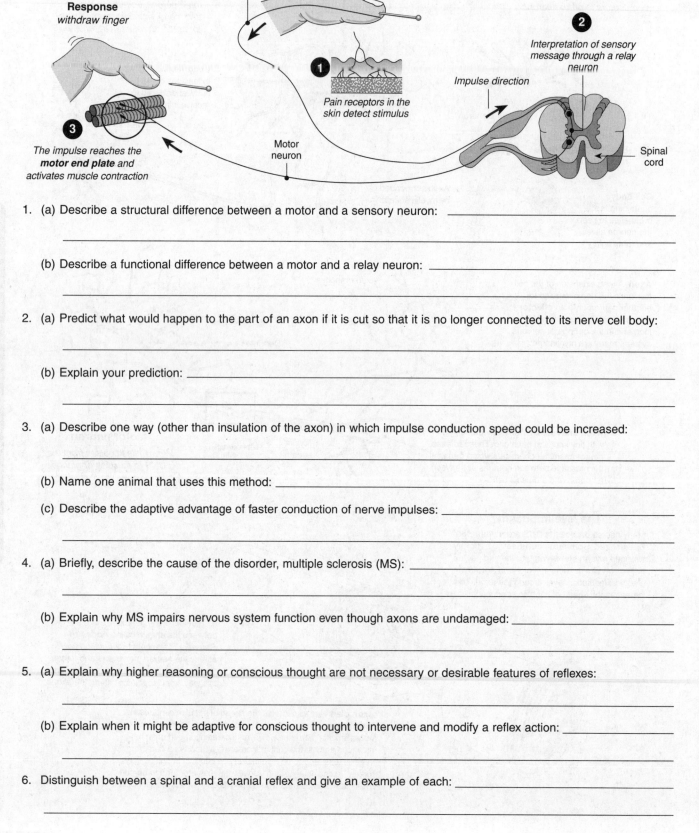

1. (a) Describe a structural difference between a motor and a sensory neuron: _____

    _____

    (b) Describe a functional difference between a motor and a relay neuron: _____

    _____

2. (a) Predict what would happen to the part of an axon if it is cut so that it is no longer connected to its nerve cell body:

    _____

    (b) Explain your prediction: _____

    _____

3. (a) Describe one way (other than insulation of the axon) in which impulse conduction speed could be increased:

    _____

    (b) Name one animal that uses this method: _____

    (c) Describe the adaptive advantage of faster conduction of nerve impulses: _____

    _____

4. (a) Briefly, describe the cause of the disorder, multiple sclerosis (MS): _____

    _____

    (b) Explain why MS impairs nervous system function even though axons are undamaged: _____

    _____

5. (a) Explain why higher reasoning or conscious thought are not necessary or desirable features of reflexes:

    _____

    (b) Explain when it might be adaptive for conscious thought to intervene and modify a reflex action: _____

    _____

6. Distinguish between a spinal and a cranial reflex and give an example of each: _____

    _____

Transmission of Nerve Impulses

Neurons, like all cells, contain ions or charged atoms. Those of special importance include sodium (Na⁺), potassium (K⁺), and negatively charged proteins. Neurons are **electrically excitable** cells: a property that results from the separation of ion charge either side of the neuron membrane. They may exist in either a resting or stimulated state. When stimulated, neurons produce electrical impulses that are transmitted along the axon. These impulses are transmitted between neurons across junctions called **synapses**. Synapses enable the transmission of impulses rapidly all around the body.

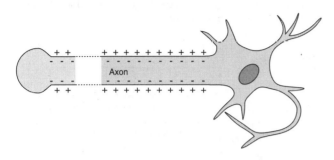

Impulse travels in this direction

Na⁺ Na⁺

Area of impulse

Next area to be stimulated

Area returning to resting state

The Resting Neuron

When a neuron is not transmitting an impulse, the inside of the cell is negatively charged compared with the outside of the cell. The cell is said to be electrically polarized, because the inside and the outside of the cell are oppositely charged. The potential difference (voltage) across the membrane is called the resting potential and for most nerve cells is about -70 mV. Nerve transmission is possible because this membrane potential exists.

The Nerve Impulse

When a neuron is stimulated, the distribution of charges on each side of the membrane changes. For a millisecond, the charges reverse. This process, called **depolarization**, causes a burst of electrical activity to pass along the axon of the neuron. As the charge reversal reaches one region, local currents depolarize the next region. In this way the impulse spreads along the axon. An impulse that spreads this way is called an **action potential**.

The Action Potential

The depolarization described above can be illustrated as a change in membrane potential (in millivolts). In order for an action potential to be generated, the stimulation must be strong enough to reach the **threshold** potential; this is the potential (voltage) at which the depolarization of the membrane becomes "unstoppable" and the action potential is generated. The action potential is **all or none** in its generation. Either the **threshold** is reached and the action potential is generated or the nerve does not fire. The resting potential is restored by the movement of potassium ions (K⁺) out of the cell. During this **refractory period**, the nerve cannot respond.

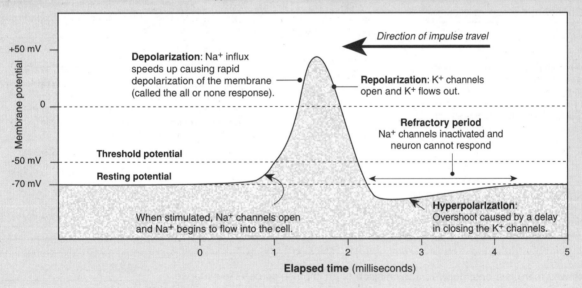

1. Explain how an action potential is able to pass along a nerve: _____

2. Explain how the refractory period influences the direction in which an impulse will travel: _____

3. Action potentials themselves are indistinguishable from each other. Explain how the nervous system is able to interpret the impulses correctly and bring about an appropriate response:

Related activities: Chemical Synapses   RA 2

Nerves, Muscles and Movement

Chemical Synapses

Action potentials are transmitted between neurons across synapses: junctions between the end of one axon and the dendrite or cell body of a receiving neuron. **Chemical synapses** are the most widespread type of synapse in nervous systems. The axon terminal is a swollen knob, and a small gap separates it from the receiving neuron. The synaptic knobs are filled with tiny packets of chemicals called **neurotransmitters**. Transmission involves the diffusion of the neurotransmitter across the gap, where it interacts with the receiving membrane and causes an electrical response. The response of a receiving cell to the arrival of a neurotransmitter depends on the nature of the cell itself, on its location in the nervous system, and on the neurotransmitter involved. Synapses that release acetylcholine (ACh) are termed **cholinergic**. In the example below, ACh causes membrane depolarization and the generation of an action potential (termed excitation or an excitatory response).

A Cholinergic Synapse

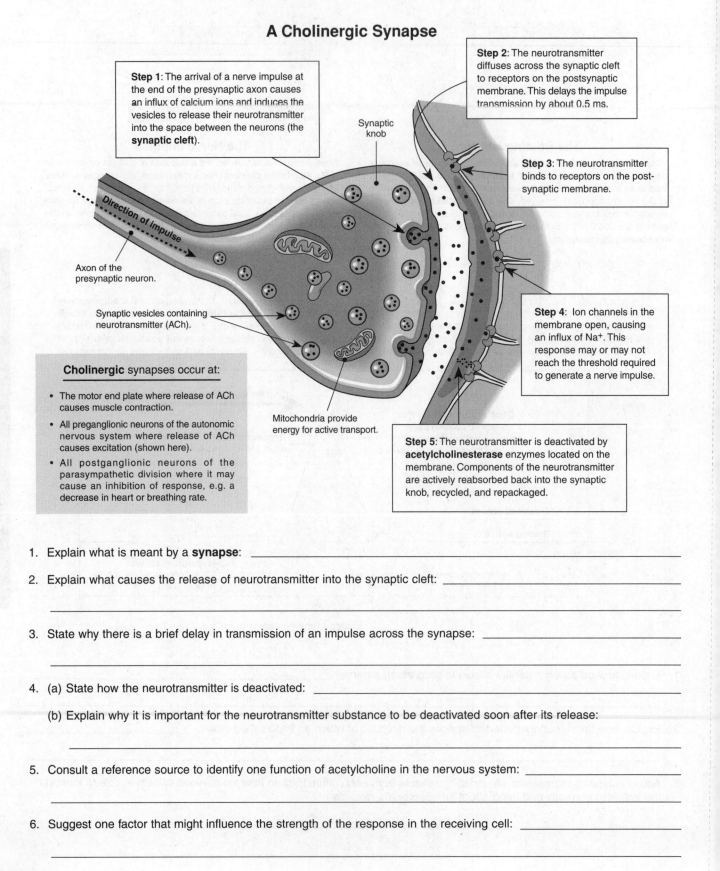

Step 1: The arrival of a nerve impulse at the end of the presynaptic axon causes an influx of calcium ions and induces the vesicles to release their neurotransmitter into the space between the neurons (the **synaptic cleft**).

Step 2: The neurotransmitter diffuses across the synaptic cleft to receptors on the postsynaptic membrane. This delays the impulse transmission by about 0.5 ms.

Step 3: The neurotransmitter binds to receptors on the post-synaptic membrane.

Step 4: Ion channels in the membrane open, causing an influx of Na^+. This response may or may not reach the threshold required to generate a nerve impulse.

Step 5: The neurotransmitter is deactivated by **acetylcholinesterase** enzymes located on the membrane. Components of the neurotransmitter are actively reabsorbed back into the synaptic knob, recycled, and repackaged.

Synaptic knob

Direction of impulse

Axon of the presynaptic neuron.

Synaptic vesicles containing neurotransmitter (ACh).

Mitochondria provide energy for active transport.

Cholinergic synapses occur at:

- The motor end plate where release of ACh causes muscle contraction.
- All preganglionic neurons of the autonomic nervous system where release of ACh causes excitation (shown here).
- All postganglionic neurons of the parasympathetic division where it may cause an inhibition of response, e.g. a decrease in heart or breathing rate.

1. Explain what is meant by a **synapse**: _____

2. Explain what causes the release of neurotransmitter into the synaptic cleft: _____
_____

3. State why there is a brief delay in transmission of an impulse across the synapse: _____
_____

4. (a) State how the neurotransmitter is deactivated: _____

   (b) Explain why it is important for the neurotransmitter substance to be deactivated soon after its release:
   _____

5. Consult a reference source to identify one function of acetylcholine in the nervous system: _____
_____

6. Suggest one factor that might influence the strength of the response in the receiving cell: _____
_____

Related activities: Transmission of Nerve Impulses, The Autonomic Nervous System

Integration at Synapses

Synapses play a pivotal role in the ability of the nervous system to respond appropriately to stimulation and to adapt to change. The nature of synaptic transmission allows the **integration** (interpretation and coordination) of inputs from many sources. These inputs need not be just excitatory (causing depolarization). Inhibition results when the neurotransmitter released causes negative chloride ions (rather than sodium ions) to enter the postsynaptic neuron. The postsynaptic neuron then becomes more negative inside (hyperpolarized) and an action potential is less likely to be generated. At synapses, it is the sum of **all** inputs (excitatory and inhibitory) that leads to the final response in a postsynaptic cell. Integration at synapses makes possible the various responses we have to stimuli. It is also the most probable mechanism by which learning and memory are achieved.

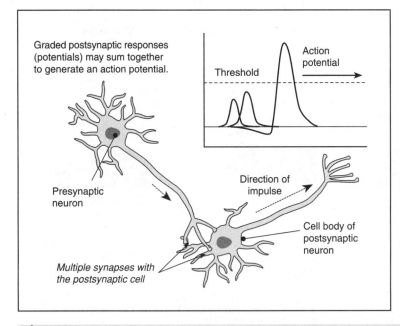

Graded postsynaptic responses (potentials) may sum together to generate an action potential.

Threshold

Action potential

Presynaptic neuron

Direction of impulse

Cell body of postsynaptic neuron

Multiple synapses with the postsynaptic cell

Synapses and Summation

Nerve transmission across chemical synapses has several advantages, despite the delay caused by neurotransmitter diffusion. Chemical synapses transmit impulses in one direction to a precise location and, because they rely on a limited supply of neurotransmitter, they are subject to fatigue (inability to respond to repeated stimulation). This protects the system against overstimulation.

Synapses also act as centers for the **integration** of inputs from many sources. The response of a postsynaptic cell is often graded; it is not strong enough on its own to generate an action potential. However, because the strength of the response is related to the amount of neurotransmitter released, subthreshold responses can sum to produce a response in the post-synaptic cell. This additive effect is termed **summation**. Summation can be **temporal** or **spatial** (below). A neuromuscular junction (photo below) is a specialized form of synapse between a motor neuron and a skeletal muscle fiber. Functionally, it is similar to any excitatory cholinergic synapse.

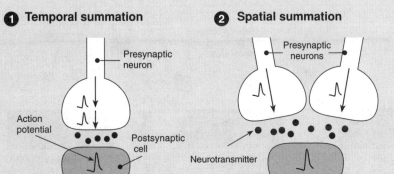

1 Temporal summation

Presynaptic neuron

Action potential

Postsynaptic cell

Neurotransmitter

2 Spatial summation

Presynaptic neurons

Several impulses may arrive at the synapse in quick succession from a single axon. The individual responses are so close together in time that they sum to reach threshold and produce an action potential in the postsynaptic neuron.

Individual impulses from spatially separated axon terminals may arrive **simultaneously** at different regions of the same postsynaptic neuron. The responses from the different places sum to reach threshold and produce an action potential.

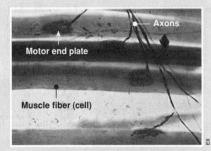

3 Neuromuscular junction

Axons

Motor end plate

Muscle fiber (cell)

The arrival of an impulse at the neuromuscular junction causes the release of acetylcholine from the synaptic knobs. This causes the muscle cell membrane (sarcolemma) to depolarize, and an action potential is generated in the muscle cell.

1. Explain the purpose of nervous system integration: _____

_____

2. (a) Explain what is meant by **summation**: _____

_____

   (b) In simple terms, distinguish between temporal and spatial summation: _____

_____

_____

3. Describe two ways in which a neuromuscular junction is similar to any excitatory cholinergic synapse:

   (a) _____

   (b) _____

Related activities: Chemical Synapses

RA 3

Nerves, Muscles and Movement

Drugs at Synapses

Synapses in the peripheral nervous system are classified according to the neurotransmitter they release; **cholinergic** synapses release acetylcholine (**Ach**) while **adrenergic** synapses release adrenalin or noradrenaline (**NA**). The effect produced by these neurotransmitters depends, in turn, on the type of receptors present on the postsynaptic membrane. Ach receptors are classified as nicotinic or muscarinic according of their response to nicotine or muscarine (a fungal toxin).

Adrenergic receptors are also of two types, alpha (α) or beta (β), classified according to their particular responses to specific chemicals. **Drugs** exert their effects on the nervous system by mimicking (**agonists**) or blocking (**antagonists**) the action of neurotransmitters at synapses. Because of the small amounts of chemicals involved in synaptic transmission, drugs that affect the activity of neurotransmitters, or their binding sites, can have powerful effects even in small doses.

Drugs at Cholinergic Synapses

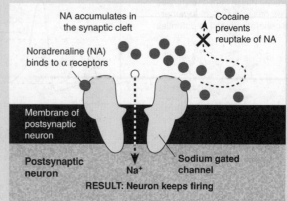

Nicotine binds to Ach receptors and opens Na⁺ gates
Synaptic cleft
Ach
Membrane of postsynaptic neuron
Postsynaptic neuron
Na⁺
Sodium gated channel
RESULT: Depolarization and impulse generation

Nicotine acts as a **direct agonist** at nicotinic synapses. Nicotine binds to and activates acetylcholine (Ach) receptors on the postsynaptic membrane. This opens sodium gates, leading to a sodium influx and membrane depolarization. Some agonists work indirectly at the synapse by preventing Ach breakdown. Such drugs are used to treat elderly patients with Alzheimer's disease.

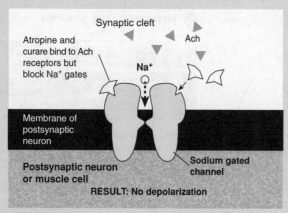

Synaptic cleft
Atropine and curare bind to Ach receptors but block Na⁺ gates
Ach
Na⁺
Membrane of postsynaptic neuron
Postsynaptic neuron or muscle cell
Sodium gated channel
RESULT: No depolarization

Atropine and **curare** act as antagonists at some cholinergic synapses. These molecules compete with Ach for binding sites on the postsynaptic membrane, and block sodium influx so that impulses are not generated. If the postsynaptic cell is a muscle cell, muscle contraction is prevented. In the case of curare, this causes death by flaccid paralysis.

Drugs at Adrenergic Synapses

NA accumulates in the synaptic cleft
Cocaine prevents reuptake of NA
Noradrenaline (NA) binds to α receptors
Membrane of postsynaptic neuron
Postsynaptic neuron
Na⁺
Sodium gated channel
RESULT: Neuron keeps firing

Under normal circumstances, the continued activity of the neurotransmitter noradrenaline (NA) at the synapse is prevented by reuptake of NA by the presynaptic neuron. **Cocaine** and **amphetamine** drugs act indirectly as agonists by preventing this reuptake. This action allows NA to linger at the synapse and continue to exert its effects.

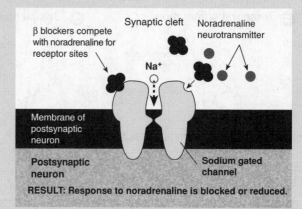

β blockers compete with noradrenaline for receptor sites
Synaptic cleft
Noradrenaline neurotransmitter
Na⁺
Membrane of postsynaptic neuron
Postsynaptic neuron
Sodium gated channel
RESULT: Response to noradrenaline is blocked or reduced.

Therapeutic drugs called **beta (β) blockers** act as direct antagonists at adrenergic synapses (sympathetic nervous system). They compete for the adrenergic β receptors on the postsynaptic membrane and block impulse transmission. Beta blockers are prescribed primarily to treat hypertension and heart disorders because they slow heart rate and reduce the force of contraction.

1. Providing an example of each, outline two ways in which drugs can act at a cholinergic synapse:

   (a) _____

   (b) _____

2. Providing an example, outline one way in which drugs can operate at adrenergic synapses: _____

   _____

3. Explain why atropine and curare are described as direct antagonists: _____

   _____

4. Suggest why curare (carefully administered) is used during abdominal surgery: _____

   _____

Related activities: Chemical Synapses
Web links: The Science of Addiction

The Basis of Sensory Perception

Sensory receptors are specialized to detect stimuli and respond by producing an electrical discharge. In this way they act as **biological transducers**, converting the energy from a stimulus into an electrochemical signal. Stimulation of a sensory receptor cell results in an electrical impulse with specific properties. The frequency of impulses produced by the receptor cell encodes information about the strength of the stimulus; a stronger stimulus produces more frequent impulses. Sensory receptors also show **sensory adaptation** and will cease responding to a stimulus of the same intensity. The simplest sensory receptors consist of a single sensory neuron (e.g. free nerve endings). More complex sense cells form synapses with their sensory neurons (e.g. taste buds). Sensory receptors are classified according to the stimuli to which they respond (for example, photoreceptors respond to light). The response of a simple **mechanoreceptor**, the Pacinian corpuscle, to a stimulus (pressure) is described below.

The Pacinian Corpuscle

Pacinian corpuscles are pressure receptors occurring in deep subcutaneous tissues all over the body. They are relatively large and simple in structure, consisting of a sensory nerve ending (dendrite) surrounded by a capsule of layered connective tissue. Pressure deforms the capsule, stretching the nerve ending and leading to a localized depolarization. Once a **threshold** value is reached, an **action potential** propagates along the axon.

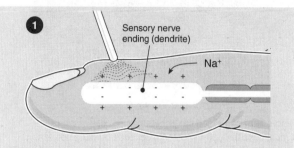

Deforming the corpuscle leads to an increase in the permeability of the nerve to sodium. Na^+ diffuses into the nerve ending creating a localized depolarization. This depolarization is called a **generator potential**.

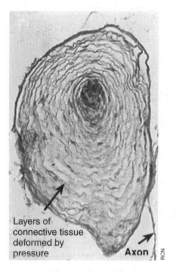

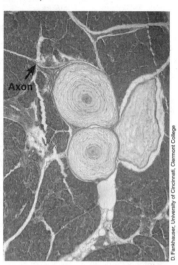

Pacinian corpuscle (above, left), illustrating the distinctive layers of connective tissue. The photograph on the right shows corpuscles grouped together in the pancreas. Pacinian corpuscles are rapidly adapting receptors; they fire at the beginning and end of a stimulus, but do not respond to unchanging pressure.

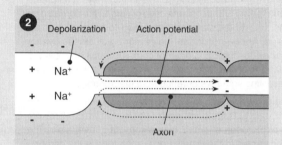

A volley of **action potentials** is triggered once the generator potential reaches or exceeds a **threshold value**. These action potentials are conducted along the sensory axon. A strong stimulus results in a high frequency of impulses.

1. Explain why sensory receptors are termed 'biological transducers': _____

_____

_____

2. Explain the significance of linking the magnitude of a sensory response to stimulus intensity: _____

_____

_____

3. Explain the physiological importance of sensory adaptation: _____

_____

4. (a) Describe the properties of a generator potential: _____

_____

(b) Suggest why a simple mechanoreceptor, such as the Pacinian corpuscle, does not fire action potentials unless a stimulus of threshold value is reached:

_____

_____

_____

Related activities: The Physiology of Vision
Web links: Neuron Information Coding & Transfer, Sensory Systems, Hearing

RA 2

Nerves, Muscles and Movement

The Structure of the Eye

The eye is a complex and highly sophisticated sense organ specialized to detect light. The adult eyeball is about 25 mm in diameter. Only the anterior one-sixth of its total surface area is exposed; the rest lies recessed and protected by the **orbit** into which it fits. The eyeball is protected and given shape by a fibrous tunic. The posterior part of this structure is the **sclera** (the white of the eye), while the anterior transparent portion is the **cornea**, which covers the colored iris.

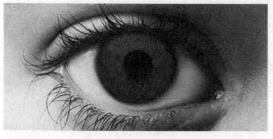

The Structure and Function of the Mammalian Eye

The human eye is essentially a three layered structure comprising an outer fibrous layer (the sclera and cornea), a middle vascular layer (the choroid, ciliary body, and iris), and inner **retina** (neurons and **photoreceptor cells**). The shape of the eye is maintained by the fluid filled cavities (aqueous and vitreous humors), which also assist in light refraction. Eye color is provided by the pigmented iris. The iris also regulates the entry of light into the eye through the contraction of circular and radial muscles.

Forming a Visual Image

Before light can reach the photoreceptor cells of the retina, it must pass through the cornea, aqueous humor, pupil, lens, and vitreous humor. For vision to occur, light reaching the photoreceptor cells must form an image on the retina. This requires **refraction** of the incoming light, **accommodation** of the lens, and **constriction** of the pupil.

The anterior of the eye is concerned mainly with **refracting** (bending) the incoming light rays so that they focus on the retina (below left). Most refraction occurs at the cornea. The lens adjusts the degree of refraction to produce a sharp image. **Accommodation** (below right) adjusts the eye for near or far objects. Constriction of the pupil narrows the diameter of the hole through which light enters the eye, preventing light rays entering from the periphery.

The point at which the nerve fibers leave the eye as the optic nerve, is the **blind spot** (the point at which there are no photoreceptor cells). Nerve impulses travel along the optic nerves to the visual processing areas in the cerebral cortex. Images on the retina are inverted and reversed by the lens but the brain interprets the information it receives to correct for this image reversal.

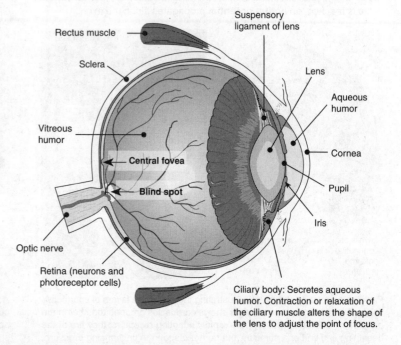

Ciliary body: Secretes aqueous humor. Contraction or relaxation of the ciliary muscle alters the shape of the lens to adjust the point of focus.

Normal vision	Accommodation for near and distant vision

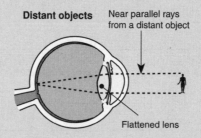

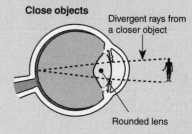

In normal vision, light rays from an object are bent sufficiently by the cornea and lens, and converge on the central fovea. A clear image is formed. Images are focused upside down and mirror reversed on the retina. The brain automatically interprets the image as right way up.

The degree of refraction occurring at each surface of the eye is precise. The light rays reflected from an object 6 m or more away are nearly parallel to one another. Those reflected from near objects are divergent. The light rays must be refracted differently in each case so that they fall exactly on the central fovea. This is achieved through adjustment of the shape of the lens (**accommodation**). Accommodation from distant to close objects occurs by rounding the lens to shorten its focal length, since the image distance to the object is essentially fixed.

1. Identify the function of each of the structures of the eye listed below:

   (a) Cornea: _____

   (b) Ciliary body: _____

   (c) Retina: _____

   (d) Iris: _____

Related activities: The Physiology of Vision
Web links: Anatomy of the Eye

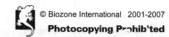

The Physiology of Vision

Vision involves essentially two stages: formation of the image on the retina (see previous activity), and generation and conduction of nerve impulses. When light reaches the retina, it is absorbed by the photosensitive pigments associated with the membranes of the photoreceptor cells (the rods and cones). The pigment molecules are altered by the absorption of light in such a way as to lead to the generation of nerve impulses. It is these impulses that are conducted via nerve fibers to the visual processing centre of the cerebral cortex (see the activity *The Human Brain* for the location of this region).

The Structure and Arrangement of Photoreceptor Cells in the Retina

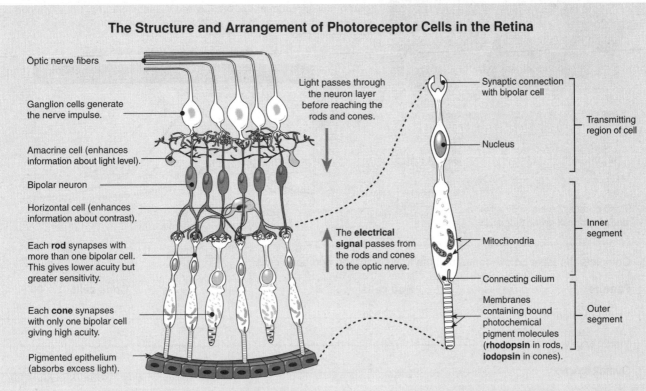

Optic nerve fibers

Ganglion cells generate the nerve impulse.

Light passes through the neuron layer before reaching the rods and cones.

Amacrine cell (enhances information about light level).

Bipolar neuron

Horizontal cell (enhances information about contrast).

The **electrical signal** passes from the rods and cones to the optic nerve.

Each **rod** synapses with more than one bipolar cell. This gives lower acuity but greater sensitivity.

Each **cone** synapses with only one bipolar cell giving high acuity.

Pigmented epithelium (absorbs excess light).

Synaptic connection with bipolar cell

Nucleus

Transmitting region of cell

Mitochondria

Inner segment

Connecting cilium

Membranes containing bound photochemical pigment molecules (**rhodopsin** in rods, **iodopsin** in cones).

Outer segment

Arrangement of photoreceptors and neurons in the retina

Structure of a rod photoreceptor cell

The photoreceptor cells of the mammalian retina are the **rods** and **cones**. Rods are specialized for vision in dim light, whereas cones are specialized for color vision and high visual acuity. Cone density and visual acuity are greatest in the **central fovea** (rods are absent here). After an image is formed on the retina, light impulses must be converted into nerve impulses. The first step is the development of **generator potentials** by the rods and cones. Light induces structural changes in the **photochemical pigments** (or photopigments) of the rod and cone membranes. The generator potential that develops from the pigment breakdown in the rods and cones is different from the generator potentials that occur in other types of sensory receptors because stimulation results in a **hyperpolarization** rather than a depolarization (in other words, there is a net loss of Na+ from the photoreceptor cell). Once generator potentials have developed, the graded changes in membrane conductance spread through the photoreceptor cell. Each photoreceptor makes synaptic connection with a bipolar neuron, which transmits the potentials to the **ganglion cells**. The ganglion cells become **depolarized** and initiate nerve impulses which pass through the optic chiasma and eventually to the visual areas of the cerebral cortex. The frequency and pattern of impulses in the optic nerve conveys information about the changing visual field.

1. (a) The first stage of vision involves forming an image on the retina. Explain what this involves (see the previous activity):

_____

_____

   (b) Explain how accommodation is achieved (see the previous activity for help): _____

_____

_____

_____

2. Contrast the structure of the blind spot and the central fovea: _____

_____

_____

_____

Related activities: The Structure of the Eye, The Human Brain
Web links: Eye Structure and Function

RA 3

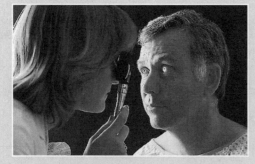

The Basis of Trichromatic Vision

There are three classes of **cones**, each with a maximal response in either short (blue), intermediate (green) or long (yellow-green) wavelength light (coded B, G, and R below). The yellow-green cone is also sensitive to the red part of the spectrum and is often called the red cone (R). The differential responses of the cones to light of different wavelengths provides the basis of trichromatic color vision.

Cone response to light wavelengths

| Violet | Blue | Green | Yellow | Orange |

Electrical response

B   G   R

450   500   550   600   650   700
Wavelength (nm)

Synaptic connection   Nucleus   Mitochondrion

Membranes containing bound **iodopsin** pigment molecules.

Each **cone** synapses with only one bipolar cell giving high acuity.

3. Complete the table below, comparing the features of rod and cone cells:

Feature	Rod cells	Cone cells
Visual pigment(s):		
Visual acuity:		
Overall function:		

4. Account for the differences in acuity and sensitivity between rod and cone cells: _____

_____

_____

_____

5. (a) Explain clearly what is meant by the term photochemical pigment (photopigment): _____

_____

_____

(b) Identify two photopigments and their location: _____

_____

6. In your own words, explain how light is able to produce a nerve impulse in the ganglion cells: _____

_____

_____

_____

_____

_____

7. Explain the physiological basis for color vision in humans: _____

_____

_____

_____

Animal Support and Movement

Most animals support themselves in their environment and move around. In animals, support systems (skeletons) are adapted to methods of locomotion and feeding. Movement in water and on land requires different adaptations because of the very different properties of these two media. In vertebrates, limbs are usually modified for different modes of locomotion. Invertebrate methods of propulsion are more diverse, partly a reflection of their more diverse range of support systems.

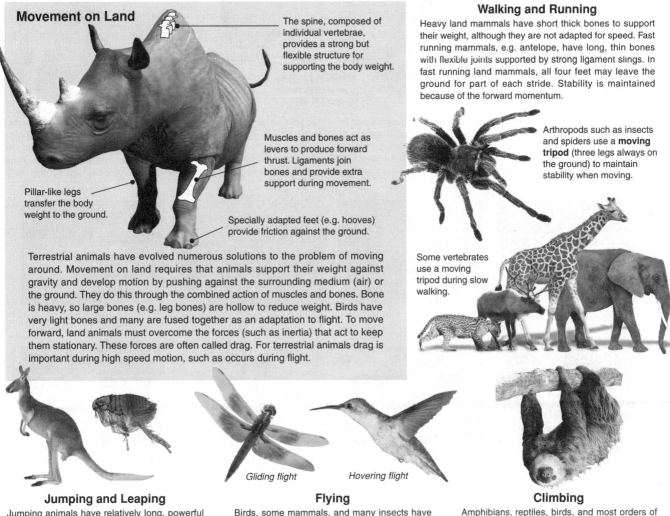

Movement on Land

The spine, composed of individual vertebrae, provides a strong but flexible structure for supporting the body weight.

Muscles and bones act as levers to produce forward thrust. Ligaments join bones and provide extra support during movement.

Pillar-like legs transfer the body weight to the ground.

Specially adapted feet (e.g. hooves) provide friction against the ground.

Terrestrial animals have evolved numerous solutions to the problem of moving around. Movement on land requires that animals support their weight against gravity and develop motion by pushing against the surrounding medium (air) or the ground. They do this through the combined action of muscles and bones. Bone is heavy, so large bones (e.g. leg bones) are hollow to reduce weight. Birds have very light bones and many are fused together as an adaptation to flight. To move forward, land animals must overcome the forces (such as inertia) that act to keep them stationary. These forces are often called drag. For terrestrial animals drag is important during high speed motion, such as occurs during flight.

Walking and Running

Heavy land mammals have short thick bones to support their weight, although they are not adapted for speed. Fast running mammals, e.g. antelope, have long, thin bones with flexible joints supported by strong ligament slings. In fast running land mammals, all four feet may leave the ground for part of each stride. Stability is maintained because of the forward momentum.

Arthropods such as insects and spiders use a **moving tripod** (three legs always on the ground) to maintain stability when moving.

Some vertebrates use a moving tripod during slow walking.

Gliding flight   *Hovering flight*

Jumping and Leaping

Jumping animals have relatively long, powerful hind limbs. In mammals the forelimbs are often reduced in size and used for slow movement and food handling. Jumping mammals need a long tail to help to centre the weight over the back legs. Jumping results in rapid acceleration and is often used for prey capture or escape. For some animals (e.g. kangaroos), jumping is also an energy efficient means of sustained locomotion.

Flying

Birds, some mammals, and many insects have mastered flight. Flying is a very rapid but energy expensive mode of locomotion. Flying animals have wings shaped like an airfoil (curved up on the top surface and thicker in the front). This reduces drag and increases lift. Wings have different origins: arthropod wings are extensions of the thorax exoskeleton, while vertebrate wings are modifications of the limbs.

Climbing

Amphibians, reptiles, birds, and most orders of mammals have climbing representatives. Adaptations for climbing involve structures and mechanisms for maximizing grip on surfaces, e.g. foot pads, claws, and grasping feet. Many of the expert climbers, such as primates, have elongated, flexible limbs for reaching and swinging. Others, e.g. rodents such as squirrels, combine agile climbing with leaping.

Nerves, Muscles and Movement

1. Explain the significance of the 'moving tripod' to movement in terrestrial animals: _____

_____

2. (a) Describe the advantages of flight to a land animal: _____

_____

_____

(b) Describe two main problems that need to be overcome by an animal if it is to fly: _____

_____

(c) State how the shape of a wing assists in this: _____

3. Describe the situation in which jumping is normally used and explain why: _____

_____

Related activities: The Human Skeleton   **A 1**

Movement in Water

Fat, oil and gas filled structures are lighter than water and give buoyancy.

Bone, cartilage and muscle are denser than water and cause sinking.

Fins and flippers can be used for control, maneuvering and braking.

Gas filled swim bladder

Tail fins are important in generating thrust against the water.

Some aquatic invertebrates have jelly filled bodies and/or gas filled floats to provide buoyancy.

The backward displacement of water generates forward movement.

Path of the tail through the water

Streamlined body shape reduces drag through the water.

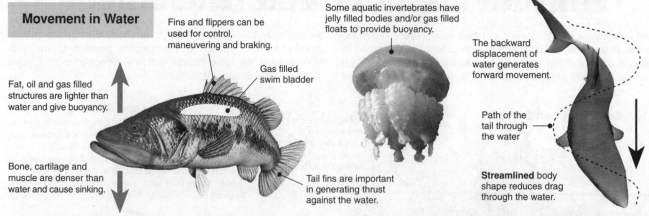

Animals show a wide range of adaptations to movement through water. In **invertebrates** propulsion can be generated by a huge range of mechanisms, from jointed limbs to adhesive tube feet (below). Where movement is across a substrate, a hard skeleton (external in arthropods, internal in echinoderms) or shell provides weight. Where buoyancy is required, air or gas chambers are usually used. **Vertebrates** have adapted to movement underwater by adapting limbs into paddles or fins. Birds have webbed feet to provide propulsion in water while also allowing for reasonable mobility on land. The fastest vertebrate swimmers (dolphins, whales and fish) use a powerful tail to provide thrust against the water.

Backswimmer

Feathered limbs in aquatic insects give effective rowing with paddles.

Marine snail

A large muscular foot allows snails to glide smoothly over the substrate.

Starfish

Adhesive tube feet in echinoderms provide slow but strong movement.

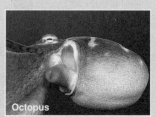

Octopus

Water jet propulsion in cephalopods allows rapid escape from danger.

Green sea turtle

In sea turtles, powerful strokes from broad flippers provide propulsion.

Fish

Powerful tail fin in fish gives thrust, other fins provide lift and control.

Penguin

Webbed feet and flightless, paddle like wings in penguins provide thrust.

Dolphins

Strong fins and horizontal tail fluke in dolphins give strong propulsion.

4. Water provides most of the support for aquatic animals. Describe the main problem for animals moving through water:

_____

_____

5. (a) Explain what is meant by **streamlining** with respect to body shape: _____

_____

_____

(b) Explain why streamlining is a characteristic of the fastest swimmers: _____

_____

6. Describe some of the methods by which animals remain buoyant in the water: _____

_____

_____

_____

7. Many marine invertebrates (e.g. snails, starfish) do not require a buoyancy mechanism. Explain why this is the case:

_____

_____

The Human Skeleton

The skeletal system consists of bones and their associated connective tissues (cartilage, tendons, and ligaments). The skeletal system performs five basic functions: it provides support and protection; it allows for movement; and it is involved in storing minerals and producing red blood cells. It also has a role in the conduction of sound in the middle ear. The human skeleton consists of two main divisions: the **axial skeleton**, which comprises the bones of the head and torso (skull, spine, sternum, and ribs), and the **appendicular skeleton** (the limbs and limb girdles).

Word list: *humerus, patella, scapula, tibia, clavicle, sternum, vertebra, femur, phalanges, mandible, metacarpals, rib, ilium, fibula.*

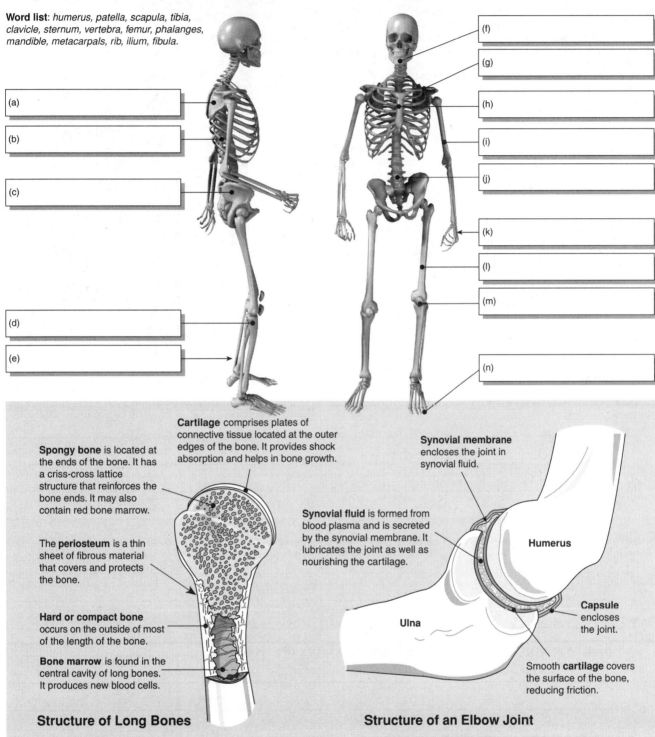

Structure of Long Bones

Spongy bone is located at the ends of the bone. It has a criss-cross lattice structure that reinforces the bone ends. It may also contain red bone marrow.

The periosteum is a thin sheet of fibrous material that covers and protects the bone.

Hard or compact bone occurs on the outside of most of the length of the bone.

Bone marrow is found in the central cavity of long bones. It produces new blood cells.

Cartilage comprises plates of connective tissue located at the outer edges of the bone. It provides shock absorption and helps in bone growth.

Structure of an Elbow Joint

Synovial membrane encloses the joint in synovial fluid.

Synovial fluid is formed from blood plasma and is secreted by the synovial membrane. It lubricates the joint as well as nourishing the cartilage.

Humerus

Ulna

Capsule encloses the joint.

Smooth cartilage covers the surface of the bone, reducing friction.

Nerves, Muscles and Movement

1. Use the word list provided to label the bones (a)-(n) of the skeleton in the diagram above.

2. Briefly describe the functions of a mammalian skeleton (bone tissue) under the following headings:

(a) Movement: _____

_____

(b) Protection: _____

_____

Related activities: The Mechanics of Locomotion

A 2

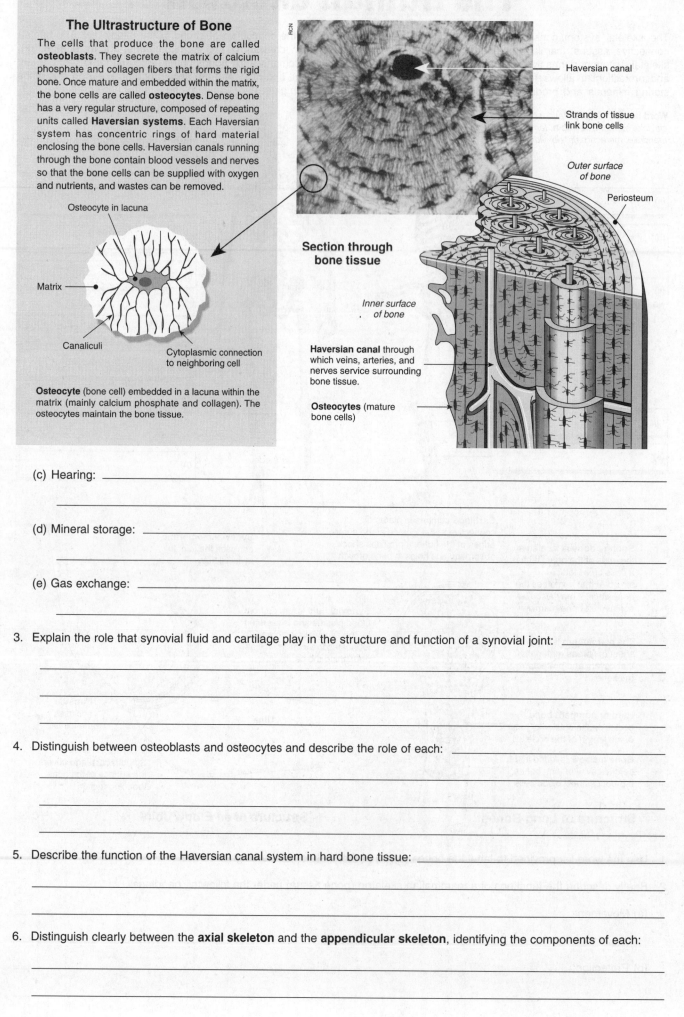

The Ultrastructure of Bone

The cells that produce the bone are called **osteoblasts**. They secrete the matrix of calcium phosphate and collagen fibers that forms the rigid bone. Once mature and embedded within the matrix, the bone cells are called **osteocytes**. Dense bone has a very regular structure, composed of repeating units called **Haversian systems**. Each Haversian system has concentric rings of hard material enclosing the bone cells. Haversian canals running through the bone contain blood vessels and nerves so that the bone cells can be supplied with oxygen and nutrients, and wastes can be removed.

Haversian canal

Strands of tissue link bone cells

Outer surface of bone

Periosteum

Osteocyte in lacuna

Matrix

Canaliculi

Cytoplasmic connection to neighboring cell

Section through bone tissue

Inner surface of bone

Haversian canal through which veins, arteries, and nerves service surrounding bone tissue.

Osteocytes (mature bone cells)

Osteocyte (bone cell) embedded in a lacuna within the matrix (mainly calcium phosphate and collagen). The osteocytes maintain the bone tissue.

(c) Hearing: _____

_____

(d) Mineral storage: _____

_____

(e) Gas exchange: _____

_____

3. Explain the role that synovial fluid and cartilage play in the structure and function of a synovial joint: _____

_____

_____

_____

4. Distinguish between osteoblasts and osteocytes and describe the role of each: _____

_____

_____

5. Describe the function of the Haversian canal system in hard bone tissue: _____

_____

_____

6. Distinguish clearly between the **axial skeleton** and the **appendicular skeleton**, identifying the components of each:

_____

_____

The Mechanics of Locomotion

Bones are too rigid to bend without damage. To allow movement, the skeletal system consists of many bones held together at **joints** by flexible connective tissues called **ligaments**. All movements of the skeleton occur at joints: points of contact between bones, or between cartilage and bones. Joints may be classified according to the amount of movement they permit: none (sutures); slight movement (symphyses), and free movement in one or more planes (e.g. **synovial joints**). Bones are made to move about a joint by the force of muscles acting upon them. The muscles are attached to bone by **tendons**. Many muscles act in **antagonistic** pairs, one set causing the joint to

move one way, the other set causing its return. The skeleton of an animal works as a system of levers. The joint acts as a fulcrum, the muscles exert the force, and the weight of the bone being moved represents the load. Contraction causes a muscle to shorten and this shortening moves attached bones. When only a few fibers in a muscle contract, the muscle will tighten but not produce movement. This partly contracted state is responsible for **muscle tone** and is important in maintaining **posture**. The amount of muscle contraction is monitored by sensory receptors in the muscle called **muscle spindle organs**. These provide the sensory information necessary to adjust movement as required.

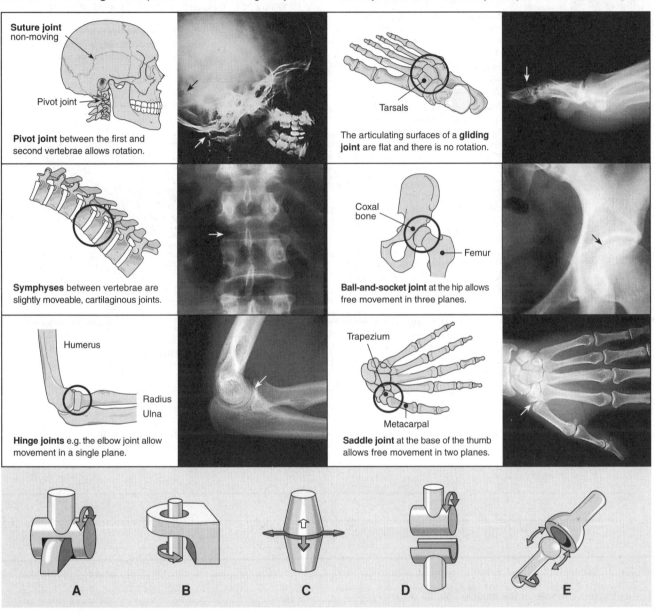

Nerves, Muscles and Movement

1. Classify each of the models illustrating movement in synovial joints (**A-E** above), according to the labels given below:

   (a) Pivot: _____ (b) Hinge: _____ (c) Ball-and-socket: _____ (d) Saddle: _____ (e) Gliding: _____

2. Briefly describe the role of each of the following in human locomotion:

   (a) Ligament: _____

   (b) Tendon: _____

   (c) Antagonistic muscles: _____

   (d) Bones: _____

   (e) Joints: _____

The Action of Antagonistic Muscles

The flexion (bending) and extension (unbending) of limbs is caused by the action of **antagonistic muscles**; muscles that work in pairs and whose actions oppose each other. Every coordinated movement in the body requires the application of muscle force. This is accomplished by the action of agonists, antagonists, and synergists. The opposing action of agonists and antagonists also produces muscle tone. Note that either muscle in an antagonistic pair can act as the prime mover, depending on the movement (flexion or extension).

Biceps brachii

Agonists or prime movers: muscles that are primarily responsible for the movement and produce most of the force required.

Antagonists: muscles that oppose the prime mover. They may also play a protective role by preventing overstretching of the prime mover.

Synergists: muscles that assist the prime movers and may be involved in fine-tuning the direction of the movement.

During flexion of the forearm at the elbow, (left) the **biceps brachii** acts as the prime mover, and the antagonist, the **triceps brachii** at the back of the arm, is relaxing. During extension, their roles are reversed.

Quadriceps

Hamstrings

Movement of the leg is accomplished through the action of several large groups of muscles, collectively called the **quadriceps** and the **hamstrings**.

The hamstrings are actually a collection of three muscles, which act together to flex the leg. The quadriceps at the front of the thigh (a collection of four large muscles) opposes the motion of the hamstrings and extends the leg. When the prime mover contracts very forcefully, the antagonist also contracts very slightly. This prevents any overstretching and allows greater control over thigh movement.

The Role of the Muscle Spindle

Changes in length of a muscle are monitored by the **muscle spindle organ**, a stretch receptor located within skeletal muscle, parallel to the muscle fibers themselves. The muscle spindle is stimulated in response to sustained or sudden stretch on the central region of its specialized intrafusal fibers. Sensory information from the muscle spindle is relayed to the spinal cord. The motor response brings about adjustments to the degree of stretch in the muscle. These adjustments help in the coordination and efficiency of muscle contraction. Muscle spindles are important in the maintenance of muscle tone, postural reflexes, and movement control, and are concentrated in muscles that exert fine control over movement.

Sensory nerves monitor stretch in the non-contractile region of the spindle and send impulses to the spinal cord.

Motor nerves send impulses to adjust the degree of contraction in the intrafusal and extrafusal fibers.

Striated appearance of contractile elements

The spindle is surrounded by the muscle fibers of the skeletal muscle.

Nucleus of muscle fiber

The **muscle spindle organ** comprises special **intrafusal fibers** which lie parallel to the muscle fibers within a lymph-filled capsule. Only the regions near the end can contract.

3. Using appropriate terminology, explain how antagonistic muscles act together to raise and lower a limb:

_____

_____

_____

_____

_____

4. (a) Explain the role of the muscle spindle organ: _____

_____

(b) With reference to the following, describe how the structure of the muscle spindle organ is related to its function:

Intrafusal fibers lie parallel to the extrafusal fibers: _____

_____

Sensory neurons are located in the non-contractile region of the organ: _____

_____

Motor neurons synapse in the extrafusal fibers and the contractile region of the intrafusal fibers: _____

_____

Muscle Structure and Function

There are three kinds of muscle: **skeletal, cardiac**, and **smooth** muscle, each with a distinct structure. The muscles used for posture and locomotion are skeletal (striated) muscles. Their distinct striped appearance is the result of the regular arrangement of contractile elements within the muscle cells. Muscle fibers are innervated by motor neurons, each of which terminates in a specialized cholinergic synapse called the **motor end plate**. A motor neuron and all the fibers it innervates is called a **motor unit**.

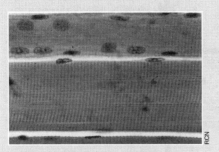

Skeletal muscle
Also called striated or striped muscle. It has a banded appearance under high power microscopy. Sometimes called voluntary muscle because it is under conscious control. The cells are large with many nuclei at the edge of each cell.

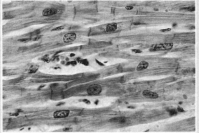

Cardiac muscle
Specialized striated muscle that does not fatigue. Cells branch and connect with each other to assist the passage of nerve impulses through the muscle. Cardiac muscle is not under conscious control (it is involuntary).

Smooth muscle
Also called involuntary muscle because it is not under conscious control. Contractile filaments are irregularly arranged so the contraction is not in one direction as in skeletal muscle. Cells are spindle shaped with one central nucleus.

Structure of Skeletal Muscle

Skeletal muscle is organized into bundles of muscle cells or **fibers**. Each fiber is a single cell with many nuclei and each fiber is itself a bundle of smaller **myofibrils** arranged lengthwise. Each myofibril is in turn composed of two kinds of **myofilaments** (thick and thin), which overlap to form light and dark bands. It is the alternation of these light and dark bands which gives skeletal muscle its striated or striped appearance. The **sarcomere**, bounded by the dark Z lines, forms one complete contractile unit.

Longitudinal section of a sarcomere

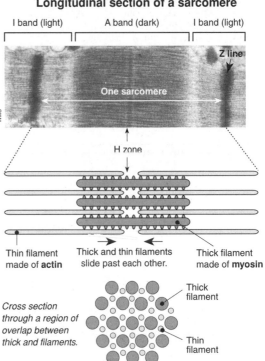

The photograph of a sarcomere (above) illustrates the distinctive banding pattern of skeletal muscle. The pattern, which arises because of the arrangement of thin and thick filaments, is shown in schematic form below the photograph. A representation of the region of overlap is also illustrated.

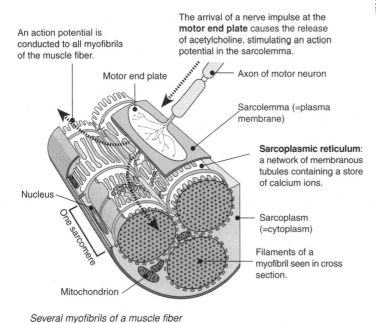

Several myofibrils of a muscle fiber

The Banding Pattern of Myofibrils

Within a myofibril, thin filaments, held together by the **Z lines**, project in both directions. The arrival of a nerve impulse sets in motion a series of events that cause the thick and thin filaments to slide past each other. This **contraction** results in shortening of the muscle and is accompanied by a visible change in the appearance of the myofibril: the I band and the sarcomere shorten and H zone shortens or disappears.

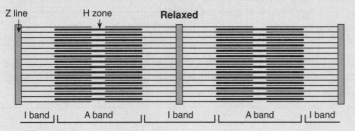

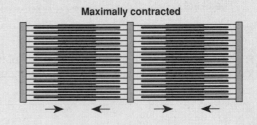

Nerves, Muscles and Movement

Footnote text from the left diagram:

An action potential is conducted to all myofibrils of the muscle fiber.

The arrival of a nerve impulse at the **motor end plate** causes the release of acetylcholine, stimulating an action potential in the sarcolemma.

Motor end plate

Axon of motor neuron

Sarcolemma (=plasma membrane)

Sarcoplasmic reticulum: a network of membranous tubules containing a store of calcium ions.

Nucleus

Sarcoplasm (=cytoplasm)

Filaments of a myofibril seen in cross section.

Mitochondrion

One sarcomere

Labels from sarcomere diagram:

I band (light)　A band (dark)　I band (light)

Z line

One sarcomere

H zone

Thin filament made of **actin**

Thick and thin filaments slide past each other.

Thick filament made of **myosin**

Thick filament

Thin filament

Cross section through a region of overlap between thick and filaments.

Banding pattern diagram labels:

Z line　H zone　**Relaxed**　**Maximally contracted**

I band　A band　I band　A band　I band

The Sliding Filament Hypothesis

Muscle contraction requires calcium ions (Ca^{2+}) and energy (in the form of ATP) in order for the thick and thin filaments to slide past each other. The steps are:

1. The binding sites on the **actin** molecule (to which myosin 'heads' will locate) are blocked by a complex of two molecules: tropomyosin and troponin.

2. Prior to muscle contraction, ATP binds to the heads of the myosin molecules, priming them in an erect high energy state. Arrival of an action potential causes a release of Ca^{2+} from the sarcoplasmic reticulum. The Ca^{2+} binds to the troponin and causes the blocking molecules to move so that the myosin binding sites on the actin filament become exposed.

3. The heads of the cross-bridging myosin molecules attach to the binding sites on the actin filament. Release of energy from the hydrolysis of ATP accompanies the cross bridge formation.

4. The energy released from ATP hydrolysis causes a change in shape of the myosin **cross bridge**, resulting in a bending action (*the power stroke*). This causes the actin filaments to slide past the myosin filaments towards the centre of the sarcomere.

5. (Not illustrated). Fresh ATP attaches to the myosin molecules, releasing them from the binding sites and repriming them for a repeat movement. They become attached further along the actin chain as long as ATP and Ca^{2+} are available.

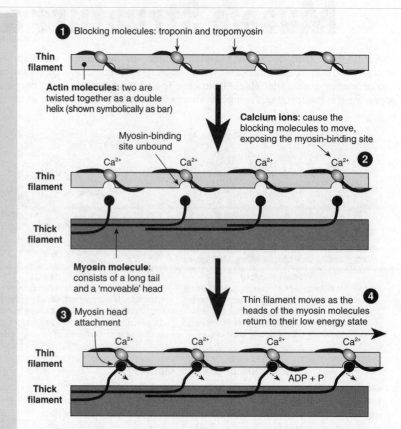

1. Distinguish between **smooth muscle**, **striated muscle**, and **cardiac muscle**, summarizing the features of each type:

_____

_____

_____

_____

2. Match the following chemicals with their functional role in muscle movement (draw a line between matching pairs):

(a) Myosin • Bind to the actin molecule in a way that prevents myosin head from forming a cross bridge

(b) Actin • Supplies energy for the flexing of the myosin 'head' (power stroke)

(c) Calcium ions • Has a moveable head that provides a power stroke when activated

(d) Troponin-tropomyosin • Two protein molecules twisted in a helix shape that form the thin filament of a myofibril

(e) ATP • Bind to the blocking molecules, causing them to move and expose the myosin binding site

3. (a) Explain the cause of the banding pattern visible in striated muscle: _____

_____

_____

(b) Explain the change in appearance of a myofibril during contraction with reference to the following:

The I band: _____

The H zone: _____

The sarcomere: _____

4. **Rigor mortis** is a state of partial contraction of the muscle that occurs after death. During rigor mortis, the muscles are locked and the body is stiff. From what you understand of muscle contraction, suggest why the muscle enters this state:

_____

_____

Energy and Exercise

Exercise places an immediate demand on the body's energy supply systems. During exercise, the metabolic rate of the muscles increases by up to 20 times and the body's systems must respond appropriately to maintain homeostasis. The ability to exercise for any given length of time depends on maintaining adequate supplies of ATP to the muscles. There are three energy systems operating to do this: the ATP-CP system, the glycolytic system, and the oxidative system. The ultimate sources of energy for ATP generation in muscle via these systems are glucose, and stores of glycogen and triglycerides. Prolonged intense exercise utilizes the oxidative system, and relies on a constant supply of oxygen to the tissues. The VO_2 is the amount of oxygen (expressed as a volume) used by muscles during a specified interval for cell metabolism and energy production. **VO_2max** is the maximum volume of oxygen that can be delivered and used per minute and therefore represents an individual's upper limit of aerobic metabolism. VO_2max is used as a measure of fitness, and is high in trained athletes. At some percentage of VO_2max (the **anaerobic threshold**) the body is unable to meet its energy demands aerobically and an **oxygen debt** is incurred.

CP provides enough energy to fuel about 10 s of maximum effort (e.g. a 100 m race).

The ATP-CP System

The simplest of the energy systems is the **ATP-CP system**. CP or **creatine phosphate** is a high energy compound that stores energy sufficient for brief periods of muscular effort. Energy released from the breakdown of CP is not used directly to accomplish cellular work. Instead it rebuilds ATP to maintain a relatively constant supply. This process is anaerobic, occurs very rapidly, and is accomplished without any special structures in the cell. CP levels decline steadily as it is used to replenish depleted ATP levels. The ability of the ATP-CP system to maintain energy levels is limited to 3-15 seconds during an all out sprint. Beyond this, the muscle must rely on other processes for ATP generation.

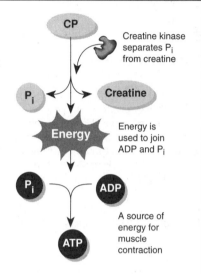

The Glycolytic System

ATP can also be provided by glycolysis: the first phase of cellular respiration. The ATP yield from glycolysis is low (only net 2ATP per molecule of glucose), but it produces ATP rapidly and does not require oxygen. The fuel for the glycolytic system is glucose in the blood, or glycogen, which is stored in the muscle or liver and broken down to glucose-6-phosphate. Glycolysis provides ATP for exercise for just a few minutes. Its main limitation is that it causes lactic acid ($C_3H_6O_3$) to accumulate in the tissues. Indirectly, it is the accumulation of lactic acid that gives the feeling of muscle fatigue. The lactic acid must transported to the liver and respired aerobically. The extra oxygen needed for this is the **oxygen debt**.

Rugby and other field sports demand brief intense efforts with recovery in-between.

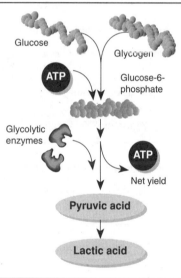

The Oxidative System

In the oxidative system, glucose is completely broken down to yield (about) 36 molecules of ATP. This process uses oxygen and takes place within the mitochondria. Aerobic metabolism has a high energy yield and is the primary method of energy production during sustained high activity. It is reliant on a continued supply of oxygen and therefore on the body's ability to deliver oxygen to the muscles. The fuels for aerobic respiration are glucose, stored glycogen, or stored **triglycerides**. Triglycerides provide free fatty acids, which are oxidized in the mitochondria by the successive removal of two-carbon fragments (a process called β-oxidation). These two carbon units enter the Krebs cycle as acetyl coenzyme A (acetyl CoA).

Prolonged aerobic effort (e.g. distance running) requires a sustained ATP supply.

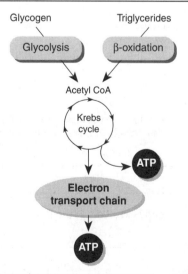

Nerves, Muscles and Movement

Related activities: Muscle Physiology and Performance
Web links: Effects of Training

DA 2

Oxygen Uptake During Exercise and Recovery

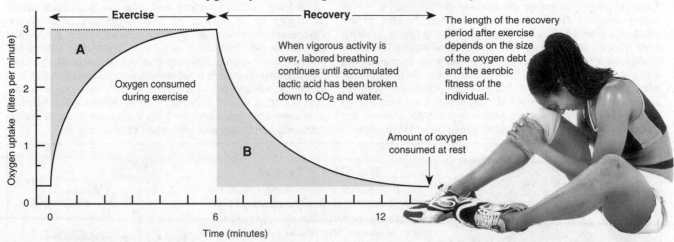

The graph above illustrates the principle of oxygen debt. In the graph, the energy demands of aerobic exercise require 3 liters (dm³) of oxygen per minute. The rate of oxygen uptake increases immediately exercise starts, but the full requirement is not met until six minutes later. The **oxygen deficit** is the amount of oxygen needed (for aerobic energy supply) but not supplied by breathing. During the first six minutes, the energy is supplied largely from anaerobic pathways: the ATP-CP and glycolytic systems (opposite). After exercise, the oxygen uptake per minute does not drop immediately to its resting level. Extra oxygen is taken in despite the drop in energy demand (the **oxygen debt**). The oxygen debt is used to replace oxygen reserves in the body, restore creatine phosphate, and break down the lactic acid (through various intermediates) to CO_2 and water.

1. Explain why the supply of energy through the glycolytic system is limited: _____

   _____

   _____

2. Summarize the features of the three energy systems in the table below:

	ATP-CP system	Glycolytic system	Oxidative system
ATP supplied by:			
Duration of ATP supply:			

3. Study the graph and explanatory paragraph above, then identify and describe what is represented by:

   (a) The shaded region **A**: _____

   _____

   (b) The shaded region **B**: _____

   _____

4. With respect to the graph above, explain why the rate of oxygen uptake does not immediately return to its resting level after exercise stops:

   _____

   _____

5. The rate of oxygen uptake increases immediately exercise starts. Explain how the oxygen supply from outside the body to the cells is increased during exercise:

   _____

   _____

6. Lactic acid levels in the blood continue to rise for a time after exercise has stopped. Explain why this occurs:

   _____

   _____

Muscle Physiology and Performance

The overall effect of **aerobic training** on muscle is improved oxidative function and better endurance. Regardless of the type of training, some of our ability to perform different types of activity depends on our genetic make-up. This is particularly true of aspects of muscle physiology, such as the relative proportions of different fiber types in the skeletal muscles. Muscle fibers are primarily of two types: **fast twitch** (FT) or **slow twitch** (ST). Fast twitch fibers predominate during anaerobic, explosive activity, whereas slow twitch fibers predominate during endurance activity. In the table below, note the difference in the degree to which the two fiber types show fatigue (a decrease in the capacity to do work). Training can increase fibre size and, to some extent, the makeup of the fiber, but not the proportion of ST to FT, which is genetically determined.

The Effects of Aerobic Training on Muscle Physiology

Improved oxidation of glycogen. Training increases the capacity of skeletal muscle to generate ATP aerobically.

An increased capacity of the muscle to oxidize fats. This allows muscle and liver glycogen to be used at a slower rate. The body also becomes more efficient at mobilizing free fatty acids from adipose tissue for use as fuel.

Increased myoglobin content. Myoglobin stores oxygen in the muscle cells and aids oxygen delivery to the mitochondria. Endurance training increases muscle myoglobin by 75%-80%.

Increase in lean muscle mass and decrease in body fat. Trained endurance athletes typically have body fat levels of 15-19% (women) or 6-18% (men), compared with 26% (women) and 15% (men) for non-athletes.

The size of **slow twitch fibers** increases. This change in size is associated with increased aerobic capacity.

An increase in the size and density of mitochondria in the skeletal muscles and an increase in the activity and concentration of Krebs cycle enzymes.

An increase in the number of capillaries surrounding each muscle fiber. Endurance trained men have 5%-10% more capillaries in their muscles than sedentary men.

Fast vs Slow Twitch Muscle

Feature	Fast twitch	Slow twitch
Color	White	Red
Diameter	Large	Small
Contraction rate	Fast	Slow
ATP production	Fast	Slow
Metabolism	Anaerobic	Aerobic
Rate of fatigue	Fast	Slow
Power	High	Low

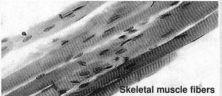

Skeletal muscle fibers

There are two basic types of muscle fibers. Slow twitch (type I) muscle and fast twitch (type II) muscle fiber. Human muscles contain a genetically determined mixture of both slow and fast fiber types. On average, we have about 50% slow and 50% fast fibers in most of the muscles used for movement.

The slow twitch fibers contain more mitochondria and myoglobin than fast twitch fibers, which makes them more efficient at using oxygen to generate ATP without lactate acid build up. In this way, they can fuel repeated and extended muscle contractions such as those required for endurance events like a marathon.

Both fiber types generally produce the same force per contraction, but fast twitch fibers produce that force at a higher rate, so fast fibers are important when there is a limited time in which to generate maximal force (as in a sprint)

1. Explain three ways in which aerobic (endurance) training improves the oxidative function of muscle:

(a) _____

_____

(b) _____

_____

(c) _____

_____

2. Contrast the properties of fast and slow twitch skeletal muscle fibers, identifying how these properties contribute to their performance in different conditions:

_____

_____

_____

Related activities: The Human Respiratory System, Exercise and Blood Flow,
Web link: Muscle Fatigue, Effects of Training

RA 2

Nerves, Muscles and Movement

Animal Behavior

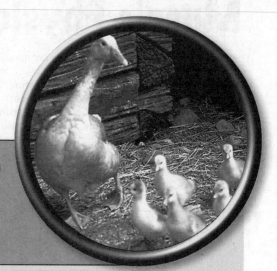

IB SL	IB HL	IB Options	AP Biology
Not applicable to core	Not applicable to core	Complete: Option E: SL/HL: 1-12, 15-19 HL: 13-14, 20-26, 29	Complete: 1-34 Some numbers extension as appropriate

Learning Objectives

☐ 1. Compile your own glossary from the **KEY WORDS** displayed in **bold type** in the learning objectives below.

Introduction to Behavior (page 312 and see the TRC: Behavior Supplements)

☐ 2. Appreciate that the behavior of animals is related to the **environmental context**. Explain the role of **natural selection** in the development of behavior patterns; behavior is fine-tuned by microevolutionary processes in the same way as structure and physiology.

☐ 3. Contrast the dependence (or otherwise) of **innate** and **learned behavior** on the environmental context.

☐ 4. Describe, using species of birds or non-human mammals, specific examples of each of the following types of behavior. See the objective numbers provided for activities and details to help with your explanation:
- **Migration** see numbers 11-12
- **Grooming** see number 33
- **Courtship** see numbers 28-29
- **Communication** see numbers 22, 26
- **Mate selection** see numbers 29, 34

☐ 5. Explain the need for **quantitative data** in studies of behavior. Suggest how these data could be obtained.

Innate Behavior (page 312)

☐ 6. Distinguish **innate** from **learned behavior**. With respect to innate behavior, explain the terms **stereotyped, fixed action pattern**, and **sign stimuli**.

☐ 7. Explain the role of **orientation** in the survival of an organism. Distinguish between **migration** and orientation behavior, and other innate behaviors.

Taxes and kineses (pages 313-314)

☐ 8. Define the terms: **taxis** (*pl.* taxes) and **kinesis** (*pl.* kineses), distinguishing clearly between them. Distinguish between **positive** and **negative** responses.

☐ 9. Describe the role of **pheromones** in animal orientation, including their role as sexual attractants and as signalling molecules to coordinate activities in social species such as ants.

☐ 10. Explain, using named examples, the adaptive value of taxes and kineses. Typical examples of **taxes** include the response of *Euglena* toward light, flatworms towards food, and blowfly larvae away from light. Typical examples of **kineses** include the response of woodlice to humidity and body lice to temperature.

Migration & dispersal (pages 317-319 & the TRC)

☐ 11. Using examples, distinguish between **migration** and **dispersal**. Identify the broad environmental cues important for migratory and dispersal behaviors. Identify how and why they might be different.

☐ 12. Explain what is meant by **navigation**. Describe how migratory birds navigate and identify the internal and external stimuli that trigger the migration.

Biological Rhythms (page 320 and the TRC)

☐ 13. Describe what is meant by a **biological rhythm**, explain what governs these rhythms, and comment on the predictable nature of the environmental cues. Describe examples of biological rhythms in plants and animals and identify the events governed by the rhythm in each case.

☐ 14. Providing examples, describe the characteristics of the following biological rhythms: **daily** rhythm, **tidal** rhythm, **lunar** rhythm, **annual** rhythm. Name the cues that establish and maintain the rhythm in each case.

Learned Behavior (pages 315-316)

☐ 15. Recall the difference between innate and **learned behaviors**. Name examples of learned behaviors, identifying their adaptive role in each case.

☐ 16. Explain what is meant by **habituation** and distinguish it clearly from sensory adaptation. Understand the basic characteristics of habituation and its adaptive value.

☐ 17. Identify the basic characteristics of **imprinting** and its adaptive value. Outline **Lorenz**'s experiments on imprinting in geese. Include reference to the role of **sign stimuli**, **species-specific behavior**, and **innate releasing mechanisms** in the imprinting behavior.

☐ 18. Explain what is meant by **classical conditioning**, and outline the work of **Pavlov** that illustrates this. Include reference to the **unconditioned stimulus**, **conditioned stimulus**, **unconditioned response** and **conditioned response**. Using examples, discuss how this form of learning improves the chances of survival.

☐ 19. Explain what is meant by **operant conditioning** and distinguish it from classical conditioning. Outline the work of **Skinner** that investigated this type of learning. Include reference to the following in your explanation: **operant response**, **reinforcement**, and **reward**.

Sociality and Communication (pages 319-322)

☐ 20. Describe the benefits and problems associated with **social behavior**. Appreciate that most social behaviors are innate but may be modified by experience (learning).

☐ 21. Identify some important social behaviors, identifying the role of the behavior in each case. List examples of social animals and describe the behavior involved.

☐ 22. Describe the types of auditory, visual, and olfactory signals used by animals to **communicate**. Distinguish between types of **displays** and their purposes. Describe the role of communication in reproduction and in maintaining social systems.

Social Organization *(pages 323-325 and the TRC)*

☐ 23. Outline the benefits to survival of **group behavior**. Distinguish between true **social organization** and large, rather loose groupings or **aggregations** (such as occur in flocks and schools).

☐ 24. Explain what is meant by **altruistic behavior**. Discuss the role of altruistic behavior (**altruism**) in social organizations, using two examples (examples follow):

Helpers at the nest: Describe altruism in birds (e.g. some species of jays), where **helper birds** assist in rearing the offspring of a single pair. Discuss the benefits of this behavior to the helpers, the parents, and the offspring, and suggest how the behavior might be explained in an evolutionary sense.

Alarm calls in Belding's ground squirrel: Belding's ground squirrels will stare at a predator while giving an alarm call, even though this increases their chance of being attacked. Females with female relatives in the area are more likely to give these alarm calls. Explain the selective benefits of this behavior and identify any disadvantage to the individual.

☐ 25. In general terms, describe the survival value of group cooperative behavior in detection and defense against danger, food acquisition, and reproduction.

☐ 26. Describe social organization of honey bee colonies as an example of sociality in insects. Include reference to the **caste systems** and methods of **communication**. Appreciate why a social insect colony is sometimes termed a super-organism.

Reproductive Behavior *(pages 319, 326-329)*

☐ 27. Describe examples of **breeding behavior**. Explain the role of these behaviors suspending aggression between competing individuals.

☐ 28. Describe **courtship** behavior in a named example, e.g. mallard duck, peacock, identifying its role in breeding.

Include reference to the **male display**, **stereotyped** fixed action patterns, and duration of display. Discuss whether the behaviors are learned or innate.

☐ 29. Explain the basis of **mate selection**, identifying aspects of male behavior important in female choice. Recognize the role of **territories**, **male displays**, or **combat** in this process.

☐ 30. Explain what is meant by **parental care** and appreciate how it is different from altruism. Account for the variability observed in the degree of parental care in different species. Describe the nature of parental care in named examples to show this variation.

☐ 31. Describe examples of **sign stimuli** used by offspring to elicit parental care behaviors in the adults.

Aggressive Behavior *(pages 319-321, 328-330)*

☐ 32. Distinguish between **aggression** and **agonistic behavior**. Identify examples of agonistic behavior in the following behaviors: sexual, parent-offspring, territorial, competitive, sibling, and dominance.

☐ 33. Identify the purpose of **hierarchies** in social animals and describe an example of a hierarchical social structure. In your example, describe behaviors used to maintain **rank** and consolidate relationships in the hierarchy (e.g. **grooming**, **displays**, **appeasement behavior**, vocalizations, or **ceremonies** that may be **aggressive** or **submissive**). Appreciate the role of auditory or visual signals in the recognition of individuals and maintenance of social position.

☐ 34. Distinguish between **territory** and **home range**. Describe the benefits and disadvantages of territories and explain how territorial behavior may change seasonally. Describe the types of auditory, visual, and olfactory signals used to mark and maintain territories.

See the 'Textbook Reference Grid' on pages 8-9 for textbook page references relating to material in this topic.

Supplementary Texts

See page 6 for additional details of this text:
- Murray, P. and N. Owens, 2001. **Behavior and Populations** (Collins), pp. 6-27.
- Helms, D.R. *et al.*, 1998. **Biology in the Laboratory** (W.H. Freeman), #42.

See page 6 for details of publishers of periodicals:

STUDENT'S REFERENCE

- **Migration** New Scientist 12 Sept. 1992 (Inside Science). *An excellent overview of migration in a number of different animal species.*
- **No Way Out** New Scientist, 26 January 2002, pp. 34-38. *A study of repetitive behaviors in captive animals indicates a high level of frustration.*
- **All for One** New Scientist, 13 June 1998, pp. 32-35. *Social insects such as ants and termites all show cooperative behavior: workers are altruistic and the colony functions as a superorganism.*

- **Monkey Business** New Scientist 5 Nov. 2005. *Examining patterns of primate behavior, such as the sense of 'fairness' and how monkeys work together for mutual benefit.*
- **Evolution of Parental Care** Biol. Sci. Rev., 17(2) Nov. 2004, pp. 13-16. *An account of the varied strategies for parental care. Why do parents improve offspring survival at a cost to themselves?*
- **The Social Life of Foxes** Biol. Sci. Rev., 13(2) Nov. 2000, pp. 15-18. *Social organization in a canid, including an examination of dominance relationships and the benefits of cooperative care.*

TEACHER'S REFERENCE

- **Oh Brother!** New Scientist, 19 Feb. 2000, pp. 36-39. *This article looks at the reason for siblicide in animal species and suggests it is a mechanism for manipulating sex ratios in the offspring.*
- **Child Care among the Insects** Scientific American, Jan. 1999, pp. 50-55. *An account of parental care in insects and its costs and benefits.*
- **Divided We Fall: Cooperation Among Lions** Scientific American, May 1997, pp. 32-39. *Lions cooperate for both group and individual benefit.*
- **Africa's Wild Dogs** National Geographic, May 1999, pp. 36-63. *The ecology and behavior of wild dogs, including the role of territoriality.*
- **How Females Choose their Mates** Scientific American, April 1998, pp. 46-51. *The methods by which females choose their reproductive mates.*
- **Disturbing Behaviours of the Orangutan** Scientific American, June 2002, pp. 46-51. *Studies of these great apes show that subordinate male adolescents remain in a state of arrested development with respect to their secondary sexual characteristics, but copulate forcibly with females.*

This behavior represents an evolutionary strategy aimed at maximizing reproductive success.
- **Mouse Behavior** The Am. Biology Teacher 63(5), May 2001, pp. 346-350. *A how-to-do-it study on the behavior of mice to illustrate adaptation.*
- **A Directed Research Project Investigating Territoriality and Aggression in Crickets** The Am. Biology Teacher 63(1), Jan. 2001, pp. 44-47. *The outline of an animal behavior experiment investigating aggression in crickets.*
- **Using Artificial Nests to Study Nest Predation in Birds** The Am. Biology Teacher, 67 (2), Feb. 2005, pp. 105-110. *A how-to-do-it series of field exercises demonstrating factors affecting predation on bird nests. Hypotheses about nesting behavior can be formulated and examined.*

See pages 10-11 for details of how to access **Bio Links** from our web site: **www.thebiozone.com** From Bio Links, access sites under the topics: **ANIMAL BEHAVIOR:** • Animal behavior • Innate behavior • Ken's bioweb resources: Animal behavior • Pavlovian conditioning • Sign stimuli and motivation... *and others*

Software and video resources for this topic are provided on the **Teacher Resource CD-ROM**

Animal Behavior

The Components of Behavior

Behavior in animals can be attributed to two components: **innate behavior** that has a genetic basis, and **learned behavior**, which results from the experiences of the animal. Together they combine to produce the total behavior exhibited by the animal. It should also be noted that experience may modify certain innate behaviors. Animals behave in fixed, predictable ways in many situations. The innate behavior follows a classical pathway called a **fixed-action pattern** (FAP) where an innate behavioral program is activated by a stimulus or **releaser** to direct some kind of behavioral response. Innate behaviors are generally adaptive and are performed for a variety of reasons. Learning, which involves the modification of behavior by experience, occurs in various ways.

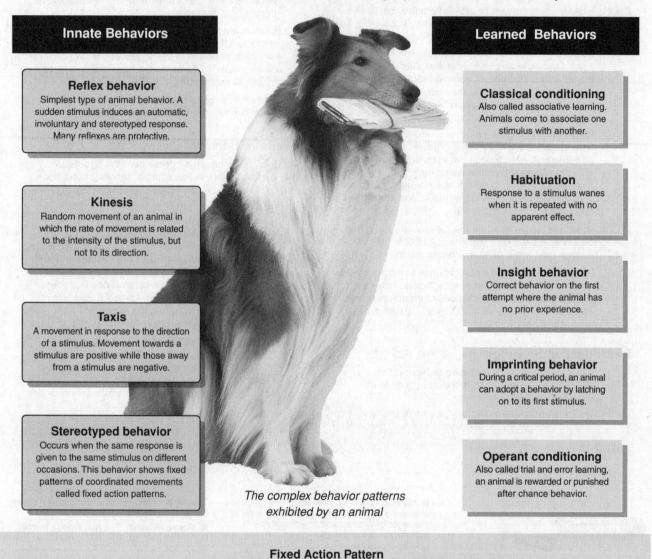

Innate Behaviors

Reflex behavior
Simplest type of animal behavior. A sudden stimulus induces an automatic, involuntary and stereotyped response. Many reflexes are protective.

Kinesis
Random movement of an animal in which the rate of movement is related to the intensity of the stimulus, but not to its direction.

Taxis
A movement in response to the direction of a stimulus. Movement towards a stimulus are positive while those away from a stimulus are negative.

Stereotyped behavior
Occurs when the same response is given to the same stimulus on different occasions. This behavior shows fixed patterns of coordinated movements called fixed action patterns.

Learned Behaviors

Classical conditioning
Also called associative learning. Animals come to associate one stimulus with another.

Habituation
Response to a stimulus wanes when it is repeated with no apparent effect.

Insight behavior
Correct behavior on the first attempt where the animal has no prior experience.

Imprinting behavior
During a critical period, an animal can adopt a behavior by latching on to its first stimulus.

Operant conditioning
Also called trial and error learning, an animal is rewarded or punished after chance behavior.

The complex behavior patterns exhibited by an animal

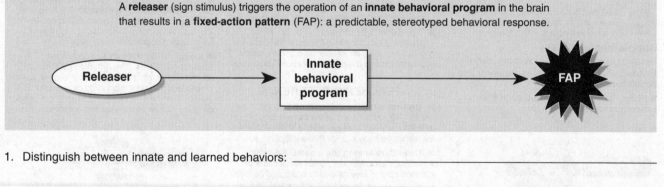

Fixed Action Pattern
A **releaser** (sign stimulus) triggers the operation of an **innate behavioral program** in the brain that results in a **fixed-action pattern** (FAP): a predictable, stereotyped behavioral response.

Releaser → Innate behavioral program → FAP

1. Distinguish between innate and learned behaviors: _____

_____

2. (a) Explain the role of releasers in innate behaviors: _____

_____

(b) Name a releaser for a fixed action pattern and the animal involved, and describe the behavior elicited: _____

_____

_____

Related activities: Simple Behaviors, Learned Behavior
Web links: Animal Behavior Record

Simple Behaviors

Taxes and kineses are examples of **orientation behaviors**. Such behaviors describe the way in which motile organisms (or gametes) **position** themselves and move in response to external cues (stimuli). Common stimuli are gravity, light, chemicals, and temperature. Some animals and many protozoa respond to certain stimuli simply by changing their rate of movement or by randomly turning without actually orientating to the stimulus. These movements are called **kineses** (*sing.* kinesis). In contrast, **taxes** (*sing.* taxis) involve orientation and movement directly to or away from one or more stimuli, such as temperature. Taxes often involve moving the head (which carries the sensory receptors) from side to side until the sensory input from both sides is equal (a **klinotaxic response**). Note that many taxic responses are complicated by a simultaneous response to more than one stimulus. For example, fish orientate dorsal side up by responding to both light and gravity. Male moths orientate positively to **pheromones**, but use the wind to judge the direction of the odor source (the female moth).

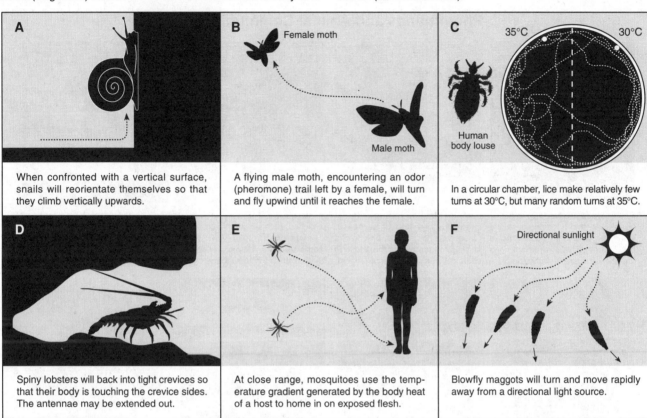

A When confronted with a vertical surface, snails will reorientate themselves so that they climb vertically upwards.

B Female moth / Male moth. A flying male moth, encountering an odor (pheromone) trail left by a female, will turn and fly upwind until it reaches the female.

C 35°C / 30°C. Human body louse. In a circular chamber, lice make relatively few turns at 30°C, but many random turns at 35°C.

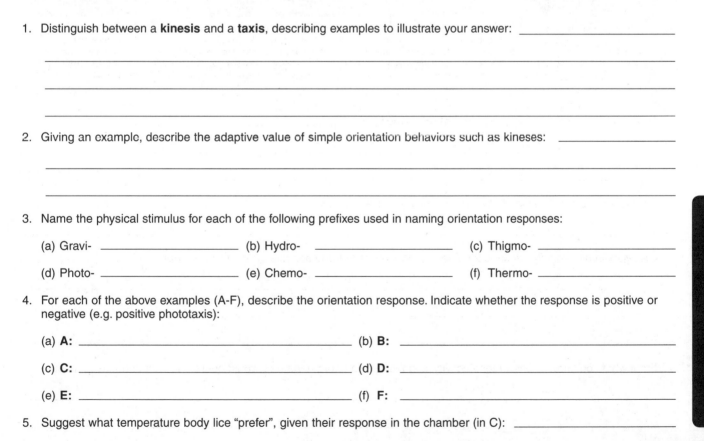

D Spiny lobsters will back into tight crevices so that their body is touching the crevice sides. The antennae may be extended out.

E At close range, mosquitoes use the temperature gradient generated by the body heat of a host to home in on exposed flesh.

F Directional sunlight. Blowfly maggots will turn and move rapidly away from a directional light source.

1. Distinguish between a **kinesis** and a **taxis**, describing examples to illustrate your answer: _____

_____

_____

_____

2. Giving an example, describe the adaptive value of simple orientation behaviors such as kineses: _____

_____

_____

3. Name the physical stimulus for each of the following prefixes used in naming orientation responses:

   (a) Gravi- _____   (b) Hydro- _____   (c) Thigmo- _____

   (d) Photo- _____   (e) Chemo- _____   (f) Thermo- _____

4. For each of the above examples (A-F), describe the orientation response. Indicate whether the response is positive or negative (e.g. positive phototaxis):

   (a) **A:** _____   (b) **B:** _____

   (c) **C:** _____   (d) **D:** _____

   (e) **E:** _____   (f) **F:** _____

5. Suggest what temperature body lice "prefer", given their response in the chamber (in C): _____

Related activities: The Components of Behavior, Pheromones
Web links: Assessing Habitat Preference

RA 2

Animal Behavior

Pheromones

A **pheromone** is a chemical produced by an animal and released into the external environment where it has an effect on the physiology or behavior of members of the same species. Hundreds of pheromones, some of which are sex attractants, are known. They are especially common amongst insects and mammals, and commonly relate to reproductive behavior. Many mammals, including canids and all members of the cat family, commonly use scent marking to mark territorial boundaries and to advertise their sexual receptivity to potential mates. Other mammals, including rabbits, release a mammary pheromone that triggers nursing behavior in the young. Pheromones are also used as signalling molecules in social insects such as bees, wasps, and ants. They may be used to mark a scent trail to a food source or to signal alarm. Species specific odor cues are now widely used as bait in traps when controlling insect or mammalian pests or to capture animals for study.

Pheromones and Animal Communication

Pheromones produced by a honey bee queen and her daughters, the workers, maintain the social order of the colony. The pheromone is a blend of unsaturated fatty acids.

Like mammals, reptiles detect chemicals with the vomeronasal (Jacobson's) organ. The flicking of a snake's tongue allows the snake to chemically sample its environment.

In mammals, pheromones are used to signal sexual receptivity and territorial presence, or to synchronize group behavior. Pheromone detection relies on the vomeronasal organ (VNO), an area of receptor tissue in the nasal cavity. Mammals use a flehmen response, in which the upper lip is curled up, to better expose the VNO to the chemicals of interest.

Photo courtesy of Cereal Research Centre, AAFC

Communication in ants and other social insects occurs through detection of pheromones. Foraging ants will leave a trail along the ground which other ants will follow and reinforce until the food source is depleted. Ants also release alarm substances, which will send other ants in the vicinity into an attack frenzy. These signals dissipate rapidly if not reinforced.

The feathery antennae of male moths are stereochemically specialised to detect the pheromone released by a female moth. Male moths can detect concentrations as low as 2ppm and will fly upwind toward the source to mate with the female. This sex attractant property of pheromones is exploited in pheromone traps, which are widely used to trap insect pests in orchards.

1. (a) Distinguish between hormones and **pheromones**: _____

_____

_____

(b) Explain the significance of pheromones being species specific: _____

_____

2. Giving examples, briefly describe the role of pheromones in three aspects of animals behavior:

(a) _____

(b) _____

(c) _____

3. From what you know of pheromone activity, suggest how a pheromone trap would operate to control an insect pest:

_____

_____

Related activities: Simple Behaviors, The Endocrine System
Web links: Cichlid Response to Pheromones

Learned Behavior

Imprinting occurs when an animal learns to make a particular response only to one type of animal or object. Imprinting differs from most other kinds of learned behavior in that it normally can occur only at a specific time during an animal's life. This **critical period** is usually shortly after hatching (about 12 hours) and can last for several days. While a critical period and the resulting imprinted behavior are normally irreversible, they are not considered rigidly fixed. There are examples of animals that have had abnormal imprinted behaviors revert to the 'wild type'. There are two main types of imprinting using visual and auditory stimuli: filial and sexual imprinting. Breeding ground imprinting uses olfactory (smell) stimuli.

Filial (Parent) Imprinting

Filial imprinting is the process by which animals develop a social attachment. It differs from most other kinds of learning (including other types of imprinting), in that it normally can occur only at a specific time during an animal's life. This **critical period** is usually shortly after hatching (about 12 hours) and may last for several days. Ducks and geese have no innate ability to recognize *mother* or even their own species. They simply respond to, and identify as mother, the first object they encounter that has certain characteristics.

Breeding Ground Imprinting

Salmon undertake long migrations in the open ocean where they feed, grow and mature after hatching in freshwater streams. Some species remain at sea for several years, after which each fish returns to its exact home stream to spawn. Research has shown that this ability is based on **olfactory imprinting** where the fish recognize the chemical odors of their specific stream and swim towards its source. Other animals (bears, humans, etc.) have learned to exploit this behavior.

Sexual Identity Imprinting

Individuals learn to direct their sexual behavior at some stimulus objects, but not at others. Termed **sexual imprinting**, it may serve as a species identifying and species isolating mechanism. The mate preferences of birds have been shown to be imprinted according to the stimulus they were exposed to (other birds) during early rearing. Sexual imprinting generally involves longer periods of exposure to the stimulus than filial imprinting (*see left*).

Habituation

Habituation is a very simple type of learning involving a loss of a response to a repeated stimulus when it fails to provide any form of reinforcement (reward or punishment). Habituation is different to fatigue, which involves loss of efficiency in a repeated activity, and arises as a result of the nature of sensory reception itself. An example of habituation is the waning response of a snail attempting to cross a platform that is being tapped at regular time intervals. At first, the snail retreats into its shell for a considerable period after each tap. As the tapping continues, the snail stays in its shell for a shorter duration, before resuming its travel.

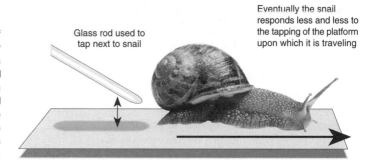

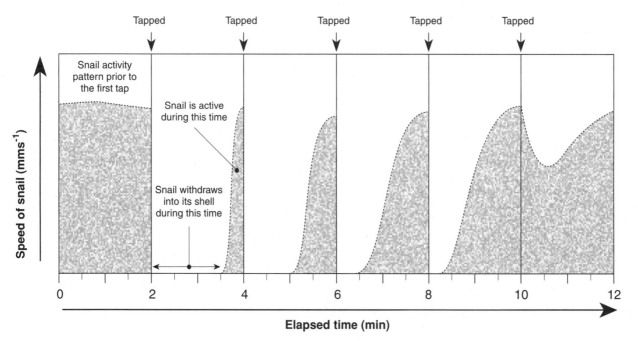

Related activities: The Components of Behavior
Web links: Optimal Foraging, Learning to Sing

A 1

Animal Behavior

Classical (Pavlovian) Conditioning

Classical conditioning, founded by **Ivan Pavlov**, describes a type of **associative learning** in which behavior that is normally triggered by a certain stimulus comes to be triggered by a substitute stimulus that previously had no effect on the behavior. Between 1890 and 1900, Pavlov noticed that the dogs he was studying would salivate when they knew they were to be fed. It was determined that the dogs were alerted by a bell that rung every time the door into the lab was opened. Through experimentation, Pavlov discovered that the ringing of the bell initially brought about no salivation, but the dogs could be **conditioned** to relate the ringing of the bell to the presentation of food. Eventually the ringing of the bell elicited the same salivation response as the presentation of food, indicating that the dog was conditioned to associate the two stimuli.

❶ A bell is rung, immediately prior to feeding. The bell alone produces no salivary response in the dog.

❷ Food is introduced after the bell has rung. Steps one and two are repeated a number of times (association of bell and food).

❸ Eventually the dog becomes conditioned to salivate whenever the bell is rung, even when no food is presented.

Operant Conditioning

Operant conditioning is used to describe a situation where an animal learns to associate a particular behavioral act with a **reward** (as opposed to a stimulus in classical conditioning). This behavior determines whether or not the reward appears. **Burrhus Skinner** studied operant conditioning using an apparatus he invented called a **Skinner box** *(see right)*. Skinner designed the box so that when an animal (usually a pigeon or rat) pushed a particular button it was rewarded with food. The animals learned to associate the pushing of the button with obtaining food (the reward). The behavioral act that leads the animal to push the button in the first place is thought to be generated spontaneously (by accident or curiosity). This type of learning is also called **instrumental learning** because the spontaneous behavior is instrumental in obtaining the reward. Operant conditioning is the predominant learning process found in animals.

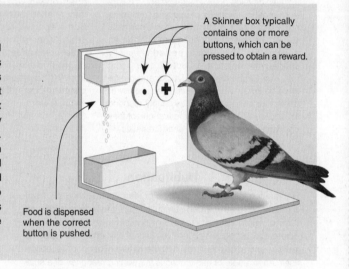

A Skinner box typically contains one or more buttons, which can be pressed to obtain a reward.

Food is dispensed when the correct button is pushed.

1. Explain what is meant by **filial imprinting**: _____

_____

_____

2. For the example of filial imprinting (see previous page), identify which parts of the behavior can be attributed to:

   (a) Innate behavior: _____

   (b) Learned behavior: _____

3. In relation to human behavior, describe an example of the following:

   (a) Habituation: _____

   _____

   (b) Imprinting: _____

   _____

   (c) Classical conditioning: _____

   _____

   (d) Operant conditioning: _____

   _____

Migratory Navigation in Birds

Navigation is the process by which an animal uses various cues to determine its position in reference to a particular goal. Migrating birds must be able to know their flight direction and when they have reached their destination (goal). They use a wide range of environmental stimuli to provide navigational cues.

These include stellar and solar cues, visible landscape features, prevailing wind direction, low frequency sounds generated by winds, polarized light, the Earth's magnetic field, gravitational 'contours', and the smell of pungent sea bird colonies or the sweet smell of meadows. Some of these are examined below:

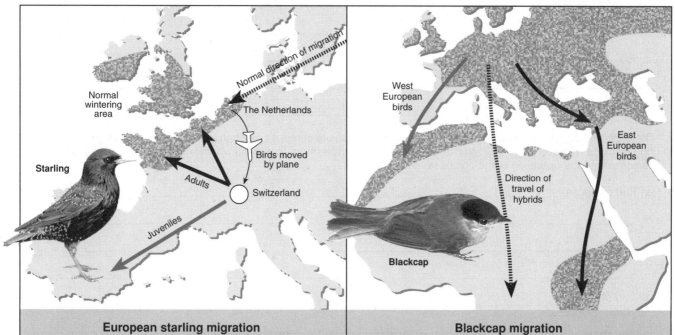

European starling migration

An experiment with starlings investigated the roles of **genetics** and **experience** in navigating during migration. Birds caught in the autumn leg of their migration were caught in the Netherlands and taken to Switzerland and released. The juveniles, which had not migrated before, flew to Spain. The more experienced birds reached their winter homes in France, Britain and Ireland.

Blackcap migration

Blackcaps are divided in their migration paths. Birds breeding in eastern Europe fly via Turkey to eastern Africa. Those from western Europe fly across the Strait of Gibralta to north Africa. In an experiment to test their genetic memory for navigation, birds from both populations were crossed. The hybrids tried to fly south but on a course that takes them over the Alps and the widest part of the Mediterranean.

Sun compass

Experiments have been carried out to investigate the existence of a sun compass and its importance for daytime migrations. Caged birds were placed in circular enclosures with four windows. Mirrors were used to alter the angle at which light entered the enclosures. At migration time, in natural conditions, these birds clearly showed a preferred flight direction (left). When mirrors bent the suns rays through 90°, the birds turned their preferred direction (middle and right).

Magnetic compass

An experiment that investigated the possibility of a magnetic compass being used by migratory birds used magnetic coils to mimic the Earth's magnetic field. The birds detect magnetic north, the direction of their spring migration. When the magnetic field was twisted so that north was in the east-southeast position, the birds kept their original path for the first two nights. By the third night, they had detected the change and altered their path accordingly.

Star compass

An experiment that investigated the use of star positions in the night sky used an ink pad at the base of a cone of blotting paper. Nocturnal migrants flutter in their preferred direction of travel as the amount of ink shows. In a planetarium that projected the real sky, Indigo Buntings located the Pole Star and used it to find north, the direction of their spring migration. When the sky in the planetarium was rotated 90° counter-clockwise the birds altered their direction accordingly. Simulating a cloudy night, the obscured sky confused the birds.

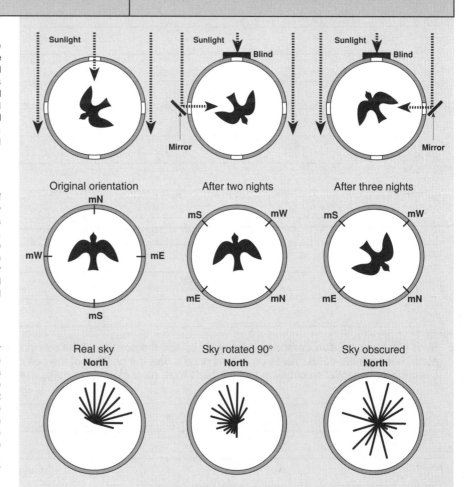

Animal Behavior

Related activities: Migratory Patterns
Web links: Bird Migration

RA 2

1. Making reference to the information on the **European starling** and **blackcap** migrations opposite, discuss the contributions of innate behavior (genetic programing) and learned behavior on navigation in these migratory birds:

_____

_____

_____

_____

_____

2. The experiments on the opposite page investigate three possible compass mechanisms used by migratory birds in the long dictance migration flights. Discuss the results of each experiment to explain whether the experiment effectively demonstrated the operation of the compass:

(a) Sun compass: _____

_____

_____

_____

_____

_____

(b) Magnetic compass: _____

_____

_____

_____

_____

_____

(c) Star compass: _____

_____

_____

_____

_____

_____

3. Birds that rely on a **sun compass** to navigate by use the position of the sun in the sky as a reference point to determine north. Because the earth rotates on its axis once a day, the position of the sun in the sky is constantly changing. Describe an essential mechanism that the birds must have in order to make use of this type of compass:

_____

_____

_____

318

Migration Patterns

In many animals, migration is an important response to environmental change. True migrations are those where animals travel from one well-defined region to another, for a specific purpose such as overwintering, breeding, or seeking food. Migrations often involve very large distances and usually involve a return journey. They are initiated by the activity of internal clocks or timekeepers in response to environmental cues such as change in temperature or daylength. Some mass movements of animals are not truly migrations in that they do not involve a return journey and they are governed by something other than an internal biological clock (e.g. depletion of a food resource). Such movements are best described as dispersals and are typical of species such as 'migratory' locusts and some large African mammals which relocate in response to changing food supplies.

Dispersal: one-way migration

Some migrations of animals involve a one-way movement. In such cases, the animal does not return to its original home range. This is typical of population dispersal. This often occurs to escape deteriorating habitats and to colonise new ones.

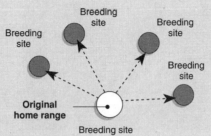

Dispersal: muskrat

Return migration

Animals that move to a winter feeding ground are making one leg of a return migration. The same animals return to their home range in the spring which is where they have their breeding sites. Sometimes they follow different routes on the return journey.

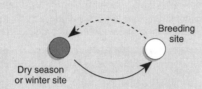

Return migration: caribou

Nomadic migration

Similar to one-way migration but individuals may breed at several locations during their lifetimes. These migrations are apparently directionless, with no set pattern. Each stopover point is a potential breeding site. There may also be temporary non-breeding stopovers for the winter or dry season.

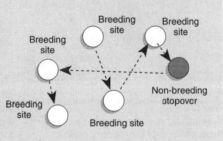

Nomadic Inuit

Nomadic Bedouin

Remigration circuits

In some populations, the return leg of a migration may have stopovers and may be completed by one or more subsequent generations. In addition to winter or dry season areas, there may be stops at feeding areas by juveniles or adults. Also included are closed circuits where animals die after breeding.

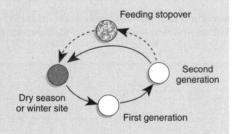

Remigration circuit: Pacific salmon

1. Giving an example, describe the conditions under which nomadic migration behavior might be necessary:

_____

_____

2. Identify which of the above forms of migration would lead to further dispersal of a population. Explain your answer:

_____

3. Describe an environmental cue important in the regular migratory behavior of a named species:

_____

4. Discuss the adaptive value of migratory behavior: _____

_____

_____

_____

Related activities: Migratory Navigation in Birds, Home Ranges and Resources

RA 2

Animal Behavior

Biological Rhythms

Environmental cues, such as daylength, timing and the height of tides, temperature, and phase of the moon are often used by plants and animals to establish and maintain a pattern of activity. Regular environmental cues assist in survival by synchronizing important events in the life cycle of an organism; events such as pollination, mating, birth, germination, rearing of offspring, collection and storage of food reserves and body fat, and periods of torpor. **Biological rhythms** (biorhythms) in direct response to environmental stimuli are said to be **exogenous**, because the rhythm is controlled by an environmental stimulus that is external to the organism. Those rhythms that continue in the absence of external cues are said to be **endogenous**.

TIDAL: mud crab

Rhythm: tidal.
Period: ~ 12.4 h (coincident with tidal flows).
Examples: In mud crabs, locomotion and feeding occurs when covered by tidal waters.

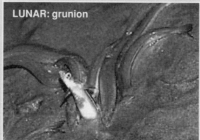

LUNAR: grunion

Rhythm: lunar.
Period: ~ 29.5 days (a month).
Example: In grunions, egg laying above the high water mark coincides with a new moon.

DAILY: kokako

Rhythm: daily
Period: ~ 24 h.
Examples: In kokako, general activity and feeding occurs during daylight hours.

ANNUAL: sheep

Rhythm: annual.
Period: ~ a year.
Example: In many domestic livestock and antelope species, young are born in spring.

ANNUAL: NZ long tailed bat

Rhythm: annual.
Period: ~ a year.
Example: NZ long-tailed bats hibernate for 4-5 months during the autumn and winter.

INTERMITTENT: shiner

Rhythm: intermittent.
Period: does not apply.
Example: In some shiners (a minnow-like fish), reproduction is triggered by flooding.

1. Use the examples provided above to determine a definition of each of the following terms describing biological rhythms. For each type of rhythm describe one other example to illustrate how the behavior follows the astronomical cycle:

   (a) **Daily** rhythm: _____

   Example: _____

   (b) **Lunar** rhythm: _____

   Example: _____

   (c) **Annual** rhythm: _____

   Example: _____

   (d) **Tidal** rhythm: _____

   Example: _____

2. For each of the examples below, describe an **environmental cue** that might be used to induce or maintain the activity:

   (a) Hedgehog's hibernation in winter: _____

   (b) Blackbird's foraging and social behavior during daylight: _____

   (c) Kiwi's activity of hunting for soil organisms at night: _____

   (d) Coordinated flowering of plants in spring: _____

3. Explain what is meant by an exogenous rhythm: _____

Related activities: Breeding Behavior
Web links: Biological Clocks Animations

Animal Communication

Communication (the transmission of (understood) information) between animals of the same species is essential to the survival and reproductive success of animals. Effective communication enables animals to avoid predators, coordinate foraging and hunting activity, maintain social behaviors, and attract mates.

Messages can be passed between animals using a range of signals that commonly include visual, chemical, auditory, and tactile perception. Which of these signals is adopted will depend on the activity pattern and habitat of the animal. Visual displays, for example, are ineffective at night or in heavy undergrowth.

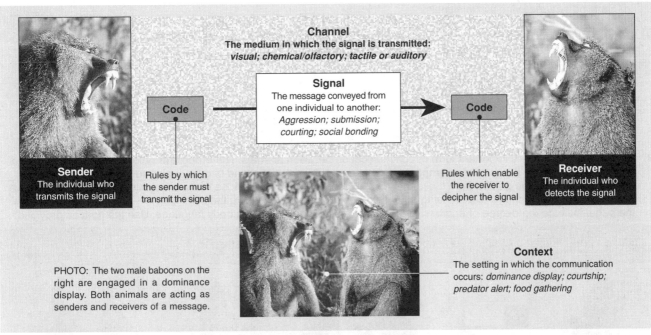

Channel
The medium in which the signal is transmitted:
visual; chemical/olfactory; tactile or auditory

Signal
The message conveyed from one individual to another:
Aggression; submission; courting; social bonding

Code

Code

Sender
The individual who transmits the signal

Rules by which the sender must transmit the signal

Rules which enable the receiver to decipher the signal

Receiver
The individual who detects the signal

Context
The setting in which the communication occurs: *dominance display; courtship; predator alert; food gathering*

PHOTO: The two male baboons on the right are engaged in a dominance display. Both animals are acting as senders and receivers of a message.

Olfactory Messages
Some animals produce special scents that are carried considerable distance by the wind. This may serve to advertise for a potential mate, or warn neighboring competitors to keep out of a territory. In some cases, mammals use their urine and feces to mark territorial boundaries. Sniffing genitals is common among mammals.

Tactile Messages
The touching of one animal by another may be a cooperative interaction or an aggressive one. Grooming behavior between members of a primate group communicates social bonding. Vibrations sent along a web by a male spider communicates to a potential female mate not to eat him.

Auditory Messages
Sound may be used to communicate over great distances. Birds keep rivals away and advertise for mates with birdsong. Fin whales are able to send messages over thousands of kilometers of ocean. Calls made by mammals may serve to attract mates, keep in touch with other members of a group or warn away competitors.

Visual Messages
Many animals convey information to other members of the species through their body coverings and adornment, as well as through gestures and body language. Through visual displays, it is possible to deliver threat messages, show submission, attract a mate and even exert control over a social group.

Warning
Animals may communicate a warning to other animals through visual displays. Many wasp species (like those above) have brightly colored black and yellow markings to tell potential predators that they risk being stung if attacked.

Deception
Animals may seek to deceive other animals about their identity. As an alternative to camouflage, animals may use visual markings that startle or deter potential predators. The eye spots on this moth may confuse a predator.

Attraction
Some animals produce a stunning visual display in order to attract a mate. The plumage of some bird species can be extremely colorful and elaborate, such as the peacock (above), the birds of paradise, and the lyrebird.

Animal Behavior

Related activities: Social Organization, Cooperative Behavior, Breeding Behavior, Aggressive Behavior

A 2

1. Describe a **benefit** an animal may receive as a result of being able to communicate information that facilitates:

   (a) Maintaining social structures: _____

   (b) Coordinating foraging and hunting: _____

   (c) Advertising suitability as a mate: _____

   (d) Sending and receiving alarm signals: _____

2. Describe the communication methods best suited to **nocturnal** animals in a forest habitat and explain how these are different to those used by **diurnal** animals living in open grassland:

   _____

   _____

   _____

3. Postures provide a very important form of communication between animals. The **ethogram** below illustrates the various postures exhibited by the **purple swamphen** (*Porphyrio porphyrio*), a wetland bird belonging to the rail family. Social behaviors can often be graded from those that display overt aggression to those that are submissive. Swamphens have a **graded range** of displays of increasing aggression or submission. By using the symbols (+, − and 0) at the bottom of the page, indicate the degree of aggressiveness, submissiveness, or neutral body language. Use the spaces provided:

Ethogram for Swamphen Behavior

1B

1A

Fighting. One bird jumping with feet ready for clawing and beak open for pecking.

2A   2B

Fighting. One bird in aggressive upright posture with wings and tail raised and feet raised. The other bird is in the aggressive upright but not attacking.

3

Full bow. Submissive wings and tail fully up.

4A   4B

Fighting. Both birds in aggressive uprights and using feet to attack.

5A   5B

Facing away. Submissive display to an aggressive upright bird.

6A   6B

Fighting. Both birds jumping with feet ready for clawing and beak open for pecking.

7

Aggressive upright. Wings down. Tail horizontal.

8

Move away. Submissive display. Wings exaggerated. Tail fully up to uncover white feathers.

9A   9B

Crouch. Submissive display to an aggressive upright bird.

10

Horizontal forward. Aggressive display but not as aggressive as an upright.

11A   11B

Head flagging. Submissive display. Head held low and moved from side to side.

12

Head flick. Submissive display. Usually at end of encounter. Wings exaggerated, tail fully up. Beak held too high to peck at other bird.

Range of aggressive/submissive behaviors

| + + very aggressive | + slightly aggressive | 0 neutral | − slightly submissive | − − very submissive |

Social Organization

All behavior appears to have its roots in the underlying genetic program of the individual. These innate behaviors may be modified by interactions of the individual with its environment, such as the experiences it is exposed to and its opportunities for learning. The behavioral adaptations of organisms affect their fitness (their ability to survive and successfully reproduce) and so are the products of natural selection. A behavior that leads to greater reproductive success should become more common in a species over time. Few animal species lead totally solitary lives. Many live in cooperative groups for all or part of their lives. Social animals comprise groups of individuals of the same species, living together in an organized fashion. They divide resources and activities between them and are mutually dependent (i.e. they do not survive or successfully reproduce outside the group).

Tigers are solitary and territorial animals, living and hunting alone. A male will remain with a female for 3-5 days during the mating season. A female may have 3 or 4 cubs which will stay with their mother for more than 2 years.

Many invertebrates (e.g. hermit crabs) are solitary animals, with occasional, random encounters. Some animals may be drawn together at feeding sites. Wind or currents may also cause aggregations.

Schooling fish and herds of mammals are examples of animals that form groups of a loose association. There is no set structure or hierarchy to the group. The grouping is often to provide mutual protection.

Family groups may consist of one or more parents with offspring of various ages. The relationship between parents may be a temporary, seasonal one or may be life-long.

Some insects (e.g. ants, termites, some wasp and many bee species) form colonies. The social structure of these colonies ranges from simple to complex, and may involve castes that provide for division of labor.

Primates such as chimpanzees and baboons have evolved complex social structures. Organized in terms of dominance hierarchies, higher ranked animals within the group have priority access to food and other resources.

Advantages of large social groupings

1. Protection from physical factors
2. Protection from predators
3. Assembly for mate selection
4. Locating and obtaining food
5. Defense of resources against other groups
6. Division of labor amongst specialists
7. Richer learning environment
8. Population regulation

Possible disadvantages of large social groupings

1. Increased competition between group members for resources as group size increases.
2. Increased chance of the spread of diseases and parasites.
3. Interference with reproduction (e.g. cheating in parental care; infanticide by non-parents).

1. Briefly describe two ways in which behavior may be passed on between generations:

    (a) _____

    (b) _____

2. Explain how large social groupings confer an advantage by providing:

    (a) Richer learning environment: _____

    _____

    _____

    _____

Animal Behavior

Related activities: Cooperative Behavior

DA 2

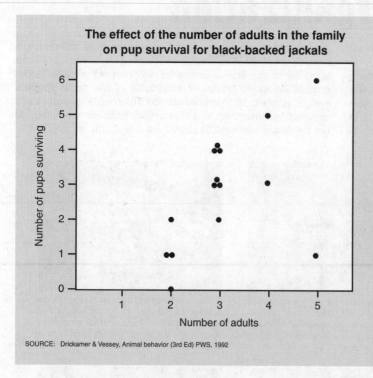

The effect of the number of adults in the family on pup survival for black-backed jackals

SOURCE: Drickamer & Vessey, Animal behavior (3rd Ed) PWS, 1992

Black-backed jackal *(Canis mesomelas)*

Black-backed jackals live in the brushland of Africa. Monogamous pairs (single male and female parents) hunt cooperatively, share food and defend territories. Offspring from the previous year's litter frequently help rear their siblings by regurgitating food for the lactating mother and for the pups themselves. The pup survival results of 15 separate jackal groups are shown in the graph on the left.

(b) Division of labor among specialists: _____

_____

_____

_____

(c) Assembly for mate selection: _____

_____

_____

_____

_____

3. The graph at the top of this page shows how the survival of black-backed jackal pups is influenced by the number of adult helpers in the group.

   (a) Draw an approximate 'line of best fit' on the graph (by eye) and describe the general trend: _____

   _____

   (b) Describe two ways in which additional adult helpers may increase the survival prospects of pups:

   _____

   _____

   _____

   _____

4. Explain how a social behavior that is beneficial to individuals in a species may become more common over time:

   _____

   _____

   _____

   _____

   _____

Cooperative Behavior

Individuals both within and between species may cooperate with each other for many reasons: for mutual defense and protection, to enhance food acquisition, or to rear young. To explain the evolution of cooperative behavior, it has been suggested that individuals benefit their own survival or the survival of their genes (offspring) by cooperating. **Kin selection** is a form of selection that favors altruistic (self-sacrificing) behavior towards relatives. In this type of behavior an individual will sacrifice its own opportunity to reproduce for the benefit of its close relatives. Individuals may also cooperate and behave altruistically if there is a chance that the "favor" may be returned at a later time. **Altruistic behavior** towards non-relatives is usually explained in terms of trade-offs, where individuals weigh up the costs and benefits of helpful behavior. Cooperation will evolve in systems where, in the long term, individuals all derive some benefit.

Many mammalian predators live in well organized social groups. These are formed for the purposes of cooperative hunting and defense and they facilitate offspring survival. In the gray wolves above, territories are marked by scent. Howling promotes group bonding and helps to keep neighboring packs away.

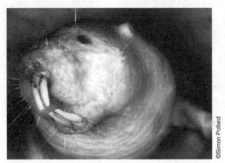

Naked mole rats, from the arid regions of Kenya, are unique among mammals in having a social organization similar to that of social insects. Up to 300 of the rodents spend their lives underground in a **colony** with a **caste system**, with workers, soldiers, infertile females, and one breeding queen.

The males of many species help their mates collect enough food to meet reproductive needs. In some species, especially amongst birds, non-breeding individuals, e.g. older siblings, may assist in rearing the offspring by protecting or feeding them. This type of altruism may arise through **kin selection**.

Herding is an effective defensive behavior, providing a great number of eyes to detect approaching predators. Although they have horns for defense, when wildebeest (above) detect danger, their first reaction is to run as a group (at up to 80 kmh^{-1}).

South African meerkats live in communities in earth burrows. They are vulnerable to attack from land and aerial predators (especially vultures). The group maintains a constant surveillance by posting sentinels to warn the rest of the group of danger.

Cooperative (mutualistic) associations can occur between different species. Cape buffalos are warned of approaching predators by cattle egrets and maribou storks which in turn feed on insects disturbed by the buffalo as it grazes.

1. Using examples, discuss the difference between **altruistic behavior** and **kin selection**: _____

_____

_____

_____

_____

2. Explain (in evolutionary terms) why an animal would raise the offspring of a close relative rather than their own:

_____

_____

_____

3. Describe two ways in which members of a herd or a shoal reduce their likelihood of being attacked by a predator:

(a) _____

_____

(b) _____

_____

Related activities: Parental Care

A 2

Animal Behavior

Parental Care

As with mating systems, there is a wide variation in the degree to which animals care for their young. Animals have a certain amount of energy that they are prepared to put into reproduction. This is called the **reproductive effort**. The amount of care given by parent(s) will depend on how much of this reproductive effort is allocated before birth (in producing the young) and how much is allocated to the period after the young are born (the parental care period). Some animals, such as birds, fish, and reptiles, give birth to their young in eggs with a supply of food in the form of yolk. This provides some nourishment during the early stages of development. Mammals carry young internally until they have reached a more developed stage. After birth or hatching, the parents of many mammals and birds care for their young by providing food, protection, and warmth.

Giant clam

Shield bug

Canada geese

Sheep

Many invertebrates offer no parental care whatsoever. The giant clam (above left) is in the process of releasing millions of eggs into the surrounding water (arrowed). These will be fertilized by sperm released by other clams in the area. The massive numbers of resulting planktonic larvae will be severely reduced by plankton feeding animals. The shield bug (above right) is in the process of laying eggs. It will then abandon them to an uncertain future, risking their loss to predators.

Both mammals and birds are well known for their high levels of parental care. Other vertebrates, such as some amphibians, fish, and reptiles also provide intensive care until the offspring are capable of fending for themselves. Bird parents are required to incubate their eggs in a nest and then feed the chicks until they are independent. Although most mammals give birth to well developed offspring, they are dependent (to various degrees) on their mother for nourishment via suckling milk, as well as learning valuable behaviors.

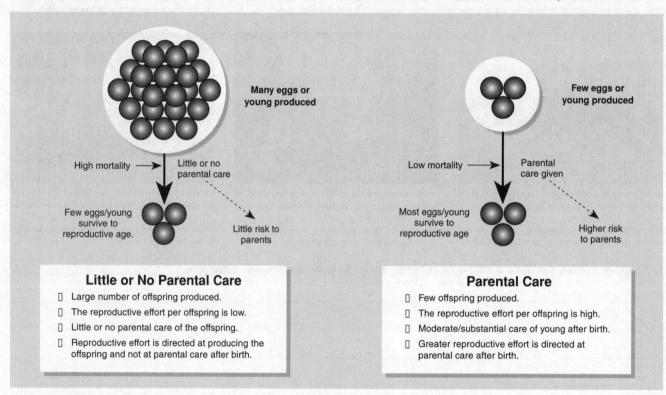

Many eggs or young produced

High mortality → Little or no parental care

Few eggs/young survive to reproductive age. ⤑ Little risk to parents

Few eggs or young produced

Low mortality → Parental care given

Most eggs/young survive to reproductive age ⤑ Higher risk to parents

Little or No Parental Care
☐ Large number of offspring produced.
☐ The reproductive effort per offspring is low.
☐ Little or no parental care of the offspring.
☐ Reproductive effort is directed at producing the offspring and not at parental care after birth.

Parental Care
☐ Few offspring produced.
☐ The reproductive effort per offspring is high.
☐ Moderate/substantial care of young after birth.
☐ Greater reproductive effort is directed at parental care after birth.

1. Explain how animals with little or no parental care compensate for not caring for their young:

_____

_____

2. Name two quite different animals with little or no parental care. _____

3. Name two quite different animals with considerable parental care: _____

4. Describe three ways in which a young bird may benefit by having a high degree of parental care:

(a) _____

(b) _____

(c) _____

Related activities: Animal Reproductive Strategies

Breeding Behavior

Many of the behaviors observed in animals are associated with reproduction, reflecting the importance of this event in an individual's life cycle. Many types of behavior are aimed at facilitating successful reproduction. These include **courtship** behaviors, which may involve attracting a mate to a particular breeding site (often associated with high availability of resources such as food or nesting sites). Courtship behaviors are aimed at reducing conflict between the sexes and are often **stereotyped** or ritualistic. They rely on **sign stimuli** to elicit specific responses in potential mates. Other reproductive behaviors are associated with assessing the receptivity of a mate, defending mates against others, and rearing the young.

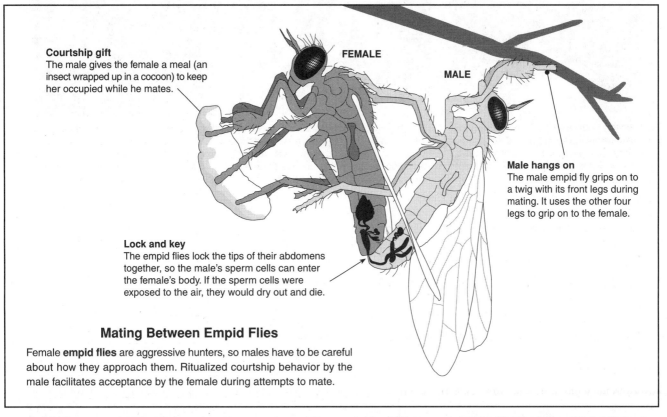

Courtship gift
The male gives the female a meal (an insect wrapped up in a cocoon) to keep her occupied while he mates.

FEMALE

MALE

Male hangs on
The male empid fly grips on to a twig with its front legs during mating. It uses the other four legs to grip on to the female.

Lock and key
The empid flies lock the tips of their abdomens together, so the male's sperm cells can enter the female's body. If the sperm cells were exposed to the air, they would dry out and die.

Mating Between Empid Flies

Female **empid flies** are aggressive hunters, so males have to be careful about how they approach them. Ritualized courtship behavior by the male facilitates acceptance by the female during attempts to mate.

Courtship behavior occurs as a prelude to mating and is most common in vertebrates and insects. One function of courtship is to synchronize the behaviors of the male and female so that mating can occur, and to override attack or escape behavior. Here, a male greater frigatebird calls, spreads its wings, and inflates its throat pouch to court a female.

It is common in some birds (and many arthropods) for the male to provide an offering, such as food or nesting material, to the female. These **rituals** reduce aggression in the male and promote appeasement behavior by the female. For some **monogamous** species, e.g. the blue-footed boobies mating above, the pairing begins a long term breeding partnership.

Many marine birds, such as the emperor penguins above, form breeding colonies where large numbers of birds come together to lay their eggs and raise their young. The adults feed at sea, leaving the young unattended for varying lengths of time. Penguin chicks congregate in large, densely packed groups to conserve body heat while their parents are away.

1. (a) Explain what is meant by **courtship behavior**: _____

_____

(b) Suggest a reason why courtship behavior may be necessary prior to mating: _____

_____

(c) Explain why courtship behavior is often ritualized and involves stereotyped displays: _____

_____

_____

Related activities: Aggressive Behavior

RA 2

Animal Behavior

Territorial Behavior and Courtship Displays

A territory is any area that is defended against members of the same species. Territories are usually defended by clear acts of aggression or ritualized signals (e.g. vocal, visual or chemical signals).

Birds often engage in complex courtship behavior. Males display in some way and females select their mates. These courtship displays are usually species specific and include ritualized acts such dancing, feeding, and nest-building.

Resource availability often determines territory size and the population becomes spread out accordingly. Gannet territories are relatively small, with hens defending only the area they can reach while sitting on their nest.

(d) Describe one example of a courtship behavior: _____

_____

2. Using an example, describe an advantage of cooperation during breeding: _____

_____

3. (a) Explain the nature and purpose of the courtship display in empid flies: _____

_____

(b) Identify the **sign stimulus** in this behavior: _____

_____

4. (a) Explain what is meant by the formation of a **pair-bond**: _____

_____

(b) Using an example, describe an advantage of pair-bonding behavior: _____

_____

_____

5. (a) Explain what is meant by a **territory**: _____

_____

(b) Explain why a male will defend a particular breeding territory against other males: _____

_____

(c) Suggest how a female in this situation would select a mate: _____

_____

6. Discuss the advantages and disadvantages of maintaining a territory: _____

_____

_____

_____

_____

_____

_____

Aggressive Behavior

Aggression is a complex phenomenon often associated with competition for resources but also including predatory behavior (hunting for prey). An associated but more precise term is **agonistic behavior**: behavior that is associated with **conflict** situations among members of the same species. Agonistic behavior includes all aspects of conflict, such as threats, submissions, chases and physical combat, but it specifically excludes predatory aggression for obtaining food. Conflicts between members of the same species are usually resolved without serious injury. Often, ritualized behavior (e.g. submissive behavior or ritualized threat) within a hierarchy will resolve conflict without physical combat being necessary.

Two male African elephants (above) are fighting. Confrontations like this seldom end in very serious physical injury and the contest is more one of establishing strength than inflicting wounds.

Aggression can occur between different species when they are competing for the same resources. In the photograph above, vultures are competing with hyenas for a carcass. The hyenas may also have been competing with lions and jackals.

Competing for the right to mate with a harem of females, two stags are locked antler to antler. While the antlers provide effective weapons to repel predator attacks and protect the herd, they seldom inflict serious injury on other stags.

Two wave albatrosses are engaged in ritualized aggression with wings spread to provide an intimidating display. These encounters may include a few harmless pecks.

Hooker's (New Zealand) sealion forms breeding colonies on several subantarctic islands. A bull will set up a territory on one of the breeding beaches, defend it against challenges from other bulls, and attract females as mates to the site.

Disputes between zebra stallions can get serious. The fighting is less ritualized than in many species and the force of the kick from the hind legs can cause serious injury. Face to face fighting may also result in serious bite injuries.

1. Distinguish between aggressive behavior and agonistic behavior: _____

   _____

   _____

   _____

2. In social species, aggression between groups (e.g. one group invading another's territory) is usually less ritualized and more inclined to lead to injury than aggression within the same social grouping. Explain why this is the case:

   _____

   _____

   _____

3. Describe how the following behaviors reduce the risk of injury to individuals in a population:

   (a) Dominance hierarchies: _____

   _____

   _____

   (b) Ritual aggression: _____

   _____

   _____

Related activities: Breeding Behavior

RA 2

Animal Behavior

Home Ranges and Resources

Olive baboons (*Papio anubis*) live in the African savannah and have a highly organized social structure. Within each troop there is an orderly hierarchy. The hierarchy promotes division of labor and maximizes the efficiency with which the troop can search for food and defend itself against predators and other troops. Each of the different baboon troops occupies a distinct **home range**. This is the area regularly utilized by the troop, and it provides all the resources the troop needs for its survival. Home ranges differ from territories in that they may overlap in places and are not necessarily defended exclusively.

Baboon Home Ranges in Nairobi Park

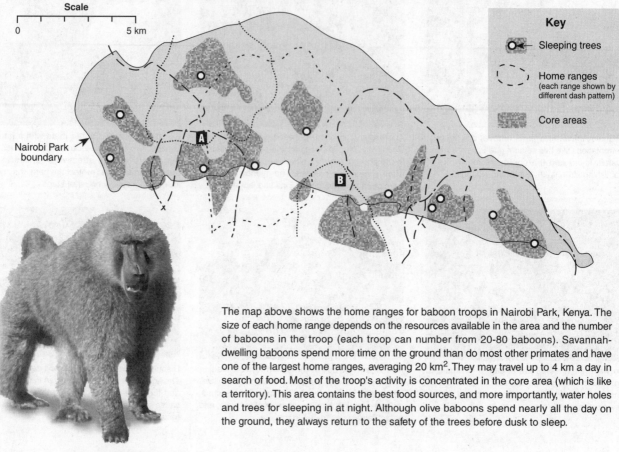

The map above shows the home ranges for baboon troops in Nairobi Park, Kenya. The size of each home range depends on the resources available in the area and the number of baboons in the troop (each troop can number from 20-80 baboons). Savannah-dwelling baboons spend more time on the ground than do most other primates and have one of the largest home ranges, averaging 20 km^2. They may travel up to 4 km a day in search of food. Most of the troop's activity is concentrated in the core area (which is like a territory). This area contains the best food sources, and more importantly, water holes and trees for sleeping in at night. Although olive baboons spend nearly all the day on the ground, they always return to the safety of the trees before dusk to sleep.

1. Describe one advantage to a baboon troop in having a troop hierarchy: _____
   _____

2. Describe the factors that might determine the size of the home range in any given area: _____
   _____

3. Distinguish between a territory and a home range: _____
   _____

4. Baboons defend the core areas aggressively. Suggest why they would do this: _____
   _____

5. (a) State how many home ranges are represented on the map: _____

   (b) State how many home ranges overlap at the following points on the map: Point A: _____   Point B: _____

   (c) Contrast the distribution of **home ranges** and **core areas** of neighboring troops: _____
   _____

6. Provide an example of a territorial animal and suggest a purpose for the territoriality: _____
   _____
   _____

RA 2   **Related activities**: Breeding Behavior, Aggressive Behavior

Plant Structure and Adaptation

IB SL	IB HL	IB Options	AP Biology
Not applicable to core	Complete: 1-16	Not applicable to options	Complete: 1-16 Some numbers extension as appropriate

Learning Objectives

☐ 1. Compile your own glossary from the **KEY WORDS** displayed in **bold type** in the learning objectives below.

The Pivotal Role of Plants *(pages 332-336)*

☐ 2. Recall the pivotal role of plants as producers in ecosystems and in the global carbon budget. If required, outline the importance of plants to humans, providing examples to illustrate your answer.

☐ 3. Outline plant diversity as illustrated by the structural differences between **bryophytes**, **ferns**, **conifers**, and **angiosperms** (flowering plants).

☐ 4. Explain how **plant (primary) productivity** can be measured in terms of **relative growth rate**, **harvestable dry biomass**, and **net assimilation rate**. Describe factors affecting plant productivity.

Basic Plant Structure *(pages 333, 339-341, 344-348 and see the TRC: Plant Diversity)*

☐ 5. Describe the external structure of a named dicot (dicotyledonous) plant. Identify the location and function of **root**, **stem**, **leaf**, and **axillary** and **terminal buds**.

☐ 6. Using labeled **plan diagrams**, describe the distribution of tissues in a dicot **stem**, **root**, and **leaf**. Note that plan diagrams show regions of tissues (e.g. xylem, phloem) and not individual cells.

☐ 7. Explain the relationship between the distribution of tissues (e.g. phloem, xylem, parenchyma) in a leaf and the functions of these tissues. Include reference to: light absorption, gas exchange, support, water conservation, and transport. Describe the adaptations of leaves to maximize photosynthesis in different environments.

☐ 8. Describe the role of **stomata** and explain the movement of gases into and out of the **spongy mesophyll** of the leaf. Recognize the role of lenticels in gas exchange in woody plants.

Plant Transport *(pages 337-338, 342-345, 349-353)*

☐ 9. Describe the roles of **cell turgor**, transport tissues, and cellulose in supporting the plant. Recall the structure and function of the **xylem** and **phloem** in angiosperms.

☐ 10. Recall the structure of a dicot **primary root**. Explain how the root system provides a large surface area for uptake of water and mineral ions, identifying the role of the **root hairs** and the cell walls of the **root cortex**.

☐ 11. Describe water uptake in plant roots. Include reference to the role of **osmosis**, gradients in **water potential**, the **symplastic** and **apoplastic pathways**, and the role of the **endodermis**.

☐ 12. Describe passive and active uptake of minerals in plant roots. Identify the role of some of the mineral ions important to plants, including: nitrate (NO_3^-), phosphate (PO_4^{3-}), and magnesium (Mg^{2+}) ions.

☐ 13. Recognize **transpiration** as an inevitable consequence of gas exchange and identify the role of **stomata** in these processes. Identify two benefits of transpiration.

☐ 14. Explain how water and dissolved minerals are moved up the plant from the roots to the leaves, identifying the roles of xylem, **cohesion-tension**, **transpiration pull** and **evaporation**, and **root pressure**. Explain the effect of humidity, light, air movement, temperature, and water availability, on transpiration rate.

☐ 15. Explain translocation in the phloem, identifying **sources** and **sinks** for sucrose. Evaluate the evidence for and against the **mass flow (pressure-flow) hypothesis** for the mechanism of translocation.

Plant Adaptations *(pages 354-359)*

☐ 16. Describe structural and/or physiological adaptations in **xerophytes** and/or **hydrophytes**. In each case, explain how the adaptation enhances survival in the environment. Describe some modifications of leaves, roots, or stems for different functions, e.g. for support, as **food storage** organs, or for food capture.

See the 'Textbook Reference Grid' on pages 8-9 for textbook page references relating to material in this topic.

Supplementary Texts
See page 6 for additional details of this text:
■ Clegg, C.J., 2003. **Green Plants: The Inside Story**, (John Murray), entire text as required.
■ Helms, D.R. *et al.*, 1998. **Biology in the Laboratory** (W.H. Freeman), #28, #29, #30.

See page 6 for details of publishers of periodicals:
STUDENT'S REFERENCE
■ **How Trees Lift Water** Biol. Sci. Rev., 18(1), Sept. 2005, pp. 33-37. *Cohesion-tension theory and others on how trees lift water.*

■ **High Tension** Biol. Sci. Rev., 13(1), Sept. 2000, pp. 14-18. *Cell specialization and transport in plants: an excellent account of the mechanisms by which plants transport water and solutes.*

■ **Temperature and Wind Effect on Plant Transpiration** The Am. Biology Teacher, 63(6) Aug. 2001, pp. 420-421. *A how-to-do-it lab for students on plant transpiration.*

See pages 10-11 for details of how to access **Bio Links** from our web site: **www.thebiozone.com** From Bio Links, access sites under the topics:
PLANT BIOLOGY: • Plant biology for non-science majors ... *and others* **Structure and Function:** • Plant structure * Plant structure II ...*and others* > **Nutrition and Gas Exchange:** • Gas exchange in plants • Mineral requirements • Photorespiration and C_4 plants ... *and others* > **Support and Transport:** • LAB measuring transpiration • Plant structure and growth • Plant transport lecture

The Importance of Plants

Via the process of photosynthesis, plants provide oxygen and are also the ultimate source of food and metabolic energy for nearly all animals. Besides foods (e.g. grains, fruits, and vegetables), plants also provide people with shelter, clothing, medicines, fuels, and the raw materials from which innumerable other products are made.

Plant tissues provide the energy for almost all heterotrophic life. Many plants produce delicious fruits in order to spread their seeds.

Plant tissues can be utilized to provide shelter in the form of framing, cladding, and roofing.

Many plants provide fibers for a range of materials including cotton (above), linen (from flax), and coir (from coconut husks).

Plant extracts, including rubber from rubber trees (above), can be utilized in many ways as an important manufacturing material.

Coal, petroleum, and natural gas are fossil fuels which were formed from the dead remains of plants and other organisms. Together with wood, they provide important sources of fuel.

Plants produce many beneficial and not so beneficial substances (e.g. the cannabis plant above). Over 25% of all modern medicines are derived from plant extracts.

1. Using examples, describe how plant species are used by people for each of the following:

    (a) Food: _____

    _____

    (b) Fuel: _____

    _____

    (c) Clothing: _____

    _____

    (d) Building materials: _____

    _____

    (e) Aesthetic value: _____

    _____

    (f) "Recreational" drugs: _____

    _____

    (g) Therapeutic drugs (medicines): _____

    _____

2. Outline three reasons why the destruction of native forests is of concern:

    (a) _____

    (b) _____

    (c) _____

Related activities: Fruits
Web links: Ethnobotany

The General Structure of Plants

The support and transport systems in plants are closely linked; many of the same tissues are involved in both systems. Primitive plants (e.g. mosses and liverworts) are small and low growing, and have no need for support and transport systems. If a plant is to grow to any size, it must have ways to hold itself up against gravity and to move materials around its body. The body of a flowering plant has three parts: **roots** anchor the plant and absorb nutrients from the soil, **leaves** produce sugars by photosynthesis, and **stems** link the roots to the leaves and provide support for the leaves and reproductive structures. Vascular tissues (xylem and phloem) link all plant parts so that water, minerals, and manufactured food can be transported between different regions. All plants rely on fluid pressure within their cells (turgor) to give some support to their structure.

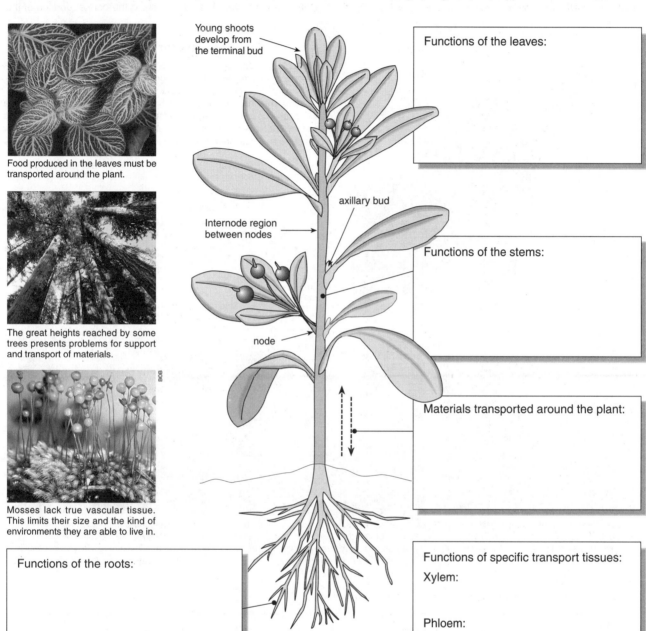

Food produced in the leaves must be transported around the plant.

The great heights reached by some trees presents problems for support and transport of materials.

Mosses lack true vascular tissue. This limits their size and the kind of environments they are able to live in.

Young shoots develop from the terminal bud

axillary bud

Internode region between nodes

node

Functions of the leaves:

Functions of the stems:

Materials transported around the plant:

Functions of specific transport tissues:
Xylem:

Phloem:

Functions of the roots:

1. In the boxes provided in the diagram above:

   (a) Describe the main functions of the leaves, roots and stems (remember that the leaves themselves have leaf veins).

   (b) List the materials that are transported around the plant body.

   (c) Describe the functions of the transport tissues: xylem and phloem.

2. Name the solvent for all the materials that are transported around the plant: _____

3. Identify the processes involved in the transport of sap in the following tissues:

   (a) The xylem: _____

   (b) The phloem: _____

Related activities: Xylem, Phloem, Uptake in the Root, Translocation

RA 1

Plants as Producers

Life on earth is solar-powered; it runs on energy from the sun. Plants, algae, and some bacteria capture this solar energy and convert it into sugars. They achieve this through a process called **photosynthesis**. Each year these organisms produce more than 200 billion tonnes of food. The chemical energy stored in this food fuels the reactions that sustain life (metabolism). Producers are **autotrophs** (self-feeding). Organisms that cannot make their own food are **heterotrophs** and rely on producers either directly or indirectly for their energy. The photosynthesis that occurs in the oceans is vital to the Earth's functioning, providing oxygen and absorbing carbon dioxide. The oceans cover nearly three quarters of the globe. The evaporation from oceans provides most of the Earth's rainfall and ocean temperatures have a major effect on the world's climate. Despite its importance, humans have harvested the ocean heavily and used it to dump waste. Only in recent years have we realized the consequences of this.

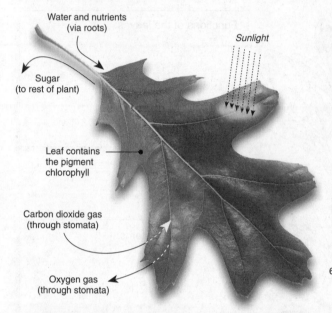

Water and nutrients (via roots)

Sunlight

Sugar (to rest of plant)

Leaf contains the pigment chlorophyll

Carbon dioxide gas (through stomata)

Oxygen gas (through stomata)

Requirements for Photosynthesis

In order to produce their own food, plants need only a few raw materials, light energy from the sun, and the pigment chlorophyll, which is contained in chloroplasts (in the leaves and stems of higher plants). Photosynthesis is summarized in the chemical equation below. It is important to note that this equation is a deceptively simple summary of a more involved process. Photosynthesis is not a single process but two complex processes (the light dependent and light independent reactions) each with multiple steps.

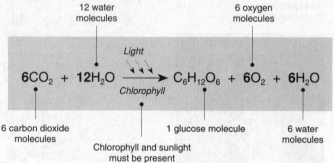

12 water molecules

6 oxygen molecules

$$6CO_2 + 12H_2O \xrightarrow[\text{Chlorophyll}]{\text{Light}} C_6H_{12}O_6 + 6O_2 + 6H_2O$$

6 carbon dioxide molecules

1 glucose molecule

6 water molecules

Chlorophyll and sunlight must be present

The photosynthesis of marine algae supplies a substantial portion of the world's oxygen. The oceans also act as sinks for the absorption of large amounts of carbon dioxide.

Macroalgae, like this giant kelp, are important marine producers. Algae living near the ocean surface get access to light used in photosynthesis (the red wavelength).

On land, vascular plants (such as trees with transport vessels) are the main producers of food. Plants at different levels in a forest receive different intensity and quality of light.

1. Write the overall chemical equation for photosynthesis using:

   (a) Words: _____

   (b) Chemical symbols: _____

2. Describe the role of producers to the functioning of the Earth's ecosystems: _____

_____

3. Explain how light limits the distribution of algae in the ocean: _____

_____

4. Describe the effects of deforestation on the Earth's climate and/or level of the gases oxygen and carbon dioxide:

_____

_____

_____

Related activities: Modes of Nutrition

Plant Productivity

The energy entering ecosystems is fixed by producers in photosynthesis. The rate of photosynthesis is dependent on factors such as temperature and the amount of light, water, and nutrients. The total energy fixed by a plant through photosynthesis is referred to as the **gross primary production** (GPP) and is usually expressed as Jm^{-2} (or kJm^{-2}), or as gm^{-2}. However, a portion of this energy is required by the plant for respiration. Subtracting respiration from GPP gives the **net primary production** (NPP). The **rate** of biomass production, or net primary productivity, is the biomass produced per area per unit time.

Measuring Productivity

Primary productivity of an ecosystem depends on a number of interrelated factors (light intensity, nutrients, temperature, water, and mineral supplies), making its calculation extremely difficult. Globally, the least productive ecosystems are those that are limited by heat energy and water. The most productive ecosystems are systems with high temperatures, plenty of water, and non-limiting supplies of soil nitrogen. The primary productivity of oceans is lower than that of terrestrial ecosystems because the water reflects (or absorbs) much of the light energy before it reaches and is utilized by producers. The table below compares the difference in the net primary productivity of various ecosystems.

Ecosystem Type	Net Primary Productivity	
	kcal m^{-2} y^{-1}	kJ m^{-2} y^{-1}
Tropical rainforest	15 000	63 000
Swamps and marshes	12 000	50 400
Estuaries	9000	37 800
Savanna	3000	12 600
Temperate forest	6000	25 200
Boreal forest	3500	14 700
Temperate grassland	2000	8400
Tundra/cold desert	500	2100
Coastal marine	2500	10 500
Open ocean	800	3360
Desert	< 200	< 840

* Data compiled from a variety of sources.

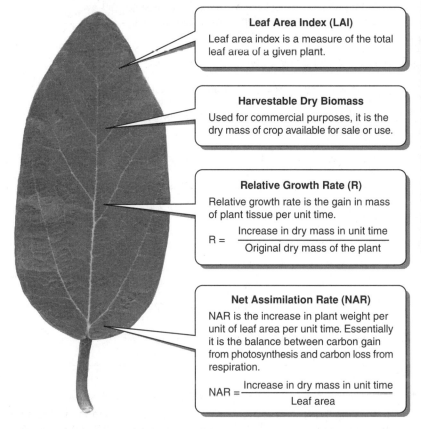

Leaf Area Index (LAI)
Leaf area index is a measure of the total leaf area of a given plant.

Harvestable Dry Biomass
Used for commercial purposes, it is the dry mass of crop available for sale or use.

Relative Growth Rate (R)
Relative growth rate is the gain in mass of plant tissue per unit time.

$$R = \frac{\text{Increase in dry mass in unit time}}{\text{Original dry mass of the plant}}$$

Net Assimilation Rate (NAR)
NAR is the increase in plant weight per unit of leaf area per unit time. Essentially it is the balance between carbon gain from photosynthesis and carbon loss from respiration.

$$NAR = \frac{\text{Increase in dry mass in unit time}}{\text{Leaf area}}$$

Net Primary Productivity of Selected Ecosystems (figures are in kJ m^{-2} y^{-1})

< 2500	< 12 500 – 42 000	< 42 000 – 105 000	2500 – 42 000
Arid desert	Temperate forest	Tropical rain forest	Continental shelf waters
Polar tundra and ice desert	Grassland agriculture	Intensive horticulture	Open ocean

1. Briefly describe three factors that may affect the primary productivity of an ecosystem:

   (a) _____

   (b) _____

   (c) _____

2. Explain the difference between **productivity** and **production** in relation to plants: _____

   _____

   _____

3. Suggest how the LAI might influence the rate of primary production: _____

_____

_____

4. Using the data table on the previous page, choose a suitable graph format and plot the differences in the net primary productivity of various ecosystems (use either of the data columns provided, but not both). Use the graph grid provided, right.

5. With reference to the graph:

(a) Suggest why tropical rainforests are among the most productive terrestrial ecosystems, while tundra and desert ecosystems are among the least productive:

_____

_____

_____

_____

_____

(b) Suggest why, amongst aquatic ecosystems, the NPP of the open ocean is low relative to that of coastal systems:

_____

_____

_____

6. Estimating the NPP is relatively simple: all the plant material (including root material) from a measured area (e.g. 1 m^2) is collected and dried (at 105°C) until it reaches a constant mass. This mass, called the **standing crop**, is recorded (in kg m^{-2}). The procedure is repeated after some set time period (e.g. 1 month). The difference between the two calculated masses represents the *estimated* NPP:

(a) Explain why the plant material was dried before weighing: _____

_____

(b) Define the term **standing crop**: _____

(c) Suggest why this procedure only provides an estimate of NPP: _____

_____

(d) State what extra information would be required in order to express the standing crop value in kJ m^{-2}: _____

_____

(e) Suggest what information would be required in order to calculate the GPP: _____

_____

7. Intensive horticultural systems achieve very high rates of production (about 10X those of subsistence systems).

(a) Outline the means by which these high rates are achieved: _____

_____

(b) Comment on the sustainability of these high rates (summary of a group discussion if you wish): _____

_____

_____

_____

Support in Plants

Plants support themselves in their environment and maintain the positions that enable them to carry out essential processes. All plants are provided some support by **cell turgor**. For very small plants, this is sufficient. Terrestrial vascular plants have

strengthening tissues that may be hardened with lignin, and many also produce secondary growth (wood). For aquatic plants the water provides support, and adaptations are primarily to maintain the plant in the photic zone and to remain anchored.

Aquatic Environment

Large air spaces in the leaves provide buoyancy

Reproductive parts may be supported by cell turgor or, if submerged, by the water itself.

Water lily

Single leaves may be large enough to float, supporting the weight of the rest of the plant.

While some aquatic plants have roots that are simply suspended in the water, others have stems that attach to roots or rhizomes anchored firmly in the sediment.

Some aquatic plants, like **water hyacinth**, have swollen petioles that act as floats. Many form floating mats which block water ways and are serious weeds e.g. *Salvinia* and alligator weed.

Marine and freshwater **algae** are not plants but have plant like qualities (e.g. chlorophyll). They lack vascular tissue and are supported by the water. Buoyancy may be assisted by airfilled floats or projections of the cell wall, which increase surface area (as in the case of diatoms).

Many floating or semi-aquatic plants, such as **water lilies**, have expanded leaves that provide a large surface area for flotation and photosynthesis. Such floating leaves support the submerged parts of the plant. These plants have roots that are attached to the bottom sediment.

Terrestrial Environment

Vascular plants with secondary thickening (woody tissue) can reach an enormous size. The Australian *Eucalyptus regnans* is reputed to grow to over 140 m in height. Their structural tissues (e.g. **xylem** and **wood**) provide support against gravity. Leaves and reproductive parts are supported by **cell turgor**.

Roots anchor the plant in the ground, forming a stable base for growth. The roots of large hard-wood trees can form **buttresses**, providing extra support in poor soils.

Moss

Bryophytes (mosses and liverworts) lack any vascular tissue: the plant body is supported by **cell turgor**. As a consequence, they are small and their upward growth is restricted. Although there are no true roots, filamentous rhizoids anchor the plant in the ground.

Liverwort

Liverworts are simpler in structure than mosses. The gametophyte (the main plant body) is a flattened structure that may be a lobed thallus or leaf-like, depending on the species. The plant lies flat against the substrate, rising just a centimeter or two above the ground.

Fern

Ferns are tracheophytes (vascular plants). They have well developed vascular tissues that provide support and allow transport of nutrients and water around the plant. Because of this, they are able to grow to considerable heights (e.g. tree ferns).

The **Lord Howe Island fig** has ten or more trunks that develop and form aerial roots. These grow downwards and once anchored in the ground, they provide extra support for the heavy weight of the trunks, allowing them to cover a wide area. Without such support, the trunks would collapse.

Strangler figs begin life high in the forest canopy as epiphytes. They develop roots that grow towards the forest floor. Once rooted in the soil they grow rapidly, embracing the trunk of a host tree with roots and shading it. As the host tree increases in girth, the fig cuts off the sap supply to its roots, killing it.

Mangroves grow on mudflat shorelines. The root system cannot penetrate far into the mud due to the lack of oxygen. Support is provided by roots that are sent out in all directions just below the surface. Pneumatophores or breathing roots, (seen above) arise from these shallow lateral roots.

Related activities: Stem Structure

A 1

Support in Woody Plants

Secondary xylem which consists of massed xylem vessels and fibers, makes up the bulk of the stem as **wood**, providing considerable strength.

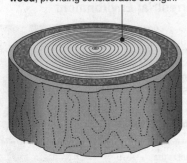

The strengthening of cells with lignin gives support to stems in all vascular plants. Lignin, together with cell turgor, is particularly important in non-woody (herbaceous) plants.

Support in Herbaceous Plants

Turgor pressure inside the parenchyma cells provides a strong inflating force that pushes against the epidermal layer.

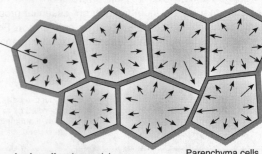

Parenchyma cells

Vascular bundles (comprising xylem and phloem) enhance the ability of herbaceous stems to resist tension and compression.

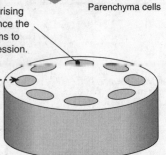

Xylem vessel with spiral thickening produced as a result of **lignin** deposition.

1. Contrast the main problems experienced by aquatic and terrestrial plants in supporting themselves:

   _____

   _____

   _____

2. Describe how the following are achieved in the aquatic protists and plants named below:

   (a) Maintaining a stationary position in seaweeds: _____

   (b) Keeping the fronds of kelp near the surface: _____

   (c) Keeping water lily pads floating on the surface: _____

3. Describe the function of **buttresses** on the trunks of large rainforest hardwood trees: _____

   _____

   _____

4. Explain the role of the following in providing support for vascular plants:

   (a) Lignin: _____

   _____

   (b) Turgor pressure: _____

   _____

   (c) Vascular bundles: _____

   _____

   (d) Secondary xylem: _____

   _____

5. Describe how strangler fig trees overcome support problems during the early stage of their development:

   _____

   _____

   _____

Leaf Structure

The main function of leaves is to collect the radiant energy from the sun and convert it into a form that can be used by the plant. The sugars produced from photosynthesis have two uses: (1) they can be broken down by respiration to release the stored chemical energy to do cellular work or (2) they can provide the plant with building materials for new tissues (growth and repair). The structure of the leaf is superbly adapted to collecting the sun's energy. To an extent, a leaf is also able to control the amount of carbon dioxide entering and the amount of water leaving the plant. Both the external and internal morphology of leaves are related primarily to habitat, especially the availability of water and light (see the activity on the next page). Regardless of their varying forms, foliage leaves comprise epidermal, mesophyll, and vascular tissues. The mesophyll (the packing tissue of the leaf) may be variously arranged according to the particular photosynthetic adaptations of the leaf.

Angiosperm Leaves

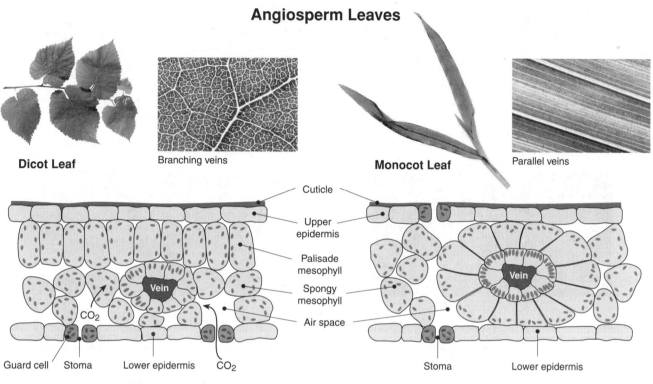

Dicot Leaf   Branching veins   **Monocot Leaf**   Parallel veins

Cuticle
Upper epidermis
Palisade mesophyll
Spongy mesophyll
Air space
Vein
CO₂
Guard cell   Stoma   Lower epidermis   CO₂   Stoma   Lower epidermis

1. The internal arrangement of cells and tissues in typical monocot and dicot leaves are illustrated above. Describe two ways in which the internal leaf structure of the dicot differs from that of the monocot:

   (a) _____

   _____

   (b) _____

   _____

2. (a) Explain the purpose of the waxy cuticle that coats the leaf surface: _____

   _____

   (b) Explain why the leaf epidermis is transparent: _____

   _____

   (c) Explain why leaves are usually broad and flat: _____

   _____

3. (a) Identify the region of a dicot leaf where most of the chloroplasts are found: _____

   (b) Name the important process that occurs in the chloroplasts: _____

4. (a) Explain the purpose of the air spaces in the leaf tissue: _____

   _____

   (b) Describe how gases enter and leave the leaf tissue: _____

   _____

Related activities: Adaptations for Photosynthesis, Gas Exchange and Stomata

RA 1

Adaptations for Photosynthesis

In order to photosynthesize, plants must obtain a regular supply of carbon dioxide (CO_2) gas; the raw material for the production of carbohydrate. In green plants, the systems for gas exchange and photosynthesis are linked; without a regular supply of CO_2, photosynthesis ceases. The leaf, as the primary photosynthetic organ, is adapted to maximize light capture and facilitate the entry of CO_2, while minimizing water loss. There are various ways in which plant leaves are adapted to do this. The ultimate structure of the leaf reflects the environment of the leaf (sun or shade, terrestrial or aquatic), its resistance to water loss, and the importance of the leaf relative to other parts of the plant that may be photosynthetic, such as the stem.

Sun plant

A **sun leaf**, when exposed to high light intensities, can absorb much of the light available to the cells.

Palisade mesophyll layer often 2 or 3 cells thick

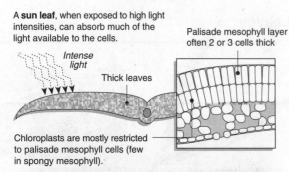

Chloroplasts are mostly restricted to palisade mesophyll cells (few in spongy mesophyll).

Sun leaves

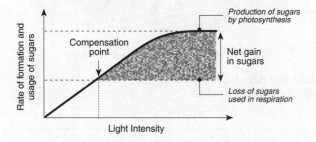

Plants adapted for full sunlight have higher levels of respiration and much higher **compensation points**. **Sun plants** include many weed species found on open ground. They expend much more energy on the construction and maintenance of thicker leaves than do shade plants. The benefit of this investment is that they can absorb the higher light intensities available and grow more quickly.

Shade plant

A **shade leaf** can absorb the light available at lower light intensities. If exposed to high light, most would pass through.

Palisade mesophyll layer only 1 cell thick

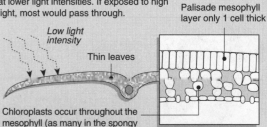

Chloroplasts occur throughout the mesophyll (as many in the spongy as in the palisade mesophyll).

Shade leaves

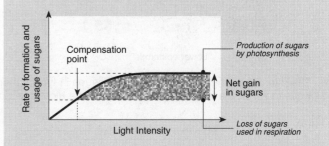

Shade plants typically grow in forested areas, partly shaded by the canopy of larger trees. They have lower rates of respiration than sun plants, mainly because they build thinner leaves. The fewer number of cells need less energy for their production and maintenance. As a result, shade plants reach their compensation point at a low light intensity; much sooner than sun plants do.

---

1. (a) From the diagrams above, determine what is meant by the **compensation point** in terms of sugar production:

_____

_____

(b) State which type of plant (sun or shade adapted) has the highest level of respiration: _____

(c) Explain how the plant compensates for the higher level of respiration: _____

_____

2. Discuss the adaptations of leaves in **sun** and **shade plants**: _____

_____

_____

_____

_____

DA 2   **Related activities**: Adaptations of Xerophytes, Adaptations of Hydrophytes

Stem Structure

The stems of most plants are the primary organs for supporting the plant. Stems have distinct points, called **nodes**, at which leaves and buds attach. The region of the stem between two nodes is called the **internode**. Regardless of their shape or location, all stems can be distinguished as such by the presence of nodes and internodes. Stems, like most parts of the plant, contain vascular tissues. These take the form of bundles containing the xylem and phloem and strengthening fibres. The arrangement of these bundles in the stem depends on the plant type (e.g. monocot or dicot). The growth that leads to the young, flexible stem is called **primary growth**. The increase in the girth (diameter) of the stem is the result of **secondary growth** and is caused by the production of wood. All plants have primary growth but only some plants show secondary growth.

Dicot Stem Structure

In dicots, each vascular bundle contains **xylem** (to the inside) and **phloem** (to the outside). Between the phloem and the xylem is the **vascular cambium**; a layer of cells that divide to produce the thickening of the stem. The middle of the stem, called the **pith**, is filled with thin-walled parenchyma cells. The vascular bundles in dicots are arranged in an orderly way around the periphery of the stem (below).

Monocot Stem Structure

The main features of monocot stem structure are illustrated below. The ground tissue of the stem comprises large parenchyma cells (there is no distinction between cortex and pith). Note how the vascular bundles are scattered randomly through the stem. Contrast this with the orderly arrangement of the vascular bundles in the dicot stem.

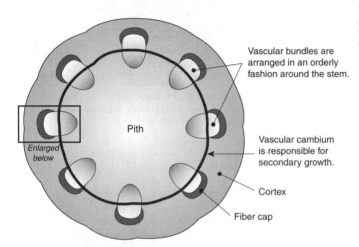

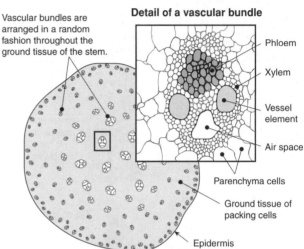

Cross section through a typical dicot stem

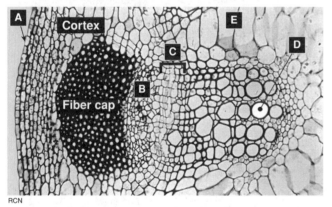

Cross section through a corn stem

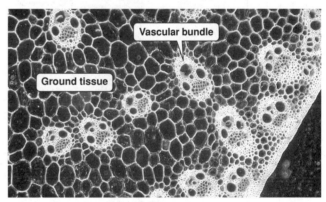

RCN

1. Use the information provided to identify the structures labelled **A-E** in the photograph of the dicot stem above:

   (a) A: _____ (b) B: _____ (c) C: _____

   (d) D: _____ (e) E: _____

2. Identify the feature that distinguishes stems from other parts of the plant: _____

   _____

3. (a) Identify a distinguishing feature of stem structure in dicots: _____

   (b) Contrast the arrangement of the vascular bundles in monocots and dicots: _____

   _____

   _____

4. Describe the role of the vascular cambium: _____

   _____

Xylem

Xylem is the principal **water conducting tissue** in vascular plants. It is also involved in conducting dissolved minerals, in food storage, and in supporting the plant body. As in animals, tissues in plants are groupings of different cell types that work together for a common function. Xylem is a **complex tissue**. In angiosperms, it is composed of five cell types: tracheids, vessels, xylem parenchyma, sclereids (short sclerenchyma cells), and fibers. The tracheids and vessel elements form the bulk of the tissue. They are heavily strengthened and are the conducting cells of the xylem. Parenchyma cells are involved in storage, while fibers and sclereids provide support. When mature, xylem is dead.

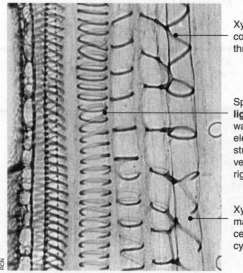

Xylem vessels form continuous tubes throughout the plant.

Spiral thickening of **lignin** around the walls of the vessel elements give extra strength allowing the vessels to remain rigid and upright.

Xylem is dead when mature. Note how the cells have lost their cytoplasm.

The Structure of Xylem Tissue

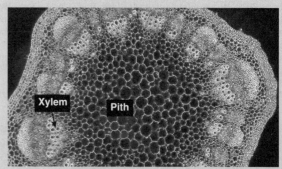

Xylem   Pith

This cross section through the stem, *Helianthus* (sunflower) shows the central pith, surrounded by a peripheral ring of vascular bundles. Note the xylem vessels with their thick walls.

Fibers are a type of sclerenchyma cell. They are associated with vascular tissues and usually occur in groups. The cells are very elongated and taper to a point and the cell walls are heavily thickened. Fibers give mechanical support to tissues, providing both strength and elasticity.

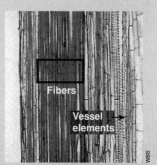

Fibers

Vessel elements

Vessel elements are found only in the xylem of angiosperms. They are large diameter cells that offer very low resistance to water flow. The possession of vessels (stacks of vessel elements) provides angiosperms with a major advantage over gymnosperms and ferns as they allow for very rapid water uptake and transport.

Vessel elements

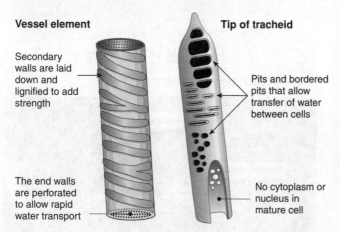

Vessel element

Secondary walls are laid down and lignified to add strength

The end walls are perforated to allow rapid water transport

Tip of tracheid

Pits and bordered pits that allow transfer of water between cells

No cytoplasm or nucleus in mature cell

Vessel elements and tracheids are the two conducting cells types in xylem. Tracheids are long, tapering hollow cells. Water passes from one tracheid to another through thin regions in the wall called **pits**. Vessel elements have pits, but the end walls are also perforated and water flows unimpeded through the stacked elements.

1. Describe the function of **xylem**: _____

_____

2. Identify the four main cell types in xylem and explain their role in the tissue:

(a) _____

(b) _____

(c) _____

(d) _____

3. Describe one way in which xylem is strengthened in a mature plant: _____

4. Describe a feature of vessel elements that increases their efficiency of function: _____

_____

Phloem

Like xylem, **phloem** is a complex tissue, comprising a variable number of cell types. Phloem is the principal **food (sugar) conducting tissue** in vascular plants, transporting dissolved sugars around the plant. The bulk of phloem tissue comprises the **sieve tubes** (sieve tube members and sieve cells) and their companion cells. The sieve tubes are the principal conducting cells

in phloem and are closely associated with the **companion cells** (modified parenchyma cells) with which they share a mutually dependent relationship. Other parenchyma cells, concerned with storage, occur in phloem, and strengthening fibers and sclereids (short sclerenchyma cells) may also be present. Unlike xylem, phloem is alive when mature.

LS through a sieve tube end plate

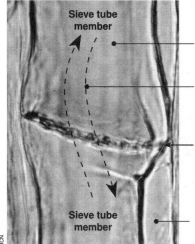

Sieve tube member

The sieve tube members lose most of their organelles but are still alive when mature

Sugar solution flows in both directions

Sieve tube end plate
Tiny holes (arrowed in the photograph below) perforate the sieve tube elements allowing the sugar solution to pass through.

Sieve tube member

Companion cell: a cell adjacent to the sieve tube member, responsible for keeping it alive

TS through a sieve tube end plate

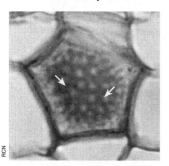

Adjacent sieve tube members are connected through **sieve plates** through which phloem sap flows.

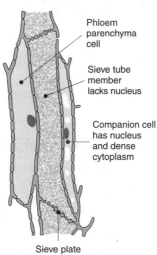

Phloem parenchyma cell

Sieve tube member lacks nucleus

Companion cell has nucleus and dense cytoplasm

Sieve plate

The Structure of Phloem Tissue

Phloem is alive at maturity and functions in the transport of sugars and minerals around the plant. Like xylem, it forms part of the structural vascular tissue of plants.

Fibers are associated with phloem as they are in xylem. Here they are seen in cross section where you can see the extremely thick cell walls and the way the fibers are clustered in groups. See the previous page for a view of fibers in longitudinal section.

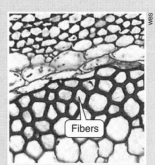

Fibers

In this cross section through a buttercup root, the smaller companion cells can be seen lying alongside the sieve tube members. It is the sieve tube members that, end on end, produce the **sieve tubes**. They are the conducting tissue of phloem.

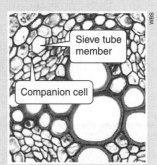

Sieve tube member

Companion cell

In this longitudinal section of a buttercup root, each sieve tube member has a thin **companion cell** associated with it. Companion cells retain their nucleus and control the metabolism of the sieve tube member next to them. They also have a role in the loading and unloading of sugar into the phloem.

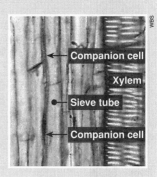

Companion cell

Xylem

Sieve tube

Companion cell

1. Describe the function of **phloem**: _____

2. Describe two differences between xylem and phloem: _____

_____

3. Explain the purpose of the **sieve plate** at the ends of each sieve tube member: _____

_____

4. (a) Name the conducting cell type in phloem: _____

(b) Explain two roles of the companion cell in phloem: _____

_____

5. State the purpose of the phloem parenchyma cells: _____

6. Identify a type of cell that provides strengthening in phloem: _____

Root Structure

Roots are essential plant organs. They anchor the plant in the ground, absorb water and minerals from the soil, and transport these materials to other parts of the plant body. Roots may also act as storage organs, storing excess carbohydrate reserves until they are required by the plant. Roots are covered in an epidermis but, unlike the epidermis of leaves, the root epidermis has only a thin cuticle that presents no barrier to water entry. Young roots are also covered with **root hairs** (see below). Much of a root comprises a cortex of parenchyma cells. The air spaces between the cells are essential for aeration of the root tissue. Minerals and water must move from the soil into the xylem before they can be transported around the plant. Compared with stems, roots are relatively simple and uniform in structure. The structure of monocot and dicot roots is compared in the photographs below.

The Structure of a Dicot Root

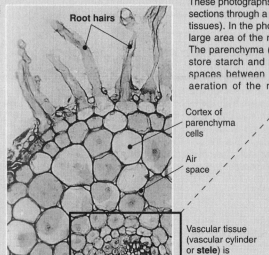

Root hairs

Cortex of parenchyma cells

Air space

Vascular tissue (vascular cylinder or **stele**) is enlarged in the photo on the right.

These photographs (left and below) show cross sections through a young dicot root (i.e. primary tissues). In the photograph to the left, note the large area of the root occupied by the cortex. The parenchyma (packing) cells of the cortex store starch and other substances. The air spaces between the cells are essential for aeration of the root tissue, which is non-photosynthetic. The vascular tissue, xylem (X) and phloem (P) forms a central cylinder through the root and is surrounded by the **pericycle**, a ring of cells from which lateral roots arise. The primary xylem of dicot roots forms a star shape in the center of the vascular cylinder with usually 3 or 4 points. Unlike monocots, there is no central pith of parenchyma cells.

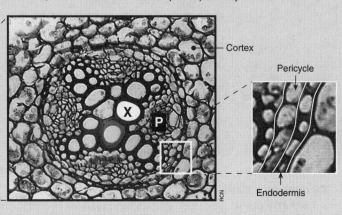

Cortex

Pericycle

Endodermis

Root cap   **Root tip**

Root hairs are located behind the region of cell elongation in the root tip. They are single celled extensions of the epidermal cells that increase the surface area for absorption. Individual root hairs are short lived, but they are produced continually. The root tip is covered by a slimy **root cap**. This protects the dividing cells of the tip and aids the root's movement through the soil.

Monocot roots (right) vary from dicot roots in several ways. As in dicots, there is a large cortex but the **endodermis** is very prominent and heavily thickened. The stele (ring of vascular tissue) is large compared with the size of the root and there are many xylem points. There is a central pith inside the vascular tissue that is absent in dicot roots.

The Structure of a Monocot Root

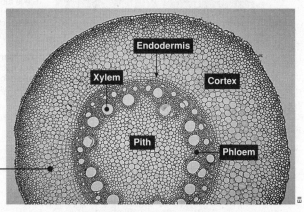

Endodermis

Xylem

Cortex

Pith

Phloem

Cross section through an old root of corn (Zea mays), a typical monocot.

---

1. Explain the purpose of the root hairs: _____

    _____

2. Explain why the root tip is covered by a cap of cells: _____

    _____

3. Describe two features of internal anatomy that distinguish monocot and dicot roots:

    (a) _____

    (b) _____

4. Describe one feature that monocot and dicot roots have in common: _____

5. Describe the role of the parenchyma cells of the cortex: _____

Uptake in the Root

Plants need to take up water and minerals constantly to compensate for water losses and obtain the materials they need to manufacture food. The uptake of water and minerals is mostly restricted to the younger, most recently formed cells of the roots and the root hairs. Some water moves through the plant via the plasmodesmata of the cells (the **symplastic route**), but most passes through the free spaces between cell walls (the **apoplast**). Water uptake is assisted by root pressure, which arises because the soil and root tissue has a higher water potential than other plant tissues. Uptake by the roots is largely a passive process, although some mineral uptake involves active transport. Note: An alternative version of this activity, without reference to water potential, is available in *Uptake in the Root* on the TRC (or see web links below).

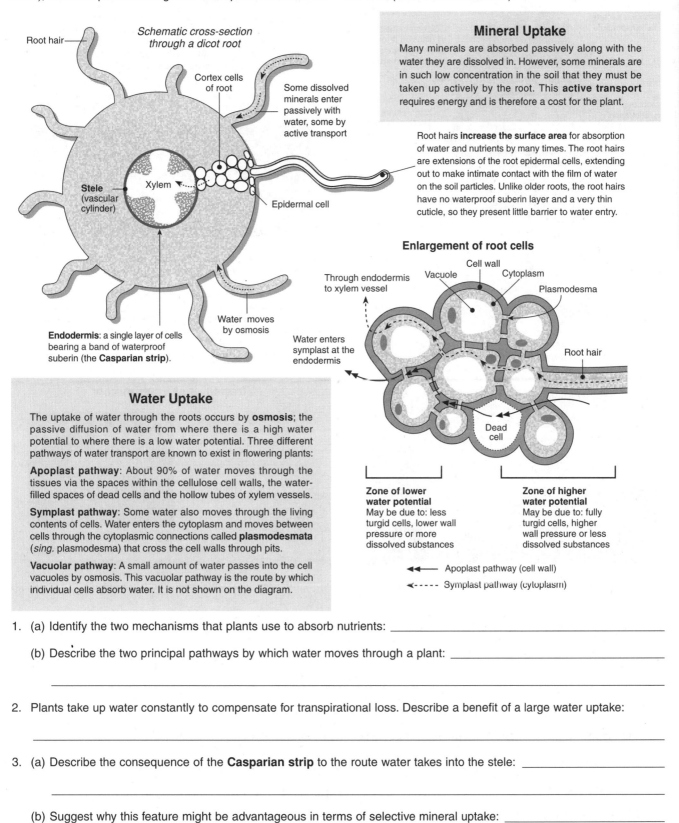

Mineral Uptake

Many minerals are absorbed passively along with the water they are dissolved in. However, some minerals are in such low concentration in the soil that they must be taken up actively by the root. This **active transport** requires energy and is therefore a cost for the plant.

Root hairs **increase the surface area** for absorption of water and nutrients by many times. The root hairs are extensions of the root epidermal cells, extending out to make intimate contact with the film of water on the soil particles. Unlike older roots, the root hairs have no waterproof suberin layer and a very thin cuticle, so they present little barrier to water entry.

Schematic cross-section through a dicot root

Root hair
Cortex cells of root
Some dissolved minerals enter passively with water, some by active transport
Stele (vascular cylinder)
Xylem
Epidermal cell
Endodermis: a single layer of cells bearing a band of waterproof suberin (the **Casparian strip**).
Water moves by osmosis

Enlargement of root cells

Through endodermis to xylem vessel
Vacuole
Cell wall
Cytoplasm
Plasmodesma
Water enters symplast at the endodermis
Root hair
Dead cell

Water Uptake

The uptake of water through the roots occurs by **osmosis**; the passive diffusion of water from where there is a high water potential to where there is a low water potential. Three different pathways of water transport are known to exist in flowering plants:

Apoplast pathway: About 90% of water moves through the tissues via the spaces within the cellulose cell walls, the water-filled spaces of dead cells and the hollow tubes of xylem vessels.

Symplast pathway: Some water also moves through the living contents of cells. Water enters the cytoplasm and moves between cells through the cytoplasmic connections called **plasmodesmata** (*sing.* plasmodesma) that cross the cell walls through pits.

Vacuolar pathway: A small amount of water passes into the cell vacuoles by osmosis. This vacuolar pathway is the route by which individual cells absorb water. It is not shown on the diagram.

Zone of lower water potential
May be due to: less turgid cells, lower wall pressure or more dissolved substances

Zone of higher water potential
May be due to: fully turgid cells, higher wall pressure or less dissolved substances

◄◄─── Apoplast pathway (cell wall)
◄----- Symplast pathway (cytoplasm)

1. (a) Identify the two mechanisms that plants use to absorb nutrients: _____

   (b) Describe the two principal pathways by which water moves through a plant: _____

   _____

2. Plants take up water constantly to compensate for transpirational loss. Describe a benefit of a large water uptake:

   _____

3. (a) Describe the consequence of the **Casparian strip** to the route water takes into the stele: _____

   _____

   (b) Suggest why this feature might be advantageous in terms of selective mineral uptake: _____

   _____

   _____

Related activities: Root Structure, Plant Nutritional Requirements
Web links: Uptake in the Root

Gas Exchange in Plants

Respiring tissues require oxygen, and the photosynthetic tissues of plants also require carbon dioxide in order to produce the sugars needed for their growth and maintenance. The principal gas exchange organs in plants are the leaves, and sometimes the stems. In most plants, the exchange of gases directly across the leaf surface is prevented by the waterproof, waxy cuticle layer. Instead, access to the respiring cells is by means of **stomata**, which are tiny pores in the leaf surface. The plant has to balance its need for carbon dioxide (keeping stomata open) against its need to reduce water loss (stomata closed).

Terrestrial Environment

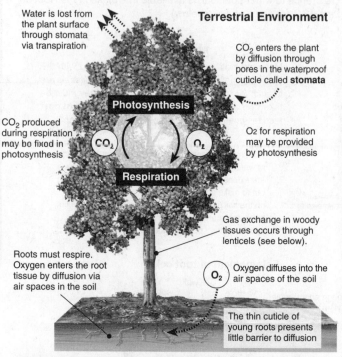

Water is lost from the plant surface through stomata via transpiration

CO_2 enters the plant by diffusion through pores in the waterproof cuticle called **stomata**

CO_2 produced during respiration may be fixed in photosynthesis

O_2 for respiration may be provided by photosynthesis

Gas exchange in woody tissues occurs through lenticels (see below).

Roots must respire. Oxygen enters the root tissue by diffusion via air spaces in the soil

Oxygen diffuses into the air spaces of the soil

The thin cuticle of young roots presents little barrier to diffusion

Most gas exchange in plants occurs through the leaves, but some also occurs through the stems and the roots. The shape and structure of leaves (very thin with a high surface area) assists gas exchange by diffusion.

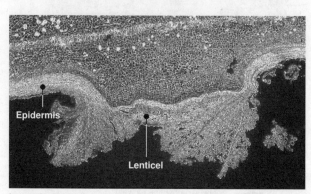

Epidermis

Lenticel

In woody plants, the wood prevents gas exchange. A lenticel is a small area in the bark where the loosely arranged cells allow entry and exit of gases into the stem tissue underneath.

Aquatic Environment

The aquatic environment presents special problems for plants. Water loss is not a problem, but CO_2 availability is often very limited because most of the dissolved CO_2 is present in the form of bicarbonate ions, which is not directly available to plants. Maximizing uptake of gaseous CO_2 by reducing barriers to diffusion is therefore important.

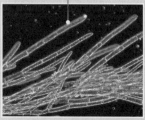

Absorption of CO_2 by direct diffusion

Gas exchange through stomata on the upper surface

Algae lack stomata but achieve adequate gas exchange through simple diffusion into the cells.

Floating leaves, such as the water lilies above, generally lack stomata on their lower surface.

With the exception of liverworts, all terrestrial plants and most aquatic plants have stomata to provide for gas exchange. CO_2 uptake is aided in submerged plants because they have little or no cuticle to form a barrier to diffusion of gases. The few submerged aquatics that lack stomata altogether rely only on diffusion through the epidermis. Most aquatic plants also have air spaces in their spongy tissues (which also assist buoyancy).

Transitional Environment

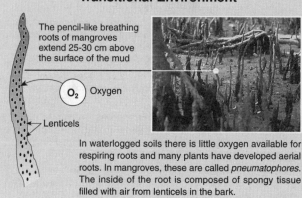

The pencil-like breathing roots of mangroves extend 25-30 cm above the surface of the mud

O_2 Oxygen

Lenticels

In waterlogged soils there is little oxygen available for respiring roots and many plants have developed aerial roots. In mangroves, these are called *pneumatophores*. The inside of the root is composed of spongy tissue filled with air from lenticels in the bark.

1. Name the gas produced by cellular respiration that is also a raw material for photosynthesis: _____

2. Describe the role of lenticels in plant gas exchange: _____
_____

3. Identify two properties of leaves that assist gas exchange: _____

4. With respect to gas exchange and water balance, describe the most important considerations for:

    (a) Terrestrial plants: _____

    (b) Aquatic plants: _____

5. Describe an adaptation for gas exchange in the following plants:

    (a) A submerged aquatic angiosperm: _____

    (b) A mangrove in a salty mudflat: _____

Related activities: Gas Exchange and Stomata, Adaptations of Hydrophytes

Gas Exchange and Stomata

The leaf epidermis of angiosperms is covered with tiny pores, called **stomata**. Angiosperms have many air spaces between the cells of the stems, leaves, and roots. These air spaces are continuous and gases are able to move freely through them and into the plant's cells via the stomata. Each stoma is bounded by two **guard cells**, which together regulate the entry and exit of gases and water vapor. Although stomata permit gas exchange between the air and the photosynthetic cells inside the leaf, they are also the major routes for water loss through transpiration. Note: An alternative version of this activity, without reference to water potential, is available in *Gas Exchange and Stomata* on the TRC (or see web links below).

Gas Exchanges and the Function of Stomata

Gases enter and leave the leaf by way of stomata. Inside the leaf (as illustrated by a dicot, right), the large air spaces and loose arrangement of the spongy mesophyll facilitate the diffusion of gases and provide a large surface area for gas exchanges.

Respiring plant cells use oxygen (O_2) and produce carbon dioxide (CO_2). These gases move in and out of the plant and through the air spaces by diffusion.

When the plant is photosynthesizing, the situation is more complex. Overall there is a net consumption of CO_2 and a net production of oxygen. The fixation of CO_2 maintains a gradient in CO_2 concentration between the inside of the leaf and the atmosphere. Oxygen is produced in excess of respiratory needs and diffuses out of the leaf. These **net** exchanges are indicated by the arrows on the diagram.

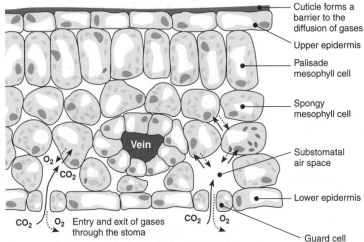

- Cuticle forms a barrier to the diffusion of gases
- Upper epidermis
- Palisade mesophyll cell
- Spongy mesophyll cell
- Substomatal air space
- Lower epidermis
- Guard cell

Entry and exit of gases through the stoma

Net gas exchanges in a photosynthesizing dicot leaf

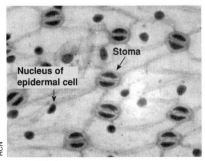

A surface view of the leaf epidermis of a dicot (above) illustrating the density and scattered arrangement of stomata. In dicots, stomata are usually present only on the lower leaf surface.

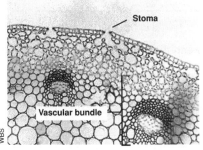

The stems of some plants (e.g. the buttercup above) are photosynthetic. Gas exchange between the stem tissues and the environment occurs through stomata in the outer epidermis.

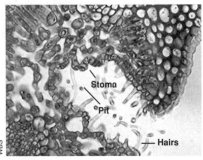

Oleander (above) is a xerophyte with many water conserving features. The stomata are in pits on the leaf underside. The pits restrict water loss to a greater extent than they reduce CO_2 uptake.

The cycle of opening and closing of stomata

The opening and closing of stomata shows a daily cycle that is largely determined by the hours of light and dark.

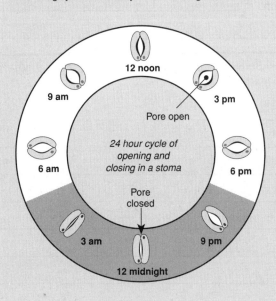

24 hour cycle of opening and closing in a stoma

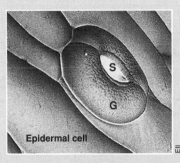

The image left shows a scanning electron micrograph (SEM) of a single stoma from the leaf epidermis of a dicot.

Note the guard cells (G), which are swollen tight and open the pore (S) to allow gas exchange between the leaf tissue and the environment.

Factors influencing stomatal opening

Stomata	Guard cells	Daylight	CO₂	Soil water
Open	Turgid	Light	Low	High
Closed	Flaccid	Dark	High	Low

The opening and closing of stomata depends on environmental factors, the most important being light, carbon dioxide concentration in the leaf tissue, and water supply. Stomata tend to open during daylight in response to light, and close at night (left and above). Low CO_2 levels also promote stomatal opening. Conditions that induce water stress cause the stomata to close, regardless of light or CO_2 level.

Related activities: Gas Exchange in Plants, Transpiration
Web links: Gas Exchange and Stomata

A 2

The guard cells on each side of a stoma control the diameter of the pore by changing shape. When the guard cells take up water by osmosis they swell and become turgid, making the pore wider. When the guard cells lose water, they become flaccid, and the pore closes up. By this mechanism a plant can control the amount of gas entering, or water leaving, the plant. The changes in turgor pressure that open and close the pore result mainly from the reversible uptake and loss of potassium ions (and thus water) by the guard cells.

Stomatal Pore Open

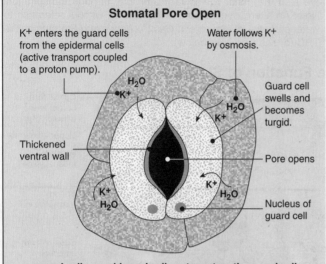

K^+ enters the guard cells from the epidermal cells (active transport coupled to a proton pump).

Water follows K^+ by osmosis.

H_2O

K^+

H_2O

Guard cell swells and becomes turgid.

Thickened ventral wall

K^+

Pore opens

K^+

H_2O

K^+

H_2O

Nucleus of guard cell

ψguard cell < ψepidermal cell: water enters the guard cells

Stomata open when the guard cells actively take up K^+ from the neighboring epidermal cells. The ion uptake causes the water potential (ψ) to become more negative in the guard cells. As a consequence, water is taken up by the cells and they swell and become turgid. The walls of the guard cells are thickened more on the inside surface (the ventral wall) than the outside wall, so that when the cells swell they buckle outward, opening the pore.

Stomatal Pore Closed

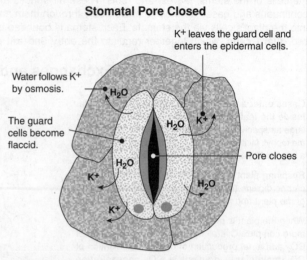

K^+ leaves the guard cell and enters the epidermal cells.

Water follows K^+ by osmosis.

H_2O

H_2O

K^+

The guard cells become flaccid.

H_2O

K^+

Pore closes

H_2O

K^+

ψepidermal cell < ψguard cell: water leaves the guard cells

Stomata close when K^+ leaves the guard cells. The loss causes the water potential (ψ) to become less negative in the guard cells, and more negative in the epidermal cells. As a consequence, water is lost by osmosis and the cells sag together and close the pore. The K^+ movements in and out of the guard cells are thought to be triggered by blue-light receptors in the plasma membrane, which activate the active transport mechanisms involved.

1. With respect to a mesophytic, terrestrial flowering plant:

    (a) Describe the **net** gas exchanges between the air and the cells of the mesophyll in the dark (no photosynthesis):

    _____

    (b) Explain how this situation changes when a plant is photosynthesizing: _____

    _____

    _____

2. Identify two ways in which the continuous air spaces through the plant facilitate gas exchange:

    (a) _____

    (b) _____

3. Briefly outline the role of stomata in gas exchange in an angiosperm: _____

    _____

    _____

4. Summarize the mechanism by which the guard cells bring about:

    (a) Stomatal opening: _____

    _____

    _____

    (b) Stomatal closure: _____

    _____

    _____

Transpiration

Plants lose water all the time, despite the adaptations they have to help prevent it (e.g. waxy leaf cuticle). Approximately 99% of the water a plant absorbs from the soil is lost by evaporation from the leaves and stem. This loss, mostly through stomata, is called **transpiration** and the flow of water through the plant is called the **transpiration stream**. Plants rely on a gradient in water potential (ψ) to move water through their cells. Water flows passively from soil to air along a gradient of decreasing water potential. The gradient in water potential is the driving force in the ascent of water up a plant. A number of processes contribute to water movement up the plant: transpiration pull, cohesion, and root pressure. Transpiration may seem to be a wasteful process, but it has benefits. Evaporation cools the plant and the transpiration stream helps the plant to maintain an adequate mineral uptake, as many essential minerals occur in low concentrations in the soil. Note: An alternative version of this activity, without reference to water potential, is available in *Transpiration* on the TRC (or see web links below).

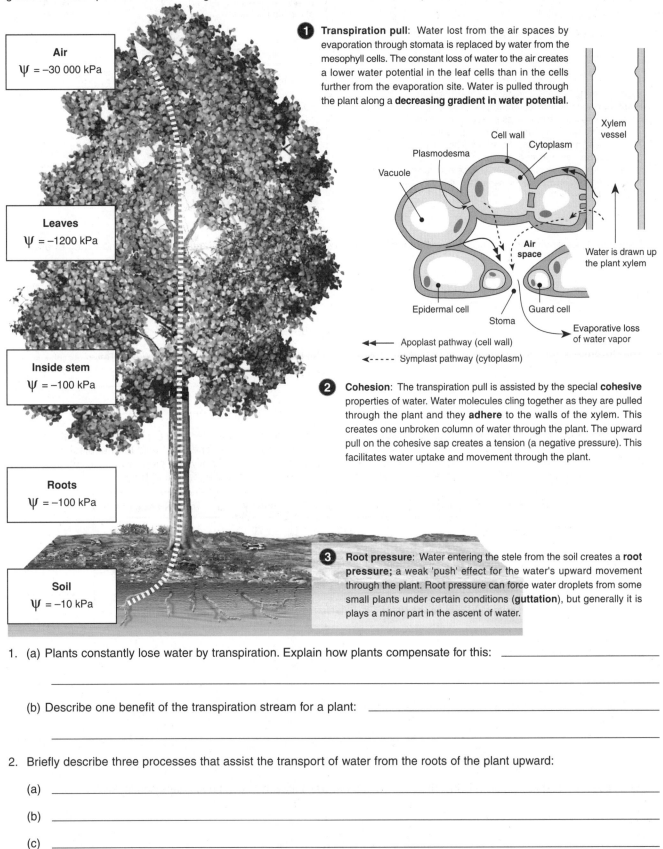

Air
ψ = –30 000 kPa

Leaves
ψ = –1200 kPa

Inside stem
ψ = –100 kPa

Roots
ψ = –100 kPa

Soil
ψ = –10 kPa

1 **Transpiration pull**: Water lost from the air spaces by evaporation through stomata is replaced by water from the mesophyll cells. The constant loss of water to the air creates a lower water potential in the leaf cells than in the cells further from the evaporation site. Water is pulled through the plant along a **decreasing gradient in water potential**.

Cell wall
Cytoplasm
Plasmodesma
Vacuole
Xylem vessel
Air space
Water is drawn up the plant xylem
Epidermal cell
Guard cell
Stoma
Evaporative loss of water vapor

◄◄── Apoplast pathway (cell wall)
◄----- Symplast pathway (cytoplasm)

2 **Cohesion**: The transpiration pull is assisted by the special **cohesive** properties of water. Water molecules cling together as they are pulled through the plant and they **adhere** to the walls of the xylem. This creates one unbroken column of water through the plant. The upward pull on the cohesive sap creates a tension (a negative pressure). This facilitates water uptake and movement through the plant.

3 **Root pressure**: Water entering the stele from the soil creates a **root pressure**; a weak 'push' effect for the water's upward movement through the plant. Root pressure can force water droplets from some small plants under certain conditions (**guttation**), but generally it is plays a minor part in the ascent of water.

1. (a) Plants constantly lose water by transpiration. Explain how plants compensate for this: _____

_____

(b) Describe one benefit of the transpiration stream for a plant: _____

_____

2. Briefly describe three processes that assist the transport of water from the roots of the plant upward:

(a) _____

(b) _____

(c) _____

The Potometer

A potometer is a simple instrument for investigating transpiration rate (water loss per unit time). The equipment is simple and easy to obtain. A basic potometer, such as the one shown right, can easily be moved around so that transpiration rate can be measured under different environmental conditions.

Some of the physical conditions investigated are:

- Humidity or vapor pressure (high or low)
- Temperature (high or low)
- Air movement (still or windy)
- Light level (high or low)
- Water supply

It is also possible to compare the transpiration rates of plants with different adaptations e.g. comparing transpiration rates in plants with rolled leaves vs rates in plants with broad leaves. If possible, experiments like these should be conducted simultaneously using replicate equipment. If conducted sequentially, care should be taken to keep the environmental conditions the same for all plants used.

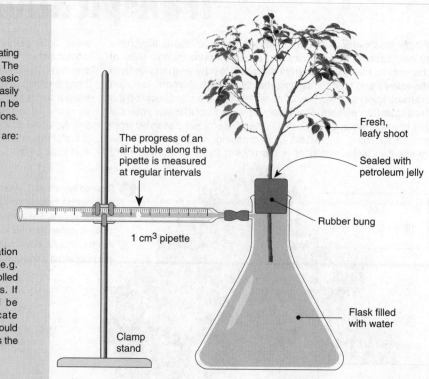

The progress of an air bubble along the pipette is measured at regular intervals

1 cm^3 pipette

Clamp stand

Fresh, leafy shoot

Sealed with petroleum jelly

Rubber bung

Flask filled with water

3. Describe three environmental conditions that increase the rate of transpiration in plants, and explain how they operate:

(a) _____

(b) _____

(c) _____

4. The **potometer** (above) is an instrument used to measure transpiration rate. Briefly explain how it works:

_____

_____

5. An experiment was conducted on transpiration from a hydrangea shoot in a potometer. The experiment was set up and the plant left to stabilize (environmental conditions: still air, light shade, 20°C). The plant was then subjected to different environmental conditions and the water loss was measured each hour. Finally, the plant was returned to original conditions, allowed to stabilize and transpiration rate measured again. The data are presented below:

Experimental conditions	Temperature (°C)	Humidity (%)	Transpiration (gh^{-1})
(a) Still air, light shade, 20°C	18	70	1.20
(b) Moving air, light shade, 20°C	18	70	1.60
(c) Still air, bright sunlight, 23°C	18	70	3.75
(d) Still air and dark, moist chamber, 19.5°C	18	100	0.05

(a) Name the control in this experiment: _____

_____

(b) Identify the factors that increased transpiration rate, explaining how each has its effect: _____

_____

_____

(c) Suggest a possible reason why the plant had such a low transpiration rate in humid, dark conditions:

_____

_____

Translocation

Phloem transports the organic products of photosynthesis (sugars) through the plant in a process called **translocation**. In angiosperms, the sugar moves through the sieve elements, which are arranged end-to-end and perforated with sieve plates. Apart from water, phloem sap comprises mainly sucrose (up to 30%). It may also contain minerals, hormones, and amino acids, in transit around the plant. Movement of sap in the phloem is from a **source** (a plant organ where sugar is made or mobilized) to a **sink** (a plant organ where sugar is stored or used). Loading sucrose into the phloem at a source involves energy expenditure; it is slowed or stopped by high temperatures or respiratory inhibitors. In some plants, unloading the sucrose at the sinks also requires energy, although in others, diffusion alone is sufficient to move sucrose from the phloem into the cells of the sink organ. (See the *TRC: Translocation* for an alternative version of this activity without reference to water potential or the web links below.)

Transport in the Phloem by Pressure-Flow

Phloem sap moves from source (region where sugar is produced or mobilised) to sink (region where sugar is used or stored) at rates as great as 100 m h⁻¹: too fast to be accounted for by cytoplasmic streaming. The most acceptable model for phloem movement is the **pressure-flow** (bulk flow) hypothesis. Phloem sap moves by bulk flow, which creates a pressure (hence the term "pressure-flow"). The key elements in this model are outlined below and in steps 1-4 right. For simplicity, the cells that lie between the source or sink cells and the phloem sieve-tube have been omitted.

1 Loading sugar into the phloem from a source (e.g. leaf cell) increases the solute concentration (decreases the water potential, ψ) inside the sieve-tube cells. This causes the sieve-tubes to take up water from the surrounding tissues by osmosis.

2 The water absorption creates a hydrostatic pressure that forces the sap to move along the tube (bulk flow), just as pressure pushes water through a hose.

3 The gradient of pressure in the sieve tube is reinforced by the active unloading of sugar and consequent loss of water by osmosis at the sink (e.g. root cell).

4 Xylem recycles the water from sink to source.

Measuring Phloem Flow

Experiments investigating flow of phloem often use aphids. Aphids feed on phloem sap (left) and act as natural **phloem probes**. When the mouthparts (stylet) of an aphid penetrate a sieve-tube cell, the pressure in the sieve-tube force-feeds the aphid. While the aphid feeds, it can be severed from its stylet, which remains in place in the phloem. The stylet serves as a tiny tap that exudes sap. Using different aphids, the rate of flow of this sap can be measured at different locations on the plant.

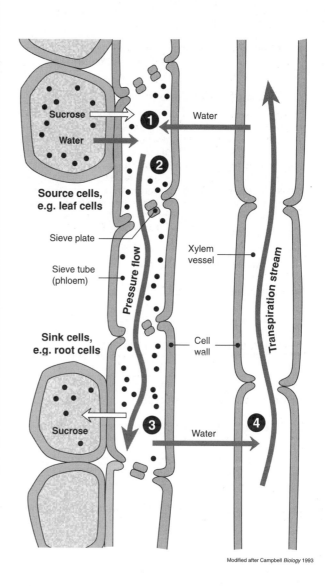

Modified after Campbell *Biology* 1993

---

1. (a) Explain what is meant by '**source to sink**' flow in phloem transport: _____

_____

(b) Name the usual **source** and **sink** in a growing plant:

Source: _____ Sink: _____

(c) Name another possible **source** region in the plant and state when it might be important: _____

_____

(d) Name another possible **sink** region in the plant and state when it might be important: _____

_____

2. Explain why energy is required for translocation and where it is used: _____

_____

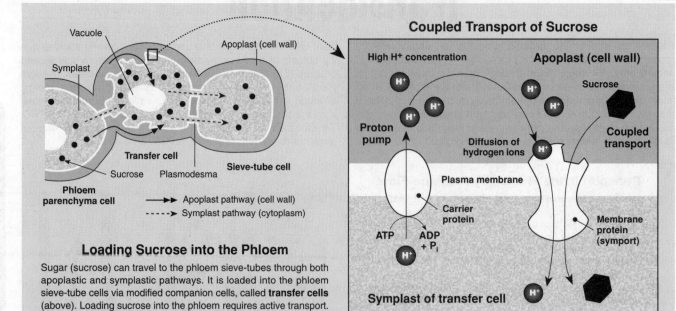

Loading Sucrose into the Phloem

Sugar (sucrose) can travel to the phloem sieve-tubes through both apoplastic and symplastic pathways. It is loaded into the phloem sieve-tube cells via modified companion cells, called **transfer cells** (above). Loading sucrose into the phloem requires active transport. Using a **coupled transport** (secondary pump) mechanism (right), transfer cells expend energy to accumulate the sucrose. The sucrose then passes into the sieve tube through plasmodesmata. The transfer cells have wall ingrowths that increase surface area for the transport of solutes. Using this mechanism, some plants can accumulate sucrose in the phloem to 2-3 times the concentration in the mesophyll.

Above: Proton pumps generate a hydrogen ion gradient across the membrane of the transfer cell. This process requires expenditure of energy. The gradient is then used to drive the transport of sucrose, by coupling the sucrose transport to the diffusion of H^+ back into the cell.

3. In your own words, describe what is meant by the following:

(a) Translocation: _____

_____

(b) Pressure-flow movement of phloem: _____

_____

(c) Coupled transport of sucrose: _____

4. Briefly explain why water follows the sucrose as the sucrose is loaded into the phloem sieve-tube cell:

_____

_____

5. Explain the role of the companion (transfer) cell in the loading of sucrose into the phloem: _____

_____

_____

6. Contrast the composition of phloem sap and xylem sap (see the activities on xylem and phloem if you need help):

_____

_____

_____

7. Explain why it is necessary for phloem to be alive to be functional, whereas xylem can function as a dead tissue:

_____

_____

_____

8. The sieve plate represents a significant barrier to effective mass flow of phloem sap. Suggest why the presence of the sieve plate is often cited as evidence against the pressure-flow model for phloem transport:

_____

_____

_____

_____

Plant Nutritional Requirements

Plants normally obtain minerals from the soil. The availability of mineral ions to plant roots depends on soil texture, since this affects the permeability of the soil to air and water. Mineral ions may be available to the plant in the soil water, adsorbed on to clay particles, or via release from humus and soil weathering. **Macronutrients** (e.g. nitrogen, sulfur, phosphorus) are required in large amounts for building basic constituents such as proteins. **Trace elements** (e.g. manganese, copper, and zinc) are required in small amounts. Many are components of, or activators for, enzymes. After being absorbed, mineral ions diffuse into the endodermis and may diffuse, or be actively transported, to the xylem for transport to other regions of the plant.

Plant Macronutrients

CARBON (as CO_2):

A component of all organic compounds.

NITROGEN (as NO_3^- or NH_4^+):

POTASSIUM (as K^+):

MAGNESIUM (as Mg^{2+}):

CALCIUM (as Ca^{2+}):

SULFUR (as SO_4^{2-}):

Mycorrhizal Associations

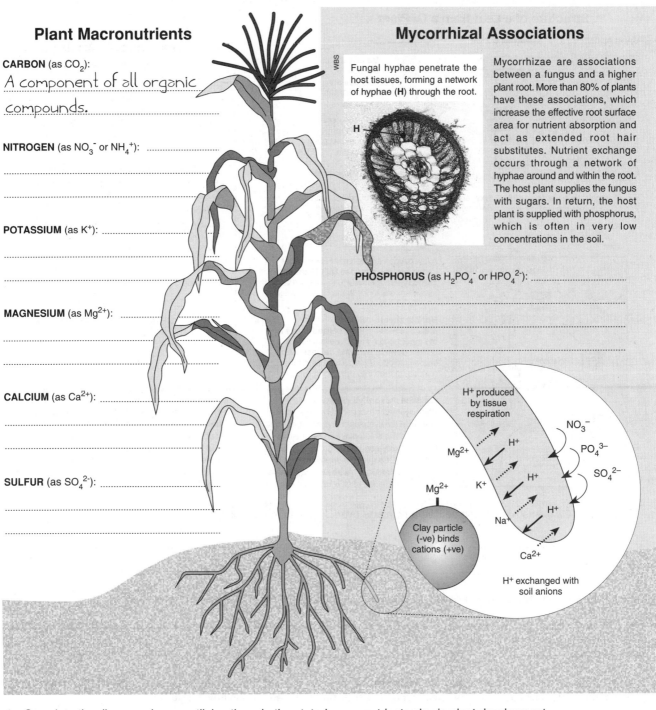

WBS

Fungal hyphae penetrate the host tissues, forming a network of hyphae (**H**) through the root.

H

Mycorrhizae are associations between a fungus and a higher plant root. More than 80% of plants have these associations, which increase the effective root surface area for nutrient absorption and act as extended root hair substitutes. Nutrient exchange occurs through a network of hyphae around and within the root. The host plant supplies the fungus with sugars. In return, the host plant is supplied with phosphorus, which is often in very low concentrations in the soil.

PHOSPHORUS (as $H_2PO_4^-$ or HPO_4^{2-}):

H^+ produced by tissue respiration

Mg^{2+}
H^+
NO_3^-
PO_4^{3-}
SO_4^{2-}
K^+
H^+
Mg^{2+}
H^+
Na^+

Clay particle (-ve) binds cations (+ve)

Ca^{2+}

H^+ exchanged with soil anions

1. Complete the diagram above, outlining the role the stated macronutrients play in plant development.

2. Briefly describe the ways in which minerals are available to plants: _____

_____

3. (a) Describe the role of mycorrhizal associations in plant nutrition: _____

_____

(b) Suggest why plants without mycorrhizal associations might show poor growth: _____

_____

Related activities: Uptake in the Root

RA 2

Photosynthesis in C₄ Plants

When photosynthesis takes place, the first detectable compound which is made by a plant is usually a 3-carbon compound called GP (glycerate 3-phosphate). Plants which do this are called C₃ plants. In some plants, however, a 4-carbon molecule called oxaloacetate, is the first to be made. Such plants, which include cereals and tropical grasses, are called C₄ plants. These plants have a high rate of photosynthesis, thriving in environments with high light levels and warm temperatures. Their yield of photosynthetic products is higher than that of C₃ plants, giving them a competitive advantage in tropical climates. The high productivity of the C₄ system is also an important property of crop plants such as sugar cane and maize.

Structure of a Leaf from a C₄ Plant

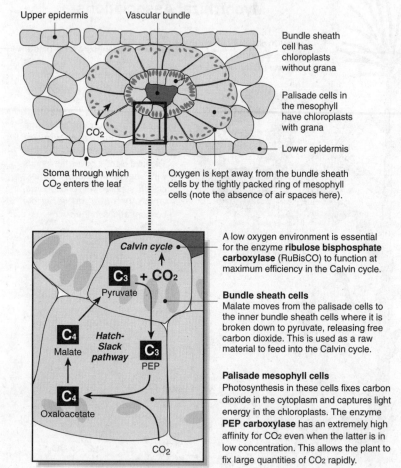

Upper epidermis

Vascular bundle

Bundle sheath cell has chloroplasts without grana

Palisade cells in the mesophyll have chloroplasts with grana

CO_2

Lower epidermis

Stoma through which CO_2 enters the leaf

Oxygen is kept away from the bundle sheath cells by the tightly packed ring of mesophyll cells (note the absence of air spaces here).

Calvin cycle

C₃ + **CO₂**

Pyruvate

C₄ *Hatch-Slack pathway* **C₃**

Malate PEP

C₄

Oxaloacetate

CO_2

A low oxygen environment is essential for the enzyme **ribulose bisphosphate carboxylase** (RuBisCO) to function at maximum efficiency in the Calvin cycle.

Bundle sheath cells
Malate moves from the palisade cells to the inner bundle sheath cells where it is broken down to pyruvate, releasing free carbon dioxide. This is used as a raw material to feed into the Calvin cycle.

Palisade mesophyll cells
Photosynthesis in these cells fixes carbon dioxide in the cytoplasm and captures light energy in the chloroplasts. The enzyme **PEP carboxylase** has an extremely high affinity for CO₂ even when the latter is in low concentration. This allows the plant to fix large quantities of CO₂ rapidly.

Examples of C₄ plants
- Sugar cane (*Saccharum officinale*)
- Maize (*Zea mays*)
- Sorghum (*Sorghum bicolor*)
- Sun plant (*Portulaca grandifolia*)

Distribution of grasses using C₄ mechanism in North America

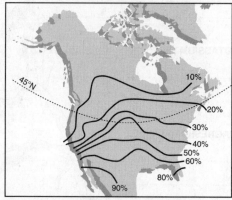

45°N

10%

20%

30%

40%

50%

60%

80%

90%

The photosynthetic strategy that a plant possesses is an important factor in determining where it lives. Because many of the enzymes of C₄ plants have optimum temperatures well above 25°C, they thrive in hot tropical and sub-tropical climates. Under these conditions, they can out-compete most C₃ plants because they achieve faster rates of photosynthesis. The proportion of grasses using the C₄ mechanism in North America is greatest near the tropics and diminishes northwards.

1. Explain why C₄ plants have a competitive advantage over C₃ plants in the tropics: _____

_____

_____

2. Explain why the bundle sheath cells are arranged in a way that keeps them isolated from air spaces in the leaf:

_____

_____

3. Study the map of North America above showing the distribution of C₄ plants. Explain the distribution pattern in terms of their competitive advantage and the environmental conditions required for this advantage:

_____

_____

4. In C₃ plants, the rate of photosynthesis is enhanced by higher atmospheric CO₂ concentrations. Explain why this is not the case for C₄ plants:

_____

_____

Related activities: Leaf Structure

Modifications in Plants

Various parts of the plant body may be modified for a specific role. Some **biennial plants**, e.g. carrots, store carbohydrates in fleshy **storage roots** during their first year of growth and use this store the following year to fuel the development of flowers, fruits, and seeds. The specialized **buttress** roots and **aerial** roots of some large tropical tree species (e.g. the banyan tree) provide support in thin tropical soils. Mangroves also have specialized aerial roots, called pneumatophores, which enable gas exchange in the water-logged substrate. In some **epiphytes**, e.g. the orchids, the aerial roots may be photosynthetic. **Parasitic** plants, such as mistletoe, produce rootlike organs that penetrate and parasitize the host's tissues. The stems of some plants also function as storage or photosynthetic organs. Horizontal underground stems, or **rhizomes**, can become swollen to provide a food store in the same way as root tubers. Similarly, **corms** are upright underground stems that become thickened with stored food. **Bulbs** are large buds with thick non-photosynthetic, food storage leaves clustered on short stems, e.g. onions. Cacti are a familiar example of stem and leaf modification. The fleshy green stems store water and photosynthesize while the leaves are modified into defensive spines. The tendrils of legumes and the traps of insectivorous plants are other familiar leaf modifications.

Plant Structure and Adaptation

Modifications of Plant Parts for Storage

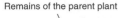
Remains of the parent plant

Tuber

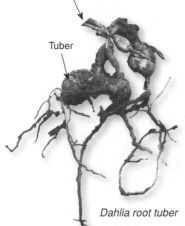

Dahlia root tuber

Root tubers, e.g. dahlias (above), lack terminal and lateral buds. Both stem and root tubers can give rise to new individuals, thereby providing a means of vegetative propagation.

Tubers are the swollen part of an underground stem or root, usually modified for storing food. The potato (below) is a **stem tuber**, as indicated by the presence of terminal and lateral buds.

Potato stem tuber

'Eye' (lateral bud)

Underground stem containing stored food

Iris rhizome

In **rhizomes**, as in corms, food is stored in the horizontal, underground stem. Rhizomes tend to be thick, fleshy or woody, and bear nodes with scale or foliage leaves and buds. Growth occurs at the buds on the ends of the rhizome or nearby nodes. Ginger, irises and lily-of-the-valley are rhizomes.

Bulbs

A true bulb is really just a typical shoot compressed into a shortened form. Fleshy storage leaves are attached to a stem plate and form concentric circles around the growing tip. New roots form from the lower part of the stem.

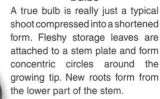

Food is stored in fleshy "scale" leaves

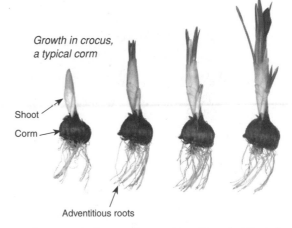
Growth in crocus, a typical corm

Shoot

Corm

Adventitious roots

In a **corm**, food is stored in stem tissue. Corms look like bulbs, but if you cut a corm in half you see a mass of homogenous tissue rather than concentric rings of fleshy leaves as in a bulb. Cyclamen, gladiolus, and crocus (above) are corms.

Supportive and Breathing Roots

istock

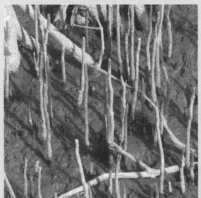
Phil Camill

istock

Many plants have specialized roots growing from the stem into the soil. These **prop roots** are seen in mangroves (above) and corn. They provide stability for the plant in the substrate.

Pneumatophores are the specialized 'breathing roots' of some types of mangroves. They grow up into the air and absorb oxygen-rich air via surface openings in the wood called lenticels.

The tropical **banyan tree** sends down rope-like aerial roots from its branches. These anchor in the soil and become very thick, forming massive columns that support the heavy branches.

Related activities: Adaptations of Xerophytes, Adaptations of Hydrophytes
Web links: Types of Roots

A 2

Leaves as Insect Traps

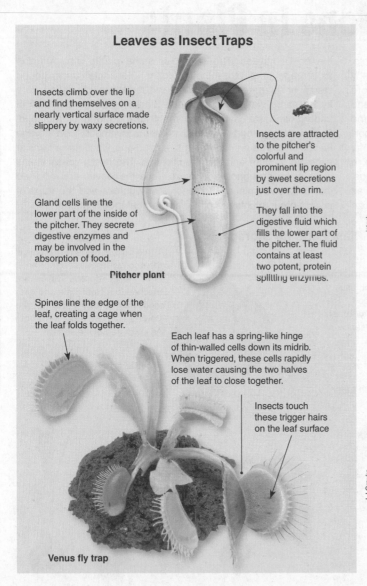

Insects climb over the lip and find themselves on a nearly vertical surface made slippery by waxy secretions.

Insects are attracted to the pitcher's colorful and prominent lip region by sweet secretions just over the rim.

Gland cells line the lower part of the inside of the pitcher. They secrete digestive enzymes and may be involved in the absorption of food.

They fall into the digestive fluid which fills the lower part of the pitcher. The fluid contains at least two potent, protein splitting enzymes.

Pitcher plant

Spines line the edge of the leaf, creating a cage when the leaf folds together.

Each leaf has a spring-like hinge of thin-walled cells down its midrib. When triggered, these cells rapidly lose water causing the two halves of the leaf to close together.

Insects touch these trigger hairs on the leaf surface

Venus fly trap

Many arid-adapted plants, like this aloe, have succulent leaves that are photosynthetic and also modified for internal storage of water.

Tendril

A tendril is a thread-like structure leaf modification that helps a plant to climb over other plants or objects to gain access to light.

Opening bud

Bud scale

In temperate climates, the buds of woody plants (e.g. **hickory**) are protected over winter by modified leaves called bud scales. The waxy scales prevent desiccation and insulate the bud against the cold.

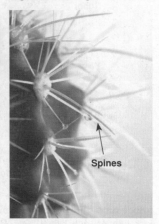

Spines

Many cacti have leaves reduced to sharp non-photosynthetic spines, which act to deter browsers. In the example above, the spines (leaves) grow from shortened shoots that arise from the photosynthetic stem.

1. For each of the following, identify the plant part that has been modified, and describe the modification and its purpose. Give an example in each case. The first one has been completed for you:

   (a) Bulb: Leaves are modified for food storage in the dormant plant. The leaf bases are fleshy and tightly packed together on a shortened stem. Example: onion, garlic, tulip, lily.

   (b) Corm: _____

   _____

   (c) Bud scales: _____

   _____

   (d) Tendrils: _____

   _____

   (e) Venus flytrap 'trap': _____

   _____

2. Discuss the role of aerial roots in named examples, explaining how they benefit the plant in each case:

   _____

   _____

   _____

   _____

Adaptations of Xerophytes

Plant Structure and Adaptation

Without sufficient water plant cells lose **turgor** and the tissue wilts. If a plant passes its **permanent wilting point** it will die. Water is lost from the plant by **transpiration**: the loss of water vapor, primarily through the stomata. Water balance is not a problem for aquatic plants; they allow water to flow in by osmosis until the cell wall stops further expansion. Plants adapted to dry conditions are called **xerophytes** and they show structural (xeromorphic) and physiological adaptations for water conservation. Some of these are outlined below. **Halophytes** (salt tolerant plants) and alpine species may also show xeromorphic features in response to the scarcity of obtainable water and high transpirational losses in these environments.

Tropical Forest Plant

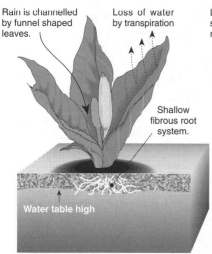

Rain is channelled by funnel shaped leaves.

Loss of water by transpiration

Shallow fibrous root system.

Water table high

Tropical plants live in areas of often high rainfall. There is also a corresponding high transpiration rate. Water availability is not a problem in this environment.

Dry Desert Plant

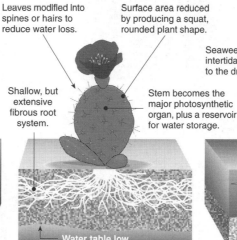

Leaves modified into spines or hairs to reduce water loss.

Surface area reduced by producing a squat, rounded plant shape.

Shallow, but extensive fibrous root system.

Stem becomes the major photosynthetic organ, plus a reservoir for water storage.

Water table low

Desert plants, e.g. cacti, must cope with low rainfall and high transpiration rates. They have strategies to reduce water loss, store water, and access available water supplies.

Ocean Margin Plant

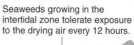
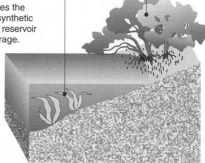

Mangrove trees take in brackish water, excreting the salt through glands in the leaves.

Seaweeds growing in the intertidal zone tolerate exposure to the drying air every 12 hours.

Land plants that colonize the shoreline (e.g. mangroves) must cope with high salt content in the water. Seaweeds below low tide do not have a water balance problem.

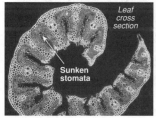

Grasses living in dry areas curl their leaves and have sunken stomata.

Mosses are poor at obtaining and storing water, restricting distribution.

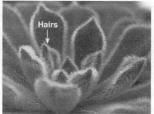

Hairs on leaves trap air close to the surface, reducing transpiration rate.

Excess water is forced from leaves (guttation) during high humidity.

Methods of water conservation in various plant species		
Adaptation for water conservation	**Effect of adaptation**	**Example**
Thick, waxy cuticle to stems and leaves	Reduces water loss through the cuticle.	*Pinus* sp. ivy (*Hedera*), sea holly (*Eryngium*), prickly pear (*Opuntia*).
Reduced number of stomata	Reduces the number of pores through which water loss can occur.	Prickly pear (*Opuntia*), *Nerium* sp.
Stomata sunken in pits, grooves, or depressions Leaf surface covered with fine hairs Massing of leaves into a rosette at ground level	Moist air is trapped close to the area of water loss, reducing the diffusion gradient and therefore the rate of water loss.	**Sunken stomata:** *Pinus* sp., *Hakea* sp. **Hairy leaves:** lamb's ear. **Leaf rosettes:** dandelion (*Taraxacum*), daisy.
Stomata closed during the light, open at night	CAM metabolism: CO_2 is fixed during the night, water loss in the day is minimized.	**CAM plants**, e.g. American aloe, pineapple, *Kalanchoe*, *Yucca*.
Leaves reduced to scales, stem photosynthetic Leaves curled, rolled, or folded when flaccid	Reduction in surface area from which transpiration can occur.	**Leaf scales:** broom (*Cytisus*). **Rolled leaf:** marram grass (*Ammophila*), *Erica* sp.
Fleshy or succulent stems Fleshy or succulent leaves	When readily available, water is stored in the tissues for times of low availability.	**Fleshy stems:** *Opuntia*, candle plant (*Kleinia*). **Fleshy leaves:** *Bryophyllum*.
Deep root system below the water table	Roots tap into the lower water table.	Acacias, oleander.
Shallow root system absorbing surface moisture	Roots absorb overnight condensation.	Most cacti

Related activities: Transpiration

A1

Adaptations in halophytes and drought tolerant plants

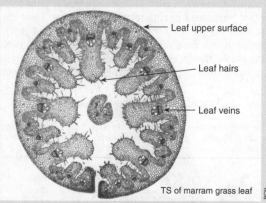

TS of marram grass leaf

Ice plant (*Carpobrotus*): The leaves of many desert and beach dwelling plants are fleshy or succulent. The leaves are triangular in cross section and crammed with water storage cells. The water is stored after rain for use in dry periods. The shallow root system is able to take up water from the soil surface, taking advantage of any overnight condensation.

Marram grass (*Ammophila*): The long, wiry leaf blades of this beach grass are curled downwards with the stomata on the inside. This protects them against drying out by providing a moist microclimate around the stomata. Plants adapted to high altitude often have similar adaptations.

Ball cactus (*Echinocactus grusonii*): In cacti, the leaves are modified into long, thin spines which project outward from the thick fleshy stem (see close-up above right). This reduces the surface area over which water loss can occur. The stem takes over the role of producing the food for the plant and also stores water during rainy periods for use during drought. As in succulents like ice plant, the root system in cacti is shallow to take advantage of surface water appearing as a result of overnight condensation.

1. Explain the purpose of **xeromorphic** adaptations: _____

_____

2. Describe three xeromorphic adaptations of plants:

   (a) _____

   (b) _____

   (c) _____

3. Describe a physiological mechanism by which plants can reduce water loss during the daylight hours:

_____

_____

4. Explain why creating a moist microenvironment around the areas of water loss reduces transpiration rate:

_____

5. Explain why seashore plants (halophytes) exhibit many desert-dwelling adaptations: _____

_____

_____

Adaptations of Hydrophytes

Hydrophytes are a group of plants which have adapted to living either partially or fully submerged in water. Survival in water poses different problems to those faced by terrestrial plants. Hydrophytes have a reduced root system, a feature that is often related to the relatively high concentration of nutrients in the sediment and the plant's ability to remove nitrogen and phosphorus directly from the water. The leaves of submerged plants are thin to increase the surface area of photosynthetic tissue and reduce internal shading. Hydrophytes typically have no cuticle (waterproof covering) or the cuticle is very thin. This enables the plant ability to absorb minerals and gases directly from the water. In addition, being supported by the water, they require very little in the way of structural support tissue.

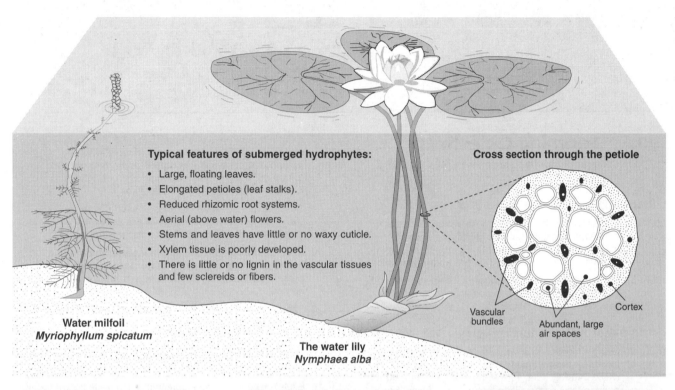

Typical features of submerged hydrophytes:

- Large, floating leaves.
- Elongated petioles (leaf stalks).
- Reduced rhizomic root systems.
- Aerial (above water) flowers.
- Stems and leaves have little or no waxy cuticle.
- Xylem tissue is poorly developed.
- There is little or no lignin in the vascular tissues and few sclereids or fibers.

Cross section through the petiole

Vascular bundles
Cortex
Abundant, large air spaces

Water milfoil
Myriophyllum spicatum

The water lily
Nymphaea alba

Myriophyllum's submerged leaves are well spaced and taper towards the surface to assist with gas exchange and distribution of sunlight.

The floating leaves of water lilies (*Nymphaea*) have a high density of stomata on the upper leaf surface so they are not blocked by water.

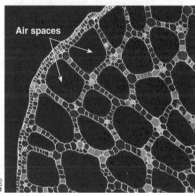

Air spaces

Cross section through oxygen weed (*Potamogeton*), showing the large air spaces which assist with flotation and gas exchange.

1. Explain how the following adaptations assist hydrophytes to survive in an aquatic environment:

   (a) Large air spaces within the plant's tissues: _____

   _____

   (b) Thin cuticle: _____

   _____

   (c) High stomatal densities on the upper leaf surface: _____

   _____

2. Explain why hydrophytic plants have retained an aerial (above water) flowering system: _____

   _____

Related activities: Support in Plants, Pollination and Fertilization

A 2

Plant Responses and Reproduction

IB SL	IB HL	IB Options	AP Biology
Not applicable to core	Complete: 1, 4, 7, 10, 12-13, 14(a)-(e) Extension: 2-3, 5-6, 8-9, 11, 14(f), 15	Not applicable to options	Complete: 1-15 Some numbers extension as appropriate

Learning Objectives

☐ 1. Compile your own glossary from the **KEY WORDS** displayed in **bold type** in the learning objectives below.

Plant Life Cycles *(pages 368-370)*

☐ 2. With reference to angiosperm life cycles, describe **alternation of generations**. Identify the life cycle stages, and the nature and significance of the **haploid (gametophyte)** and **diploid (sporophyte)** generations.

☐ 3. Contrast the relative importance of the sporophyte and gametophyte generations in non-angiosperm plants: mosses, ferns, gymnosperms.

Angiosperm Reproduction *(pages 368, 371-376)*

☐ 4. Using a labeled diagram, describe the structure of a typical **insect-pollinated** dicot **flower**, including: **sepal**, calyx, **petal**, corolla, **anther**, **filament**, stamen, **stigma**, **style**, **ovary**, carpel. State the function of each part.

☐ 5. Using a labeled diagram, describe the structure of a typical monocot **wind pollinated** flower, as seen with the naked eye and with a hand lens.

☐ 6. Distinguish between the typical adaptations of wind-pollinated and insect-pollinated flowers, identifying the significance of the differences.

☐ 7. Distinguish between **pollination**, **fertilization**, and **seed dispersal**. If required, describe **pollination** and the events leading to **fertilization**. Include reference to the development of the pollen tube, the role of the **polar nuclei**, and the significance of the **double fertilization**.

☐ 8. Explain what is meant by **cross pollination** and explain its significance. Describe mechanisms in angiosperms for ensuring cross pollination.

☐ 9. Explain the purpose of the fruit and describe stages in **fruit** development. Name the structure from which the fruit usually develops and discuss variations on this.

☐ 10. Explain the purpose of a **seed**. Describe the structure of a named dicot, non-endospermic seed, including reference to the **testa**, **micropyle**, **embryo shoot (plumule)**, **embryo root (radicle)**, and **cotyledons**. Explain the function of these structures.

☐ 11. Describe four common methods of **seed dispersal**. Using named examples, compare and contrast methods (and efficiency) of seed dispersal.

☐ 12. Describe the metabolic events in the **germination** of a typical starchy seed. Include reference to the role of water absorption, the formation of gibberellin in the cotyledon, and the production of amylase.

☐ 13. Explain the environmental conditions important in triggering **germination** in a typical seed.

Plant Growth Regulators *(pages 361-367, 377-378 and the TRC: Plant Hormones and Applications)*

☐ 14. Explain why plants need communication systems to respond to environmental stimuli. Describe responses in plants and their physiological basis, including the commercial significance of these. Include reference to:

(a) The nature of **tropisms**, especially phototropism.

(b) The role of **auxins** in tropic responses (particularly phototropism). Evaluate the experimental evidence for the role of auxins in regulating plant growth.

(c) The role of **auxins** in **apical dominance**, explaining how pruning promotes bushiness.

(d) The role of **cytokinins**, **ethene**, **gibberellins** and **abscisic acid** on plant growth and development.

(e) The control of flowering in **long-day** and **short-day plants**, and the role of **phytochrome** in this.

(f) The responses of plants to temperature changes.

☐ 15. Describe the techniques used in cloning plants by **micropropagation** (tissue culture), including reference to the use of **plant growth regulators**. Appreciate the applications of micropropagation in modern horticulture.

 Textbooks

See the 'Textbook Reference Grid' on pages 8-9 for textbook page references relating to material in this topic.

Supplementary Texts

See page 6 for additional details of these texts:
■ Clegg, C.J., 2003. **Green Plants: The Inside Story** (John Murray), reading as required.

Software and video resources for plant structure and function topics are provided on the TRC

 Periodicals

See page 6 for details of publishers of periodicals:
STUDENT'S REFERENCE
■ **An Explosive Start for Plants** New Scientist, 2 Jan. 1993, pp. 35-37. *Seed dispersal often involves the explosion of the seeds from the fruit.*
■ **Flower Power** New Scientist, 9 Jan. 1999, pp. 22-26. *Pollination and fertilisation in angiosperms, and the place of pollen competition.*
■ **How Plants Know Their Place** Biol. Sci. Rev., 17(3), Feb. 2005, pp. 33-36. *Plants receive vital cues for their growth, development, and ecology from signals in the light environment. This account explores the mechanisms behind these responses.*

 **Internet**

See pages 10-11 for details of how to access **Bio Links** from our web site: **www.thebiozone.com** From Bio Links, access sites under the topics:
BIOTECHNOLOGY > Applications of Biotechnology > Cloning and Tissue Culture: • Tissue culture in the classroom
PLANT BIOLOGY: • Plant biology for non-science majors ... *and others* **Structure and Function:** • Plant hormones and nutrition ...*and others* > **Reproduction:** • Flower structure • Flowers and reproduction • Seed germination > **Hormones and Responses:** • Plant hormones and growth regulators • Plant hormones and directional growth ... *and others*

Plant Responses

Even though most plants are firmly rooted in the ground, they are still capable of responding and making adjustments to changes in their external environment. This ability is manifested chiefly in changing patterns of growth. These responses may involve relatively sudden physiological changes, as occurs in flowering, or a steady growth response, such as a **tropism**. Other responses made by plants include nastic movements, circadian rhythms, photoperiodism, dormancy, and vernalization.

TROPISMS
Tropisms are growth responses made by plants to directional external stimuli, where the direction of the stimulus determines the direction of the growth response. A tropism may be positive (towards the stimulus), or negative (away from the stimulus). Common stimuli for plants include light, gravity, touch, and chemicals.

LIFE CYCLE RESPONSES
Plants use seasonal changes in the environment as cues for the commencement or ending of particular life cycle stages. Such changes are mediated by **plant growth factors**, such as phytochrome and gibberellin. Examples include flowering and other **photoperiodic responses**, dormancy and germination, and leaf fall.

RAPID RESPONSES TO ENVIRONMENTAL STIMULI
Plants are capable of quite rapid responses. Examples include the closing of **stomata** in response to water loss, opening and closing of flowers in response to temperature (photo, below right), and **nastic responses** (photos, below left). These responses often follow a circadian rhythm.

PLANT COMPETITION AND ALLELOPATHY
Although plants are rooted in the ground, they can still compete with other plants to gain access to resources. Some plants produce chemicals that inhibit the growth of neighboring plants. Such chemical inhibition is called **allelopathy**. Plants also compete for light and may grow aggressively to shade out slower growing competitors.

PLANT RESPONSES TO HERBIVORY
Many plant species have responded to grazing or browsing pressure with evolutionary adaptations enabling them to survive constant cropping. Examples include rapid growth to counteract the constant loss of biomass (grasses), sharp spines or thorns to deter browsers (acacias, cacti), or toxins in the leaf tissues (eucalyptus).

Shoots are **positively phototropic** and grow toward the light.

Roots are positively gravitropic and grow towards the Earth's gravitational pull.

Plant Responses and Reproduction

Some plants, such as *Mimosa* (above), are capable of **nastic responses**. These are relatively rapid, reversible movements, such as leaf closure in response to touch. Unlike tropisms, nastic responses are independent of stimulus direction.

The growth of tendrils around a support is a response to a mechanical stimulus, and is called thigmomorphogenesis.

The opening and closing of this tulip flower is temperature dependent. The flowers close when it is cool at night.

1. Identify the stimuli to which plants typically respond: _____

2. Explain how plants benefit by responding appropriately to the environment: _____

_____

_____

Related activities: Investigating Phototropism, Investigating Gravitropism, Plant Rhythms, Photoperiodism in Plants   Web links: Plants in Motion

A 2

Investigating Phototropism

Phototropism in plants was linked to a growth promoting substance in the 1920s. A number of classic experiments, investigating phototropic responses in severed coleoptiles, gave evidence for the hypothesis that **auxin** was responsible for the tropic responses of stems. Auxins promote cell elongation. Stem curvature in response to light can therefore result from the differential distribution of auxin either side of a stem. However, the mechanisms of hormone action in plants are still not well understood. Auxins increase cell elongation only over a certain concentration range and, at certain levels, auxins stop inducing elongation and begin to inhibit it. Note that there is *some* experimental evidence to contradict the original auxin hypothesis and the early experiments have been criticized for oversimplifying the real situation. Some of the early experiments investigating the phototropic response, and the role of hormone(s) in controlling it, are outlined below.

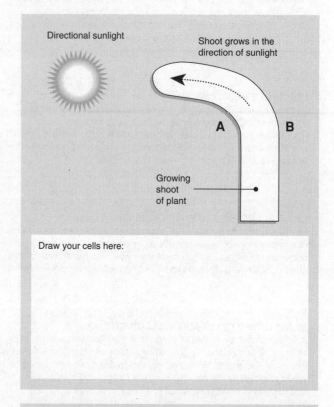

1. **Directional light**: A pot plant is exposed to direct sunlight near a window and as it grows, the shoot tip turns in the direction of the sun. If the plant was rotated, it adjusted by growing towards the sun in the new direction.

   (a) Name the hormone that regulates this growth response:

   _____

   (b) Give the full name of this growth response:

   _____

   (c) State how the cells behave to cause this change in shoot direction at:

   Point A: _____

   Point B: _____

   (d) State which side (A or B) would have the highest concentration of hormone:

   _____

   (e) Draw a diagram of the cells as they appear across the stem from point A to B (in the rectangle on the right).

2. **Light excluded from shoot tip**: With a foil cap placed over the top of the shoot tip, light is prevented from reaching it. Under these conditions, the direction of growth does not change towards the light source, but continues straight up. State the conclusion you could make about the source and activity of the hormone that controls the growth response:

   _____

   _____

   _____

   _____

   _____

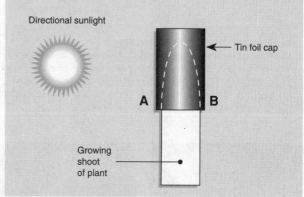

3. **Cutting into the transport system**: Two identical plants were placed side-by-side and subjected to the same directional light source. Razor blades were cut half-way into the stem, interfering with the transport system of the stem. Plant A had the cut on the same side as the light source, while Plant B was cut on the shaded side. Predict the growth responses of:

   Plant A: _____

   _____

   Plant B: _____

   _____

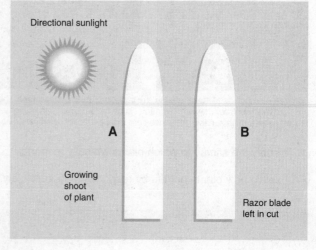

Related activities: Plant Tropisms; Auxins, Gibberellins and ABA

Investigating Gravitropism

Although the response of shoots and roots to gravity is well known, the mechanism behind it is not at all well understood. The importance of auxin as a plant growth regulator, as well as its widespread occurrence in plants, led to it being proposed as the primary regulator in the gravitropic response. The basis of auxin's proposed role in **gravitropism** is outlined below. The mechanism is appealing in its simplicity but, as noted below, has been widely criticized, and there is not a great deal of evidence to support it. Many of the early plant growth experiments (including those on phototropism) involved the use of coleoptiles. Their use has been criticized because the coleoptile (the sheath surrounding the young shoot of grasses) is a specialized and short-lived structure and is probably not representative of plant tissues generally.

Auxins and Gravitropic Responses

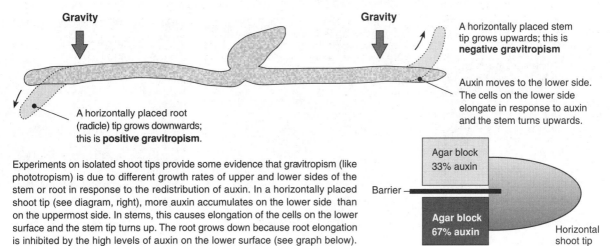

Gravity

A horizontally placed root (radicle) tip grows downwards; this is **positive gravitropism**.

Gravity

A horizontally placed stem tip grows upwards; this is **negative gravitropism**

Auxin moves to the lower side. The cells on the lower side elongate in response to auxin and the stem turns upwards.

Experiments on isolated shoot tips provide some evidence that gravitropism (like phototropism) is due to different growth rates of upper and lower sides of the stem or root in response to the redistribution of auxin. In a horizontally placed shoot tip (see diagram, right), more auxin accumulates on the lower side than on the uppermost side. In stems, this causes elongation of the cells on the lower surface and the stem tip turns up. The root grows down because root elongation is inhibited by the high levels of auxin on the lower surface (see graph below).

Agar block 33% auxin

Barrier —

Agar block 67% auxin

Horizontal shoot tip

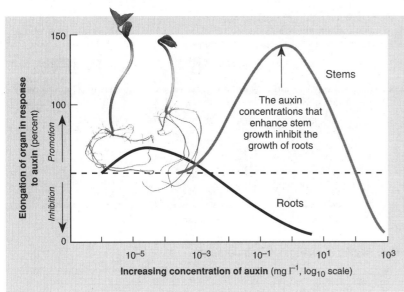

The auxin concentrations that enhance stem growth inhibit the growth of roots

Stems

Roots

Elongation of organ in response to auxin (percent)

Promotion / Inhibition

Increasing concentration of auxin (mg l^{-1}, log$_{10}$ scale)

Auxin Concentration and Root Growth

In a horizontally placed seedling, auxin moves to the lower side of the organ in both the stem and root. Whereas the stem tip grows upwards, the root tip responds by growing down. Root elongation is inhibited by the same level of auxin that stimulates stem growth (see graph left). The higher auxin levels on the lower surface cause growth inhibition there. The most elongated cells are then on the upper surface and the root turns down. This simple auxin explanation for the gravitropic response has been much criticized: the concentrations of auxins measured in the upper and lower surfaces of horizontal stems and roots are too small to account for the growth movements observed. Alternative explanations suggest that growth inhibitors are also somehow involved in the gravitropic response.

Plant Responses and Reproduction

1. Explain the mechanism proposed for the role of auxin in the gravitropic response in:

(a) Shoots (stems): _____

(b) Roots: _____

2. (a) From the graph above, state the auxin concentration at which root growth becomes inhibited: _____

(b) State the response of the stem at this concentration: _____

3. Briefly state a reason why the gravitropic response in stems or roots is important to the survival of a seedling:

(a) Stems: _____

(b) Roots: _____

Related activities: Investigating Phototropism; Auxins, Gibberellins and ABA

DA 2

Plant Rhythms

Plants are capable of marked physiological responses to a wide range of environmental variables. Some plant activities, such as the daily opening of flowers, follow **daily rhythms**, others are seasonal. Gardeners are well aware of the seasonal effects of temperature on plant growth and development. Woody plants are able to survive freezing temperatures because of metabolic changes that occur in the plant between summer and winter. This process of **acclimation** involves the production of thicker cell walls and accumulation of growth inhibitors in the plant tissues. Cold hardiness is genetically determined but can be influenced by horticultural practices that mimic seasonal changes. Alternation of periods of growth with periods of **dormancy** allows the plant to survive water shortages and extremes of hot or cold. When dormant, growth will not resume until the right combination of environmental cues are met. Such cues include exposure to cold, dryness, and suitable photoperiod. **Annuals** produce dormant seeds, whereas in **biennials** and **perennials** the shoots may die back while the overwintering structures become dormant. Low temperature stimulation of flowering (**vernalization**) and seed germination (**stratification**) are common in many species. These temperature responses are usually associated with increased activity in plant growth regulators such as gibberellic acid.

Dormancy is a condition of arrested growth in which the entire plant, or its seeds or buds, do not renew growth without certain environmental cues.

In many plants, after the seeds have taken up water, exposure to a period of low temperature (5°C) will break dormancy. This is called **stratification**.

Bud burst and flowering follow exposure to a cold period in many plants, including bulbs and many perennials. This process is called **vernalization**.

Daily Rhythm in Tulips

Many flowers, including tulips, show **sleep movements**. In many species, these are triggered by daylength, but in tulips the environmental cue is temperature. This series of photographs show the sleep movements of a single **tulip** flower over one 12 hour period during spring

All photos: RA

| 7.00 am | 9.30 am | 11.00 am | 5.00 pm | 7.00 pm |

1.   Describe two physiological responses of plants to seasonal changes in temperature:

(a) _____

(b) _____

2.   (a) Explain the adaptive value of **stratification** in plants: _____

_____

(b) State whether this response is endogenous or exogenous: _____

3.   Suggest why evergreen trees have a growth advantage in regions with a very short growing season: _____

_____

4.   (a) Describe the sleep movements of tulips in response to temperature: _____

_____

(b) Explain the adaptive value of these movements: _____

_____

Related activities: Photoperiodism in Plants; Auxins, Gibberellins and ABA

Photoperiodism in Plants

Photoperiodism is the response of a plant to the relative lengths of daylight and darkness. Flowering is a photoperiodic activity; individuals of a single species will all flower at much the same time, even though their germination and maturation dates may vary. The exact onset of flowering varies depending on whether the plant is a short-day or long-day type (see next page). Photoperiodic activities are controlled through the action of a pigment called **phytochrome**. Phytochrome acts as a signal for some biological clocks in plants and is also involved in other light initiated responses, such as germination, shoot growth, and chlorophyll synthesis. Plants do not grow at the same rate all of the time. In temperate regions, many perennial and biennial plants begin to shut down growth as autumn approaches. During

unfavorable seasons, they limit their growth or cease to grow altogether. This condition of arrested growth is called **dormancy**, and it enables plants to survive periods of water scarcity or low temperature. The plant's buds will not resume growth until there is a convergence of precise environmental cues in early spring. Short days and long, cold nights (as well as dry, nitrogen deficient soils) are strong cues for dormancy. Temperature and daylength change seasonally in most parts of the world, so changes in these variables also influence many plant responses, including germination and flowering. In many plants, flowering is triggered only after a specific period of exposure to low winter temperatures. As described in the previous activity, this low-temperature stimulation of flowering is called **vernalization**.

Photoperiodism

Photoperiodism is based on a system that monitors the day/night cycle. The photoreceptor involved in this, and a number of other light-initiated plant responses, is a blue-green pigment called **phytochrome**. Phytochrome is universal in vascular plants and has two forms: active and inactive. On absorbing light, it readily converts from the inactive form (P_r) to the active form (P_{fr}). P_{fr} predominates in daylight, but reverts spontaneously back to the inactive form in the dark. The plant measures daylength (or rather night length) by the amount of phytochrome in each form.

Summary of phytochrome related activities in plants

Process	Effect of daylight	Effect of darkness
Conversion of phytochrome	Promotes $P_r \rightarrow P_{fr}$	Promotes $P_{fr} \rightarrow P_r$
Seed germination	Promotes	Inhibits
Leaf growth	Promotes	Inhibits
Flowering: long day plants	Promotes	Inhibits
Flowering: short day plants	Inhibits	Promotes
Chlorophyll synthesis	Promotes	Inhibits

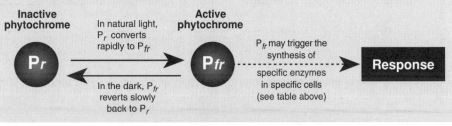

Inactive phytochrome — In natural light, P_r converts rapidly to P_{fr} — **Active phytochrome** — P_{fr} may trigger the synthesis of specific enzymes in specific cells (see table above) — **Response**

In the dark, P_{fr} reverts slowly back to P_r

Day length and life cycle in plants (Northern Hemisphere)

The cycle of active growth and dormancy shown by temperate plants is correlated with the number of daylight hours each day (right). In the southern hemisphere, the pattern is similar, but is six months out of phase. The duration of the periods may also vary on islands and in coastal regions because of the moderating effect of nearby oceans.

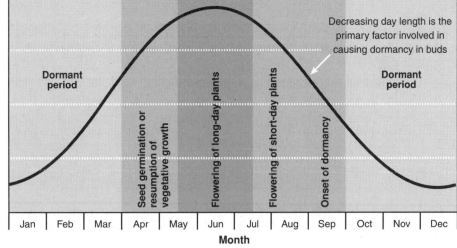

Decreasing day length is the primary factor involved in causing dormancy in buds

1. Describe two plant responses, initiated by exposure to light, which are thought to involve the action of phytochrome:

   (a) _____

   (b) _____

2. Discuss the role of phytochrome in a plant's ability to measure daylength: _____

   _____

   _____

   _____

   _____

Long-day plants

When subjected to the light regimes on the right, the 'long-day' plants below flowered as indicated:

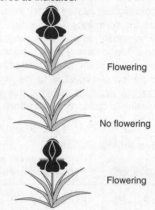

Flowering

No flowering

Flowering

Examples: *lettuce, clover, delphinium, gladiolus, beetscorn, coreopsis*

Photoperiodism in Plants

An experiment was carried out to determine the environmental cue that triggers flowering in 'long-day' and 'short-day' plants. The diagram below shows 3 different light regimes to which a variety of long-day and short-day plants were exposed.

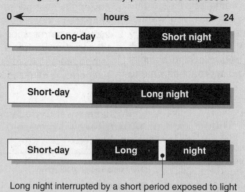

0 ◄——— hours ———► 24

| Long-day | Short night |

| Short-day | Long night |

| Short-day | Long | night |

Long night interrupted by a short period exposed to light

Short-day plants

When subjected to the light regimes on the left, the 'short-day' plants below flowered as indicated:

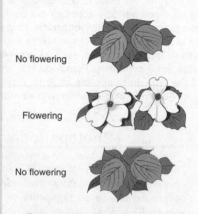

No flowering

Flowering

No flowering

Examples: *potatoes, asters, dahlias, cosmos, chrysanthemums, pointsettias*

3. (a) Identify the environmental cue that synchronizes flowering in plants: _____

   (b) Describe one biological advantage of this synchronization to the plants: _____

   _____

   _____

4. Discuss the role of environmental cues in triggering and breaking **dormancy** in plants:

   _____

   _____

   _____

   _____

5. Discuss the adaptive value of **dormancy** and **vernalization** in temperate climates: _____

   _____

   _____

   _____

   _____

   _____

6. Study the three light regimes above and the responses of short-day and long-day flowering plants to that light. From this observation, describe the most important factor controlling the onset of flowering in:

   (a) Short-day plants: _____

   (b) Long-day plants: _____

7. Using information from the experiment described above, discuss the evidence for the statement "*Short-day plants are really better described as long-night plants.*"

   _____

   _____

   _____

   _____

Auxins, Gibberellins, and ABA

Auxin was the first substance to be identified as a plant hormone. Charles Darwin and his son Francis were first to recognize its role in stimulating cell elongation, while Frits W. Went isolated this growth-regulating substance, which he called auxin. **Indole-acetic acid** (IAA) is the only known naturally occuring auxin. Shortly after its discovery it was found to have a role in suppressing the growth of lateral buds. This inhibitory influence of a shoot tip or apical bud on the lateral buds is called **apical dominance**. Two Japanese scientists isolated **gibberellin** in 1934, eight years after the isolation of auxin, and more than 78 gibberellins have now been identified. Gibberellins are involved in stem and leaf elongation, as well as breaking dormancy in seeds. Specifically, they stimulate cell division and cell elongation, allowing stems to 'bolt' and the root to penetrate the testa in germination. During the 1960s, Frederick T. Addicott discovered a substance apparently capable of accelerating **abscission** in leaves and fruit (which he called abscisin), and which is now called **abscisic acid** (ABA). Although it now seems that ABA has very little to do with leaf abscission, it is a growth inhibitor and also stimulates the closing of stomata in most plant species. It is also involved in preventing premature germination and development of seeds.

Auxins, Gibberellins, and Abscisic Acid (ABA) and Plant Responses

ABA stimulates the closing of stomata in most plant species. Its synthesis is stimulated by water deficiency (water stress).

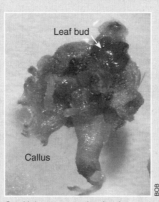

Cytokinins promote the development of leaf buds in calluses (above). In contrast, increased auxin levels will promote the development of roots.

Gibberellins are responsible for breaking dormancy in seeds and promote the growth of the embryo and emergence of the seedling.

ABA promotes seed dormancy. It is concentrated in senescent leaves, but it is probably not involved in leaf abscission except in a few species.

Gibberellins cause stem and leaf elongation by stimulating cell division and cell elongation. They are responsible for **bolting** in brassicas.

Gibberellins are used to hasten seed germination and ensure germination uniformity in the production of barley malt in brewing.

ABA is produced in ripe fruit and induces fruit fall. The effects of ABA are generally opposite to those of cytokinins.

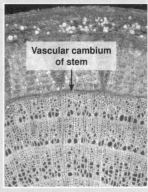

Auxins promote the activity of the vascular cambium (above), stem length, differentiation of tissues, and **apical dominance**.

Plant Responses and Reproduction

1. Describe the role of **auxins** in apical dominance: _____

_____

_____

2. Describe the role of **gibberellins** in stem elongation and in the germination of grasses such as barley:

_____

_____

_____

3. Describe the role of abscisic acid in closure of stomata: _____

_____

Related activities: Plant Responses

RA 2

Angiosperm Reproduction

The primary method of reproduction for flowering plants is by seeds, which develop after fertilization of the female parts of the flower, and contain the protected plant embryo together with a store of food. The typical life cycle of a flowering plant such as the bean (below) involves the formation of gametes (egg and sperm) from the haploid gametophytes, the fertilization of the egg by a sperm cell to form the zygote, the production of fruit around the

seed, and the germination of the seed and its growth by mitosis. The eggs and sperm are housed within the female and male gametophytes (embryo sac and pollen grain respectively). Each mature pollen grain contains two sperm nuclei and each mature embryo sac contains the egg and two polar nuclei. The leafy plant bearing the flowers represents the sporophyte generation of the life cycle.

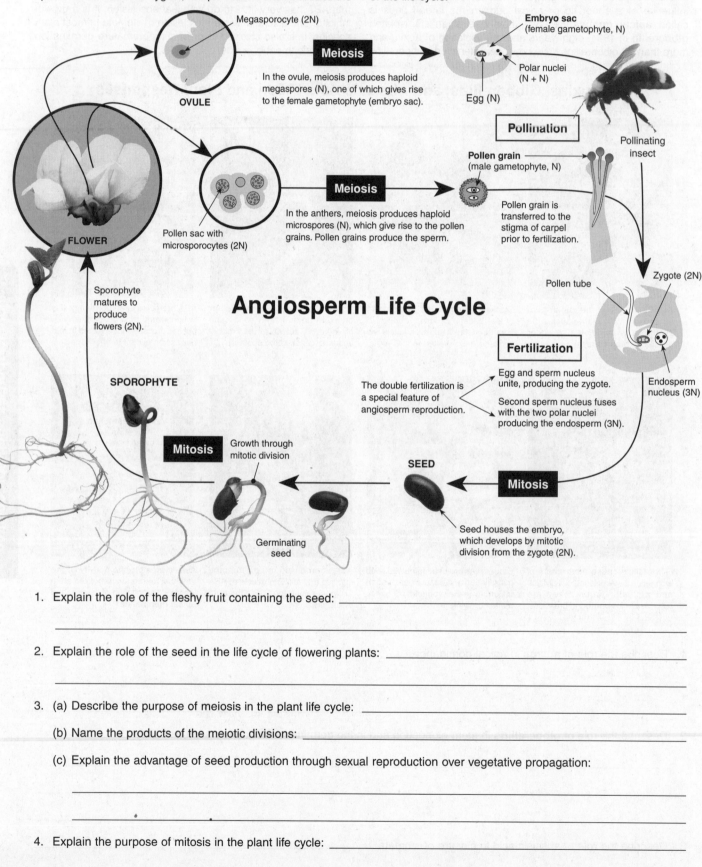

Angiosperm Life Cycle

Megasporocyte (2N)

Meiosis

In the ovule, meiosis produces haploid megaspores (N), one of which gives rise to the female gametophyte (embryo sac).

OVULE

Embryo sac (female gametophyte, N)

Polar nuclei (N + N)

Egg (N)

Pollination

Pollinating insect

Meiosis

In the anthers, meiosis produces haploid microspores (N), which give rise to the pollen grains. Pollen grains produce the sperm.

Pollen sac with microsporocytes (2N)

FLOWER

Sporophyte matures to produce flowers (2N).

Pollen grain (male gametophyte, N)

Pollen grain is transferred to the stigma of carpel prior to fertilization.

Pollen tube

Zygote (2N)

Fertilization

The double fertilization is a special feature of angiosperm reproduction.

Egg and sperm nucleus unite, producing the zygote.

Second sperm nucleus fuses with the two polar nuclei producing the endosperm (3N).

Endosperm nucleus (3N)

SPOROPHYTE

Mitosis — Growth through mitotic division

Germinating seed

SEED

Mitosis

Seed houses the embryo, which develops by mitotic division from the zygote (2N).

1. Explain the role of the fleshy fruit containing the seed: _____

_____

2. Explain the role of the seed in the life cycle of flowering plants: _____

_____

3. (a) Describe the purpose of meiosis in the plant life cycle: _____

   (b) Name the products of the meiotic divisions: _____

   (c) Explain the advantage of seed production through sexual reproduction over vegetative propagation:

   _____

   _____

4. Explain the purpose of mitosis in the plant life cycle: _____

_____

Related activities: Alternation of Generations, Seed Structure and Germination
Web links: Life Cycle of an Angiosperm

Alternation of Generations

The life cycles of all plants include a gametophyte generation (haploid or N phase) and a sporophyte generation (diploid or 2N phase). The two generations alternate, each giving rise to the other (commonly termed **alternation of generations**). The two plant forms (sporophyte and gametophyte) are named for the type of reproductive cells they produce. Gametophytes produce gametes by mitosis, whereas sporophytes produce spores by meiosis. Spores develop directly into organisms. Gametes (egg and sperm) unite during fertilization to form a zygote which gives rise to an organism.

Plant Responses and Reproduction

Algae

The sea lettuce *Ulva*, a green alga, has a life cycle alternating between two generations that seem to be the same. Although they appear identical, the cells of the sporophyte generation contain **26** chromosomes, while the gametophyte cells contain only **13** chromosomes. The sporophyte produces spores that settle on rock surfaces to grow into male and female gametophytes. These in turn mature and release gametes into the water. In fertilization, two gametes fuse and grow into a sporophyte.

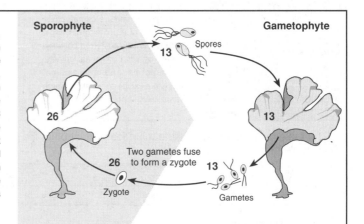

Moss

Most moss species have separate male and female gametophytes. A sperm swims through a film of moisture to the female gametophyte (archegonium) and fertilizes an egg. The resulting zygote develops into an embryonic sporophyte on top of the female gametophyte. It grows a long stalk that has a spore-producing capsule (sporangium) at the tip. When the sporangium matures, it bursts, scattering the spores. Those landing on moist soil will germinate to form a new gametophyte.

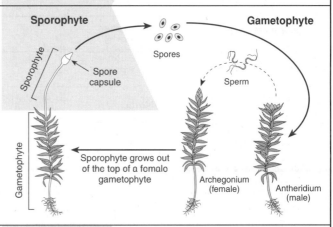

Fern

Ferns are sporophytes. Spores are formed on the back of the fronds and are released into the air to be dispersed by the wind. If a spore lands on moist soil, it will germinate into a very small **prothallus**. On this flat, heart-shaped gametophyte, male and female organs develop, but at different times. As with mosses, fern sperm use flagella to swim through moisture to the female cells to fertilize them. A new sporophyte grows out of the female organ (archegonium) and matures into a fern.

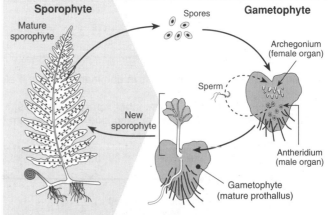

Gymnosperm

Trees are sporophytes. Most gymnosperm species produce both pollen cones and ovulate (female) cones. Male cones produce hundreds of pollen grains (male gametophytes). A female cone contains many scales, each with two ovules. Wind blown pollen falls on the female cone and is drawn into the ovule through a tiny opening called the micropyle. The pollen grain germinates in the ovule and grows a pollen tube that seeks out the female gametophyte and fertilizes the egg cell within it.

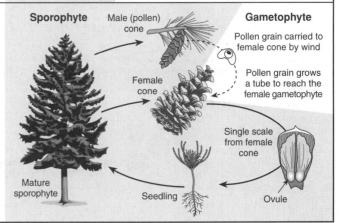

Related activities: Angiosperm Reproduction

A 2

Angiosperm

Angiosperms, or flowering plants, are the most successful plants on Earth today. They reproduce sexually by forming flowers, fruits, and seeds. The sporophyte generation is clearly dominant, and the gametophyte generation is reduced in size to just a small number of cells (there are no archegonia or antheridia). Anthers develop an immature gametophyte in the form of a pollen grain. Most often, pollen is transferred between flowers by wind or animal activity; angiosperms and their animal pollinators exhibit coevolution. Some plants are self-pollinating.

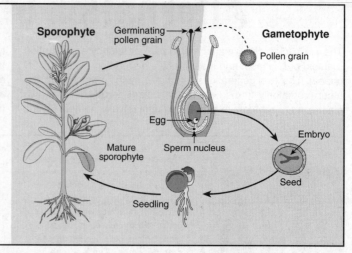

1. The table below summarizes the main features of plant life cycles. Using brief explanations, complete the table (the first example has been completed for you):

Life cycle feature	Group				
	Algae	Mosses	Ferns	Gymnosperms	Angiosperms
Dominant generation	Gametophyte				
Alternate generation	Sporophyte (zygospore)				
Movement of sperm	Needs water				
Gametophyte reliance on sporophyte	None				
Sporophyte reliance on gametophyte	None				
Ecological niche with respect to reproduction	Water needed				

2. One of the principal trends evident in plant life cycles is the increasing independence on water for reproduction. Explain what feature of the male gamete (sperm or pollen) illustrates this:

_____

_____

3. State which generation increases in dominance from the algae to the angiosperms: _____

4. In the schematic diagram below, label: **spores**, **gametes**, and **zygote**. Beside each, indicate the chromosome state: haploid (**N**) or diploid (**2N**). Label each side of the diagram (gray and white) with haploid or diploid as appropriate:

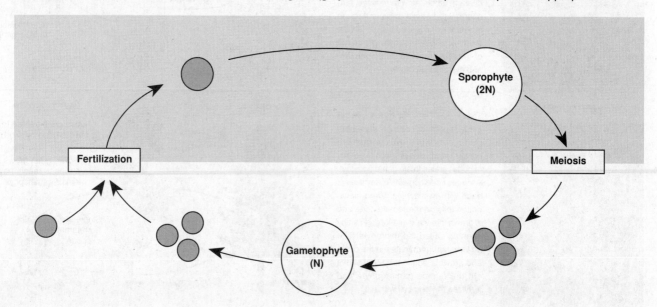

The Structure of Flowers

Flowering plants (**angiosperms**) are highly successful organisms. The egg cell is retained within the flower of the parent plant and the male gametes (contained in the **pollen**) must be transferred to it by **pollination** in order for fertilization to occur. Most angiosperms are **monoecious**, with male and female parts on the same plant. Some of these plants will self-pollinate, but most have mechanisms that make this difficult or impossible. The female and male parts may be physically separated in the flower, or they may mature at different times (in **protandrous** plants the male matures first, whereas in **protogynous** plants the female matures first). **Dioecious plants** avoid this problem by carrying the male and female flowers on separate plants. Different methods of pollination (animal, wind, and water pollination) also help to ensure that **cross-pollination** occurs. Common animal pollinators include insects, bats, birds, and small reptiles. Animals are able to transfer pollen between plants very effectively and often over large distances, so much so that many plants have come to depend on only one or two animal pollinators.

Insect Pollinated Flowers

In most angiosperms the flower has both male and female parts. The flowers are temporary structures, often produced in large numbers. Those that are pollinated by insects typically offer an attraction such as nectar or edible flower parts and their pollen is relatively large and heavy. In general, each flower consists of a stem, bearing sepals, petals, stamens, and carpels. Such flowers may be able to self pollinate although there are often mechanisms to prevent this. In **dioecious** plants, the male and female flowers occur on separate plants and cross pollination is assured.

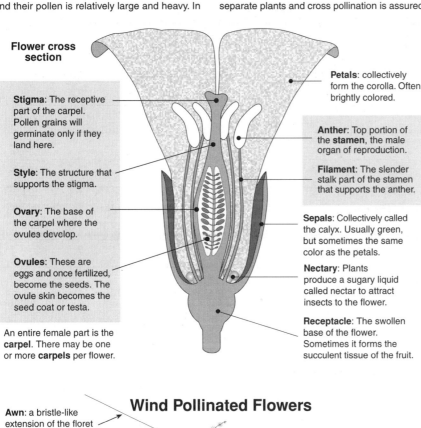

Flower cross section

Stigma: The receptive part of the carpel. Pollen grains will germinate only if they land here.

Style: The structure that supports the stigma.

Ovary: The base of the carpel where the ovules develop.

Ovules: These are eggs and once fertilized, become the seeds. The ovule skin becomes the seed coat or testa.

An entire female part is the **carpel**. There may be one or more **carpels** per flower.

Petals: collectively form the corolla. Often brightly colored.

Anther: Top portion of the **stamen**, the male organ of reproduction.

Filament: The slender stalk part of the stamen that supports the anther.

Sepals: Collectively called the calyx. Usually green, but sometimes the same color as the petals.

Nectary: Plants produce a sugary liquid called nectar to attract insects to the flower.

Receptacle: The swollen base of the flower. Sometimes it forms the succulent tissue of the fruit.

Wind Pollinated Flowers

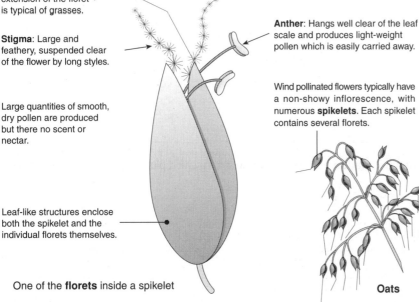

Awn: a bristle-like extension of the floret is typical of grasses.

Stigma: Large and feathery, suspended clear of the flower by long styles.

Large quantities of smooth, dry pollen are produced but there no scent or nectar.

Leaf-like structures enclose both the spikelet and the individual florets themselves.

One of the **florets** inside a spikelet

Anther: Hangs well clear of the leaf scale and produces light-weight pollen which is easily carried away.

Wind pollinated flowers typically have a non-showy inflorescence, with numerous **spikelets**. Each spikelet contains several florets.

Oats

Petals form 'guides' for insects that visit for nectar or pollen. In this way, wandering insects transfer pollen.

Stigma

Anther

Here, the stigma and anthers are separated to reduce self-pollination.

Pollen on bee leg

Pollen can be transported from flower to flower on the hairs of insects.

Most grasses are wind pollinated. The feathery appearance of their flowers is typical of wind pollinated plants.

Plant Responses and Reproduction

Related activities: Angiosperm Reproduction, Pollination and Fertilization

RA 2

1. Using the diagram on the previous page to help you, identify the parts of the flower labeled (a)-(g) on the diagram below.

(a)

(b)

(c)

Flower cross section

(d)

(e)

(f)

(g)

RCN

2. (a) Name the male structures on a flower: _____

   (b) Name the female structures on a flower: _____

3. Distinguish between **monoecious** and **dioecious** plants and explain how each type of plant avoids self pollination:

   _____

   _____

   _____

   _____

4. Describe two adaptations of insect pollinated flowers:

   (a) _____

   (b) _____

5. Describe two adaptations of wind pollinated flowers:

   (a) _____

   (b) _____

6. Describe one advantage and one cost to the plant of insect pollination:

   (a) Advantage: _____

   (b) Cost: _____

7. Describe two ways in which plants manage to attract animal pollinators:

   (a) _____ (b) _____

8. Contrast the efficiency of wind and animals as pollinating agents, giving a reason for your answer:

   _____

   _____

9. Describe the main the advantage of **cross pollination** and discuss the ways in which plants can ensure this occurs:

   _____

   _____

   _____

   _____

   _____

Pollination and Fertilization

Before the egg and sperm can fuse in fertilization, the pollen (which contains the male gametes) must be transferred from the male anthers to the female stigma in **pollination**. Plants rarely self-pollinate, although they can be made to do so. Most often the stigma of one plant receives pollen from other plants in **cross-pollination**. After pollination, the sperm nuclei can enter the ovule and fertilization can occur. In angiosperms, there is a double fertilization: one to produce the embryo and the other to produce the endosperm nucleus. The endosperm nucleus gives rise to the endosperm: the food store for the embryonic plant.

Growth of the pollen tube and double fertilization

Pollen grains are immature male gametophytes, formed by meiosis in the microspore mother cells within the pollen sac. Pollination is the actual transfer of the pollen from the stamens to the stigma. Pollen grains cannot move independently. They are usually carried by wind (**anemophily**) or animals (**entomophily**). After landing on the sticky stigma, the pollen grain is able to complete development, germinating and growing a pollen tube that extends down to the ovary. Directed by chemicals (usually calcium), the pollen tube enters the ovule through the **micropyle**, a small gap in the ovule. A **double fertilization** takes place. One sperm nucleus fuses with the egg to form the zygote. A second sperm nucleus fuses with the two polar nuclei within the embryo sac to produce the endosperm tissue (3N). There are usually many ovules in an ovary, therefore many pollen grains (and fertilizations) are needed before the entire ovary can develop.

Different pollens are variable in shape and pattern, and genera can be easily distinguished on the basis of their distinctive pollen. This feature is exploited in the relatively new field of forensic botany; the tracing of a crime through botanical evidence. The species specific nature of pollen ensures that only genetically compatible plants will be fertilized. Some species, such as *Primula*, produce two pollen types, and this assists in cross pollination between different flower types.

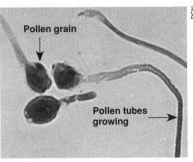
Germinating pollen grains

SEM: *Primula* (primrose) pollen

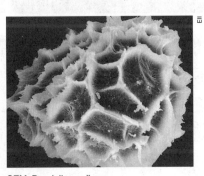
SEM: Dandelion pollen

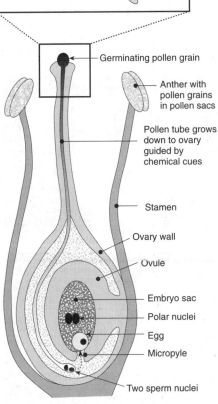

1. Distinguish clearly between **pollination** and **fertilization**: _____

_____

_____

_____

2. Describe the role of the double fertilization in angiosperm reproduction: _____

_____

3. Name the main chemical responsible for pollen tube growth: _____

4. Suggest a reason for the great variability seen in the structure of pollen grains: _____

_____

_____

5. Pollen can be used as an indicator of past climates and vegetation. Give two reasons why pollen is well suited to this use:

(a) _____

(b) _____

Fruits

A **fruit** is a mature, ripened ovary, although other plant parts, in addition to the ovary, may contribute to the fleshy parts of what we call the fruit. As a seed develops, the ovary wall around it enlarges to become the fruit wall or **pericarp**. The pericarp has three regions: the outer exocarp, central mesocarp, and inner endocarp. Fruits may open to release the seeds or they may retain the seeds and be dispersed whole. They are classified according to the number of ovaries involved in their formation and the nature of the fruit wall (dry or fleshy). Succulent fruits are usually dispersed by animals and dry fruits by wind, water, or mechanical means. Fruits occur only in angiosperms. Their development has been a central feature of angiosperm evolution.

Type of fruit	Description	Type of fruit	Description
Berry	A fleshy fruit with soft tissues throughout. The single seed or seeds are scattered through flesh.	Aggregate fruit	Formed from a single flower that has many carpels (ovaries) fused to form a single fruit.
Drupe	The fruit wall is fleshy but the endocarp surrounding the single seed forms a hard stone.	Multiple fruit	Formed from the ovaries of many flowers, fused together at maturity (e.g. fig, pineapple).
Legume	A simple fruit. Fruit wall is dry when mature and splits open along two seams to release the seeds.	False fruit	The fleshy part is formed from tissues other than the ovary, often the flower base.
Grain	A simple dry, one seeded fruit. The fruit wall and seed coat are joined and cannot be separated.	Nut	A simple, one-seeded dry fruit with a hard fruit wall (the nut shell). The nut is the seed.

False fruit (pseudocarp), e.g. apple

Specialized berry, e.g. citrus fruits

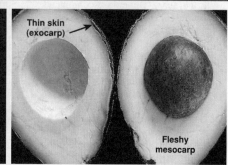

Drupe, e.g. avocado

Berry, e.g. kiwifruit

Legume or pod, e.g. bean

Drupe: fleshy with a single seed, e.g. peach

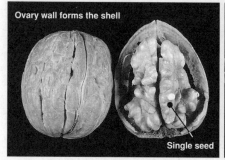

Nut: a dry, hardshelled fruit, e.g. walnut

Aggregate fruit, e.g. strawberry

Grain: a dry, single seeded fruit, e.g. corn

1. Describe the two main purposes of fruits in the life cycle of flowering plants:

   (a) _____

   (b) _____

2. Using the table and the examples above to help you, classify the following fruits:

   (a) Plum: _____ (b) Pea: _____

   (c) Raspberry: _____ (d) Watermelon: _____

 Related activities: Seed Structure and Germination, Seed Dispersal

Seed Structure and Germination

After fertilization has occurred, the ovary develops into the fruit and the ovules within the ovary become the **seeds**. Recall that in plants there is double fertilization. One sperm fertilizes the egg to form the embryo, but another sperm combines with the diploid endosperm nucleus to form a large triploid cell which gives rise to the endosperm. The development of the endosperm is important and begins before embryonic development in order to produce a nutrient store for the young plant. A seed is an entire reproductive unit, housing the embryonic plant in a state of dormancy. During the last stages of maturing, the seed dehydrates until its water content is only 5-15% of its weight. The embryo stops growing and remains **dormant** until the seed germinates. At germination, the food store is mobilized to provide the nutrients for plant growth and development. An activity, *Events in Germination*, which covers the metabolic events of germination in more detail, is available on the TRC and as a web link.

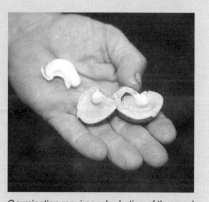

Dicot seeds: soy (above) cashew (below)
There are two fleshy cotyledons. These store food that was absorbed from the endosperm.

Germination requires rehydration of the seed and reactivation of the metabolism. The seed absorbs water through the seed coat (testa) and micropyle. As the dry substances in the seed tissue take up water, the cells expand, metabolism is reactivated, and embryonic growth begins. Activation begins with the release of gibberellin (GA) from the embryo. GA enhances cell elongation, making it possible for the root to penetrate the testa. It also stimulates the synthesis of enzymes, which hydrolyze the starch to produce sugars. The mobilized food stores are then delivered to the developing roots and shoots.

Seed Structure and Formation

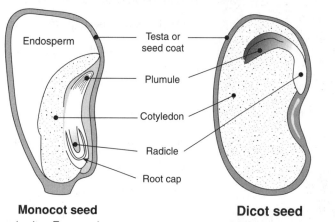

Monocot seed
(maize: *Zea mays*)

Dicot seed
(garden bean: *Phaseolus vulgaris*)

Every seed contains an embryo comprising a rudimentary shoot (plumule), root (radicle), and one or two cotyledons (seed leaves). The embryo and its food supply are encased in a tough, protective seed coat or **testa**. In monocots, the endosperm provides the food supply, whereas in most dicot seeds, the nutrients from the endosperm are transferred to the large, fleshy cotyledons.

Germination in a Dicot Seed
(garden bean: *Phaseolus vulgaris*)

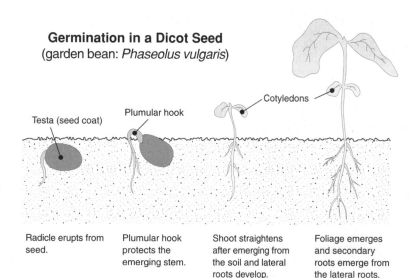

Radicle erupts from seed.

Plumular hook protects the emerging stem.

Shoot straightens after emerging from the soil and lateral roots develop.

Foliage emerges and secondary roots emerge from the lateral roots.

1. Explain the purpose of a **seed**: _____

_____

2. (a) State the function of the endosperm in angiosperms: _____

(b) State how the endosperm is derived: _____

3. Explain the role of the testa in seeds: _____

4. Explain why the seed requires a food store: _____

_____

5. Explain why stored seeds must be kept dry: _____

Related activities: Pollination and Fertilization, Fruits
Web links: Events in Germination

A 2

Plant Responses and Reproduction

Seed Dispersal

Flowering plants have evolved many ways to ensure that their seeds are dispersed. This has given them greater opportunities to expand their range. If a seed is carried into an area suitable for its germination, it will become established there. In some cases the seed itself is the agent of dispersal, but often it is the fruit. The chief agents of seed dispersal are wind, water, and animals. Many seeds are readily dispersed by water, even when they lack special buoyancy mechanisms. Wind also spreads the seeds of many plants. Such seeds have wing-like or feathery structures that catch the air currents and carry the seeds long distances. Plants that rely on animals to spread their seeds may have hooks or barbs that catch the animal hair, sticky secretions that adhere to the skin or hair, or fleshy fruits that are eaten leaving the seed to be deposited in faeces some distance from the parent plant. Other dispersal mechanisms rely on explosive discharge or shaking from pods or capsules (e.g. legumes, poppy).

For each of the examples below, describe the method of dispersal and the adaptive features associated with the method:

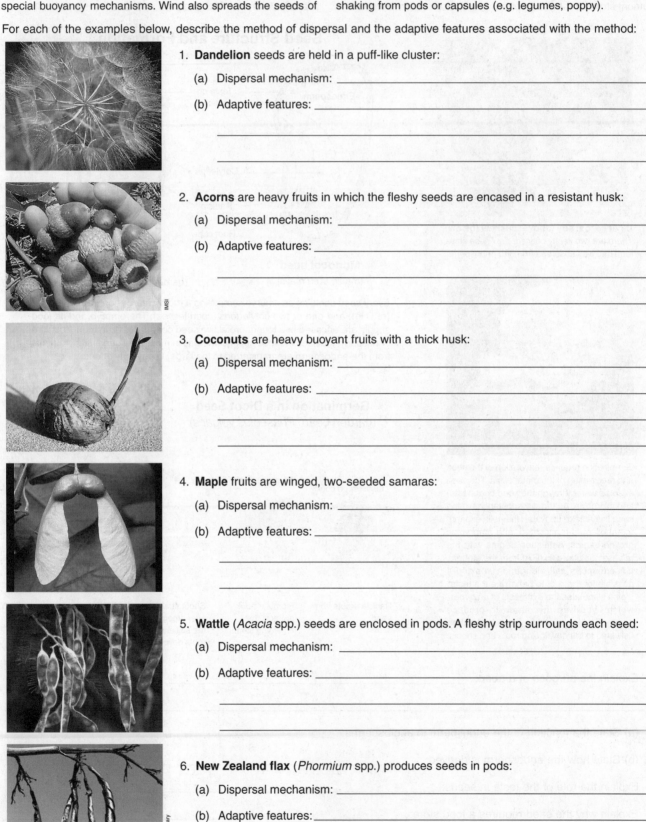

1. **Dandelion** seeds are held in a puff-like cluster:

   (a) Dispersal mechanism: _____

   (b) Adaptive features: _____

   _____

   _____

2. **Acorns** are heavy fruits in which the fleshy seeds are encased in a resistant husk:

   (a) Dispersal mechanism: _____

   (b) Adaptive features: _____

   _____

   _____

3. **Coconuts** are heavy buoyant fruits with a thick husk:

   (a) Dispersal mechanism: _____

   (b) Adaptive features: _____

   _____

   _____

4. **Maple** fruits are winged, two-seeded samaras:

   (a) Dispersal mechanism: _____

   (b) Adaptive features: _____

   _____

   _____

5. **Wattle** (*Acacia* spp.) seeds are enclosed in pods. A fleshy strip surrounds each seed:

   (a) Dispersal mechanism: _____

   (b) Adaptive features: _____

   _____

   _____

6. **New Zealand flax** (*Phormium* spp.) produces seeds in pods:

   (a) Dispersal mechanism: _____

   (b) Adaptive features: _____

   _____

   _____

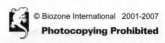

Plant Tissue Culture

Plant tissue culture, or **micropropagation**, is a method used for **cloning** plants. It is used widely for the rapid multiplication of commercially important plant species with superior genotypes, as well as in the recovery programs for endangered plant species. Plant productivity and quality may be rapidly improved, and resistance to disease, pollutants, and insects increased. Continued culture of a limited number of cloned varieties leads to a change in the genetic composition of the population (genetic variation is reduced). New genetic stock may be introduced into cloned lines periodically to prevent this reduction in genetic diversity. Micro-propagation

is possible because differentiated plant cells have the potential to give rise to all the cells of an adult plant. It has considerable advantages over traditional methods of plant propagation (see table below), but it is very labor intensive. In addition, the optimal conditions for growth and regeneration must be determined and plants propagated in this way may be genetically unstable or infertile, with chromosomes structurally altered or in unusual numbers. The success of tissue culture is affected by factors such as selection of **explant** material, the composition of the culturing media, plant hormone levels, lighting, and temperature.

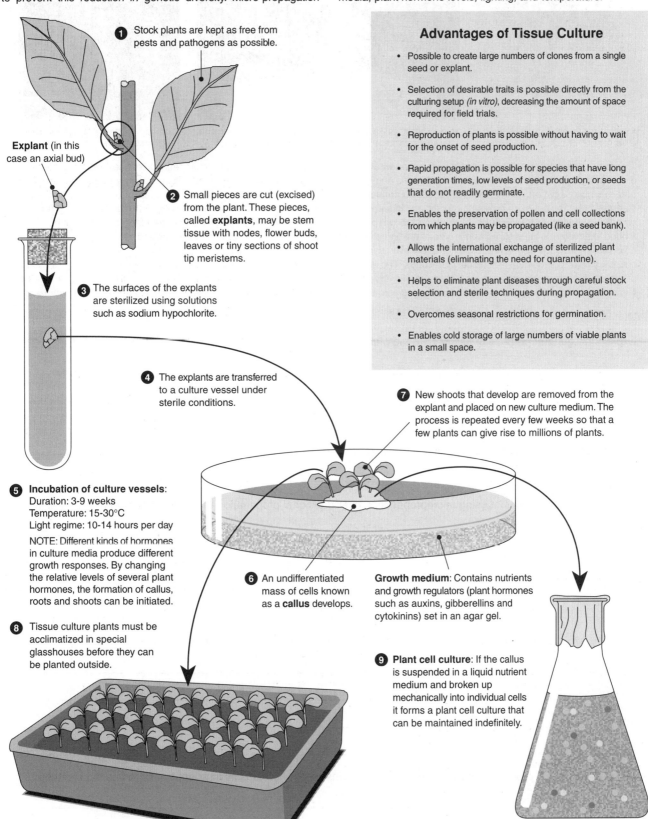

1 Stock plants are kept as free from pests and pathogens as possible.

Explant (in this case an axial bud)

2 Small pieces are cut (excised) from the plant. These pieces, called **explants**, may be stem tissue with nodes, flower buds, leaves or tiny sections of shoot tip meristems.

3 The surfaces of the explants are sterilized using solutions such as sodium hypochlorite.

4 The explants are transferred to a culture vessel under sterile conditions.

5 **Incubation of culture vessels**:
Duration: 3-9 weeks
Temperature: 15-30°C
Light regime: 10-14 hours per day

NOTE: Different kinds of hormones in culture media produce different growth responses. By changing the relative levels of several plant hormones, the formation of callus, roots and shoots can be initiated.

6 An undifferentiated mass of cells known as a **callus** develops.

7 New shoots that develop are removed from the explant and placed on new culture medium. The process is repeated every few weeks so that a few plants can give rise to millions of plants.

Growth medium: Contains nutrients and growth regulators (plant hormones such as auxins, gibberellins and cytokinins) set in an agar gel.

8 Tissue culture plants must be acclimatized in special glasshouses before they can be planted outside.

9 **Plant cell culture**: If the callus is suspended in a liquid nutrient medium and broken up mechanically into individual cells it forms a plant cell culture that can be maintained indefinitely.

Advantages of Tissue Culture

- Possible to create large numbers of clones from a single seed or explant.

- Selection of desirable traits is possible directly from the culturing setup (in vitro), decreasing the amount of space required for field trials.

- Reproduction of plants is possible without having to wait for the onset of seed production.

- Rapid propagation is possible for species that have long generation times, low levels of seed production, or seeds that do not readily germinate.

- Enables the preservation of pollen and cell collections from which plants may be propagated (like a seed bank).

- Allows the international exchange of sterilized plant materials (eliminating the need for quarantine).

- Helps to eliminate plant diseases through careful stock selection and sterile techniques during propagation.

- Overcomes seasonal restrictions for germination.

- Enables cold storage of large numbers of viable plants in a small space.

Plant Responses and Reproduction

RA 2

Micropropagation of the Tasmanian blackwood tree (*Acacia melanoxylon*)

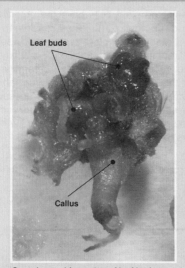
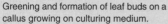

Leaf buds

Callus

Greening and formation of leaf buds on a callus growing on culturing medium.

Culture medium

Normal shoots with juvenile leaves growing from a callus on media. They appear identical to those produced directly from seeds.

Photos: BOB

Seedling with juvenile foliage six months after transfer to greenhouse.

Micropropagation is increasingly used in conjunction with genetic engineering to propagate transgenic plants. Genetic engineering and micropropagation achieve similar results to conventional selective breeding but more precisely, quickly, and independently of growing season. The **Tasmanian blackwood** (above) provides a good example of a plant suited to this type of manipulation. It is a versatile hardwood tree now being extensively trialled in some countries as a replacement for tropical hardwoods. The timber is of high quality, but genetic variations between individual trees invariably lead to differences in timber quality and color. Tissue culture allows the multiple propagation of trees with desirable traits (e.g. uniform timber color). Tissue culture could also facilitate solutions to other problems that cannot be solved by forestry management. When combined with genetic engineering (introduction of new genes into the plant) problems of pest and herbicide susceptibility may be resolved. Genetic engineering may also be used to introduce a gene for male sterility, thereby stopping pollen production. This would improve the efficiency of conventional breeding programs by preventing self-pollination of flowers (the manual removal of stamens is difficult and very labor intensive).

Information courtesy of Raewyn Poole, University of Waikato (Unpublished Msc. thesis).

1. Explain the general purpose of tissue culturing plants: _____

_____

2. (a) Explain what a **callus** is: _____

_____

(b) Explain how a callus may be stimulated to initiate root and shoot formation: _____

3. Describe two advantages of using micropropagation over traditional propagation methods such as cutting or grafting:

(a) _____

_____

(b) _____

_____

4. Describe two disadvantages of using micropropagation over traditional propagation methods such as cutting or grafting:

(a) _____

_____

(b) _____

_____

5. Discuss a potential problem with micropropagation in terms of long term ability to adapt to environmental changes:

_____

_____

Microbes and Biotechnology

IB SL	IB HL	IB Options	AP Biology
Not applicable to core	Not applicable to core	Complete: Option F: SL/HL: 1, 3-5, 8-11	Not applicable

Learning Objectives

☐ 1. Compile your own glossary from the **KEY WORDS** displayed in **bold type** in the learning objectives below.

Introduction to Biotechnology

☐ 2. Provide a definition of **biotechnology**. Identify areas traditionally associated with biotechnology and outline the areas now encompassed by the term. Appreciate the role of biotechnology in providing employment and trade, and in improving productivity and quality of life in the modern world. Recognise the important role of microorganisms and genetic engineering in much of modern biotechnology.

Microorganisms and Food Production (pages 380-386 and the TRC: Cheese Making)

☐ 3. Outline the history of traditional biotechnology practices including the use of yeast in bread production, the production of alcoholic beverages, and the manufacture of cultured milk products.

☐ 4. Explain the role of biotechnology in the large scale production of fermented foods and beverages (e.g. soy sauce, cheese, yoghurt, bread, wine, or beer) and tenderised meat. In each case, outline the processes and stages involved, the microorganisms used, and any features of importance (e.g. microbial metabolism, genetic modifications).

☐ 5. Describe the production of **chymosin** (rennin) from genetically modified (GM) microbes (yeast or bacteria) and describe its use in the dairy industry. Discuss any benefits and disadvantages of using enzymes, such as chymosin, from a GM source, and compare these with the benefits and disadvantages of traditional methods.

☐ 6. Appreciate the social, economic, ethical, and environmental implications of biotechnology and gene manipulation (especially the manipulation of organisms used in food production).

Microorganisms and Medicine (pages 391-392)

☐ 7. Recognise the importance of genetically modified microorganisms in the large scale production of human proteins (e.g. **insulin**, **human growth hormone**, **factor VIII**). Explain the reasons for using microorganisms in these cases. Describe in detail the steps involved in the production of a human protein by microorganisms.

Gene therapy (pages 387-390)

☐ 8. Outline the principles of **gene therapy**. Identify the criteria that must be met before gene therapy can be considered as a potentially viable treatment. Distinguish between using gene therapy to cure a disease and its use to relieve symptoms of a disease.

☐ 9. Describe the genetic basis of **cystic fibrosis** (CF) and the symptoms of the disease that arise as a result of this defect. In terms of its genetic basis, explain the potential for CF to be treated/cured using gene therapy.

☐ 10. Using an appropriate example, explain the techniques involved in **gene therapy**, including the **vectors** used, and delivery systems for these vectors. With reference to your specific example, discuss the difficulties currently encountered in improving the success of gene therapy and explain why successful gene therapy has, to date, been largely unsuccessful.

☐ 11. Identify types of **vectors** used in gene therapy and discuss the advantages and disadvantages of each. Include reference to **viral vectors** and **liposomes**.

 See the 'Textbook Reference Grid' on pages 8-9 for textbook page references relating to material in this topic.

Supplementary Texts

See pages 5-6 for additional details of these texts:

■ Adds, J. *et al.*, 1999. **Tools, Techniques and Assessment in Biology** (NelsonThornes), pp. 56-71.

■ Adds, J., *et al.*, 2004. **Genetics, Evolution and Biodiversity**, (NelsonThornes), chpt. 9.

■ Barnum, S.R., 2005. **Biotechnology: An Introduction** (Thomson Brooks/Cole).

■ Clegg, C.J., 1999. **Genetics and Evolution** (John Murray), pp. 48-59.

■ Jones, N., *et al.*, 2001. **Essentials of Genetics** (John Murray), pp. 235-260.

See page 6 for details of publishers of periodicals:

STUDENT'S REFERENCE

■ **Lactic Acid Bacteria** Biol. Sci. Rev., 11(3) Jan. 1999, pp. 10-12. *Lactic acid bacteria: their metabolism and central role they play in the production of fermented foods.*

■ **The Science of Bubbly** Scientific American, January 2003, pp. 68-73. *The science behind champagne production.*

■ **Genes Can Come True** New Scientist, 30 Nov. 2002, pp. 30-33. *An overview of the recent state of gene therapy, and a note about future directions in this controversial new area of medicine.*

■ **Human Gene Therapy** The Am. Biology Teacher, 64(4), April 2002, pp. 264-270. *The latest advances and setbacks in gene therapy.*

See pages 10-11 for details of how to access **Bio Links** from our web site: **www.thebiozone.com** From Bio Links, access sites under the topics:

BIOTECHNOLOGY > General Biotechnology Sites: • ABelgoBiotech • Molecular genetics ... *and others* > **Applications in Biotechnology**: access sites under > *Food biotechnology* > *Medical biotechnology* > *Industrial biotechnology* ... *and others*

Presentation MEDIA to support this topic:
GENES & INHERITANCE
• Gene Technology

Beer Brewing

Brewing is one of the oldest forms of traditional biotechnology. 5000 years ago, the ancient Sumerians and Babylonians used yeast (without knowing what it was) to brew beer, which they flavored with cinnamon. Today, most beers are made from barley and hops. Brewing is divisible into seven stages, with finishing being an important final part of the whole process. At this stage, bacterial proteases are added to break down the yeast and prevent cloudiness. Amyloglucosidases are used to break down sugars in the production of low calorie beers. Traditional beers are stored in barrels and allowed to condition to develop their characteristic qualities. Modern beers are pasteurized, and standardised for color and flavor before bottling.

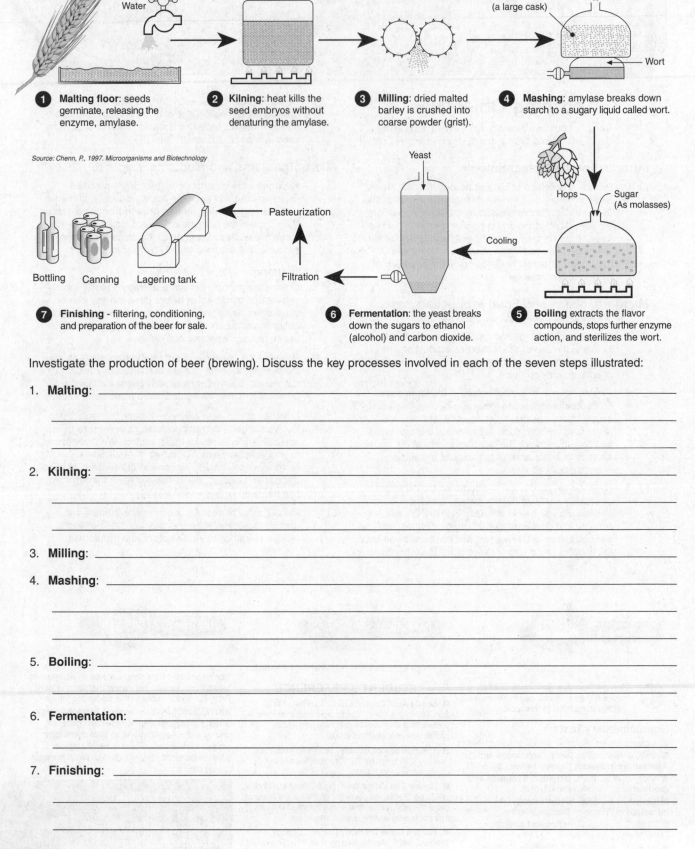

The Commercial Production of Beer

Barley

Water

1. **Malting floor**: seeds germinate, releasing the enzyme, amylase.

2. **Kilning**: heat kills the seed embryos without denaturing the amylase.

3. **Milling**: dried malted barley is crushed into coarse powder (grist).

Grist   Hot water

Mash tun (a large cask)

Wort

4. **Mashing**: amylase breaks down starch to a sugary liquid called wort.

Source: Chenn, P., 1997. Microorganisms and Biotechnology

Yeast

Hops   Sugar (As molasses)

Cooling

Pasteurization

Bottling   Canning   Lagering tank

Filtration

7. **Finishing** - filtering, conditioning, and preparation of the beer for sale.

6. **Fermentation**: the yeast breaks down the sugars to ethanol (alcohol) and carbon dioxide.

5. **Boiling** extracts the flavor compounds, stops further enzyme action, and sterilizes the wort.

Investigate the production of beer (brewing). Discuss the key processes involved in each of the seven steps illustrated:

1. **Malting**: _____
_____
_____

2. **Kilning**: _____
_____
_____

3. **Milling**: _____

4. **Mashing**: _____
_____
_____

5. **Boiling**: _____
_____

6. **Fermentation**: _____
_____

7. **Finishing**: _____
_____
_____

Red Wine Production

Red wine is made from red (or black) grapes, but its red color is bestowed by the skin being left in contact with the juice during fermentation. The grape varieties used for red wines vary tremendously in their characteristics, most importantly color, flavor, and tannins. Many of the basic steps in red wine production are similar to those outlined for making white wines (see the web link below), but there are important differences related to the extent of crushing, pressing (grapes are always pressed in white wine production), maceration, and alternative fermentation processes.

Harvest: The condition of the grapes at the time of harvest is crucial to wine quality. Overripe or underripe grapes have too much or too little sugar and this affects alcohol content and wine quality.

Vine trimming: This is done to improve the light penetration to the grapes. It can carried out at various stages during the growing season and may be done by hand or using machines.

Destemming is a mechanical process that occurs immediately prior to crushing. Although it is not always necessary, destemming prevents excessive tannins in the wine.

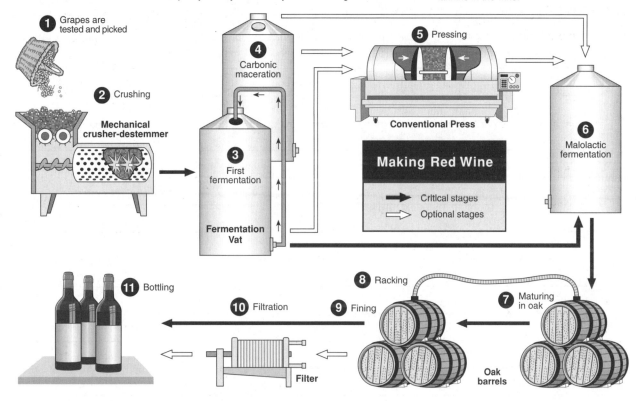

1. Grapes are tested and picked as for white wine production.

2. The grapes are **crushed** and **destemmed**. Destemming is not always necessary and bunches may be crushed whole. Stems are removed if the winemaker wishes to avoid high levels of tannin in the wine.

3. While many red wines are still fermented in vats made of oak, stainless steel vats are increasingly popular as they are easy to cool and so offer better control over the fermentation temperature. High temperatures reduce the fruit flavors in the wine. **Maceration** is the period during which the grapes skins are left in contact with the juice. Usually lasting 5-7 days, the length of time given to maceration determines the depth of color and tannin of the wine.

4. **Carbonic maceration** is an alternative fermentation process in which the fruit is allowed to ferment spontaneously under a protective layer of CO_2. The weight of the grapes is sufficient to crush the fruit and release the juice without mechanical pressure. These wines are soft and for drinking without ageing (e.g. Beaujolais Nouveau).

5. Pressing the grape mass (called pomace) is carried out after the 'free run' juice has been removed from the fermentation vat.

6. **Malolactic fermentation** is almost always encouraged in red winemaking. This secondary (bacterial) fermentation softens the acidity, while adding complexity and stability to the wine.

7. High quality red wines are almost always matured in oak barrels. Maturing in **oak** contributes wood tannin and vanilla flavors.

8. The wine is **racked** every few months by transferring it to a clean, sterile barrel, gently aerating it and leaving any sediment in the old barrel.

9. The wine is clarified (a process called fining) by pouring egg white or bentonite clay on to the surface.

10. A fine filter may be used to ensure stability and 'brightness' of the wine. Some winemakers believe this strips the wine of its character.

11. Because wines are susceptible to air and bacteria, the bottles are sterilized and filled in the absence of air.

Microbes and Biotechnology

Web links: White Wine Production, Industrial Microbiology

RA 2

Aging: The wine is aged in oak barrels, where changes in the aroma and flavors occur. The extent and type of barrel ageing varies depending on wine type and quality.

Monitoring the wine: The wine is tested regularly in the barrel as it ages to check sugar and alcohol content. Here, the winemaker uses a **hydrometer** to measure the specific gravity of the wine.

Bottling: Quality control and sterile conditions during the bottling process are very important. Bottle aging before release is still important for some red wines but is becoming less common.

1. Using the information above and on the previous page for guidance, investigate the wine making process for a named red wine. Note that in the diagram shown on the previous page, obligatory processes in the production are indicated by black arrows and white arrows indicate alternative or additional stages. Summarize the important points in the process in the spaces provided below:

(a) Name of red wine and winemaker (if relevant): _____

(b) Steps in production, including any special processes and the reasons for these: _____

_____

_____

_____

_____

_____

_____

_____

_____

_____

_____

_____

_____

_____

_____

_____

_____

(c) Special features of the process for this example: _____

_____

_____

_____

_____

_____

Bread Making

Using yeast to make foods and drinks is probably the oldest form of biotechnology. Modern methods of bread making use varieties of the yeast *Saccharomyces*. When the raw ingredients are mixed, the proteins in the flour (called gluten) are hydrated and they coalesce to form a sticky, elastic dough. Enzymes, having survived the milling process when grains are made into flour, act on the starch in the dough to make a mixture of sugars. During the leavening or proving process, yeast uses the sugars (anaerobically) and produces ethanol and carbon dioxide gas which causes the bread to rise. *Lactobacilli* may grow during the early stages of proving, producing lactic acid which contributes to the final flavor and inhibits growth of other organisms. Baking inactivates the yeast, evaporates the ethanol, and stops the enzymatic reactions as it cooks the flour. Bakeries may add other ingredients such as vitamin C, whiteners, raising agents, stabilizers, and flavorings.

The Commercial Production of Bread

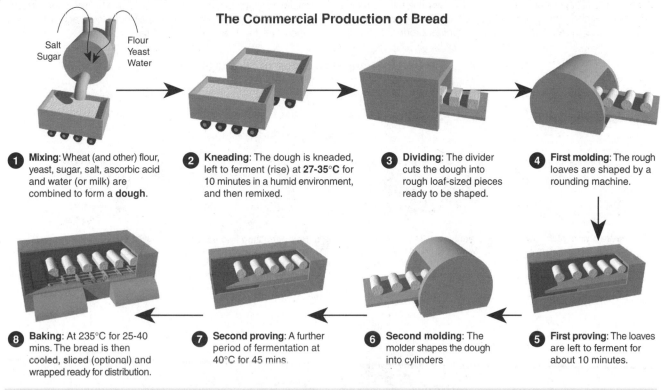

1 **Mixing**: Wheat (and other) flour, yeast, sugar, salt, ascorbic acid and water (or milk) are combined to form a **dough**.

2 **Kneading**: The dough is kneaded, left to ferment (rise) at **27-35°C** for 10 minutes in a humid environment, and then remixed.

3 **Dividing**: The divider cuts the dough into rough loaf-sized pieces ready to be shaped.

4 **First molding**: The rough loaves are shaped by a rounding machine.

8 **Baking**: At 235°C for 25-40 mins. The bread is then cooled, sliced (optional) and wrapped ready for distribution.

7 **Second proving**: A further period of fermentation at 40°C for 45 mins.

6 **Second molding**: The molder shapes the dough into cylinders

5 **First proving**: The loaves are left to ferment for about 10 minutes.

Bread making is one of the oldest and simplest of biotechnologies, involving mixing of wheat flour, water, and yeast to form a **dough**.

Kneading results in the physical and chemical changes in the gluten (flour proteins) which give the dough its elastic and resilient texture.

During **proving**, the dough is left to ferment and the yeast metabolizes sugars to produce ethanol and CO_2. The CO_2 causes the dough to rise.

Baking kills the yeast, evaporates the ethanol, and cooks the flour. Modern bakeries can produce about 10 000 loaves per hour.

1. Explain the role of each of the following in the bread-making process:

   (a) Sugar: _____

   (b) Yeast: _____

   (c) Water (or milk): _____

2. (a) Explain what happens to the dough during the fermentation (or proving) stages: _____

   _____

   (b) Suggest why the dough goes through two fermentations: _____

   _____

3. Suggest why gluten free bread is flat and dense: _____

   _____

Web links: Industrial Microbiology

RA 2

Microbes and Biotechnology

Yoghurt Making

The biochemistry of yoghurt production is similar to that of cheese: suitable lactic acid **bacteria** are inoculated into milk and the **lactic acid** they produce coagulates the milk proteins and thickens the yoghurt. The starter culture for yoghurt contains roughly equal amounts of two **symbiotic** bacteria, *Lactobacillus bulgaricus* and *Streptococcus thermophilus*. *L. bulgaricus* metabolizes lactose in the milk anaerobically to produce the lactic acid responsible for the formation of the yoghurt. *L. bulgaricus* also produces peptidases, which break down the milk proteins into peptides and amino acids. These stimulate the growth of the *Streptococcus* in the culture. *S. thermophilus* produces carbon

dioxide and methanoic acid, which together lower the pH and, in turn, stimulate the growth and metabolism of the *Lactobacillus*. Natural yoghurt's characteristic flavor comes from the lactic acid and from **ethanal**, a metabolic by-product released by both bacteria. Traditional yoghurt was much thinner and more acidic than the commercially available yoghurt today. The addition of flavoring, coloring and fruit pulp have been developed to cater for modern tastes and recently so-called 'bio' yoghurts produce a milder tasting, sweeter, creamier yoghurt. 'Bio' yoghurts use *L. acidophilus* and *Bifidobacterium bifidum* incubated at a lower temperature for a longer period of time.

The Commercial Production of Yoghurt

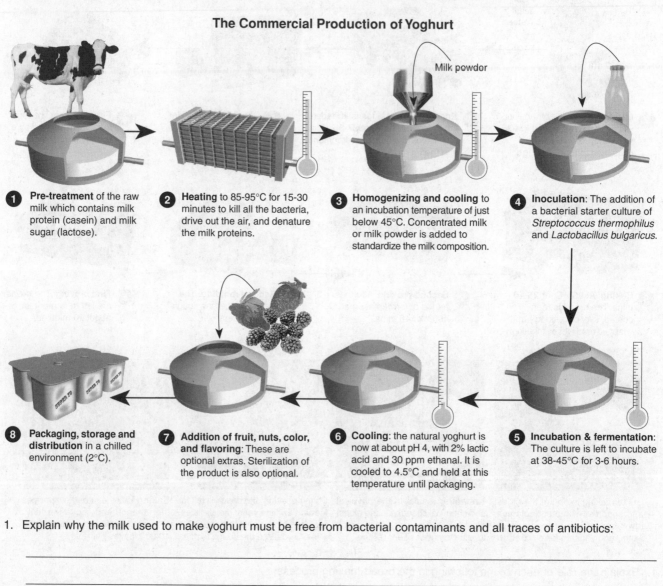

Milk powder

1 **Pre-treatment** of the raw milk which contains milk protein (casein) and milk sugar (lactose).

2 **Heating** to 85-95°C for 15-30 minutes to kill all the bacteria, drive out the air, and denature the milk proteins.

3 **Homogenizing and cooling** to an incubation temperature of just below 45°C. Concentrated milk or milk powder is added to standardize the milk composition.

4 **Inoculation**: The addition of a bacterial starter culture of *Streptococcus thermophilus* and *Lactobacillus bulgaricus*.

8 **Packaging, storage and distribution** in a chilled environment (2°C).

7 **Addition of fruit, nuts, color, and flavoring**: These are optional extras. Sterilization of the product is also optional.

6 **Cooling**: the natural yoghurt is now at about pH 4, with 2% lactic acid and 30 ppm ethanal. It is cooled to 4.5°C and held at this temperature until packaging.

5 **Incubation & fermentation**: The culture is left to incubate at 38-45°C for 3-6 hours.

1. Explain why the milk used to make yoghurt must be free from bacterial contaminants and all traces of antibiotics:

_____

_____

2. Describe the mutualistic association between the two starter bacteria, *L. bulgaricus* and *S. thermophilus*:

_____

_____

_____

_____

3. Explain why the pH falls during the incubation stage: _____

4. The packed yoghurt is stored at 2-4°C which keeps the bacteria alive but inactive. Explain why it is not necessary to kill the bacteria before eating the yoghurt:

_____

Soy Sauce Production

Soy sauce manufacture originated in China 2500 years ago. The traditional fermentation process takes months to complete, and conditions during fermentation are carefully monitored to ensure the final product has the correct flavor characteristics. There are three main steps in the traditional **soy sauce fermentation** process: **Koji-making**, **brine fermentation**, and **refinement**. During Koji-making, a soy and wheat mixture is cooked, cooled, and inoculated with a fungus, usually ***Aspergillus oryzae*** or ***Aspergillus sojae***. Enzymes produced by the mold break down the starch and proteins to simple sugars and peptides. These are used as fuel by the microorganisms in the brine fermentation stage. In this stage, which can take up to 11 months, lactic acid

bacteria ferment the sugars to lactic acid which lowers the pH. Yeasts also produce alcohols, which contribute to the flavor of soy sauce. Salt provides flavor and establishes a favorable chemical environment for the lactic acid bacteria and yeast. Salt also helps to protect the finished product from spoilage. The final stage of refinement involves separating the liquid from the more solid by-product, and pasteurization to kill microorganisms. Some modern manufacturing techniques use a **chemical hydrolysis method** (rather than fermentation) to produce soy sauce in a matter of days rather than months. Soy sauce produced by these chemical methods are considered inferior to the traditional fermented product and may contain potentially harmful residues.

The Traditional Production of Soy Sauce

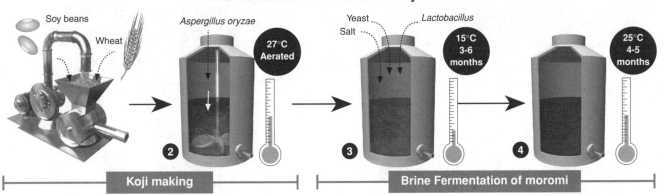

Koji making

In the first stage of the koji-making process, soy beans and wheat are crushed and **mixed** together with water to produce a mash.

The mash is cooked, cooled to 27°C, **inoculated** with the mold ***Aspergillus*** and matured in large aerated vats for three days. The mash is now called **koji**.

Brine Fermentation of moromi

The koji is fermented with salt in deep tanks. ***Lactobacillus*** and **yeast** enhance fermentation. The mixture is now called **moromi**. This fermentation takes 3-6 months at 15°C.

A second fermentation at 25°C for 4-5 months ages the soy sauce. Brine fermentation utilizes the sugars and peptides produced during the koji making stage.

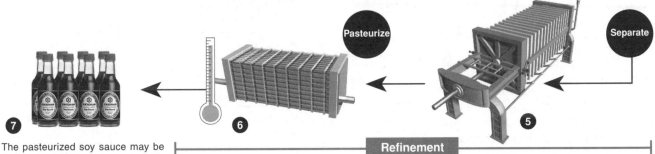

Refinement

The pasteurized soy sauce may be filtered a second time to improve clarity. Alcohol, sodium benzoate or benzoic acid may be added as preservatives before the soy is bottled.

The liquid is pasteurized to kill any microorganisms and enhance the flavour profile of the soy sauce.

The mixture is now a thick paste. The liquid soy sauce is **separated** from solid material using a filter press. A hydraulic press pushes the liquid through layers of cloth filters.

1. How would crushing the soy beans and wheat before inoculation enhance the Koji-making process:

   _____

2. Explain the contribution of each of the following microorganisms to the production of fermented soy sauce:

   (a) Fungus (*Aspergillus* spp.) _____

   (b) Lactic acid bacteria: _____

   (c) Yeasts: _____

3. (a) Suggest why the soy sauce produced using chemical hydrolysis is regarded as inferior to the fermented product:

   _____

   _____

   (b) Suggest why commercial producers might choose to use this method anyway: _____

   _____

RA 2

Microbes and Biotechnology

Using Recombinant Bacteria

In 1990 Pfizer, Inc. produced one of the first two products of recombinant DNA technology to enter the human food supply; the "CHY-MAX" brand of chymosin. This was a protein purified from bacteria that had been given a copy of the chymosin gene from cattle. Traditionally extracted from "chyme" or stomach secretions of suckling calves, chymosin (also called rennin) is an enzyme that digests milk proteins. Chymosin is the active ingredient in rennet, used by cheesemakers to clot milk into curds. CHY-MAX extracted from bacteria grown in a vat is identical in chemical composition to the chymosin extracted from cattle. Pfizer's product quickly won over half the market for rennet because cheesemakers found it to be a cost-effective source of high-quality chymosin in consistent supply. A recombinant form of the fungus, *Mucor*, is also used to manufacture chymosin.

Chymosin Production using Recombinant Bacteria

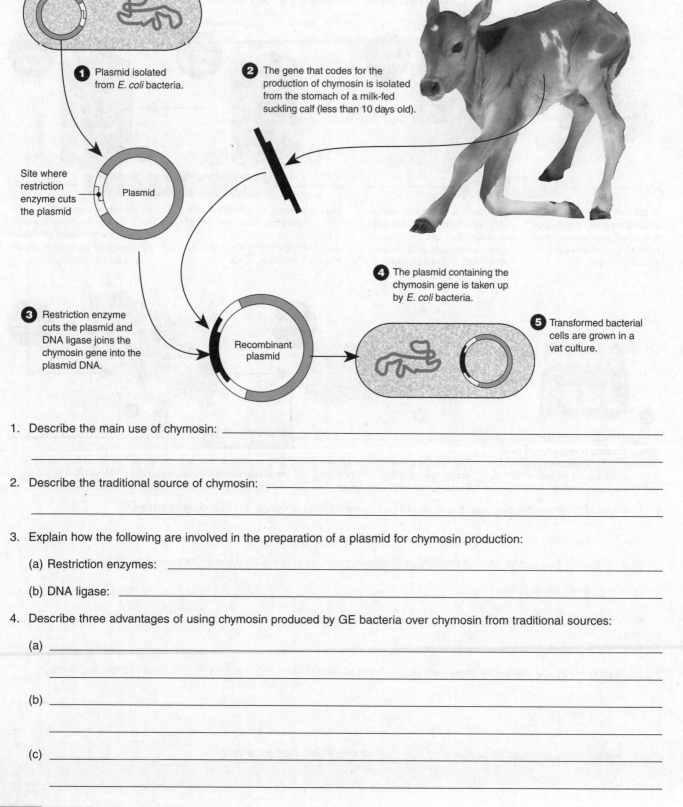

1 Plasmid isolated from *E. coli* bacteria.

2 The gene that codes for the production of chymosin is isolated from the stomach of a milk-fed suckling calf (less than 10 days old).

Site where restriction enzyme cuts the plasmid

Plasmid

4 The plasmid containing the chymosin gene is taken up by *E. coli* bacteria.

3 Restriction enzyme cuts the plasmid and DNA ligase joins the chymosin gene into the plasmid DNA.

Recombinant plasmid

5 Transformed bacterial cells are grown in a vat culture.

1. Describe the main use of chymosin: _____

    _____

2. Describe the traditional source of chymosin: _____

    _____

3. Explain how the following are involved in the preparation of a plasmid for chymosin production:

    (a) Restriction enzymes: _____

    (b) DNA ligase: _____

4. Describe three advantages of using chymosin produced by GE bacteria over chymosin from traditional sources:

    (a) _____

    _____

    (b) _____

    _____

    (c) _____

    _____

Related activities: Production of Human Proteins

Gene Therapy

Gene therapy refers to the application of gene technology to correct or replace defective genes. It was first envisioned as a treatment, or even a cure, for genetic disorders, but it could also be used to treat a wide range of diseases, including those that resist conventional treatments. Gene therapy may operate by providing a correctly working version of a faulty gene or by adding a **novel gene** to perform a corrective role. In other cases, gene expression may be blocked in order to control cellular (or viral) activity. About two thirds of currently approved gene therapy procedures are targeting cancer, about one quarter aim to treat genetic disorders, such as cystic fibrosis, and the remainder are attempting to provide relief for infectious diseases. Gene therapy requires a **gene delivery system**; a way to transfer the gene to the patient's cells. This may be achieved using a infectious agent such as a virus; a technique called **transfection**. A promising development has been the recent approval for gene therapy to be used in treating tumors in cancer patients. Severe combined immune deficiency syndrome (SCIDS) has also shown improvement after gene therapy. Infants treated for this inherited, normally lethal condition have become healthy young adults (see below). Gene therapy involving **somatic cells** may be therapeutic, but the genetic changes are not inherited. The transfection of **stem cells**, rather than mature somatic cells, achieves a longer persistence of therapy in patients. In the future, the introduction of corrective genes into **germline cells** will enable genetic corrections to be inherited.

Gene Delivery Using Extracted Cells

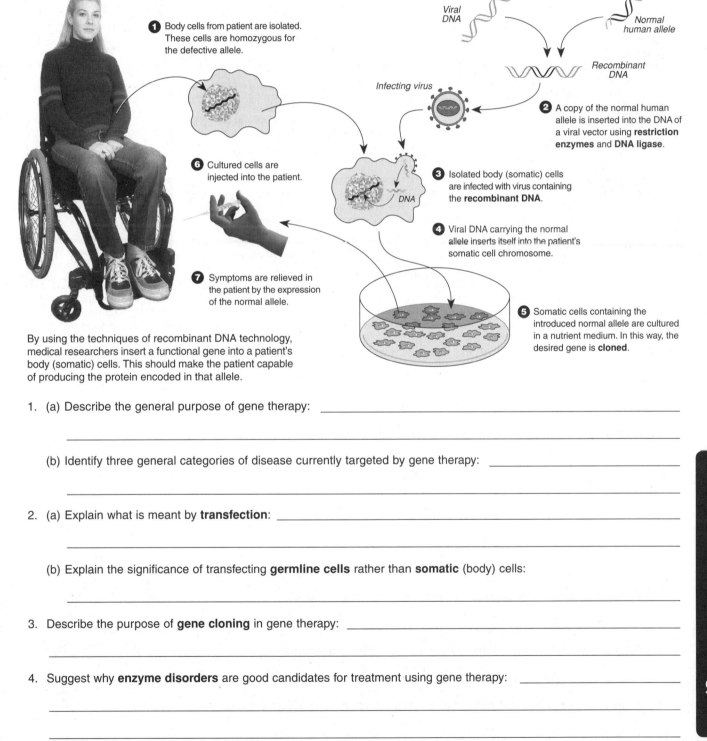

1. Body cells from patient are isolated. These cells are homozygous for the defective allele.

6. Cultured cells are injected into the patient.

7. Symptoms are relieved in the patient by the expression of the normal allele.

Viral DNA

Normal human allele

Recombinant DNA

Infecting virus

2. A copy of the normal human allele is inserted into the DNA of a viral vector using **restriction enzymes** and **DNA ligase**.

3. Isolated body (somatic) cells are infected with virus containing the **recombinant DNA**.

DNA

4. Viral DNA carrying the normal allele inserts itself into the patient's somatic cell chromosome.

5. Somatic cells containing the introduced normal allele are cultured in a nutrient medium. In this way, the desired gene is **cloned**.

By using the techniques of recombinant DNA technology, medical researchers insert a functional gene into a patient's body (somatic) cells. This should make the patient capable of producing the protein encoded in that allele.

1. (a) Describe the general purpose of gene therapy: _____

_____

(b) Identify three general categories of disease currently targeted by gene therapy: _____

_____

2. (a) Explain what is meant by **transfection**: _____

_____

(b) Explain the significance of transfecting **germline cells** rather than **somatic** (body) cells: _____

_____

3. Describe the purpose of **gene cloning** in gene therapy: _____

_____

4. Suggest why **enzyme disorders** are good candidates for treatment using gene therapy: _____

_____

_____

Related activities: Gene Delivery Systems
Web links: Gene Therapy

RA 2

Microbes and Biotechnology

Vectors for Gene Therapy

Gene therapy usually requires a **vector** (carrier) to introduce the DNA. The majority of approved clinical gene therapy protocols (63%) employ **retroviral vectors** to deliver the selected gene to the target cells, although there is considerable risk in using these vectors (below). Other widely used vectors include adenoviral vectors (16%), and liposomes (13%). The remaining 8% employ a variety of vector systems, the majority of which include injection of naked plasmid DNA.

Vectors That Can Be Used For Gene Therapy

	Retrovirus	Adenovirus	Liposome	Naked DNA
Insert size:	8000 bases	8000 bases	>20 000 bases	>20 000 bases
Integration:	Yes	No	No	No
***In vivo* delivery:**	Poor	High	Variable	Poor
Advantages	• Integrate genes into the chromosomes of the human host cell. • Offers chance for long-term stability.	• Modified for gene therapy, they infect human cells and express the normal gene. • Most do not cause disease. • Have a large capacity to carry foreign genes.	• Liposomes seek out target cells using sugars in their membranes that are recognized by cell receptors. • Have no viral genes that may cause disease.	• Have no viral genes that may cause disease. • Expected to be useful for vaccination.
Disadvantages	• Many infect only cells that are dividing. • Genes integrate randomly into chromosomes, so might disrupt useful genes in the host cell.	• Viruses may have poor survival due to attack by the host's immune system. • Genes may function only sporadically because they are not integrated into host cell's chromosome.	• Less efficient than viruses at transferring genes into cells, but recent work on using sugars to aid targeting have improved success rate.	• Unstable in most tissues of the body. • Inefficient at gene transfer.

In the table above, the following terms are defined as follows: **Naked DNA**: the genes are applied by ballistic injection (firing using a gene gun) or by regular hypodermic injection of plasmid DNA. **Insert size**: size of gene that can be inserted into the vector. **Integration**: whether or not the gene is integrated into the host DNA (chromosomes). **In vivo delivery**: ability to transfer a gene directly into a patient.

1. (a) Describe the features of viruses that make them well suited as **vectors** for gene therapy: _____

   _____

   _____

   (b) Identify two problems with using viral vectors for gene therapy: _____

   _____

   _____

2. (a) Suggest why it may be beneficial for a (therapeutic) gene to integrate into the patient's chromosome: _____

   _____

   _____

   (b) Explain why this has the potential to cause problems for the patient: _____

   _____

3. (a) Suggest why naked DNA is likely to be unstable within a patient's tissues: _____

   _____

   (b) Suggest why enclosing the DNA within liposomes might provide greater stability: _____

   _____

Related activities: Gene Therapy, Gene Delivery Systems
Web links: Gene Therapy Primer

Gene Delivery Systems

The mapping of the human genome has improved the feasibility of gene therapy as a option for treating an increasingly wide range of diseases, but it remains technically difficult to deliver genes successfully to a patient. Even after a gene has been identified, cloned, and transferred to a patient, it must be expressed normally. To date, the success of gene therapy has been generally poor, and improvements have been short-lived or counteracted by adverse side effects. Inserted genes may reach only about 1% of target cells and those that reach their destination may work inefficiently and produce too little protein, too slowly to be of benefit. In addition, many patients react immunologically to the vectors used in gene transfer. Much of the current research is focused on improving the efficiency of gene transfer and expression. One of the first gene therapy trials was for **cystic fibrosis** (CF). CF was an obvious candidate for gene therapy because, in most cases, the disease is caused by a single, known gene mutation. However, despite its early promise, gene therapy for this disease has been disappointing (below).

Gene Therapy as a Potential Treatment for Cystic Fibrosis (CF)

In cystic fibrosis, a gene mutation causes the body to produce an abnormally thick, sticky mucus that accumulates in the lungs and intestines. The identification and isolation of the CF gene in 1989 meant that scientists could look for ways in which to correct the genetic defect rather than just treating the symptoms using traditional therapies.

In trials, normal genes were isolated and inserted into patients using vectors such as **adenoviruses** and **liposomes**.

In order to prevent the progressive and ultimately lethal lung damage, the main target of CF gene therapy is the lung. The viral vector was piped directly into the lung, whereas the liposomes were inhaled in a spray formulation. The results of these trials were disappointing; on average, there was only a 25% correction, the effects were short lived, and the benefits were quickly reversed. Alarmingly, the adenovirus used in one of the trials led to the death of one patient.

Source: Cystic Fibrosis Trust, UK.

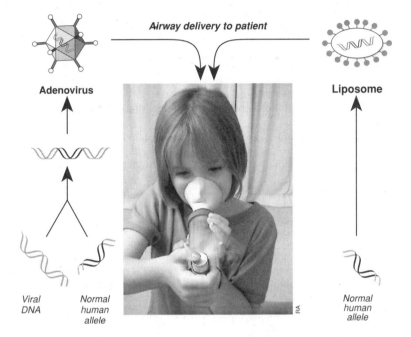

Viral DNA   *Normal human allele*   **Airway delivery to patient**   *Normal human allele*

Adenovirus   **Liposome**

An **adenovirus** that normally causes colds is genetically modified to make it safe and to carry the normal (unmutated) CFTR ('cystic fibrosis') gene.

Liposomes are tiny fat globules. Normal CF genes are enclosed in liposomes, which fuse with plasma membranes and deliver the genes into the cells.

Gene Delivery Systems Used In Human Patients

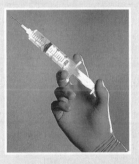

Hypodermic needle injection

► Injection of the vectors directly into the bloodstream or organs of the patient. Vectors injected into the blood travel through the body and may be taken up by the target cells.

► Injections of plasmid DNA into thymus, skin, cardiac muscle and skeletal muscle have already proved successful in non-human trials (mice and primates).

Aerosol delivery

► Aerosols and nebulizers offer an effective spread and efficient delivery of the vector to the site of certain target cells (especially in the respiratory tract).

► Used in trials of gene therapy for cystic fibrosis, but effective only on epithelial cells that can be reached by the aerosol.

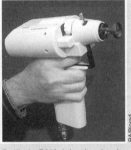

Ballistic DNA injection is also called microprojectile gene transfer, the gene-gun, or particle bombardment method.

Ballistic DNA injection

► Plasmid DNA with the gene of interest is coated onto microbeads. These are 'fired' at the target cells using gas pressure or a high voltage discharge.

► Used to transfer genes to a wide variety of cell lines *(ex vivo)* or directly into surgically exposed tissue *(in vivo)*.

► May be used in DNA-based vaccines to prevent infectious diseases or cancer.

► Allows precise DNA dosages to be delivered, but the genes are expressed transiently and there is considerable cell damage at the delivery site.

An incubator for culturing cell lines (ex-vivo).

©1999 University of Kansas Office of University Relations

Gene delivery to extracted cells and cell culture

► Target cells are isolated from tissue. Genes are delivered non-specifically to the cell population or as a microinjection of DNA into the nucleus of a single cell.

► Cells that have taken up the normal allele are cultured outside the body and re-injected into the patient.

► The expression of the normal allele relieves symptoms of the disease.

Microbes and Biotechnology

Related activities: Vectors for Gene Therapy   **RA 2**

1. A great deal of current research is being devoted to discovering a gene therapy solution to treat **cystic fibrosis** (CF):

   (a) Describe the symptoms of CF: _____

   _____

   _____

   (b) Explain why this genetic disease has been so eagerly targeted by gene therapy researchers: _____

   _____

   _____

   _____

   _____

   (c) Outline some of the problems so far encountered with gene therapy for CF: _____

   _____

   _____

   _____

   _____

   _____

2. Identify two vectors for introducing healthy CFTR genes into CF patients. For each vector, outline how it might be delivered to the patient and describe potential problems with its use:

   (a) Vector 1: _____

   Delivery: _____

   Problems: _____

   _____

   _____

   (b) Vector 2: _____

   Delivery: _____

   Problems: _____

   _____

   _____

3. Changes made to chromosomes as a result of gene therapy involving somatic cells are not inherited. Germline gene therapy has the potential to cure disease, but the risks and benefits are still not clear. For each of the points outlined below, evaluate the risk of germline gene therapy relative to somatic cell gene therapy and explain your answer:

   (a) Chance of interfering with an essential gene function: _____

   _____

   _____

   _____

   (b) Misuse of the therapy to selectively alter phenotype: _____

   _____

   _____

   _____

Production of Human Proteins

Transgenic microorganisms are now widely used as **biofactories** for the production of human proteins. These proteins are often used to treat metabolic protein-deficiency disorders. **Type I diabetes mellitus** is a metabolic disease caused by a lack of insulin and is treatable only with insulin injection. Before the advent of genetic engineering, insulin was extracted from the pancreatic tissue of pigs or cattle. This method was expensive and problematic in that the insulin caused various side effects and was often contaminated. Since the 1980s, human insulin has been mass produced using genetically modified (GM) bacteria (*Escherichia coli*) and yeast (*Saccharomyces cerevisiae*). Similar methods are used for the genetic manipulation of both microorganisms, although the size of the bacterial plasmid requires that the human gene be inserted as two, separately expressed, nucleotide sequences (see below). The use of insulin from GM sources has greatly improved the management of Type I diabetes, and the range of formulations now available has allowed diabetics to live much more normal lives than previously.

Synthesis of human insulin using recombinant DNA technology

Type I diabetes is treated with regular injections of insulin according to daily needs (right). Since the 1980s, human insulin has been mass produced using genetically modified (GM) microorganisms and marketed under various trade names. Various methodologies are employed to produce the insulin, but all involve inserting a human gene into a plasmid (bacterial or yeast), followed by secretion of a protein product from which the active insulin can be derived.

1 Identify and synthesize the human gene

Insulin is a small, simple protein. It comprises a total of 51 amino acids in two polypeptide chains (A and B). The two chains are linked by disulfide bonds. The nucleotide sequence of the gene for human insulin has been determined from the amino acid sequence. The first step in insulin production is to chemically synthesize the DNA chains that carry the specific nucleotide sequences for the A and B chains of insulin (the A and B 'genes').

2 Insert the synthetic DNA into plasmids

Using a tool kit of restriction enzymes and DNA ligase, the synthetic A and B nucleotide sequences are separately inserted into the gene for the bacterial enzyme, β-galactosidase, which is carried on the bacterial plasmid. In *E. coli*, β-galactosidase controls the transcription of genes. To make the bacteria produce insulin, the insulin gene needs to be tied to the gene for this enzyme.

3 Insert plasmid into the bacterial cell

The recombinant plasmids are then introduced to *E. coli* cells in culture conditions that favor the bacterial uptake of plasmid DNA. In practical terms, the synthesis of human insulin requires millions of copies of bacteria whose plasmid has been combined with the insulin gene. The insulin gene is expressed as it replicates with the β-galactosidase in the cell undergoing mitosis.

4 Make the functional protein

The protein formed consists partly of β-galactosidase, joined either to the A or B chain of insulin. The A and B chains are then extracted from the β-galactosidase fragment and purified. The two chains are then mixed and reconnected in a reaction that forms the disulfide cross bridges and the functional human protein, insulin. The final purified product is made suitable for injection and provided in a number of different formulations.

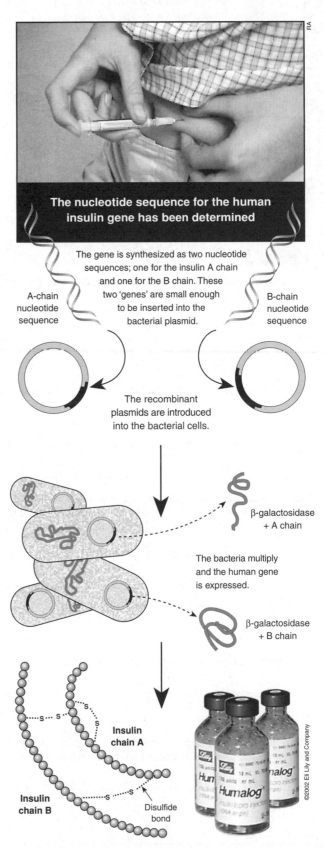

The nucleotide sequence for the human insulin gene has been determined

The gene is synthesized as two nucleotide sequences; one for the insulin A chain and one for the B chain. These two 'genes' are small enough to be inserted into the bacterial plasmid.

A-chain nucleotide sequence

B-chain nucleotide sequence

The recombinant plasmids are introduced into the bacterial cells.

β-galactosidase + A chain

The bacteria multiply and the human gene is expressed.

β-galactosidase + B chain

Insulin chain A

Insulin chain B

Disulfide bond

©2002 Eli Lily and Company

Microbes and Biotechnology

Related activities: Diabetes Mellitus, Gene Therapy

A 3

Human Proteins Produced Using Genetic Engineering

Human protein and biological role	Traditional production method	Current production
Erythropoetin A hormone, produced by kidneys, which stimulates red blood cell production. Used to treat anemia in patients with kidney failure.	Not applicable. Previous methods to treat anemia in patients with kidney failure was through repeated blood transfusions.	Cloned gene grown in hamster ovary cells
Human Growth Hormone Pituitary hormone promoting normal growth in height (deficiency results in dwarfism). Injection used to treat pituitary dwarfism.	Extracted from the pituitary glands of corpses. Many patients developed Creutzfeldt-Jacob disease (CJD) as a result. CJD is a degenerative brain disease, transmitted via infected tissues or their extracts.	Genetically engineered bacteria
Insulin Regulates the uptake of glucose by cells. Used (via injection) in the treatment of Type I (insulin-dependent) diabetes mellitus.	Physical extraction from the pancreatic tissue of pigs or cattle. Problems included high cost, sample contamination, and severe side effects.	Genetically engineered bacteria or yeast
Interferon Anti-viral substance produced by virus-infected cells. Used in the treatment of hepatitis B and C, some cancers, and multiple sclerosis.	Not applicable. Relatively recent discovery of the role of these proteins in human physiology.	Genetically engineered bacteria
Factor VIII One of the blood clotting factors normally present in blood. Used in the treatment of hemophilia caused by lack of factor VIII.	Blood donation. Risks of receiving blood contaminated with infective viruses (HIV, hepatitis), despite better screening procedures.	Genetically engineered bacteria

1. Describe the three major problems associated with the traditional method of obtaining insulin to treat diabetes:

   (a) _____

   (b) _____

   (c) _____

2. Explain why the insulin gene is synthesized as two separate A and B chain nucleotide sequences: _____
   _____

3. Explain why the synthetic nucleotide sequences ('genes') are inserted into the β-galactosidase gene: _____
   _____

4. Yeast (*Saccharomyces cerevisiae*) is also used in the production of human insulin. It is a eukaryote with a larger plasmid than *E. coli*. Its secretory pathways are more similar to those of humans and β-galactosidase is not involved in gene expression. Predict how these differences might change the procedure for insulin production with respect to:

   (a) Insertion of the gene into the plasmid: _____
   _____

   (b) Secretion and purification of the protein product: _____
   _____

5. Describe the benefits to patients of using GMOs to produce human proteins: _____
   _____
   _____

6. When delivered to a patient, artificially produced human proteins only alleviate disease symptoms; they cannot cure the disease. Describe how this situation might change in the future:
   _____
   _____
   _____

Index

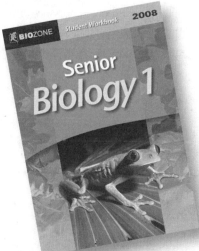

Senior Biology 1

A companion title to
Senior Biology 2
provides coverage of:

- experimental design
- forming hypotheses
- data analysis
- experimental write-up
- cell structure
- cell function
- biochemistry

- cellular energetics
- molecular genetics
- inheritance
- gene technology
- ecology
- classification
- conservation

Model Answers

Model Answers books are available for both
Senior Biology 1 and Senior Biology 2.
Each provides suggested answers to nearly
all of the activities in the workbook.